Virginia's Cattle Story

THE FIRST FOUR CENTURIES

Katharine L. Brown
Nancy T. Sorrells

Kenneth E. Koons, editor

Commissioned by
The Virginia Cattlemen's Foundation
and the
Dairy Foundation of Virginia

Lot's Wife Publishing
Staunton, Virginia

Dustjacket design by Cheryl Lyon. Photographs, clockwise from top left, Courtesy Fallings Springs Farm, Bath County; Tenants at the grazing place, Blue Ridge Mountains, courtesy Darwin Lambert; Courtesy Plimoth Plantation, Plymouth, Massachusetts; Mount Vernon Ladies' Association; Cattle auction, western Virginia, courtesy Virginia Cattle History Project Advisory Board; Holstein cattle, courtesy Betty Jo Hamilton; Courtesy Marvin Meek, Burke's Garden; and Courtesy Historic St. Mary's City, St. Mary's City, Maryland.

Interior layout and design Betty Jo Hamilton.   Printing by Good Printers, Inc., Bridgewater, Virginia.

Library of Congress Catalog Card Number 2004113247
ISBN 0975274511

Lot's Wife Publishing
P. O. Box 1844
Staunton, VA 24402
lotswife@rica.net

Layout & Design by
Cowpoke Productions
P.O. Box 51
Middlebrook, Virginia
24459
goodnews@rica.net

Dedication

*For Virginia's cattle
and their keepers --
past, present, and future*

Contents

Preface — vi

Acknowledgments — vii

Virginia... At Daybreak — 1

Virginia's First Cattle — 19

Cattle and the Colonists — 35

Revolutionary Times — 51

The New Republic — 61

A War on All Fronts — 76

The Great Cattle Drives — 98

Riding the Rails of Progress — 112

Caring for Cattle — 131

A Fat Cattle Kingdom — 143

In Pursuit of Excellence — 161

Milk Goes Modern — 187

Dairy Turns to Milk Specialists — 227

Beef Industry Comes of Age — 247

Promoting Quality in Seedstock — 281

The Future is Now — 311

Epilogue — 335

Endnotes and Illustration Credits — 339

Index — 348

Preface

The cattle story of the Old Dominion is, for the first time, documented in this book. History should be one of every American's favorite subjects, though many would simply prefer to look forward and plan for the future with little knowledge of the past. Virginia is steeped in history, much of which is well known to most of us. The important role of cattle and cattle people, however, may be one of her best-kept secrets.

The idea and plan for publishing the history of Virginia's cattle industry and its people evolved out of deliberations of the board of directors of the newly-established Virginia Cattlemen's Foundation in 2001. The fact that a comprehensive history had never been written justified the need for one. Also, looking ahead to the 400th anniversary of the 1607 founding of Jamestown, the board wished to sponsor a project that would increase public awareness of the significant role that cattle and cattle-related enterprises have played in the history of the colony and the Commonwealth of Virginia. Thus, this book became the first important project of the foundation.

Early in the planning stages the board decided that the book would encompass the history of both the beef and dairy industries. Both the sixty-year-old Virginia Cattlemen's Association and the ninety-seven-year-old Virginia State Dairymen's Association agreed to sponsor the endeavor jointly; the Dairy Foundation of Virginia, Inc. would work in tandem with the Virginia Cattlemen's Foundation, Inc. The mission of both foundations is to procure, manage, and distribute funds for the purposes of education, scientific discovery, leadership training, and industry enhancement and development.

The next step to move the project forward was to identify experienced and talented authors to research and write the book. Good fortune was just around the next bend in the road when Betty Jo Hamilton, a beef producer and newspaper publisher, recommended Katharine Brown and Nancy Sorrells of Lot's Wife Publishing to undertake the task. In due time they were commissioned as authors and publishers. One of their largest tasks was to sort through and winnow the large volume of historical data and the many human-interest stories and photographs turned up by research. The good news is that all the material, whether used in this volume or not, is catalogued and saved for posterity.

The total cost of the project, including research, writing, and printing, was underwritten by gifts from corporations, organizations, individuals, and other foundations. Over 150 contributions were received. Proceeds from the sale of the book will come back to the coffers of the two foundations to be used to fund scholarships and other projects benefiting individuals and families in Virginia's beef and dairy industries.

The beef and dairy industries in Virginia have both risen to national prominence in the twentieth century, based on innovation and achievement. Research for this book has uncovered the main ingredients for such an accomplishment – a strong work ethic, superior leadership skills, and a vigorous spirit of cooperation. Cooperation has been the watchword among producers, marketers, researchers, educators, and corporations as both cattle industries in Virginia have matured and developed. A strong cooperative spirit has characterized relations among the state beef and dairy associations, Virginia Tech (Virginia's land-grant university), the Virginia Department of Agriculture and Consumer Services, and a host of other infrastructure-support industries and organizations. As this book amply demonstrates, Virginians have fostered this cooperative spirit as well or better than peoples of other states.

The Virginia Cattlemen's Foundation is pleased to present this work to the members of its constituent organizations and fellow producers, but also to those whose work and interests bear upon the continuing success and vitality of Virginia's beef and dairy industries. Too, we invite members of the general reading public to open the pages of this book and learn about the history of forms of entrepreneurship that place beef and dairy products on their tables.

A.L. (Ike) Eller, Jr.
Advisor, Editorial Board
Virginia Tech professor emeritus

Acknowledgments

In January of 2002, the foundation organizations for the Virginia Cattlemen's Association and the Virginia State Dairymen's Association jointly recognized the importance and timeliness of recording the fascinating history of cattle in Virginia and the people who tended them.

The story begins four centuries ago at Jamestown with the arrival of a few cattle from England on a wind-powered sailing vessel. This book tells how those Virginia cattle and their keepers evolved during the next four centuries as this great nation developed.

Grateful acknowledgment is made to the following members of the Editorial Board for their vision and their practical assistance in bringing this volume to fruition: James Bennett and Ernie Reeves from the Virginia Cattlemen's Association, Nelson Gardner and William Harrison from the Virginia State Dairymen's Association, and Dr. A.L. Eller, Jr., editorial board advisor and Virginia Tech professor emeritus. Debbie Snead, marketing director for the project, has skillfully promoted the book with her contagious enthusiasm for agriculture and life in Virginia. Patty Douglas, recording secretary for the editorial board, has coordinated and guided our effort with her wealth of experience about Virginia cattle breeders and their cattle. The Editorial Board was commissioned to initiate the project and direct the work necessary for its completion. Individually and collectively board members worked diligently with patient determination to ensure that this history of our industry be recorded with accuracy and in the colorful way that is was lived.

Katharine Brown and Nancy Sorrells, historians and publishers, are the principals of Lot's Wife Publishing and have been recognized for the excellent works they have authored and published. *Virginia's Cattle Story: The First Four Centuries* is a product of their writing the history of the past in order to preserve it as a foundation of knowledge to serve future generations.

Dr. Kenneth E. Koons, historian and distinguished author, has been very effective and helpful as editor of the work. The layout and graphics design was the result of the creative vision and hard work of Betty Jo Hamilton. The beautiful cover and creative jumpstart comes from Cheryl Lyon.

Dr. Alfred W. Stuart, Professor Emeritus of Geography, University of North Carolina at Charlotte, helped set the tone for the book with his patient advice regarding the introduction. Patrick Jones of the Cartography Lab, University of North Carolina at Charlotte Department of Geography and Earth Sciences, created a number of maps that helped to tell the story.

An Advisory Board provided valuable advice, counsel, and support throughout the project. Members included Dr. R. Michael Akers, head of Dairy Science at Virginia Tech; Carlton Courter, Commissioner of Virginia Department of Agriculture and Consumer Services; A.L. Eller, Jr., Virginia Tech professor emeritus; Dale Gardner, executive secretary, Virginia State Dairymen's Association; Dr. Mark McCann, head of the Department of Animal and Poultry Services; Rodney Phillips, administrator of the Virginia State Milk Commission; Reggie Reynolds, executive secretary of the Virginia Cattlemen's Association; and Dr. Andy Swiger, Dean Emeritus, Virginia Tech.

Lastly, but importantly, on behalf of the two foundations, I wish to acknowledge the help of many individuals who encouraged and supported this effort by sharing their personal experiences and family histories, photographs, artifacts, and documents which, now recorded, tell the story of cattle in Virginia.

John B. Mitchell, Sr.
Chairman Editorial Board
September 2004

Virginia... at daybreak

Four hundred years ago, cattle and the Old World settlers who transported them in the holds of their tiny, creaking ships first set tentative hooves and feet on Virginia's shores as newcomers to a very ancient land. Life in the New World was harsh, and Virginia's earliest populations of cattle struggled to survive in an environment that featured a different climate, strange foods, new diseases, and predators. This book tells the story of how the first foothold of cattle in the new colony evolved into the modern cattle industry of the Commonwealth of Virginia.

But first there was the land. The Virginia of 400 years ago was a long time in coming. Even Native Americans, who had inhabited the area for nearly 11,000 years by the time the English established Jamestown, had been present for only a few seconds of geologic time. Virginia's coastal plain, where the first Europeans settled, was the last part of the state to be formed. The core of the continent we know today as North America had been in place for several billion years but, as recently as 600 million years ago, Virginia's coast was near present-day Richmond. Farther east, and still under the ocean, were layers of sedimentary rock created after rivers dumped thousands of feet of sand and mud into the sea, which then mingled with the remains of marine creatures that for eons had died and drifted to the ocean floor.

At that time, the modern-day map of Virginia and of the world was far from complete. Near the South Pole lay another giant continent known to geologists as Gondwanaland. It contained fragments of land that would eventually form the southeast coast of North America, as well as South America, Africa, Australia, and Antarctica. About 400 million years ago, forces deep within the earth caused those two supercontinents – Gondwanaland and the core of present-day North America – to begin a slow movement toward one another. Eventually they met, and for millions of years after their initial contact, the landmasses ground slowly into each other in a titanic demonstration of power far beyond our ability to imagine. Sedimentary rock layers from beneath the ocean floor buckled and cracked under the heat and pressure from the collision, forming a high chain of mountains that resembled the current Himalayas.

Two hundred million years ago, the continents reversed the direction of their movement. The giant landmasses separated, then retreated from each other, leaving behind the southeastern coast of the United States from eastern Virginia to Florida. Over the ensuing eons, the high mountains formed by the continental collision were worn down by erosion so that, as the continents drifted away from each other, oceans again covered the area. The weathering of the mountains sent tiny sediment particles off their slopes and into the expanse of eastern Virginia now known as the Coastal Plain. During those years, ocean levels rose and fell because of the shifting of continents and the periodic ice ages that locked up much of the earth's surface water in massive ice sheets. Although those glaciers never reached modern-day Virginia, they substantially affected the level of the seas. Thus, when the last glaciers retreated 10,000 years ago, they created the modern coast line of Virginia including the enormous Chesapeake Bay, and the peninsula known as the Eastern Shore.

Six hundred million years of geological sculpting created five distinct regions that define the landscape of Virginia:

1. *The Coastal Plain*, also known as the Tidewater, is the sandy low-lying area that, once an ocean floor, was left behind after the ocean receded. It is located in the easternmost part of the state.

2. *The Piedmont* is the rolling plateau that occupies the site of the ancient high mountain ranges. It straddles the heart of the state from the Blue Ridge foothills on the west to the Coastal Plain on the east.

3. *The Blue Ridge Mountains* were formed as the heat and pressure of the continental collision metamorphosed limestone, shale, and sandstone into quartzite, slate, and marble, rocks more highly resistant to erosion than the once-high mountains of the Piedmont. As such, they wore down more slowly than the land to the east, leaving today's weathered ridges.

4. *The Valley and Ridge Province* arose farther inland where the force of the continental collision caused layers of earlier sedimentary rocks to fold and buckle. Subsequent erosion of these folded layers led to the formation of a series of parallel ridges and valleys, the largest and most famous of which is the Shenandoah Valley.

5. *The Appalachian Plateau*, the most western geologic region of the state, is comprised of the same layers of sedimentary rocks found in the Valley and Ridge Province but, being farther removed from the continental collision, they were left largely undisturbed by that event. Subsequent erosion has dissected the still horizontal layers of rock into a terrain of hills and valleys.

Today Virginia encompasses almost 40,600 square miles. In size, it places thirty-sixth among the fifty states. It has 112 miles of Atlantic coastline, 230 miles of Chesapeake coastline, and 3,315 miles of tidal coastline (the points up the many rivers and streams where waterlines rise and fall with the ebb and flow of tides). The mean altitude is 950 feet above sea level with some terrain ranging to considerably higher elevations. Mount Rogers, for example, in the southwest part of the state is, at 5,729 feet, the highest point in Virginia.

The low-lying lands of the eastern part of Virginia comprise the Coastal Plain, where land meets sea or, in this case, the Chesapeake Bay. The Bay is North America's largest estuary – that transitional zone between land and sea where fresh water becomes brackish and then salty, where tides create an ebb and flow of water levels, and where some 2,700 species of animals and plants form an intricate web of life that keeps a large, multi-state ecological system in balance. The Atlantic Ocean becomes the Chesapeake Bay and breaches the sandy soils of Virginia at Cape Charles. From there the Bay reaches northward all the way to Baltimore, Maryland, and even into Pennsylvania as it takes the shape of a full-fingered glove. Protecting the Bay on the east is the Delmarva Peninsula, which is sheltered, in turn, on its eastern flank by a chain of barrier islands that, under relentless buffeting from the ocean, constantly shift location and change size. The narrow Delmarva Peninsula, encompassing all or parts of Delaware, Maryland, and Virginia, is known as the Eastern Shore. Its southern-most portion – the Virginia counties of Accomack and Northampton – as well as an island in the Bay called Tangier, belongs to the Old Dominion. English settlement came to the area quite early. Plantation owners here found that the narrow peninsula and the barrier islands formed a natural "fence" for livestock. As a result, large numbers of livestock were raised here early in the seventeenth century.

Waters draining New York, Pennsylvania, Maryland, and the Virginias, pour into the immense Chesapeake Bay estuary. The Old Dominion's four major rivers that flow into the Bay include the Potomac, which arises in western Virginia and the state of West Virginia. At Harpers Ferry the eastward-flowing Potomac converges with the north-flowing Shenandoah and then flows on to pass through Washington, D.C., before entering the Bay.

South of the Potomac, the Rappahannock arises from the eastern foothills of the Blue Ridge Mountains and flows eastward to the Bay. The peninsula of land between the two rivers is known as the Northern Neck. Between the Rappahannock and the York River lies the Middle Peninsula. The expanse of land between the York and the mighty James River, which drains eastward from deep within the Great Valley of Virginia, is known simply as the Peninsula. These three fat fingers of land created by four rivers, as well as the coastal, often marshy, landscape that extends to the North Carolina border, define the western side of the Chesapeake Bay. Geographically and culturally they form Virginia's Tidewater.

Early settlers moving west from Tidewater soon reached a transitional area between the coast and the mountains. This rolling landscape with its red and yellow clay soils and fast flowing rivers is known as the Piedmont, a word that means "foot of the mountains." In southern Virginia, a region called the Southside encompasses Tidewater and Piedmont counties situated between the James River and the North Carolina state line.

The geographic boundary between Tidewater and the Piedmont is known as the Fall Line. Fall lines are upriver places where swift waters and waterfalls block passage of ocean-going ships. In Virginia, the Fall Line also restricted the inland passage of small boats and barges during the colonial period. Faster currents at the Fall Line allowed water-powered industry to flourish in past times. Historically, then, trade and manufacturing centers were often located on the Fall Line in places like Richmond and Washington, D.C. Because this geographic boundary represented a "break of bulk" point where boat cargo had to be unloaded and reloaded on wagons for transportation further inland, settlements along the Fall Line were natural places for stores, warehouses, livery stables, and wagoners. Soon, cities grew up around the sites of these early entrepreneurial activities. Although colonial navigation upstream from the Fall Line was nearly impossible, dugouts and flatboats could ride the currents downstream during certain times of the year. Thus, industrial products from the colony's interior were often shipped, by water, to Fall Line trade centers.

The Piedmont, which begins along the Fall Line, is composed of igneous and metamorphic rocks that were interior parts of those earlier high mountains removed by erosion over eons. Super-hardened rocks underlie the Virginia landscape almost to the ocean, but in the more coastal areas, the period of oceanic inundation has left layers of soft, sandy material much like that of the ocean floor. In the Piedmont, the rocks are closer to the surface and jut up more sharply. As the landscape around them erodes over time, their hard and slower-to-erode surfaces eventually make them the higher points in the landscape. Millions of years of weathering have created a reddish, iron-rich clay soil called sapprolite.

The red-yellow, acidic clay soils that predominate in Virginia's Piedmont and the sandy soils of the Coastal Plain were easily worked and bore profitable crops, especially tobacco, when properly fertilized by adding manure to them. Tobacco culture, which took root in Tidewater, influenced the evolution of settlement and the nature of Virginia government. Tobacco was so important to Virginians that at times it functioned as the official currency. In the seventeenth, eighteenth, and early nineteenth centuries, farmers and planters grew tobacco until the soil was stripped of its nutrients. After wearing out a piece of land, the tobacco farmer moved west to another tract of land. A few urban areas developed along the coast but inland there were very few towns because most buying and selling of trade goods took place on the large plantations. Tobacco culture accompanied and even encouraged the spread of settlement west through the Piedmont. Huge tobacco estates, some larger than 10,000 acres, dominated the landscape. Tobacco was a labor-intensive crop. Thus, in addition to the landed elites who owned massive estates, the migration westward included laborers who worked the land. A shipload of Africans forcibly brought to Jamestown in 1619 helped define who those laborers would be. Slave labor meshed well with a crop requiring long hours of work in cultivation and preparation. Within three-quarters of a century, a harsh system of slavery had been codified into the fabric of life in Virginia as a direct response to the need for labor to produce tobacco.

At the western edge of the Piedmont, rolling hills give way to the Blue Ridge Mountains. These weathered ridges – the easternmost elevations of the Allegheny Mountains – extend in a southwestward direction from Pennsylvania to northern Georgia and are part of the even larger Maine-to-Georgia Appalachian Chain. North of Roanoke, Virginia, the peaks of the Blue Ridge appear softer than the rugged mountains west of the Valley of Virginia, and push upward in a band only a dozen or so miles wide. South of Roanoke, however, the mountains rise higher and spread out as far as the eye can see. These hills, which are thought to be among the oldest in the world, count 125 million more birthdays than the youthful Rockies of America's West.

The upheaval produced by the collision of the earth's tectonic plates formed the Great Valley of Virginia as well as the Atlantic Coast. Being further from the crash zone, however, the region that became the valley was subject to less buckling, pressure, and intense heat. The layers of sedimentary rock rippled, rolled, and fractured, but were usually not transformed into harder stone like quartzite or marble. And so when the retreat of the continental plates began, the sedimentary layers of limestone and sandstone from the ocean floor remained behind, weathering and eroding for millions of years. Of the two, limestone is water-soluble and erodes relatively quickly, leaving behind bedrock that resembles Swiss cheese and is lower in elevation than areas underlain by sandstone. Erosion-resistant sandstone, by contrast, remained as cliffs, gorges, hills, and mountains – Massanutten Mountain is one example of this. The geologic word for such a landscape is karst – meaning an area defined by limestone outcroppings, abundant springs, sinkholes, and caverns. Unusual landmarks such as Natural Bridge in Rockbridge County and Natural Chimneys in Augusta County are above-ground remnants of collapsed limestone caverns.

The Great Valley of Virginia lies west of the Blue Ridge Mountains. The valley is actually a series of smaller valleys, each of which is separated by parallel ridges and defined geographically by the river that drains it. The Shenandoah, perhaps the most storied of Virginia's rivers, arises in southern Augusta County at an elevation of about 2,500 feet and flows northward to lower elevations down the valley until it merges with the Potomac at Harpers Ferry. The fifty-mile-long ridge of erosion-resistant sandstone known as Massanutten Mountain juts up prominently from the floor of the Valley and divides the Shenandoah River into two forks.

The James River, much larger than the Shenandoah, also originates in the mountains and valleys of western Virginia. One series of tributaries arises in southern Augusta County and northern Rockbridge, while the others begin in Highland County and drain through Bath County. The confluence of the Cowpasture and the Jackson Rivers in northern Botetourt marks the beginning of the James River proper. As the river flows through

Rockbridge, it receives a series of creeks into its waters, the largest of which is the Maury that merges with the James at Glasgow. From there the mighty James makes its way east to Richmond and eventually the Chesapeake Bay. South of the headwaters of the James, the valleys narrow and widen and the rugged Alleghenies loom large, dividing the continent. Waters of the Roanoke River flow southeastward to the Atlantic Ocean. The gap that the Roanoke River cut through the Blue Ridge was a route followed by colonial settlers who encountered a steep rise in the valley south of Roanoke. Traveling south from Pennsylvania, they often elected instead to move through the Roanoke River gap, out on to the Piedmont and down into the Carolinas. The New River, by contrast, wends northwestward from North Carolina, through Southwest Virginia and West Virginia until it eventually joins the Ohio, and from there the Mississippi and eventually the Gulf of Mexico. The river's name carries with it a touch of irony, because, geologically, it is one of the oldest rivers in the world.

The Blue Ridge presented a formidable barrier to westward migration into the Great Valley. Settlers had to traverse the mountains through water gaps where the Potomac, James, and Shenandoah Rivers broke through on their journey to the ocean, or through wind gaps such as Swift Run Gap, where Governor Alexander Spotswood may have first looked into the Shenandoah Valley in 1716. The Appalachians also act as an orographic barrier, which is a technical way of saying that the mountain slopes catch winds from the west and as the rising air cools, it dumps rain on the windward side. Thus the westward slopes of these taller ridges are some of the wettest places in the eastern United States. The Native Americans knew this, as did the first settlers. Long before European settlement, Indians had created openings in the forest or had further encouraged, through the use of fire, natural clearings in the mountains as attractive grazing areas for game. The first European settlers called these clearings balds or sods. From the early eighteenth century until the mid-twentieth century, cattle were driven up to the mountains in the summer, where they grazed on the grasses that thrived in those well-watered clearings. In Southwest Virginia, all the factors of abundant rainfall, rich limestone-based soils, and luxuriant stands of bluegrass came together to produce a fat cattle export business that was unrivaled in the world.

Geographically, the Great Valley of Virginia offered a way to breach the mountains, and acted much like a giant funnel -- its wide end extending northward toward central Pennsylvania and its small end offering a route further west into Tennessee and Kentucky. Settlers of German and Scotch-Irish extraction, encouraged by a relaxed attitude toward laws requiring strict adherence to the established Anglican church, began migrating into the Valley of Virginia in the 1720s. Early settlers entered the funnel around present-day Winchester, Virginia, where elevations range from 600 to 800 feet. Mountains to the west were high enough to deter movement further in that direction, and so settlement pushed southwestward, following the valley floor. Settlers in the valley sought agricultural prosperity and yet were too far removed from coastal docks to successfully market tobacco. Instead they quickly began planting cash crops of hemp (for rope), flax (for linen), and wheat (for flour) which could be more easily transported over long distances. The rich limestone soils, particularly along the river bottoms, were among the best in the state. For farmers, this helped to compensate for the relative lack of rainfall; the valley was the driest region in the state. Very little of the English plantation culture transferred into the valley, where thriving market towns like Winchester and Staunton, and later New Market and Harrisonburg, developed along the Great Wagon Road (today U.S. Route 11). Towns east of the Blue Ridge were few in number, small, and widely

Land Regions of Virginia

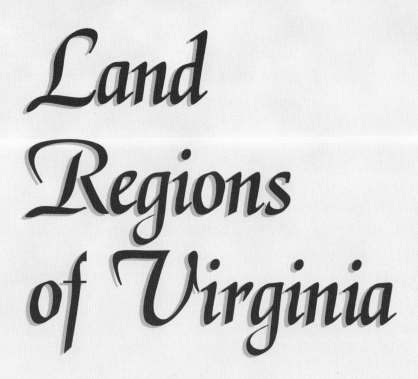

Appalachian
Plateau

Blacksburg

New River

Valley & Ridge   Blue Ridge Mountains

Winchester

Shenandoah River

Arlington

Staunton

Charlottesville

Rappahannock River

Chesapeake Bay

James River

York River

Richmond

Lynchburg

Roanoke River

Norfolk

Atlantic Ocean

Danville

Piedmont

Coastal Plain

scattered over the landscape due to the prevalence of tobacco culture. By the mid-nineteenth century, the valley had become one of the leading wheat-producing regions in the country. Valley farmers sent flour eastward through those wind and water gaps, and northward on the Valley Pike to domestic and international destinations. From the beginning, cattle, too, figured into the valley's agricultural economy as farmers found ways to successfully mix cash crop production with animal husbandry. Within a few years of settlement, great cattle drives wended their way down the valley to Philadelphia. As the Valley served as a natural corridor for the migration of people – a funnel – it was also a natural corridor for the movement of cattle.

Across the Blue Ridge, on the east side of the "funnel" opening, is the part of the Commonwealth known today as Northern Virginia. The northwestern reaches of the Northern Neck blend into the northern sections of the Piedmont near Washington, D.C. This area was the focus of much of the English gentry's territorial expansion in the seventeenth and early eighteenth centuries. Large plantations producing cash crops of tobacco or wheat characterized agriculture there. Many handsome estates, such as Mount Vernon, were located along the banks of the Potomac and had their own private docks for the shipping and receiving of water-borne goods. From these "inland" ports, seafaring vessels could export agricultural goods, including cattle, and import Old World finery such as fancy china or expensive textiles.

In Southwest Virginia, at the narrow tube of the Valley of Virginia's geographic funnel, is an area known as the Appalachian Plateau. The underlying rocks in this upland region are sandstone and shale, and they are thinly covered with a gray-brown soil. Cool temperatures in these mountains create less bacterial activity in the forest humus resulting in poor, highly acidic soil, lacking many minerals useful for agriculture. Bituminous coal, historically this region's most valuable resource, lies beneath the surface of the earth. Millions of years ago when the area was tropical and lush, plant life flourished. Plant remains trapped between layers of sedimentary rock and under pressure from the build-up of subsequent layers became coal. The mining of bituminous coal has been a dominant economic activity in this region of Virginia.

From the Tidewater's coastal estuaries to Southwest Virginia's rugged mountains, from the rolling hills and clay soils of the Piedmont to the rich limestone soils in the Valley of Virginia, the Old Dominion is geologically, geographically, and culturally, a diverse land. Four hundred years ago when the first cattle came to Virginia's shores, no one could be certain that these four-legged immigrants would survive, much less thrive. As Virginia's settlers focused on the cultivation of tobacco, cattle were forced to fend for themselves in marshlands and newly-cleared pastures. Amazingly, within a few decades cattle were so numerous that colonists developed a significant export trade. How did bovines, once so endangered that it was a capital offense to kill them, become, within a few years, too numerous to count accurately? According to one idea being postulated at Colonial Williamsburg's faunal archaeology lab, possibly the answer might lie in stowaway hitchhikers; the seeds clinging to cattle coats and hiding in animal feed changed the landscape. Few people realize today that plants such as chicory, Queen Anne's lace, bluegrass, and many clovers were not native to North America. Rather, they came as stowaways with the first settlers. One theory holds that once the Old World forage sources became established in the New World, cattle began to thrive. By the end of their first century in the New World, cattle were everywhere and at a size only slightly smaller than typical bovines of the twentieth century.

Cattle became common in Virginia but nowhere in the Commonwealth, before the late nineteenth century, were they ever considered the primary agricultural focus. And, yet, cattle were valuable. They provided meat, dairy products, and draft power; too, they were valued for their leather, horn, and tallow by-products so vital to everyday living. The value of leather alone can hardly be overestimated. It served as the raw material for shoes, aprons, gloves, and shoelaces, as well as harness, bridles, and saddles. Leather connected the parts of flails, needed to thresh grain, and was used to fashion blacksmiths' bellows, as well as the belts needed to run mill machinery.

Bovines helped to shape Virginia's landscape. Today the names of approximately eighty villages, landforms, waterways, and even churches symbolize the importance of cattle in the history of the Commonwealth. Such places are widely dispersed across the state map from Dickenson and Montgomery to Fauquier and Loudoun, from Accomack and Northampton to Hanover and Amelia, from Mathews and Lancaster to Augusta and Rockingham. Accomack leads the way with seven different cattle-related placenames and Buchanan is second with five. Some of the names are familiar places in American history. Bull Run Creek near

Manassas in Prince William County is where two bloody Civil War battles were fought; on the slopes of Bullpasture Mountain, in Highland County, the Battle of McDowell was waged in 1862. In Accomack and Northampton on the Eastern Shore, the names of places such as Bull Cove, Bulls Dock, Calfpen Bay, and Bulls Landing indicate that water was the most efficient means of transportation on the peninsula during the colonial period. Cow Island in York and Cowpen Neck in Gloucester suggest two different ways to confine animals using natural landforms. Cowcamp in Amherst probably derives from the practice of driving animals to pasture in the mountains during the summer. Other intriguing names include Cow Gut Flat in Accomack, Cowbone Ridge in Alleghany, and Cow Swamp in James City County. How those places acquired their names will probably never be known, but they symbolize the significance of cattle to the history of the Commonwealth of Virginia. This is the story of Virginia and its settlement, of the mixture of cultures and the development of economies, of wars, of education, and of technology. It is the story of Virginia and it is the story of cattle. The two are inseparable. We invite you to turn the pages of this book and begin a journey into the history of Virginia and the history of her cattle. ◖

Information for this introduction was taken from the following sources: James W. Clay, Paul D. Escott, Douglas M. Orr, Jr., and Alfred W. Stuart, *Land of the South* (Birmingham, Alabama: Oxmoor House, Inc., 1989); Keith Frye, *Roadside Geology of Virginia* (Missoula, Montana: Mountain Press Publishing Company, 1990); *The Hornbook of Virginia History*, ed. Emily J. Salmon and Edward D. C. Campbell, Jr. (Richmond: The Library of Virginia, 1994); Thomas H. Biggs, *Geographic and Cultural Names in Virginia, Information Circular 20* (Charlottesville: Commonwealth of Virginia, Department of Conservation and Economic Development, Division of Mineral Resources, 1974.

Virginia's First Cattle

Virginians have always taken particular pride in being first. Thus it seems important to begin with an attempt to determine when the first cattle came into Virginia. However, even with intense scrutiny of the documentary evidence and the exciting new archaeological work being conducted on Jamestown Island, the question of when the first cattle arrived is more complex than it first appears and efforts to answer it only lead to an educated guess. In English documents of the late sixteenth and early seventeenth-century, the word cattle referred to any hoofed animal — cattle, horses, donkeys, sheep, swine, and goats — and so a reference to cattle being transported to Jamestown does not provide certain evidence of bovines in the new world. Only if the cattle were referred to as "neat cattle" or "kine" do we know for certain that the writer was speaking of bovines. Both "neat" and "kine" are old-fashioned words meaning bovine.

We know that English settlers brought bovines to the Roanoke Island colony in the late sixteenth century, an area then in Virginia, but now on North Carolina's Outer Banks. That colony disappeared without a trace. It is doubtful that any of the cattle from the Roanoke colony survived and multiplied into feral herds. Even before the Roanoke settlement, there is evidence indicating the establishment of a Spanish Jesuit mission — called Ajacan — along Virginia's York River in 1570. The mission came to an abrupt end in February of 1571 when a Native-American attack left all the inhabitants dead except one. Any cattle that might have been at the site were presumably killed in the complete destruction of that settlement.

That leaves another possibility for the existence of feral cattle herds in Virginia at the time of the Jamestown settlement. Some historians have conjectured that the cattle Columbus brought to the New World on his second voyage, or those from sixteenth-century Spanish settlements in Florida, might have escaped and wandered northward. However, the agricultural historian Lewis

A milk cow was a valuable possession to leave by will to a daughter, granddaughter, or godchild in seventeenth-century Virginia.

Cecil Gray dismisses all notions that wild cattle existed in the Chesapeake region before permanent English settlement. According to Gray, none of the records of early explorers or records pertaining to settlement in Virginia or Maryland contains even a hint of wild cattle, hogs, or horses.[1]

All evidence indicates that the first surviving cattle in Virginia were associated with Jamestown. Nonetheless, dating the arrival of the very first bovine remains difficult. Researchers at Jamestown have always surmised that the ships carrying the first settlers in 1607 also brought livestock as a source of food and draft power, but there is no documentary evidence to support this. Two early accounts mention livestock at the settlement in 1609 and documents tell of efforts to erect a palisade to protect livestock from Indians and wolves, but no record specifically mentions cattle although chickens, pigs, horses, goats, and sheep are listed. That these species were listed and cattle were not leads researchers to the conclusion that there were no bovines at the Jamestown settlement in 1609.[2] Yet, the hiring of a "cowkeeper" at Jamestown in 1609 could suggest the presence of cows. In any case, even if there were cattle at the colony in late 1609 they had long ago been consumed when the British ships dropped anchor in the spring of 1610. The winter of 1609-1610 is known as the "Starving Time" in the annals of Virginia history. Since its establishment in 1607, the fledgling Jamestown settlement's foothold in the New World had been tenuous, at best. Then came the winter of 1609, when confrontations with Native Americans, disease, and famine decimated the colony. When Lieutenant Governor Thomas Gates and a shipload of new settlers arrived in May of 1610, only 90 colonists within the entire colony were alive out of an original number between 270 and 300. In desperation they had killed and eaten every animal they could find, including the livestock.

One month later, in June of 1610, the governor of Virginia, Thomas West, Baron De la Warr, arrived with additional supplies, including cattle. Afterward, cattle were regularly shipped to the colony. The timeline of cattle in Virginia, therefore, stretches continuously from 1610.

America's first cattle

Virginia, then, has no claim as the site of where the first cattle entered what is now the United States. That honor goes to Spanish explorer Francisco Vasquez de Coronado, whose 1519 expedition in search of the mythical Seven Cit-

ies of Gold included 500 head of cattle. Although many of those animals escaped into what is now Texas, Arizona, and New Mexico, they were killed by Native Americans and did not survive. Cattle did not establish a permanent foothold in the Southwest until the 1690s.[3]

In 1611, at least two ships brought cattle to Virginia. These bovines, owned by the London Company rather than individual colonists, were not intended for human consumption. Indeed, at this time, Virginia authorities prohibited the butchering of cattle unless they were injured or diseased. Rather,

Artist's rendering of cattle arriving in the West Indies from a voyage by explorer Christopher Columbus

these cattle were to be used as draft animals, for breeding, and for dairy production. Archaeological evidence shows that the first colonists relied heavily on the local wildlife as a food source – fish, turtle, deer, waterfowl, and small mammals. This trend contrasts sharply with the period from 1625 to 1650 when the settlers consumed less wild game and more beef.[4]

Protected by law

Increasing numbers of cattle in the settlement created concerns both about the well-being of the livestock and about the possibility of crop damage. In 1611 deputy governor Sir Thomas Dale ordered the construction of a block house on Jamestown Island to protect the cattle. It was hoped that greater attention paid by settlers to agricultural pursuits would result in an increase of livestock as is evidenced by the February 1611 council declaration: ". . . Wth garden seeds and feed grounde the first yeare besides pasture, feeding, and mastage for his cattell. . . .And as god shall blesse the increase of cattle, hereafter, enye house shal be allowed a cowe, and two Goats."[5]

Still, convincing the colonists to protect their livestock for breeding purposes was not easy. In 1612 the governor found it necessary to make the killing of any livestock a capital offense. Whether the animal was owned by the individual or the Virginia Company did not matter.[6] Perhaps the official intimidation worked, for by 1614 one observer counted 200 cattle in the colony. In 1616 John Rolfe found only 144, but he was very specific in identifying their types: he counted 83 cows, heifers, and calves, 41 steers, and 20 bulls.[7]

Colonists' preoccupation with tobacco cultivation, their conflicts with Native Americans, and depredations of wolves (something husbandmen in England had not worried about since the 1400s), caused the number of cattle to increase only very slowly. The colony's leaders, recognizing the problem, declared in the summer of 1619:

> No man, without leave of the Governor, shall kill any Neatt cattle whatsoever, young or olde, especially kine, Heyfurs or cow-calves, and shal be careful to preserve their steers and oxen, and to bring them to the plough and such profitable uses, and without having obtained leave as aforesaid, shall not kill them, upon penalty of forfeiting the value of the beast so killed.[8]

It must have been difficult for men and women plagued with almost constant pangs of hunger to refrain from eating their breeding stock.

As the Virginia Company struggled to survive in the New World, efforts to import more livestock increased. One hundred and twelve cattle arrived in Virginia in 1619, including those on the vessel "Triall." Government records noted that "the Cattle in the Triall came exceeding well, and gave the Colony much ioy [joy] and greate incouragemt."[9] In September of 1619 one writer noted that "For cattle, they do mightily increase here, both kine, hogges, & goates, and are much greater in stature, then the race of them first brought out of England. . . ."[10] In the fall of 1619, the company proposed importing twenty heifers for each 100 new settlers with the hope that the heifers would reproduce quickly and replenish herds of livestock.[11]

Despite the continuing imports of cattle, the bovine presence in the New World remained tenuous. Cattle numbers had increased to only 500 by 1620.[12] At one meeting of the council in that year, a proposal to send 500 more tenants for company land, 100 cattle for use by the new colonists, and an additional 100 cattle for perpetuating the herd on company land, met with favor. Unfortunately, the Virginia Company's treasury was nearly empty.[13] With an

This intact calf leg, found in the 1610 remains of a cellar within the walls of James Fort, represents the first documented bovine in Virginia.

eye toward greatly increasing the number of cattle, in 1620 the company contracted with Daniel Gookin, an Irish sea captain and merchant who was probably already trading with Virginia, to import cattle into the colony. Gookin was to import cattle to Virginia payable at the rate of £11 sterling or 130 pounds of tobacco per heifer on evidence of their safe arrival on Virginia soil. Another contract the following year authorized Gookin to sell cattle privately to individual settlers as well as to the London Company.[14]

Shipping lists for 1621 indicate that forty cattle came on the *Flying Hart*, another forty on the *White Lion*, and eighty on the *James*. It is not certain, however, whether these "cattle" were bovines or other livestock.[15] Gookin was not the only captain looking to make money from the livestock trade. In October of 1621, the company encouraged outlying settlements beyond Jamestown proper to take advantage of the same trade opportunity come spring.

Notice was also given that ther were certaine sufficient men come out of Ireland would undertake to transporte many hundreds of Cattle to Virginia this Springe upon the same Condicons that mr Gookin had donne; Itt was therefore moved that Southampton Hundred, Martins Hundred, Berkleys Hundred, and all other private Plantacons that desired to have Cattle would be pleased out of hand to give speedy notice what numbers of Cattle they would have. . . .[16]

By 1621 about 2,000 humans inhabited the colony, along with about 800 cattle. Livestock numbers likely rose as cattle importation continued into the spring of 1622. In March, Gookin's ship had arrived with forty young cattle. Any colonist "encouraged upon this good newes to transport Cattle out of Ireland," could enter into a private contract with Gookin by promising him 100 pounds of tobacco for every heifer "safely delivered in Virginia."[17]

Within a few weeks of Gookin's shipment, Jamestown suffered a massive setback. An attack by the Powhatan Indians on March 22, 1622, left 347 people (more than a sixth of the English population) dead and the remainder thoroughly disheartened. Much of the surrounding countryside had also been ravaged in the attack and the livestock scattered and killed.

Cattle gain a foothold

The massacre in the spring of 1622 dealt a grave blow to the livestock populations of the struggling colony, but it was not a death knell. Unfortunately, however, the situation worsened before it improved. The winter following the massacre, 1622-1623, brought more disease and death among man and beast. "...Our people as our Cattle have dyed, that we are all undone," wrote one man.[18] William Rowlsley of James City wrote to his brother, "As you know this land hath felt the affliction of Warr, sense of sickness and death of a great number of men, likewise among the Cattle for dogs have eaten in this winter more flesh then the men. . . . . and for tame Cattle there have so many died and ben killd otherwayes that there is no more to be had."[19] To prevent slaughter of the remaining stock, the governor declared martial law. Stealing "any Beaste or Birde of Domesticall or tame nature, that is to say, Horses, Mares, Colts, Oxen, Kine, Calfes, Sheeps, Lambs, Goats, Kidds, Swine, Piggs, Hens, Geese, Ducks, Peacocks, Turkeys, or any of like sorte" was a felony. If the value of the animal exceeded twelve pence, the thief could be executed. Otherwise the offender could be whipped or punished in a man-

The Characteristics of Virginia's Early Cattle

Until the late eighteenth and early nineteenth centuries, no recognizable breeds of livestock existed anywhere in the world, although, numerous isolated populations of animals had interbred and developed distinct regional characteristics. Cattle in a given geographic region had developed certain color patterns and horn lengths distinctive from those of other areas. Adaptation to forage or terrain produced still other differences such as size and

degree of hardiness. Selective breeding of livestock to create improved, more homogeneous animals was not undertaken until the late 1700s when an English farmer named Robert Bakewell began experimenting with selective breeding of cattle, sheep, and horses. Before then, most husbandmen thought that the best way to improve an animal was to feed it more. Most farmers sent the biggest and best animals to market in order to obtain more money, and kept the small, poorer quality animals for breeding.

Although no specific livestock breeds existed when importation of cattle to Virginia began in the early seventeenth century, scholars know enough about the characteristics of these animals to tie them to several modern breeds. Today most of those are classified as minor breeds whose global population numbers have plummeted. Some have even become extinct. Most of those early animals were notably hardy; they could forage in difficult terrain and endure bad weather. Also, they were triple-purpose cattle, meaning that they were used for draft power, dairy products, and meat.

In the modern world of quality animal housing, new veterinary medicines, and scientifically-engineered foods, cattle that can survive and thrive under the harshest

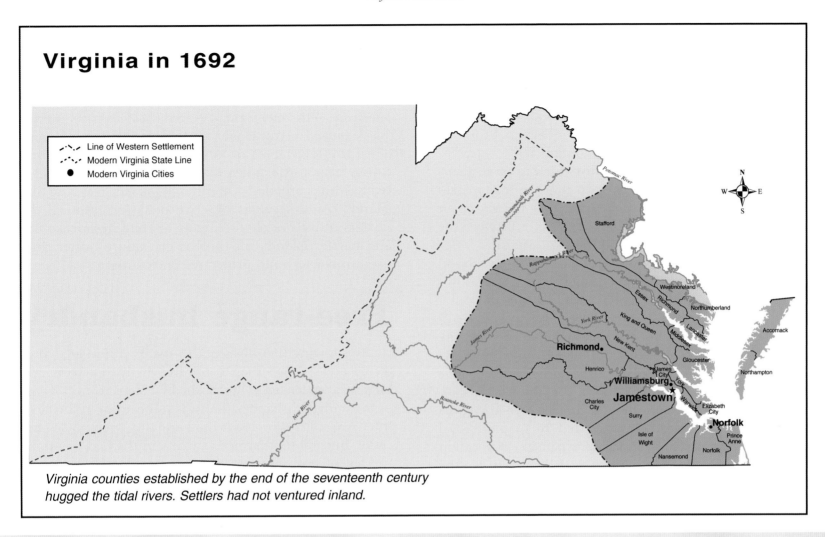

Virginia in 1692

Line of Western Settlement
Modern Virginia State Line
● Modern Virginia Cities

Virginia counties established by the end of the seventeenth century hugged the tidal rivers. Settlers had not ventured inland.

conditions are no longer needed. Cattle breeds have been developed that outproduce any of the old triple purpose breeds. Specialization of purpose between dairy and beef production have made those old types of cattle obsolete. They were good for three purposes, but not outstanding for any. Gradually in the nineteenth century, new breeds like the Holstein, Hereford, and Angus replaced English regional types like the Devon, Alderney, Shorthorn, Kerry, Suffolk Dun, and Gloucester. The older types fell into disfavor and their numbers plunged downward. The Suffolk Dun and the Alderney are extinct, two of seven English cattle breeds that disappeared in the twentieth century.

The rise of domesticated cattle

Tracing the origin of cattle breeds makes an interesting detective story. Inhabitants of the Mediterranean region first domesticated cattle more than 10,000 years ago, even before the horse. All modern breeds descend from *Bos primigenius*. From that ancient animal, four modern strains developed: Hamitic Longhorn, Hamitic Shorthorn, Humped Longhorn, and Humped Shorthorn. All modern bovines descend from one or more of those types. The cattle brought to early Virginia

came from either western Europe or the British Isles. In Spain, the strongest genetic link is to the Hamitic Longhorn that spread across Europe four thousand years ago. Modern descendants of that strain include the Irish Kerry, Welsh Black, Scottish Highland, White Park, Camargue, and the Longhorn. The horn spread of these animals is wide and their horns curve upward. Fossil remains of

ner deemed proper by the local magistrate.[20] For breaking this law, several hungry settlers found themselves facing a future as indentured servants. "Two or 3 freemen that wanted flesh must needs goe into the woods to kill a deere but in stead of the deere they shott yor Calfe, but they are confined to serve the Colony 7 yeares for it."[21]

After the losses of 1622, colonists tried to protect surviving livestock more carefully. Soon after the 1622 massacre, colonists were ordered to draw together and have their "grounds impailed for the keeping of Cattle."[22] Between the Starving Time of 1609-1610 and the 1622 Massacre, colonists had constructed a series of palisaded rings around the animals and crops. The first ring enclosed the houses and other buildings of settlements, while the second, outer ring, provided a secure grazing area for livestock. By 1613 at Rochedale Hundred, for example, a palisaded enclosure allowed "our Hogs and cattell [to] have twentie miles circuit to graze in securely." By 1624, Virginia had become a royal colony under the direction of the king and his appointed governor; the private, stockholder-owned Virginia Company of London no longer existed. In 1630 the royal governor, John Harvey, planned an expansive fortification consisting of a paling fence many miles long between the James and the York Rivers. The idea was to "add safety, strength, plenty, and increase of cattle to the plantation

and greate advantage from that place to assaile the enemy."[23] Work began on the giant fence in early 1634, and the enclosure dramatically altered the appearance of the landscape. A traveler soon observed that Governor Harvey "hath caused a strong palisade to be builded . . . whereby all of the lower part of Virginia have a range for their cattle, near fortie miles in length and in most places twelve miles broade."[24] In other instances, realizing that islands could serve as effective pens for animals, the settlers moved cattle to islands in the Chesapeake Bay and barrier islands off the Eastern Shore rather than use lumber to build protective enclosures.

Free-range husbandry

By allowing their livestock to roam within large, protected areas rather than confining them to a barnyard, Virginia's settlers were taking the first steps toward a type of free-range husbandry that was unheard of in England. Intensive cultivation made draft animals, both horses and cattle, integral to a farmer's success in the Old World. By the seventeenth century, dairying was also an important economic activity (usually performed by women) within a yeoman household. The yeoman and his wife kept milk

these animals have been found in Neolithic sites across Great Britain.

The short-horn and polled gene, which descended mostly from the Hamitic Shorthorn, did not reach Britain until the Iron Age (circa 250 B.C. to 400A.D.). At that time, animals from the Germanic regions of Europe enlarged the genetic pool of cattle in the British Isles. Those animals reinforced the short or medium-horned characteristic and added a predominantly red color. Many red-colored British beef breeds, like the Danish Red and the Lincoln Red, originated in this line.

The Vikings (or Norse), who migrated to England in the eighth and ninth centuries, introduced new characteristics into the island's bovine gene pool. These included a polled gene, dun coloring, and a black and white pattern. Scholars think that many of the Channel Island breeds such as the Jersey, the Irish Moiled, the Shetland, the Shorthorn, and the Red Poll, came from the blood of bovines brought to the British Isles by the Vikings.

Geographic isolation influenced this gene pool over time as cattle in specific regions of England and Ireland

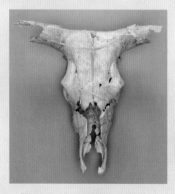

The archaeology lab at Colonial Williamsburg houses this skull of a Devon cow from about 1650 excavated from a well in Portsmouth.

developed characteristics that differed from cattle in other regions. In the midlands, the predominant color was red with varying degrees of white markings. Animals tended to be darker red and have less white in the south of the island. Eight or ten red-colored British breeds, including the Shorthorn (originally called Durham), Red Poll, Hereford, Gloucester, and the Devon, originated in the south of England.

Virginia's early cattle

The modern breed that most closely matches the animals brought to the Virginia colony in the first half of the seventeenth century is probably the dark red Devon. In the geographically isolated counties of Somerset, Devon, and Cornwall, there arose a very early type of cattle that was as close to a breed as existed in that time. By the 1760s, animals with those particular characteristics from that geographic region had become recognized as a specific breed called Devon although their distinctiveness had been created several hundred years earlier. Like all colonial-era cattle, Devons were triple-purpose animals,

Finchback or lineback cattle were a type that may have accompanied seventeenth century settlers to Virginia.

but they were most prized as oxen. In 1623 the Massachusetts colony imported a bull and three heifers from Devonshire. An intact cattle skull unearthed in a 1650 well by Colonial Williamsburg's archaeological team is identical in appearance to known Devon skulls.

The Durham emerged near the Tees River in England. By the mid-seventeenth century a recognizable type of animal called the Teeswater arose in that region. This red, red and white, or roan animal with short horns, could easily have been among those brought to the Tidewater settlements. One hundred and fifty years later, back in England, these animals would provide the genetic stock for the development of one of the first true breeds of cattle, which came to be called Durham and then, eventually, Shorthorn.

Today's modern Red Poll breed also has its roots in older British types of animals. During the seventeenth century, settlers arriving in Virginia from England's eastern shires of Norfolk and Suffolk brought small, dun-colored polled animals called Suffolk Duns and larger, red horned animals called Norfolks. The mixture of these animals produced red "muley" cattle that were common in colonial Virginia. The word "muley" is a corruption of the Celtic

word moile, which means hornless. Although the Suffolk Dun is extinct, its lineage continues in the Red Poll.

The cattle of early Virginia were varied. Many may have had red coloring, others black. Some had longhorns, others short, and a significant number would have been naturally polled (muley) cattle. The absence of documentary evidence providing adequately specific descriptions of Virginia's early cattle makes it impossible to be definitive about their appearance and characteristics. Given such vague early descriptions, it is not possible to be more definitive about the appearance and characteristics of Virginia's early bovine inhabitants. ~

Lawrence Alderson, in his book *The Chance to Survive* (London: Christopher Helm, 1989) traces the genetic history of cattle as well as any other source. Alderson's work was sponsored by Great Britain's Rare Breeds Survival Trust. Specific breed histories for animals that were imported to America can be found in the *American Minor Breeds Notebook*, compiled by Laurie Heise and Carolyn Christman of the American Livestock Breeds Conservancy in Pittsboro, N.C. Otis L. Fisher of Augusta County, has probably gathered more Shorthorn research than anyone. His volume, *Shorthorns Around the World*, details much of that information. Ralph E. Ward's research report, "Appropriate Rare Breeds of Cattle," which he produced for the Colonial Williamsburg Foundation in 1985, helped sort out the similarities and connections between modern breeds and their eighteenth-century counterparts.

cows under close supervision, often housed them in barns, and fed them well. For a number of reasons, a similar agricultural system did not transfer to Virginia. The shift to free-range husbandry is one of the most significant developments in the early history of cattle in Virginia.

In England, a principal reason for owning and caring for cattle was to use them as draft animals in plowing fields. But in Virginia the colonists concentrated on cultivating tobacco and corn rather than cereal grains such as wheat and barley, and, following Native American practice, they did so with hoes, not plows. Eight years after the founding of Jamestown, leaders only "hoped" that three or four plows would start being used to till the soil. Captain John Smith said the problem was not the lack of oxen, but the lack of trained plowmen.[25] As late as 1650, with a white population of around 12,000, only 150 plows were to be found in Virginia. In 1686, a visiting Frenchman wrote that Virginians "do not know what it is to work the land with cattle."[26] Little need for plows reduced the need for draft power, one of the three main uses for cattle.

Although dairying provided important dietary supplement in the first century of Chesapeake settlement, it never received the attention that it did in England. Traditionally, dairying probably received little emphasis as an economic activity because of the relatively few women in the settlements. Dairy production also suffered under the hotter Virginia climate and the poorer forage available to cows. During the summer, the typical cow produced one or two quarts of low-butterfat milk. Late in the century an Anglican minister living in the colony noted that the people refrained from milking cows at all in the winter for fear it would kill the animals. With such low production levels in comparison to New England or England and without cold streams in which to chill cream and butter, it was little wonder that inferior products resulted.[27]

Dairy production was the second of three qualities for which cattle were prized. The third was for meat. Even after early restrictions on the slaughter of cattle had been lifted, many years passed before cattle other than excess bulls and worn-out oxen and milk cows

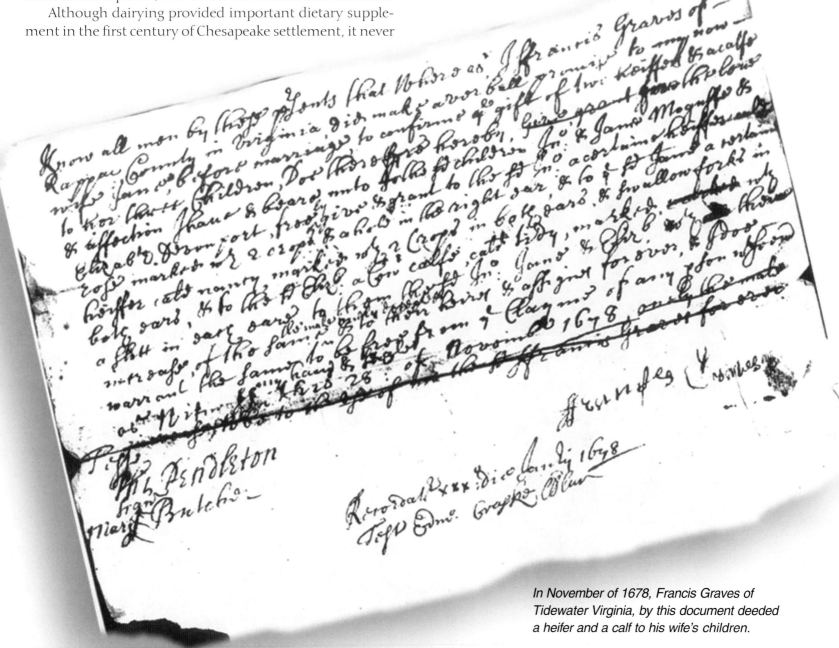

In November of 1678, Francis Graves of Tidewater Virginia, by this document deeded a heifer and a calf to his wife's children.

were killed and eaten. As late as 1630 the legislature cautioned the colonists to curtail the slaughter of female cattle unless they were past breeding age or "likely to dye by some infirmity."[28] The beef on the dinner table then would hardly have been the tender steak we have come to savor in the twenty-first century.

Hoe cultivation of crops and free-range livestock created an agricultural system very different than that prevailing in England. This newly evolved system soon received legislative recognition and sanction, for between 1632 and 1646 the assembly passed what was probably the first free-range laws in North America. A Virginia statute of 1632 declared that "every man shall enclose his ground with sufficient fences or else to plant, upon theire own peril."[29] Thus, colonists were required to fence their crops to protect them from free-ranging animals. Three years later, an effective fence was defined as being four-and-a-half feet high and "substantiall close downe to the bottom." If a stray animal breached such a fence, its owner, if one could be identified, could be held liable for damages. Land owners with less substantial fences had no legal grounds for complaint when livestock damaged their crops.[30] Virginia statutes thus reversed the English practice of holding livestock owners responsible for crop damages.

The free-range livestock practice in colonial Virginia also created a different landscape. The English countryside demonstrated neatness and order with animals penned near the barnyard or grazing under the supervision of a cowherd or shepherd. The Virginia landscape, by contrast, featured small pockets of settlement where crops of tobacco and corn were fenced in for protection amid giant swatches of unimproved land, both forested and open. Roaming through those forests, pastures, and swamps were domestic animals that were hardly more tame than the land on which they foraged.

Native scrub cattle

The effects of indiscriminate breeding, severe climate and lack of proper diet on unsupervised, mongrel cattle, which Virginians would come to call "native scrub," were obvious to European visitors. Throughout the seventeenth century, visitors to the colony aimed more than a few barbs at Virginia farmers for their careless animal husbandry. As early as 1613, one settler noted that the livestock would thrive "if they might bee provided for." But close supervision of the colony's animals was not to be. In the 1670s Thomas Glover explained that the small size of the ani-

Cattle in seventeenth-century Virginia were triple purpose: beef, dairy, and draft.

27

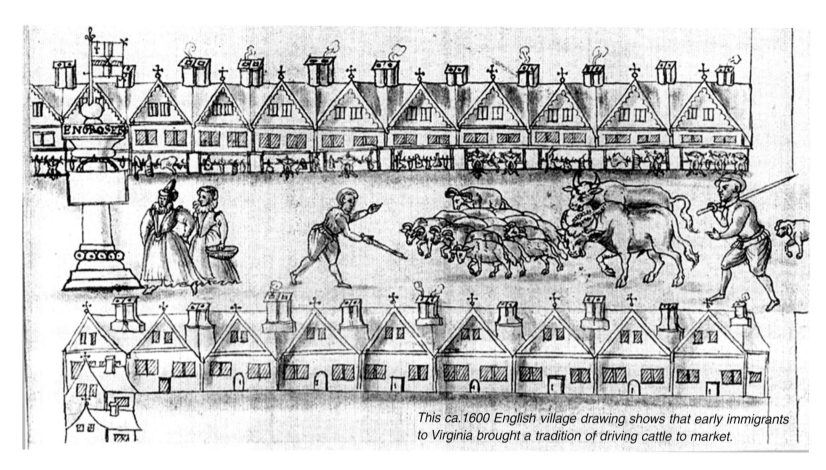

This ca.1600 English village drawing shows that early immigrants to Virginia brought a tradition of driving cattle to market.

mals resulted from their lack of care: "[the cattle] might be much larger than they are, were the Inhabitants as careful in looking after them and providing fodder for them as they in *England* are." He added that even in the winter the cattle were given only corn husks, which forced them to search for food in "marshy grounds and swamps . . . where very many are lost."[31] A French visitor in 1686 was one of many observers who noted that the colonists gave their animals nothing to eat or drink and devoted no time to putting up hay for winter foodstocks. He further criticized Virginians for having no mercy upon their cattle even in the thick of winter when he said, "I saw the poor beasts of a morning all covered with snow and trembling with the cold, but no forage was provided for them. They eat the bark of the trees because the grass was covered." His final comment regarding the colonists' poor animal husbandry practices testifies to the hardiness of cattle in the New World. "Despite this treatment. I saw no dead cattle."[32] These visitors were viewing cattle in light of Old World husbandry while the cattle themselves were adapting to New World conditions and agricultural practices.

The New World

Archaeological evidence from hundreds of Tidewater sites also reveals, surprisingly, that these scrub animals grew to almost modern size late in the seventeenth century despite a less-than-superior attendance to livestock needs by planters and yeomen alike. The

reason, theorize some archaeologists, is that even as the cattle were adapting to the New World, so, too, were the plants that had been part of bovine diets in the Old World for generations. Those seeds hitchhiked to Virginia via animal fur and human clothing as well as in straw bedding and hay packed in ships. Populations of those Old World plants took root and spread across the countryside even as cattle were doing the same. Once more suitable forage was available in the colony, the cattle populations prospered despite inadequate attention from human caretakers.[33]

Although the conditions of free-range husbandry remained far from ideal, cattle began to multiply. At first the increase was slow. In 1625, at 365 head, cattle numbers were barely above pre-massacre levels. By 1649, however, Virginians owned about 20,000 head of cattle and they had started shipping surplus animals to other English colonies, especially those in New England and Barbados.[34]

Cowpenning

Late in the seventeenth century, Virginia colonists adapted their free-range system of cattle husbandry to improve productivity of their tobacco and grain farming. Occasionally planters rounded up their cattle and turned them onto a field — probably luring them with grain or fodder — allowing them to graze the remnants of a recently harvested crop. Cowpenning also led to improved care for animals but this was probably incidental. Early adherents of this practice urged its wider adoption. John Clayton, rector of the church at Jamestown from 1684 to 1686, recommended to one of his parishioners that she "sow her Wheat as early as possible" so that in the spring of the year she could turn her winter-weakened cattle upon it for nourishment. He also recommended that she plant sainfoin (a beanlike plant used as fodder) on the field where the cattle were to be penned so that the animals could be nourished and the fields fertilized simultaneously, which the English had done very successfully. The French visitor, Durand of Dauphiné, who complained of the colonists' ill treatment of their livestock, observed some rudimentary cowpenning in 1687: "As to wheat at M. Wormeley's plantations I saw the cows, horses & sheep grazing on it. It was Christmastime when I was there, & I told him they would spoil it. The servants replied that they left the cattle there until the fifteenth of March."[35]

Cowpenning for tobacco was practiced at least as early as 1688. By the 1790s, it had become a general practice. Tobacco wears out the soil quickly. Consequently, colonists let fields lie fallow for many years and faced the constant need to clear new fields or find a way to revitalize the soil through fertilization. All three methods were used, but as new lands became increasingly difficult to find, ever increasing numbers of farmers began penning cattle on tobacco and grain fields so that soils could be revitalized by animal manure. Obviously, following free-ranging animals around in order to collect manure was impractical and penning animals in a barnyard meant that feed had to be hauled to the animals and manure then had to be hauled to the field. So the practice of cowpenning was born. The owner of the cattle was reimbursed per head for the manure that his animals provided the farmer. The cost to the tobacco farmer was often more than that of opening up a new piece of land, but the cost was worth it once land had become scarce and therefore expensive. As late as 1800 an agricultural manual recommended that half a dozen cattle be penned on small blocks of tobacco land each night and that the pens be moved slowly until "a sufficient quantity of manure is deposited." The pens were made of split rails and so they were easily built and dismantled for moving. The split-rail fences came to be called zig-zag or Virginia worm fences. Cowpenning and free-range husbandry continued well into the nineteenth century, when it was recommended that 100 cattle be penned in an area of tobacco land where 1,000 plants were to be raised. The pens were moved weekly.[36]

Despite their free-ranging existence and lack of close human contact, each animal, in principle at least, had an owner, who counted that animal among his wealth. When possible, animals were marked by ear crops or brands, or they wore bells to identify them as belonging to a particular owner. Customarily, an individual's wealth was counted in land first, slaves second, and cattle third. Cattle were a sign of wealth and civility. Very telling is a 1656 statute passed by the Virginia House of Burgesses that rewarded with a cow, any Indian who turned in a wolf pelt to government authorities. The motive of the Burgesses was twofold: the countryside would be rid of a carnivore that preyed upon livestock and the colony would have taken "a step to civilizing" the Native Americans "and to making them Christians."[37]

> *Cattle were a sign of wealth and civility. Very telling is a 1656 statute passed by the Virginia House of Burgesses that rewarded with a cow, any Indian who turned in a wolf pelt to government authorities.*

Settlement Expansion

During the 1630s and 1640s English colonists expanded settlement to areas beyond the bottomlands along the James and York Rivers. In early Virginia, land could be acquired by purchasing a "bill of adventure" (similar to a stock share) in the London Company, or by having performed some meritorious service for the colony, or by headright. This last method granted fifty acres in fee simple to anyone who paid his passage to Virginia and another fifty acres for each additional person, such as family members or servants, that he brought over to Virginia.[38]

One early field of migration for expanded settlement was the Eastern Shore, that narrow neck of land between the Chesapeake Bay and the Atlantic Ocean. Salt extraction and fishing had been the major economic activities of the region in the days of the Virginia Company. Little land had been patented and settled by yeoman farmers, although Sir Thomas Dale, the governor in 1616, patented some 1,500 acres, and later his widow, Lady Elizabeth Dale, acquired an additional 3,000 acres. Governor George Yeardley and Ensign Thomas Savage also received large Eastern Shore grants, but most mid-century grants were in small amounts. In the 1630s, the average grant was for 482 acres, and for 345 acres in the 1640s.[39]

Eastern Shore settlers realized early the value of raising cattle. Lady Dale (although she was an absentee owner) was one of English-America's first large-scale cattle producers. As Lady Dale was in England, she engaged men in the

1620s and 1630s to manage the plantation, including an extensive herd of cattle. In 1636, she authorized her overseer to sell all but one hundred of her cattle, instructing him that "I would have you reserve a hundred kine and young cattle together for my use and breed although you should be offered a very great price for them."[40] The barrier islands in the Atlantic and islands in the Chesapeake offered a protected area for cattle to range. The 500 acres of Smith Island, first patented in 1636, eventually came into the hands of John Custis, who guarded his cattle there jealously. In 1675 he threatened to sue anyone who came to the island to hunt game. The owners of Hog Island's 3,350 acres posted a similar notice in 1681.[41]

Eastern Shore settlers realized early the value of raising cattle.

Another Eastern Shore cattle entrepreneur later in the seventeenth was the Reverend Thomas Teackle. He was parish minister of the established Church of England for both St. George's Parish in Accomack County and Northampton Parish in Northampton County, for forty-four years from 1652 to his death in1696. Teackle, one of the wealthiest ministers in the colonies, amassed a considerable fortune in land and slaves. His wealth derived from his activities as a farmer and a merchant, as well as his salary from tithes. Teackle was a partner in trading ventures with the West Indies that could well have involved cattle. He owned eleven slaves at the time of his death. Most of them assisted him in cultivating the two glebes, or farms, provided by the two parishes Teackle served, as well as his own land. Cattle-raising operations formed a significant part of his farming. In 1672, he and his business partners complained to the county court that wild or stray cattle had damaged their enclosure or cattle pens.[42]

A seafaring trade

As early as the 1630s, planters on the Eastern Shore developed a significant ocean borne trade with other colonies, especially New England, New Netherlands (modern-day New York), and the West Indies, trading first in corn, but soon in cattle as well. In 1633, for example, a Dutch sea captain encountered an Eastern Shore trader, John Stone, bound for Boston with a cargo of corn and cattle. The trade must have grown so extensive that there was some alarm about depletion of Virginia's livestock base. The 1639-1640 session of the Virginia General Assembly passed a law limiting export of cattle from Virginia to one-seventh of a herd.[43]

Besides the trade in cattle on the hoof, some Virginians began to develop a trade with Barbados in barrelled pork and beef. One observer remarked that "the Virginians cannot have a better market to sell them; for an Oxe 5£. [pound] price at Virginie, will yield 25£. there." A later observer noted that the Virginians could do as well by increasing their trade in cattle, beef, pork, and provisions with Barbados as the New Englanders do with the Sugar Islands, but that "all their thoughts run upon Tobacco," so that they fail to take advantage of such opportunities.[44]

Another aspect of the flourishing cattle trade that took place on the Eastern Shore was the tanning of leather from cowhides. A shortage of labor may have prevented this from becoming a more significant trade, however. In the 1660s, complaints from two entrepreneurs highlight this problem. One large landowner bemoaned that his currier had left the job with more than one hundred hides ready for him and fourteen shoemakers were thus left with no work for lack of finished leather. Another entrepreneur complained that he had five hundred hides ruined because they lacked "timely tanning." [45]

Settlers in Tidewater

The rapid dispersal of the Virginia population not only to the Eastern Shore but throughout the Tidewater region of Virginia, is generally attributed to the spread of tobacco culture, which depleted the soil and necessitated the fallowing of fields. In recent years, agricultural historians, reassessing this interpretation, have suggested that the needs of the livestock, especially cattle, may have played the paramount role in the dispersed settlement pattern.

Caring for the cows and dairy products was an important aspect of women's work on a seventeenth century Virginia plantation.

With the relatively infrequent use of oxen for tilling, with the limited success of dairying in Virginia, and with the adoption of free-range animal husbandry, Virginia settlers needed more and more land for their agricultural practices. Experts estimate that a single free-range cow needed five acres of pinewoods in summer and fifteen in winter to sustain itself. Cows or steers foraging in the woods damage the undergrowth, so that in time more forest acreage would be needed to sustain the same herd. This was not a problem for the very wealthy planters who had amassed several thousand acres, most of which they left in woodland for their livestock. It was a major problem, however, for those who owned less than 500 acres – the majority of the planters. These small planters typically had perhaps 10 cattle and 10 swine, which would have required 150 to 200 acres of woodland to sustain them. Such small operators depended on access to unpatented public lands for their livestock to forage.[46]

One area of significant expansion of settlement was the land between the York and the Rappahannock Rivers. Captain John Smith had sailed along the junction of the two rivers in an exploratory trip to the upper Chesapeake in 1608, but it was not until the 1640s that the area opened for settlement. Although this land was set aside for Indians in the treaty following the second major Native American uprising, which occurred in 1646, it did not remain theirs for long. In that very year the first "settlement" of the lands along the Piankatank River in present Middlesex County occurred with the transportation of cattle there by boat. They were left to graze on the river's meadows. Two years later, owners, claiming that their cattle and hogs had overgrazed the area, needed more land, so the treaty terms were set aside and the area opened for settlement.[47]

The Northern Neck, that area between the Rappahannock and Potomac Rivers, also opened for settlement in the 1640s. Although this area was later to be the domain of Lord Fairfax and the home base of the powerful Carter family, its early settlers were mainly small planters. John Taylor in the Fleets Bay area, for example, worked his 400-acre plantation with one servant boy and his wife. At his death in 1653, Taylor's modest estate included six milk cows, a bull, a calf, three "young beasts" and a couple dozen hogs.[48]

As new lands became available for settlement, they offered the possibility for unscrupulous settlers to help themselves to the free-ranging cattle of others and take them off to the frontier. This caused the House of Burgesses to legislate in 1658 that persons planning to leave a settled area for the frontier must give notice of their intention, pay their debts, and have four neighbors certify that any cattle they planned to take with them actually belonged to them.[49]

A wealth of cattle

Ralph Wormeley, a man whose descendants were significant cattle breeders in the area that became Middlesex County, arrived in 1649 to stake out 3,000 acres on Rosegill Creek. Wormeley soon died and his widow, Agatha Eltonhead Wormeley, remarried to Henry Chichley. Agatha Chichley exemplified the significance of cattle as valuable, prized possessions in seventeenth-century Virginia. She deeded a "black-browed cow" by the name of Thacker to her niece, Eltonhead Connoway, daughter of her sister, Martha, who lived across the Rappahannock in Lancaster County. Agatha mentioned "the love and affecion I beare unto my neece" as the reason for her gift, which was of sufficient value to be recorded in a deed with the clerk of the county court.[50]

Presenting a cow, a cow and a calf, or a cow and her increase was an important means of trying to guarantee financial security for a daughter, a grandchild, or a godchild in colonial Virginia. This was particularly true in the middle of the seventeenth century, before slavery became entrenched in Virginia. Later, the gift of a slave, or a female slave and her increase, would replace the gift of a cow among wealthier Virginians, but smaller planters and their wives continued the gift of cattle to cherished family members and friends.

Another early example of bestowing a cow as a gift appears in the deed to Bartram Obert, a Dutch settler in Virginia, from Sir John Harvey, governor of Virginia, made on May 3, 1640. Obert accompanied Harvey to England in the "good ship the Planter of London," attending the governor while he took a cure in Bath. His reward was the gift of a "negro woman," the remaining year's service of a young indentured servant, and "one milch cow called Goulding" that was on Jamestown Island. Harvey further stipulated that in case that particular cow "shal by misfortune dye or be lost" then Obert could have any other out of "the stock of cattle belonging to me in this Colony of Virginia."[51]

When Obert died nineteen years later in January 1660, his own will made careful provision for the disposal of his cattle so that each of his four children would be remembered. His elder son, Bartram, received land and a cow called Cole with her calf and a yearling heifer. The elder daughter, Lettice, received land, a cow, a calf, and a yearling heifer. The younger daughter, Agatha, received land and two cows called Sloe and Starr. The younger son, Chichester, received a slave instead of a cow, while the remainder of Obert's land, cattle, and chattels went to his widow Ann.[52] This will is typical of dozens of others probated in Virginia in the mid-seventeenth century. What stands out clearly is that in spite of free range practices prevailing in Virginia, many planters knew their stock well enough to name individual animals and divide them thoughtfully among their children to provide for their future well-being.

A cow as inheritance could make a difference in the life of a woman far less well-placed in colonial Virginia society than the Obert daughters. Hannah Provert began life as the illegitimate daughter of a servant woman in Middlesex County. As a ward of the parish, she was bound out as a servant to Nicholas West. He proved to be a generous master and left her seventy-five acres and a heifer. When she married William Provert, who had also been a servant, they had land of their own and a cow to help them get started as small planters.[53]

In Warwick County, between the James and the York Rivers, in 1660 a widow, Temperance Oxwicke, in making good the intentions of her late husband, noted that "out of a motherly affecion [I] bequeath unto my eldest daughter Temperance Oxwicke foure cowes. . . knowne formerly by these names the one Dainty the second Glow, the third Crump the fourth whitefoot." This document is one of many in a volume called *Warwick County Cattle (Livestock) Accounts 1656-1685*. The purpose of the book was to record the livestock that had been left to orphans, and for which their guardians had to provide annual accounting to the county court.[54] Its existence indicates the great value early Virginians placed upon cattle.

Guardians of the orphan children of the late Captain Thomas Harwood of Warwick County reported in 1656 that the children had seven draft oxen, six steers between four and five years of age, three steers between three and four years, one steer and a bull between two and three years old, three cows, three young cows that had their first calves, five heifers that were four years old, one yearling heifer and a bull, six weaned calves, and one "steare seene at springe but not yet found." By the next year, the guardians reported

that the missing steer was still roaming, that one old ox had died in the winter as well as one old cow and two calves. The children's inheritance seemed to be dwindling.[55]

Another legal instrument that featured the use of cattle to provide a measure of financial security was the prenuptial agreement. Before Francis Graves of Old Rappahannock County married the widow Jane McGuffe [McGuffey], he promised to give a cow to each of her children, John, Jane, and Elizabeth, at some point in the future. In November, 1678, Graves made good on his promise, providing two heifers and a calf for that purpose in a deed of gift. The earmarks for each of the animals were carefully listed in the document, which was recorded at the courthouse in January 1679, perhaps at the time Graves died.[56]

As the first century of English settlement in Virginia drew to a close, the colony that had survived starvation, near-extinction from a massacre, and political upheaval, was firmly established as a successful venture. From one struggling settlement behind a paling fence on Jamestown Island in 1607, Virginians had spread north, south, east, and west. They had settled the eastern part of the present state, from the Eastern Shore to the Potomac River in the north, to the Dismal Swamp in the south, and to the fall line of the great Tidewater rivers in the west. Twenty-four counties had been carved out of territory taken or otherwise acquired from the Native American tribes. Each county in turn had been settled with an assortment of large planters, small planters, tenant farmers, craftsmen, indentured servants, and slaves. Except for a few enclaves, the Native Americans had been pushed west. The New World crop of tobacco had created great wealth for the few and great hopes for the many. The system of chattel slavery imposed on Africans imported to Virginia expanded rapidly as the seventeenth century drew to a close, creating a New World society unlike England, and tying agriculture to the production of one major cash crop produced for a European market.

English emigrants who endured the long Atlantic voyage to Virginia included four-legged creatures as well as the men, women, and children. Foremost among the livestock were cattle. Just as the settlers had to develop new ways of taming the land, adapting to the soil and climate, and developing a new kind of agriculture, they also had to develop new methods for their livestock. The careful handling, feeding, and housing of cattle that characterized the gentry, yeomen, and husbandmen of Elizabethan and Jacobean England had to be abandoned in Virginia. The adoption of a cash crop, tobacco, that did not require draft animals, and the shortage of labor and poor climate for dairying led Virginians to adopt a free-range system for their cattle. In Virginia, cattle became principally a source of beef. Yet cattle were clearly prized in seventeenth-century Virginia, being considered one of the principal measures of wealth and a significant means of granting financial security to children and loved ones through wills, deeds of gift, and prenuptial agreements. The numerous laws regulating the protection and marking of cattle stand as testimony to their value in the Virginia economy, even as it matured and developed in ways far different from those familiar back in England.

Cattle and the Colonists

In the seventeenth century, cattle operations in Virginia were restricted to the narrow band of land comprising the Eastern Shore and the Tidewater. During the new eighteenth century, however, Virginians expanded to the west, opening new lands to settlement. The lands included western parts of Lord Fairfax's Northern Neck Proprietary, the Piedmont region south of the James, and the Great Valley of Virginia. This expansion increased the settled area of Virginia, promoted population growth, and brought ethnic diversity to the colony.

The population of seventeenth-century Virginia was racially diverse, composed of Native Americans, English, and Africans. In the eighteenth century, however, the number of Native Americans shrank, while numbers of Europeans increased. The introduction of colonies of French Huguenots at Manakin in 1705 and German Reformed and Lutheran colonies at Germanna in 1714 and 1717 marked the first influx of non-English populations in the colony. Large numbers of German and Scotch-Irish dissenters settled the Great Valley of Virginia starting in the late 1720s. New cultures brought new agricultural methods as well as livestock varieties from different gene pools. Those factors, combined with growing urban markets, periodic warfare, and new interest in scientific breeding and care of livestock helped shape the development of cattle farming in Virginia in the eighteenth century.

Beef on the Dinner Plate!

Beef and dairy products played an increasingly significant role in the diet of eighteenth-century Virginians. An important source of information about the diets of eighteenth-century Virginians comes from the work of archaeologists. The bones of cattle, swine, game, and poultry that are found in archaeologi-

The plow came slowly to Virginia agriculture, as most fields were worked by hoe. When plows appeared in the eighteenth century, they were usually pulled by oxen.

cal digs can tell us a great deal about the diet of Virginians of all classes and races. Two important kinds of information are found this way. One comes from the comparative numbers of bones of the various animals that are found at a site in consideration of the amount of meat on those bones. A rabbit leg, a chicken leg, a pig leg, and a steer leg include different amounts of meat. Finding one leg of each at a site would not mean that the residents there ate equal amounts of the four kinds of meat. When viewed comparatively, it is possible to obtain a more accurate sense of the role beef played in the diet of early residents of the site in comparison with other available meats. This is especially helpful for locations for which there may be little written record, as with small planters or at plantation quarters inhabited only by slaves and an overseer. Slaves, for instance, consumed more meat, including beef, than had commonly been assumed.[1] Another interesting way in which archaeology can provide insights into the foodways of colonial Virginians, and especially in their consumption of beef, comes from the cut of the bones and the butcher's tool marks on them. These show a range of beef cuts that are not in common use today, but were very popular in Virginia 300 years ago. One of the most unusual is ox cheek, a meat pie dish virtually unknown today, but much loved by early Virginians. Archaeologists at Colonial Williamsburg have found ample evidence of this cut of bones with the butcher's tool marks, indicating that it was a deliberate method of cutting the animal's head to prepare it for consumption.[2]

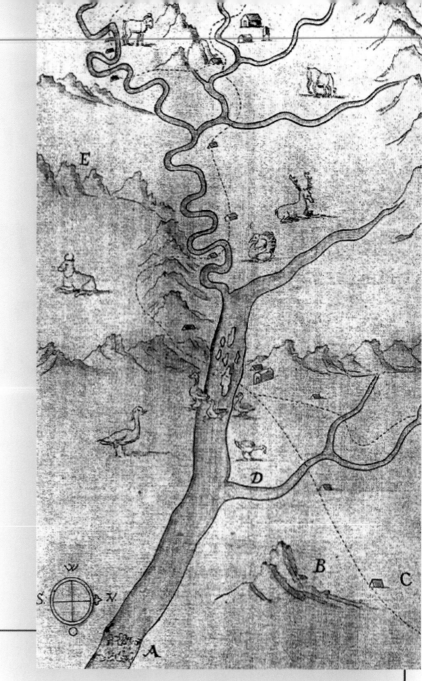

The first map of the Shenandoah Valley, by Franz Ludwig Michel, included cattle.

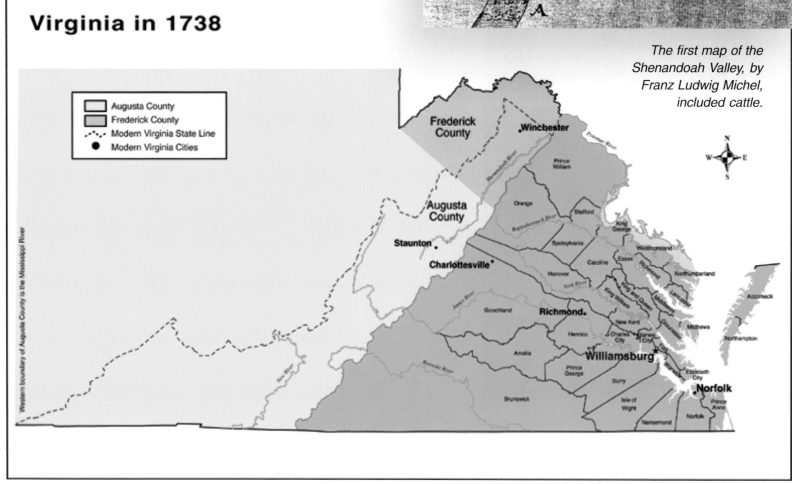

Virginia in 1738

- Augusta County
- Frederick County
- Modern Virginia State Line
- ● Modern Virginia Cities

William Byrd II (1674-1744), owner of Westover, the magnificent plantation on the James River in Charles City County, exhibited a fondness for ox cheek. In his diary for the years 1739 to 1741 he indicated that he ate ox cheek on March 25, and August 23, 1740, and on March 24, 1741.[3] These dates suggest that this dish may have been traditional for New Year's, as the old style (Julian) calendar turned the year over on March 25 rather than January 1.

William Byrd could hardly be considered a typical Virginian. He wrote to a British friend, Lord Dunkellan, "the Estate I have in Virginia consists in above 43,000 acres of Land, about 220 Negroes, with a vast stock of every kind upon it" which he estimated was worth £33,000.[4] Clearly, he was among the small class of extremely wealthy and influential planters who dominated the political, social, and economic life of colonial Virginia. His diary, kept for a two-year period in the mid-eighteenth century, provides remarkable insights into the foodways of members of his class, and makes it possible to discern the role and relative importance of beef in their diet.

Byrd recorded faithfully the meat dish he ate at dinner, the principal meal of the day, which was served in the mid-afternoon (in the evenings he ate a light supper, the menu of which he mentioned only occasionally). He recorded his main dish for 630 days in the period from August 12, 1739 through August 31, 1741. In that period, he consumed a beef dish on 140 days, or twenty-two percent of the total.

The range and variety of beef cuts and cooking methods used in Byrd's time differ considerably from modern preferences and practices. Veal played a greater role in Byrd's diet than it does in our diets today. Veal (served broiled, boiled, stewed, minced, but most often roasted) comprised thirty-two of Byrd's 140 beef-related dinners. Byrd did not prefer steak, a favorite cut of beef today; in the two-year period, he ate "beefsteak" only twice. Roast beef accounted for twenty of Byrd's dinners, or ten per year. Boiled beef, mentioned fifteen times, was another favorite. Many of Byrd's dinners featured cold beef, either boiled or roasted. Dried beef also appeared often in the diary, but with no explanation as to its method of preparation. Another favorite is a cut unfamiliar today, called chine. This is a section of spine with meat clinging to it. Byrd ate this either boiled or roasted sixteen times.[5]

Specialty cuts and miscellaneous parts rarely consumed today also appealed to Byrd. One day Byrd ate a calf's head, several times he had tripe (stomach), and ox cheek appeared on his list. Tongue was a great favorite, served hot either boiled or roasted, and also served cold with "sallet" or salad. The most unusual use of tongue occurred one day shortly before Christmas in 1739, when Byrd, after a game of billiards, reported that "I ate tongue and udder."[6]

If Byrd ate ox tongue and cheek, he probably ate ox palate, the roof of the mouth, as well. He was not alone – English on both sides of the Atlantic enjoyed the dish. One of the most popular cookbooks in England and Virginia in the eighteenth century was Hannah Glasse's *The Art of Cookery Made Plain and Easy*. The book went through several printings. This recipe "To Fricasey Ox Palates" comes from her 1747 edition:

> After boiling your ox Palates very tender (which you must do by setting them on in cold Water, and letting them do softly) then blanch them and scrape them clean, take mace, nutmeg, Cloves, and Pepper beat fine, rub them all over with those, and with Crumbs of Bread; have ready some Butter in a Stew-pan, and when it is

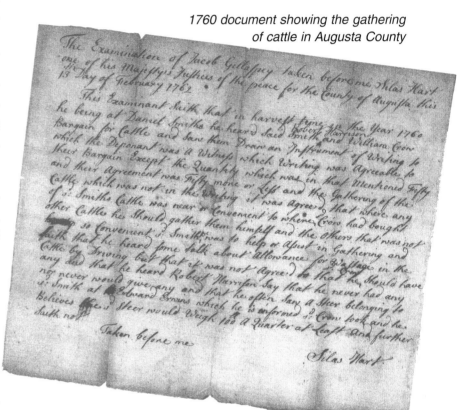

1760 document showing the gathering of cattle in Augusta County

> hot put in the Palates, fry them Brown on both Sides, then pour out the Fat, and put to them some Mutton or Beef Gravy, enough for Sauce, an Anchovy, a little Nutmeg, a little Piece of Butter rolled in Flour, and the Juice of a Lemon; let it simmer all together for a Quarter of a Hour, dish it up, and garnish with Lemon.[7]

Beef was the main dish for only one-fourth of Byrd's dinners. The main dishes for his other dinners included a remarkable variety of meats. Pork was used heavily, as roasts, spareribs, sausage, bacon, griskins (chops), sow's head, and souse. Boiled mutton was another favorite, and lamb appeared occasionally as well. Chicken could be fricasseed, stewed, or roasted, but only once in the two years did Byrd have fried chicken. Byrd ate roast goose as often as he ate chicken. He was fond of fish and occasionally ate oysters. A variety of wild game, including venison, sheldrake (canvasback duck), turkey, rabbit, and roast pigeon, rounded out the Byrd table.[8]

Bones and Teeth
Reveal Cattle History

Documenting the history of cattle in Virginia often calls for creative detective work using some rather unusual resources. In particular, the first two centuries of cattle history in the Commonwealth represent quite a challenge to the historian. There were no established breeds, no refined methods of animal husbandry, and few records of any sort – cattle or otherwise – that managed to survive into the modern age. In the near-absence of written records, historians look to ox cheeks, bovine skulls, drawers full of cattle scapulas, and even bovine teeth. Rooms full of bones, taken from more than one hundred archaeological sites in Tidewater Virginia, hold the secrets of bovine life during the first two hundred years in Virginia. The key is reading the story held in those faunal remains and unlocking their secrets. Joanne Bowen, head archaeologist at the Colonial Williamsburg faunal lab, and her team of experts, study written documents that survive from the seventeenth and eighteenth centuries, and then they study the bones and begin piecing together the puzzle.

Marks on bones, for instance, reveal the nature of diet and butchering techniques. What cuts of meat were being consumed (ox cheek for instance) and by whom are questions that have been answered in Bowen's laboratory. The results of analysis performed by Bowen and her colleagues forced the revision of a number of scholarly interpretations: slaves ate more beef than

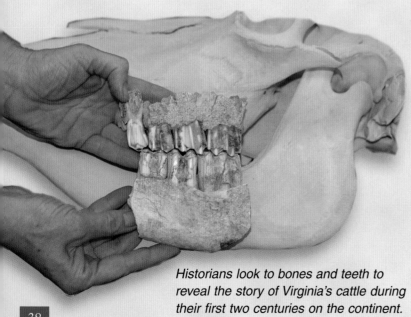

Historians look to bones and teeth to reveal the story of Virginia's cattle during their first two centuries on the continent.

"Things go very well"

Byrd took an interest in his livestock. In addition to the home plantation at Westover, Byrd owned land along the Roanoke River and several farms – or "quarters" as they were called – in Hanover County where slaves worked under the supervision of white overseers.[9] Brief diary entries indicate regular shipment of animals from outlying farms back to Westover. Sometimes cattle were driven from outlying quarters where slaves tended them, but sometimes they were put on a cart and brought to Westover.[10] In August of 1739, Byrd recorded, "A calf came from Hanover, where things go very well, thank God." Apparently, he had the calf slaughtered, because four days later he ate broiled veal for dinner and two days after that, minced veal.[11]

The cattle seem to have been transported by boat on the river as often as driven by land. In December of 1739, Byrd recorded that "after dinner the people went over the river to bring the beef and brought four very late."[12] Two weeks later, he noted that "we killed one of the Roanoke steers."[13] Nearly a year later he indicated that "the steers were brought over the river in good order, thank God," and several days later, "we began to kill our beef from Roanoke." Two days later, "we continued to grind our corn and kill our beef." The following day he recorded that "in the evening we killed another beef from Roanoke."[14] Whether these steers were being slaughtered and butchered for the Williamsburg market or solely for consumption at Westover is not known.

Cattle of eighteenth-century Virginia – even those owned by wealthy planters – suffered when the weather turned brutally cold. The winter of 1740-1741, for example, was especially severe, causing apprehension about the well-being of the livestock. Byrd pleaded with the Almighty, "God grant this cruel weather may pass away for the sake of the poor dumb creatures," on one occasion, and on another, it was exceedingly cold. God be merciful to his creatures."[15]

The helplessness of even the wealthiest planter in the face of brutal weather conditions was a problem in colonial Virginia. Robert Carter's diary entries reveal concern for the welfare of his cattle in severe winters of the 1720s that was mirrored half a century later in the diary of his son, Landon Carter of Sabine Hall (in Richmond County on the Northern Neck). The younger Carter wrote, "this day snowing and I fear it will be a deep one. . . . I have ordered my Cattle to be well taken care of which is all we can do." After seven more days of rain & snow, he wrote "yet I thank god we have lost no creatures; but they must be prodigeously wasted and perhaps in this month, March, or April they will begin to die."[16]

The Carters and Byrds of colonial Virginia represented only a very small segment of the colony's rural landholders, making it important to investigate the use of cattle among middling farmers of the Tidewater. Cattle were owned nearly universally in the Tidewater region, but the emphasis on stock raising shifted over time as the agricultural economy changed. In the two decades before the Revolution, tobacco dominated the landscape and thus little attention was given to the care or breeding of cattle. Tobacco was cultivated with a hoe, not a plow, creating little need for draft animals. Middling farmers tended to use horses rather than oxen. Cattle were valued for their manure. Also, a few were butchered in the fall and the meat was dried, salted, or pickled.[17]

Revolutionary Change

The Revolutionary War changed the nature of the agricultural economy. By the end of the century, the importance of tobacco had declined in favor of grain, a crop that required plows and draft animals and that encouraged more diversified farming practices. The change produced a new emphasis on cattle and gave rise to an important export economy in the coastal areas. In Elizabeth City County, (present-day Hampton) for example, the economy was driven by the ability of all planters to supply beef and corn to ships bound for the West Indies. An analysis of estate inventories for the county shows that cattle were the only form of agricultural wealth common to nearly every household. In addition, more than three-fourths of the herds were larger than needed for home consumption. Amazingly, Elizabeth City County had almost four times as many cattle per capita as the more traditional port supply areas, such as the Philadelphia region.[18]

Not only did the local farmers supply barreled meat for export, but the ships' crews purchased fresh meat for their own consumption directly from local farmers, usually a quarter of beef at a time. Farmers, both large and small, could turn a nice profit in the ship provisioning business. In 1788, the crews of the *Liberty* and the *Patriot* made beef purchases over several months in amounts ranging from 46 to 260 pounds. Among the suppliers were Joseph Needham, a large farmer who sold 386 pounds, and John Drewry, a tenant farmer, who sold 130 pounds.[19]

Got Milk!

A small dairy industry also emerged during this period. Ownership of butter pots, churns, pails, scales, cheese presses, and the like are obvious indicators of dairy production. In Yorktown, thirty percent of the inventories from the 1780s show no evidence of dairy production. Middling households

The study of marks left on bones in the butchering process provides information about how cattle were used in Virginia's first two centuries.

previously thought and cattle increased in size in the late seventeenth century before again diminishing.

The use of bovine teeth to learn about the dietary history of cattle – a technique still in its experimental stage – is one example of creative investigation and rethinking of historical data and archaeological resources by experts at the faunal laboratory. While pondering the adage, "you are what you eat," researchers at the lab decided to examine cattle teeth in search of carbon and nitrogen stable isotopes that will help map the diet of colonial cattle. During photosynthesis, plants incorporate chemical variants of particular elements, called isotopes, into their structures. As those plants are consumed, the isotopes are passed up the food chain and incorporated into the bones, including teeth, of the animals that ate them. Tracking stable isotopes in old bones can aid in reconstructing diets from long ago. Because, at Carter's Grove in Tidewater, bovine teeth exist from archaeological sites that span two hundred years from the 1620s until the early nineteenth century, initial Colonial Williamsburg experiments are focusing on that collection. For comparison, additional teeth from modern animals with known diets are being examined.

Teeth, then, might hold answers to the questions of why cattle numbers in Virginia rose exponentially after a period when they survived only in small numbers, and why the animals increased in size throughout the seventeenth century. Could it be that European grasses were established and naturalized almost as quickly as the introduction of Old World cattle? Joanne Bowen believes the answers to these and similar questions might lie in something as simple as a couple of cow teeth. ~

owned a disproportionate share of the dairy equipment which suggests that surplus from those farms supplied the poorer and wealthier families with milk, butter, and occasionally, cheese.[20] Anne Dunford, who died around 1780, was probably one such local supplier. Two cows and calves valued at £300, one cow worth £100, a heifer worth £75, and a yearling calf worth 40 shillings were far and away the most valuable items in her estate inventory. She also owned eight butter pots and a pair of scales and weights. Mary Timson, who died by 1783, owned eight cows and three calves, two stone butter pots, and four jugs.[21]

Colonial milkhouse

For a variety of reasons, including a warmer climate and emphasis on tobacco production, dairying never dominated the rural economy of Tidewater Virginia as it did in England, New England, and the Mid-Atlantic. Also in Virginia, dairying was devoted almost exclusively to the production of milk and butter rather than cheese. Very few estate inventories in Virginia mention cheese-making equipment, and great quantities of English cheese were imported into the colony.[22]

Despite the relative unimportance of dairying, many farmers set aside a room or a small outbuilding as was traditional in England, called variously a milkhouse or a dairy, for storage of dairy products. From the seventeenth century to the nineteenth century these buildings changed little. Most were small one or two-room structures that were from ten to twelve feet square. Coolness and ventilation were essential so most were located under a shade tree or near a spring. Most milkhouses featured latticed windows, shelves, deep eaves, and brick floors.

Great Cattle Drives

While Byrd and other Tidewater planters, large and small, had settled into an agricultural system based on the cultivation of tobacco and small grains by the mid-eighteenth century, an entirely different system of farming was developing west of the Blue Ridge Mountains. In the Valley of Virginia, where the high cost of transportation made tobacco cultivation unprofitable, a significant concentration on livestock production emerged almost simultaneously with settlement. Geographically the Great Valley was a natural transportation corridor, funneling people and animals southwestward from Pennsylvania into the backcountry of Virginia and be-

yond. By the 1720s, encouraged by Virginia's colonial government, people of Scotch-Irish and German extraction began migrating into that region west of the Blue Ridge Mountains. Although these settlers created farms in relatively isolated frontier regions, they strove to establish commercial linkages with eastern seaboard cities such as Philadelphia and Baltimore. Winchester, in the northern, or lower valley, and Staunton, at the southern end, also called the upper valley, became key market towns. By 1740 or so, settlement extended into southwest Virginia, the Carolinas, and Kentucky. Tying the entire region together was the Great Wagon Road, an Indian path used initially by settlers on foot and then by wagon. It was also the road used to drive cattle into and out of the region. Modern-day U.S. Route 11 follows generally the same route as the original Great Wagon Road.

The agricultural economy that first developed in the valley, called "general" or "mixed" farming, featured a diversity of crops and large numbers of horses, cattle, and swine. An examination of estate inventories shows that eighty-three percent of them in Frederick County contained cattle, while in Augusta County eighty percent included cattle. In the upper valley, cattle outnumbered all other domestic animals. They outnumbered horses, for example, by a margin of three to two. Livestock-related items, like milk, butter, and cheese, appeared frequently in the inventories of early settlers. In the Beverley Manor settlement around Staunton, butter was second only to horses as the item that appeared most frequently in estate inventories. Beef and tallow were seen less frequently in the inventories. Although horses, not oxen, constituted the draft animal of choice west of the Blue Ridge Mountains, six Augusta and three Frederick inventories taken before 1760 mentioned oxen. A yoke of oxen was generally valued at about £6.[23]

Many of the cattle products – meat, butter, cheese, and tallow – were used locally. The only description of an eighteenth-century meal consumed in the valley was produced in the 1770s by visitor, Philip Vickers Fithian. "They have not, it is true, Coffee, Chocolate, nor many other of what is allow'd to be needful in polite Life — But they have Bread, Meat of many kinds, Milk, Butter, and Cheese, and all in great Plenty, and the best Quality. . . Large Platters covered with Meat of many Sorts; Beeff; Venison; Pork. . ."[24]

An examination of estate inventories shows that eighty-three percent of them in Frederick County contained cattle, while in Augusta County eighty percent included cattle.

Very early in the settlement of the backcountry, large numbers of cattle were exported to the urban markets, particularly Philadelphia, for consumption there or for export to the West Indies. Fall cattle drives were among the earliest commercial contacts established with the eastern markets. Large drives from deep in the Carolinas passed through the valley so often that in 1742 – just four years after Augusta County was established and three years before there was a working local government in Staunton – the county petitioned the Virginia legislature to impose a duty "on all Horses and cattle drove thro' the said Inhabitants, from the Northern or Southern Provinces."[25]

In the upper valley, enterprising men began to organize cattle drives to the northern markets, particularly Philadelphia. James Patton, for example, tried to round up 200 cattle for a drive by requesting payment of debts owed to him in the form of "Black or Fatt cows" instead of money. Probably the most important cattle trader in the Upper Valley in the 1750s and 1760s was William Crow, a Staunton merchant. He often organized droves of 150 to 200 animals that went to Winchester or on to Philadelphia if the market was not favorable in the lower valley. For at least one drove, Crow realized a profit of 200 percent. There were some who grumbled that his herds seemed to "grow larger" as they continued down the valley to the northern markets.[26] Crow's cattle business caused him to frequent the Augusta County courts. In 1760, for example, Crow and Daniel Smith were at odds over fifty head of cattle that Smith was to add to a herd Crow was driving to market in Winchester. Crow presented a document, dated September 17, 1760, in which he informed Smith of his intention to gather cattle the following week and requested that Smith "gather what you and Company has Between the Mountons as soon as possible I would be glade to See you at the General Muster next Tuesday."[27]

Robert Preston, a surveyor who, in the 1770s and 1780s, operated in the region that is now Botetourt County, successfully combined surveying and cattle trading. Preston acquired cattle from his neighbors by direct purchase or by bartering his surveying services. Too, sometimes he included the cattle of others that he had taken on consignment. He then queried his acquaintances about what goods they might desire from the city. With his shopping list, he drove the cattle to Philadelphia where he sold them and used the profits to purchase the commodities he then carried back to the frontier.[28]

Enterprising valley farmers planned ahead for the fall passing of the drover. The average drove of cattle comprised 120 head managed by two men – one stayed at the head of the herd, often leading one animal, and one followed the herd on horseback. Cattle could walk about a dozen miles a day. In the evening the drovers located a farmer with fields of corn left to dry on the stalk or with corn already shucked, and arrangements were made for keeping the cattle overnight. Astute drovers knew that a journey of many hundreds of miles took its toll on the animals' weight and carcass quality and they were careful to give the animals the best care possible.[29]

The condition of cattle at the conclusion of a drive was at the heart of a dispute heard in the Augusta County Court in 1766. In October of 1761, while in Staunton, apparently a cattle dealer named Greer agreed to sell sixty "fat and merchantable beeves fit for Slaughter." Greer was to drive the cattle to Fredericksburg in December and deliver them to the brothers, James and Archibald Hunter. The selling price was fifteen shillings per hundredweight. According to the court records: "Sometime in the month of November & Dec. the Defendant Greer drove down to Fredbg. 40 head of Cattle. . ." James Hunter refused the cattle, deeming them "too poor for Slaughter" and turned them over to his brother, William, who slaughtered some and then randomly picked three different sized animals in order to come up with an average weight of the forty. The total payment was based on an estimated 11,046 pounds, or about 275 pounds for each animal. One man called in to describe the animals noted that "the Cattle in general were poor" and added that "a great number died before the ensuing spring."[30] The size of the cattle in dispute was small even by eighteenth-century standards when a marketable animal from the valley typically weighed between 480 and 560 pounds.[31]

Free Roaming

Several factors account for why this type of animal husbandry evolved in the eighteenth century and persisted until well into the twentieth century in western Virginia. From the earliest introduction of cattle in Virginia, colonial settlers practiced free-range methods of livestock management. Crops were fenced in, while animals were fenced out and allowed to roam freely, foraging on tree leaves and the salt marsh grasses. In the backcountry, free-range practices evolved in a more controlled manner with herds grazing in certain areas under the direction of specific individuals. In the fall livestock could be easily gathered and taken to market. These huge herds of cattle were vital to Virginia's economy, a fact recognized by the Virginia Assembly. Legislators worried that the profits from such large herds were being funneled out of Virginia when they were driven to out-of-state port cities such as Philadelphia, where the cattle were sold, butchered, and the salted beef exported. As a result, in 1748 the legislature passed an act to fund the clearing of roads over the mountains to the eastern part of the state in order that the livestock trade from the backcountry could be rerouted to Virginia ports.[32] Thus, cattle farming in western Virginia stimulated the building of east-west transportation arteries within the colony and contributed to expansion and settlement in the backcountry.

Farmers of western Virginia successfully combined two different types of agriculture – grain production and animal husbandry. The key was the summer pasturing of the animals far away from the grain fields and the fall cattle drives to market or back to the farms. The cultural roots for this agricultural system lay in the Old World. The majority of Virginians in the Tidewater and Piedmont were of English origin. West of the mountains, Scotch-Irish and Germans predominated. Both Irish and Germanic peasants had traditionally practiced systems of animal husbandry similar to those in the valley. According to Edward Wakefield's 1812 statistical and political account of Ireland, the common practice in the north of Ireland (where the Scotch-Irish originated) was to keep young cattle on the farm until around April and then send them to the high country to be grazed on rough pasture. These young cattle were called yeld cattle, probably a slurring together of the words "year old." The amount charged the farmer for the grazing depended on the quality of the pasture. Around November, the cattle were brought down out of the highlands.[33] Arthur Young's findings are similar. Around Newry, this British agriculturist who toured Ireland in the late eighteenth century noted that there were "large tracts rented by villages, the cotters dividing it among themselves, and making the mountain common for their cattle."[34] In Fermanagh (in the north of Ireland) he described a system in which farmers annually purchased year-old cattle and sold four-year-old cattle. "In summer they feed on mountains," he wrote. In Fermanagh, rent for the mountainsides was "set by the lump, according to the number of cattle they feed."[35]

Evidence for pasturing animals in the hills away from the main farm can also be found in the Germanic culture. Pennsylvania German farming practices that had been established in the eighteenth century, continued into the twentieth. Early Pennsylvania German farmers enlarged meadowland by grazing animals on newly cutover land in order to make it ready for cultivation.[36] The Germans also worked hard at improving their "upland meadows" through a primitive irrigation system described in 1754:

Robert Carter's Cattle Kingdom

Colonial Virginians called Robert Carter, "King," and for good reason; he was the colony's richest planter. The value of his holdings in land, slaves, plantation houses, ships, indentured servants, mills, mines, tobacco, crops, and livestock rivaled the wealth of some of Europe's minor rulers. His landholdings alone comprised nearly 300,000 acres.

Cattle played an important part in Carter's kingdom. When Carter died in 1732 at the age of sixty-nine, he owned 2,307 cattle divided among forty-seven different plantations in the counties of Lancaster, Northumberland, Richmond, Westmoreland, Caroline, King George, Stafford, Spotsylvania, and Prince William.

Robert "King" Carter

Here it was I first saw the method of watering a whole range of pastures and meadows on a hillside, by little troughs cut in the side of a hill, along which the water from springs was conducted, so as that when the outlets of these troughs were stopped at the end the water ran over the sides and watered all the ground between that and the other trough next below it.[37]

The appreciation of the Pennsylvania Germans for their well-tended meadows continued into the twentieth century. Those fields were never plowed and many were completely fenced. Before enclosure it was the job of both children and adults to tend the grazing animals. Cattle were usually turned out to pasture around May 1 although some believed that cattle should not be put out until after the longest day of the year, around June 21. Animals were driven home around November 1.[38]

Summer grazing in the mountains and fall cattle drives were also practiced in Augusta County. From 1775 until 1840, Augusta's clerk of court wrote detailed descriptions for 1,213 stray cattle found in the county. Of those, 723 (sixty percent) were reported from October to January with November and December being the months of most frequent reportage. Since the large drives took place in late October, November, or early December, and allowing time for an animal to wander, be found, and then reported, it is not surprising that most strays would have been reported in these months. Almost invariably, stray cattle were reported in the fall or winter when they would have wandered off from large drives. Lesser numbers of cattle were also reported in the spring, but those smaller groups of cattle were managed more easily and animals would have had less opportunity to escape the herd unnoticed. At the other end of the spectrum, only twenty-eight cattle were reported in June and twenty-one in July making those months the times of infrequent reportage. During those summer months, cattle would have already been in the mountains for summer grazing. Further evidence can be found in the fact that the majority of the cattle reported were steers or heifers, the common market animal, and most were two to four years old. Older cows and bulls were only rarely reported.

The great cattle drives of eighteenth-century western Virginia waned somewhat during the Revolution and then were revived during the years just after the war. The difference, however, was that improved roads in the Old Dominion now directed much of the livestock trade to Virginia markets, especially Richmond, in addition to the traditional outlets of Baltimore and Philadelphia. A better transportation network by the 1770s also meant that other cattle by-products, such as butter and cheese, could make their way out of the backcountry to urban markets. Between 1772 and 1776 Rockbridge County merchant William Anderson shipped more than four tons of butter, no doubt purchased from area farm families, to Richmond. He received six shillings per pound for his product, giving him £225 in income. From 1766 to 1775, a Staunton merchant shipped 11,000 pounds of butter, 812 pounds of cheese, and 200 pounds of tallow to Richmond for sale.[39]

After the Revolution, Augusta and Rockbridge Counties continued to lead the state in cattle production. In 1782, just after the close of war, there were 59,520 cattle in the valley, with more than half located in the upper valley. With 13,000 cattle, Augusta County led the state. Cattle outnumbered horses by as many as five to two in Rockbridge and Augusta and even held an edge over swine and sheep. The lower valley had developed differently than the southern valley. The introduction of larger plantations and the production of tobacco contributed to a decline in the cattle business in the countryside. In contrast to Au-

---

King Carter paid close attention to the management of each of these plantations (or "quarters" as they were sometimes called). On December 2, 1727, for example, he recorded that there had been "a deep snow, very cold wind W[est]," and that he "lost at Old House (one of his plantations) 3 steers. 1 cow died suddenly." A week later as the cold continued, he noted, "several more cows taken sick." Carter monitored the care his servants and slaves gave the cattle, and wrote scathing letters to overseers when he suspected shortcomings. To one of them he wrote that "I have a great many observations to make of your ill management."

He reminded the man that "you have 12 calves at the quarter where you live some of them very near killd with the churn stick I believe I shall have hardly butter enough from your dairy to answer the life of one of them."

Carter always remained aware of the cost of operating a cattle business. In March of 1727, he recorded that he "Bought Widow Short cattle, 30 head, gave her for 22 head 20 s[hilling] apiece & for 8 yearlings 4 £, in all 26£." He pointed out to his London agent that "as for Cattle there is no Such thing as Selling a stock together for ready Money, the common price for a young fat cow in killing time is Thirty five shillings Cash and for a Steer 7 year old Fifty shillings."

gusta and Rockbridge, cattle outnumbered horses in only a two to one ratio in Frederick and Shenandoah Counties.[40] It was the lower valley, however, at Winchester, that prospered as the central collection point for cattle drives out of the upper valley and from what is now West Virginia, and from points deep within Kentucky and Tennessee. In 1793, English emigrant Harry Toulmin said of Winchester: "you would be astonished at the multiplicity of cattle which pour through this town from the backcountry."[41]

The Great Planters

As the eighteenth century advanced, changes in agricultural practices and emphases appeared on Tidewater plantations. Examples of these new practices may be seen in the career of Carter Burwell, a grandson of Robert "King" Carter. Burwell was the builder and master of Carter's Grove plantation on the James, now a part of Colonial Williamsburg.[42] In his years at Carter's Grove, from 1738 to his death in 1756, Carter Burwell diversified his farming operations by reducing traditional dependence on the market crop of sweet-scented tobacco. He engaged a general manager to supervise overseers on each of the outlying farms or quarters and on the home farm and the mill.

In addition to tobacco, wheat and corn were key crops. Some 800 barrels of corn were grown annually on Burwell's plantation. After setting aside the amounts needed for feeding the slaves and fattening the livestock, from one-quarter to one-half of the corn could be marketed. Cattle became more important than they had been for Carter's grandfather at Corotoman on the Northern Neck. Excess cattle were sold each year and some of the stock was butchered for the Williamsburg meat market. As that town grew, sales of beef and wheat

became an increasingly important source of steady annual income. The diversification of crops, the increased use of plows, and the need to deliver more beef, grain, and flour to town markets increased the need for oxen. Slaves on the plantation diversified their work from tobacco into livestock tending and working teams of horses or oxen for the plow or the cart.[43]

Like Burwell, Landon Carter experimented with greater use of oxcarts to bring in the corn crop. He used one drawn by two oxen and another by four. It took ten hands plus the two boys leading the oxen four days to bring in the 100 barrels of corn, leaving Carter skeptical of the labor efficiency.[44] He was certain of the failure of another experiment at one plantation in 1774: using the animals for treading the wheat crop in order to thresh it. Four steers were killed in obtaining the forty bushels of wheat.[45]

Carter Burwell died in 1756 in the prime of life. His friend and brother-in-law, William Nelson, of Yorktown, served as guardian of the estate until young Nathaniel Burwell II reached his majority in 1771. Under Nelson's guidance, although tobacco production continued, the diversification of the operation increased with an emphasis on dairying and other enterprises including the production of corn, wheat, livestock, and cider.[46]

Butter production offered opportunities for women to participate in the market economy. Typically overseers' wives supervised the production of butter by slave women. As incentive, the overseer and his wife received a share of the butter. In 1776 Landon Carter recorded pleasure with a new overseer, Leonard Hill, at his Park Quarter. Hill seemed to manage cattle well and his wife had produced butter for Carter.[47] One summer Carter indicated that the various plantations were providing pots of butter weighing twenty to thirty pounds each.[48] The Burwell estate

Also, Carter arranged for teams of oxen to be properly trained as draft animals, for he wished to make more efficient the hauling of lumber, stone, wheat, corn, and tobacco on his plantations.

In addition to raising cattle for the production of beef, Carter managed extensive dairying operations. Corotoman, the home plantation where he lived in Lancaster County, featured an old dairy, a new dairy, and a new dairy store. In his diary, Carter recorded the number of tubs of butter that arrived by sloop from his distant plantations along the Rappahannock. His letters took overseers to task if they sent too few tubs. Carter was quite fond of butter and cheese, and on numerous occa-

sions he noted in his diary that he had enjoyed a simple supper of bread and butter or hominy and butter, or that his daughter sent him a gift of two pots of butter.

In the management of his beef cattle and dairying operations, Robert Carter demonstrated the skill, care, and good judgment that characterized all aspects of his career as a planter, politician, land speculator, slave trader, merchant, and church leader. ~

Sources about Robert "King" Carter include his will and estate inventory that are in Special Collections at the University of Virginia; his diary, which, transcribed by Francis Berkeley, is held at the Jessie Ball duPont Research Library at the Foundation for Historic Christ Church, along with his transcribed letter books, which contain correspondence with his merchant factor Micajah Perry in London, and with various of his overseers. His letter books are held at the Virginia Historical Society and at the University of Virginia.

produced "butter on a level equivalent to that of a middling-size Pennsylvania dairy producing for the Philadelphia market in the mid-nineteenth century."[49]

Tallow was another by-product of beef production that the labor of women turned to good use. Landon Carter reported in June of 1777 that his servant Betty had made "three gross minus eight" (424) molded tallow candles. This was fewer than usual; his fatted beeves that year were old steers fattened hurriedly, and as such made little tallow.[50]

The Burwell family exhibited an increasing sophistication in its farming that reflected, a change in the attitudes and actions of the Tidewater planter class. These changes, which included an emphasis on beef and dairy production, resulted from the introduction of English agricultural innovations. Lewis Burwell of Fairfield in Gloucester County engaged as overseer Robert Mountain, an English farmer who had expertise in raising grain and fattening livestock. The Burwells, as well as their cousins, in-laws, and neighbors, took a strong interest in the development of self-sustaining, low-ground clover meadows for the livestock.

But even the most progressive planters of colonial Virginia did not have the advantage of a body of scientific agricultural experimentation to guide them in the best methods of breeding, feeding, and tending their livestock. To assist his agricultural pursuits, Landon Carter ordered a number of books from England, including Baron von Haake's *Composition for Manuring Land*, Robert Dossie's, *Memoirs of Agriculture, and other Oeconomical Arts*, and the four-volume set entitled *The Farmer's Tour Through the East of England*.[51] While some publications from England were beginning to make their way to America, most planters and farmers relied on their own experi-

ence and that of friends to guide them. Carter, for example, recounted "a very possitive though not a very learned Contest" that he and his friends held "about the reason why some people's cows do not breed." While some of his friends asserted that a good diet of corn and hay would "make any cow wanton and take bull," Carter had observed that hot, dry weather stifled the interest of even the best-fed cows. Others in the group claimed that cattle ought to have salt, but Carter proved to them "that where I gave most salt I had the fewest Calves."[52]

Reflecting on the value of "every husbandman whether Planter or farmer" keeping a journal of observations on his management and that of others, Carter remarked that he could correct many of his errors by comparing one year with another. His case in point was his decision in the 1760s to encourage cow penning over a larger area in order to benefit from the accumulated manure. While this benefited the fields and provided nourishment to the cattle, by his observation, it also coincided with a decline in the number of calves produced. His dilemma then was to guess whether his cows produced fewer calves because it was also a time of drought, or whether his extended practice of cow penning had caused the reduction in the fertility of his cows.[53]

> *Robert "King" Carter, the colony's richest planter, arranged for teams of oxen to be properly trained as draft animals to be used for hauling wheat, corn, and tobacco on his plantation.*

Father of Our Country and American Agriculture

George Washington, the new country's most famous citizen, was also America's most famous planter. In many ways the father of our country was also the father of enlightened agricultural practices in America. Washington was one of the first farmers in the country to develop a system of selective livestock breeding, use livestock manure to fertilize fields, build a dung storage area, and construct fencing to keep animals on or off fields.[54] Many of his ideas were borrowed from the great English agriculturists for whom he had great admiration.

To Washington, the importance of livestock could not be underestimated. Mount Vernon comprised 3,000 acres of tilled soil and Washington regarded manure as a key resource for keeping cropland productive. He collected manure from cattle, horses, mules, and sheep and stored it in a "Repository for Dung." The open-sided building, which he directed his farm manager to construct, measured thirty-one by twelve feet and featured a cobblestone floor. Washington requested that discarded organic materials of all sorts from the household be raked into the repository, creating what modern gardeners would call a compost pile. In the 1990s, archaeologists located the dung building behind Mount Vernon's stable.[55]

Although Washington loved his horses, he always kept large numbers of cattle. These animals provided a strong,

Detail on fireplace mantle at Washington's Mount Vernon home

steady source of draft power and were a source of food for the Mount Vernon household. Many entries in Washington's journals from 1761 to 1765 include information on the purchase and feeding of cattle. During that time he expanded his cattle herd from 126 to 166. When Washington died in 1799, he owned 171 cattle. Washington's diary entry of November 1, 1765, recorded what were typical chores for any owner of livestock:

Sent 1 Bull 18 Cows & 5 Calves to Doeg Run in all — 24 head branded on the left Buttock GW. Sent 3 Cows, & 20 Yearlings & Calves to the Mill, wch. With 4 there makes 27 head in all viz. 5 Cows & 22 Calves & Yearlgs. Branded on the Right shoulder GW. Out of the Frederick Cattle made the Stock in the Neck up 100 head — these branded on the Right Buttock GW. Muddy hole Cattle in all [ ] head branded on the left shoulder GW.[56]

Washington prized his oxen (castrated bulls) as draft animals. Stronger than most horses and mules, oxen could remove stumps from cleared fields, haul logs from the woods, and pull carts, plows, and harrows. Washington worked his oxen for eight years and then retired them to the fields for a year of fattening before they were butchered and eaten. He developed a rotating system so that he owned oxen at all stages of training, work, and retirement. When he died, Washington owned sixty oxen.[57]

The entrepreneurial possibilities of dairying also appealed to Washington. As early as 1760, his holdings included a small dairy house built near Mount Vernon. Later he eyed the growing urban areas like Alexandria and Georgetown with hopes of turning his small plantation production into a profitable business. In 1788 he had another dairy house built at his River Farm, but plans for two more dairies at two other farms were never carried out. Dairy production at Mount Vernon probably never met Washington's expectations. His personal papers indicate that not only did dairying never reach a level necessary for selling to the urban markets, but at times the farm was hard-pressed to supply enough butter for the table at Mount Vernon. In his very last farm memorandum, Washington recorded his great disappointment over a butter shortage:

"It is hoped and will be expected, that more effectual measures will be pursued to make butter another year; for it is almost beyond belief, that from 101 Cows actually reported on a late enumeration for the Cattle, that I am obliged to *buy butter* for the use of my family."[58]

As with all of his agricultural pursuits, Washington applied the most enlightened techniques of the time to cattle husbandry, and he was willing to provide advice to others:

to tell a farmer. . . that his Cattle & ca. Ought to be regularly penned in summer and secured from bad weather in winter, and the utmost attention paid to the making of manure for the improvement of his fields at both seasons; that his oxen should be well attended to, and kept in good and fit condition, thereby enabling them to perform the labour which they must undergo; to remind him of these things would, I say be only observing what every Farmer must be thoroughly sensible of his duty enjoins. . . .[59]

Selective breeding might have been the most important agricultural practice that Washington promoted in America. The farmer-president sought the best ways to improve his livestock. While searching through British volumes on the subject, he encountered the work of Robert Bakewell (1725-1795). The son of a tenant farmer, Bakewell increased his farm production by using the latest tech-

...every Farmer must be thoroughly sensible of his duty...

George Washington

niques of manuring and irrigation for his arable land and by incorporating new ideas about housing livestock and collecting manure into his practice.[60]

Perhaps Bakewell's most important contribution to the advancement of agriculture was selective breeding, a practice that laid the groundwork for the rise of true animal breeds. Bakewell built upon the selective breeding ideas already being practiced by England's thoroughbred horse breeders since the middle of the eighteenth century. He coupled those ideas with a new one called "in-and-in" and applied them to sheep, cattle, and draft horses. Before Bakewell, most farm animals had been pastured together regardless of gender. The indiscriminate breeding that resulted led to a lack of uniformity in the appearance of the animals. Bakewell separated the males from the females and made decisions about which females would be bred by which males based on traits that he wanted to highlight. By inbreeding his stock he could enhance positive characteristics and reduce or eliminate undesirable ones so that, over time, specific breeds emerged.

Bakewell first tested his theory with old Lincolnshire sheep. His breeding program created the New Leicester breed, also known as Bakewell (Washington raised descendants of Bakewell sheep). Ever the experimenter, Bakewell soon tried his ideas out on Longhorn cattle. He had observed that Longhorns produced meat more efficiently than other breeds and he established a breeding program to enhance that characteristic. Although his experiment was successful, Longhorns soon went out of fashion. However, one of Bakewell's apprentices applied the same breeding techniques to develop the Shorthorn or Durham, the breed that probably influenced Virginia cattle more than any other.

Oxen served as draft animals for pulling wagons owned by merchants and large planters of Tidewater Virginia in the eighteenth century.

A Century of Change

Virginia planters and small farmers of the late eighteenth century produced an agricultural economy that differed greatly from that of their grandparents at the beginning of the century. No longer was the economy of the Old Dominion based solely on tobacco — the gold leaf that paved the streets of Jamestown. Cattle had played an important role in an increasingly diversified Virginia agricultural economy. From the sandy beaches of the Eastern Shore to the worn mountains of the Alleghenies, farmers turned increasingly to cattle as a market commodity. They served as sources of manure to enrich the soil for crops of wheat and corn, as draft animals, as producers of the raw material for a small but growing dairy industry, and for the objects manufactured from their horns, hides, and tallow. The increased reliance on cattle as a source of income meshed with the intellectual driving force of the eighteenth century, the Enlightenment. This world-view, which included a desire to understand and master the natural world, led the elite of eighteenth-century Virginia society to apply the new scientific knowledge to the improvement of agriculture and livestock, benefiting all Virginians, as increased productivity and improved livestock resulted.

Revolutionary Times

There is much truth to the old saying that "an army moves on its stomach." So it is that the humble bovines of Virginia were called upon during three wars of the eighteenth century to supply Virginia forces with the protein necessary to fight their enemies. Those foes were the French and their Native American allies in the French and Indian War (1754-1763), the Native American tribes in Dunmore's War of 1774, and the British armies in the American Revolution, which lasted from 1775 to 1783. The ability of Virginia's colonial leaders and later of the governments of the new Commonwealth of Virginia and new United States of America to feed their fighting forces would affect the outcome of each of those wars.

Beef and the Battlefront

The bitter lesson of failure in warfare caused by an improperly fed fighting force was brought home to Virginians on the frontier and to those making decisions in Williamsburg by the ill-fated Sandy Creek Expedition in 1756, under Major Andrew Lewis. Captain William Preston, of a distinguished Scotch-Irish family of the Valley of Virginia, set out from Fort Prince George near present-day Salem, Virginia, with twenty-five men and six officers on February 9, 1756, to answer a call to serve in this campaign against Shawnee towns. Their supplies included 200 pounds of lead and 2,000 pounds of dried beef. At Fort Frederick on the New River they joined with English-allied Cherokee fighters and other frontier fighting veterans. In all, there were about 350 men.[1]

Colonel David Stewart was Governor Robert Dinwiddie's appointee as commissary for the expedition, and he arrived with the governor's earnest plea to exert himself in the job. Whether Stewart is chiefly to blame cannot be determined, but his exertions do not appear to have been adequate. The men complained that there were only fifteen days' provisions for the journey of 300 miles. They did not reach the head of Sandy, the stream they would follow and that is now the border between Kentucky and West Virginia, until February 28, nineteen days after departure. By then the ton of dried beef had long been consumed.[2]

Arms and ammunition for the colony were stored in the powder magazine in Williamsburg, the capital. The presence of cattle in the town serves as a reminder that the lines between urban and rural life were not as sharply drawn in the eighteenth century as they are in the twenty-first century.

By March 6 their ration was down to half a pound of flour per man per day. Lewis ordered that some of the remaining butter supply be divided among the men. The horses were as short of food as the men and dropped dead with alarming frequency. Preston wrote on March 5, "this day my four pound [£4] horse expired and I was left on foot with a hungry belly, which increased my woe. Nothing but hunger and fatigue appears to us." Hunger sharpened tempers, causing dissention to break out among the men and even among the officers. In desperation, as men threatened to quit, Preston wrote, "I proposed to kill the horses to eat, which they refused. They said that might do to support them if they were on their way home but it was not a diet proper to sustain men on a long march against the enemy."[3]

Even hunting provided little food to the dispirited soldiers of the Sandy Creek Expedition. They shot two elk and a little bear and ate them, but this meat was unevenly divided, causing rancor. The camp surgeon, Dr. Thomas Lloyd, confirmed that the men finally did eat some of the remaining horses. The other physician along, Dr. William Fleming, also blamed the expedition's failure on the lack of provisions. Eventually the group turned back, reaching Fort Dinwiddie on Jackson River on April 3.[4] It was a sorry episode in frontier history, and a hard lesson about the necessity of providing an adequate supply of beef for a fighting force.

John Murray
The Earl of Dunmore

Although this episode of frontier warfare was a planning fiasco, the decade of the French and Indian War saw advances in the production of cattle in the Valley of Virginia as large cattle herds were grazed in the mountains in the summer and then driven to market outlets in the fall. By the time this war broke out, Valley farmers had some surplus that could be devoted to commercial activities and particularly to military supply.[5] The early settlers of the Greenbrier Valley, now in West Virginia, had introduced cattle to the region and were building thriving frontier farms when, in August 1755, a small party of Indians attacked a fort where nearly sixty settlers had gathered. They killed thirteen inside the fort and a dozen others outside, captured two girls, burned eleven houses, and drove off or slaughtered some 500 cattle and horses.[6]

In the French and Indian War, Winchester became a supply depot for both the ill-fated British general, Edward Braddock, and for his young colonial assistant, George Washington. Local farmers and townspeople supplied the militia and army with food, beverages, and supplies. In the upper valley, Augusta County farmers in 1757 supplied 36 cattle on the hoof, 41 beeves (whole carcasses), some 8,300 pounds of beef, 2,518 pounds of pork, 480 bushels of wheat, and 10,450 pounds of flour (from some 250 bushels of wheat) to the militia and their Indian allies. The demand for flour and beef continued through 1758, 1759, and 1760, no doubt encouraging farmers in the valley to grow more wheat and slaughter more beef.[7]

As animosity grew between the colonies and the Mother Country in the years after the Stamp Act of 1765, Virginia found itself embroiled in another military confrontation with Native Americans under the Royal Governor John Murray, the Earl of Dunmore. Settlers moving into the Trans-Allegheny region (in spite of England's efforts to prevent it), the activities of land speculators and surveyors in the Ohio Valley, and the activities of George Croghan, an Indian agent from Pennsylvania, in inflaming the Indians were among many factors that provoked several Native American tribes to launch attacks upon isolated frontier settlers from Pennsylvania to the Cumberland Mountains.[8]

Dunmore's War

In Virginia, in May of 1774, the question of western lands was hotly debated by the governor, the Council, and the House of Burgesses. Although Fincastle County had been formed from Botetourt in 1772 to take in the far southwest and Kentucky, settlers who had pushed far to the southwest along the Holsten River were demanding another new county. The government resisted their pleas. Meanwhile, dispatches from Andrew Lewis in late May notified Virginians of the beginning of a war with the Shawnees in the Ohio Valley that would be known as Dunmore's War. Then the murder of a Cherokee led to the concern that the Cherokees, traditionally friends of the British and the Virginians, would turn against them and join the Shawnees.[9]

Lord Dunmore seemed determined to engage in a war with the Indians, for motives that some have claimed were designed to distract the

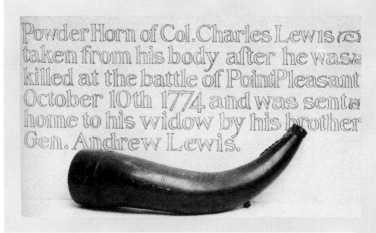

Powder Horn of Col. Charles Lewis taken from his body after he was killed at the battle of Point Pleasant October 10th 1774 and was sent home to his widow by his brother Gen. Andrew Lewis.

Charles Lewis of Bath County, Virginia, is credited with taking the first cattle across West Virginia via present-day Charleston to Point Pleasant during Lord Dunmore's war in 1774. Perhaps one of the most renowned Virginia militia men of his time, Lewis was killed at the Battle of Point Pleasant in October of 1774.

Virginians from the First Virginia Convention scheduled to meet in August in order to discuss issues of concern with England. By mid-July he had called out troops and began marching to the mountains. On July 24 he was at Winchester heading for Fort Dunmore (Pittsburgh). The governor placed Andrew Lewis in command of the frontier forces and told him he expected his brother, Charles Lewis, and William Preston to assist him. They were to meet Dunmore at the mouth of the Great Kanawha or any other point along the river and join forces to attack the Shawnees in Ohio.[10]

Charles Lewis, who resided in that part of Augusta County that eventually became Bath, lost little time collecting provisions and marching his 600 men in fourteen companies to the rendezvous at Camp Union (Lewisburg, West Virginia). Meanwhile, 300 men from the Clinch, Holsten, and New River settlements, under William Russell and William Christian, marched down the New River to the rendezvous, driving 200 head of cattle ahead of them, and losing time each morning rounding up strays. Botetourt County sent 450 men and Culpeper 100. On September 6, Lewis and his Augusta men left the camp and headed toward Mouth of Elk (Charleston, West Virginia). There they built canoes to float to the Ohio. Moving his 600 men, 54,000 pounds of flour on 400 packhorses, and 108 beeves on hoof, was no mean feat. It took them seventeen days to travel 100 miles, but this army would not suffer the hunger experienced by the men of the Sandy Creek expedition eighteen years earlier. Lewis located his forces on land that he had claimed at the mouth of the Great Kanawha called Point Pleasant. Meanwhile Governor Dunmore arrived on the river and built a stockade fifteen miles below the mouth of the Little Kanawha to protect his 170 cattle and provisions, including 50,000 pounds of flour. These three groups of cattle are said to have been the first in the Ohio Valley.[11]

A combined force of Shawnees and Mingoes under the leadership of Chief Cornstalk crossed the Ohio and attacked Lewis's men on October 9, 1774. Dunmore and his men were up the Ohio planning a march on a major Shawnee town there and did not assist Lewis. Casualty estimates varied from 49 killed and 80 wounded to 75 killed and 180 wounded. Among the wounded was

Cattle Horns: A Colonial Commodity

Rural people often declare during hog butchering time that "everything but the squeal" is eaten or otherwise used. The same frugality applied to cattle during Virginia's colonial period. Not only were cattle put to good use while they were alive – for dairy production, manure production, and as draft animals – but everything except the "moo" was used after slaughter. The meat was consumed, hoofs became glue, hide became leather, tallow became candles, and horn was fashioned into a variety of useful household items. In the seventeenth and eighteenth centu-

ries, eating utensils, combs, and drinking vessels were often made of horn. Also, horn could be softened with heat and flattened into thin translucent sheets for making a horn-book – printed text mounted on a wooden board and covered with a thin sheet of horn. The word lantern derives from the word "Lanthorn"; originally, lamp windows were covered with translucent pieces of horn, not glass.

Perhaps the best-known colonial use of cattle horns is the powder horn, used as a safe, dry storage container for gunpowder. Surviving examples of horn powder vessels dating to the fifteenth and sixteenth centuries can be found in Europe.

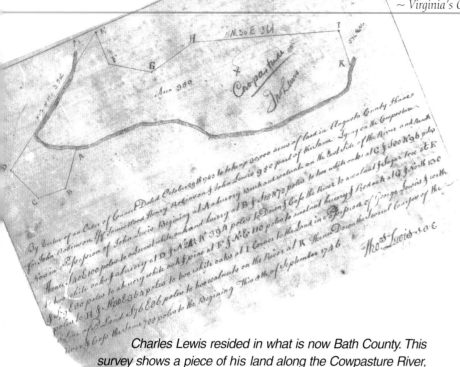

Charles Lewis resided in what is now Bath County. This survey shows a piece of his land along the Cowpasture River, one of dozens of bovine-related placenames in Virginia.

Feeding an Army

A revolution is a form of civil war pitting neighbor against neighbor, brother against brother. Although hindsight often suggests that American colonists were overwhelmingly in favor of the break with Britain, much contemporary evidence suggests otherwise. As the rhetoric of Continental Congress sharpened in the late spring of 1775, some Virginia residents decided to leave the colony and return to England. In the *Virginia Gazette* many persons announced their intention to leave and placed their property, including cattle, for sale.[12]

Supplying Virginia's Revolutionary soldiers was an enormous task, in part because of the complexity of how they were organized. Virginia soldiers in the Revolution served in four different forces: the continental line under the command of George Washington and the Continental Congress, the state troops, the county militia, and the navy. Virginia supplied fifteen regiments to the continental line. In addition, several independently raised regiments of infantry, artillery, and dragoons served the Continental Congress. The troops of the state line included an artillery regiment, three infantry regiments, the State Garrison Regiment, Dabney's State Legion, two regiments in Illinois, and the troops guarding the prisoners from the Battle of Saratoga who lived in the barracks outside Charlottesville. Militia units are more difficult to detail, as there were so many of them (from each of the seventy-five counties) and they served such a variety of commands, locales, and lengths of service.[13]

Supplying all of these troops was carried out somewhat haphazardly until late in the war when Virginia was invaded. Virginians who had fought under Washington's

William Fleming, and among the dead was Andrew Lewis' brother, Charles of Fort Lewis, Bath County. Dunmore concluded a peace with the Shawnee that quieted the western borders for a while, but many of the solders resented his lack of support at Point Pleasant, a clash some historians consider the "first" conflict of the American Revolution. These military forays set the stage for independence, but they also introduced cattle into the westerly region of Virginia and helped fuel a fundamental psychological shift in colonial thinking. Before these engagements, Virginias looked east to the Tidewater and even to the Old World. By the end the century, Americans were looking and migrating west to the great expanse of land across the Allegheny Mountains. And with civilization came agriculture and with agriculture came cattle.

These horns, however, did not retain the natural shape of the animal's horn but were, instead, flattened and carved in relief. The first known horn-shaped powder vessels appeared in Europe in the late seventeenth century. By 1724, many Germans were using a horn-shaped powder horn and hunting pouch with remarkable similarities to those used in the Virginia backwoods.

There is little doubt about the European origin of the traditionally shaped American frontier powder horn, but the carvings and decorations on America horns are uniquely New World. Makers carved initials, maps, animals, dates, flags, and geographic place names on their horns. The earliest known

American powder horn contains elaborate carvings of animals, Indians, canoes, flowers, hunters, and fish, as well as the date of 1726 and the name "Jorges Fort" – probably the same Fort George located at the mouth of the James River in Virginia. Another early horn, once owned by Virginia militiaman James Halstead, tells the story through its engraving of Halstead's adventures in the French and Indian War while on duty in New York.

No two powder horns were alike. Some were homemade and contained only crude initials and dates scratched into the outer surface; others were carved by professional horners. Professionals often made wooden utensils as well because both materials were

command in New Jersey and wintered in Valley Forge in 1777-1778 knew well the horrors of deprivation of food and clothing. Washington himself reported to Congress just before Christmas of 1777 that there was "not a single hoof of any kind to slaughter, and not more than twenty-five barrels of flour."[14] John Marshall, the future Chief Justice of the United States, who was a young soldier at Valley Forge, was enraged that "through treachery, cattle meant for the famishing patriots were driven into the already over-supplied Philadelphia."[15]

An early view of the local purchase of beef to supply the Virginia forces comes from the diary of Landon Carter of Sabine Hall, Richmond County. He recorded on Sunday, April 7, 1776, his receipt of money for beef: "Yesterday Captain Burgess Ball having sent me by Wm. Beale, Junr., my Steward, £6.16 for 403 pounds of beef at 4 which was 8d more than my due, I this day sent him a full bit in balance by his Ensign Bob Beale…. I also sold to Griffin Garland, the under contractor, two beaves more."[16] In late July of 1776, Carter noted again that a contractor, William Barber of Richmond County, had come to buy beef from him.[17]

Historians agree that the war stimulated agricultural production and that the civilian population, except only in rare isolated instances, did not suffer food deprivation during the war. One of those isolated instances was the May 1778 threat of 300 Wyandot and Mingo warriors to Fort Randolph at the mouth of the Kanawha in present West Virginia. Although no lives were lost in the verbal confrontation, the Indians slaughtered the 150 cattle grazing outside the compound, striking a blow to the food supply of those isolated frontier settlers in the midst of the war.[18] Yet, while most civilians in Virginia continued to eat well, there were numerous instances, such as at

Valley Forge, in which the army encountered food shortages. In February of 1778, George Washington released an address to the patriots about the food shortages. He reminded that his armies were now shut off by the British from access to cattle in the east (New England and New York), so he urged the people of Virginia and Maryland to fatten as many stock cattle as they could spare for the army.[19]

Virginia's efforts to comply with this request can be seen in the plans throughout the new Commonwealth to collect and drive the needed cattle north to Washington's army. On April 24, 1778, a notice appeared in the *Virginia Gazette*, the state's only newspaper, published in Williamsburg since 1738. John Hawkins announced that the governor and Council had appointed him to collect

turned on lathes. A horner also owned a device called a horn press that softened horn by heating it. Some horners made their livings by attaching themselves to military encampments.

Raw horns were obtained from tanners, and sometimes supplies of horns were requisitioned by the military. Large numbers of horns would have been needed in the Virginia backcountry during the French and Indian War, Dunmore's War, and during the Revolution. In 1778, faced with a desperate need for powder horns, authorities in the Continental Army ordered that "The Commissary of hides is hereafter Carefully to Deposit all the horns of the Cattle Kill'd for the army with the Commissary of Military Stores, who is hereby

Directed to have them Converted into Powder horns, for the use of the Troops, as fast as they are Delivered him."

Once the cartridge box was introduced during the Revolutionary War, the days of the powder horn were numbered. However, it did not disappear entirely until the Civil War. The last half of the twentieth century has seen a revival in the horner's craft and much beautiful horn work has been created as a result. The utilitarian tool of the eighteenth-century Virginia backwoodsman is today seen as a work of art. ~

Gordon Barlow, "The Traditional American Powder Horn: Its Origin and Future," unpublished article, and John S. duMont, *American Engraved Powder Horns: The Golden Age, 1755-1783* (Canaan, N.H.: Phoenix Publishing, 1978) were important sources for this sidebar.

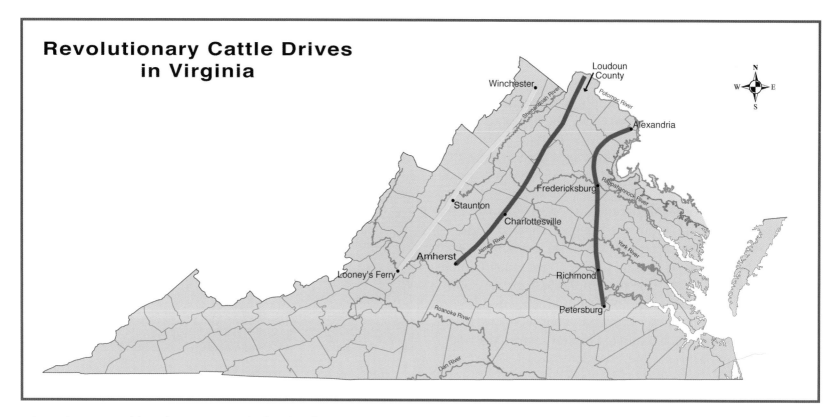

Revolutionary Cattle Drives in Virginia

In order to provide adequate protein for the Continental Army as well as the Virginia militia, the revolutionary government of the Old Dominion arranged for cattle drives. Starting at three appointed collection points for the Fall Line counties, the Piedmont, and the Valley, the cattle were driven north for slaughter and distribution to the army.

cattle for the army. Several significant collection points had been set up across the state, including Petersburg, Amherst Courthouse, Orange Courthouse, Fredericksburg, Looney's Ferry, Staunton, and Winchester.

Three large droves had been organized. One would start in Petersburg and make its way north by way of the city of Richmond, and Hanover and Caroline Counties just to the west of the fall line. The second would start in Amherst and work its way north along the eastern slopes of the Blue Ridge via Albemarle, Orange, Culpeper, Fauquier, and Loudoun Counties. The third route drove through the Valley, starting at Looney's Ferry on the James River near the present town of Buchanan in Botetourt County, stopping at Paxton's in present Rockbridge County, then at Staunton and Winchester. Hawkins assured readers that agents who were qualified to purchase cattle at the highest current local prices would accompany each drove.[20]

The Virginia legislature found numerous ways to raise funds, food, and supplies to fight the war. By October 1779, the legislature admitted that "it is found that the taxes already imposed for defraying the annual expenditure of this commonwealth, are not adequate" and a new measure was passed. This provided that, among other assessments, "an additional tax of six shillings and eight pence per head shall be paid for all neat cattle within this state."[21] That same session passed a measure to recover arms, cattle, horses, and other property belonging either to the Commonwealth or to the United States, but in the hands of private Virginia citizens, with county courts empowered to try any suits or petitions regarding such property.[22]

In July of 1780, with massive British invasion of the state pending, Virginia faced the task of raising and equipping additional troops, as well as providing troops for General Nathanael Greene's Continental Army in the southern campaign in the Carolinas. Governor Thomas Nelson sent a letter that month to the county lieutenants of each of the seventy-five Virginia counties noting that "the Harvest being over. I hope the militia which have been ordered into Service from your county will take the field with the greatest alacrity."[23]

While Pittsylvania County, to name one example, could theoretically raise 1,004 men, in reality no more than 670 were available, and 300 of them had already been sent to General Greene. Finding the resources to clothe and equip them was difficult, especially with agents of the Continental Army and of the Commonwealth competing for the same short supplies. In October 1780, the General Assembly assessed all counties for clothing and beef. Pittsylvania County's share was twenty complete suits of clothing and twenty beeves, as well as a wagon and four horses to pull it. To acquire the clothing and beef, the county was divided into twenty districts, each to provide one suit and one beef, with a person named as receiver for each district. The receiver then called a meeting of the (white male) inhabitants of his district in August and assessed each a sum in pounds, depending, apparently, upon his ability to pay. With the sum in hand, the receiver took bids in early September and awarded the contract for the clothing to several men, and bought one beef that was to weigh 300 pounds from George Herndon for £600. The goods were finally delivered in November, making the process four months from beginning to end.[24] Prince Edward County followed the same procedure for the thirty-eight suits of clothing and one good beef weighing 300 pounds that it was assessed.[25] It is little wonder that supplying the troops was difficult with such a scattered and lengthy procedure taking place in every county. Sparsely populated areas and poor transportation networks further complicated the situation.

The commissioners appointed to get provisions in the counties operated under oath and were empowered to visit farms to examine the livestock and supplies of each family. If the owners refused to sell, the commissioners had the authority to seize the goods. Commissioners

...the Harvest being over. I hope the militia which have been ordered into Service from your county will take the field with the greatest alacrity.

Governor Thomas Nelson

paid for the goods with receipts or certificates that were payable within six months at six percent interest, and that could be used as currency.[26]

The war came to Virginia in the most direct way in the summer of 1781. As General Lafayette, commander of the Continental Army in Virginia, made his way through the state, the Southside counties of Prince Edward, Charlotte, Lunenburg, Mecklenburg, and Bedford served as collection points for his ammunition and supplies. Amelia, Dinwiddie, Chesterfield, Powhatan, Cumberland, and Goochland were the source of most of the fifty barrels of flour Lafayette's army needed each day. When Lord Cornwallis' British army reached the James River in Surry County on July 8, 1781, he dispatched Lieutenant Colonel Banastre Tarleton to lead raiding parties throughout the nearby countryside. British detachments that landed at Hampton Roads led raiding parties along the James under the command of the traitor Benedict Arnold and others.[27]

As American armies pushed the British toward Yorktown, the problem of food and supplies reached the crisis stage. The governor dispatched General Robert Lawson of Virginia's Fourth Regiment into the countryside to round up supplies. He set mills to grinding flour, and requisitioned wagons and ox-carts to haul it to the army. He noted

that a large amount of beef had been sent so that "the army will not suffer on this head."[28] The American efforts, with major French army and navy assistance, finally proved successful. Cornwallis's deputy surrendered his sword to General Benjamin Lincoln acting on Washington's behalf on October 19, 1781. The Revolution was not over officially but this signaled the end of the fighting.

The costs of war

In the minds of thousands of Virginians, the Revolution would not be over until they had been compensated for their provision of food and supplies to the army. The law required that those with claims against the United States government or against the Commonwealth of Virginia submit the claim and authenticating documentary evidence to their local county court. The court would determine the validity of the claim and its fair market value, and send the claim on to Richmond to be paid. Each county court compiled its report of claims made.[29]

A detailed analysis could fill as much space as the three published volumes that have been compiled from the reports. Such an analysis is not the intention of this chapter. For purposes of this book, the claims offer the opportunity to examine a representative sampling of counties across the state to see the extent to which beef played a role in the claims.

In Accomack County on the Eastern Shore, the court certified fifty-eight claims, mainly for salt, rum, brandy, corn, bacon, and oats. Not one was for cattle. The Gloucester County court in April 1782 set its compensation rates at four pence per pound for grass beef, six pence for stalled beef, six pence also per pound for pickled beef, four pence per pound for pork, and -and-one-half pence for mutton and pickled pork.[30]

Each county court was apparently free to set its own rates of compensation. In the same month in James City County, on the south side of the York River and just a few miles from Gloucester, stalled beef was compensated at five pence per pound, grass-fed beef at three pence per pound, and smoked beef at seven-and-one-half pence per pound. The fee for a driver to service beef was five pence per day. In comparison, mutton and veal were each six pence per pound, bacon seven-and-one-half pence per pound, and a turkey was four shillings. Among the claims presented for the county was that of Colonel Nathaniel

Crops, slaves, and animals, including cattle, that the British Army took from Edward Baptist are listed here. A special commission was named to receive war damage claims from Virginia patriots for losses they suffered in the Yorktown campaign that brought the American Revolution to an end.

Burwell of Carter's Grove plantation on the James outside Williamsburg. Besides two horses, a wagon and gear for four horses, eight bushels of wheat, 360 bundles of fodder, and 1,000 pounds of hay, Burwell had provided 7,294 pounds of beef and 179 pounds of salted beef.[31]

A much smaller operator, Isham Allen, put in a claim for driving beeves and for providing 275 pounds of grass beef and two hundred pounds of fodder. James Cannaday claimed 650 pounds of beef. Five men, William Allen, Jr., William Geddy, Jr., Jeremiah Taylor, and Pinkethman Taylor each put in for fifteen days of beef driving. A representative few of the many other beef claimants and their poundage were Hudson Allen, 1,950 pounds grass beef, Cary Wilkinson, 2,776, Benjamin Warburton, 1,987, John Walker, 812 pounds beef, 25 pounds smoked beef, and Digges Cole 532 1/2 pounds beef.[32]

In Augusta County, in the heart of the Shenandoah Valley, the provisions purchased by commissioner James Culbertson in February through December of 1779, were destined for the Convention troops, part of the army that surrendered at the Battle of Saratoga, who were stationed "at or near Staunton." Of the 118 purchases made, some of them from Staunton merchants, many were for flour, some for hogs, and more than a few for whiskey. Forty-eight of the 118 claims involved purchase of beef or services relating to beef. These included £10/6 on the claim of Captain Peter Hogg to be paid to the butcher for "slatring 12 beeves," and to another butcher £69 for slaughtering Pat. Lockhart's forty-six beeves. Other payments went to John Paxton for salting and storage of meat, and to George Kile, Henry Backer, David Bell, and others for driving cattle.[33]

The purchases made in Augusta County in 1780 by commissioner Joseph Bell went for the army and militia. Bell bought from eighty-six different persons, including himself and six others with the surname Bell. He bought four beeves for £2,100 from Zachariah Johnston, who represented Augusta County in the legislature and who was to chair its important committee on religion in 1786 when Jefferson's bill for religious freedom was the landmark measure passed. The currency was greatly inflated by this time, so that animals that had cost a few pounds before the war now cost more than £400 each. He purchased a total of 275 beef cattle, paid several persons for pasturage and for driving them, and apparently took the responsibility of looking after them, for he put in a claim for "57 days guarding country cattle" and pasturage for £1,021 / 12.[34]

In the summer of 1781 Redcoat units were all over eastern Virginia. The General Assembly, warned by Jack Jouett of the British advance on their Charlottesville meeting place, had fled west over the Blue Ridge at Rockfish Gap at the end of June and met in the Augusta Parish Church at Staunton. In July, under pressure to raise more troops and supplies to turn back the British advances, Henry King, deputy commissioner for Augusta County, began purchasing provisions for "Col. White's Regt. Of Light Dragoons." He bought 32 beeves and 409 gallons of whiskey.[35]

The claims continued in this same vein in county after county all across Virginia, and continuing into 1783, two years after the Battle of Yorktown. In May 1782, three famous figures were among the 118 persons presenting claims to the Albemarle County Court. Jouett, Virginia's counterpart to Paul Revere, asked compensation for the Continental forces who occupied a house he owned and also for a bay mare impressed for the Continental line. Thomas Mann Randolph, Jefferson's son-in-law and future governor of Virginia, placed a claim for 4,000 sheaves of oats. Dr. Thomas Walker, explorer, land speculator, discoverer of the Cumberland Gap and guardian to the young fatherless Thomas Jefferson, presented a claim for 2,975 pounds of beef taken for the use of the Continental army. Jefferson himself had a long list of claims, including ten bushels of corn furnished for General Anthony Wayne, pork and corn furnished to the guards for the German General von Steuben who aided Washington, a gelding, a steer, a beef, and 825 pounds of beef taken for the state militia.[36]

The most poignant of claims were those placed by persons who suffered far more than the loss of some of their livestock and farm produce impressed by local government officials to feed the soldiers. Residents of York County, site of the Battle of Yorktown, suffered severe losses. For example, Edward Baptist presented a list of the damage done to his farm by the British army. He lost a field of corn, 3,000 fencing logs, 16 head of cattle, 8 hogs, 6 sheep, 25 gallons of brandy, a gun, a large quantity of oats in the straw, turkeys and geese, his "valuable Negroe man (Sam) abt 45" [years], a field hand, and a two year-old child. If Baptist were an ordinary farmer, a loss of this extent could be a serious blow to the well-being of his family.[37]

Far more serious were the losses of William Stevenson "by the ravages of the Enemy during the present War." He lost an entire six room house, another house, a kitchen, a dairy, a smoke house, a large hen house, his well, eleven head of cattle, a riding horse, a young slave girl, and a number of pieces of fine walnut and mahogany furniture. His total claims reached £785, a significant and serious loss. John Robinson turned in his list of losses "sustained from the depradations and several Invasions of the British Troops during the War." In addition to three slaves, two large canoes burned by the British, a fowling piece, and ten head of sheep, he lost a young bull and an ox cart with new wheels, six very fine oxen and good yokes and chains. Merritt Moore lost a canoe, two horses, a fowling piece, and four work oxen with yokes, chains, and a cart.[38] Among the many forms of loss in the war, cattle figured prominently.

By supplying the needs of the Continental and state armies throughout the Revolution, but especially in the final three years, Virginia farmers made a difference in the ability of those forces to continue the long fight. Whether the thousands of farmers sold cheerfully and voluntarily cannot always be determined. Nonetheless, it is certain that the general success of agriculture in late-eighteenth-century Virginia enabled the state to be a source of food for armies fighting to the north and to the south, as well as within the borders of the Old Dominion. That the American armies marched on bread and beef is a key theme running through all these records of food collection, so that one can safely say that Virginia beef played a significant role in the winning of the American Revolution.

In the minds of thousands of Virginians, the Revolution would not be over until they had been compensated for their provision of food and supplies to the army.

The New Republic

In many ways the era of the American Revolution marks an important transition in the history of Virginia's cattle. Markets, both foreign and domestic, were drastically redefined and agriculture changed to reflect those new trends. The development of the republican ideology of the new nation shifted the popular focus westward for growth and expansion rather than eastward toward the Old World. Nowhere was this better reflected than in the new word coined for that territory on the edge of civilization. The region west of the Blue Ridge, but especially the land west of the Alleghenies, once called the "backcountry," was now referred to as the "frontier."

Fertilizing the Earth. . . with Cattle

The changed political and economic climate also brought changes in agriculture. In the eastern-most portions of Virginia, the decades just after the war saw the completion of a shift from a tobacco-based economy to one based on corn or wheat. This change led to a rise in the importance of cattle for draft purposes and manure production and helped launch a search for ways

to increase agricultural production. For the first time, there were practical reasons to confine animals in pastures or yards. Fences prevented wandering animals from destroying crops, but, more important, penning animals allowed for the stockpiling of manure for enriching the soil. The idea for cowpenning was born in the tobacco era, but the practice became more widely known during the grain era as Enlightenment-based scientific ideas were applied to farming.

Between the presidencies of George Washington and Abraham Lincoln, Virginia agriculture underwent dramatic change. For the first time, farmers saw value in penning animals as depicted in this 1850s scene just outside Lexington. Confining livestock limited crop damage from strays while simultaneously collecting manure to replenish fields under cultivation.

Tobacco wears out the soil. Colonists had to let fields lie fallow for many years, clear new fields, or find ways to revitalize the soil more quickly than by fallowing. As new lands became scarce and difficult to obtain, increasingly farmers turned to the practice of penning cattle on tobacco fields and letting the manure revitalize the soil.

Planters who did not own enough cattle to employ this technique, rented them from others. The owner of the penned cattle was reimbursed per head for the manure that his animals provided the tobacco farmer. The first documented instance of cowpenning occurred in 1688. One hundred years later, in the 1790s, farmers practiced cowpenning widely, despite its high cost.[1]

In 1800, leading agriculturists recommended confining small numbers of cattle on small tobacco fields and shifting the cattle to a new area daily as a means of enriching the soils.[2] Cowpenning continued well into the 1800s and many nineteenth-century agricultural journals lauded its merits. Eventually farmers penned 100 cattle for a week at a time on an area of land where 1,000 tobacco plants were to be grown.[3]

Thomas Jefferson relied upon cattle to fertilize his field and garden crops.

The shift from tobacco to grain in Virginia strengthened the interdependence of cattle and plant cultivation. A common ditty from the nineteenth century summarized the connections: "Without grass you've no cattle – without cattle 'tis plain, You'll have no manure and without that no grain."[4] As noted earlier, George Washington knew full well the value of manure. The same can be said of another prominent Virginian, Thomas Jefferson. Although his international fame was based on his statesmanship, Jefferson attempted to derive his living from the land; he operated a number of plantations in Albemarle and Bedford Counties. Cattle were important to him for their meat, dairy, and leather products as well as for draft power and transportation. In his later years, Jefferson also relied upon them to

fertilize his field and garden crops. Despite his recognition of manure as a means of enriching the soil, Jefferson only slowly warmed to the idea of confining cattle for dung collection. In 1793, he wrote George Washington that he did not bother with the process "because we can buy an acre of new land cheaper than we can manure an old acre. . . ."[5]

Eighteen months later, Jefferson had apparently changed his mind as he set out in a letter an idea he had conceived for constructing ". . . a moveable airy cow house, to be set up in the middle of the field which is to be dunged, & soil our cattle in that thro' the summer as well as winter, keeping them constantly up & well littered. . . ."[6] Jefferson eventually worked his moveable cow sheds into the rotation of each of his forty-acre grain fields. In the center of each field was a granary. During the winter after a wheat crop was removed from a particular field, the temporary sheds were erected next to the granary. The cattle housed there were fed on the straw left from the harvest. In February or March the manure and straw were put on the field to enhance its fertility. Also, green manures such as clover and vetch were integrated into the rotation of crops.[7]

Selective Breeding

The progressiveness of Jefferson's views regarding the integration of cattle into his scheme for crop production did not extend to other aspects of his bovine husbandry. Unlike Washington, he did little in the way of selective breeding or importation of superior cattle. Some of the other wealthier Virginia farmers, however, were beginning to take an interest in the selective breeding experiments of Robert Bakewell and others in Britain. Improved horses, sheep, and cattle were imported first into Maryland and Pennsylvania and, shortly thereafter, Virginia. Among these Virginia planters whose agricultural practices were influenced by Enlightenment ideas were Colonel Archibald Cary of Chesterfield County, who imported some early Shorthorns, and a Mr. Hylton, who brought in blooded animals specifically as large oxen.[8]

The best-documented early importation of improved cattle occurred in 1793 when Matthew Patton of Rockingham County and Augusta County's Henry Miller began crossing large, red, long-horned and short-horned cattle imported from England, with the smaller, native scrub stock. The resulting animals, which came to be known as Patton stock, were thought by many to be larger-framed and better milk producers than the common cattle. Patton moved to Kentucky in the 1790s and took his improved cattle with him. These improved animals greatly influenced the appearance of cattle in western Virginia and Kentucky for decades.

Although no true cattle breeds existed in the 1790s, these cattle probably carried the genetic foundation for the development of both the Shorthorn and the British Long-horn breed (genetically distinct from the later Texas Long-horn) as those two breeds arose from the same area around Yorkshire in England. In 1839, Patton's grandson described the "blooded" cattle that his grandfather had used to create the Patton stock. The bull, named "Mars," was "a deep red, with a white face, of good size, of round full form, of more bone than the popular stock of the present day, his horns somewhat coarse." The heifer, named "Venice," was almost entirely white "except her ears which were red, of fine size, high form, short crumply horns turning downwards." In 1803, Patton crossed his Mars bloodline with that of an imported bull, named "Pluto," which he had purchased from Miller. According to some accounts, Pluto represented the Shorthorn breed prototype.[9] Patton's grandson described Pluto as "dark red or brindle" and as "the largest bull I have ever seen." The bull had "an uncommonly small head and neck, light, short horns, very heavy fleshed, yet not carrying so much on the most desirable points as the fashionable stock of the present day, with small bones for an animal of his weight. . . ."[10]

Although the Patton stock was technically not yet a specific breed, it represented the beginning of a trend to introduce imported animals that had been selectively bred in certain regions of Britain and Europe. Geographic isolation in the Old World had also helped create distinct gene pools within certain regions even before the application of scientific breeding techniques. The Devon is a good example of a breed created more through geographic isolation than selective breeding. These dark red animals, which had been developed in the counties of Devon and Cornwall in southwest England, represented a distinct breed by the sixteenth century. Known for their hardiness in a yoke and good milking abilities, Devon-like animals were among the first cattle imported into Virginia. Nearly two centuries of random breeding in the colony had subsequently produced a hard, compact, multi-purpose animal that, more often than not, had a red coloring. Virginians called them native scrub, common, or grade stock of the state. The Shorthorn, also known as Durham or Teeswater cattle for their geographic place of origin in Yorkshire, then, represented the first improved animals introduced into the state. For more than a century, the Shorthorn blood reigned supreme in Virginia cattle. Shorthorns ranged in color from red, red and white, to roan or any combination of those colors. The introduction of this blood would have only enhanced the dominant red color of cattle seen across Virginia's countryside. Seeing predominantly red cattle grazing in Virginia's fields would certainly be an odd sight to the modern traveler accustomed to seeing a majority of black or black and white animals as a result of Angus and Holstein importations late in the nineteenth century.

By the early nineteenth century, true breeds had emerged. Uniformity came to the process of selective breeding with the creation of herd books in which breeders recorded detailed lineages of purebred animals. The maintenance of these records and the efforts to keep stock pure eventually necessitated the formation of breed associations as well. The Shorthorn breed represents a good example of how record keeping evolved. The Shorthorn breed book was established in 1822 in England. New Yorker Lewis Allen produced the first American herd book in 1846, and in 1872 leading breeders founded the American Shorthorn Association.[11]

Once farmers understood the science of selective breeding and husbandmen knew how to enhance particular desirable characteristics, the door opened to a new age of agriculture. For the first time, farmers could specialize in dairy or beef production and imported stock

could be chosen with an eye toward a particular quality. Although it would take another half century and several important transportation and technological advances for a full emergence of cattle breeds well suited to distinctive agricultural specialties, the groundwork for this had been laid in the early nineteenth century.

Although the Shorthorn breed was the first of the early improved breeds to be introduced into North America (and proved to be the most popular), several other distinct breeds appeared before the Civil War. Ayrshires followed on the heels of the Shorthorn importations. These good milk producers developed in Scotland. Formally recognized as a breed in 1814, the first Ayrshires came to Connecticut in 1822 and quickly became popular elsewhere, including

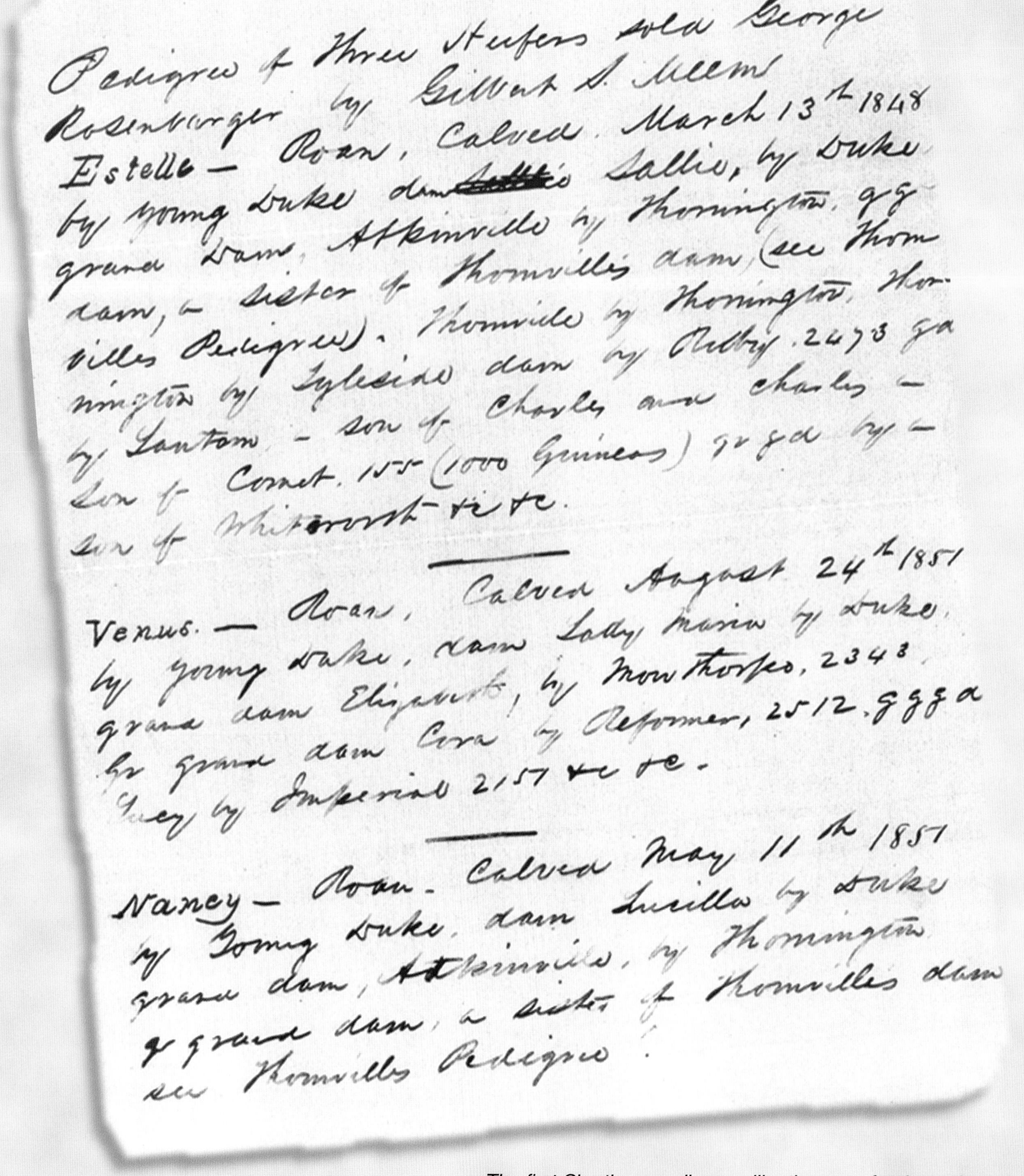

Pedigree of three Heifers sold George
Rosenberger by Gilbert S. Meem

Estelle — Roan, Calved. March 13ᵗʰ 1848
by Young Duke dam ~~Sallie's~~ Sallie, by Duke
grand Dam, Atkinville by Thornington, 9 g
dam, a sister of Thornville's dam (see Thorn
villes Pedigree). Thornville by Thornington. Thornington by Tyleside dam by Ruby. 2473 g⁴
by Santon — son of Charles and charles —
Son of Comet. 155 (1000 Guineas) 9ᵗʰ gᵈ by —
son of Whitworth &c &c.

_____

Venus. — Roan, Calved August 24ᵗʰ 1851
by young Duke, dam Lady Maria by Duke.
grand dam Elizabeth, by Mowthorpes, 2343.
gr grand dam Cora by Reformer, 2512. g g g a
Lucy by Imperial 2157 &c &c.

_____

Nancy — Roan. Calved May 11ᵗʰ 1851
by Young Duke. dam Lucilla by Duke
grand dam, Atkinville, by Thornington.
g grand dam, a sister of Thornville's dam
see Thornvilles Pedigree.

*The first Shorthorn pedigrees, like the ones for these three
heifers named Estelle, Venus, and Nancy, were handwritten.*

Virginia. A breed association was established in 1875. Guernsey cattle, from the English channel island of the same name, were brought into the United States about 1830, specifically for the golden yellow milk they produced. In contrast, Herefords, from England, were prized for their meat. Breeders introduced them in large numbers in the early 1800s.[12] Although animals resembling the black, hardy Kerry cattle of Ireland probably arrived in Virginia in the seventeenth century, the breed was not improved and imported as a recognized breed until 1818. They were popular dairy animals until the early twentieth century.[13]

It is important not to confuse the introduction of purebred stock into Virginia with the notion that most farmers had herds of purebred animals. Rather, farmers would acquire one or two blooded animals with the characteristics they were seeking and use that blood to improve their own stock. The editor of *The Southern Planter* explained this reasoning in an 1841 article: "So valuable is acclimation, that the judicious breeder seldom discards the native stock, but builds upon it by selection and crossing."[14]

George W. Rosenberger, of Tenth Legion in Rockingham County, knew that most farmers were seeking a few select animals to improve their own stock. Starting in the 1830s, Rosenberger began making contacts with Shorthorn breeders in such places as New York, Pennsylvania, and Canada. According to an 1858 article in the *Valley Democrat*, he did so at significant expense, but with considerable success as well. He "procured the finest blooded stock to be found in the country, and commenced raising and grazing his own stock, and by this means has contributed greatly to the improvement of cattle in this section. His cattle are acknowledged by all to be of the very best kind, larger, handsomer, better developed; and the cows give more, better, and richer milk than others that could be mentioned. His cattle have received premiums at all the agricultural fairs they have been, and always command a high price in the market."[15]

"Christmas Duke" was the prize bull of Rosenberger's barnyard. Rosenberger had purchased him as a yearling from a breeder in Auburn, New York, in the spring of 1860. Negotiations at such distances included detailed descrip-

tions and drawings. A letter from the breeder noted that, in early 1860, the young bull was sixteen months old, weighed over 1,000 pounds and was a rich roan color.[16]

Even before the acquisition of Christmas Duke, Rosenberger's animals had a reputation of quality in the Valley of Virginia. In 1856, he sold a thirteen-year-old cow, Fleety Red, to a man in Page County for $100. The cow weighed 1,530 pounds when she was sold. In 1858, eight steers and a heifer from Rosenberger's farm brought $820 – more than a year's salary for many people.[17]

The desire of at least some Valley farmers to upgrade their stock through the introduction of a Rosenberger ani-

CHRISTMAS DUKE---2628.

mal or two was great. For example, in a letter to Rosenberger, one prospective buyer of his stock indicated that he had received a letter from his brother-in-law...

> ...in which he gives a glowing description of your improved stock, pronouncing them the best he ever seen. I should like to get one of your best bred bull calves and a cow or so with him, but having just purchased a large and high priced farm I fear I shall be short of funds, consequently will have to cut my coat with reference to the cloth. I must however strain a point to get your bull calf. I will pay you a visit – the last of August please reserve the calf until the first of September. I expect one of my neighbours, an industrious & enterprising farmer to accompany me.[18]

Of Fairs and Fodder – An Agricultural Revolution

The period between the American Revolution and the Civil War was a time of great innovation in agriculture. The selective breeding of livestock such as that undertaken on Rosenberger's farm changed the face of American farming. Much of the information about new practices was disseminated through agricultural journals, like the *American Farmer*, which was published in Baltimore, and *The Southern Planter*, published in Richmond. The latter advertised itself as "a monthly periodical devoted to Agriculture, Horticulture and Household Arts." By the 1820s and 1830s, local farming clubs began meeting. Farmers in these "self-improvement" groups would study various innovations, discuss issues, and compare notes on plant and animal varieties and agricultural techniques. Even the United States government became involved, circulating questionnaires among the more prominent farmers all across the country and publishing those replies along with a national agricultural census (first conducted in the mid-nineteenth century) containing farm-by-farm statistics on everything from numbers of animals to the bushels of grain grown.

This period also marked the beginning of the agricultural fair – an annual event still held in many rural communities – in which farm families pitted their best agricultural products against those of their neighbors for annual bragging rights. The first documented fair in Virginia took place in November of 1822 in Fredericksburg. The Fredericksburg Agricultural Society hosted the two-day event that included judging in both livestock and agricultural implements. Colonel George Love of Fauquier garnered top honors in the bull category for his animal that was the offspring of an English Lancashire bull and a crossbred milk cow.[19] By the 1840s nearly every county seat hosted a fair and many states held a large extravaganza with dozens of classes and large premiums. In 1841 the Henrico Agricultural and Horticultural Society held a fair that offered first-place prizes of ten dollars for the best bull, the best milch[20] cow and the best yoke of oxen.[21] By the next spring the society had expanded its classes to: the best bull, cow, and heifer of imported, improved stock; the best bull, cow and heifer of native stock raised by the exhibitor; and the best oxen raised by the exhibitor.[22] By contrast, the Virginia State Agricultural Society's show in 1843 offered prizes for Shorthorns, Herefords, Devons, Alderneys, Ayrshires, Holsteins, native or grade animals, working oxen, milch cows, and fat cattle. Premiums were also offered for the best butter.[23]

Ironpott, Model T, Blossom... What's in a Name?

Cattle have always been important on the family farms of Virginia. While there have always been nameless range cattle that were driven out to pasture in the summer and on to market in the fall, almost always a few head of cattle remained on the home farm. These animals, favorite milk cows, working oxen, or prize bulls, were often given names, either for a physical characteristic or a behavioral trait. We know some of those names today because the original owners called the animals by name in wills, letters, diaries, or account books.

Tidewater planter Thomas Silverthorn painstakingly named every one of the fifteen bovines in his 1798 will, but did not bother to give the name of his riding horse, or his hogs, if indeed the latter had names. Included in his list were "one cow with calf called Cherry," "Bull yearling called Buck," "one cow called Browny," as well as others called Diamond, Blossom, Rose, Damsel, and Pink.

The Poller Bull

Tracking the facts

Agricultural societies used their fairs and shows to showcase new technology and machinery as well as to judge livestock and plant produce. New plows, threshing machines, and the invention called the reaper were big crowd pleasers. One invention that is taken for granted today debuted in Virginia to considerably less fanfare in the 1830s. The cattle guard, used today as a convenience to tractor and automobile drivers, who would otherwise have to leave their vehicles to open and close gates, was patented on March 11, 1837, by Thomas J. West of Whitehall, Virginia, in Caroline County. West's intended use for his invention was the railroad. In fact he described his invention as a "road-stop for preventing cattle, &c, from crossing railroads." West's accompanying drawing shows a cattle guard based upon the same principle as today's guards with open slats that the animals would not cross.[24] Although West's patent places him in Caroline County, there is no Whitehall in that county although a farm by that name might have existed. There is a Whitehall in Albemarle County and some very hazy folklore links a resident West family and the invention of the cattle guard. Dr. James Hoy, a folklorist who has written a book on the cattle guard, suggests that West's Whitehall was the one in Albemarle County and, further, that he might have borrowed his patent idea from the area's most prominent

citizen – Thomas Jefferson. In order to protect the lawn around Monticello from grazing animals, Jefferson had his laborers construct a ha-ha, which is a deep, steep-sided ditch over which the grazing animals would have been afraid to jump. The ha-ha was not unique to Monticello; George Washington had one at Mount Vernon and many English country manors used this technique to keep livestock off their main lawns. Jefferson's innovation was to place a series of split rails across the ha-ha. Humans could walk across the rails, but cattle could not. Although its purpose was slightly different than the cattle guard in that the rails were not meant to deter animals (that was the job of the ha-ha) the crossway looked like a cattle guard and could have provided inspiration for West's patent. Hoy argues that maybe Jefferson, not West, should be given the real credit for the invention of the cattle guard.[25]

The cattle guard's impact was slight compared to other scientific and technological advances. In addition to the introduction of improved breeds, some important advances came in regard to diet and nutrition for cattle. As the nineteenth century progressed, the days of allowing cattle to forage for themselves were slowly disappearing. Farmers were making the connection between supplementing the diets of their animals and increased weight gain in beef animals and better milk production in dairy cows. With

Roger Chew, who lived near Winchester in the part of Virginia that became West Virginia after the Civil War, kept lists in his diary of when he put certain cows in with bulls to be bred. Sometimes the names he gave the animals were simply descriptive, as in "Cow no. 3," "yellow white-faced cow," or "Broken horned cow." However, he also owned animals named Cherry, Rose, Pink, and Plumb." In the early 1880s he often mentioned cows named Bossie, Spottie, Reddie, White, and Bush.

While many of Chew's bovine names were obviously created out of affection for the animals, George Rosenberger, of Rockingham County, had another reason for naming his purebred Shorthorn cattle.

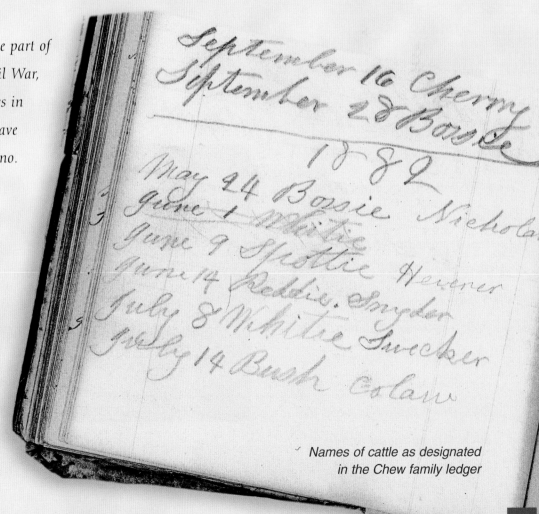

Names of cattle as designated
in the Chew family ledger

an increased emphasis on wheat and corn production, it did not take long to realize that animals could eat straw, and even better, they could eat the corn stalks and leaves. Soon a rudimentary box with a blade was being marketed so that cornstalks could be chopped into more palatable fodder for cattle. Leading agriculturalists also pushed the idea of growing hay especially for over-wintering animals. Some even grew timothy. Beets, mangelwurtzels, potatoes, carrots, turnips, and pumpkins were all used to fatten cattle. Jefferson noted in his farm book that "in fattening cattle they will eat from 1/3 to 1/4 of their weight of turneps per day besides hay. they will fatten in 4 months on turneps & hay alone, or in 3 months on a change of food. They prefer carrots to turneps. lots of them will suffice & fatten faster."[26] Jefferson was also known to feed his cattle wheat straw, corn tops and shucks, corn, pumpkins, and potatoes.

The agricultural journals from the period were filled with new ideas and advice on supplementing the bovine diet. In 1840 the Cumberland Agricultural Society heard an address recommending Silesian sugar beets as cattle food, while a representative of a veterinary school lauded a fermented potato and bran mixture, particularly for dairy cows, to his audience. In 1843, readers of the *Southern Planter* learned that tomatoes, either raw or mixed with meal, increased "the quality and richness of the milk" in dairy animals. And farmers who fed hay to their animals over the winter were reminded of the well-known axiom: "Count your cattle, and then your hay stocks, and if the one shall exceed the other, then either sell, eat, give away, or kill the surplus to keep them from dying."[27]

By tradition, farmers are conservative and so they did not adopt many of the newest ideas and techniques espoused in agricultural journals, at fairs, and within clubs until many years after their introduction. In many cases it was often the outsider who took to innovation more quickly. In 1837, upstate New Yorker Lewis Bailey, Sr., bought extensive tracts of land in an area of Fairfax County today known as Baileys Cross Roads. The Baileys operated a circus and they needed land on which to winter the circus animals. Lewis Bailey, Jr., decided to put down roots in the area and he purchased a worn-out farm of 150 acres from his father. Bailey applied the most modern scientific practices to his farm and within ten years some observers judged his farm to be the most prosperous one in the area. His cattle earned many prizes at local and state fairs in Maryland and Virginia. Bailey was among the first of a wave of northern transplants who migrated to Fairfax and applied advanced agricultural techniques to create prosperous farms.[28]

He wanted to keep track of their lineage through registered names. Thus, Christmas Duke was "calved December 25, 1858; got by Double Duke…out of Lady Sale Third…" Some of the other purebred animals that he owned were Estelle, Venus, and Nancy.

Sometimes the fancy registered names were shortened to more affectionate nicknames. During the last forty years, the Kindig family of Stuarts Draft, in Augusta County, built a national reputation for its Charolais cattle. The key to that reputation was ACR Alfalfa John 075, who was only six weeks old when they purchased him in 1970. The Poller Bull, as they nicknamed the gentle giant, was a

Cherry… Buck… Browny… Diamond, Blossom, Rose, Damsel, and Pink…

homozygous polled bull, which meant his offspring would always be polled. Similarly, the Wampler family from the village of Dayton in Rockingham County became nationally known for their Angus cattle. In the 1960s their record-breaking, prize bull was Eileenmere's Model T.H., but the family just called him Model T.

And while there have always been animals named Bossie and Flossie, a few unique names have also been placed upon Virginia's bovines. Heading that list might be the calf, "Iron Pott," which Amy Palmer of Lancaster County inherited from Mary Phipps in 1709. ~

Twentieth-century information about cattle names came from interviews with Earl Kindig (April 2002) and Bill Wampler (November 2002). Sources about nineteenth-century cattle naming practices include the Chew and Rosenberger Family Collections held at the archives at the Virginia Military Institute in Lexington. The best eighteenth-century sources for cattle names are wills and estate inventories. Thomas Silverthom's 1798 will can be found in Elizabeth City County Deed and Will Book 34, while the 1709 will of Mary Phipps is found in the Lancaster County Deed and Will Book.

Cash Cattle

The agricultural revolution spurred by scientific advances trickled down slowly to small and middling farmers. A study of post-revolutionary war changes in York County from 1783 to 1820 shows that relatively few small planters used improved agricultural tools or fed their livestock better and larger quantities of fodder and cultivated grasses. Nonetheless, a shift from tobacco production to grain production had occurred, although the grain of choice in the fields tended to be corn for animal food, not wheat. The same can be said of Elizabeth City County where the years after the Revolution witnessed the emergence of a farm economy based on provision trade – pork, corn, beef, and butter to supply ships trading within the Chesapeake Bay and with the West Indies – but saw very little attention paid to innovation. Although much of the ship provisions on which the rural economy was based went through middleman merchants in Hampton and Norfolk, farmers sold large amounts directly from the farm to procurement agents representing specific ships. In a relatively cash poor economy, slaughtered steers created a good cash flow to the farmer, as they were worth about twice as much dead as they were on the hoof.[29] Beef animals coming out of Elizabeth City and fattened on the salt marshes were as large as any in the country, each yielding, on average, 436 pounds of meat. At about four cents a pound, the average carcass sold for $17.44. The hide was worth an additional $1.20 and the tallow would have brought in still more income. An analysis of the trade items mentioned above, as listed in Elizabeth City inventories, shows clearly that the pivotal item within this economy was cattle. Three-fourths of the inventories of farmers from all income levels had herds larger than needed for home consumption.[30]

Some historians argue that the large numbers of animals grazing in the salt marshes along the mouth of the Chesapeake Bay, eating sedges and reeds, rivaled in numbers the size of the herds coming out of the mountains and valleys of western Virginia.[31] At least one traveler, Johann Schoepf from Germany, commented in the 1790s that the forage of sedge and reeds provided a better quality meat.[32] Better meat or not, this type of grazing continued long after the West Indies trade had bottomed out and long after more scientific feeding methods were catching on in other parts of the state. One writer in 1842 noted that the salt marshes provided "extensive and luxuriant grazing, and in some situations the cattle are raised exclusively upon them, having never tasted a grain of corn, or blade of fodder."[33] The West Indies trade connection, in particular, boomed until the end of the Napoleonic Wars in 1815 and

Blennerhassett's Cattle Drives from Western Virginia

Cattle drives through the Great Valley of Virginia were common from at least the 1740s, but a half a century passed before settlement and agriculture in the Ohio Valley advanced to the point that farmers of that region, which was then the western part of Virginia, could drive cattle to eastern urban markets.

The first recorded cattle drive from the Ohio Valley headed not across the Allegheny Mountains, but to Detroit. In 1785, Isaac Zane and George Green of Wheeling, situated on the Ohio River in present-day West Virginia, drove cattle to Detroit and brought back "a great pile of money." The venture was dangerous, however. On a subsequent trip as they were returning with fourteen packhorses loaded with furs, Indians killed them.

The person credited with initiating cattle drives from the Ohio Valley to markets in Alexandria was a fascinating Irish aristocrat who settled in the Ohio Valley in 1797. Harman

Blennerhassett from Castle Conway, County Kerry, graduated from Trinity College, Dublin, and was admitted to the Irish bar. While in France at the time of the French Revolution he became a Deist. In Ireland he joined the Society of United Irishmen in 1793, a group that hoped to bring independence and republicanism to Ireland. Although Blennerhasset inherited Castle Conway and a small fortune when his father died in 1792, and he could have lived in customary comfort, he chose to emigrate. Part of the reason may have been that in 1794 he had married his own niece, Margaret Agnew, daughter of his older sister.

Blennerhassett purchased an island in the Ohio River near the mouth of the Little Kanawha River at present-day Parkersburg, West Virginia. There he constructed an elegant Georgian mansion house with dependencies. He purchased ten slaves and established a plantation where his economic

then crashed dramatically, forcing farmers to reduce their ship provisioning activities to vessels plying the Chesapeake waters and expand cultivation of new crops like sweet potatoes rather than concentrating on livestock.[34]

Although nearly every Elizabeth City County farmer, large or small, participated in the beef provisioning trade, commercial dairy production was usually the economic niche of farmers with thirty or more cattle. Butter, both for the ships and for urban markets such as Norfolk, was the main product. Probably the biggest producer was John Lowry. With his fifty-three cows, it is estimated that he made a surplus of 730 pounds of butter annually, well above and beyond the demands of his family. Lowry had thirty milk pots and fifteen butter pots in his inventory – further proof of the large-scale dairying operation. Such a set-up would have brought about $121 a year to the farm, or more than $1,200 in modern-day figures.[35]

A glimpse of urban meat production practices in the coastal region during the period just after the American Revolution and in the early republic comes from the pen of a French Creole, Moreau de St. Méry. This native of the French Caribbean island of Martinique was a lawyer, judge, and participant in the French revolution who settled in the new United States in

Harman Blennerhassett

the 1790s.[36] He observed of Norfolk, his first American place of residence, that "the slaughterhouses are on the outskirts of the town. The beeves are killed with a sledge hammer, their throats cut with a knife, and almost before they have stopped breathing they are skinned. In ordinary times one beef suffices for the town's daily needs."[37]

The arrival in Norfolk of a large number of French colonial and Creole refugees from Santo Domingo after the slave rising there, followed by the arrival of the French fleet, increased the demand for meat. After the arrival of the convoy from Santo Domingo, "two or three had to be killed daily; but when the French fleet anchored in the Chesapeake, from eight to twelve had to be slaughtered each day. Other foods were needed in similarly increased proportions."[38]

A Hardy Draft Animal

The shift in cultivation emphasis from tobacco to grains evident in the coastal areas occurred in varying degrees throughout the state. As a result of wider grain cultivation, even small farmers had an increased need for draft animals for plowing and harvesting. The shift from more expensive, faster, but less hardy horses to oxen as the preferred draft animal was dramatic in York County.

With Woodbridge and another associate, Joseph Lewis, Blennerhassett developed a cattle business. The animals they raised or purchased from others were driven east across the Allegheny Mountains for sale in Alexandria markets. Theirs was said to have been the first Trans-Allegheny cattle drive from the Ohio Valley. On the route east, the drovers and cattle had an ideal resting and grazing area along the South Branch of the Potomac River.

Land along the South Branch of the Potomac River was settled by the 1750s and this region soon emerged as the premier cattle-raising area of the Allegheny Mountains. Those cattle grazed in fields and were fed unhusked corn, and in the summer they pastured on the rich grasses in the Allegheny Glades. This region of bogs, swamps, and heath, which stretches from present Terra Alta, West Virginia, to Altamont, Maryland, includes the popular Canaan Valley ski area today.

activities included the raising of cattle. The $30,000 Blennerhassett spent constructing and stocking his idyllic retreat stimulated economic growth in the locale. The main nearby settlement at that time was Marietta, Ohio. There Blennerhasset entered a partnership with Dudley Woodbridge to establish a string of stores in Ohio in which imported European wares would be offered for sale and furs would be purchased for sale in Europe.

"This trend was most pronounced among non-slaveowners and on farms with five or fewer working hands. The incidence of oxen in inventories of non-slaveowners jumped from thirty-eight percent at the end of the eighteenth century to over half in the early nineteenth century, and among small slaveowners from fifty-eight percent just after the war to ninety-four percent after the War of 1812. . . . Small planters clearly selected the cheapest, albeit slowest, available draft animals when they began to use plows more systematically."[39]

Although an increase in the use of oxen occurred in the Tidewater region, the shift to oxen was not universal. West of the Blue Ridge Mountains, the draft animal of choice remained the horse, although oxen made occasional appearances in estate inventories. The estray books from Augusta County show this quite dramatically as well. John Skinner, the editor of the *American Farmer*, criticized Shenandoah Valley farmers for their indifference toward oxen after he toured the region in 1821: "farmers of this country make little use of them; they ought to be more in use. In fact, where negroes are the entire labourers, reliance ought to be placed on the ox for draft – the saving in their graizing and tackling is vast . . . ."[40]

The two-wheeled oxcart was a common form of farm transport in nineteenth-century Virginia.

Early settlers had found that its sedges and other plants provided ideal summer grazing. A national forest trail in the region still bears the name "Cow Pasture Trail."

Cattlemen of this region were already experienced in driving their cattle to markets in Baltimore and Alexandria. By 1800 a number of men raised on the South Branch had moved to the Ohio Valley, taking their cattle methods and their knowledge of eastern markets with them. Some members of the Renick, Inskeep, Patton, Gay, and Sanders families migrated to the Ohio Valley, while others remained along the South Branch. In the early nineteenth century the entrepreneurial projects of these families led to the full development of a trade that linked the Valley of Virginia and the Allegheny Glades to the cities of Baltimore, Alexandria, and the new federal capital at Washington. It is likely that Blennerhassett worked with some of these men in developing his cattle trade.

Unfortunately, the idyllic life that Blennerhassett tried to build for himself and his family on his frontier island, supported by agriculture, trade, and boat-building, came crashing down around him. Blennerhassett had the misfortune and misjudgment to become closely involved with Aaron Burr and his schemes for the southwest. As a result, President Thomas Jefferson ordered the arrests of Blennerhassett and Burr. The Irish aristocrat and frontier entrepreneur was to have been tried for treason in Richmond, but was freed when Burr was acquitted. As a result of this ill-fated political partnership, Blennerhassett's financial empire and his reputation were ruined. He then departed his island in the Ohio Valley. ~

The historian Ray Swick has devoted careful scholarship to the life of Harman Blennerhassett. Most of the material for this sidebar can be found in his dissertation, "Harman Blennerhassett: An Irish Aristocrat on the American Frontier" and on the website www.blennerhassett.org. Otis Rice's book, *The Allegheny Frontier: West Virginia Beginnings, 1730-1830* is a source for cattle raising in the South Branch of the Potomac. Information on the Allegheny Glades is available from the West Virginia Native Plant Society and *Geologic Map of West Virginia, Slightly Revised*, 1986 by Dudley Cardwell, et. al.

Mr. Shanghai tries another kind of Work. Finds the Odor unpleasant.

Is driven off from his work by an attack of Wild Beasts.

Makes one more Experiment. Close of Second Day.

Undertakes to yoke and drive the "Team." Slight mistake in the Gender.

This being rectified, he drives off;—a Reminiscence of the "Avenue."

After due meditation, Mr. Shanghai concludes to give up the Idea of being a Farmer.

This 1850s cartoon in a popular national magazine poked fun at a city slicker who tried his hand at farming. Among his many clumsy actions, he yoked two milk cows to draw the ox cart to market.

'Milch' Cows Move In

Virginians had always relied upon cattle for home dairy production in the form of milk, butter, and soft and hard cheese, but attempts at commercial production had been unsuccessful through the colonial period. The more profitable dairy operations in the colonies were in the Pennsylvania and New Jersey region around Philadelphia, and in New England. Part of Virginia's lack of success was due, no doubt, to the hot and humid climate, but some of the blame certainly fell on farmers who let their animals roam the countryside, fending for themselves. When Virginians recognized the need to confine animals for manure production, this attitude changed. Animals kept close to home for manure collection could also be milked regularly and given better care. The slow move toward modern dairy operations began around the Revolution when farmers began counting "milch" cows separately from their other cattle. The first agricultural census in 1840 had separate categories for the two types of bovines. The transportation boom of the first half of the nineteenth century contributed greatly to the rise in dairy production. Macadamized roads, canals, and railroads meant that farm surplus could be marketed in distant urban areas.

The potential that could be realized with improved husbandry was evident by the early nineteenth century. In 1809, Leila Skipworth Tucker of Williamsburg wrote the following to Frances Bland Coalter:

> Will you believe that I make every day a good plate of butter from my two cows, who have lately had calves, and give me, the two between 3 & 4 gallons of milk a day – This I atribute to the pains I have myself bestowed on them, and to my change of dairy maid, Judy being now in that capacity, and one of the best I ever saw –. . .I have Mash boiled for my cows in the kitchen, at the door of which they are milked 3 times a day – and I have plenty of butter with every day. It is impossible to say how much pleasure I feel every morning when the making of the day before comes to the Table. . . .[41]

The efforts made by Mrs. Tucker were obviously not commonplace across the state. On the eve of the Civil War, an article in the *Staunton Spectator* offered advice on the care and management of small dairies where, regrettably, "owners do not often study that close economy in feeding their cows, and the disposal of their products. . . . " The keys to increased dairy production, particularly in the winter, were, according to the newspaper, "succulent and nutritious food," especially carrots, pumpkins, and apples, and stabling animals, "especially at night and in stormy weather."[42]

Despite the conservative nature of most farmers and opinions of many writers such as the one above, the agricultural revolution had affected Virginians by mid-century. Improved bloodlines and better animal husbandry

A farmer ca.1910 milking a Shorthorn cow out in the field.

techniques produced an amazing change from centuries past, even within the state's limited dairy operations. In medieval times, cows were milked only four months a year, but agricultural advances in the seventeenth century meant that animals coming into Jamestown could be depended upon for milk production eight months of the year. By the nineteenth century, a good milk cow was dry only two months per year, although daily milk production had risen dramatically as well. In 1800 an average cow might produce only four or five quarts a day.[43]

The extra effort of maintaining a few animals for dairy production paid high dividends by the mid-1800s. Although Virginia never competed with the more traditional dairy areas in the United States, the state did outrank all other southern states in butter production per capita and total pounds in both 1850 and 1860.[44] Extra butter made on the farm could be salted and sold locally or shipped to Richmond where it was exported to the Caribbean. The increased emphasis on butter led Rockbridge County farmer, Henry Boswell Jones, to declare in 1851: "Our milk and butter are equal to any in the world." He added: "Fine butter is made, but there are few farmers who give their entire attention to dairy husbandry. Our surplus butter finds at Richmond a ready market at a price varying from 15 to 25 cents per pound, according to quality. The little cheese that is made, finds a home market at 10 cents a pound."[45]

Augusta County makes a good case study of the rising butter trade. In 1850, ninety-eight percent of the farms had milk cows with an average of 4.2 cows per farm. Herds of nine or ten were rare, although one man owned forty-eight. Most farms had five or fewer milk cows. Thirty-three percent of Augusta's farms made only enough butter for home consumption, while fifty-eight percent of Augusta's farms produced surplus butter in amounts ranging from 200 to 599 pounds. Only ten percent can be considered as specializing in dairy production. Those farms made between 600 and 1,999 pounds annually.[46] At twenty-five cents a pound, the average farm then could have realized seventy-five dollars worth of goods or cash annually for 300 pounds of surplus butter. Seventy-five dollars in 1860 is equal to about $1,440 today.[47]

The production of hard cheese was the least significant economic segment of what was still a fledgling Vir-ginia dairy industry. Local housewives and dairy maids had always produced soft cheeses, such as cottage cheese, for home consumption, but it was highly perishable and, thus, never a good market product before the advent of refrigeration. Hard cheeses, on the other hand, could be shipped long distances and remained edible for months if not years. For a variety of reasons, again including climate, poor animal husbandry practices, and a simple lack of interest, Virginians never produced and marketed cheese in large quantities. Even the small quantity of cheese produced received almost universal criticism. However, some farmers persisted and in 1847 *The Southern Planter* noted that a number of Fauquier farmers had launched flourishing cheesemaking operations. Such was their success – farmers reported making three or four pounds of cheese a day from each cow – that several more plantation owners of the county considered dividing up their farms and converting them to specialized dairy operations.[48]

A nineteenth-century photograph of the Rotunda at The University of Virginia shows a barrier built on The Lawn to protect the area from livestock.

Great Cattle Drives Continue

For most Virginia farmers, dairying was a sideline or part of a mixed farming operation. Fattened cattle continued to be the way to make extensive profit with bovines. Across the state, improved stock had increased the size of beef cattle, which were still driven to market from places deep in southwest Virginia, Kentucky, and the Carolinas. Significant numbers of cattle were imported from the Cherokee Nation in North Carolina. In 1828 this Native American tribe exported almost forty percent of the cattle they raised and large herds went to Virginia, South Carolina, and Georgia as well as to Tennessee. Tennessee speculators then incorporated those animals into cattle droves that went through the Valley of Virginia to markets in the northeast, like Philadelphia and Baltimore.[49]

In Albemarle County, many of the agricultural practices discussed in this chapter came to fruition during the 1850s. An article in *The Southern Planter* noted that as many as 2,000 cattle a year were driven from western Virginia, Kentucky, and Tennessee and fattened on corn over the winter in Albemarle before being sold to markets in Richmond, Washington, Baltimore, and other northern markets. The author further explained that many of those fattening the cattle were tobacco and wheat farmers who then applied the accumulated manure to their fields with positive results. In some years Albemarle farmers realized a profit when their fat cattle were sold, while in other years they suffered a loss. In all cases, however, the crop production was improved because of the additional accumulation of manure.[50]

The six decades between George Washington's presidency in the 1790s and the inauguration of Abraham Lincoln in 1861 saw a remarkable transformation in agriculture in Virginia and throughout the new nation. For Virginia farmers interested in cattle, methods underwent such a sharp change — with the reliance on manuring, the introduction of breeds, the spread of scientific information through publications and fairs, and the increased understanding of nutrition for livestock — that the animals taken to market in Lincoln's day bore little resemblance even to those of an advanced farmer such as George Washington. Judged by its ultimate impact, the word revolution does not exaggerate the nature and importance of this transformation.

A War on All Fronts

The tragedy of the American Civil War changed the United States forever. The nation that ushered in the new year in 1861 was deeply divided – more urban and manufacturing oriented in the North, more agricultural in the South. Within the borders of the eleven states that eventually joined the Confederacy and four of the states that remained in the Union, were more than three million African Americans in bondage. The war's causes, including slavery, which plunged the nation into such a bloody struggle across those five Aprils from 1861 to 1865 were complicated enough that historians today, almost 150 years later, continue to reexamine and reinterpret them. Never listed among those causes, however, is a single word about cattle. Nonetheless, cattle played an integral role in the war effort on both the battlefield and the homefront. Soldiers had to eat, as did civilians, thus beef, butter, milk, and cheese were important. Tallow was used to make candles and grease wagon wheels, and hides were used for shoes, worn out by marching soldiers, as well as for harnesses, belts, and straps for guns, canteens, and knapsacks. Early in the war, the Confederacy even relied upon cattle as draft animals to pull artillery in the western reaches of Virginia.[1]

On November 28, 1864, Union General Philip Sheridan sent General Wesley Merritt into Loudoun and Fauquier Counties with orders to "consume and destroy all forage and subsistence, burn all barns and mills and their contents, and drive off all stock in the region."

Never before or since has America suffered such total war and no state witnessed more action or destruction in that war than Virginia, the most populous state in the Union in 1861, with 1.5 million people. For the Commonwealth, the conflict began at the mouth of the York River on May 9, 1861. There, at Gloucester Point, southern shore batteries exchanged fire with a Union ship. Within two weeks, Virginia voted to secede from the Union. Almost four years later, Confederate General Robert E. Lee surrendered to Union General Ulysses Grant at Appomattox Courthouse on April 9, 1865. In between, there were 2,154 battles, skirmishes, or actions in Virginia, more than in any other state. The costs of such a total war are beyond accounting, but in 1877 the Virginia House of Delegates put a price tag of $457 million on the economic devastation[2] – $7.4 billion in 2002 dollars.[3]

A Wealth of Cattle

Taking the full brunt of the war's devastation were the Virginia's family farms, where fields and pastures became battlefields and barns and farmhouses were looted and burned. Even farms out of harm's way became overgrown and less productive without men to work them. The change wrought in four years was dramatic. Virginia's agricultural system in 1861 was marked by diversity and mixed farming and cattle played an important role. Many farmers owned milk cows, producing butter for urban and foreign markets, as well as beef animals that were driven to city markets such as Philadelphia, Alexandria, Richmond, and Norfolk. Farmers also used manure collected from their livestock to enrich their fields, particularly in grain-producing regions of the state such as the Piedmont and the Valley of Virginia. In the Tidewater and Eastern Shore areas, cattle were also vital as draft animals. In 1861, Texas was the leading cattle producer in the South, with Georgia and Virginia, close together at second and third. The U.S. Census of 1860 showed Virginia with about 228,300 milk cows (excluding those counties that became part of West Virginia), 433,600 beef cattle, and 75,400 working oxen. The leading dairy counties were grouped in different sections of the state, either around urban areas, such as Halifax, Loudoun, and

Fauquier, or in areas that had established trade routes to those urban markets. State leaders included Halifax with 8,609 milk cows, Augusta with 6,441, Rockingham with 6,011, Loudoun with 5,809, Fauquier with 5,489, Pittsylvania with 5,401, Bedford with 5,305, Albemarle with 4,498, Washington with 4289, Rockbridge with 4,046, and Tazewell with 4,002. The counties and cities with the smallest numbers of milk cows were usually those with single crop-agricultural economies, often based on tobacco, or those urban areas without the open space necessary for extensive dairy operations, such as: Warwick 480, Alexandria (Arlington County) 506, James City 636, Lancaster 802, Matthews 838, Charles City 847, Elizabeth City 900, Middlesex 916, Craig 973, Greenville 976, Surry 982, and Alleghany 996.[4]

Leading the way in market cattle were the following counties, many of which were among the dairy leaders as well: Fauquier 23,192, Loudoun 14,504, Augusta 14,206, Rockingham 13,999, and Tazewell 11,291. People in the following counties possessed the fewest beef cattle: Alexandria 170, Warwick 896, Charles City 926, Middlesex 1060, Elizabeth City 1,094, Matthews 1,249, James City 1,284, Prince George 1,308, Greene 1,345, Henrico 1,396, and New Kent 1,442. The working oxen in the state were concentrated in Caroline with 2,228, Albemarle 2,252, Halifax 2,104, and Louisa 2,058. The areas obviously relying on horses or mules as draft animals were: Craig with only 16 oxen, Alexandria with 19, Shenandoah 31, Rockingham 50, Page 73, Warren 80, Alleghany with 84, Frederick 85, Buchanan 94, Botetourt 135, Highland 178, Giles 170, and Augusta 198.[5]

When the war broke out, the Confederacy began looking at Virginia's extensive livestock resources and drawing up plans. In order to supply meat (pork and beef) to the Southern soldiers, Confederate Commissary General, Lt. Col. Frank Ruffin had packing plants built in Richmond and at Thoroughfare Gap in Prince William County. He then created substation commissaries at Danville in Pittsylvania County, Lynchburg in Campbell County, Dublin in Pulaski County, Boykins in Southampton County, Milford in Caroline County, Charlottesville in Albemarle County, and Staunton in Augusta County. All of the commissaries were located on railroad lines and all received regular cattle and hog shipments. The Thor-

*The village of Occoquan is seen in the background of this illustration "Army Beef Swimming the Occoquan River, Virginia," which ran in **Harper's Weekly** on June 4, 1863.*

oughfare Gap facility was the largest in the South. Ruffin chose the Prince William site because of its accessibility to the railroad and because Loudoun and Fauquier, the neighboring counties, were the two largest cattle-producing counties in Virginia. Unfortunately operations at the facility were short-lived. In the spring of 1862, Confederate general Joseph Johnston abandoned Manassas Junction and its railroad connections to the commissary where Ruffin had stockpiled two million pounds of meat. During the withdrawal of troops, the packing house burned, making the air for twenty miles around smell like bacon frying.[6]

The Richmond packing house and most of the substations operated throughout the war. Confederate agents contracted with local farmers for supplies of animals and for the care of animals shipped into the area. The contract between J.W. Curtis of Williamsburg and the Confederate government is probably typical of agreements between the government and local individuals. In the undated contract, Curtis agreed to board 500 cattle on his Skiffs Creek farm. He was to be reimbursed ninety cents for each bushel of feed that he used.[7]

The purpose of the agreement was to supply 14,600 Confederate soldiers while they were encamped on the Peninsula in the winter of 1861-1862. Such an army required 250 steers a week. Rations for armies – both North and South – consisted of pork or beef, hardtack, beans, and coffee. Additional foodstuffs were often sent from home, especially early in the war. In May of 1861, Augusta County's William B. Gallaher wrote home to his brothers, Clinton and Charles, about soldier life in the vicinity of Harpers Ferry. "We get plenty of good bread coffee & beef to eat besides butter molasses & apple butter. I wish you were both here to see the soldiers. . . . I suppose you are getting along very well tanning butchering & if you attend to it well you can make some money."[8] Gallaher wrote from an encampment where fresh beef was common. For armies

on the move, pork would have been more common. Salt pork and salt beef were also standard rations for campaigning armies, the former being much more palatable than the latter. Some observers, however, linked disease to fresh beef. "The command were getting sick from the use of fresh beef only, and many of them preferred doing without beef rather than increase the disease (diarrhea) brought on by its use without bread or salt," noted Union general T.A. Morris of the Indiana militia in a report.[9]

Major troop movements usually included a herd of cattle in addition to supply trains of salted meat. The animals were driven by hired drovers or the soldiers.[10] In planning for his Manassas campaign in the summer of 1862, Union general Irvin McDowell arranged to have a herd of beef with each wagon train of rations.[11] In 1864 as Union general Franz Sigel maneuvered his army out of West Virginia and into the Valley of Virginia, he ordered the 12th West Virginia Infantry to act as drovers for a herd of 250 cattle. The regiment drove the mobile "meal train" in advance of the army for forty-two miles from Webster to Beverly, West Virginia. The trek was in vain as Sigel soon changed his plans and the West Virginia cowboys were forced to return by the same route, this time in the rain and mud, to Webster.[12]

> *Union and Confederate forces often depended upon the surrounding countryside to replenish their food supplies. Sometimes farmers were reimbursed for the surrender of their livestock, but just as often the confiscation of property was a hostile act.*

Living Off the Land

Both sides often depended upon the surrounding countryside to replenish their herds. Sometimes farmers were reimbursed for the surrender of their livestock, but just as often the confiscation of property was a hostile act. In April of 1861, Robert E. Lee helped create a strategy for raising and equipping an army from scratch. He suggested to General Philip St. George Cocke that "that the valley of Virginia will naturally suggest itself to you as the point from which this part of the ration [beef and mutton] must be obtained."[13] Northern commander General Irvin McDowell planned to reimburse the residents of the territory he occupied when he confiscated their cattle. "If the supply trains do not come up in time, division commanders will procure beef from the inhabitants, paying for it at the market rates by orders of the Chief of the Commissary Department," he wrote in his general orders.[14] As he moved toward

The Union army's "traveling food supply" crossing the Long Bridge at Washington, D.C., was captured in this **Harper's Weekly** illustration published September 16, 1861.

Confederate Cunning Enabled Beefsteak Raid

Perhaps the most famous of the military cattle raids occurred in September of 1864. Wade Hampton's Great Beefsteak Raid briefly helped boost the sagging Confederate morale and filled the bellies of some hungry soldiers. General Hampton was the dashing cavalry officer appointed to lead Lee's army after the death of General J.E.B. Stuart in May of 1864. Like Stuart, he had a fondness for exploits of surprise and daring. When scouts reported seeing a lightly guarded corral filled with nearly 3,000 cattle, he began hatching a scheme. There is no doubt that the beef were needed as the Union siege of Petersburg was into its third month and General Grant was shutting down the supply lines to Lee's Army of Northern Virginia that was guarding the city.

The cattle, guarded by just 120 soldiers and 30 unarmed civilians, were spotted by the scouts at Coggin's Point on the James River. On September 15, Hampton took 3,000 men including, apparently, several well-experienced cattle rustlers, and circled the entire Union army. Before dawn on the 16th, they were in position to attack. The cavalry turned back the tough, but short-lived, Federal resistance and rounded up 2,486 cattle. Three hours later they were headed back home

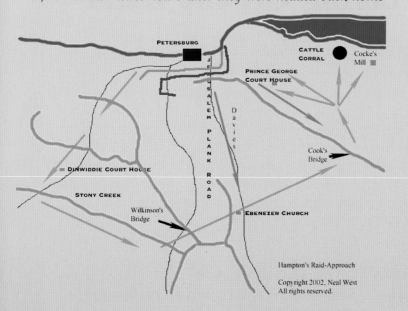

Hampton's Raid-Approach

Manassas and a showdown at that railroad junction in 1861, he noted that "in addition to the supplies in wagons, I took charge of, from Alexandria, ninety head of beef cattle, at estimated gross weight equal to 48,600 rations."[15]

In the mountains of western Rockingham County, a Confederate scout later wrote of having "appropriated" a few dozen cattle from the Union army in 1862. With the intention of making some money off their sale, he began driving the animals to Harrisonburg, but his plan went awry due to an abandoned road and troop movements leading up to the battles of Cross Keys and Port Republic just outside of Harrisonburg.

> On the 1st day of June I started and drove them by a back way through the mountains until we reached a Mr. Wilkins, on what was then called Wilkin's run. Mr. Wilkins had plenty of good grass, we kept the cattle here for two days waiting to hear from the Valley, but could get nothing definite. . .On the morning of the third day we started to drive to Harrisonburg by way of Brock's Gap. On reaching a kind of public stopping place well down the gap, kept by a man by the name of Fishwaters. This route, to us for the present, must be abandoned. It now began to look very much as though in our cattle deal [we would] draw a blank and very possibly Gen. Fremont might get his own back again. We were really at a loss to know what to do with our stock. Mr. Fishwaters advised us to drive them back several miles to a large cave at the base of Shenandoah Mountain where a man by the name of Whitacre had a fine grazing farm and leave them until we could get them away; this we finally concluded to do.
>
> After disposing of our cattle, we remained in the neighborhood for a day or two, then ventured toward the mouth of the gap.[16]

Supplying an Army

For the Union, the logistics of moving a massive army and its supply train through enemy territory was a daunting task. Many historians think that General George McClellan's failed attempt to capture Richmond during the Peninsula Campaign of 1862 was because of supply problems. There was never a time during that military action when McClellan had to feed fewer than 100,000 men. The supply train began with a line of steamers and schooners that stretched from New York, Philadelphia, Baltimore, Annapolis, and Alexandria all the way up the York River in Virginia to the town of West Point. From there it stretched another forty-five miles up the Pamunkey River, then inland another fifteen miles to the Chickahominy until it was about six miles from Richmond. The fodder for the 17,000 horses and 8,000 mules needed to pull wagons and artillery amounted to 313 tons daily.[17] McClellan withdrew his Army of the Potomac in late June of 1862 after an unsuccessful campaign. Clogging the few roads along the Peninsula were soldiers and vehicles as well as 2,500 head of cattle, creating so much chaos that it took three days to retreat just fifteen miles.

In the border counties between Virginia and West Virginia as well as those in the lower valley, fear of raiding parties from both sides was constant. In June of 1861, John Ruckman of Pocahontas County, Virginia (now West Virginia) wrote to Confederate President Jefferson Davis:

> Will you help us? Can you help us in time? One short week, and I fear it will be too late. Many of our best families have their carriages in readiness to move; many more are having their wagons prepared. All that can go I fear will soon be on the move. Then woe to those who are left. Nothing but destruction awaits our houses and barns. Our waving fields of grain and grass, our thousands of cattle, they will soon possess. On my own grass I have from one hundred and fifty to two hundred head of good beef cattle. I have no hope of anything being saved unless you can send a large force at once.[18]

Ruckman's fear was not unfounded. In 1861, for instance, Confederate forces operating in the vicinity west of Winchester – in what is now West Virginia – were told to strip the countryside of horses and beef cattle in Unionist areas.[19] At the same time, the Federal forces were reporting good supplies of beef and forage in the region.[20]

Raiding Armies

Further south, the main transportation route from the Upper Shenandoah Valley to the Ohio River was the Staunton-Parkersburg Turnpike. This engineering marvel, completed in 1848, was the superhighway of its time. During the war, it became a key corridor for opposing armies. Several significant battles and campaigns were conducted along its length and small skirmishes and raids carried out by Confederate partisan soldiers into what was now Union territory were commonplace. Perhaps the most significant partisan raid occurred in April of 1863. Approximately 4,700 Confederates launched a mission to destroy key railroad lines and capture supplies in the area of Burning Springs. The torching of 150,000 oil barrels there marked the first time in military history that an oil installation had been burned. On the way back into Virginia, the raiders rounded up 3,000 cattle and 1,200 horses and drove them through Beverly and back across the turnpike into the Valley. The vast herd was the largest group of animals ever to pass at one time over the turnpike.[21]

General Lee was as pleased as anyone with the cattle raids occurring along the Virginia-West Virginia border. And he had very specific ideas about what should be done with the war booty. On June 1, 1863, he sent the following memo to James Seddon, the Confederate Secretary of War:

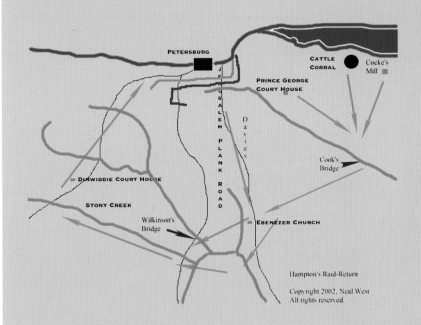

across the Blackwater River. The advance Confederate guard met and held off a Union force of 2,100 while the cattle crossed two miles below. The Southerners arrived back at camp on the 17th having accomplished their mission. Of the raid, Hampton wrote:

> the command returned to their old quarters after an absence of three days, during which they had marched upward of 100 miles, defeating the enemy in two fights, and bringing from his lines in safety a large amount of captured property, together with 304 prisoners. Of the 2,486 cattle captured 2,468 have been brought in, and I hope [to] get the few remaining ones. Three flags were taken and eleven wagons brought in safely, several others having been destroyed. Three camps of the enemy were burned, after securing from them some very valuable stores, including quite a number of blankets. My loss was 10 killed, 47 wounded, and 4 missing.[25]

The Beefsteak Raid lifted the spirits of the sagging Confederacy and embarrassed the United States. One Southern soldier wrote home that "we are now having Yankee beef everyday." Adding further insult were the raucous comments shot across the lines by the Confederates. Some yelled "Hey, Yanks, want any fresh beef?" while others simply mooed. In the White House, President Abraham Lincoln could only admire Hampton's daring, calling the raid "the slickest piece of cattle-stealing" he had ever known. And General Grant, when asked about a time table for starving out Lee's forces, replied, "Never, if our armies continue to supply him with beef-cattle."[26]

Sir: General Imboden reports that 3,176 head of cattle were brought out of Western Virginia by the recent expedition. I am very anxious to keep these cattle, if possible, exclusively for the use of this army. Twelve hundred and fifty were brought out by General Samuel Jones' commissary, and are in Greenbrier. There are reported 3,000 head of cattle in Greenbrier and Monroe besides these. I think, therefore, that General Jones could readily spare the 1,250 brought in by the expedition, or, if he wishes to keep them, the 3,000 reported to be in Greenbrier and Monroe might be collected for this army. The remaining cattle brought out by Generals Jones and Imboden are in Pocahontas and Augusta. I hope these will be secured for the Army of Northern Virginia.[22]

West Virginians near the Virginia border faced incredible hardship during the war. Along French Creek in Upshur County, loyalties were divided and soldiers of both armies were commonly seen. The area changed hands twelve times during the war and raiders from both sides confiscated food, livestock, and other material goods such as

shoes and blankets. On September 28, 1864, sixteen-year-old Sirene Burton recorded the exciting events that she had witnessed that day and the day before:

> There was eleven rebels ate supper here last night. There was one Lieut. here and he kept his men straight. I do not know how many there is but I do not think they will stay long. That Lieut. tried very hard to make Harry and I rebels but he had to give it up. They camped down at E.G. Burr's last night. Late. There was about six hundred rebels passed here today, they were driving cattle and I just expected they would take ours (cow) but they did not. They took Chet's but the girls got them back. It was a curious body of soldiers, they were dressed in all colors. They robbed the stores and houses all along the road. They took one blanket from us.[23]

Although much of the cattle rustling that occurred throughout the war was little more than depredation against the civilian population, there were often daring cattle raids that took place between the regular armies. In July of 1864, a young New Yorker named Joseph Lonsway

Confederate General Jubal Early's troops travel south across the Potomac River at White's Ford. Early resupplied his army with captured horses and beef cattle on a failed foray to capture the Federal capital.

found himself caught up in just such a raid near Hopewell, Virginia. The plot began to unfold in late June when Southern forces successfully stampeded a herd of 500 Union beef cattle and were driving them back to their lines. Lonsway's unit was ordered to recapture the cattle if possible and so set off on the morning of the Fourth of July in pursuit of the Confederate raiders. The Federals pushed the Confederates back into a stand of woods near the Blackwater River and set about destroying some train cars filled with food. They also captured a boat and crossed the river to continue the search for cattle. Somehow Lonsway became separated from his unit and, while wandering on a country road, heard the sounds of cattle being driven. The herd was guarded by several unarmed elderly men who quickly surrendered their animals to the young Union soldier after he slapped them with the flat of his sword. Lonsway bunched the animals together and started them back to the Union lines. For his daring exploits, the New Yorker was presented a bronze medal and offered a commission, which he declined.[24]

For Virginians who remained at home on the farm while loved ones went off to war, life was anything but normal. And yet it was up to those older men, young children, and women to operate farms as profitably as possible in order to provide the necessary food and material goods for their homes and for the cause. Far away from the farm, farmers who had taken up arms felt the frustration of not being at home where they could direct agricultural operations. William Gallaher of Augusta County wrote home to his family, offering suggestions in the spring of 1861: "If you could buy some small cattle next month for 12 or 15 dollars and sell altogether for cash you can make some money. Mr Slough can buy them."[27]

Tinsley Allen of Amherst had similar concerns in late 1861 when he wrote his brother, Henry. "You will please attend to my cattle best you can. Mr. Johnston will tend to the cattle until Christmas. You will see to them after that time. See that my fodder and stacks are not destroyed and also see that my horses are well treated. You shall not lose for your trouble. You know it is out of my power to see to them."[28]

Jesse Rolston, Jr., a farmer in Mt. Solon in northern Augusta County, also worried about his wife, Mary Catharine Cromer Rolston, supervising farm operations alone. Rolston was thirty-seven years old with five children when he entered the military. His letters home, always ending with the same affectionate and misspelled phrase "until seperated by death," usually included simple instructions and words of advice regarding the farm. In November of 1861 he wrote his wife that "there is only the one head of caltel missing yet and that is the cherrys calf. it is a dark read sides white on the back and belly with rite ear crop and the left split and has a little bell on it when i seen it last some white in its fase."[29] The next day Rolston again wrote his wife with a touch of concern: "i wish you would let me no how you are getting along and how all the stalk[stock] is doing as i don't know when i will get a chance to come home."[30]

June of 1862 brought an additional degree of worry to the family. Soldiers from both sides passed through the area as General Stonewall Jackson's famous Valley Campaign played out its final scenes in Highland, Augusta, and Rockingham Counties. A surviving letter from one relative to another on June 1 tells of the vandalism wrought by the visiting Federals in Harrisonburg:

> thay Just come and broke the smoke hous opened and took what bacon they wanted and robed the spring hous of all milk and butter. Thay dident take nothing from us compared with what thay took from uther people. . . thay took a grate deal from Cromers. took there cattle. Corn oats bacon and ever thing that was eatable. Tay Jusdt run about braking opened the spring houses and robbing the hen nests like a parsel of starved houns. I think our boys gave them such a whipen that they wont come back direcly.[31]

Later that month, Rolston wrote to his wife with specific instructions regarding their cattle: "about the cows i leave that with you as to selling of them. i think the hufman will make a good cow from the looks of her. if you think

you cant or haint got a nough grass to keep them coiws sell. If you have keep them. . . . Cattel is very high prise."[52] A year later, in April of 1863, Rolston offered his wife advice on driving the cattle to the mountains for summer grazing. "I spoke to Rusmisel about them caves[calves] you have their, he said he would take ours with his and tend to them for you. A. Staubus and Rusmisel drives to the mountain to gether. if you don't make no other arrangements I am afraid you cant keep them on the place to keep in order but any way you fix it will suit me." Catharine apparently heeded her husband's advice regarding sending the livestock to the mountains, because in late September he wrote his wife the following question: "have you got the cattel all from the mountains?"[33] Rolston's wife must have managed the farm adequately. For example, she was able at least once to send her husband butter to supplement his camp rations.

In Augusta County just outside Staunton, Jacob Hildebrand kept the farm running as best he could while his two sons were away in the army. The effects of the war, however, were all too evident in his diary. In 1863 Hildebrand attended a sale of cattle, horses, and mules nearby Fishersville. The sellers had brought the animals south from Clarke County, but were able to sell only the yearling cattle at eighty to one hundred dollars each. As the war continued, shortages became more commonplace. In September, Hildebrand went to a tanyard to buy shoe leather but found it was only available wholesale. Leather was a concern again in January of 1864 when he went to G.W. Hall's tanyard to pick up the hide he had left to be tanned on shares. Later the same month he dropped off two hides, one which weighed fifty-nine pounds, to be tanned on the same share arrangement. In March of the same year, his wife took twenty-five pounds of butter to Staunton and sold it for a whopping ten dollars a pound. The price, however, reflected the inflated Confederate currency. By comparison, Mrs. Hildebrand had to pay $125 for a bunch of cotton yarn.[34]

Troop movements and news from the battlefield often interrupted the normal routine of the farm. In Janu-

Cattle were sometimes harnessed by the Confederacy to provide a means to move artillery.

ary of 1864, Hildebrand wrote in his diary: "Gen Fitz Hugh Lee returned from western Va a few days ago with his Brigade of cavelry & brot several Hundred prisoners & some cattle & destroyed a good many wagons."[35] In June of 1864 when the Union army passed through en route to Lexington, Hildebrand's son took the livestock over the mountain to Nelson County. Their safe return was noted in the diary on June 13, 1865.[36]

Deadly Diseases

When war came to Virginia in 1861, it brought several invading forces. More insidious than the bullets and cannonballs, however, were the diseases. The war's opening volley brought a mass of humanity together into opposing armies the likes of which had never been seen in North America. Men mustered into the army from all parts of the country including city slums and isolated mountain hollows. And they brought with them diseases and germs to which men from other sections of the nation had never been exposed. Mumps, measles, cholera, and typhoid fever felled far more men over the course of the war than did bullets. And the epidemics were not confined to human victims. "In the supply of horses, cattle, and hogs for the contending armies, the worst livestock diseases in the nation fell upon Virginia," noted historian G. Terry Sharrer. "Equine glanders and hog cholera, which seem not to have appeared in Virginia before 1860, and cattle fever, which had been negligible for forty years, became rampant by 1865, and probably inhibited agricultural recovery even more so than labor problems."[37]

In the case of cattle fever, also called Carolina distemper, Georgia murrain, and Spanish fever, the invasion was from within the Confederacy. The troublemaker in cattle fever is the protozoa, *Babesia bigemina*, which hitches a ride in the cattle tick, *Babesia boophilus*. The northern-most range of the tick is South Carolina and Georgia and herds in the deep south had developed enough resistance to cattle fever that they appeared quite healthy. When those carriers mingled with more northern animals, however, the effects were often devastating. Virginians and North Carolinians, although oblivious to the existence of the protozoa, knew that prohibiting cattle from crossing into North Carolina between April 1 and November 1 (the time period when the tick is alive and active) would stymie the spread of the disease. Thus, from the 1790s onward, North Carolina had policed its borders during those months. Because of this, cattle fever was virtually non-existent in Virginia before 1860.[38]

Concoctions yielded from recipes like this one were mostly ineffective in treating cattle fever or murrain, as it was often called.

Original expectations by the Confederacy's commissary general were that rations for the Army of Northern Virginia could be supplied from within the state. As the war effort expanded and resources from the countryside were exhausted, the Confederacy began railroading cattle in from the south, especially from Tennessee, the Carolinas, and Georgia. With the animals came cattle fever. The ensuing epidemic boggled the minds of many. One physician in Cumberland County was certain that the disease must be some particularly virulent strain introduced from another country. In Gloucester, the "bloody murrain" infected four-fifths of the cattle and killed ten percent. In all parts of the state, from Fauquier just outside of Washington, D.C., to Washington County in southwest Virginia, the reports were equally gloomy. It was many years before the disease was brought under control. In the meantime, recovery of Virginia agriculture after 1865 was all the more difficult. Not only did dairy and beef production drop, but so did crop production in many areas (although not in the Shenandoah Valley) because supplies of manure to fertilize the fields were limited.[39]

A Terrible, Total War

The introduction of animal diseases was accidental and the cattle raids across the countryside were spontaneous and random, but there were several periods during the war in which planned, total destruction of Virginia's agriculture occurred. In April and May of 1863, the armies were struggling for control of the Peninsula. In the course of the many skirmishes, the Union soldiers attempted to eliminate as many enemy supply points as possible. The 4th Delaware Volunteers reported having "destroyed a large amount of stores of the rebel army, consisting of grain, cotton, bacon, flour. . . and quinine; also collected and drove within the lines 57 head of horned cattle, 260 sheep, and 8 horses and mules."[40] By late May, the Delaware soldiers were in Mathews County operating under instructions to ". . .inflict as much injury as possible on armed enemies. . . capture and bring in all animals and supplies needful to our troops that may be found, but will not wantonly burn or pillage anywhere." A few days later, in the same area, they rounded up 300 horses and mules, 150 cattle, and 150 sheep. Some grain was destroyed and five mills filled with grain and flour were burned.[41] One soldier, Stephen Buckson, wrote home to his wife:

Here the boys made another raid on the rebs and captured a lot of poultry and meat and molasses, and tobacco, and a little of everything.

. . . The next day we came down east river and burnt 2 mills full of corn and flour and several barns and then went up the north river again to meet with the other force there they had a lot of stock and sheep. We took the sheep on board [a gunboat] and laid there till night and took the drafted men on board and the cavalry drove the horses and cattle to camp where we all arrived this morning. The cavalry burnt the mill belonging to the rebs. . . .It done me good to think we could burn the property of one reb that lived in Delaware. The amount of horses brought in were 550 or 600 and 500 head of cattle and 300 sheep and there is no telling all that was brought in but you may depend all soldiers knows how to provide for theirselves.[42]

The Burning

As the grim conflict continued into 1864, it became clear to Federal military leaders that the only way to subdue the Confederacy was to institute a policy of total destruction, aimed at separating the military from its supply lines of food, munitions, and other military items. This meant targeting the Valley of Virginia, also known as the Breadbasket of the Confederacy. The valley, with its iron foundries and tanneries, also contributed mightily to the military's industrial needs.

In late May of 1864, General David Hunter took command of the Union forces and blazed up the valley with a vengeance. After winning a lively battle at Piedmont, in Augusta County, on June 5, his path was open. During the next two days, Union troops burned and looted their way through Staunton. By June 7, most of the occupiers had left Staunton and headed south toward Lexington, skirmishing and plundering as they went. In all, 37,000 Union troops moved in parallel lines between the two towns. Along the way they confiscated livestock, burned mills and bridges, and caused great unrest among the local inhabitants. "This is a day of great excitement," wrote the Rev. Francis McFarland in his diary on June 7. "I am pretty calm. There have been in all eleven Yankees here. . . . took my horse Squire 14 years old a saddle & bridle & a few bushels of oats."[43]

Just a few miles south of McFarland's home, in southern Augusta County, Nancy Emerson's household was also visited by the enemy. She wrote: "The Yankees took from this plantation several hundred weight of bacon (nearly all there was) a hundred bushels of corn, a quantity of flour, oats, &c. & all the horses." A few days later she added:

...the deliberate, planned devastation of the Shenandoah Valley [during the Civil War] deservedly ranks as one of the grimmest episodes of a sufficiently grim war...

On the 10th of June we received another visit from our invaders, at least, several thousand of them passed our house on their way from Staunton to Lexington. . . . Some went in the spring house however, & helped themselves to milk & one went off with a large panfull in each hand. Ellen called after him to "Bring back those pans," but he only laughed & went on. Another who had been taking a cool draught from a pan, came out with his chin covered & some on the end of his nose, like a cat from the cream pot. E. accosted him with "Ar'nt you ashamed?" putting as much emphasis as she well could & adding, "Who do you think is going to drink that milk, after you have put your nose in it!" The fellow made no reply but walked off.[44]

When the Union forces converged on Lexington, the plundering and looting escalated. Virginia Military Institute, where General Jackson had taught and from where a corps of cadets had arrived to help win victory at New Market only weeks earlier, symbolized everything bad about the Southern rebellion. In addition, it housed a weapons arsenal. As a result, the school was destroyed. David Hunter Strother, a soldier with Hunter's army and a journalist, described the chaos of the countryside as he watched from Lexington:

We saw a great deal of smoke in the mountains eastward and were told it came from the camps of the refugees who were hiding from us with their Negroes and cattle. Their campfires had fired the dry leaves and the air was misty with smoke. Our cavalry also burned some extensive iron works in that direction. The satisfaction of these people in regard to their Negroes is surprising. They seem to believe firmly that their Negroes are so much attached to them that they will not leave them on any terms. Thus when running off their cattle, horses, and the goods into the mountains, they take their Negroes with them. The Negroes take the first opportunity they find of running into our lines and giving information as to where their masters are hidden and conduct our foragers to their retreats. In this way our supply of cattle has been kept up.[45]

Finally in late June, Hunter's army was pushed out of the upper valley and calm returned. For the people of the Shenandoah Valley, however, the worst was yet to come. As bad as Hunter's visit to the area had been, when Generals Philip Sheridan and George Armstrong Custer visited the central and lower valley from August until October of 1864, the lifeblood was drained from this agricultural jewel. For thirteen days in September and October, four counties – Augusta, Rockingham, Page, and Shenandoah – probably suffered more devastation than the famous Georgia march by General William Sherman when he burned that state from Atlanta to the sea. Sheridan intended to devastate the Breadbasket of the Confederacy and end the war. To those who witnessed the invasion and to the generations that followed, it became known as "The Burning." One historian noted that "the deliberate, planned devastation of the Shenandoah Valley has deservedly ranked as one of the

In this August 1862 photo, a slave family gains emancipation after crossing the Rappahannock River in an oxcart. The family was ensured its freedom there by the presence of an encampment of Federal troops.

grimmest episodes of a sufficiently grim war. Unlike the haphazard destruction caused by Sherman's bummers in Georgia, it was committed systematically, and by order."[46]

The invaders went as far south as Staunton and Waynesboro where they destroyed rail lines, a government tannery, and large stores of leather. The Richmond newspaper reported that the fleeing populace left the roads between Waynesboro and Richmond a mass of ambulances, carriages, buggies, horses, mules, cattle, and African Americans. Sheridan's report from Waynesboro concluded with the vow that he would "go on and clean out the Valley."[47] The Federals plundered their way northward, gathering up what cattle the area residents had not hidden in the mountains, and breaking into springhouses for fresh milk and butter. The damage in Augusta by the Union's reckoning was $3,270,650, nearly $46 million in today's dollars.[48]

The damage in Augusta was small compared to that in Rockingham and Page – the heart of the burnt district. Obvious targets for Union wrath included a Confederate commissary at Bridgewater, a large flour mill, many barns, a tannery in Elkton, and a large tannery near Luray. Peter Borst, the tannery owner, was a native New Yorker who had married a Virginian and moved to the Valley in the 1850s. His enterprise, which supplied large quantities of leatherwork to the Confederacy, included tanning pits, storage buildings holding finished hides, a leaching house, and large buildings to store the tanbark. The officer who ordered the business burned on October 6 noted in his report that it had been "used for the exclusive benefit of the rebel army. Unfinished leather to the value of about $800,000 was destroyed here."[49] The burning of that much leather must have left an acrid stench in the air.

REMARKS.

He sent his son John through the lines to the North to keep him out of the rebel Army, And in the fall of '64 he took his family & went off with Sheridan's Army & went to Ohio where he staid till the close of the war—

The testimony of his witnesses has an air of truth that convinces one of the loyalty of clmt.

We find him loyal.

The Cattle were driven off in Sheridan's raid in Oct '64 & probably sent to Penna. & sold & the proceeds put in the Treasury— The other property was taken for Army use & used by the Army.

Whole Amt. allowed is — $556.00 — 565.00

But the son Frederick was disloyal & his share must be deducted, There were 7 children, all loyal but Fredk.

Deducting one seventh for Fredk's share — 80.71 (79.42)

And it leaves — $484.29 (476.51)

to be divided among the other heirs. 76.57

We therefore allow $484.29 to the Adm. for those legally entitled to the allowance —

A. O. Aldis, J. B. Howell, O. Ferriss — Commrs of Claims

In an effort to receive at least some small compensation for agricultural losses suffered during "The Burning," members of the Rhodes family of Rockingham County testified before the Southern Claims Commission.

Under the Act of Congress of March 3, 1871, Washington, D. C.:

The Petition of [1] *John Rodes*

respectfully represents :

That he *is a* citizen of the United States, and resides at present at or near
[2] *Mount Crawford, Rockingham County Virginia*

and that he resided when this claim accrued at or near [3] *the same place*

That he *has* a claim against the United States for property [4] *taken*

for the use of the army of the United States during the late rebellion at (or near)

Mount Crawford, in the county of *Rockingham*, and State of
Virginia

That the said claim, stated by items, and excluding any and all items of damage, destruction, and loss, (and not use,) of property ; of unauthorized or unnecessary depredations by troops and other persons upon property, or of rent or compensation for the use or occupation of buildings, grounds, or other real estate, is as follows :

No. of Item	QUANTITIES AND ARTICLES.	VALUE.	
1	Eight Cattle (8) 3200 lbs of Beef Net a 12¢ p lb	$ 384	00
2	Thirteen (13) Hogs, 1825 lb " Pork " a 15¢ " "	273	75
3	Thirteen (13) Sheep 975 lb " Mutton " a 10¢ " "	97	50
4	Thirty (30) Bushels Potatoes $1.00 p Bushl	30	00
5	Fifteen Gallons Molasses $1.00 p Gal	15	00
6	Four (4) Bushels of Salt a $1.50	6	00
7	One black Horse worth	125	00
8	One bay Mare "	100	00
9	One bay Mare "	100	00
10	One bay Mare "	25	00
11	Seventy (70) Bushels of Oats a 60¢ p Bushl	42	00
12	Thirty (30) " " Corn $1.00	30	00
13	Three (3) Saddles 25$, 2 Bridles 3$	28	00
	Total,	$ 1256	25

On or about 10 day of Oct 1864

Note 1. Give full names of all the petitioners.

While most valley residents could only watch helplessly as their homes, barns, smokehouses, and springhouses were ransacked and then burned, some tried to defend themselves, usually to no avail. Mrs. Mullins was one person who managed to put the enemy in its place. Union soldiers visited her farm near Harrisonburg in late September. As the soldiers helped themselves to the bounty from her farm they ignored her pleas to leave something behind for the family. However, when the soldiers put a rope on her milk cow and led it back to their camp she had seen enough. She retrieved her shotgun from its hiding place, loaded it, and went off in search of the cow. Once she had located the animal, she approached the men, squinted down the barrel of her gun, and said, "You gimme my cow or I'll kill every one of ya! I gotta have her to feed my children or they'll starve!" The soldiers must have felt Mrs. Mullins meant business because they relinquished the cow and avoided her farm after that.[50]

> *The federal government created a Southern Claims Commission in an attempt to compensate those people who had suffered damage from United States military action despite their loyalty to the Union.*

Lean times

Although Sheridan wanted to destroy the agricultural vitality of the area, he also shrewdly used what plunder he could to feed his own army. As a consequence, livestock that could be rounded up, particularly cattle, but also horses and sheep, were driven back to the quartermaster near New Market. More often than not, hogs were easier to shoot than to drive. In Page County, one farmer named John R. Burner knew from the progression of the smoke that the enemy was approaching. Hoping to avoid contact with the soldiers, he herded his cattle into a ravine. Unfortunately, after he had done so, men from the Second Pennsylvania Cavalry passed close by, driving cattle they had confiscated from a neighbor. The lowing of the animals and the jingling of their bells apparently sounded welcoming to Burner's animals in the ravine. Before he knew what was happening, his cattle had left their hiding place to join their captured brethren. Later one old yellow cow of his did return home, giving him a supply of milk for the rest of the war.[51]

When the herds of livestock became too unwieldy, Sheridan issued orders to simply destroy the animals. Such was the case with a large drove on the Valley Pike north of Harrisonburg. The animals were driven to the top of a broad hill and shot. The carcasses were then dragged into a pile, covered with tinder, soaked with turpentine and lamp oil, and burned. The intense fire sent streams of grease running down the hillside.[52]

In the rampage, family farms were targeted as often as mills and government buildings. Typical was the Garber family near Timberville. When the Yankees arrived, the father had escaped with some of the livestock, leaving his wife and two young boys to defend the farm. The soldiers lit torches from the kitchen fire and proceeded to burn the barn, stable, and grain house. They then rounded up three horses, forty-seven cattle, eighty sheep, and shot two hogs. At the nearby Shoup farm, five barns filled with wheat and fodder were torched and 2,000 bushels of wheat were destroyed. Sheds were broken open, farm machinery including a threshing machine, grain drill, fodder cutter, a wheat fan, and harness were burned. The men left with four horses, eight cattle, and ten sheep.[53]

When the Federal forces finally left Rockingham, the newspaper reported the horrific damages: 30 homes, 450 barns, 31 mills, 3 factories, and 1 iron furnace burned; 100 miles of fence, 100,000 bushels of wheat, 50,000 bushels of corn, and 6,232 tons of hay destroyed. Livestock losses included 3,350 hogs, 4,200 sheep, 1,750 horses, and 1,750 cattle.[54] A few days later, Sheridan halted at Woodstock and sent Grant the following dispatch:

> The whole country from the Blue Ridge to the North Mountain has been made untenable for a rebel army. I have destroyed over two thousand barns filled with wheat, hay, and farming implements, over seventy mills filled with wheat and flour. Four herds of cattle have been driven before the army, and not less than three thousand sheep have been killed and issued to the troops. This destruction embraces the Luray and Little Fork [Fort] valleys as well as the main valley. Tomorrow I will continue the destruction of wheat, forage, etc., down to Fishers Hill. When this is completed, the Valley from Winchester up to Staunton, ninety-two miles, will have little in it for man or beast.[55]

Caught up in the ravages of war in the Valley was a group of peaceful farmers of German descent. Religious principles of these Brethren and Mennonite families prevented them from participating in war and most abhorred the fracture of the Union and its bloody outcome of Civil War. Such pacifist views were not welcome, particularly when the young men of those denominations began evading the draft. In several cases persecution turned violent. Nonetheless, these families often fared no better than their neighbors when Sheridan's troops rampaged through the valley in 1864. Years later, the federal government created a Southern Claims Commission in an attempt to compensate those people who had suffered damage from United States military action despite their loyalty to the Union. The Rockingham County claims, in particular, help paint the fine strokes on the larger canvas of human suffering. John and Fannie Rhodes lived near Pleasant Valley in Rockingham. Their religious view put them squarely against slavery and secession, and eventually war itself. Members of the Rhodes family were verbally and physically abused by those strongly in support of the Confederacy, but they held to their principles. During the war the family assisted potential draftees, including their teenage son, who needed to flee the area to escape military service. Nonetheless, when Sheridan's army came through in 1864, the losses to the Rhodes farm were so great that they were forced to temporarily abandon their farm and spend the remainder of the war in Ohio. Testimony before the claims commission indicates the following losses: 8 milk cows, 3,200 pounds of beef, 13 hogs, 1,875 pounds of pork, 13 sheep, 975 pounds of mutton, 30 bushels of potatoes, 15 gallons of molasses, 4 bushels of salt, 4 horses, 70 bushels of oats, 30 bushels of corn, 3 saddles, and 2 bridles. According to the deposition, "the cattle were driven off in Sheridan's raid in Oct '64 & probably sent to Penna. & sold & the proceeds put in the Treasury – The other property was taken for Army use & used by the Army." All told, the estate of John Rhodes (who died in 1870) submitted a claim for $1,256.25. In March of 1877, over twelve years after Sheridan visited the valley and seven years after Rhodes' death, the federal government paid the Rhodes family $476.57 in reparations.[56]

With the destruction of the valley complete in 1864, Sheridan could set his sights on settling another score. Back in August, Grant had asked Sheridan to retaliate against General John Mosby's partisan raids in the Loudoun-Fauquier area of northern Virginia. He wanted his cavalry officer to destroy crops, livestock, fields, and barns, and seize all slaves and able-bodied men under fifty. In late November, Sheridan sent General Wesley Merritt to fulfill those orders and "consume and destroy all forage and subsistence, burn all barns and mills and their contents, and drive off all stock in the region. . . This order must be literally executed, bearing in mind, however, that no dwellings are to be burned and that no personal violence be offered to the citizens."[57] In a five-day burning raid, 1,000 hogs were slaughtered, 6,000

cattle, 4,000 sheep, and 700 horses were driven off, 230 barns, eight mills, and a distillery were burned, and 10,000 tons of hay and 25,000 bushels of grain were destroyed.[58]

As telling as the cold tally of numbers is, it is the personal accounts of Sheridan's campaigns that put a face on the human suffering. Ida Blanche Haley's mother, also Ida, was a teenager when the raiders came to her family's home near Upperville, burned the mill of her grandfather, John Milton Reed, ransacked the farmhouse, and took most of her family's livestock. After the war was over, Ida passed on the story of the Yankee invasion to her daughter, Ida Blanche Haley, who wrote it down and also painted a watercolor of the mill ruins.

Now Sheridan comes back on his burning trip to leave our country so if a crow would fly over he would have to take his rations with him. This is his own words and he did it. All large mills, barns and some homes were burned. The first thing he did was to have the covered wagon loaded with meal, flour and meat. He shot the chickens, turkeys, killed the hogs & took wheat. After he had gotten all wagons loaded then he burned this large fine mill full of wheat and corn. My grandfather had just gotten home from Alexandria and had on a new hat. One of the Yankees rode up and asked him to come to the fence. He took his good hat and put his old one on my grandfather's head and when my grandfather threw it on the ground the Yankee rode off and laughed saying, "You had better keep it old man it's getting cold now it will be hard for you to get another soon." Mr. Reed sat down on the hog pen or what had been the hog pen with nothing in it. Now while he was sitting here a hen came out from under the pen & looked around. Grandfather said, "They are gone and so this is all we have." When the old hen found the coast clear she called out 12 chickens. Mr. Reed named her Stonewall and she had the best of care the rest of her life and is buried at Clifton. That night an old cow came back and she had a real young calf and they had nothing to feed her. Stonewall and this cow and one calf was all they had with 8 children to feed and Mr. and Mrs. Reed, a colored boy named Joe and another colored woman.[59]

In a five-day burning raid, 1,000 hogs were slaughtered, 6,000 cattle, 4,000 sheep, and 700 horses were driven off, 230 barns, eight mills, and a distillery were burned, and 10,000 tons of hay and 25,000 bushels of grain were destroyed.

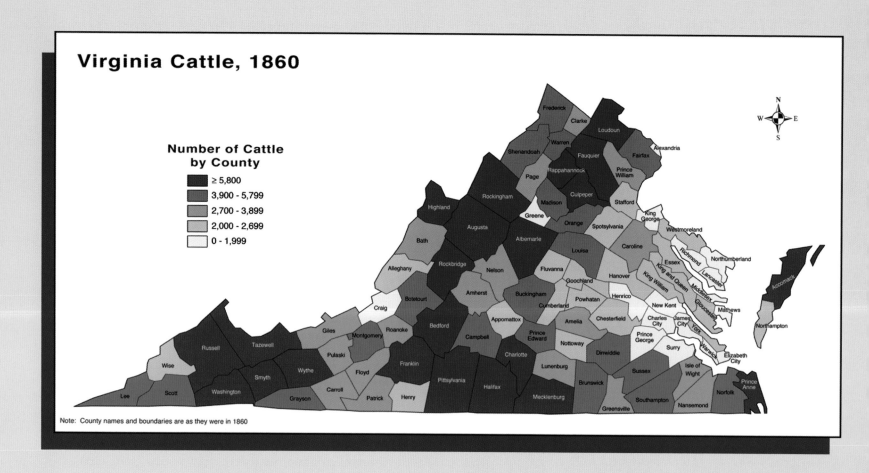

Virginia Cattle, 1860

Number of Cattle by County

- ≥ 5,800
- 3,900 - 5,799
- 2,700 - 3,899
- 2,000 - 2,699
- 0 - 1,999

Note: County names and boundaries are as they were in 1860

Tracking the facts

Counting Cows: The U.S. Agriculture Census

Beginning in 1790, and every decade since that year, the United States has kept statistics on its people and its lands. Because the majority of Americans were farmers, it seems only natural that government officials would have begun to compile agricultural statistics. But not until the fourth "counting of heads," in 1820, did the census takers tabulate the numbers of Americans engaged in farming. And it was not until 1840 that a more sophisticated agricultural schedule was added to the census. This new set of statistics looked at production numbers for those involved in forestry, animal husbandry, and crop cultivation. The second agricultural census, in 1850, included statistics on the number and size of farms. The census recorded the number of animals on hand as of June 1 of the census year, and the amounts of crops produced (bushels of grain, tons of hay, and the like) during the previous crop year.

The agricultural census is an amazing resource for the study of agricultural history. Trends and patterns can be studied farm-by-farm, county-by-county, state-by-state, or for the entire country. Twenty or thirty pieces of statistical information were recorded for every farmer in the country. For example, in 1860 Francis McFarland of Augusta County had 100 acres under cultivation. He produced corn, wheat, oats, Irish potatoes, and hay; the exact amounts of each are included in the census table. McFarland had three horses, four milk cows, and sixteen pigs. He converted his surplus milk to butter and cheese, which he then sold for a profit.

As technological and scientific advances came to the farm, the types of questions asked of individual farmers changed as well. Questions about chemical fertilizer,

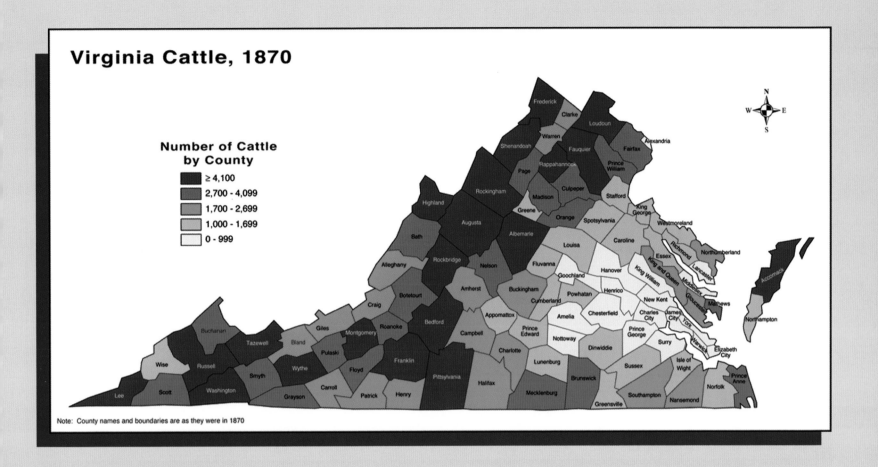

Virginia Cattle, 1870

Number of Cattle by County

- ≥ 4,100
- 2,700 - 4,099
- 1,700 - 2,699
- 1,000 - 1,699
- 0 - 999

Note: County names and boundaries are as they were in 1870

tractors, electricity, pesticides, and irrigation were added in the late nineteenth and early twentieth centuries. By 1920, markets had changed rapidly enough that trends needed to be analyzed more frequently than once a decade. Starting in that year, the agricultural census was conducted every five years.

In the middle of the twentieth century, the agricultural census was moved to years ending in four and nine. The system was reworked again in 1976 so that the data would mesh with other regular economic surveys. Today the census is conducted in years ending in seven and two, for example 1987 and 1992. The 1987 census was the twenty-third agricultural census conducted in the United States.

Today's census contains more than 115 categories ranging from size of farms, to market value of products and from livestock numbers to crop production levels. Any agricultural operation having more than one thousand dollars worth of total sales during the year is included in the census. Some of the questions, like those concerning pineapple production, are not applicable in the Old Dominion. Others are vitally important. In 1997, for instance, there were 28,325 farms in Virginia with cattle. There were 1.5 million cattle in the state, down about 100,000 from the previous two censuses. In 1997 Virginians owned about 580,000 beef cattle and 157,000 milk cows, and sold 860,000 cattle and calves. The last number was up slightly from 1992, but down significantly from 1987. Whether the statistics are used for historical research or to analyze market patterns, the U.S. Agriculture Census is a valuable resource. ~

Information from the 1987, 1992, 1997 Census of Agriculture, www.agcensus.mannlib.cornell.edu; "Explanatory notes from U.S.A. Agricultural Census 1987, Food and Agricultural Organization of the United Nations website, www.fao.org; *Factfinder for the Nation* (U.S. Census Bureau), May 2000; and U.S. Bureau of the Census, Eighth Census, 1860, Augusta County, Virginia, agricultural schedule (manuscript, Augusta County courthouse).

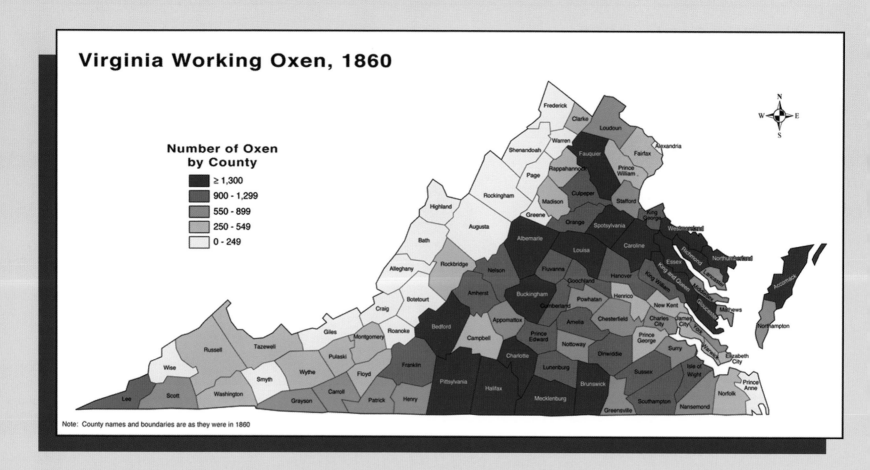

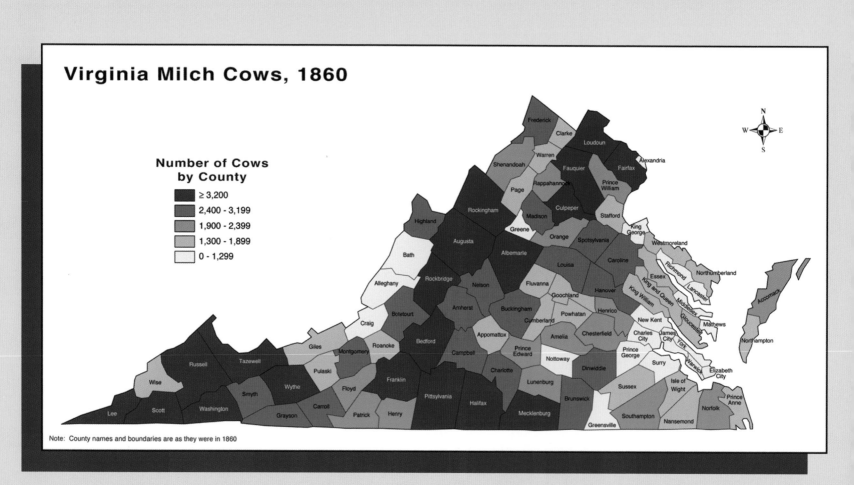

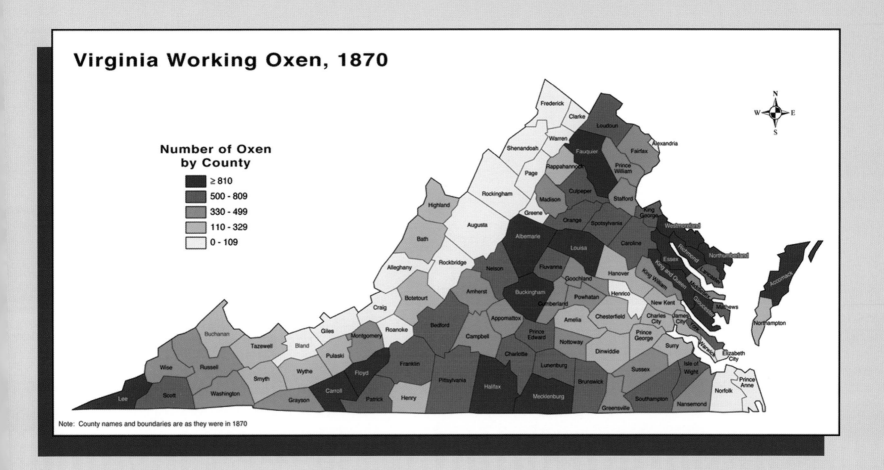

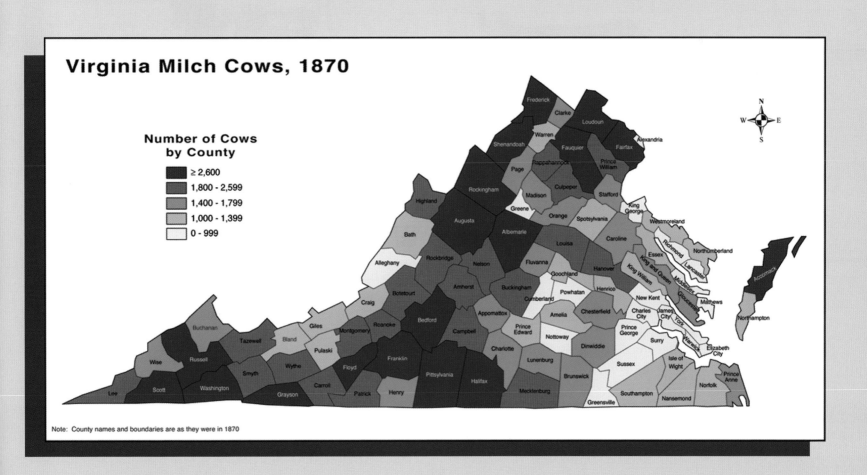

A Long Winter

Although the Union soldier who mocked Reed and warned him about holding onto the old hat because winter was coming was only referring to the fact that it was late November, his words were prophetic. It was indeed a long, hard winter for the Confederacy. In fact it would be many seasons before Virginia farms and farmers could recover. When the war ended in April of 1865, a whole generation of young men had perished. The state's agriculture and industry were crippled, its labor system forever changed, and its resources plundered. The loss of fences – chopped up for the campfires by the hundreds of thousands of soldiers

who had criss-crossed the state – and the loss of farm animals changed the way livestock was handled. The war marked the end of the open range system, in which crops were fenced in and animals were allowed to roam freely. As the South's agriculture clawed its way back, the remaining animals were fenced into smaller fields.

In a way, Virginia's cattle provided a glimpse of what was happening throughout the state's agricultural system. The sheer numbers of cattle driven off by raiding armies and commandeered by the government war effort were staggering enough, but post-war Virginia also faced cattle

diseases where there had been none before. Even five years after the conflict had concluded, the numbers of cattle in Virginia were nowhere near the antebellum years. In 1870 there were 188,471 milk cows, down from 228,347 in 1860. The numbers of beef cattle (217,285) were only half the 433,666 total in 1860, and the number of working oxen in 1870 was only 45,787 compared to 75,405 in 1860. Four of Virginia's leading cattle producing counties in 1860 – Loudoun, Fauquier, and Augusta and Rockingham – were also four of the counties that suffered under Sheridan's

scorched earth policy. The comparison of the cattle populations in 1860 and 1870 makes that all too clear. Loudoun's numbers were 5,809 milk cows and 14,504 beef cows in 1860 and only 5,719 and 10,855 in 1870. Fauquier was 5,489 and 23,192 in 1860 and 5,325 and 13,910. Augusta counted 6,441 milk cows and 14,206 beef cattle before the war and 6,232 and 11,323 after the war, while Rockingham had 6,011 milk and 13,999 beef cattle before the war and only 5,401 and 9,295 in 1870.[60] For Virginians, the end of the war meant, indeed, that a long winter lay ahead. ✿

The Great Cattle Drives

When the road swept in a bold curve around the base of a
cliff, now advanced with slow and stately tread, in all the
pomp of bovine majesty, the vanguard of one of those
monstrous herds of cattle wending their way from the rich
pastures of Monroe and Greenbrier to the eastward.[1]

Porte Crayon

In the fall of 1853 when the artist and journalist, Porte Crayon (David Hunter Strother), wrote those words for *Harpers Weekly*, he described a scene he had witnessed in Augusta County, Virginia, just west of Staunton. The illustration accompanying his words shows a well-dressed African American drover on foot, whip in hand, leading a large bovine. Behind him the road was clogged with cattle of all shapes and sizes, and horsemen crowded up behind them in the distance. Porte Crayon's sketch depicts the practice of driving animals to the mountains in the spring for summer pasturage and then driving them out of the mountains in the fall.

From the 1730s to the 1930s, farmers of the Great Valley of Virginia drove their cattle to the cool, open pastures of the Allegheny Mountains to the west, or the Blue Ridge Mountains to the east, to graze all summer. Today the practice has all but disappeared. Although it is not impossible to find families that continue this practice on a small scale, generally only the oldest residents of the valley remember the days of drovers and cow bells.

Tradition holds that the practice of grazing cattle herds was once so common that the names of three rivers in western Augusta, Bath, and Highland Counties called the Calfpasture, Cowpasture, and Bullpasture, derive from it. According to one of the legends, when herds of cattle were driven out to those well-watered pastures, the endurance of the younger animals gave out first, so drovers separated them and left them to graze near the Calfpasture River. The mature cows were stronger, so made it over the next mountain to be summered along the Cowpasture River, while the steers and bulls possessed the power to cross yet another mountain, so they spent the summer grazing along the Bullpasture River.

Pounding the Streets

During any period of Virginia's history, the sight of hundreds of animals pounding through the streets of western Virginia towns on their journey to and from summer grazing must have been awe-inspiring and maybe a little frightening. Damage and injury were sometimes the consequence when the animals spooked. At Harrisonburg, in Rockingham County, one early nineteenth-century resident remembered stampeding cattle that ripped off the front porches of houses. Maria Carr, who was born in 1812 and lived her early years in Harrisonburg, or Rocktown as it was called then, recalled

> In the Fall thousands of cattle passed through the town on their way to market. There was a stampede of cattle near the Court House, they ran around and around and broke for the houses, tore down the porches, running over the people, not killing any one, but injuring many. I with my aunt was sitting on the porch; she

*A magazine correspondent for **Harper's Weekly** created this illustration in 1853 of a fall cattle drive just west of Staunton.*

seeing what was going on, ran into the house dragging me with her, slamming the door to – they broke all the porch railing down and part of the floor of the porch – it was a long time before the cattle were gotten under control. My aunt was almost frightened to death, and was sick a long time afterwards.[2]

One man, who told of his cattle herding experiences from his youth during the 1930s, remembered helping drive a herd of twenty-five or so animals in the Fishersville area of Augusta County. "A dog got in them and spooked them and they all ran up in the woods and we had a tough time finding them and getting them back together."[3] In Winchester, in Frederick County, the problem in 1821 was not so much any danger but that drovers ran their animals through the city streets on the Sabbath:

> A drove of upwards of 200 cattle passed through the main street on Sunday last for the District of Columbia, another of the same number on Monday, and a third of about 100 on Wednesday. Soon after the drove passed on Sunday, several team-wagons from below passed in a contrary direction. These things are certainly improper for the Sabbath. If they must be tolerated, confine to the by streets, so public an example of profanation may be avoided.[4]

In Clarke County, a northern schoolteacher who was a newcomer to the area, described the scramble to get out of the way of a herd in October of 1854. "M came on the bank calling that a drive of cattle was coming down the bank we just escaped them & climb the broken bridge. The cattle were very small. . . at last a horseman fording the stream with out wetting his saddle cloth sent the long roped boat over for little Jennie & we after the herd had drunk their fill & been turned into a field had a race up the hill home." The next morning she and her friends returned to see the drive get going again. "We to see the drive cross the ford. 2 men on one horse prevented their going upstream others below & Mr. M. urged them behind. They crossed in a close body very gently . . ."[5] Later that fall the same diarist remarked that "9 cattle drovers spent the night, 700 cattle not beef but stock cattle, for the VA market." She added an interesting description of the whips used by the drovers to maintain order among the animals as the drive proceeded. "Their whips were 1½ to 2 yards long in lash, large as a 25 ct. piece in the middle, handles only one foot."[6]

The diary of a Bridgewater shoemaker, Henry Smals, shows that even after the railroad reduced distances drovers had to travel to market, large herds were common sights in western Virginia towns and villages in the spring and fall. In early October 1871 two droves of sheep and a drove of hogs had already come through his Rockingham County village when, on October 23, " a drove Cattle Came through the town." On October 31, 1871, "A drove of Cattle Came to town to be Weighed. . . . " A herd of cattle came through on November 6, a drove of cattle and horses passed through the next day, on November 9 a drove of "fine hogs" and a drove of cattle passed through, and on November 10 a herd

came through to be weighed by John Hevins who apparently operated the cattle scales. Five more herds came through Bridgewater in November, one in December and two in January of 1872. Livestock matters quieted down in the town until the spring when Smals noted on March 7, 1872 that "a drove of Cattle Came through town today." On April 26, he noted that "a drove of stock cattle Came through town Going to West Virginia." Then on May 8, 1872 he wrote: "A drove of Cattle went thray [sic] our town to day to W.V. to graze." At some other time in the spring he added "a drive of the fatest Cattle went through our town I ever saw." Finally, on May 14 he noted that "a drove of Cattle went through with bells on."[7]

A Valley of Grain

In the eighteenth century much of the beef exported from Virginia went to the West Indies. By the middle of the nineteenth century, however, the market had shifted to domestic consumption in America's urban markets. By this time, the Valley of Virginia had become a grain belt where large amounts of wheat and corn were grown. Throughout the middle decades of the century, Baltimore and Richmond vied as the top two milling cities in the country. Wheat grown in the valley was ground into flour, shipped around the tip of South America and up to California where the California Forty-niners baked it into sourdough bread. During the Civil War, of course, the valley earned the reputation as the "Breadbasket of the Confederacy." Despite the large quantities of wheat grown, the production of corn far surpassed the cereal grain. However, corn was con-

Beef cattle in Augusta County, ca. 1905

Smal's diary, October 29, 1879, records a drove of 547 cattle passing through the town of Bridgewater.

sumed locally, either by man or beast, while the wheat was shipped all over the world. Beef and grain production complemented one another in the agriculture system that evolved in the Great Valley. One historian described the partnership that evolved between a grain producing economy and cattle grazing in this way:

> Large numbers of cattle from the Appalachian Mountains were driven into farming districts, such as the Valley of Virginia, the valleys of east Tennessee, and the piedmont sections of Maryland, Virginia, and the Carolinas, where they were sold to grain raising farmers who fattened them for market. . . . The mountain cattle were customarily purchased when three or four

years of age, "roughed" through the first winter on cornstalks and wheat straw, fattened in the summer and fall on clover pasture and grain, and then driven to the markets of Baltimore and Philadelphia. About 1850 some 2,000 head were driven from the mountains into Albemarle County alone. This constituted an economical way to market the corn of the piedmont areas.[8]

In 1851 a Rockbridge County farmer witnessed the practice of pasturing and cattle drives first hand. In 1851 he reported to the United States Commissioner of the Patents that from his area "vast herds of the finest beeves are driven to Richmond, Baltimore and Philadelphia markets."[9] The *Journal of Agriculture*, a New York farming periodical from the 1840s, made some observations about the methods of cattle production in western Virginia during the same period (western Virginia at that time included all of West Virginia). The author wrote that grazing cattle to fatten for market was pursued more in the Valley than east of the Blue Ridge Mountains and that many farmers owned fifty to one hundred stock cattle. The cattle were driven to the mountains in the late spring or early summer and then brought back in September or October. They were fattened over the winter on wheat straw and hay and were also "mealed"

Cropping, Belling, Branding

Ownership Marks through the Years

How did Virginians of the past identify and separate their cattle from the hundreds and even thousands of animals that often foraged untended through the countryside? Some of the many methods, like bells and brands, might seem quite familiar to modern-day readers, while other methods, like ear cropping and horn branding, have all but disappeared from common usage. The free-range livestock

The unknown nineteenth-century artist who painted this group of animals resting in a field knew enough about ownership of livestock to accurately depict crop marks on the animals' ears.

(given grain) and salted twice a week. Salting was thought to promote rapid weight gains. The ones that were considered fit to be sold in the spring averaged about 500 pounds and brought about fourteen dollars. The animals that were too young or too poor were returned to pasture between April 15 and May 1.[10] Alma Hibbard in her Clarke County diary noted in 1854 that she was told that more than 10,000 cattle were driven from the valley floor to a point in the mountains about ten miles away.[11]

Many men sought to profit from this system of stock raising. In June of 1842 Caswell Freeman, a drover from Jacksborough, Tennessee, wrote to David Flook of Rockingham County concerning the price of cattle:

Mr David Flook Sir After my Best Respects to you I know [now?] sit down to Address a few lines to let you know that I have not forgotten you and to let you know that I am well and have enjoyed good health since I saw you last hoping this few lines may find you and family enjoying the same Blessing Dear Sir I have taken this method and wish you to wright to me and to let me know how you think cattle will do this season as I have one hundred and fifty head and Expects to Drive them this season an expects to start Abought the same time I started last season and I wish you to wright that such cattle as I sold you last season will sell for this season and how times is in your contry [?] and how you think

The ledger book of Rockingham County's John H. Reed included expenses for driving a lot of cattle in November 1849. Most of the expenses were for road tolls, animal feed, and lodging.

husbandry that developed in Virginia by the mid-seventeenth century left a legacy that affects agriculture as it is practiced in the state today. One element of that legacy is ownership marking. Whether farmers wanted to locate their animals for the market or the dinner table, or whether the finder of a stray animal was trying to identify its owner, a means of matching owners with animals was needed.

A good identification system also thwarted cattle rustling, something easily accomplished by simply not reporting stray livestock that had wandered onto one's land. Although numbers of cattle remained small in the first half of the seventeenth century, by mid-century approximately 20,000 cattle were in the colony. Most of those animals were probably free-range animals, making it easy for unscrupulous individuals to take strays as their own. Very early the House of Burgesses enacted legislation to combat this weakness in the Chesapeake

system of husbandry. A law, established in 1656 and modeled after English law, was designed to curtail the practice of people making free use of the animals that had wandered onto their property. The law was designed "for remedie of the great abuse and wrong done in taking up stray horses [and] cattell . . . not only in concealing of them, but in useinge and employing them; to the hurt and damage of the owners."

cattle will sell this season as all the men I have seen that Drove last season says they will not drive this season as times were so hard last season and how crops is in your contry [?] as crops is fine in this contry [?] so fare Pleas[e] Wright a soon as you get this and your compliance will much oblige your friend Direct your letter to Jackborough Post Office Campbell County east Tenessee Yours respectfully Caswell [12]

Farmers who lived along major thoroughfares profited by supplying feed to the drovers. Shenandoah County farmer Levi Pitman recorded all the herds that stopped at

Drovers, such as these in Southwest Virginia, were often on horseback. Others walked with the animals or led one animal. Large cattle drives needed both mounted men and those on foot to control the cattle. Drovers of both sorts usually carried whips to crack over the heads of the cattle. Close examination of this picture indicates that at least two of the men, the one in the middle and one on the right, have whips.

Virginia authorities encouraged colonists to mark their livestock and to record those marks at the county courthouse. Descriptions of stray animals, including approximate age, color, size, and ownership marks, were displayed in newspaper advertisements and, later, in estray books maintained by the county clerk of court. Because earmarks were the most common means of marking an animal in the seventeenth century, county clerks often recorded the particular marks or combinations of marks used by an individual. A person

his farm in late 1852. A sampling of his diary entries reveals how this form of enterprise worked:

> Nov. 17, 1852: This afternoon, we took in a drove of fat cattle, 111 head, M.J. Miles manager, had his son along fed the cattle our cornstocks yet standing in the field.
> Nov. 24, 1852: Late this afternoon I took in a drove of fat cattle, of Mr. Morris, manager. . . . I sold him 30 bushels of my corn at 45 cents per bushel amount $13.50.
> Dec. 7, 1852: We took in two large droves in three lots of fat cattle. . . I sold them 60 bushels of my corn, took all my corn at 40 cents per bushel.[13]

Jedediah Hotchkiss had been Confederate General Thomas "Stonewall" Jackson's cartographer. As a Staunton businessman he published *Virginia: A Geographical and Political Summary in 1876* in order to attract commercial ventures to the Commonwealth. Hotchkiss noted the economic potential of the grazing lands:

> There are vast tracts of mountain land in Virginia that furnish a "range" for young cattle, enabling the grazier to rear them at but little expense. These tracts of land are covered by a growth of timber, more or less heavy, beneath which is an undergrowth of rich-weed, wild grasses, &c., that are highly nutritious, and on which cattle can subsist from April to November. The stock raising capacity of the State can hardly be estimated, so great is it.[14]

accused of stealing an animal that had already been slaughtered, then, was required to produce the ears of the animal in order to prove innocence or guilt. A lack of ears meant guilt. A legislative act of 1658 further reinforced the use of ownership marks by making it illegal for Virginians to move cattle into Maryland for resale without first having four neighbors examine the marks on their livestock. By 1662 anyone moving was required to have his marks registered before departing. This was to discourage families from pulling up stakes and taking someone else's livestock with them.

For more than two centuries, starting with that 1656 law, Virginia authorities continued to refine statutes concerning Virginia's estrays (wandering livestock) in order to keep a step

Gathering, Grazing

More than two centuries ago settlers in the region west of the Blue Ridge Mountains worked out the logistics of gathering animals from Valley farms, grazing them in the mountains for the summer, then returning them in the fall. In the mid-nineteenth century, for example, drover Jacob Zimmerman took nine cattle to Pocahontas County. The animals were taken on May 31 and Zimmerman was paid "50 ct per month pasturage – $1 per head to carry them & return them to me." Zimmerman was also given four dollars in expenses for his travel to Pocahontas. The animals were described in great detail, probably for easy identification when it came time to return the animals in the fall. For instance, one yearling was described as follows: "one red Heifer white spots on top of rump middle of tail white – most of belly & breast bone white – white behind horns white on inside of each leg at Knee joint." In addition "all of above cattle have a small clip from each ear & branded with [a mark was drawn in here] on right shoulder [illegible word, maybe mark?] of above was branded on left shoulder."[15] These practices described by Zimmerman persisted until well into the twentieth century.

According to Leon "Mose" Kiracofe, when he was a child in the 1920s and 1930s, the cost of a summer of pasturing was still fifty cents a head and most of the money went to the forest service. Kiracofe is quite familiar with the practices around the Sangerville area where he was born and reared. That mountain grazing area was about fifteen miles long and not quite fifteen miles wide. The animals were let loose in forest clearings. Those openings in the forest, sometimes called balds by the local residents, were more often known in the German areas as sods. "There were hundreds of sods, some were little bitty and one cow could take it in one day. Some were fifty acres or more," Kiracofe said. The origin of the mountain sods has always been somewhat of a mystery. Some contend that the forest clearings are natural, others argue that the Native Americans first created them by burning. Some were documented as having been cleared by settlers who used some of the wood as firewood to heat their houses and burned the rest. The sods were scattered all through the ridges. The larger ones

Until well into the twentieth century, cattle that were fattened on pasture were Shorthorn or Shorthorn crosses.

ahead of violators. Illegal deceit took a variety of forms, from concealing strays to reporting and subsequently advertising them with "false and imperfect descriptions," so that the real owners could not recognize their own animals. A law passed in 1762 established "a more effectual method to prevent frauds committed by persons taking up strays." This statute required that animals other than horses (which had to be brought to the courthouse) be examined and appraised by neighbors who presented a description, under oath, that was recorded by the county clerk. Most important, the law also required that the clerk enter the same descriptions "in a book to be by him kept for that purpose." These official records became known as the estray books.

The "finder" of wandering livestock, who for many years could only be a white, male, landowner, reported found animals, complete with detailed descriptions, to the clerk of the county where the animal was found. The finder bore the costs of advertising the found animals during quarterly court sessions and in the newspaper. Owners could claim the livestock at any time, but they had to reimburse finders for their payments to the court and for their advertising expenses. Also owners were expected to give rewards to finders.

Ownership marks and identification methods took several different forms as a variety of documents and illustrations from the 1640s until the early 1900s show. The best sources of information, however, are the estray books, which contain elaborate descriptions of animals. These ledgers reveal a

were named, for example, Click's Hacking, Goolsby Sod, and Shull's Sod, while the smaller ones remained nameless.

Typically one man oversaw the grazing of a collection of sods. In mid-May he would go from farm to farm, gathering cattle, three or four here and two or three there, until he had about thirty-five animals. The cattle were a mixture of breeds and colors. "Most had Shorthorn in them or were what we called blue dun. There was some Hereford in there too," he said. The bulls, which went out in the mountains too, were the only ones that sometimes were pure bred. Those cattle that were born without horns were called "muley," Kiracofe said. After the drover had rounded-up all the cattle, he herded them fifteen or so miles into the mountains and then allowed them to roam freely. The animals, accustomed to the routine, would meander off in search of grass. "One fellow had rented some land in Sugar Grove Valley. They said he would drive his cattle up to the top of the ridge and start 'em down the road. Then he'd just turn around and go back home. The cattle knew what to do," he said.

The drovers checked on the cattle once a week, to put out salt and make sure bears had not gotten into them. The cattle roamed from sod to sod, sometimes traveling ten miles or more in search of good grass and water. In severe drought, some cattle were brought home so they would not

The Dwyer family were tenants at the Varner grazing place at Spiencop in Rappahannock County (now Shenandoah National Park). The man on the right with the small boy is believed to be Jake Dwyer. In the center are Mr. and Mrs. Jeff Dwyer. The young ladies are Dwyers too.

remarkable record of marks and methods of livestock identification from the eighteenth to the twentieth century. Belling — of sheep and horses, as well as cattle — was one way to show ownership. Estray book entries often included detailed descriptions of animal bells, with a listed valuation of the bell itself. In 1787, an Augusta County mare had on a "three shilling Bell with a double strap," for example. According to Leon "Mose" Kiracofe, who grew up in the predominantly German area of Sangerville, along the Augusta-Rockingham County border in the Shenandoah Valley, belling was the ownership mark of choice among the people grazing animals in his neighborhood in the 1930s: "all of 'em had to be belled," he recalled. "The bells had the owner's initial on it. Those old boys could listen to a bell and say 'that's on so-and-so's white heifer. They could listen to a bell and tell what animal it was and whose it

was." He added that bull bells were larger and had a different tone.

Branding, another means of ownership identity, was used on all types of livestock, but horses most often. When cattle were branded in colonial Virginia, it was often on the ear cushion. After the Civil War, brands were more typically found on the hips. Additionally, cattle were often branded on their horns or their horns were drilled with holes. The red and white steer that Elias Craun of Rockingham County found in 1868 was "branded on each horn with letter the 'H'."

Today in Virginia, branding is a common form of identification and the practice is regulated under the Code of Virginia. A brand is considered any means (except tattooing) of applying an identification mark on an animal's hide. Heat, freezing, or chemicals can create brands. Applications for brands are made to the Virginia State Veterinarian and are

starve. As a youngster, Kiracofe witnessed the grazing practices first hand and was sometimes called upon to help bring the cattle home in the fall. Cattle were retrieved from the higher elevations by the first of September. "Up on the high mountains the oaks would start maturing and dropping their acorns. When cattle eat acorns it cuts their insides, so the cattle were brought back before the acorns matured," he remembered. He recalled helping drive the cattle off Shenandoah Mountain and remembered that it took three men and two dogs to accomplish the task. "We would get up there early and get all the cattle in a little corral," he recalled. That evening, the men would feast on hams and homemade pies that their wives had packed. "Those meals at those cattle camps were something," he said with a grin. "The next morning we would get the rest together and if we were lucky we could get away by 10 o'clock. They were always getting cattle mixed up when they drove 'em out. They would just drop those others off at a farm and the owners would come and get them. It was a nice cooperative effort." Once the cattle were home, those that were finished out might be driven on into Harrisonburg or Staunton to be sold. "A lot of times people would come by the farms and buy them," Kiracofe added.[16]

In the fall when the animals were returned, some merry mix-ups often occurred as attempts were made to

By the 1910s and 1920s, the dominance of the Shorthorn had faded, only to be replaced by the Hereford.

put the right animals back at the correct farms. Until the use of silos and ensilage became widespread in the late nineteenth and early twentieth centuries, the majority of those pastured animals that had attained a marketable size at three or four years of age were driven straight to markets in the fall. In the eighteenth and through three-quarters of the nineteenth century, the drovers brought the animals out of the mountains and continued to push them many miles to urban markets such as Philadelphia, Richmond, Baltimore, and Alexandria.

Kiracofe's experiences bear striking similarities to other valley men who recalled driving cattle up into the cool pas-

maintained in a register kept by the Virginia Department of Agriculture and Consumer Services. In Virginia, brands can include any of the twenty-six letters of the alphabet, numerals from two to nine, and any one of nine recognized symbols such as a triangle or an arrow. Every registered brand must have at least two of the three types of characters but not more than three. The characters have to be positioned so that they can be read from left to right or top to bottom. The brand can be located only on shoulders, hips, or ribs.

Dewlapping, or slitting pieces of skin on an animal's dewlap (that loose fold of skin under an animal's throat) was a less common means of marking cattle. Several animals in the Augusta County estray books were described as being "dewlapped," and a white and black spotted heifer found in Rockingham County in 1898 had a "crop off left ear; slit in right and dew lap." An 1854 diary entry of a northern

woman visiting the Shenandoah Valley provides further evidence of this unusual marking system. Alma Hibbard observed a drove of cattle that had been "marked by cutting a strip of skin, one, two, or three from the neck & leaving it to grow pendent some the upper some the lower one the longest."

Probably the most common type of identifying marks were ear notches. Many ears had three or four different holes, slits, underkeels, notches, and swallow forks cut out of them. In 1786 a brindle cow in Augusta County sported "a hole in each ear & a half penny cut of the right ear on the uper side."

A 1678 document from the Northern Neck describes "a certain heiffer and cafe marked wth a cropd & a hole in the right ear," another heifer "marked wth a Crops on both ears & swallow fork on both ears," and a cow and calf "marked with a Slitt in each eare."

In an even earlier document from 1657 in Warwick County, Robert Elie described the cattle belonging to his siblings. This

tures of the mountains for the summer. In 1980, John V. Heatwole of Rockingham County recalled that:

> In the summers, around 1900, us boys would be sent into the mountains with our cattle and the neighbors'. We drove them to Richland Mountain [west of Union Springs in Rockingham County] where my father and Potter John [Tom Heatwole and John D. Heatwole] had 600 acres of land. It was me and my brother John was sent with the cattle. They'd send along enough food for us for a week. Being growing boys we'd bolt it all down in two or three days and then starve until they brought us more food. We had to watch out for rattlesnakes and Briery Branchers [rough folks from Briery Branch]. We'd avoid them if we heard them coming. We went barefoot and slept in a shack on the mountain.

Heatwole always resented being sent to the mountains while other boys were out of school at home along Dry River. It soured him on farm life altogether.[17] Some of the best grazing lands for cattle were in what became West Virginia. Both Rockingham and Augusta Counties border West Virginia, and the state line meanders along the ridge tops in the very area where the cattle were grazing. In 1997 William Miller of Mossy Creek in northern Augusta County recalled that West Virginia connection along with some other interesting stories.

> When I was a boy I used to help my father herd cattle from Pocahontas County to the railroad at Bridgewater. We drove the cattle to Pocahontas in the spring and left them with a farmer over there to graze for the summer. In the fall we would get together a team of drovers and go get them. We drove them through Highland County to Palo Alto Gap in Pendleton County, West Virginia where we spent the night before driving the cattle on into the valley. My father always arranged with a woman there to provide pasturage for the cattle for the night. She fed us drovers and we slept in the barn. What I remember most is that the woman always served us mutton broth with a little wool floating around in it. It was nasty. I hated that soup.[18]

A 1997 interview with William H. Sipe of eastern Rockingham County is remarkably similar to the others, and makes the same point as Kiracofe about removing the cattle before the acorns began falling. The difference in this interview is that Sipe's cattle drives took place in the Blue Ridge Mountains, not the Alleghenies.

> We used to drive cattle from Island Ford. We'd stop at Swift Run at J.E.F. Hughes' store to have something to drink; Elk Run Soda or ginger ale. Then on to Cedar Falls to the north [actually more to the east] of Swift Run Gap, about halfway up the mountain. The cattle would be left for the summer with the Burke family. They would pas-

document is remarkable for the detail with which it describes the crops, slits, and other marks in the ears of the cattle.

> *My Sister Elizabeth 2 Cowes and 2 Calves and one heyfer of a yeare old; My sister Annas cattle 1 Cow &Calfe & 1 steere of a yeer old and one heyfer of 2 yeares old; my Brother Wills Cattle 1 Cow & a bull calfe & a yeerlinge heifer; my Brother Edward 1 heifer 2 yeeres old/2 Cows have a halfe Moone under the right ear and a halfe moone under the left the heifer is Cropt in the right and halfe Cropt in ye Left 2 Cow Calves 1 halfe moone cropt in ye right and under the Left and Slitt in ye Left, 2 Cow Calves 1 halfe moone cropt in ye right and under the Left and Slitt in ye Left, 1 Cow calfe Cropt in both eares and slitt; my Sister Anne 1 Cow cropt in ye left and halfe moone and nicke in The right 1 heyfer Cropt in the right & halfe Crop in the left 1 steere of a yeere old, halfe moon[e] in the right & slitt and halfe moone in ye left 1 calfe of the Same marke 1 Cow with 2 halfe moones on each eare 1 yearling and Calfe of the Same Marke, one 2 yeere old heifer wth 2 halfe moones under boath eares*

This common method of marking the animals' ears persisted into the twentieth century as evidenced by one of the last entries in the Rockingham Estray book. Interesting, too, is that a new type of identification, introduced a few years earlier, was also in use: "15 June 1919 Mrs. Virginia Heversly - heifer; 650 lbs.; 2 yrs. old; roan; beef type; right ear cropped and slightly slit; left ear bearing a leather tag attached with hog ring; $60"

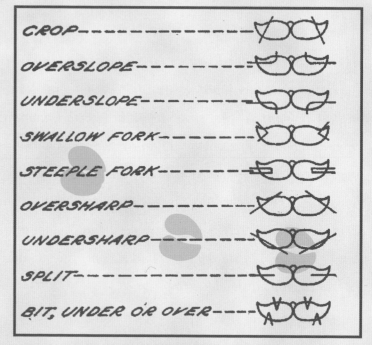

The combination of crops, forks, splits, and sharps used to mark an animals' ears was as specific to a particular owner as was a brand.

Another identification technique introduced in the twentieth century and still practiced today is tattooing, used mostly for registered purebred cattle. Westmoreland Davis, Virginia governor

ture the cattle for so much per head. There was good grass and cool air and we'd take salt for them. We had to get them off before the acorns fell because the cattle would browse on them and get poor; get skinny as snakes.[19]

Waldo Whistleman grew up in the Crimora-Dooms area of northeastern Augusta County. Whistleman, in a 2002 interview, remembered as a boy in the early 1930s helping drive cattle from the Barger estate, which was a collection of nine farms in the area, up into the Blue Ridge Mountains above Waynesboro to graze for the summer. He was one of those who went on foot to help drive the cattle to pasture. Periodically through the summer, someone would go to the mountains, check on the animals, and salt them. Whistleman's father grew up in the western part of Augusta County at Augusta Springs where he kept the tollhouse at Jennings Gap. His father often recalled the many drovers passing through from Highland County and driving "cattle, pigs, even turkeys...whatever they could drive." They would spend the night at the tollhouse and then drive on into Staunton where they would sell the animals.[20]

Janet Baugher Downs has less-than-fond memories of helping her father drive ten to fifteen head of cattle from their farm in Goods Mill (Rockingham County) to her grandfather's farm a few miles away. By driving the ani-

mals to the farm every spring, her father, Wilmer K. Baugher, was carrying on a scaled-down droving tradition that he had known all his life. Earlier in the twentieth century, Baugher had been hired to take large numbers of cattle to the mountains in the summer and then transport them by truck through Harpers Ferry to the Baltimore market in the fall. At that time the only bridge that spanned the river at Harpers Ferry was for the railroad, so when the coast was clear, Baugher drove the big cattle truck across the railroad bridge and through the railroad tunnel.

For his own cattle, Baugher and his son, Wayne, would drive the animals to summer pasture in the spring, while Janet and her mother, Louise, followed behind in a car to watch for stragglers. "I hated every minute of this activity," remembered Janet. "I was in my early teens and, of course, I wore a skirt because this was before jeans or shorts were popular or permitted. Most fields were fenced and we would have to watch at the turn in on the roads and watch them at the openings in the fields as there were few gates."

The three-mile route wound over paved and unpaved roads and even crossed several small streams. The cattle drive concluded at Scott and Leannah Baugher's farm. The animals grazed there all summer and were driven home again in the fall.[21]

from 1918 until 1922, developed a large herd of Guernsey milk cows at Morven Park, his estate in Loudoun County. A 1921 letter from the Morven Park farm manager to the governor in Richmond discussed some tattooing problems at Morven Park.

> As to tattooing the calves, I never tatood [sic] one until he was at least six months old. I would have tattooed them all however at any age if had been so that Mr. Weschler could have been with me. It so happened that we were not ready at the same time, and I waited for him thinking that it would be best for him to see it done. If Mr. Weschler cannot Tattoo the calves I will go out some day and help him. He told me however that he could. As to the two young bulls, they were both Tattood when calves but I got hold of a bad bottle of ink and it did not stand.

According to one historian, the handling of animals to mark them helped keep them domesticated. The reversion of cattle to a feral state, one of the dangers of a free-range system, was less likely because of such regular human contact.

The system of marking animals also brought order to the landscape. People accepted that the animals wandering the hills and marshes had owners who could be determined through a system of identification that had been implemented during Virginia's first decades of settlement. So

common were the notches, crops, and holes in the ears of cattle that when an unknown artist painted a bucolic scene in nineteenth-century western Virginia, he or she included the ragged edges of the ears of the group of cattle depicted. ~

A variety of primary and secondary sources helped draw together the history of livestock ownership marks in Virginia. The Code of Virginia as outlined in William Waller Hening's, *Statutes at Large; Being a Collection of all the Laws of Virginia from the 1st session of the Legislature in the year 1619* helped track the evolution of estray laws, while the Code of Virginia, 1950, provided information about modern branding practices. Extant estray books from Augusta County and Rockingham County can still be found in their respective courthouses. The thousands of ledger entries are rich with details about ownership marks. Transcriptions from the colonial records of the now-defunct Warwick County can be found in *Warwick County, Virginia: Colonial Court Records in Transcription*, by Richard Dunn (Williamsburg, Va.: The Jones House Association, Inc., 2000). Other primary sources that reinforced the idea of ownership marks include Alma Hibbard's journal from the mid-1850s that is located in the Special Collections Library, Duke University; a 1678 statement by Francis Graves of Rappahannock County found in the Virginia Historical Society; and a 1921 letter from Westmoreland Davis to a Mr. Turnbull can be located in the archives at Morven Park, Leesburg, Virginia. As always, the comprehensive, two-volume set by Lewis Cecil Gray, *History of Agriculture in the Southern United States to 1860*, proved invaluable. Also helpful were journal articles by Virginia DeJohn Anderson ("Animals into the Wilderness: The Development of Livestock Husbandry in the Seventeenth-Century Chesapeake," *William and Mary Quarterly* 3, vol. 59, April 2002) and Nancy Sorrells ("Muley Cows & Brock Faced Ewes: Delving into the Ulster Roots of the Augusta County Estray Books, 1775-1840," *The Journal of Scotch-Irish Studies*, vol. 1, Summer 2001). Thanks must be given to Peggy Dillard for transcribing the Rockingham estray records and to Pamela H. Smith for allowing the painting of cattle to be photographed.

Boost to the Economy

The tradition of cattle drives and summer grazing created an economic link between the people of the mountains and those in the valley. Even tavern keepers and toll collectors along drovers' routes realized an economic benefit from the system. Before the creation of the Shenandoah National Park in the 1930s, at least fifty square miles of grassland was used as summer grazing. Among the German communities, a well-established system of animal husbandry involved a combination of lowland farmers and their tenants who lived in the highlands. [22] The lowland families owned vast acreage on the ridges and hollows just above where the cattle were taken for the summer. On that mountain land were less refined dwellings and barns that were used by tenants who watched over the animals at the "grazing places." Louise Varner Long grew up in a family that summered cattle in three great mountain pastures in Page, Madison, and Rappahannock Counties. As a child she accompanied her grandfather in a buckboard wagon when they went to check on the cattle. Lambert described the journey up into the mountains and the business partnership of the family.

"[Upon the arrival of Louise and her grandfather] They were greeted by Jake and Jeff Dwyer, tenants on the grazing property, and their families. The Dwyer children gave Louise hazelnuts they'd gathered. . . . Three Varner brothers, "Grandpa, Uncle Jake and Uncle Martin," put cattle on this rich pasture. Earlier, the pastureland had belonged to great-grandfather Hamilton Varner. Sometime before park establishment, a fourth partner . . . joined the ownership." In a log barn there each of the four had places for their horses. They also had a bedroom each. The different owners would sometimes stay for weeks, enjoying the cool mountains and gathering chestnuts while they looked after the cattle. [23]

Mrs. Long's husband, Arthur, grew up in a family that summered cattle along two ridgetops above Hawksbill Creek. As an adult Arthur Long "had a fine grazing place on Thorofare Mountain between Skyland and Nicholson Hollow. The tenant was Charlie "Buck" Corbin. . . . About fifty of Long's cattle grazed there, and Corbin kept a watchful eye on them." The Long brothers grazed another portion of the mountains outside the park boundaries in partnership just as the Varners had done. Because the land was not part of Shenandoah National Park, the grazing tradition continued there for a number of years after the creation of the park. Each April the Longs would gather about 300 of their cattle and move toward their mountaintop pasture in the early morning hours. The drive required men on horseback to keep the cattle off neighboring lands as well as flagmen at the front and back of the herd to warn passing motorists. In more recent times, Long's elderly father would drive a truck and give a ride to any young calves that tired during the ten-mile journey. The trip to the grazing lands was finished by noon. The tenants on the Long pasture were Carrie and Joe Thomas. They reserved one room of their house for the Longs to use. Every week one of the Longs rode up to the mountains to check the condition of their cattle, which were mostly Shorthorns. [24]

Although the tenant system in the Blue Ridge Mountains had more structure than the system described by Kiracofe of families living in the sods of the Alleghenies, there are many similarities. One author has compared the lives of the Blue Ridge tenants to the tenants of the English gentry.

There wasn't any formal agreement of tenancy; everyone seemed to understand the relationship already. The tenants would "salt the cattle"—that is, they'd notice if the salt the owners had put out was gone and they'd

put a new supply on rocks where the cattle could lick it up. The salt was fine then, like table salt, not big cubes of rock salt. . . A tenant and family lived in the cabin and took care of it. They grew vegetables, often with separate patches for potatoes and corn, and orchard fruit. It was customary, though not required, for the tenant family to make small gifts of wild nuts or berries, or maybe a few heads of the superior cabbage that grew in mountain gardens, to the owner family when they came, perhaps also to feed and lodge them occasionally unless the owners had a summer house for their own use as many did. The owners, too, would bring small gifts, maybe toys, maybe coffee or sugar. . . . The tenant paid no rent, either in cash or a set share of production. The owner paid nothing for the regular watching and emergency coping.[25]

Sometime in the years before World War II the practice of driving cattle to the mountains for the summer's grazing and then bringing them home in the fall disappeared. In the case of much of the Blue Ridge grazing it was the creation of Shenandoah National Park that forced the end of the tradition. A more intensely managed national forest in the western part of the valley and in places like southeastern Augusta County had a similar effect. In other areas it was a combination of factors. By the outbreak of World War II the Shenandoah Valley was no longer intensively producing grain. This meant that pastureland on the valley floor was open for grazing. Much of Virginia's land had been enclosed by that time so that the days of open range had all but disappeared. With a shift from small grain production to hay and more corn, and with the building of silos, more animal feed could be grown and stored. Animals could be pastured or stall-fed and not forced to fend for themselves on open range. A growing human population and the ris-

ing popularity of the automobile meant that people could now live in remote places in the mountains and commute to the valley. The resulting urban sprawl meant that houses were built in some of the more remote grazing areas. And finally, in the newer era of more managed, intensive farming, the idea of turning a herd of heifers out to indiscriminately mate and to calve away from watchful supervision was not appealing to farmers desiring to improve their herds.

After two centuries the tradition of driving cattle up to the mountains to graze freely for the summer has disappeared. For the most part, only the old-timers retain a memory of those days when cattle were belled and, for half a dollar, were released in the woods for the summer.[26] However there are still a few scattered families holding on to the tradition.

Each year the Cash family continues to drive a few head of cattle from their home about six miles away to a summer pasture higher up in the Blue Ridge Mountains called Mag Lot, presumably named for the old woman called Maggie Coffey who used to live on the property. Doris and Ralph Cash continue the cattle drive in the spring and the fall because that is what their families have done for generations. Mrs. Cash remembered her grandparents driving cattle all the way from Spottswood in southern Augusta County to grazing ground near the Mill Creek Schoolhouse near Montebello. The trip took an entire day. In the 1940s, her parents continued driving cattle to a place about six miles distant. Since 1952 when Doris and Luther Cash were married, she has participated in the Cash cattle drive. Several generations later the tradition continues with a six-mile drive in the spring. The tradition continued by the Cash family is among the last of its kind in the Old Dominion.

Riding the Rails of Progress

German artist Edward Beyer depicted progress of the day – the railroad – in his 1850s lithograph of Bedford County near the town of Liberty (now Bedford), with the Peaks of Otter in the background and cattle grazing peacefully in the foreground.

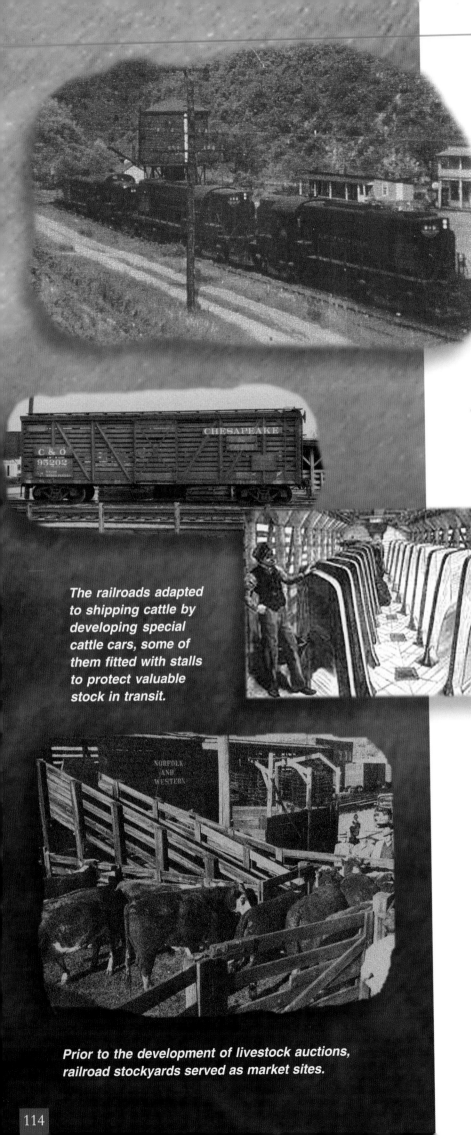

The grimmest era in the history of the United States came to a close in the spring of 1865. Although the Civil War devastated the entire South, arguably, no state experienced more destruction than Virginia. At war's end, the Old Dominion lay in shambles. No state had witnessed more military action or suffered such ruin. A generation of men had been silenced on the battlefield, while at home farm fields had reverted to wilderness and industrial complexes were nothing more than smoldering wreckage. Diseases, both human and livestock, plagued the countryside with unprecedented force. As the Confederacy imploded, so too did Virginia's economy. In 1865, under the load of a massive war debt and with a shattered economic infrastructure, the Old Dominion began the long task of rebuilding.

Out of the smoke of war chugged the steam locomotive. If any good had come from the war, it was that the potential of the railroad for economic development had been demonstrated. The lessons learned about moving men and supplies in war could easily be applied to moving goods to market. A modern transportation system would lure Northern investors who would, in turn, build more railroads, which would aid the state's economic recovery. The railroad could pull the South out of its economic abyss.

For Virginia's farmers, the railroad represented the path to economic recovery, as it ushered in a new era of marketing options. Keeping pace with the new age of industrial technology was a rise in scientific medicine – again a positive gain wrung from the death and suffering experienced on and off the battlefield during the conflict. An understanding of the germ theory and the ability to peer into the microscopic world of disease meant that farmers could abandon their mostly useless homemade concoctions and look toward prevention rather than just treatment. Improved methods of testing for disease, better vaccines, and other proactive ideas such as dipping to prevent tick infestation, meant healthier livestock and production levels less affected by fate.

In 1830, three decades before the Civil War, the iron horse quietly ushered in a new era when Peter Cooper's railroad steam engine, the Tom Thumb, rattled forward for thirteen miles. A decade later, the nation boasted 3,000 miles of track but none of the lines connected products and markets over long distances. Within another decade, however, major trunk lines crossed the Appalachian Mountains, effectively tying urban markets to production sources. By 1860, 30,000 miles of rail criss-crossed the nation.[1] One of the most significant east-west railroads in the Old Dominion, the Virginia Central (later the C&O), breached the Blue Ridge Mountains and extended to Staunton in 1854, thus connecting the upper valley to the state capital in Richmond. On the eve of the Civil War, Richmond served as the hub for Virginia's railroads. In that city alone, seven businesses specialized in the production of railroad cars.[2]

The railroads adapted to shipping cattle by developing special cattle cars, some of them fitted with stalls to protect valuable stock in transit.

Prior to the development of livestock auctions, railroad stockyards served as market sites.

The war ended rail expansion for a time but military strategists relied on rail as a quick and efficient means of transportation. When war ended, farmers quickly put their land back into production and entrepreneurs wasted little time in finding ways to get agricultural products to market. By 1876, eleven railroad lines laced the state. Some lines were but a few miles long while others, like the Atlantic, Mississippi and Ohio, stretched almost 400 miles from Norfolk to Saltville. The Chesapeake and Ohio, with 421 miles of track, connected Richmond to Huntington, West Virginia. The Richmond and Danville and Piedmont comprised almost 300 miles of rail connecting Richmond to Charlotte, North Carolina, and the Valley Railroad (part of the Baltimore and Ohio) connected Staunton and Baltimore with just over 200 miles of line.[3] The age of the railroad had arrived.

Market Changes

The importance of the steam locomotive to Virginia agriculture cannot be overestimated. The acceptance of this new transportation source by the farming community expanded markets for farm products and even altered what farmers produced. Virginia agriculture faced a crisis in the last quarter of the nineteenth century. Traditionally the state had been one of the leading wheat producing regions in the nation, but farmers found it increasingly difficult to match the production levels of the Midwest. Increasingly, farmers began to seek profits by grazing animals on grass and hay. The rise of the fat cattle export business in western and southwestern Virginia resulted directly from railroad expansion and the development of industry-specific equipment. Refrigerated cars, developed in the 1870s, meant that fresh meat and dairy products could be shipped longer distances and livestock cars meant live animals could be congregated in massive stockyards in cities such as Norfolk, Richmond, and Baltimore.[4] Live cattle, fresh beef, salted beef, butter, cheese, condensed milk, hides, leather, tallow, and neat's foot oil (derived from the feet and shinbones of cattle and used for dressing leather) from deep within the state's interior could now be marketed internationally. No longer could farmers in Elizabeth City County corner the fresh beef market as they had in the past by supplying crews from ocean-going vessels.

Although the large railroads in Virginia focused heavily on mining and timbering, the companies realized the opportunities presented by the fertile farmland that their lines traversed. Railroad trade magazines pushed the idea of locating potentially profitable agricultural operations along rail lines. "Stock raising in Virginia is more than an ordinary pursuit, and settlers locating in this state are realizing her advantages in this respect and are profiting thereby," noted one such journal in 1913.[5]

Railroads developed forty-foot long, slatted stock cars, very similar in external appearance to coke cars but with adaptations for transporting livestock. Except for technological additions such as air brakes, and replacement of some wooden parts with metal, the appearance of the stock cars changed little between the 1890s and the 1950s.[6] There was a short-lived movement to create so-called palace stock cars with an internal feeding and watering system that allowed for non-stop fast freight service. The railroads disliked palace cars for the simple reason that troughs and hayracks took up valuable interior space that prevented the filling of cars with different freight once the animals had been unloaded. Hauling empty cars on a return trip reduced a company's profit margin. In the 1890s, groups urging the adoption of humane practices accused companies of not properly servicing the palace cars. Eventually the U.S. government settled disputes between these groups, the private stock car companies, and the railroads. The resulting compromise led to regulations concerning livestock densities within stock cars and requirements for siderailing animals for feed and watering.[7]

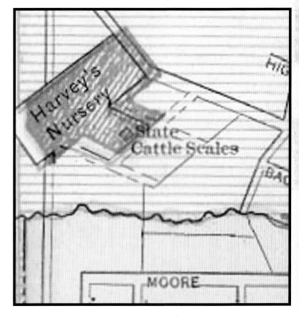

The livestock business provided an economic boon to the state capital, where road and rail brought cattle to the city and ships took them away, across the ocean. The official state cattle scales can be seen on this 1890s map of Richmond.

A National System

By the early twentieth century, three lines traversed the entire Old Dominion and the railroad was fast becoming a principal means by which farmers got their products to market. For cattlemen, the advantages of the new system were obvious. The time necessary to get animals to market was dramatically reduced, while animals arrived at their final destination in better health since they were not being driven on foot.

Isaac Acker of Rockingham County quickly incorporated the railroad into his agricultural pursuits. That cattle were an important part of the Ackers' mixed farming operation near Broadway is reflected in the diary that he kept from

1880 to 1896. During the last two decades of the nineteenth century, he produced a small quantity of butter for sale both locally and through the railroad, engaged the local tanner to make leather from his cattle hides, regularly drove animals away from Broadway for summer grazing, bought and sold cattle locally, and used the railroad to market cattle in cities such as Baltimore and Philadelphia. Acker's brother, John, apparently operated a cattle scales and was a livestock dealer who utilized the railroad to market animals in cities.

In late February of 1881, Acker recorded: "took my cattle to the depot. They averaged 1141 lbs." In late February of 1883 he recorded that he and his son took their cattle to Linville Station. In December of the same year he made at least two trips to local stations, once to sell a heifer and once to see another man's cattle weighed on the scales. On January 15, 1885, he noted "took 4 cattle to Linville for John Acker to ship to Philadelphia. John Kline helped me drive them up." Nine days later he wrote: "took my cattle to Cowan's Station for John Acker to ship to Baltimore. He shipped 2 loads from Cowan's and one load from Linville."[8]

John Acker's cattle scales appear to have been used for more than just recording livestock weights in preparation for railroad shipping. Isaac Acker regularly notes instances where animals were taken to the scales for weighing before sending them to summer pasture or trading them locally. In October of 1895 Acker recorded in his diary the routine of going to West Virginia to get the cattle that had grazed there during the summer. Two days later, before daybreak, Acker weighed his cattle while they were still in the mountains and then started them home. In late December he weighed them again and sold them. He concluded that for the year he ultimately took a loss: "Delivered my cattle at Brother John Acker's scales to John Hoover. Weighed in the mountains, 1293. Weighed at home, 1215. Weighed today, 1314. Got 3 ½ cents gross, one dollar per head off. Paid in the mountains, 4 cents gross. Loss per head $6.70 beside the corn I fed."[9]

Although the scales might have had a multiplicity of uses, their construction in close proximity to the railroad was for the convenience of shipping livestock by rail. Acker kept his diary through 1896. During that time, the railroad was a vital economic link between him, his brother, and the cattle industry. Perhaps his November 12, 1889, diary entry sums up that relationship as well as any: "rode over to Cowan's Depot this morning. Helped John Acker load a car load of hogs and cattle."[10]

The efficiency of the railroad for moving cattle long distances contributed to the rise of the fat cattle export business in southwest Virginia. One railroad trade magazine published the following testimonial about raising beef cattle for the export market: "it need hardly be added that a country possessed of the fine grazing lands found in Virginia has also a source of great length in cattle raising. This industry of last years has assumed immense proportions, and thousands of head of cattle are now shipped abroad from this state."[11]

Cattle were also shipped into the state. In the early twentieth century, farmers in Rappahannock County, on the east side of the Blue Ridge Mountains, purchased two-year-old stock cattle that had arrived by train from as far west as Texas, but also from North Carolina, southwest Virginia, and even Highland County. Dealers who knew the quality of cattle desired by the Rappahannock stockmen hand-selected the animals and shipped them to Culpeper by rail. Buyers would arrive at the railhead with drovers to help them select animals for purchase, and drive them home. Locals knew from experience that the wild cattle from Texas were best worked by drovers on horseback rather than on foot.[12]

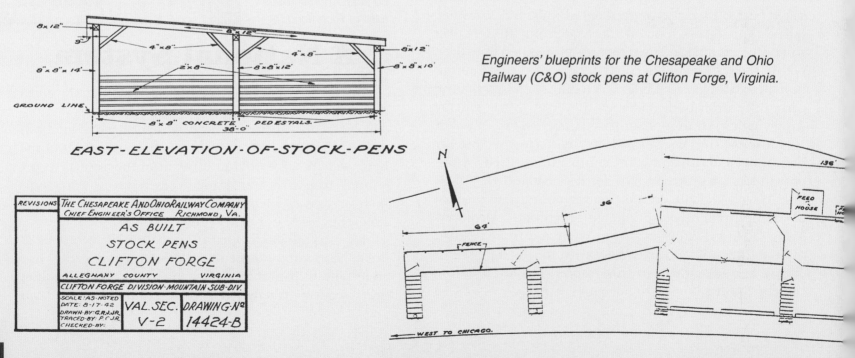

Engineers' blueprints for the Chesapeake and Ohio Railway (C&O) stock pens at Clifton Forge, Virginia.

Scales, Chutes, and Cattle Cars

The days of drovers driving animals hundreds of miles to urban markets were gone. Instead, animals were driven relatively short distances to railroad depots where cattle scales and stockyards quickly sprang up to facilitate the new marketing strategies that accompanied the advent of railroads. Livestock facilities were necessary not only because local farmers and regional dealers were bringing their animals to regional centers for shipping, but because the United States Department of Agriculture required that animals traveling for longer than twenty-eight hours be rested, watered, and fed, although shippers could sign a release giving the railroads up to thirty-six hours. Violators were fined.[13]

Thus many depots were equipped with livestock yards where the animals (twenty-two to twenty-seven cattle in a regular car and eight to ten in the special cars) were unloaded, rested, and watered. As a matter of convenience, stock cars were located either directly behind the locomotive or directly in front of the caboose so they could easily be cut from the train. More often than not, according to railroad folklore, the stock cars were located to the rear of the train because of their offensive odor.[14]

Railroad stock pens and chutes were remarkably similar throughout the country, varying more in size than in detail of construction. Stock chutes, both mobile and fixed, were nearly universal in rural farming regions. In 1948, ninety-three C&O stations from Newport News to Cincinnati had facilities where trains could load, unload, feed, and water livestock. Of the nine largest, two were in Virginia, three in West Virginia, two in Kentucky, one in Indiana, and one in Ohio. The cattle yard at Staunton, which was part of the Staunton Livestock Market facility, was the second largest on the entire line with two regular and two double loading chutes, seventy-five lots,

seventy-five sheds, and available water. Charlottesville was Virginia's second largest facility with six chutes, twelve lots, six sheds, and watering capabilities.[15]

Oversight of such stockyards was handled by a "yarder" who reported directly to the Superintendent of Stockyards. The yarder made sure that animals were unloaded, under the direction of herdsmen armed with canvas snappers (like whips), into their resting pens where they were given water, hay, and grain. Young calves were fed a warm milk formula from buckets with special nipples. With the cattle penned, the stock crew swept and flushed out the cars. In the morning the animals were reloaded into the cars and a crew arrived to clean out the stockyards in preparation for the next evening's animals.[16]

Livestock was never a primary concern of any of the Virginia railroads. The C&O's peak year for transporting livestock was 1890 and even then live animals represented only one percent of the company's total freight, which consisted mostly of mineral resources such as coal. That percentage declined steadily until 1948, the last year the statistic was calculated, when livestock represented only .06 percent of the company's tonnage. Despite the steady decline in percentage of livestock business on the C&O, the actual tonnage of livestock doubled between World War I and 1948.[17]

Most of the livestock shipped on the C&O originated from farms along the company's lines. That made good business sense to railroad managers who could capitalize on a ready-made market with only a minimal financial investment. And, while the financial returns were

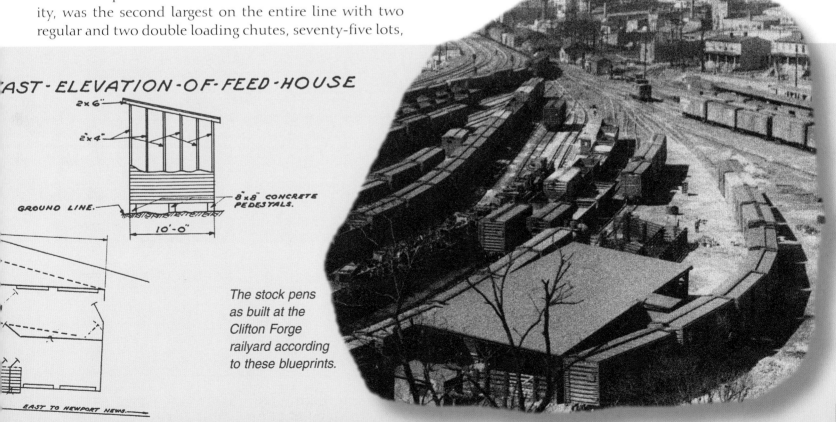

The stock pens as built at the Clifton Forge railyard according to these blueprints.

EAST · ELEVATION · OF · FEED · HOUSE

2 x 6"

2"x 4"

GROUND LINE.

8"x 8" CONCRETE PEDESTALS.

10'-0"

EAST TO NEWPORT NEWS.

miniscule to the railroad moguls, the market connections were vital to the remote, rural communities along the lines. In 1919, the C&O Company published an "Official Industrial and Shippers Directory." Of the nearly 200 livestock dealers and shippers on the line that stretched to Indiana, thirty-eight were Virginians. By 1925, the number of dealers had dropped to 159, but the number of Virginians involved in the livestock business along the C&O had risen to fifty-four. In that year the railroad also published a list of related businesses dealing in hides, tallow, or meat packing, and nine additional Virginia businesses were listed.[18] Dairy products and fresh meats were also marketed through the railroad after the development of the refrigerated car. In 1931, the C&O carried over 32,000 tons of live cattle and calves, over 64,000 tons of fresh meat, almost 95,000 tons of other packing house products, nearly 11,000 tons of butter and cheese, and almost 20,000 tons of hides and leather. All of those numbers, with the exception of the fresh meats and butter and cheese, represented a decrease in tonnage from 1930.[19]

A photo taken in Orange County shows the effects of the 1929-1930 drought on a Jersey cow.

Possibly the Norfolk and Western Railway paid even more attention to the agricultural connections made possible through its line than did the C&O. In 1916 the company published a "List of Leading Farmers, Stock Raisers and Stock Dealers Along the Norfolk and Western Railway, Alphabetically Arranged by Stations." A total of 1,853 stock dealers, farmers, and dairymen used the 147 stations along the line, which ran from the Tennessee border through the Valley of Virginia and east through Petersburg to Norfolk.[20]

Farmers used railroads for purposes other than taking animals to market. In the devastating drought of 1929, cattle were shipped into southwest Virginia where the grazing was still good. Members of the Purcell family in Russell County

1,853 stock dealers, farmers, and dairymen used the 147 stations along the Norfolk & Western line, which ran from the Tennessee border through the Valley of Virginia and east through Petersburg to Norfolk.[2]

remembered cattle coming to the area by rail from Texas and other drought stricken areas during the Dust Bowl era of the late 1920s and 1930s.[21] To Virginia's farmers, the 1929-1930 drought had far greater impact than anything that happened on Wall Street during that year. In Fairfax County, where wells and springs went dry and crops for animal feed withered in the fields, the railroad brought drought relief in the form of 727 railroad cars of animal feed.[22]

O. Winston Link, an imaginative and innovative Virginia photographer who captured images of life along the N&W railroad lines in the 1950s and 1960s, took this photo at night using special equipment he designed. "Cow 13, Norvel Ryan and his Son Bringing in the Cows, Train No. 3 in the background," was taken in 1955 in Shawsville.

Progress and Politics

The railroad brought political headache as well as economic progress to Virginia. Railroad speculation drove up land prices and contributed to a nationwide financial crisis in 1873. The opinion that politicians and capitalists were out "to get" the farmer was as strong in Virginia as it was anywhere in the nation. Realizing strength in numbers, many Virginia farmers joined granges – local politically active chapters of the Patrons of Husbandry. By 1876 there were more grange members in Virginia – 18,000 – than in any other south Atlantic state. Grangers challenged the railroad monopolies and, in Virginia, the fertilizer companies. Again harkening to the idea of strength in numbers, farmers in the Old Dominion began forming cooperatives to sell fertilizer and, in northern Virginia they formed at least four creamery cooperatives.[23]

Although the grange movement was short-lived in the state, the ideas remained to be rolled over into other organizations. In 1885 the newly-formed Farmers' Assembly lobbied for political reforms that included the creation of a railroad commission with real authority to regulate. Instrumental in the assembly's creation was Virginia aristocrat Colonel Robert Beverley, a plantation owner on the Rappahannock River. Almost simultaneously, Colonel Gabriel Barbee and J.J. Silvey, agricultural reformers in Bridgewater, Virginia, formed the first Virginia chapter of the National Farmers' Alliance in Rockingham County in 1887. Soon nearly 1,400 chapters sprang up across the state. By December 1889 the assembly and the alliance had joined forces as the Farmers' Alliance. The alliance formed supply stores, labor exchanges, and cooperatives, forced fertilizer prices down by twenty-five percent, and launched a series of agriculture lectures.[24]

Beverley continued his agricultural lobbying for many years. In the 1920s, he had seats on committees dealing with fertilizer, transportation, and rates in the Essex County Farmers Education and Cooperative Union. Charged with studying legislation adversely affecting farmers, Fertilizer Committee Chairman Beverley issued the following report:

1st Whereas, the transportation situation has become intolerable, the huge losses that agriculture has suffered from extortionate freight rates and no appreciable reduction has been made to correspond with the tremendous slump in farm products the railroad rates being practically at or near war prices we appeal to our members in Congress to urge a substantial reduction in freight rates as recommended by the recent Congressional Investigation Committee in their Report on Transportation in Congress. We believe temporary relief may be secured through the repeal or the substantial amendment of Cumming Esch Act the restoration of the Rate making and regulatory power to the State Railway Commission.

2nd We reiterate again that the hauling by the railroads of fertilizer to the farms is to a great extent compensated for by the subsequent hauling of the increased production by the railroads from the farms to the markets, we therefore, urge that all freights on fertilizers be reduced to the rates which existed prior to the war.

3rd Resolved that a copy of these Resolutions be sent by the Secretary to each of our Senators and Representatives in Congress and we appeal to every member of the Union to write a personal letter to his Congressman urging a reduction in transportation rates.[25]

Ultimately, the railroad gave and the railroad took away. In 1890 the Virginia Commissioner of Agriculture complained that "the production of beef has become unprofitable; a sufficiency for local consumption is still produced, but competition with the Chicago stock-yards, with low transportation on inferior beef, has crippled this great industry of Valley and Southwest, and checked the growth of the fine herds of short horns in those sections.[26] Many stockmen, who were outmaneuvered by the railroad and the giant Midwest meat packing companies in the beef market, turned to dairying, especially if they had a rail connection to an urban area that required large and fresh supplies of dairy products.

Although railroads and agriculturalists were often at odds, each needed the other to survive. At times real cooperation occurred. A case in point was the railroad classroom designed to take the new agricultural ideas being developed at the Agricultural Experiment Station in Blacksburg to the masses of poorly educated farmers. At the time, few farmers had more than an eighth-grade education, and the state as a whole had a twenty-three percent illiteracy rate. The railroad classroom rolled out in 1908 with Professor Walter Quick giving lectures on dairy husbandry. Crowds turned out to hear the lectures; in some places five and six hundred attended. In twelve days in March and April of 1911, the train made thirty-two stops and 8,745 persons heard the lecture.[27]

The Iron Horse Fades

In the late 1930s and early 1940s, railroad management's control of the railroad loosened considerably. Squabbles over high freight charges, the rise of regional livestock markets and auction houses, and improvements in roads and automobiles all contributed to the change. On the whole the shift from railroad to truck was gradual, but for one farmer and livestock dealer from Stuarts Draft, in the Shenandoah Valley, the love affair with the railroad ended almost overnight. In a 2002 interview, Earl Kindig remembered the exact incident that triggered his father's change of heart back in the 1930s. His father, John Kindig, had a Model A 1932 Ford truck with mule wheels (metal rims) and a twelve-foot cattle rack. That contraption allowed him to dabble in the contract cattle business in order to supplement his regular farm income. He would put cattle out onto farms for farmers to fatten on silage and grain for 90 to 120 days. Then he would take his truck around and buy back the cattle at 2.5 cents more per pound than the amount for which he had sold them. In addition, he bought fat cattle from other farmers even when he had not personally placed the animals. Those cattle were then shipped by railroad to Baltimore where they were sold. Recalled Earl Kindig:

Dad was really fond of the railroads. He said railroads were what made this country as strong as it is. We had three places in the eastern part of Augusta County that he loaded cattle: Stuarts Draft, Lyndhurst, and Weyers Cave. One of the things my dad loved to do when he wasn't so busy was to go to Waynesboro on Sunday night after he had sent cattle to Baltimore. He would board the passenger train there at 6 o'clock Monday morning and he would be at the stock yard in time to see his animals sold. Even though trailer trucks were available and that freight was a little cheaper, he still liked to patronize the railroad.

Kindig changed his practices, however, when one of his cattle shipments went awry. Kindig recalled that story:

One time he shipped two loads of cattle from Stuarts Draft on Friday and went to Baltimore. When he entered the hotel, one of the brokers asked him, 'Mr. John are you planning on buying some feeders today?' He said, 'no, I don't think so. I just came up to see my cattle sold.' And he said, 'you don't have any cattle here.' Well much to my dad's disappointment the cattle were unhooked somewhere during the transfer from one rail company to another and they failed to get picked up and the rule was if the cattle didn't reach their destination in forty hours then they had to be unloaded and fed and rested and watered so they were

A contemporary building mural in Tazewell depicts cattle from an earlier time being driven through the town beside the railroad tracks.

YESTERDAY

TODAY

VIRGINIA BEEF CATTLE NO LONGER WALK
TO MARKET--THEY ARE TRANSPORTED

TODAY BEEF IS BETTER

unloaded in Maryland and they didn't make it for the Monday sale. My dad was really disappointed from the service he got from the railroad that time. That was the last time we ever loaded any cattle on the railroad. They always went on trucks from there on.[28]

The railroad witnessed one final peak before fading from sight as the nation's main livestock mover. Just prior to World War II, an Indiana farmer and Church of the Brethren member named Dan West founded an organization called Heifers for Relief. The idea was to provide poor people of foreign countries with bred livestock – cattle and horses – to help families in need. As those animals produced offspring the recipients of the animals were, in turn, supposed to give animals to others in need. West's idea crystallized and his organization enjoyed one small success during the war with a shipment of seventeen heifers to Puerto Rico in June of 1944.

Following the war, the United Nations Relief and Rehabilitation Administration connected with the Heifer Project in an effort to revitalize Europe's agricultural economy. Virginia and the railroad played an important role in that effort as cattle and horses were shipped by railroad to Newport News, Baltimore, and other port cities. The capacity of the cars and the livestock holding pens along the C&O were severely strained by the large numbers of animals shipped to Poland, Greece, Italy, Czechoslovakia, Yugoslavia, and parts of the Soviet Union under the auspices of the United Nations Relief effort. Tens of thousands of animals were gathered at the Newport News terminus to be shipped overseas.[29] In this cooperative effort between the UN and the Heifer Project, the former agreed to supply the ships and crews, while the latter supplied the animals and the men to care for the animals during their voyage. The sea cowboys, as the young men came to be called, were

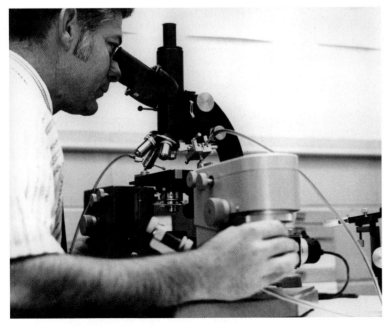

The germ theory – the idea that a microscopic world of creatures affects human and animal health – turned biological thinking on its head.

part of the Church of the Brethren Volunteer Service. Maynard Garber of Staunton served as a sea cowboy on voyages to Greece and South Africa. Although his experience was with horses (thirty-two sea cowboys, one veterinarian, and 750 horses in the hold of the ship), he witnessed first-hand the good that heifers were doing. After unloading their horses in Greece, they happened upon some Greek children tending cattle they had received from the Heifer Project. The cattle still had the Brethren Volunteer Service ear tags. "People in Europe practically worshipped livestock after the war. Cattle provided milk and horses provided labor," Garber remembered of his experience.[30]

Microscopic Changes

The railroad represented just one element of great change in the new age of science and technology that reworked every facet of American society in the late nineteenth century. Perhaps more far-reaching in its importance to animal husbandry was medical, or biotechnology as it later came to be called, advances. The germ theory – the idea that a microscopic world of creatures affects human and animal health – turned biological thinking on its head. The theory challenged the very foundation of traditional medicine, which operated on the notion of the spontaneous generation of disease. Much of the development of the germ theory took place in Europe through the research of Louis Pasteur and German botanist Anton deBary. Whether they were looking at diseases in plants, humans, or livestock, their theories held true time and again. In 1882 Robert Koch isolated the organism that causes tuberculosis and in 1883 he did the same for cholera. Once the microscopic puzzle was unlocked, work moved rapidly into the vaccination and testing stages. In just a few years vaccines for fowl cholera, anthrax, and rabies had been developed; diagnostic tests for tuberculosis and glanders had been created; water could be filtered to prevent cholera; and milk was pasteurized.

Virginia, as much as any state or region in the nation, needed to take the war against disease to a new level. The devastation of the Civil War was obvious to the naked eye, but the war also left a lingering mark at the microscopic level. The mass of humanity and livestock that crossed and recrossed the state as the tide of war surged and ebbed brought human and livestock disease, the likes of which had never before been seen. Farm boys from all parts of the nation unleashed localized germs and diseases to which they probably had developed resistance, but troops and civilians from elsewhere were susceptible. When introduced to populations with no immunity, the effects were catastrophic. Livestock suffered the same fate. Cattle, horse, and hog diseases rarely seen in the state became epidemic by the war's end. Nationwide systems of transportation, particularly the railroad, meant that isolated disease outbreaks could quickly become rampant when diseased animals were transported from one place to another in a matter of hours. Because of this, physicians, veterinarians, and farmers were probably as open to accepting biotechnology as they ever could have been. Nonetheless, the transition was difficult for many. Tick fever makes a good example. This disease, caused by a microorganism that attacks and destroys an animal's red blood corpuscles, plagued the South for years. Although this disease had been rare in Virginia before the war, it reached epidemic proportions in the Commonwealth after 1865. The fever, known by many names, including Spanish fever, Carolina distemper, bloody murrain, or Texas fever, was little understood. For the average farmer who had never peered into a microscope it was hard to accept that microscopic protozoa inside a tick caused their cattle to sicken and die. In fact, it was hard for the scientific community as well. In the decade after the Civil War one Virginia doctor still prescribed a homemade concoction of golden rod and sheep mint tea mixed with one tablespoon of salt petre per gallon for murrain.[31]

Winning a War on Ticks

Success against tick fever proved difficult because of the complicating factor of the disease-carrying organism (*Babesia bigemina*) being hosted by a parasite and transmitted through that tick (*Boophilus*) to the bovine. The true warrior in the fight against tick fever was Dr. Cooper Curtice, a disciplined researcher from New York who not only embraced the new "germ theory," but agreed to be part of the research team at the U.S. Bureau of Animal Industry (BAI), in Washington, D.C. Established in 1884 with the goal of eradicating pleuropneumonia, the agency quickly expanded its fight to encompass all animal disease. Curtice's research helped expand the front on a number of livestock diseases, but he became obsessed with unlocking the mysteries of cattle fever. Although the microscopic organism causing cattle fever was identified in 1889, researchers were still baffled as to how that organism infected animals. Was it air-borne? Did it pass from one animal to another? When Curtice declared his belief that the tick was the culprit, he found very few who supported his theory. He took the germ theory to the next level with the idea that a host (in this case the tick) would take a disease from an infected animal and carry it to an uninfected animal. Even Robert Koch initially rejected what came to be called "the vector theory" and fellow scientists joked about Curtice's obsession with raising ticks.[32] Proving his theory meant unlocking the life cycle of the tick itself. Eventually he would leave the BAI to carry on the fight privately or in cooperation with other agencies.

One group of researchers who listened to Curtice and believed in his theories – the scientists at the Agricultural Experiment Station in Blacksburg – conducted their own experiments to prove that the disease was passed by ticks and not from animal to animal. They concluded that disease could be prevented by keeping the ticks away. As a result, in 1896 Virginia Governor Charles O'Ferrall drew a quarantine line through the state:

> All counties in Virginia south of a line beginning on the boundary between Virginia and North Carolina, at a point coinciding with the summit of the Blue Ridge Mountains, thence following the

In the years just after the Civil War, and before there was a broad understanding of the microscopic world of germs, farmers and livestock breeders had to combat disease with medicinal aids such as those advertised in this Rockingham County newspaper.

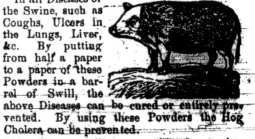

summit...northeasterly to the southern boundary of Bedford county; thence following the southern and eastern boundaries of Bedford county to the James river; thence following the James river to the southeastern corner of Charles City county; thence northerly and easterly along the eastern and northern boundaries to James City, Gloucester, Mathews and Accomac counties to the Atlantic ocean. . . .

O'Ferrall's proclamation added seasonal restrictions in accordance with the life cycle of the tick.

From the 15th day of February to the 15th day of November of each year no cattle are to be transported from said area or below said State quarantine line above described to any portion of the State above said line, except by rail or boat, and then only for immediate slaughter. . . .

As a further precaution, animals arriving for slaughter or those unloaded for rest and watering, were to be quarantined in separate pens.[33]

Quarantining helped contain tick fever, but it did little to eradicate it. That would fall back on Curtice's shoulders. In 1906, the man who had declared war on ticks returned to the BAI where he was put in charge of tick eradication. When an area was cleared of ticks, it could be released from quarantine. He helped develop an arsenic bath into which cattle could be dipped. The bath killed the ticks, thus eliminating the disease. Much of his experimental tick dipping

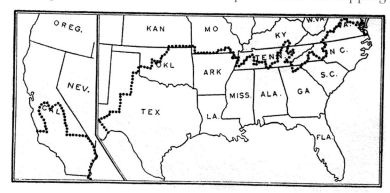

This map shows areas quarantined in 1906 due to tick fever. The dotted line shows the northern boundary of the infected area at the beginning of the tick eradication program.

took place in Virginia and North Carolina. The program was so successful that the United States Department of Agriculture began issuing pamphlets entitled: "Kill That Seed Tick in March," and "Dip That Tick Now." Within one year of Curtice's appointment, 40,000 acres in Virginia and North Carolina had been released from quarantine.[34]

Although success against tick fever was listed among the early biotechnical successes in agriculture, it was not the first. The catalyst for the establishment of the BAI was the farming losses due to bovine pleuropneumonia. The eradication of that disease from the United States in 1892 marked the first contagious animal or human disease ever successfully eradicated.[35]

Extension agents taught new medical and sanitary practices to farmers. Here an agent demonstrates a method to reduce mastitis in cows.

To Be TB Free

The next disease to be targeted by both the BAI and Virginia's experiment station was tuberculosis. Here there would not be a total victory, only a series of advances complicated by a long-standing disagreement among scientists and farmers about whether bovine tuberculosis could be passed to humans and vice versa. Work on TB began in earnest in 1882 when Robert Koch identified the specific germ, *Mycobacterium tuberculosis*. Ten years later the Koch Test was being used to identify infected animals. The problem – and it was an immense one considering that in turn-of-the-century Virginia tuberculosis killed one in every 500 people – was the various forms of the disease could cross from one species to another and the pathogen could survive for years in damp, dark corners of barns and barnyards. With no effective drug treatments or vaccines, the war had to be waged on other fronts: by sanitizing barns and outbuildings, pasteurizing milk, and testing and destroying infected cattle. Virginia lawmakers reacted to TB in much the same way as they had to tick fever, by passing legislation meant to control the spread of the disease. In 1909, all cattle coming into the state were required to be tuberculin tested. However, cattle traded internally were unregulated. To combat that problem, by World War I, most of Virginia's local governments had passed laws requiring pasteurization of milk sold to cities and/or certification that milk had originated from TB-free herds. It was a slow, but successful battle. From 1909 to 1911, over fifteen percent of Virginia milk supplied to Washington, D.C. showed a TB infection. Between 1917 and 1922, that number plummeted to under three percent.[36]

Banishing Blackleg

More complete success came early in the battle against blackleg, a soil-borne organism. Blackleg kills the organs and muscles of infected cattle, causing gases to build up in the body tissue, and leading to gangrene and death within twelve hours. Dead animals were usually found on their sides, bloated, with upper legs rigidly extended. In Virginia, blackleg had been persistent among cattle since the Civil War. French veterinarians developed the first blackleg vaccine in 1883, but it was not always effective or safe. The BAI developed a better vaccine in 1895, using ground-up tissue from infected carcasses. Two years later the USDA distributed the vaccine free of charge to cattlemen while simultaneously reinforcing the need to vaccinate with a flood of promotional literature and instructions on how to use the four-dollar vaccination kit. Farmers quickly embraced the medicine and by 1901 blackleg was no longer a worry in Virginia as long as vaccination of animals occurred regularly.[37] Of the thirty or so counties that had regularly received distributions of the vaccine from 1897 until the spring of 1901, the average losses from blackleg dropped from 11.07 percent to 0.89 percent. In Montgomery County where more than one animal in four had died from the disease, losses had dropped to zero.[38]

By 1899, 18,815 doses of vaccine had been distributed to cattlemen in thirty-five counties of Virginia.[39] The degree to which cattlemen believed in the new vaccine was evident in the flood of letters received by U.S. Congressman William F. Rhea in 1900. Rhea's southwest Virginia constituents learned that the USDA planned to discontinue the free distribution of blackleg vaccine so that pharmaceutical companies could sell it. Rhea received more than a dozen letters, many with multiple signatures, begging him to continue the government distribution. The note from A.C. Beattie of Chilhowie was typical.

> I see that Pasteur Vaccine Co. & Parke, Davis & Co. have sent to all Senators & Members of congress urgent letters for the Department of agriculture to stop making Black Leg Vaccine. I speak for quite a Number of farmers in this section of state. Black leg has prevailed from 5 to 12 per cent among our cattle for 10 years or more & The goverment vaccine has been used extensively here for the Past two years with marked

results. I know of nearly a 1000 head that have been treeted with vaccine & up to this time I have only heard of but one case that died of Black Leg. The vaccine has save me 10 or 12 this year.

> If congress would put the entire mfg. of Vaccine in private hand, it would cause the firms to charge from 1200 to 2000 per cent on their good, when the acual cost of vaccine per dose is less that ¼ of a cent per dose.

> We as farmer want goverment vaccine; we are not a fraid to use it & we know of its good effects.

> If congress permits individuals entirely to mfg vaccine the farmer will be swindled out of a great deal of money. The US Department has proved of great value to the farmer I urge our senators of the 9 congressional districtic to exert their influence in maintaining the present method of the free distribution of Black Leg vaccine & other products which are of value to the stock owner

> I could get hundreds of signers to the last clause[40]

Despite the protests and fears of deregulation, sales of the vaccine were privatized. Regular vaccination throughout the century has kept the disease in check.

Contents of the first blackleg kits included powder or pellets to be reconstituted into vaccine as well as the instruments needed to mix and administer the treatment.

Bang's Disease Battle

Advances were not so quickly achieved against other bovine diseases. Infectious abortion, also called Bang's Disease and brucellosis, had plagued stockman around the world. The disease causes spontaneous abortion in the last trimester of an animal's pregnancy, with a period of infertility and poor milk production afterward. Brucellosis is found in cattle, hogs, goats, bison, and elk, and poses serious risks to human health as undulant fever.

As late as 1935, incidence of the disease in American cattle stood at 11.5 percent.[41] The disease had been recognized for years, and drew quite a bit of attention at the Virginia Agricultural Experiment Station. In 1892, the station reported that the microorganism causing the disease remained undiscovered, but

> In view of the fact that a large portion of Virginia is devoted to stock-raising and dairying, and that so little is known of this form of abortion, the Station has deemed it advisable to point out a few of the precautions to be observed when the trouble once makes its appearance in a herd of pregnant cows.[42]

This Bang's Free seal certified that the dairy herd of former Virginia Governor Westmoreland Davis was free of brucellosis.

The mysterious organism, *Bacterium abortum*, was actually discovered by Dr. Bang of Denmark in 1896. By 1900 the pathological division of the BAI launched an intensive study of the disease. By the 1910s, better testing methods had been developed and the disease and its method of spread were thoroughly understood.[43]

It was not until the late 1930s and early 1940s, however, that real success against Bang's was achieved. Today a vaccination given to calves before the age of ten months has virtually eliminated the disease in the United States although it is still a serious health problem in many other countries. Use of the vaccine reduced the incidence of Bang's in American herds to 0.5 percent by 1970.[44] The state of Virginia has been Bang's free for a number of years.

Science and Farming

Despite market problems and ongoing struggles against disease, the stockman and dairyman of Virginia in 1925 operated in a world that would have been unrecognizable to the farmer fifty years earlier. Modern transportation such as the railroad and steam ship and new refrigeration methods had literally made the entire globe a potential marketplace. Scientifically conducted experiments with food, nutrition, and crop production and advances against disease made possible agricultural yields never dreamed of a few decades before. Walter Robinson, an Extension Agent

in Marion, mused about the changes from the good old days. His father, Alex Robinson, was one of the last of the "old-style" veterinarians trained before a great deal of science was integrated into the vet's daily diagnosis and treatment methods. He remembered that his father would treat dairy cattle suffering from milk fever (a calcium deficiency created by calving) by pumping up the udder using a bicycle pump. Amazingly, the treatment worked because it built osmotic pressure and allowed the animal to retain calcium, but today a simple shot given in the vein is faster and more effective. Vets of that era were often faced with an animal that was down for unexplained reasons. In such instances, they often resorted to the "hollow tail" prescription. Robinson offered an explanation of that crude treatment: "the hollow tail cure involved splitting the animal's tail and pouring in salt and pepper and sewing it back up. Wouldn't you get up too?"[45]

The new wave of veterinarians, however, had a modern set of tools to help with diagnosis and prevention. They used the microscope and a syringe of vaccine instead of homemade folk remedies. And, just as important, scientific methods of animal husbandry were being adopted by farmers who read and saved the bulletins and pamphlets distributed by the USDA and the Virginia Department of Agriculture. Those same country folk also attended the informational lectures and their children began hearing the same message in agriculture classes and through 4-H. The transformation was remarkable. The age of scientific farming had arrived. ❦

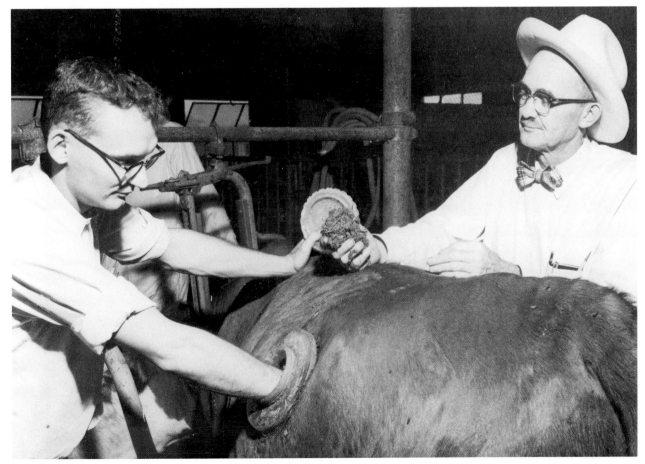

Dr. Charlie Kincaid, right, of the VPI Animal Science Department, and Dr. Kendall King, examine a fistulated cow to help reveal information regarding the multiphase digestive systems of cattle. Data from research of this nature aids cattle producers in selecting feed rations providing the most nutritive benefit to cattle.

Grandma Moses: "Shenandoah Valley: South Branch." Copyright © 1968 (renewed 1996) Grandma Moses Properties Co., New York

Folk Artist Brought Yankee Dairying to the Valley

In November of 1887, the railroad brought Anna Mary Robertson Moses, later known to the world as folk artist Grandma Moses, and her husband, Thomas, to Augusta County, Virginia. In December of 1905, the railroad took them back to their New York home. During the eighteen years the Moses family lived in Augusta County, they relied upon their Yankee ingenuity, entrepreneurial talents, and a few milk cows to provide an important supplement to the farm income needed to support a growing family. [1]

Anna and Thomas Moses were farm laborers and newlyweds when they set off by train from New York to work on a North Carolina horse farm. Weary from travel by the time they reached Staunton, they disembarked for a weekend rest. The proprietors of the boarding house where they stayed convinced them to abandon their trip south and settle in Augusta County. Within days they had rented a farm near the village of Swoope. Anna bought a cow for twenty-five dollars and her husband purchased another one for twenty-seven dollars. By May, Mrs. Moses was getting enough milk to churn butter and send it with her husband to the store as barter for groceries. Years later, Grandma Moses remembered her first venture into the butter business, at a time when most butter was bringing eight cents a pound.

> It was a hot morning, and I was afraid the butter would get warm, so I wrapped it in my best linen napkins — had put it up in 3-pound rolls — then into new tin milk pans, wrapping all with burdock leaves to keep it cool. Thomas took it in to a Mr. Spitlar and asked if he could trade it out, and Mr. Spitlar took his jack knife out of his pocket and tasted the butter and said, yes, he was getting plenty of butter but would allow me twelve cents in trade. . . . Mr. Spitlar took the butter home with him, as he said he wanted his people to see some Yankee butter. In a few days after that he sent us word to bring all the butter that we had to spare, and he would give us 15 cents a pound for it. Then when we sent in the next lot he said, "I'll give you 20 cents a pound for all of your butter this summer." So that was settled and by October 20th, I had sold butter enough to pay for our two cows. [2]

By the end of the first year, the fame of Mrs. Moses' Yankee butter had spread far and wide. Mr. Eakle, the brother-in-law of Mr. Spitlar, convinced Anna and Thomas to move to the other end of the county and operate a 600-acre dairy farm. Eakle promised fifty cents for every pound of butter they made. They moved to the new farm, called Belvidere, in November, driving their two original cows along the road to the new place. Dairy production increased dramatically at the new farm, which was outfitted with a dairy room with glass doors and running water. The couple sent to Vermont for a butter print and Thomas carved "Moses" in the wood so that every print had their trademark on it. Twenty prints filled a tray, four trays filled a crate, and Anna and Thomas tried to ship out two crates of butter per week, by rail, to White Sulphur Springs, West Virginia. They also tried to take butter to Staunton every week as well. Producing that much butter meant that Mrs. Moses was churning three or four times a day with her small churn. Soon they purchased a large barrel churn. [3]

Butter production ceased in early 1895 when the farm owner died and the Moses family had to leave Belvidere. Their new farm had no place for butter making but was much closer to the city of Staunton. So the couple decided to forego butter making and sell milk instead. Thomas and half-a-dozen men milked the cows by hand, strained the milk, bottled it, and sealed the bottles with paper. Twenty bottles filled a box. Boxes of milk and cream were loaded on a two-horse wagon that Thomas drove into town. There he delivered orders and peddled the rest of the milk and cream. Anna's role in the milk business was washing sixty to one hundred bottles every day. [4]

By the turn of the century, Anna and Thomas were increasingly homesick for their native New York and wanted to be near Thomas' parents whose health was declining. When a dairy farm became available at Eagle Bridge, New York, they decided to return home as quickly as possible. In December of 1905 they chartered a railroad car and headed north. In the car, in addition to their piano, beds, and plenty of farm produce, were chickens, the family dog, and a favorite cow. Thomas rode in the car to take care of the livestock and he smuggled in their two youngest children to ride with him without a proper ticket. The cow was tied in the corner with feed. A manure fork was nearby. In the center of the car was a kerosene stove, tied so that the jostling of the train would not tip it over. The family barely avoided disaster, however, when one jolt on the tracks sent the cow down to her knees and into the stove. The stove tipped but did not fall and, thankfully, the family arrived safely. [5]

It was not until many years later, on her seventieth birthday, that Grandma Moses picked up a brush, and without a minute's art instruction, began painting her memories of rural American life. At least thirty-eight of her primitive paintings, which took America by storm in the 1940s and 1950s, depict scenes from the nearly two decades spent in Virginia. Belvidere, where Grandma Moses had operated such a successful butter operation, appears in at least nine paintings. She also painted her family's chaotic departure from the Valley in 1905. Cattle were always an important part of her rural life and many of her paintings include them, either grazing in the fields, or, as in the "Moving Day" painting, pulling a loaded cart. In the 1950s, President Dwight Eisenhower requested that she paint his Gettysburg, Pennsylvania, farm. She complied, making sure that three Holsteins and three Angus cattle grazed in the pasture.

When Grandma Moses died in 1961 at the age of 101, she was one of the most popular folk artists in the United States. Her painted memories reminded people of a simpler time in rural America that had all but disappeared by mid-century. Many of these memories preserved by her brush were formed in the Shenandoah Valley where she and her husband, Thomas, started from scratch with two milk cows and some good old fashioned hard work. ~

Caring for Cattle

From the time the first cattle set foot on Virginia shore at Jamestown until after the Civil War, the business of breeding, raising, buying, and selling beef and dairy cattle and their products was a matter of little concern to the Virginia government. The individual planter or farmer was on his own to learn how to handle his animals and to train his children and laborers to do so. Word of mouth and conversation at court days, militia musters, and parish church gatherings were the primary means of sharing methods of animal husbandry. A few books on farming methods and animal husbandry manuals provided some information in colonial and post revolutionary Virginia. In the early nineteenth century, newspapers, almanacs, and farm journals offered additional information. By mid-century, local agricultural societies held meetings and fairs at which information was exchanged. But little or no help came from the government.

This does not mean that the government ignored cattle altogether. As previous chapters have demonstrated, the colonial House of Burgesses and later the House of Delegates of the Commonwealth passed laws regarding cattle. Most often, this legislation concerned roaming or stray cattle. In times of need, legislators enacted laws to preserve breeding stock and to provide meat for the army in wartime. But government authorities did not imagine that they had a role in assisting farmers to do a better job of breeding, raising, and marketing their animals. Nor did government officials take a role in helping farmers to raise better crops in order to produce larger, healthier cattle, or assist in the prevention and treatment of disease in cattle. Nor did the state government see that it had a role in public health issues that concerned beef and dairy products and the conditions in which they were produced and marketed. And certainly the political leaders of Virginia did not imagine that it was their responsibility to

attle stand at water's edge along the famous Seven Bends of the Shenandoah River.

Maurice and Blair Mitchell and their father and mother, Robert A. and Nanie Mitchell, pose with their ox cart in Montgomery County around 1890.

educate young men to become expert farmers and to provide a resource staff to assist them in their vocation.

In the half century after the end of the Civil War, the government of the Commonwealth embarked on an entirely different approach to Virginia cattlemen and dairymen. In that critical half century, the state government began to provide assistance to farmers to improve the breeding, raising, and marketing of their cattle. Further, the state government encouraged the treatment and prevention of cattle diseases, became concerned with public health in regard to the production and sale of meat and dairy products, and began to educate young farmers at the university level. In addition, the state government took on the responsibility to provide all farmers a statewide support system in the form of trained experts in each county. What caused this about-face regarding agricultural policy of the state government after the Civil War, and what were the means by which the Commonwealth pursued its newly recognized responsibilities for the well-being of beef and dairy cattle and the farmers who raised them?

A Chorus for Change

The end of the Civil War ushered in a period of rebuilding throughout Virginia. The destruction resulting from Virginia's role as the primary battlefield of the Civil War was vast. Sheridan's burning of the rich wheat and cattle farms of the Valley of Virginia is but one example of the devastation. Rebuilding efforts led to a change of attitudes and a rethinking of the role of government. Many political leaders, looking to the interests of farmers, came to believe that Virginia needed to be integrated more fully into the national economy and the transportation network of the rapidly urbanizing and industrializing United States. The growth of railroads and the changes that economic growth introduced to Virginia had an important impact on beef and dairy cattle. Urban growth in Richmond, Norfolk, Portsmouth, and Washington, D.C., also influenced Virginia agriculture, especially dairy farming and the production of milk for urban markets.

Yet it would be wrong to see all of the changes in attitudes and behaviors as products of reform in post Civil War Virginia. Well before the first shots were fired at Fort Sumter and Virginia responded to the federal call-up with a secession vote, various efforts had been made to involve the Virginia government in the improvement of Virginia agriculture. The 1850s had been a decade of growing interest in agricultural improvement in the Old Dominion. One of the many signs of this was the appearance of local agricultural improvement societies in county after county, and in the formation of the Virginia State Agricultural Society. The movement to improve agriculture appeared all across America at the time. The men who were members and leaders of these organizations tended to be among the best-educated and most progressive farmers in their counties. They read widely in current agricultural literature, subscribed to one or more farming journals published in Virginia or other states, and often encouraged agricultural fairs and participated in them as a means of sharing knowledge and exhibiting improved produce and livestock.

From this community of forward-looking planters and farmers came voices calling for state involvement in the improvement of agriculture. One idea that enjoyed wide appeal was that of establishing professorships in agricultural chemistry at state colleges. Governor John Floyd, a descendant of the Preston family of Smithfield plantation, now a part of the campus of Virginia Tech, was a spokesman for this plan around 1850. Floyd urged the state's two public colleges, Virginia Military Institute and the University of Virginia, to create such professorships. The Virginia State Agricultural Society also pushed for this, calling in 1854 for an experimental farm at a state agricultural college. This was one of the earliest efforts to make agricultural research and teaching at the college level a responsibility of the Virginia state government.[1]

Other voices echoed this cry. Floyd's successor, Governor Henry A. Wise, formulated a program for agricultural and mechanical education. Virginia's leading antebellum agricultural reformer, Edmund Ruffin, published an important essay, "Agricultural Education," in 1853. In this piece he called for a program of manual labor, agricultural experimentation, and military organization at an institution that would be supported by the state. Virginia's leaders could look to models in the several other states that founded agricultural colleges in the 1850s. Pennsylvania established the Farmers' High School in 1854, which evolved into Penn State University. The next year, Michigan created an agricultural school that became Michigan State University, and in 1856 the Maryland Agricultural College, later to be the University of Maryland, was chartered.[2]

Meanwhile, in the United States Congress, efforts were underway for a national plan to fund agricultural and mechanical higher education. Before any plan could be undertaken in Virginia, the Civil War intervened. While many Virginians were fighting for their cause, the U.S. Congress in Washington passed a landmark piece of legislation, the Morrill Act. This law, first proposed in 1857, well before secession, provided for the granting of public lands to fund colleges. Legislators loyal to the Union met in Alexandria in February 1864 and accepted the provisions of the Morrill Act for Virginia.[3]

After the Civil War, the Reconstruction-era legislature of the state addressed the application of the Morrill Act in Virginia. The law gave each state 30,000 acres of public land in the west for each U.S. senator and representative, based on the 1860 census figures. Income from the sale of the land was to be used to found a college. Scrip was issued for the land, and the entire Virginia issue was purchased by G.F. Lewis of Cleveland for $285,000. This was invested in 5 percent bonds, the income from which was to fund instruction. The income could not be used to buy land (except for an experimental farm) or to build buildings. It was to fund faculty and administrative salaries and similar educational expenses.[4]

Stiff competition developed over which school would receive the money. Legislators agreed that one-third of the funds would go to Hampton Normal and Agricultural Institute for black education. Several existing schools competed in a "war of the colleges" to be selected for the larger two-thirds of the income. These included the University of Virginia, Washington College in Lexington, Roanoke College, and the Virginia Military Institute.[5]

A Land Grant College

In a clever bit of political brokering, a near-defunct school, the Olin & Preston Institute, founded in the 1850s in Blacksburg was brought to the fore by some influential politicians. They arranged for the donation of the school property and for a grant of $20,000 from Montgomery County if the land grant college were placed there. The deal worked, and on March 18, 1872, Governor Gilbert Walker signed the bill creating the Virginia Agricultural and Mechanical College.[6]

An important man in Virginia education played a key role in getting the new land grant college in operation. This was William Henry Ruffner of Rockbridge County, who was then state Superintendent of Instruction. As such, he was named to the original board of visitors of the new school, and played a key role in selecting its curriculum and leaders. At least nine of the twelve members of the board of visitors had played active roles in agricultural societies around Virginia prior to the Civil War, so it was a well-informed group that guided the new college during its begin-

Virginia Tech campus, late 1800s

nings.[7] One of their early actions was to purchase a farm for the college from the estate of Robert T. Preston, whose family had long been prominent in Montgomery County. This farm, called Solitude, had been part of the Smithfield plantation. Situated near the duck pond on the present Virginia Tech campus, it included a house and some outbuildings.[8]

The board adopted a three-year program of instruction, with general subjects the first year, and surveying, agricultural engineering, agricultural physics and mechanics, and agricultural architecture and machines, the second year. The program of studies for the final year included "agricultural chemistry and geology, botany, and zoology; systems of farming, planting, gardening, dairying, fruit growing, stock raising, and farm economics, including labor, accounts, buying, selling, and renting."[9] The first students enrolled in October of 1872, at forty dollars a year tuition, under the presidency of Charles Landon Carter Minor. They received certificates of graduation in August of 1875. The college did not grant degrees until after the 1882-1883 session.[10]

The first decade saw several changes in the administration. One press attack remarked on the unfitness of one president to head this agricultural college by stating that "he knows less of practical farming than hundreds of Negro foremen in Virginia."[11] There were changes in the faculty, the curriculum, the academic calendar, experimentation with manual labor for the students as well as with military drill in the cadet corps, and questions of how and by whom the college farm should be operated. Because so few persons in Virginia, or anywhere in America, had been trained in agriculture at the collegiate level, it took some years to build up an experienced and competent faculty.[12]

While the college was sorting out its role in improving Virginia agriculture, the state government took an important step toward providing organized knowledge about farming in the Old Dominion. The Virginia General Assembly passed a bill creating the Virginia Department of Agriculture, Mining, and Manufacturing. This body began its work on July 1, 1877, and issued its first annual report later that year. That report included an assessment of the general state of agriculture in Virginia, including a census of cattle. There were just over half a million head of cattle in Virginia. Fauquier County had by far the largest number, 21,000. Augusta ranked second with slightly greater than 17,000, and Rockingham third with just under 17,000. Tazewell County, where the fat cattle export business was getting a start, counted 12,000 head, while Russell and Bedford were just under that number. While the raw numbers may seem high, they are less impressive when viewed in a comparative context.

Virginia agriculture was in need of help in the 1870s. It had not recovered its pre-war vigor. Wheat production in Virginia had averaged 10.8 bushels per capita in 1860, yet only 5.2 per capita in 1880. Beef production was 0.5 per capita in 1860 and just half that, 0.3 per capita, in 1880. Butter production was 11 pounds per capita in 1860 and only 7.6 pounds in 1880. Per capita averages of wheat, corn, beef, and butter in the United States as a whole in 1880 were nearly double those of Virginia in that year.[13]

Virginia's land grant college had opened shortly before a series of economic crises impacted sharply on the farmers of the state. These included the demonetization of silver and a banking panic caused by railroad speculation in 1873. Many farmers sought help by banding together to create local chapters of a new national farm organization, the Patrons of Husbandry, better known as The Grange.

The first local grange appeared in Virginia late in 1873, and within three years, 18,000 Virginia farmers had joined. In Virginia the movement targeted fertilizer companies and commodity middlemen as being in collusion on high prices. Grangers sought to remedy this by forming cooperatives. The organization's effectiveness in Virginia was limited and short-lived. By 1885, the Farmer's Assembly appeared, led by Col. Robert Beverley of Blandfield in Essex County, former head of the Virginia State Agricultural Society. Beverley served also as a member of the Board of Visitors of the Virginia Agricultural and Mechanical College, thereby linking the new college with the concerns of the ordinary farmers of the state. Within a few years, a new national organization, the Farmer's Alliance, succeeded the Assembly. Its state leadership came from the old planter class, with names like Beverley, Harrison, and Page dominating the officers' roster. The Alliance worked with the new Virginia Board of Agriculture on farmer education, a cause that the state government would come to embrace in a few decades.[14]

The situation of agriculture in Virginia simply reinforced the importance of the new Agricultural and Mechanical College at Blacksburg as an institution designed to educate a new generation of farm leaders and to provide better means of farming through the work of its experimental station. Under the leadership of Congressman William Henry Hatch of Kentucky, the federal government took an active role in agriculture, culminating with the elevation of the Department of Agriculture to cabinet level in 1889, with Hatch as its chair. While Congress was debating the creation of a system of agricultural experiment stations, the Virginia General Assembly forged ahead even before the federal government acted, and set up the Virginia Agricultural Experiment Station on March 1, 1886, at the state college in Blacksburg.[15]

Beef cattle research at Glade Spring, Virginia, Southwest Research Station

Experiments "Hatch"

Starting the next year, the Hatch Act, which U.S. President Grover Cleveland signed in March 1887, provided $15,000 annually to each state to establish and operate an agricultural experiment station as a department of its land grant college. The enabling legislation specified types of botanical and soil experimental work to be undertaken and types of work of specific interest to cattle and dairy farmers. These included research on "the adaptation and value of grasses and forage plants; the composition and

digestibility of the different kinds of food for domestic animals; the scientific and economic questions involved in the production of butter and cheese."[16]

At the time the Agricultural Experiment Station was founded, Lunsford Lomax, a Fauquier County farmer, was president of the college. He took an active part in establishing the station and went to Washington to meet with Department of Agriculture officials. There he met William B. Alwood, who had been the first superintendent of the Ohio Agricultural Experiment Station. Lomax enlisted Alwood to join the staff of the new Virginia station in 1888 as vice director. Lomax soon resigned as president of the college. The board secured John McLaren McBryde, who was president of the College of South Carolina and director of the South Carolina Agricultural Experiment Station, to fill both positions in Blacksburg. McBryde began to build a strong agricultural faculty of men who had advanced degrees in the field. Of interest to cattle and dairy farmers was the appointment of Edwin P. Niles, a doctor of veterinary medicine from Iowa.[17] David Oliver Nourse, who had joined the staff in 1888 as head of the Agriculture Department, had a strong interest in forage crops for livestock.

The knowledge gained through work at the Experiment Station was made available to Virginia's farmers through a publication called the *Bulletin*. This was provided free of charge to any Virginian who requested it. The early issues indicate that cattle and dairy farm concerns received a high measure of attention in the experiments that the station undertook. The third *Bulletin* issued (November 1889), for example, featured as its lead article the results of Nourse's "Feeding Experiments" for steers. Nourse expressed the concern of Virginia cattlemen of the 1880s about competition from midwestern farms and about the high cost of rail freight for domestic and export livestock. His stated goal in the experiment was to find the most economical feeds to put the greatest finishing weight on steers. This first experiment selected nine comparable pairs of steers, each to be fed a different combination of feed. From the careful records kept of cost and weight gain, Nourse concluded that the greatest gain came from a wide ration with corn as the basic grain, and that "the most economical food was corn meal, or whole corn, hay and silage."[18]

Nourse continued his feeding experiments, and eighteen months later published the results. This time he selected steers one year younger than those in the 1889 experiment. The principal issue to be examined was the difference that adding silage would produce over the control group that only received hay. Nourse concluded that "silage is very economical to give in moderate quantities to fattening animals," and that "the cost per pound increase is less with those receiving silage than those having other feeds."[19]

It is no coincidence, then, that the addition of silos to Virginia farms took off across the state as the nineteenth

century came to a close. Publishing results of experiments such as this, and using leading farmers to spread the techniques of making good ensilage helped to change the livestock feeding practices of Virginia's cattlemen and dairymen. The experiment station introduced Virginia livestock farmers to "Silos and Silage" in Nourse's 1895 *Bulletin* feature. Nourse indicated that the modern silo process was in use by 1842 in Germany and England, but not until 1875 in the United States. Virginia farmers were slower than many states in beginning to use silos. Because early silos were of stone mortared with cement and cemented inside, they allowed the mass to cool too rapidly at the walls, causing the silage to spoil. This led some farmers to turn against the method. The Agricultural Experiment Station built its first silo in 1888. The capacity was 75 tons and the material was wood. In 1893 the station staff dug a pit silo with a capacity of 125 tons. Based on the station experience, Nourse advocated wood silos as economical and practical, with little resultant loss. He indicated that the pit silo was more economical to build and featured even less loss due to spoilage than the wood silo, but he also noted the great drawback of the labor needed to move the ensilage out of the deep pit and up to the feeding level of the barn.[20]

The Agricultural Experiment Station staff was sensitive to the economic distress faced by beef and dairy cattle farmers in difficult times. The summer of 1902 was a time of drought, with almost no rain from April to September. This reduced the corn harvest by thirty-three percent and the hay harvest by ninety percent. Station staff experimented with hay substitutes that could provide

the needed roughage to keep up the milk flow in dairy cattle and to keep weight up in beef cattle. Various combinations of straw, corn stover (chopped stalks), and cotton seed hulls, both wet and dry, were used to tempt the cows to eat, with stover working well, and straw also if mixed with silage or grain. Cotton seed hulls were of limited success.[21]

Three new members who joined the staff of the Experiment Station during John McBryde's presidency of the college paid special attention in 1905 and 1907 to feed for beef and dairy cattle. Andrew McNairn Soule, John R. Fain, and Milton P. Jarnagin published *Bulletin* issues on "Stall Feeding versus Grazing," and "Finishing Beef Cattle," in which they emphasized the economic value of finishing cattle on the rich grasses of the Appalachian region of Virginia. For Virginia dairymen, they studied protein needs of dairy cattle and the use of grain to supplement skim milk for calves. In one issue about feeding dairy cattle, Soule and Fain believed so strongly in the value of silage that they wrote, "it is necessary for the dairy farmer to have a silo, and unless he is willing to build one his chances of making milk and butter at a profit will be as one to ten."[22]

The experts who got the Agricultural Experiment Station off to such a strong start in the 1880s had all retired from the staff by 1909 when the next publication about silos rolled off the press. By that time, Dr. S.W. Fletcher was director of the station, and the new staff had expanded from the original seven professional members to seventeen. This "Silo Construction" bulletin referred to publications of the U.S. Department of Agriculture for basic information, and sought to emphasize new construction techniques that had appeared in recent years, which station staff believed to be the "silos of the future." Those techniques included the use of concrete blocks, which the farmer could make inexpensively himself using a mold, a drawing of which was included with the text.[23]

Extending Education

Over the course of its first forty years the agricultural program at the college expanded dramatically. Agricultural Hall (later Price Hall) was built to house the program under McBryde's presidency of the college. Agronomy was introduced as a subject in 1907, and the first students majoring in agronomy graduated in 1919. Over time this program added graduate studies, first the Master of Science, and then the Doctor of Philosophy. Animal Husbandry became a major in 1908 and a Ph.D. program in this subject was offered beginning in 1932. In 1963, the name of this area of study was changed to Animal Science. Although courses in dairying had begun in 1872, in 1906 a full Dairying Department was added that changed its name to Dairy Husbandry in 1909. An agricultural engineering course was added in 1912, and a department of that name became a reality in 1919.[24] One remarkable and outstanding feature of the agricultural program from its early years was the very strong tie that developed between the faculty and the students they were training to be the leaders of Virginia's agricultural community.

When Paul Barringer was president of the college and S.W. Fletcher headed the experiment station, both were convinced that the college was reaching only a small part of the farming community. Both were eager to find other means of outreach and they became very enthusiastic about forming experiment stations in other parts of the state. Also, they expanded on an experimental effort involving "moving schools of agriculture," begun during the McBryde administration in cooperation with the State Department of Agriculture and Immigration. The Norfolk and Western railroad would haul some agriculture faculty members on an "institute train" to a local community to hold short-term classes in new farming techniques. However, as Barringer, Fletcher and the agriculture faculty sought means to expand agricultural education, they not only missed the potential in the farm demonstration movement that was just then developing in America, but even saw it as a threat to their outlying experiment station plan.[25]

Consequently, when the state government first became involved with extension work, it was not in connection with the college. The idea of extension work began under Dr. Seaman A. Knapp (1833-1911), the "father of extension work in America." A former head of the Iowa State College farm and president of the college, Knapp joined the U.S. Department of Agriculture to promote better farming methods in the South. In that capacity he developed the Farmers Cooperative Demonstration Work division. Dr. H.B. Frissell of Hampton Institute knew of Knapp's work and told Dr. Joseph D. Eggleston, Superintendent of Public Instruction in Virginia, about him. At Eggleston's invitation, Dr. Knapp came to Richmond in 1906 and outlined a program by which Virginia could adopt the agricultural extension concept. Governor Swanson, E.A. Alderman, president of the University of Virginia, and George W. Koiner, Virginia Commissioner of Agriculture, were among those attending the meeting with Knapp, but no one from Blacksburg was present.[26]

By the World War I era, the Commonwealth of Virginia fully embraced an active program to assist farmers in every aspect of their work.

Beef cattle on excellent pasture, ca. 1910

Agricultural Hall, now Price Hall, built in 1907 on the Virginia Tech campus.

DEPARTMENT OF

AGRICULTURE IMMIGRATION

OF VIRGINIA.

BULLETIN No. 340

1936

AUGUST

A MODERN DAIRY BARN—EASTERN SHORE OF VIRGINIA

Interest in Dairying is on the upward trend in Tidewater Virginia. Diversification on the farm is a desirable goal

QUALITY COUNTS IN ALL LINES OF FARMING

QUALITY and Good Breeding mean increased yields in the Field of Plant and Forage Life. Good Seed are essential to Good Crops.

QUALITY and Good Breeding in Livestock are Essential to a Profitable Program for the Livestock Farmer.

SELECTION of Good Land, Adaptable to the Crop to be grown, Means Better Yields and More Profits to the Farmer.

Scrub Farm Animals—Scrub Seeds—Are Not Profitable

This Bulletin is issued Monthly except January and will be sent Free upon request to
G. W. KOINER, Commissioner, Richmond, Va.

Entered as second-class matter at the postoffice at Richmond, Va., under the Act of August 24, 1912.

Tracking the facts

Virginia Department of Agriculture and Consumer Services

Despite the fact that the Virginia Department of Agriculture and Consumer Services has undergone four name changes in its century and a quarter of existence, it has remained true to its founding mission of serving the needs of the agricultural community of the state.

The Virginia General Assembly passed an act creating the Department of Agriculture, Mining, and Manufacturing in its 1877 session. The measure was signed on March 29, 1877, and went into effect on July 1, 1877. The first annual report of the Commissioner of Agriculture was published that year, starting a tradition of providing useful information to the public.

Probably no man helped shape the early department, and thus Virginia's agribusiness, more than George Wellington Koiner. Starting in

Following Knapp's leadership meeting, the extension program in Virginia got its start with donated funds. T.O. Sandy, a progressive farmer from Burkeville, in Nottoway County, became the first state agent in 1907. The first Boys' Corn Club agent was F. Southall Farrar of Amelia County. Meanwhile, Miss Ella G. Agnew developed the girls' garden, canning, and poultry clubs in Nottoway County, and became the first home demonstration agent not only in Virginia, but in America. In 1908, the Virginia General Assembly supported Extension work by appropriating $3,000 for the program.[27]

In 1913, Joseph D. Eggleston, Jr. succeeded Barringer as president of Virginia Polytechnic Institute. As a strong proponent of demonstration work, he was very pleased when in March of 1914 the Virginia General Assembly placed the responsibility for cooperative demonstration work under the wing of VPI. This change tied in well with efforts to provide federal assistance for demonstration work and require its conduct through agricultural colleges. Congress passed the Smith-Lever Act on May 8, 1914, with its implementation to commence on July 1. Eggleston himself served as initial acting director of demonstration and Extension work in a reorganized agricultural college. This was his first love in all the programs at the college. In an article he wrote for the *Southern Planter*, he concluded by stating that he hoped to make "the state of Virginia the campus of this agricultural college, and to answer promptly and effectively every reasonable call that is made by any one who wishes to improve conditions on the farm."[28]

In the half century between the end of the Civil War and the end of the First World War, the Commonwealth of Virginia had completely transformed its approach to agriculture. In 1865 the Virginia state government had almost no direct concern for the economic well-being of farmers and the quality of their crops and livestock. By the World War I era, the Commonwealth fully embraced an active program to assist farmers in every aspect of their work. Beef cattle and dairy cattle were a highly significant part of the state's agricultural prosperity. Therefore, the institutions, agencies, organizations, and professionals that made up the new network of support for farmers devoted a significant portion of their experimentation, instruction, and concern to those who cared for cattle in Virginia. ◗

1899, the Augusta County native served forty years as Commissioner of Agriculture. When he died in 1939 he was the longest serving Commissioner of Agriculture in the nation and the longest serving department head in the Old Dominion. Koiner's uncle, Virginia Senator Absalom Koiner of Augusta, actually introduced the legislation in 1877 that created the department of agriculture in which his nephew would later figure so prominently. At the commissioner's death, it was noted that "he directed all his energy towards the passage of regulatory laws for the protection and promotion of the farmer and was ever vigilant through the years in their enforcement."

In 1903, Koiner oversaw an agency reorganization, resulting in a new name, the Department of Agriculture and Immigration of Virginia, under control of a Board of Agriculture and Immigration. The inclusion of immigration addressed the changing face of labor in the state. Among the activities of the department in the 1920s and 1930s with special relevance to cattle were: the inspection and analysis of fertilizers and the supervision of state lime plants; enforcement of regulatory laws relating to the dairy industry and feeds; livestock sanitary regulation enforcement; collection and publication of farm statistics, distribution of medication to ameliorate blackleg and hemmorhagic septicemia ("shipping fever"); publication of a monthly bulletin and year book sent free to farmers for the asking; and the publication of brochures offering farms for sale to investors outside the state.

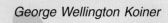

George Wellington Koiner

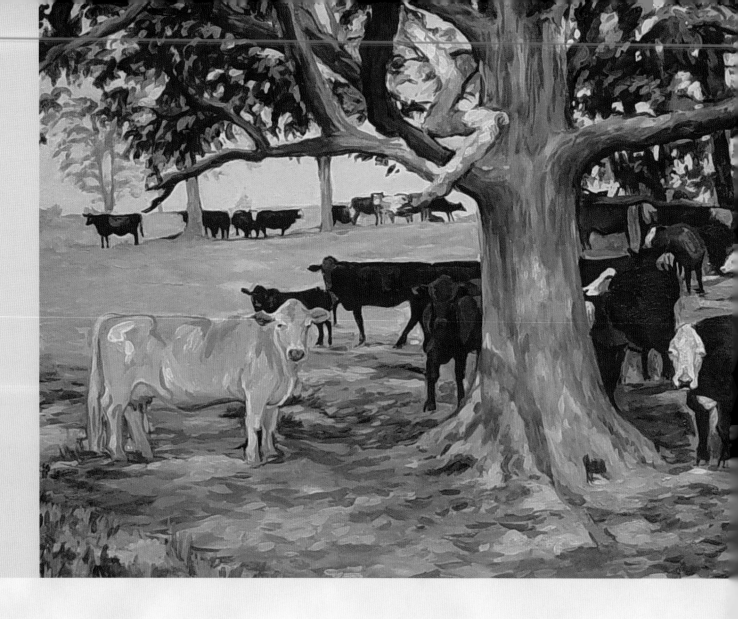

A typical example of a monthly bulletin was number 346, published in March of 1937. This contained a report of the Division of Animal Industry by Dr. H.C. Givens, State Veterinarian, regarding the department's efforts to eradicate Bang's Disease. On January of 1937 the department inspected 4,687 herds and tested 26,857 cattle. Only 374 cattle tested positive, but 414 cattle were slaughtered as a result of Bang's. In that same month, the bureau tested 2,240 cattle for tuberculosis. Also, the department inspected forty-nine public livestock auction sales. S.S. Smith, Director of the Dairy and Food Division, reported that in January, thirty-nine dairies were scored and 114 were inspected; 117 manufacturing plants and cream stations were inspected, and 1,400 gallons of cream were inspected.

In 1966 the name of the department changed to the department of Agriculture and Commerce, then in 1978 it acquired its current name, the Virginia Department of Agriculture and Consumer Services (VDACS). The body is now within the Governor's Secretariat of Commerce and Trade. The Commissioner is appointed by the governor and serves on several boards and bodies. The current Secretary of Commerce and Trade is Michael J. Schewel, while the Commissioner of Agriculture and Consumer Services is J. Carlton Courter, who grew up on an Amelia County farm his family has operated since 1737 and holds a degree in dairy science from Virginia Tech. He worked with a milk marketing cooperative and then in progressively responsible positions in the Virginia Agribusiness Council before becoming Secretary of Agriculture in 1994.

The Virginia Board of Agriculture and Consumer Services is a thirteen-member body empowered to promote the agricultural interest of Virginia, advise the governor, confer with the commissioner, and promulgate rules and

regulations necessary to administer and enforce laws relating to agriculture and commerce. L. Bruce Holland is president of the Board of Agriculture currently.

VDACS is organized into four units: Commissioner's Office, Division of Animal, Plant, and Food Industry Services, Division of Consumer Protection, and Division of Marketing. There are five regional diagnostic animal health laboratories located in Warrenton, Ivor, Lynchburg, Harrisonburg, and Wytheville. VDACS works closely with Virginia Tech, Virginia State University, and the Virginia Cooperative Extension Service.

A total of 521 carry out department responsibilities. VDACS shoulders the responsibility for enforcing fifty-seven laws and more than seventy regulations concerning consumer protection and the promotion of agriculture. ~

"About VDACS" www.vdacs.state.va.us/ ; Department of Agriculture, Mining, and Manufacturing, (1878), and Department of Agriculture and Immigration of Virginia (March 1937) Bulletin No. 346, (September 1939) Bulletin No. 374.

Dairy wagons at Virginia Tech

At 3,086 feet, the 20,000-acre bowl called Burke's Garden is Virginia's highest valley.

A Fat Cattle Kingdom

There is an old saying, "it's an ill wind that blows no one some good." An ill wind in Britain blew a lot of good in southwest Virginia, especially in Tazewell and Russell counties, after the Civil War. There it swept in a storybook era of giant "fat cattle" raised on Virginia farms that rivaled the fabled ranches of Texas. The ill wind that blew in Britain brought one of the most colorful eras in the history of cattle in Virginia.

The ill wind carried what was most likely contagious bovine pleuropneumonia (CBPP).[1] In Britain it was simply called cattle plague. This cattle lung disease, which had been around in Europe since the 1840s and had spread to South Africa, India, and later to America, hit British cattle with special severity in 1865 and 1866.[2] In 1868, the British government ordered all live cattle in Britain to be slaughtered in an effort to wipe out cattle plague.[3] It was a move that would be used again at the end of the twentieth century and the beginning of the twenty-first to eliminate two other serious bovine diseases, mad cow disease and foot and mouth disease.[4]

With the loss of their domestic supply of beef, the English turned to a new source for the roast beef dinners that are the pride of British cuisine. Fat cattle imported from America, and especially from Virginia, came under the carving knife on many a London table. This was the beginning of the "export cattle" trade that dominated the agricultural economy of several southwest Virginia counties for half a century.

To Market in Pioneer Days

Raising cattle for faraway markets was not a new idea in Tazewell County after the Civil War. In fact, some county farmers were involved in that trade shortly after the American Revolution. Tazewell at that time was not far removed from its frontier stage of development and was still a part of Russell County. One of the earliest settlers was Rees Bowen, who settled at Maiden Spring in The Cove area of the county in 1769. The Cove was actually two contiguous coves, about five miles long by four and a half miles wide, comprising some 15,000 acres at the west end of Thompson's Valley.

Rees Bowen was a son-in-law of James Smith, a partner in land speculation of the famous Scotch-Irish pioneer, James Patton. Bowen's eldest son, John Bowen, was born in 1757 and married Nancy Gillespie, of another early settler family that would play a prominent role in the cattle business. In 1789, John Bowen drove his cattle to Philadelphia to market. We can imagine that cattle drive over the mountains and through the Valley of Virginia to seek the best price in the capital of the new American nation. How heartbreaking it must have been for his wife and family to learn that he had died suddenly in a Philadelphia hotel and would never see his beautiful Cove again.[5] The seventh Rees Bowen to live on that land is currently raising both cattle and an eighth Rees Bowen.

Shorthorns seen here around 1900 in the Clinch River at Tazewell were once the dominant breed in the fat cattle business.

Other early families to settle in The Cove area of Tazewell were Barns and Ward. David Ward, the patriarch of that line, eventually acquired some 5,000 acres. His descendants married into the family of Robert Barns, a schoolteacher who came into the area in 1784 or 1785, after the American Revolution. Thomas Gillespie, who had walked from Pennsylvania to fight in the battle of King's Mountain, came to The Cove after the Revolution and married a daughter of Rees Bowen. In time they brought other connections to The Cove, including the Baylors from Montgomery County and the Thompsons. The descendants of these pioneers became involved in the fat cattle and export cattle business when it emerged, and remained leaders as long as fat cattle dominated Tazewell agriculture.[6]

The concept of fat cattle was already well developed in Virginia when the Civil War began. Smyth, Washington, Pulaski, and Montgomery Counties, and parts of the Shenandoah Valley produced these fat cattle, but it was Russell and Tazewell Counties that became a true "cattle kingdom." A history of Tazewell County published in 1850 noted that "there is nowhere to be found, a country better adapted to grazing cattle than this county. The grass is said to be superior, both in abundance and quality, by all stock dealers." At that time, of the 10,000 beef cattle in Tazewell, some 7,000 were driven annually to far-away markets. Warrenton in Fauquier County and Haymarket in Prince William County were favored destinations, each a drive of fifteen days or more. Although most of the county cattle were the unimproved native stock, the more progressive cattlemen in the county were raising the improved breeds of the day, the dual-purpose "long and short horned Durham [Shorthorn] and Devon."[7]

TAZEWELL STEER TIPS SCALES AT 2,010 LBS.

Tazewell, Oct. 4 (Special).—When a steer weighing 1,960 pounds was included in a shipment of Tazewell county export cattle from the J. S. Gillespie estate last week, he was hailed as champion for the season but among a herd from the Liberty Farm of the A. P. Gillespie estate shipped yesterday, there was one tipping the scales at 2,010 pounds. This steer was a cross-bred Hereford-Shorthorn whose weight last fall was 1,550 but the owners recognized the possibility of unusual take-on and in the face of discouraging market conditions decided to hold him over. He gained 50 pounds on winter feeding and the remaining 410 on summer pasture. The largest beef to leave Tazewell in recent years is said to have been one weighing 2,240 grazed on the farm of W. C. Thompson in Burks Garden about 15 years ago.

Yesterday's shipment from the Gillespie estates, in addition to 31 Lee county Herefords weighing an average of 1,665, and a total shipment of 81 averaging 1,606, included 30 of the same breed but of Texas nativity wearing the T bar Ranch brand, averaging 1,536. Having been selected for their uniformity as yearlings and shipped here they readily acclimated themselves.

The Perfect Place for Fat Cattle

What ingredients made it possible to raise enormous cattle whose weights regularly reached 1,600 pounds and sometimes 2,000 pounds in just a few areas of the Old Dominion? Cattle-raising families from the area who reminisced in Burke's Garden and in The Cove, agreed on the ingredients. One was bluegrass, a fine-leafed, perennial of the genus *Poa*, believed to have been introduced from the Old World. The sod-forming Kentucky bluegrass (*P. pratensis*) probably thrived in Tazewell's rich valleys before it ever reached Kentucky.

Another ingredient was climate. The cool mountain temperatures and abundant rainfall that are a part of the climate in such unusual areas as Burke's Garden and The Cove in Tazewell and in the Elk Garden area of Russell provide the ideal growing conditions for a thick crop of bluegrass that replenishes itself. Yet the temperatures are not so cool that cattle cannot stay on the pastures for eight months out of the year, nor so cool that the streams freeze often in winter.[8]

Climate works hand-in-hand with soil and topography. The reflections of one master of the fat cattle business, Sam Baylor of Wardell Farm in The Cove, said it best. "The two top counties (Tazewell and Russell) were blessed by nature with breaks in the mountain ranges and therein lay the secret of their riches."[9] At those points where the mountains broke down, the erosion of thousands upon thousands of years built up thick topsoil rich in the limestone and shale particles that make good grassland. However, the limestone bedrock that underlies the soil of Kentucky and of the Valley of Virginia is absent in these selected areas of Tazewell and Russell, so that in times of drought when grasses dry up in the Valley and in Kentucky, they remain lush and green in Tazewell and Russell. In these two counties, where the four-thousand foot mountains are topped with sandstone that does not dissolve in water, the bluegrass will grow up the slopes to a remarkable height, providing additional rich pasturelands.

A century before Sam Baylor reminisced, an important report published by the Virginia Board of Immigration in 1876 noted that "Large numbers of fat cattle are annually sent to the Eastern markets from the rich grass lands . . . where the nutritious and fattening 'blue grass' grows."[10] The following year, 1877, the General Assembly created the Department of Agriculture, Mining and Manufacturing. The first annual report of the Commissioner of Agriculture provided a cattle census for each county and commented on the soil and grasses necessary for raising fine cattle. For example, Craig County with "land well suited to the growth of the grasses, and chiefly valuable for grazing and stock," had 2,920 cattle. Many counties like Craig, in fact 51, or more than half,

A purebred Shorthorn from the Lawson herd in Burke's Garden

counted fewer than 5,000 cattle. In contrast, Russell County, called "a grazing and cattle-raising county" in the report, had 11,511 cattle. Tazewell, where "native grasses abound, and stock-raising can be profitably and cheaply prosecuted" counted 12,278 head. Only a handful of larger and more populous counties had greater numbers of cattle: Augusta, 17,401; Fauquier, 21,546; Rockingham, 16,998.[11]

But only a handful of places could produce the remarkable "fat cattle" or "export cattle" that routinely reached 1,600 pounds. They did not include Augusta, Fauquier, and Rockingham. Most remarkable is that the fattening took place solely on grass. The prevailing practice in the years before and just after the Civil War had been to drive small cattle, probably yearlings, to market in Northern Virginia. One farmer's bad experience in doing so in the Panic of 1873 led him to new methods of finishing cattle.

Sam Baylor's grandfather Thompson drove his cattle to the customary northern Virginia market. While he was underway on the month-long trip, the Panic of 1873 hit. When he reached the market, no one was buying. He had to turn his unsold cattle around and march them back to Tazewell. When he arrived home a month later, he did not have enough feed for the new cattle he had acquired at home and the old ones he brought back. So, he bought land at fifty cents an acre in Buchanan County, sent a man with his cattle to winter there, grazing on bluegrass supplemented with linden tree cuttings. The cattle did well, and the experience taught him that it was possible to put a lot of weight on the cattle after they had wintered and that they could be put on pasture. By the late 1870s, it had become general practice in the area to keep the cattle two

Tracking the facts

Straight from the horse's – umm... cow's mouth... well, almost

"Old people are like libraries on fire; we must read their books before it is too late."

This saying explains much about the significance of oral history as a resource for learning about the past. The experiences of an individual over a lifetime of work comprise a unique database in that person's brain. Those memories form a rich treasury of recollections of persons long gone, of older ways of doing things, and of new developments that transformed farming. Few people write memoirs. Therefore, oral history interviews are one way of saving these invaluable individual memories for future generations. In the writing of this book, oral history interviews with several dozen older dairy and beef cattle farmers, extension agents, professors of agriculture, auctioneers, and veterinarians have provided valuable insights about the history of cattle in Virginia.

Sometimes the interviews have been conducted one-on-one. An author or a research associate visited or called a retired dairy or beef cattle farmer. The conversation and questions may have covered a wide range of experiences. Or, the interview might have focused on only one or two aspects of the cattle industry in Virginia.

The researcher took notes and sometimes also made a tape recording of the conversation. Out of such sessions came wonderful recollections, interesting anecdotes, and usually some good

Marvin Meek of Burke's Garden holds up an ox shoe he found on his land.

years, and to experiment with a third year to reach even greater size.[12] Thompson's experiences and those of other farmers in the area set the stage for the expansion of the fat cattle business and the development of export cattle.

Cattle go to Sea

The documentary record of the first shipment of fat cattle from western Virginia to England is not clear. Several sources say that the person to develop the trade was Robert M. Lawson of Burke's Garden, Tazewell County.[13] Burke's Garden is a remarkable mountain basin, ten miles long and five miles wide, with thousands of acres of excellent grazing land surrounded by mountains. Lawson, a native of England, acquired 1,000 acres of the 3,000-acre former Governor Floyd estate in Burke's Garden.[14] He called his farm "Oak Grove" and improved it in 1888 by building a handsome twenty-two-room house in which he and his wife raised their three children.[15] In addition, he built sturdy fences, barns, and outbuildings. Perhaps it was Lawson's familiarity with England and the English beef market that caused him to think first of importing Shorthorn bulls from England, and then of exporting his cattle to England, rather than selling them in eastern markets, as had been the custom in Tazewell for several generations.

The claim for another resident of southwest Virginia as the originator of the export cattle trade is better, for he exported prior to Lawson's settlement in Burke's Garden. Certainly his claim to being the first to ship from Pulaski County is good. This was Francis Bell, a prominent cattle trader and landowner.[16] The Virginia and Tennessee Railroad had come to Pulaski County in 1854. One of the chief cattlemen in the county at that time was Major Robert Dickerson Martin, who sold land to the railroad and donated a right of way, for which the railroad built a cattle-loading switch at his farm. The railroad connection made it possible for Pulaski County residents to ship their cattle to Baltimore. This must have given Francis Bell the notion of exporting live cattle from that port city. Bell was not certain how to accomplish this transatlantic shipment, but must have received advice from someone. In the spring of 1877, Bell encouraged William Miller of Canada, who had experience with shipping stock on the Atlantic Ocean, to move to Pulaski. On July 15, 1878, Bell's first shipment of live cattle from southwest Virginia sailed from Baltimore. It included a number of Major Martin's cattle.[17] It had not been easy locating an appropriate ship, as this was a new kind of trade. Bell leased a Spanish vessel called the "Bonaventura" and fitted it out for its unusual cargo. The "Bonaventura" is said to have been the first ship captured by the Americans during the Spanish-American War, twenty years later.[18]

Bell's chartered ship sailed to Liverpool, where the agent, William Miller, took the cattle to the stockyards and sold them in competition with English, Irish, and Scottish cattle. They sold quite well, fattened as they were solely on grass, for Bell reported that they had consumed no grain since the previous winter. Sales through stockyards apparently came to a close after that first season, and English law subsequently required that the cattle be slaughtered on the dock. Bell noted that the Pulaski cattle gained a good reputation in both Liverpool and London markets.[19]

photographs, certificates, ribbons, programs, and the like to help illustrate the book.

On other occasions the format has been a group interview involving both authors, one or more members of the editorial board, and several older farmers. One notable example of this included two days of intensive interviews in Tazewell County with more than a dozen persons whose families had played a significant role in the raising of fat cattle for export. On another occasion, leaders of the dairy industry all over Virginia from the past fifty years gathered with the authors and members of the editorial board at a hotel conference room for a day of interviews. The discussion focused largely on the remarkable changes in the breeding and raising of dairy cattle that had resulted from scientific advances in which participants had played key roles.

A book such as this is wonderfully enriched by the human interest stories that emerge in oral history interviews. Such stories inform our understanding of the cattle industry as it developed in the last seventy-five or so years. The authors only wish that they could have interviewed persons who were cattle farmers and dairymen in Virginia 100, 200, and 300 years ago. ~

Walter "Brownie" Elswick

Jim Hoge's family was among the first settlers in Burke's Garden.

Francis Bell, a pioneer in the export of fat cattle from southwestern Virginia to England, built this handsome home, called Rockwood, in Pulaski County in 1876. It is still in the hands of Bell's descendants.

Bell's son, J.R.K. Bell, went along on the trip, perhaps starting a tradition in the export cattle business. There are still many memories and stories told in Tazewell and Russell by the sons and grandsons of men who, as young boys, accompanied their father's or uncle's cattle on the Atlantic voyage. Bell recalled lovely weather, the opportunity to see many new kinds of fish, sighting a school of whales, and coming close enough to an iceberg to feel its cold air.[20]

Not all of Bell's cattle voyages were as pleasant. In one terrible instance when the boat encountered a storm, Bell was told that they would have to push the cattle overboard in order to save the ship and the men on it. It was a horrible sight to see the poor animals struggling in the water behind the ship. It was also a calamitous loss for Bell, as this was the one time he had decided not to insure the cattle.[21]

Bell was a major cattle trader in several southwest counties, and employed several agents. The year following the loss of cattle overboard, Bell came to Tazewell County as usual to buy cattle. He reached his contracts with the cattlemen early in the season. Then, as the season progressed, the price of cattle rose sharply. When the time came for the cattle to be taken up, the story of the loss of Bell's cattle in the Atlantic had circulated, and the cattlemen of Tazewell assumed that

he was broke and would pay them in worthless checks or sharply depreciated paper money. Many probably wished to be relieved of their early low price contract with Bell and welcomed an excuse. Joseph S. Gillespie, Sr., then a very young man, was acting as agent for Frank Bell in the county. He wrote to Bell that the Tazewell cattlemen would only accept gold. He received no reply, and assumed that he would not actually take up any cattle for Bell in the county the next day.

At dusk, Jim Bell, another of Frank Bell's agents, rode up to Joe Gillespie's house and handed him his saddlebags. Gillespie reeled under the weight, and thought that Bell might have bottles of whiskey in them. When Gillespie inquired what was in them, Bell showed him that both sides of the bags were filled with gold. The next morning as the farmers brought their cattle to the scales, it was clear they intended to refuse paper money and to take the cattle back home. As each animal was weighed, Jim Bell gave the farmer a paper with the weight written on it. Then he told them that they could come to be paid. When he went to the saddle bags to count out the gold for the first man, all the farmers realized that their early season, low price contracts with Frank Bell were good as gold. They went home, disappointed men with gold in their pockets, but unable to take advantage of the season's higher prices. Bell later told Joe Gillespie that his profit on these cattle more than made up for his losses in pushing the cattle overboard.[22]

The life of a cattle dealer in Virginia could be just as colorful as the movies depicting the lives of western cattlemen. In July of 1877, M.B. Furr of Fauquier County, a cattle dealer, was riding the westbound express train to West Virginia to buy cattle. The train was nearly to Staunton when three men approached him to play three-card monte. In the course of play, one of the men made off with Furr's roll of $1,000 in greenbacks with which he had planned to buy cattle, and jumped from the train near Pond Gap by way of a window. The distraught Furr encountered General Echols on the train and told him of his predicament. Echols telegraphed the Staunton police, who set out along the Valley Pike to look for the robbers. On the tip of a woman who kept a tollgate, the robbers were apprehended. One carried a pistol and had $6,600 in cash, the equivalent of $165,000 in today's dollars. They claimed to be cattle dealers themselves who had been in West Virginia, but they soon found themselves lodged in the county jail at Staunton and scheduled for a speedy trial.[23]

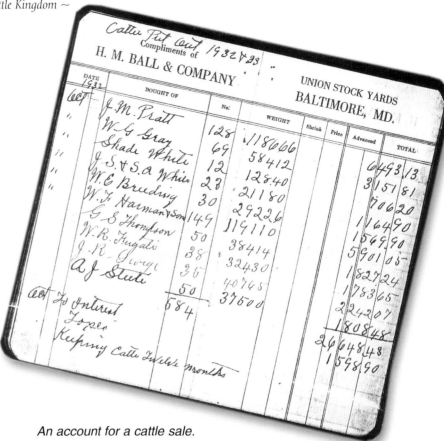

An account for a cattle sale.

Big Business

The activities of Furr, the robbers, Bell, and his agents all point to the fact that cattle dealing was a bigtime business in Virginia. The purchasing of cattle from other areas was a common practice among the fat cattle farmers. Some went to West Virginia to obtain stock, while others went to Tennessee or North Carolina. James Hoge of Burke's Garden recalled that his grandfather, Frank Moss and Frank's brother, George, drove small, tough types of cattle that they bought in Grayson County up the valley for sale in Northern Virginia in the years after the Civil War. On one such drive, Moss was able to get the cattle to cross a river by walking across their backs to reach the lead steer.[24] Sam

Baylor of The Cove recollected that Ashe County, North Carolina, was a source for feeder cattle, two-year olds who had reached a weight of 1,000 to 1,300 pounds. It would not be possible for them to gain more weight on the farms outside the special bluegrass areas. In fact, in many areas the grass simply was not good enough for the yearling cattle to reach the basic 1,000-pound feeder cattle weight, so they were sold young. In Tazewell and Russell these cattle could reach 1,500 pounds or more on the rich bluegrass diet.[25]

The export cattle trade had developed sufficiently that the first commissioner of agriculture called attention in 1878 to the great value of the export cattle market to the economy of Virginia. He reported that the London Meat Importation Company stated that meat prices in England had climbed twenty-five to thirty-three percent in just a few years. The exportation of cattle products from the United States to Europe, including live cattle, fresh beef, salted beef, butter, cheese, and condensed milk exceeded $46 million in 1877 and $49 million in 1878. Virginia provided a significant portion of the live cattle. The 1877 figure would be nearly $747 million and the 1878 exports would be worth $795 million in today's dollars. Passenger liners had even begun adding space for livestock in their holds.[26]

Just as the Tazewell farms in Burke's Garden and The Cove were developing the fat cattle business, another remarkable farming

Cattle Scene in Lebanon Valley, Va.

This circa 1900 postcard of cattle grazing on the hills of Lebanon Valley included an interesting observation from the sender which reads: "This is the main 'crop' of this country besides coal."

149

operation that would play a significant role in export cattle was forged in the Elk Garden area of Russell County. This was the mountain empire built by Henry Carter Stuart that is known today as the Stuart Land and Cattle Company, the largest landholding east of the Mississippi. The seeds for this cattle empire were sown by Stuart's great grandfather, Harry Smith, who acquired a significant landholding. Stuart's father, William Alexander Stuart, who was a prominent cattleman, built a handsome mansion on the land in the 1840s. When Virginia became embroiled in the Civil War, the Stuart men, including the famous cavalryman, General J.E.B. Stuart, uncle of Henry Carter Stuart, all served in the Confederate army. In the economic woes of war and reconstruction, the estate passed from the hands of the Stuart family.[27]

Henry Carter Stuart, who was only a lad of six when the war opened, grew up in the trying postwar years, graduated from Emory and Henry in 1874, and completed his law education at the University of Virginia in 1875. He was determined to restore the family's fortune, land, and status, and in 1880 gained control of about half of the former estate. This coincided with the emergence of the fat cattle export trade, and Stuart participated in it enthusiastically. He prospered at the fat cattle business and in 1899 was able to acquire the other half of the earlier Stuart estate. His land covered about 50,000 acres, or seventy-eight square miles, a tract that was larger than many counties, and that reached beyond its Russell County base into parts of Washington, Smyth, and Tazewell counties.[28]

In 1928, Rees Bowen V and his son Rees Bowen VI of Ward's Cove in Tazewell County stood among the special variety of corn called Spotted Buck, which was developed to fatten export cattle.

Managing a Fat Cattle Operation

Although the climate, the topography, and the bluegrass combined to create the special conditions by which cattle could reach fat cattle proportions, the other ingredient in the success of the fat cattle trade was not part of nature; it was the skillful management by the owners of these large farms and of the foremen, tenants, and hands who provided the labor.

The routine for managing the fat cattle was well developed early in the trade and modified only slightly over the decades. In October, after the fat cattle were driven to the railroad for shipping abroad, the cattlemen bought two-year-old feeder cattle at 1,000 to 1,200 pounds from their favorite sources in southwest Virginia, North Carolina, and Tennessee. These were driven to the bluegrass farms. Sam Baylor remembered that his Uncle Sam Thompson bought most of his Shorthorns in Ashe County, North Carolina. The drive to The Cove in Tazewell took four or five days

and passed through long stretches of wilderness where there were no fences along the roads. As the cattle got strung out, it was easy for some to wander off and not be missed until "counting time" at sundown. It might take the boys who were sent back to look for the strays two or three days to find them. Some were never found. Each night's stopping off place had been carefully selected in advance for its grass, water, and shelter for the drivers.[29]

Before these drives, each farmer's cattle had to be road-marked. This was done by dipping a paddle a couple of inches wide into a tar bucket and slapping a particular mark on each steer's flank. Such a temporary mark would last for the drive and eventually wash off. A wonderful story is often told about Governor Henry Stuart and those marked cattle. He had bought a string of feeders in Scott County one fall and had sent Hatcher, the son of one of his foremen, to lead the drive. Stuart rode out to the end of his

In southwest Virginia fat cattle and sheep, like these belonging to Joe Moss of Lawson & Moss in Burke's Garden, were pastured together quite successfully. This field provided fine grazing for both Hereford cattle and Hampshire sheep.

property the afternoon the feeders were expected to see how they had stood the journey. The weary animals, strung out single file appeared, with the drive leader in front on his horse, sitting sidewise to relieve saddle soreness. The governor expected all his cattle to be carefully road marked, so said "Hatcher, are all these cattle tarred?" The driver answered, "Yes, Governor, they sure are and I'm plumb wore out myself."[30]

The feeder cattle were put into the rich bluegrass pastures or areas called "boundaries" in October and remained there until the first winter cold spell in late November. They were kept on thick, well-drained sod and fed about a gallon of corn in the shock daily. Their powerful jaws easily crushed the corn and the cob. The farmers in Tazewell developed a special variety of red and white speckled corn, which they felt put weight on the cattle most efficiently. They called it Spotted Buck corn and the stalks usually reached a height well above ten feet. Many farmers fed sheaf oats and hay as well as corn until late April. The corn, oats, and hay were distributed from a wagon and spread so that all of the cattle had an equal chance at feeding. Shoats of eighty to one hundred pounds were turned in with the cattle to eat the corn that passed right through. By April, they had become hogs of two hundred to three hundred pounds. Meanwhile, by turning out time in April, the cattle had usually gained fifty to seventy-five pounds on their winter diet. Then from April until October, these mature three-year-old cattle grazed on the rich bluegrass and added two or three hundred pounds to their weight.[31]

One of the striking aspects of the fat cattle farmers in southwest Virginia is that, unlike the cattle ranchers of the west, they had no qualms about raising sheep along with their cattle. Bill Adams, who also participated in the 1976 oral history interview of Sam Baylor of The Cove, remarked that "both of them will do better together than

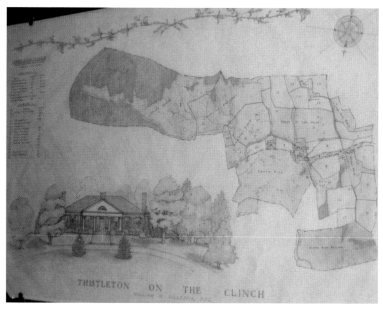

An artist rendering of William M. Gillespie's Thistleton on the Clinch carefully delineated the arable and grazing land so important to a livestock breeder.

either one of them will do individually." He noted that seventy-five percent of the grass that sheep eat is spurned by cattle, and that sheep will eat weed sprouts, but cattle will not.[32] In fact, an export sheep market developed at the same time as the cattle export. In July 1877, a steamer of the Old Dominion line loaded 400 live sheep in Philadelphia for export to Europe, the first from the City of Brotherly Love, although Montreal and New York had been ports of departure for earlier loads of sheep.[33]

There are a number of significant examples of the value of raising the sheep and fat cattle together in this blue grass region. Robert M. Lawson, who had pioneered fat cattle and export cattle in Burke's Garden was also a pioneer in the introduction of Hampshire sheep. The Moss and Meek families were also heavily involved in the raising of Hampshires in The Garden in the early and middle twentieth century.[34] On the Stuart land in the late 1920s, there were typically about 2,200 ewes and 2,500 lambs bound for market in Jersey City.[35] Speculators had contracted for them by the head a year in advance by gentleman's agreement. When shipping time came in the days before paved roads and pickup trucks, men on horses, accompanied by stock driving dogs, drove the lambs to the nearest railroad loading point.[36]

Toward the end of the nineteenth century, changes were occurring in the export trade. The British homegrown beef market was reviving from the devastation of the plague, giving housewives the option of fresh local beef. Technological advances made refrigerated ships possible, so that fresh beef butchered in America could be shipped to Britain. An investigator in 1890, Samuel Plimsoll, believed that this was better quality beef than that from stressed animals who had endured horrible conditions aboard ship. The cattle ships have been compared to the slave ships earlier in the century. Six hundred to a thou-

A group of Hereford cattle ready for shipment stand in a pen as the two gentlemen in the background shake hands to seal the deal.

Beloved extension agent George W. Litton and youngster Marvin Meek show off four prize animals in the mid-1930s.

sand head of cattle were tightly packed aboard, and sometimes given scant rations of food and water. Storms rocked ships, causing animals to fall and break bones or horns, and crowded conditions led to the spread of disease.[37]

It was because of these conditions that export cattle producers of southwest Virginia always tried to send some of the teenage boys in their families along on the voyage to guarantee that these prized fat cattle were properly treated. Bill Gillespie recalled that his father had made two trips to England in his teens. The first was miserable, as he was seasick and was stuck in the hold with the cattle most of the time. Once the cattle were sold, there was opportunity to see a little of England, and then return in comfort in a first class cabin. It was not unusual for the cattleman himself to make the voyage.[38]

Changing Times

By the turn of the twentieth century, the domestic sale of the fat cattle was expanding. Many of the Tazewell and Russell cattle were sold in New York, often for Kosher markets. The big red and roan Shorthorns continued to domi-

nate until the time of the First World War, although the packing houses began to show a preference for Herefords, and housewives began to demand smaller cuts of beef. A sirloin steak from a Shorthorn might be two feet long, according to Bill Adams, Tazewell interviewee. Herefords finished at a somewhat lower weight than Shorthorns. Because 300 pounds was the best that they could put on grazing the bluegrass, Herefords were less profitable than the Shorthorns that gained 350 to 400 pounds. Breeders also began breeding smaller cattle to produce the smaller cuts of beef in demand. When Herefords were introduced, they could attain 1,600 pounds as three-year olds, but over time they dropped in size so that they finished at 1,300 or 1,400 pounds.[39]

At the end of the First World War, the cattle business boomed, but in 1921 the bottom fell out of the market. Feeders bought for twelve cents a pound in 1920 sold for only seven cents a pound in 1921 when finished as fat cattle. Another story about Governor Stuart has him going to New York with a load of cattle in 1921. The commission man, who always handled the sale of Stuart's cattle, reported to the governor that the Jewish buyer had offered seven cents a pound. Stuart asked the commission man's permission to speak directly with the buyer. "I understand that you have only offered seven cents for these fine cattle of mine." "Yes sir, that is correct." "Hell fire, man," the governor said, "you could pay a lot more than that." "Yes, replied the buyer, "we could, but Governor, it wouldn't be good business."[40]

Around 1920 the export cattle business to Britain came to an end. This did not mean the end of fat cattle, for they continued to flourish, with Herefords as the dominant breed. The large national packing houses like Swift and Armour became the principal markets. They sent their representatives into the field to strike deals with the cattlemen for direct sales to the packing house, with no commission man. This arrangement continued through the end of World War II. Prices recovered slowly in the early 1920s, but rose more quickly later in the decade. By 1926, the price was ten cents a pound. In 1928 it rose to fourteen cents, the best price for fat cattle. After that came the financial crash, followed by the Depression. From 1929 to 1937 cattle prices sank, reaching an all-time low of three cents a pound. Surveying the calamitous drop, Irene Bowen Wendell recalled that her father, Rees Bowen VI, said "Hell is at Wardell [a nearby community] and headed this way. A pound of beef will only buy a postage stamp." Losses were great. The three cent price,

compared with the sixteen cents a pound a dozen years earlier in World War I represented an eighty percent decline in income. Some cattlemen went broke in spite of efforts of local banks to work with them. The largest fat cattle producer in The Cove was Harry Thompson, who had 300 to 400 head. Rees Bowen VII reported that his grandfather kept eighty cattle on his 600 acres. Bill Adams said they had 110 at Wardell, and Al Gillespie said his family had 100. To get only forty-five or fifty dollars per steer on operations of this size was disastrous.[41]

The Depression was hard for the cattlemen and also for the families that worked for them. Often several tenant families lived on the big farms, in some cases for several generations. The families were large, often including seven to ten children, many of whom also worked on the farm. They felt as though the farm was theirs and they took good care of the pastures and boundaries. Some seventy-five families lived on the Stuart estate, growing crops and selling feed to the company on a share basis. The Stuarts provided a company store and also built a chapel.

Prosperity returned during and after World War II, but the days of the fat cattle were numbered. There was an

On hand to load cattle in Chilhowie, Virginia, in this 1947 photo were Dr. Dean Cole, C.T. "Buster" Barnes, Mr. Buchanan, Jesse Felty of Valleydale Packers, Ballard Huff, Gwyn Richardson, Bob Foster, C.C. Clark, Mr. Shumate, and Sherman Foster.

Harry Thompson in Ward's Cove was the last man to give up on the fat cattle business. This was the last herd he drove out of The Cove in the 1960s.

increasing interest in Angus as a replacement for Hereford. With their smaller frames, they could never be fattened on grass to the large and profitable weights of the heyday of fat cattle. The preferences of housewives continued to change, and white fat was in fashion. The grass finished cattle of southwest Virginia produced a yellow fat that did not appeal to the postwar consumer.

The grand era of fat cattle came to a sad end at a meeting that has been likened to a funeral. George Litton, former Extension agent in Tazewell and head of VPI animal husbandry department, was the organizer of this effort to assess the changes that had occurred in the production and marketing of fat cattle. For that reason, he brought together some 125 major fat cattle producers, representatives of the packing houses that bought from them, chain grocery store representatives, economists, and extension service staffers. The scene was at the Martha Washington Inn in Abingdon. The date was January 22, 1952. The message was a eulogy for the great beasts that had grown and flourished on the rich bluegrass. An era came to an end, and with it a way of life that had brought to southwest Virginia an exciting age that still lives on in the memories of the last of the cattlemen who raised the fat cattle, and in their children and grandchildren.

Tazewell's Clifton Farm is Nation's Oldest Ranch

In 1774 Henry Smith was rewarded by Patrick Henry, then Colonial Governor of Virginia, with a vast tract of land along the Clinch River in return for building a fort for the protection of his fellow settlers. It is said he was able to ride his horse from his Clifton Farm to Castlewood, a distance of nearly thirty miles without ever leaving his own land. Today Clifton Farm still grazes beef cattle, making it the oldest continuously operated cattle ranch in the nation.

Henry Smith's granddaughter Eliza C. Smith married Dale Carter, an astute businessman, and their combined land holdings are said to have exceeded 80,000 acres. Their eldest daughter Mary Taylor Carter married William Alexander Stuart who owned and operated the salt works in Saltville,

Virginia. To his own substantial properties Stuart added the extensive lands his wife inherited from her parents and founded the Stuart Land and Cattle Company of Virginia, Inc. in 1884.

The steep mountain land and lush valleys were perfect for grazing large herds of cattle. By the turn of the century, the company was fattening cattle on the bluegrass pasture there and shipping the live animals to England. At that time, the Stuart family, under the leadership of Henry Carter Stuart, who served as Governor of Virginia, specialized in Shorthorns and many of he three-to-five-year-old steers they sent to Liverpool weighted in at more than 2,000 pounds.

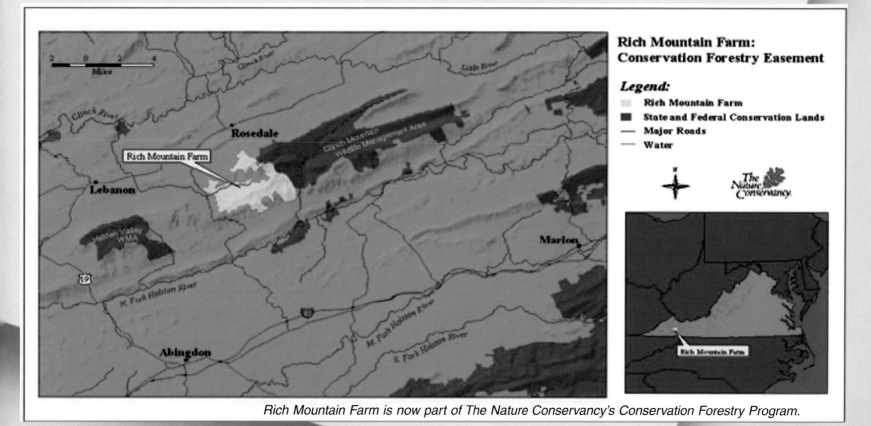

Rich Mountain Farm is now part of The Nature Conservancy's Conservation Forestry Program.

By the 1930s the Stuarts had replaced their Shorthorns with Herefords and had switched from the fat cattle export business to a cow-calf feeder operation. The ownership of the operation changed in the 1930s. The governor's nephew, Virginia Senator Harry Stuart, who managed the holdings, and his wife took over a portion of the operation as the Elk Garden Farm Products Company. William Alexander Stuart and his brother Walter Stuart, with outside investors, operated the larger portion of the original tract as the Stuart Land and Cattle Company of Virginia, Inc. with a board of directors and a manager. The manager since 1953 has been William Alexander "Zan" Stuart, Jr.

In the late 1950s Senator Stuart at Elk Garden and the Stuarts of SLC implemented crossbreeding on many of their Herefords with Black Angus. Those were later crossed with Red Angus, then Simmental. Eventually German Gelbvieh became the favored breed on the ranch. However, from the 1950s to the 1980s the SLC supplied Herefords for the USDA Foot and Mouth Disease research project at Plum Island, New Jersey. The registered Holstein dairy that SLC operated for many years was phased out in the 1970s as beef cattle became the focus of the operation.

Although the cattle operation is still thriving under Zan Stuart's management, times have changed. Much of the ranch is now managed timber and wildlife is abundant. In the 1960s, 18,000 acres of the ranch in Tazewell County were sold to the Commonwealth of Virginia. That became the Clinch Mountain Wildlife Management Area.

Prominent Virginia cattleman State Senator Harry Carter Stuart, standing, and three of his employees are pictured here about 1960 on land upon which the Stuart concerns raised beef cattle in Russell County.

More recently, Stuart found another way to protect the land so long associated with his family and continue a strong agricultural heritage into the future. The corporation permanently enrolled over 10,000 forested acres on its Rich Mountain and Clifton Farms into The Nature Conservancy's new Conservation Forestry Program.

Under this first-of-its-kind agreement, the conservancy will conduct ecologically sustainable forestry on the property to generate annual payments to the company while protecting wildlife habitat. The Rich Mountain tract subject to the agreement is located in Russell and Washington Counties and adjoins the Clinch Mountain Wildlife Management Area.

"By showcasing management practices that will enhance the forests, protect water quality, and provide a reliable stream of income to sustain a working farm, we hope to encourage other landowners to enroll and to spur the creation of similar programs across the country," noted Bill Kittrell of The Nature Conservancy.

Zan Stuart, who still manages 1,600 head of beef cattle on three separate farms, sees the agreement as one part of the puzzle that he needs to assemble to ensure the future of the operation. "This is a mutually beneficial arrangement that allows us to retain ownership of the land, while being guaranteed an annual income in perpetuity. At the same time, the conservancy will manage the timber land in an environmentally sound manner that will protect both the ecological health and the natural diversity of the landscape." ~

The Nature Conservancy website, www.tnc.org; Robert C. Snyder, "Stuart Family are Pioneers in Raising Export Cattle," The Journal Virginian, 25 June 1959; Chicago Drovers Journal, 27 November 1959; "Beautiful Elk Garden Estate," Bluefield Daily Telegraph, 10 July 1927; information supplied by Ike Eller, and author's conversation with W.A. "Zan" Stuart, Jr.

In
Pursuit of
Excellence

The remarkable growth of the dairy industry in twentieth-century Virginia and the astonishing success and expansion of beef cattle are due, of course, to the thousands of hard-working farm families across the Commonwealth and their dedication to breeding and marketing outstanding livestock. Also the efforts of every Virginia beef cattle or dairy family is supported by a large number of organizations, institutions, clubs, associations, extension agents, agricultural education programs, and fairs. This network of support provides training for the cattlemen and dairymen of the next generation. Agricultural programs in the public schools, 4-H clubs, Future Farmers of America (FFA) clubs, and agricultural courses and degrees at Virginia Tech and Virginia State, are designed for educating youth. For adults actively operating dairy or beef farms, this support network provides a wealth of services. These include the latest information about scientific advances that can improve the quality of the cattle; about government programs and initiatives that impact the operation of beef and dairy farms; about new products, new machinery, and new techniques; and about new and improved means of marketing dairy products and beef cattle. A third type of support involves the organization of shows, sales, expos, and fairs to showcase beef and dairy cattle competitively.

An Era of Education

Public school agricultural education is often associated with the passage of the Smith-Hughes National Vocational Education Act. However, Virginia provided for vocational agriculture before the Smith-Hughes Act. The person responsible for this was Joseph Dupuy Eggleston, Jr., who from 1906 to 1912 served as the first elected, not appointed, superintendent of public education. Eggleston was a great believer in rural education. During his term in office, the Virginia General Assembly passed a law providing for Congressional District Agricultural Schools in each of the state's eleven congressional districts. These schools taught agriculture and home economics. Each campus included a dormitory and a farm or agricultural experiment station. The principal of each school functioned as an extension agent, organizing clubs and farmer training sessions, and supervising farm projects.

Manassas Agricultural School, built in 1908, was the first. It was later called Bennett School to honor Dr. Maitland Bennett, who donated the land. Professor Button, the principal, chose milk testing and seed-corn se-

lection for the focus of his work in local schools, because "all farmers keep cows and raise corn."

A decade after these Virginia agricultural high schools were established, the Smith-Hughes Act of 1917 provided for agricultural education in all American high schools. As the agricultural courses became a part of the curriculum in high schools across Virginia, the special agricultural schools were phased out and absorbed into local school systems. The Bennett School, for example, became an elementary school in the Prince William County school system until replaced by a new structure of the same name in 1969 and then a third in 1996.[1] It is unlikely that any of the 700 students there today have any idea of the agricultural heritage of their school, for Manassas has become a bedroom community for Washington, D.C., and few of those children today have any experience with a farm.

Future Farmers

The Smith-Hughes Act to introduce agricultural courses in high schools was not always implemented promptly, but in due course all counties in the Commonwealth came into compliance. In Augusta County, for example, vocational agriculture became part of the curriculum in 1924.

In 1925, Walter S. Newman (VPI '19) became State Supervisor of Agricultural Education. He believed that a statewide organization for boys enrolled in vocational agriculture courses was vital to help these youngsters build self-confidence and pride in farming at a time that many of their contemporaries were moving off to city jobs and abandoning the farm. In September of 1925 Newman met at VPI with H.W. Sanders, Henry C. Groseclose, and E.C. Magill, members of the agricultural education faculty there, to discuss the formation of such an organization. Newman asked Groseclose to draft a plan for the organization. Groseclose came up with the name Future Farmers of Virginia and, with advice from many agriculture teachers, drafted a constitu-

CL 6
OLD BENNETT SCHOOL

In 1908 the General Assembly authorized ten agricultural high schools, one in each congressional district. The first such school was built in Manassas in 1908 - 1909 and named for Dr. Maitland C. Bennett, who donated the land. During construction, workers discovered the graves of unknown Civil War soldiers. Union veteran George Round, a Manassas school district trustee, and Confederate veteran George Tyler, school superintendent, decided to erect the school over the burials as a monument to the fallen. The school housed teacher training and elementary classes, and students conducted agricultural experiments on the grounds. The building remained a Prince William County public school until 1969.

DEPARTMENT OF HISTORIC RESOURCES 1994

Educating Horses on the Farm
The Feeding of Steers
Fall Care of Poultry

Taking Honey from the Comb
Student's Judging Contest
Fruit Exhibits of Virginia

Volume XXII.

OCTOBER, 1908

Number 4

Modern Farming

MODERN FARMING PUBLISHING CO.

163

tion and a plan for conducting meetings. Groseclose, with help from Newman and others, incorporated the organization under the laws of Virginia on September 5, 1928.[2]

For the organization to become a reality, Future Farmers of Virginia chapters had to be organized and put into action. Two chapters vied for the distinction of being the first in Virginia, Rural Retreat and Weyers Cave. The former may have begun first, but the latter completed its organization, and obtained the first charter and with it the official honor of being Chapter No. 1. The year was 1927, the school was Weyers Cave High School, and the ag teacher who served as the advisor was E.B. Craun. Future Farmers of Virginia became a quick success in the state.

Robert Maltby, southern regional agent for vocational agriculture, invited Newman to talk about the FFV at the Southern Regional Conference of Vocational Agriculture Workers in San Antonio, Texas. Attendees were impressed and wanted to pursue the plan in their states. The VPI staff was overwhelmed with requests for information. Groseclose was charged with responding to them. He and Newman worked with the Federal Board of Vocational Education in Washington to draft a constitution for a National Future Farmers of America organization. Meanwhile, on November 20, 1928, at a National Livestock Judging Contest in Kansas City, thirty-three students from eighteen states banded together to form the national organization and adopted the Groseclose draft for their constitution.[3]

In 1929 the official colors of national blue and corn gold were adopted. Delegates at the 1930 convention restricted membership to boys only by constitutional amendment. When the Fredericktown, Ohio, FFA members arrived at the national convention wearing blue corduroy jackets with the gold emblem on the back, the delegates voted to adopt this as the official dress of the FFA. By 1934, forty-seven states – all but Rhode Island – had chartered associations. Meanwhile, in Virginia in 1927 a similar organization for African-American boys had been formed, the New Farmers of Virginia. In 1935, this organization went national as New Farmers of America and soon it spread to thirteen states. In 1965 the NFA merged with the FFA. The creation of the National FFA Foundation, Inc., in 1944 to raise funds for FFA activities put business, foundations, government, and private individuals behind the organization's programs. Currently, the FFA Foundation raises more than $7 million annually.[4]

Molding Leaders

In the hands of thoughtful and energetic young ag teachers, FFA chapters were established across Virginia in the 1930s. Such a teacher was L.O. Brumback, who in 1934 launched chapters at two Augusta County high schools,

Beverley Manor and Middlebrook. He also taught ag classes at two other Augusta County high schools, Stuarts Draft and Spottswood. Teaching at four high schools was a lot for one teacher to handle, but during the Great Depression, county teachers had to accept a reduction in pay. Brumback was told he would not be reduced in salary if he would teach at an additional school.

FFA activities often opened doors to a wider world for young boys. From its strong early start in Augusta County,

Augusta County has the distinction of being home to the only family in the nation to provide three generations of presidents to a state FFA. O. Beverley Roller, center, was Virginia state president of FFA in 1942. His son, B. Randolph Roller, right, was state FFA president in 1971, and his grandson, Jason Roller, left, held the office in 1997.

FFA moved from strength to strength. For example, in 1932 Lurty Craun won a scholarship to VPI worth $100, a considerable sum in those days, when his project received top honors among all the counties in Virginia served by the B&O Railroad. The American Farmer Degree, the highest honor in FFA, was awarded to William Brooks of Stuarts Draft in 1933, R.W. Moffett of Stuarts Draft in 1937, and Ralph Hamilton of Churchville in 1939. The chapter at Fishersville in 1937 and that at Beverley Manor in 1939 won the state Degree Team contest. The excellent Stuarts Draft chapter under the leadership of T.J. Horne tied for third place in the state in 1935, then won second place in 1936. In 1937 the chapter won the state contest and placed second in the United States.

International exchange programs began in 1948. Congress granted FFA a federal charter in 1950 and stipulated that a U.S. Department of Education staffer be the national FFA advisor. In 1959 the FFA national headquarters was moved to Alexandria, Virginia, on land that once belonged to George Washington. FFA week had long been celebrated in February around Washington's birthday because of his pioneering contributions to agriculture in America. Women and girls, finally admitted in 1969, comprised thirty-five percent of the membership by 2000. In 1988 the national convention delegates changed the official name from Future Farmers of America to the National FFA Organization. Ten years later the headquarters left Virginia and moved to Indianapolis, Indiana. Membership is nearly half a million at the turn of the twenty-first century and the annual national convention draws nearly ten percent of the membership.[5]

Many young Virginians rose to prominence in the FFA beginning in the 1950s and running through the 1990s. Dwight Houff of Mt. Sidney was active in FFA in the 1950s and became state vice president. He went on to leadership roles in the Virginia Polled Hereford Association, the Virginia Angus Association, and the Virginia Cattleman's Association. Augusta County has the distinction of being home to the only family in the nation to provide three generations of presidents to a state FFA. O. Beverley Roller was Virginia state president of FFA in 1942 and went on to serve as national vice-president. His son, B. Randolph Roller, was state FFA president in 1971, and his grandson, Jason Roller, was state president in 1997.[6] Ernest S. Reeves of Mt. Solon, one of the first eight national recipients of a Charolais scholarship, was an active FFA member. He later became a leader in the Virginia Cattleman's Association. In 1974, Alpha Everette Trivette, a nineteen-year-old farmer from Ladysmith, Virginia, from the C.T. Smith FFA Chapter at Ladysmith High School, was elected the national president of the National Future Farmers of America.[7]

FFA activities can be found across Virginia in all aspects of promoting agricultural education among youngsters who intend to become farmers or work in agribusiness. Recent programs and competitions of FFA include agricultural issues forum, crops judging, agricultural mechanics, production proficiency, floriculture proficiency, horse judging, and

A group of 4-Hers exhibit cattle at a show in downtown Pulaski in this early 1900s photo. Note that the exhibitors knelt beside their animals to pose for the picture.

livestock and dairy judging. The annual state convention at Virginia Tech in June draws over 1,200 FFA members and their advisors from across the Commonwealth. The meeting includes competitions for teams from each chapter. The first-place individuals and teams may attend the national convention in October to compete with teams from across the country. Many of those activities pertain to cattle, both beef and dairy, so that FFA continues its role of providing practical educational experience, a healthy sense of competition, camaraderie, and pride in work well done for the beef and dairy breeders and producers of the future.

The Four Hs

It is a rare farm youngster in Virginia in the past sixty years who has not been a member of 4-H, the informal youth development education program of Virginia Cooperative Extension, formerly Virginia Agricultural Extension Service. The traditional four-leaf clover emblem representing head, heart, hands, and health is one of the first icons rural children encountered before the days of television and computers.

The roots of 4-H nationally go back to Illinois in 1898 when Will B. Otwell, president of the Farm Institute, organized a corn growing contest for teenage boys with modest monetary prizes and to Clark County, Ohio in 1901 when school superintendent Albert B. Graham began to organize after school experimental clubs. Otwell demonstrated that young people would respond to encouragement through incentives, and Graham had shown that there was an interest in clubs focused on agricultural science. A third ingredient in the 4-H recipe was the formation of tomato canning clubs among girls through the encouragement of USDA. In 1911, two USDA workers, O.H. Benson and O.B. Marting developed the club idea around the four Hs and came up with the four-leaf clover emblem. When the Smith-Lever Act (1914) created extension services through every state's land grant college, staff members were given funds for dissemination of information. Clubs for boys and girls also proved to be an effective means for agents to reach their parents.

In Virginia, F.S. "Southall" Farrer began work in 1907 organizing boys' corn clubs in Dinwiddie and Chesterfield Counties. In 1910, Ella G. Agnew organized canning clubs for girls in Halifax and Nottoway Counties. Lizzie Jenkins began work with African-American girls' canning clubs based from Hampton Institute in 1913, while boys' work began with field staff agent Jessie M. Jones in 1915. As clubs formed around Virginia between 1918 and 1920, the boys and girls were organized into the same clubs, called agriculture and home economics clubs at first, and then in the 1920s, called 4-H.[8]

Projects were an important component of 4-H, and for a great many boys and girls over the past seventy years that has meant raising an animal to show and sell. The lessons in nutrition, health, record keeping, grooming, and economics that resulted from this stood young dairymen and cattlemen in good stead in their adult lives. Furthermore, many of the leaders of the dairy and beef industries in Virginia had 4-H leadership roles in their youth. An example of this training is Hunter R. Greenlaw of Albion Farm in Stafford County, president of his local FFA chapter, who in 1938 was chosen Star Farmer of America, the top honor in FFA. The young man was already operating a dairy herd of purebred Holsteins while in high school. Later he switched to beef cattle, and in 1966, he received the coveted Mills Award of the Virginia Hereford Association. Morris Fannon, the 1974 Mills Award recipient competed in the county fair and on livestock judging teams as a 4-H member in his native Lee County in the late 1930s. Dave E. Brower, Jr., the 1967 Mills honoree, was active in 4-H for a decade and was a member of the 4-H Livestock Judging Team that competed at the Chicago International Livestock Show.[9]

From a later generation, Virginia is proud to claim five 4-H State Livestock Judging Teams that have won the national contest at the International Livestock Exposition in Chicago in 1957, 1960, 1962, 1965, and 1983. The 1962 team, coached by John Gerken, Clarke County agent, set a record in winning every contest in which it judged. Jimmy Royston of Boyce, Clarke County, a member of that team, was the high individual in the national beef cattle judging, and was high individual at both the Atlantic Rural Exposition and the Eastern National Livestock Exposition.[10] In 1972 the Virginia 4-H Livestock Judging Team placed third out of the thirty-one teams competing nationally in Chicago, and first in the beef judging. Team members were Kathy Richardson, Riner; Allen Rhudy, Tazewell; Paula Pierce, Warrenton; and Ronnie Moore, Warrenton.[11]

When 4-H initiated a new Livestock Advancement Project in 1975, the first member in Virginia to complete all four levels was Glynn Moreland of Lucketts, president of the seventy-member Loudoun 4-H Beef Club, who had also participated in the livestock judging team and had exhibited his projects at the state fair.[12] The county agents and extension animal husbandmen who have worked with these

A 4-H member practices before trying to make the milking team in this 1942 photo taken in Rockingham County. Clubs entered teams in milking contests held at the fair each fall.

A 4-H member grooms a dairy heifer while his two younger brothers watch in this 1942 Rockingham County photograph.

young people can feel justly rewarded for their efforts in the thrill of victory that their young people experienced. These extension staff members are a significant part of the support network that has mentored and upheld several generations of dairy and cattle people in the Commonwealth from their school days on through their working lives.

Clubs include boys and girls age nine to nineteen. Club leaders are adult volunteers who work with the guidance of the extension service staff. The youngsters elect their officers and conduct their meetings according to parliamentary procedures. The 4-H program has changed significantly with the changing times, changing demographics, and changing economy in Virginia since the 1960s. Where it was thought of initially as an organization for rural children mainly living on farms and intending to become farmers, in the early years of the twenty-first century, only five percent of the membership is rural. Towns with a population under 10,000 were home to forty-one percent of the members in 2003, while cities over 50,000 and their suburbs account for thirty-eight percent of the

members. Girls outnumber boys in the organization, but only slightly, fifty-one percent to forty-nine percent. Some twenty-six percent of the 2003 membership in Virginia was of minority racial or ethnic groups, down slightly from the thirty percent in 1996. The current total membership of 4-H has grown sharply in recent years. In 1996, 114,879 boys and girls were enrolled in 4-H, while in 2003 that number had escalated to 191,645.[13]

With the expansion into urban areas, many new programs and curricula have been developed. Nonetheless, some good old standards continue as the most popular among the ten curriculum areas, including animal and poultry sciences, the heart of the traditional 4-H program. One of the remarkable aspects of Virginia's 4-H program is that Virginia 4-H has the third largest camping program in the nation.

This takes place at the six 4-H educational centers, Airfield 4-H Educational Center, Wakefield; Southwest Virginia 4-H Educational Center, Abingdon; Northern Virginia 4-H Educational Center, Front Royal; Holiday Lake 4-H Educational Center, Appomattox; Jamestown 4-H Educational

Rockingham
1993 Va. B...

Supreme Grand Champion Steer
in 4-H & F.F.A. Livestock Show.
August 1974

Presenting Livestock Conservation
illustrated talk "Crossbreeding
Cattle for More Dollar Return".
Won State Demonstration Award.
June 1972

Reserve Champion Steer in 4-H & F.F.A.
show and Sale. My Father lends me
May 1971

Center, Williamsburg; and Smith Mountain Lake 4-H Educational Center, Wirtz. Each center is unique, and the six together encompass the range of terrain in Virginia from the Tidewater and Chesapeake Bay to the rolling piedmont, to the mountains and valleys of the far southwest. One of the first to be developed was the Southwest Virginia Center in Washington County, when the county government in 1958 donated the former "poor farm" for conversion to a center and camp. Others were purpose-built throughout the 1960s and 1970s, such as that at Smith Mountain Lake, constructed in 1965 on land donated by Appalachian Power Company just as the lake was being created.[14]

Calf Parties

In the 1950s the Virginia Holstein Association developed a clever way to enable 4-H and FFA members to purchase a good quality registered calf for their projects. This was an event known as a "Calf Party" that took place during the Spring Holstein Heifer Sale. The arrangement provided for a flat fee of $150 per head for a nine-month-old heifer. Each 4-H and FFA member put his or her name in a hat. The calves available for the party were gathered. Someone drew names from the hat. The first youngster whose name was drawn got the first pick of the calves. The second name drawn chose next, and so on until each youth had the chance to select a calf.

William Harrison, former County Extension Agent in Loudoun County from 1963 through 1991, remembers purchasing his first Holstein at a "Calf Party" at a Spring Holstein Heifer Sale. The calf was named Lynnhaven Mattoax Brook, bred by Arthur Conrad of Lynnhaven, Virginia.[15]

4-H The Power of Youth

18 U.S.C. 707

1902 - 2002

Livestock Shows

A sparkling example of an outstanding activity for educating youth in the cattle business is the annual 4-H FFA Market Animal Show held at the Staunton Stockyards every May. With nearly 200 exhibitors showing sheep and hogs as well as cattle, this is now the largest such event east of the Mississippi and one of the oldest continuous events in the country. It is by no means the only show of its kind, however. Similar junior livestock shows have taken place in Bristol, Chesapeake, Virginia Beach, Roanoke, Harrisonburg, Winchester, Fredericksburg,

Virginia FFA at 75
One Mission: Student Success

Danville, South Boston, Petersburg, Lynchburg, and Marshall. A number of these shows continue annually.

In its modest beginnings in the dark days of World War II the Staunton event was called the "Fat Cattle Show" as only cattle were exhibited. One of the original participants, Bill Simmons of Sangerville, was a student at North River High School in 1944 when County 4-H Extension Agent R.L. Coffey talked with the students about raising baby beeves for the show. Simmons, as an agricultural student, showed animals for three years. Following his graduation from college, he became an agriculture instructor at North River High School. He helped to organize the annual event and encourage his students to participate. Even after retirement, Simmons continued to help with the show as a Ruritan volunteer.

Within two years the event reflected the dramatic shift that was taking place in beef cattle production in Virginia. The traditional grass-fed cattle, which took up to three years to reach slaughter weights, were being replaced with baby beeves fattened on grain so that they reached market weight in less than two years, while yielding a more tender, tastier meat. By 1947 the show was called the Baby Beef Show, and was used as a means of demonstrating to farmers the advantages of modern methods of beef cattle production.[16]

Originally the show was a one-day affair, and the exhibitors had fattened their cattle for thirty days prior. By 1952 the show lasted two days, included sheep and hogs, had 100 exhibitors, and the young exhibitors had to feed their cattle for ninety days. Simmons recalled that the first year he showed he simply used a rope halter. The next year, his instructor, E.B. Craun, told the boys they would have show halters. Craun bought leather and helped the boys make their own halters. Soon, showmanship was emphasized, and the young exhibitors were put through a showing and fitting program at school. Craun, who had helped to organize the first FFA chapter in America, expected his students to wear their blue FFA jackets and white pants when showing their animals. The animals were shown by breed at that time. The size of the classes reflected the changes taking place in breed preference, for Shorthorn classes had only three or four animals, while Angus, the rising favorite, had up to twenty in a class.[17]

In the early 1970s the name changed to Market Animal Show. The animals exhibited were classified by weight rather than by breed, and the purebred heifer show was discontinued. By the turn of the twenty-first century, this event anticipated its sixtieth anniversary. Boys and girls from the age of nine to nineteen are eligible to show. Those who are thirteen or younger may show feeder calves. Registration and weighing of the animals take place the first Saturday in November, so the youngsters have six months during which they must feed and care for their calves and keep records on the feed given and costs involved. Civic organizations such as the Chamber of Commerce, the Rotary Club, and the Ruritan Club assist in and support the event. Local businesses purchase animals at the sale. The show's organizers can look with pride on the nearly 200 youngsters who, each year, exhibit some 400 animals and experience the satisfaction of recognition for a job well done. Many of the young people who have exhibited in this event over the years have continued in agriculture, and a number of them are among leaders in the beef industry in the Shenandoah Valley.[18]

Northern Virginia Dairy Show

Virginia Polytechnic Institute
VPI & SU – Virginia Tech

Virginia's land grant college provided agricultural education for young men at the university level from its founding in 1872. The expansion in programming with the addition of the Agricultural Experiment Station multiplied the service to the Commonwealth's farmers, dairymen, and cattlemen many fold. The college entered a new period of growth on the eve of World War I that would continue throughout the twentieth century, until Virginia Tech became one of the leading universities of the southeast.

Joseph Eggleston, who ushered in the system of agricultural schools as well as oversaw remarkable strides in rural schools in Virginia during his term as superintendent of public instruction, became Chief of Field Service in Rural Education in the United States Office of Education. This was a position of considerable importance and influence, but Eggleston resigned it in six months in order to return to his native state and become the president of VPI in 1913. Blessed with "the fiery zeal of a reformer and the dauntless spirit of a sincere missionary," Eggleston set out to change VPI, including reorganizing the administration of the Agricultural Experiment Station, the Agricultural School, and Agricultural Extension Work.[19] Extension work

was his great love. He wrote in an article in *The Southern Planter* that "it is our desire and our purpose to make the state of Virginia the campus of this agricultural college, and to answer promptly and effectively every reasonable call that is made by any one who wishes to improve conditions on the farm."[20] Eggleston's mission for VPI, through the agriculture department, extension work, and the experimental station, in promoting all aspects of improved agricultural knowledge and methods, whether for crops or livestock, set a high standard. That significant role in no way diminished in later decades as the university grew and expanded into traditional liberal arts and sciences.

Another great agriculture educator ushered in a new era of growth for post-World War II VPI but ill health brought his term to a close in 1947 after just two years. This was John Redd Hutcheson, a Charlotte County native and an alumnus, who had joined the Virginia Agricultural Extension Service under Eggleston in 1914 as a livestock specialist and in 1919 became director of the service. Among the myriad problems facing Hutcheson as veterans swarmed to the campus were complaints about the school of agriculture and about the limited nature of research at the Agricultural

Experimenting to Find Fit Forage

The center photo illustrates a fertilizer experiment carried out about 1939 by the Virginia Agricultural Experiment Station on Kilmacronan, the historic farm of A.J. Huff in Washington County. The farm owner contracted with R.E. Hunt from the Experiment Station to provide grazing land that could be divided into ten plots of ten to twelve acres each and sufficient steers to graze each to capacity. VPI agreed to furnish and apply the fertilizer, using a different formula for each plot. One control plot got no fertilizer. Cattle were to be weighed at the beginning and once

Experiment Station. Both H.L. Price, dean of agriculture, and Dr. A.W. Drinkard, Jr., director of the Experiment Station, indicated willingness to give up those posts. Dr. T.B. Hutcheson, head of the agronomy department, became dean of agriculture, and Dr. H.N. Young, head of agricultural economics, became director of the Experiment Station.[21]

The dean of engineering and various faculty and students in engineering expressed concern that Hutcheson, known across the state as "Mr. Agriculture," in his plans for expanding the school would simply turn VPI into a "super cow college." Their fears were not allayed with the announcement that Dr. Walter S. Newman would become the first vice-president for VPI, as Newman was a former professor of agricultural education. When a heart attack forced Hutcheson's retirement, the board of visitors selected Newman as the next president of VPI. A native of Woodstock, Virginia, after leaving his teaching post at VPI in 1925, Newman had become state supervisor of agricultural education, and then the assistant superintendent of public instruction.[22]

Newman was not going to overlook the Agriculture College, but he had no intention of making the institute a "super cow college." He had a wide range of issues to address and had ambitious and sophisticated plans for growth. Nonetheless, significant changes took place in the agricultural arm of the school. T.B. Hutcheson, the be-loved dean of agriculture, died suddenly in 1950. H.N. Young, director of the Agricultural Experiment Station, served as interim dean during a long search that resulted in 1952 in the selection of L.B. "Deet" Dietrick, director of the Agricultural Extension Service, as dean. Young returned to the Experiment Station and W.H. "Bill" Daughtrey became associate director of the Agricultural Extension Service. Dietrick, Young, and Daughtrey worked relentlessly throughout the 1950s to see that nearly every Virginia organization related to agriculture and rural life had heard about VPI and its services. Their success in public relations worked to the great benefit of the university, for these organizations went to bat for VPI by lobbying for increased financial support in the legislature.[23]

Another important 1952 appointment had a major impact on cattle and dairy industries in Virginia. Professor R.E. Hunt retired as head of the Animal Husbandry department, and Professor George W. Litton was chosen as the new department head. Litton, an engaging man with a homespun philosophy, folksy demeanor, and rich experience as an extension agent, built his department into one of the strongest at VPI.[24] In the process, he gained the loyalty of hundreds of young men who studied under him, and he exerted significant influence on the growth of the beef cattle industry and the dairy industry in Virginia. His writings and ideas were widely dis-

each twenty-eight days throughout the grazing season, and again at the end of the experiment. Forage research has been ongoing at Virginia Tech. In more recent times, Dr. Harlen White, the forage specialist at the university, experimented with overseeding pastures. A 1969 experiment depicted in the far right photograph shows clover being seeded with a tractor and, in the far left photo, Jo Vernon, a Vietnam veteran, gets ready to pilot the helicopter which will apply fertilizer to the experimental pasture area in Tazewell County.

tributed through folksy but thoughtful columns published in numerous agricultural magazines.

Other important developments impacted the agricultural arm of VPI. In 1949 Paul Mellon donated farmland in Fauquier County and funds to enable a forage research station to be established at Middleburg. Five years later, in 1954, the McCormick family donated Walnut Grove, their family farm on the Rockbridge–Augusta border, on which the reaper had been invented in the 1830s. This farm became the Shenandoah Valley Research Station. A separate department of extension education was created in the college of agriculture. In 1952 Professor C.W. Holdaway, who had served nearly forty-eight years on the faculty, retired as head of dairy husbandry and was succeeded by Dr. G.C. Graf. That department received permission to drop its archaic name, dairy husbandry, in favor of a more modern title, department of dairy science. That same year, the department of agricultural chemistry underwent a major reorganization and emerged as the department of biochemistry and nutrition

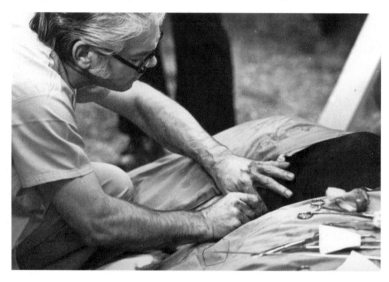

Dr. Dare McGillard, visiting from Iowa State University, performs a surgical procedure on a bovine at VPI.

under a new chair, Dr. R.W. "Charlie" Engel, former professor of animal nutrition at Alabama Polytechnic Institute.[25]

Graduate education at VPI was growing by leaps and bounds in the 1950s and 1960s. The board approved the creation of a Ph.D. in agronomy in 1958. In 1959 a Ph.D. in agricultural economics, which the board had approved in 1947, finally got underway. The department of veterinary science was finally created. This had been a dream since the 1930s; although the legislature had approved its establishment several times, it had never appropriated the funds.[26]

The team that had provided outstanding leadership in the agricultural college in the 1950s continued its excellent service in the 1960s. Dean Dietrick oversaw a complete revision of the agriculture curriculum. Harold Young oversaw a revision of the research emphasis at the Experiment Station and brought to the process a rare combination of practicality and broad perspective.

Dr. Charlie Kincaid, far right, of the VPI animal science department, conducted nutrition research with grazing animals.

Bill Daughtry's country drawl could put anyone at ease, but his sharp mind worked well to keep extension work lively and significant throughout Virginia.[27]

President Newman suffered a heart attack in March of 1961, and though he recovered well and returned to work, he determined to retire in June of 1962. His successor was Dr. Thomas Marshall Hahn, Jr. After two presidents who were homegrown leaders from the school of agriculture, a new president with no agricultural background would be a change. Hahn had been dean of the college of arts and sciences at Kansas State University, but only for three years – he had been chairman of the physics department at VPI when he left in 1959, and held his Ph.D. in physics from Massachusetts Institute of Technology.

Professor Kenneth Litton, Extension Beef Specialist, speaks at the VPI Beef Cattle Shortcourse in 1951.

A Good HEREFORD Bull Doesn't Cost...He Pays

The Bonus Breed

...ISHED BY AMERICAN HEREFORD ASSOCIATION

Virginia Tech students lead Hereford cattle in the ballroom of the Hotel Roanoke in this 1964 photo. The occasion was an educational program by VPI in cooperation with the annual meeting of the Virginia Hereford Association.

Becoming a University

The university's historian noted that while Hahn, in his opening address, mentioned teaching, research, and extension, he was the first incoming president in VPI history who failed to state that "the promotion of agricultural and engineering education" were the chief mission of VPI. Some feared that he would jettison VPI tradition and re-make the institute into a midwestern-style land grant university. Two months later, in September 1962, Dean Dietrick announced that he would retire at the end of the month. His name would be remembered on campus by new generations when a new dining facility was named Dietrick Hall for him. Dr. Wilson B. Bell ('34), associate director of the Agricultural Experiment Station, was named the new dean and welcomed with enthusiasm by the board, alumni, and agricultural leaders. W.H. Daughtrey ('27) became director of the Agricultural Extension Service, with P.H. DeHart ('29) as associate director. As he assessed the "state of the university" in his inaugural address in April of 1963, Hahn noted that the School of Agriculture was the seventeenth largest in the nation,

with its faculty members in constant demand as consultants all over the world. He also impressed upon his listeners the importance of growth and the necessity of excellence while facing the need to double enrollment by 1975, increase faculty salaries, and create a quality library.[28]

In another burst of reorganizing and re-naming, all of the schools within the institution were named colleges, and the departments of animal husbandry and poultry husbandry became the department of animal science and the department of poultry science. The word "university" crept increasingly into conversation as a description of the institution. Another change was the end of the twenty-year relationship between Radford, the largest of the state women's colleges, and VPI, the largest institution of higher learning in the state. Radford was cut loose to develop on its own in 1964. In the flurry of new buildings going up on campus a new dairy center was completed southwest of the main campus, and in 1964 a generous gift of $120,000 from the Cyrus Hall McCormick heirs endowed scholarships in agricultural sciences or agricultural engineering. But the biggest change that year was the announcement

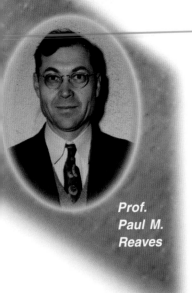

Prof. Paul M. Reaves

of a divided board decision that, beginning that fall, membership in the Corps of Cadets would be voluntary rather than compulsory for male students. The uproar that followed threatened to divide the students, alumni, faculty, and board and required a special board hearing and meeting to vote again on the issue, with the same result.[29]

A year-long institutional self-study in 1965 resulted in a detailed published report and in the decision to become a full-scale university. The board of visitors authorized a study of the administrative structure in the areas of research and extension. As a result, the legislature created a Research Division for the entire institution that consolidated the two existing units, the Virginia Agricultural Experiment Station and the Virginia Engineering Experiment Station. Dr. William B. Harrison, director of the Engineering Station, became dean of the new division and Dr. Coyt Wilson, who in 1965 succeeded Dr. H.N. Young as head of the Agricultural Experiment Station, became associate dean and director of agriculture, life sciences, and home economics research. Dr. Young devoted his early retirement to writing the history of the experiment station from its inception to

the reorganization into the Research Division in 1966. Harrison remained in the post only a short time, being succeeded by Dr. Randal M. Robertson in 1970.

At the same time the new Research Division was created, the legislature also created a new Extension Division encompassing the entire university. Dr. William E. Skelton ('40) was named dean of this division. Skelton had been the specialist in 4-H club work and had also been assistant director of agricultural extension work since 1962. William Daughtrey, the director of the extension service, retired in 1965, as did Professor R.D. Michael, who had edited all the publications of both the experiment station and the extension service. The next innovation was a name change for the Agricultural Extension Service after eighty years. Cooperative Extension Service was the new name, to comply with federal terminology. When in 1968 the popular dean of the agricultural college, Dr. Wilson B. Bell ('34), became the director of university development, Dr. James E. Martin, agricultural economics chair, succeeded him as dean. Some other retirements around 1970 took away mentors familiar to several generations of dairymen and cattlemen educated at VPI. These included Professor Paul M. Reaves in dairy science, Professor G.D. Kite ('31) in agricultural engineering, and Professor P.H. "Pat" DeHart ('29) associate dean of the extension division. [30]

Virginia Farms Have Long Histories

In 1997 the Virginia General Assembly authorized the establishment of the Century Farm program to recognize farms that have been owned by the same family for one hundred years or more. There are three requirements for inclusion in the program: the farm must have been owned by the same family for at least one hundred consecutive years, it must be lived on or actually farmed by a descendant of the original owner, and it must gross more than $2,500 annually from the sale of farm products. A certificate of recognition and an aluminum exterior sign are issued to the owner of each Century Farm. Fifty-two new farms were recognized as Century Farms in 2001 and thirty-five more in 2002. By 2003, there were 682 Century Farms scattered across eighty-seven counties and five independent cities of Virginia.

A more elite designation for Virginia's farms with a long history was formulated in the 1970s. With the approach of the Bicentennial of American Independence, the Virginia Farm Bureau board of directors created a Bicentennial Farms program to recognize farms that had been in the same family for 200 years. By 1980, ninety-six such farms had been recognized.

Smithfield, in Southwest Virginia, is a 1,260-acre farm located in the scenic valley along Elk Garden Creek near Rosedale. Its long history has earned Bicentennial Farm honors. This farming operation has been continuously owned and operated by eight generations of the Smith family since

Smithfield through the years – top, 1909; center, ca. 1960; and bottom, 2000

Dr. James R. Nichols

In 1964 Dr. James R. Nichols, a Tennessee native who was teaching at Penn State, became head of the Dairy Science Department. His undergraduate course on dairy cattle genetics brought the latest developments in that increasingly important field to the future dairy leadership of Virginia. Nichols became associate dean in 1969, but departed in 1971 to become executive vice president and general manager of Select Sires in Ohio. In 1973 he returned to Virginia Tech and in 1975 became dean of the College of Agriculture, a position he held until 1994. Virginia dairy leaders routinely comment that he built the dairy science program at Tech into one of the finest in the nation by recruiting outstanding faculty members such as Dr. R.G. Saacke, Dr. Ray Murley, Dr. Paul Chandler, and Dr. Carl Polan. Dr. Saacke's work in reproduction physiology has been widely published and recognized. Dr. Polan's research in animal nutrition, especially for dairy cattle, garnered him recognition from the Virginia Forage and Grasslands Council, among others. In 2000 the National Dairy Shrine honored "Doc Jim" Nichols as its Guest of Honor, at the World Dairy Expo, one of the dairy industry's most prestigious awards.[32]

A program that would have a significant impact on dairy education at Virginia Tech began in September of 1972. This was the Set-Aside Program, which James Nichols and Ray Cragle helped to create. Cragle approached every cooperative director in the state to obtain the organization's backing. In this voluntary program, 0.14 percent, or $1.40 out of every $1,000, of a dairy farmer's milk check is deducted by the co-op and sent to the Virginia State Dairymen's Association. The VSDA sends a significant portion of this to the Dairy Science Department at Virginia Tech to support research, technical assistance, teaching assistants, and scholarships.[33]

So many changes of organization and personnel in such a short time were difficult to absorb, especially for those who had been in the system for many years and were comfortable with it. The transformation of VPI from a college forbidden to include instruction in any areas outside agriculture, engineering, and science to a full-fledged land grant university offering undergraduate and advanced degrees in all areas, was dramatic. It went remarkably well, and those who had deep reservations about it initially generally understood that this was a more modern expression of the institute's original mission to provide service to the people of Virginia.

1774. The mid-nineteenth-century house is also a Virginia Historic Landmark and on the National Register of Historic Places.

Henry Smith (1741-1801) of Stafford County, Virginia was reputed to have been a "long hunter" and it was probably on one of his early journeys into Kentucky that he spotted the two tracts along the Clinch that he would later settle. The first two parcels of land in what is now Russell County were surveyed in 1774: one was 464 acres at the head of Mallory Hollow (this tract is on the Clifton Farm, part of the Stuart Land and Cattle Company) and the second was 214 acres where the present-day Smithfield is located. His brother, General Daniel Smith, surveyed these tracts for the Loyal Land Company. Both tracts are owned by descendents today.

In 1776, the Henry Smith family left Stafford County for the Clinch with slaves, horses, and cattle. Henry's wife Mary James was three months pregnant with their third child. In the same year they built a log house at Clifton, a couple of miles up the river

Smithfield as seen from Red Hill

175

New Times and New Directions

The Extension Division moved rapidly in new directions, responding to demands from the urban and suburban areas where Virginia's growth was occurring. Familiar titles of county agent and farm agent, used for half a century, were replaced with the term extension agent. Some extension programs, such as 4-H, began to have a major impact on urban and suburban areas. Enrollment in 4-H more than doubled, and where it had been eighty-five percent rural, its country component was now just forty percent, reflecting more accurately the population distribution in the Commonwealth.[34] Virginia Cooperative Extension, operating through Virginia Tech at Blacksburg and Virginia State University at Petersburg, has, as the Commonwealth enters the twenty-first century, 107 county extension offices, six 4-H educational centers, and thirteen Agricultural Research and Extension Centers. The center that is of special significance for the beef industry is the Shenandoah Valley Agricultural Research and Extension Center at the McCormick Farm in Steeles Tavern. The research focus there is on livestock production and forage, especially on breeding, reproduction, nutrition, and management of livestock, alternative feed for cattle, and controlled grazing and forage systems. The Middleburg Agricultural Research and Extension Center that Paul Mellon had donated in 1949 was used for dairy and beef, but mainly for beef cattle research, for forty years, but has become an equine research center.[35]

The federal government's Department Reorganization Act in 1994 impacted the Cooperative State Research Service and the Extension Service. These two USDA agencies were combined into a single agency, the Cooperative State Research, Education, and Extension Service (CSREES). Its mission was to advance knowledge of agriculture, the environment, human health and well-being, and communities by supporting research in the Land Grant Universities as well as in other federal agencies and community organizations. Competitive Funding, Formula Programs, and Congressionally Directed Funding are all aspects of the way that CSREES supports and carries out its mission.[36]

In 1989, an excellent new agricultural teaching facility was dedicated. The building was named Litton-Reaves Hall in honor of Professors George Litton and Paul Reaves, whose influence through their teaching careers had been exceptional. Reaves was present to

from the original Mallory Hollow tract. Family records state that this house was shingled with red cedar, which lasted one hundred years, and the nails for the house were wrought in Staunton. Later, they built a cabin on the 214-acre tract because of its proximity to the fort at Elk Garden and the protection from Indian attacks that it provided. Henry Smith was the first surveyor of Russell County. His handwritten notation of how he sighted a mark on House and Barn Mountain to calibrate his surveyor's compass may be found in Survey Book 1.

In the appraisal of the estate of Henry Smith, dated 21 July 1801, 122 cattle were valued at £349, 2 shillings or $9.54 each. This was the period in which the United States was gradually converting its monetary system from pounds sterling to dollars.

Smithfield passed in the following order to the present day: Henry Smith II (1774-1850); Dr. John Taylor Smith (1805-1862) built the present day house "Smithfield" in 1850; Major John Henry Anderson Smith (1847-1879); John Henry Anderson Smith II (1876-1941); William Gilkeson Smith (1908-1973); John Henry Anderson Smith III (b.1950); John Henry Anderson Smith IV (b. 1977); and William Isaac Smith (b.1979).

The Elk Garden area of Russell County where Smithfield still stands is historically known as one of the finest areas for grazing cattle in Virginia due primarily to its altitude, limestone soils, and lush bluegrass pasture. After 230 years and eight generations, quality cattle production continues there today. ~

A special thanks for this article goes to the current owner of Smithfield, John Henry Smith, who compiled the history of his homeplace. Information was also taken from "Virginia Century Farm Program Continues to Expand," *The Virginia Cattleman* (April 2003): 38; J. Hiram Zigler, and *The Virginia Farm Bureau Story: Growth of a Grassroots Organization*, (published by the Virginia Farm Bureau, 1982, 112-116 and the Virginia Department of Agriculture and Consumer Services website www.vdacs.state.va.us.

give the dedicatory address, and John L. Miller served as master of ceremonies for the occasion.

Two significant recent developments at Virginia Tech are the construction of state-of-the-art livestock facilities. The 49,260 square-foot Alphin-Stuart Multipurpose Livestock Arena has a 31,250 square-foot arena floor with seating for 800, an office, a kitchen-concession area, a livestock holding area, and classrooms. In addition to the lead gifts from Col. and Mrs. Horace E. Alphin of Clifton and the late Patricia Bonsall Stuart of Albemarle County, commodity groups, individuals, corporations, foundations, and the Virginia General Assembly provided the funding for the new facility. Located on the Animal Science Farm across the road from the Beef Cattle Center, the Livestock Judging Pavilion, and the Campbell Arena, the new facility was dedicated in April of 2004. The keynote speaker was Congressman Robert Goodlatte, Sixth District Virginia, Chairman of the House Agricultural Committee.[37] The Dairy Cattle Center was dedicated in July of 2004. The 54,542-square-foot complex replaced the school's old free stall barn, milking parlor and milk room, and research barn, with four state-of-the-art structures.[38]

Leading figures in Virginia dairy circles spoke at the ceremony, including John L. Miller; Dale A. Gardner of VSDA; State Senator John H. Chichester; J. Carlton Courter, III, Commissioner of Agriculture; David M. Hardesty of Harvue Farms; Bennet Cassell, Extension Geneticist; and Dean Sharron Quisenberry. The new facility contains a double-eight rapid-exit herringbone parlor, a freestall barn with 232 stalls, and a sophisticated, state-of-the-art manure handling system.[39]

State Fair

The fair is an institution that has a long history in the culture of the English-speaking world, since at least the time of William the Conqueror in the eleventh century. The fact that fairs are mentioned in nursery rhymes and folk songs that go back several centuries and that were brought to America with colonial settlers is an indication of their importance in the lives of ordinary rural people. One of these popular rhymes has a tune familiar to many people:

> Oh, dear, what can the matter be?
> Dear, dear, what can the matter be?
> Oh, dear, what can the matter be?
> Johnny's so long at the fair.

Another rhyme, perhaps less familiar, mentions the purchasing pleasures that a fair offered to rural folk with little access to shops:

> Gee up, Neddy, to the fair;
> What shall we buy when we get there?
> A penny apple and a penny pear;
> Gee up Neddy, to the fair.

In England the fair served as a larger market and entertainment place. In America, by contrast, fairs generally have their roots in agricultural education efforts. A fair was held in Richmond as early as the 1700s, but little information survives about its purposes and activities. Early American fairs usually featured livestock shows, demonstrations, and exhibits that highlighted excellence of crops, livestock, food preparation, and crafts.

In the 1970s, William Harrison, agriculture Extension agent from Loudoun County, gave a talk at the State Holstein Field Day at Walter McClure's farm in Rocky Mount, Virginia.

Many American fairs trace their origins to the mid-nineteenth century, when agricultural improvement organizations often sponsored them as a means to introduce new methods to local farmers. An example of such an antebellum fair was the event organized in 1854 by the Virginia State Agricultural Society in Richmond, featuring booths at which merchants could exhibit and demonstrate new manufacturing and agricultural methods. Although the Civil War interrupted the Richmond event, it resumed in 1867. In 1877, the recently elected President Rutherford B. Hayes attended the event.[40] Originally, Monroe Park was the site of this fair but later it moved to a West Broad Street location, near where the Broad Street train station was later built and that is now the Science Museum. The fair expanded at its Broad Street site, but in the depression of the 1890s could not manage its debt, so the state fair ceased in that form in 1896.[41]

The Augusta County Fair held in Staunton from 1868 is another good example of a local or regional event. Its guid-ing light was Colonel John Briscoe Baldwin, a member of the state legislature and a proponent of public education. Baldwin's Augusta Agricultural Society purchased twenty-one acres near the Virginia School for the Deaf and Blind as its fairgrounds. Colonel Matthew Fontaine Maury, "Path-finder of the Seas," and General Robert E. Lee both journeyed from Lexington to visit the 1868 fair in Staunton. The annual event continued successfully for many years, changing its name in 1873 to the Baldwin-Augusta Fair to honor its deceased founder, then in 1889 to the Baldwin District Fair. In 1913 the event moved to the city's Gypsy Hill Park, where barns, two racetracks, grandstands, cattle show rings, and other features accommodated the activities. By the 1920s, crowds attending reached 70,000. One of the most popular features at that time was the "baby beeves show" in which young boys and girls showed the beeves they had selected, fed, and prepared for show – a forerunner of today's Market Animal Show.[42]

While an excellent local fair such as that in Staunton filled the need for many, others regretted the loss of a state-

A dozen Shorthorn export cattle are judged at a fair in Tazewell County, ca. 1915.

wide fair. A stock company with a board of directors had formally incorporated in 1906 as the Virginia State Fair Association to bring back the statewide event that had folded a decade earlier. Westward growth of the city made the West Broad Street site impractical, so the association rented land from the city that had been the old Bryan estate at North Boulevard and Hermitage Road. This later became Parker Field, and is currently the Diamond. By at least the 1930s, Charles A. Somma was the general manager of the fair and owned 1,549 of the 2,640 outstanding shares of the stock. During World War II, the government took over the fairground and it served as a military transportation depot. At this time, the Virginia State Fair Association purchased the old Davenport Estate called "Strawberry Hill" for its new site. Government restrictions made it impossible for the association to undertake any improvements to the site until the war was over. Meanwhile, Somma, the principal stockholder in the association, died.[43]

There had been talk in cattle circles of the value of having a top quality exposition center to serve the growing purebred livestock interests along the Atlantic seaboard. Forward looking breeders were aware that they could not compete in size with major cattle and sheep

operations in the west, but that they could compete in the production of high quality livestock through breed improvement. The availability of a livestock exposition to host quality shows, like the centers in Denver, Chicago, Kansas City, and Fort Worth, would be a boon to that effort. One of the early proponents of this idea was Colonel John Tyssowski, a pioneering Hereford breeder at his Cobbler Mountain Farms in Fauquier County since 1926.[44]

About the time that the Virginia Beef Cattle Producers Association (VBCPA) was formed and received its state appropriation in 1944, Charles Somma died. His estate was due for probate in August of 1944. This caused a number of breeders and businessmen with livestock interests, including Colonel Tyssowski, to raise funds to purchase the Somma stock and develop the old State Fair Association into an exposition in Richmond, of which the state fair would be a part. The VBCPA played an important role in raising the initial $75,000 to purchase the stock. The Somma stock was bought at its book value of $46 per share. With control of the corporate assets that included a new 460-acre fair site on the north side of Richmond, the committee was ready to launch the Atlantic Rural Exposition (ARE).

The new organization developed plans to construct a purebred sales pavilion so that the ARE could become the center for purebred livestock sales and shows for the entire east coast. The facilities were to include meeting space for local, state, and national breed associations and other agricultural societies. To raise the funds for construction of the facilities, the additional stock in the company was offered at the same $46 per share, and purchasers were encouraged to donate their stock to a foundation for the extension of rural education that included the ARE. In Sep-

A cattle show at Gypsy Hill fairgrounds in Staunton

tember of 1944, Paul Swaffar was hired away from VPI to be executive secretary of the VBCPA and also general manager of the Atlantic Rural Exposition.[45]

On April 25 and 25, 1946, the first fat stock show took place on the new ARE grounds. Of the 434 head of fat cattle shown, 268 were 4-H club steers. The grand champion was an Angus steer shown by 4-H member Bobby Swecker of Blue Grass in Highland County. His 870-pound steer sold for $1,087 to the Country Club of Virginia. Reserve champion was a Hereford steer shown by Dale Higginbotham of Sandiges.[46] The first Atlantic Rural Exposition took place in October 1946 at the site where building construction was underway, with exhibitors from as far away as Massachusetts and Florida. The new coliseum housed 500 cattle and included a judging arena and adjoining barns. In addition to "all of the aspects of a great state fair" that were present, including automobile races that packed the new fireproof grandstand, there was "a livestock show equal in quality in its first effort equally as good as any in the east." The Aberdeen Angus show drew the greatest crowds, with the Clark ranch in Warrenton taking the grand champion bull honors.[47]

For eight years, from 1946 to 1954, Staunton was host city for a competing event, held at the Gypsy Hill fairgrounds now Gypsy Hill Park, that billed itself as the State Fair of Virginia.[48]

Leading members of the cattle industry continued to serve on the board of the state fair. An example is R. Henry Matthiessen, Jr., of Still House Hollow Farm at Hume. Matthiessen's father had been a partner of Colonel Tyssowski in their original Hereford operation. The younger Matthiessen was made a director and member of the ex-

ecutive committee of the State Fair of Virginia (ARE) and soon also chaired its livestock committee.[49]

During the 1970s and 1980s, Drs. Arden Huff and George Morrow were in charge of the agricultural programs for the September state fair. The typical shows for the cattle industry at that time included the Junior Steer, the Junior Heifer, the Angus Breeding Cattle, the FFA Bull, the Shorthorn Breeding Cattle, the Horned Hereford, the Charolais Breeding Cattle, the Belted Galloway, and the Polled Hereford Show. Besides the various beef cattle shows, there was also a comprehensive all breeds dairy cattle show and a number of junior dairy shows.[50]

In 1985, the board of directors of the Atlantic Rural Exposition came to the understanding that non-fair activities should be expanded. They concluded that a medium sized, high quality exhibition building was required and approved the building of a 67,000-square-foot facility. In 1991 the board approved a seven-million-dollar industrial bond funding for additional improvements. Two million dollars went into a classic amphitheater to seat 10,000 for a wide range of events and entertainment. Three facilities, the Home Arts and the Commonwealth buildings and the Better Living Center, were extensively renovated and a new covered ring for horse activities was built.[51]

By 1993, 1.6 million visitors were attracted annually to some 150 events at Strawberry Hill. A ten-year strategic plan looked to the development and expansion of the fair in the future, with a strong emphasis on youth. The establishment in 1994 of the merit scholarship endowment in honor of Herbert Bruce Thomson, first chairman of the Atlantic Rural Exposition, represented a commitment to the emphasis on

youth and education. The State Fair of Virginia purchased The Meadow in Caroline County in 1999. There it hopes to build a permanent home for the state fair. The principal activities regarding beef and dairy cattle that now take place at the state fair are those organized for youth. These are the Youth Dairy Competitions that include showing and fitting of all breeds, a Brown Swiss and Guernsey competition, an Ayrshire and Jersey competition, and a Holstein competition. For beef cattle, the competitions for youth are breeding cattle, feeder steers, market animals, and showmanship.[52]

In the 1950s one of the sponsors of bull shows for youngsters was the Sears Roebuck Company. Hereford bulls from a western ranch were provided to FFA chapters, then the bulls were brought to ARE for the bull show. The prize was a silver bowl provided by Sears. In 2003, as a fiftieth anniversary celebration of the event, the state fair invited everyone who had won a Sears silver bowl to come back to the fairgrounds for a reunion. Many returned to the scene of their youthful triumph, bringing their bowls with them for a charming photo opportunity.[53]

The state fair organization was streamlined in 2004 to include a twenty-five member voluntary board of directors representing all regions of Virginia, which would have oversight of all fair activities such as budgeting, strategic planning, and policy formulation. There are twenty-five staff members and 2,000 volunteers. A fund of nearly one million dollars is under management to produce income for scholarships.

"Caretakers All," the beef industry's environment kit, is being discussed in a classroom. Teachers say the educational kit encourages student participation through various activities.

Farm Bureau

The American Farm Bureau Federation was founded in Binghamton, New York, in 1911. Byers H. Gitchell of the Binghamton Chamber of Commerce realized that the city's economic well-being depended on the success of area farmers. He sought advice from the United States Department of Agriculture, Cornell University's agricultural college, and the local Delaware and Lackawanna Railroad about how best to promote the prosperity of local farmers. At the Department of Agriculture, Dr. W.J. Spillman, chief of the Office of Farm Management of the Bureau of Plant Industry, was studying how to make new scientific information available to ordinary farmers so that they could benefit from it. From a Spillman meeting with Gitchell in Binghamton came the federation motto, "Make Every Farm a Demonstration Farm," and the notion of engaging a local agricultural advisor. Gitchell employed John H. Barron in Broome County, New York, as head of the Farm Bureau of the Binghamton Chamber of Commerce, the first known farm bureau in the nation. Over the next three years, a number of other communities followed this example, usually calling the advisors county agents.[54]

Through the work of Dr. John R. Hutcheson, and the advice of Dr. Seaman A. Knapp, extension and demonstration work had begun in Virginia in 1907 under T.O. Sandy. A number of county agents were appointed, including an agent from Hampton Institute, J.B. Pierce, to work with black farmers. The passage of the Smith-Lever Act in 1914 gave official recognition to county agents and provided one-half of their salaries if the state or local community paid the other half. About 1,000 county agents were in place in 1916, but the entry of the United States into the World War brought a sudden need to maximize food production. Emergency funds put another 1,200 county agents into place by 1918. With the help of local farm bureaus, they raised much of the matching money.[55]

These county agents in Virginia and other states pushed for an organization of local farmers to systematize production and marketing of food to avoid waste. The local county organizations founded for that purpose with the help of county agents, took on the name Farm Bureau. County farm bureaus soon banded together into state farm bureaus. By the end of World War I, fourteen states had a state farm bureau organization representing nearly every county in each of those states. The functioning of the state farm bureaus led naturally to the notion of a national farm bureau. At a meeting in Chicago in March of 1920 the twenty-eight states represented organized the American Farm Bureau Federation.[56]

Virginia records are hazy but apparently the first Farm Bureau was organized in Wythe County in 1921 with Governor Henry C. Stuart of Elk Garden, Russell County, as its president. Stuart, one of the leading cattlemen in the East, had a strong interest in marketing and transportation issues pertaining to farmers and cattlemen and these were the very issues that the Farm Bureau addressed. Another Virginian interested in the Farm Bureau movement was J.S. Quisenberry, who attended the first meeting of the American Farm Bureau Federation in Chicago. Rockingham County had a Farm Bureau in 1921 and Montgomery County by 1922. D.H. Barger reported for Virginia at the 1921 national meeting and G.F. Holsinger did the same in 1923.

In 1924, Virginia had met the national requirements for a voting representative. The Virginia Farm Bureau Federation was incorporated on February 24, 1926, with "Captain" Daniel H. Barger as president. Barger, a banker and Norfolk and Western official who raised cattle on his Walnut Grove farm at Shawsville, Montgomery County, was an associate of Governor Stuart. From 1926 through 1929 Gabriel F. Holsinger of McGaheysville, president of the Rockingham Cooperative Farm Bureau and a member of the original board of directors of the Virginia Farm Bureau, represented the state federation at the national meeting and became president of the state federation in 1928. Holsinger, a dairy farmer and former high school principal, was an early advocate of scientific livestock breeding.[57]

Issues that the state Farm Bureau studied and took positions on in the difficult Depression years included taxes, freight rates, credit methods to prevent foreclosures, highway improvement taxes, soil surveys, and reforestation projects. Rockingham and Augusta Counties dominated the state organization in the early years because of the large membership and their cooperative stores, but twenty Farm Bureaus were represented at the 1938 state meeting.

The 1940s brought expansion and strengthening of the organization. The Farm Bureau Associated Women organized and met at the time of the annual meeting and beginning in 1942 had a representative on the board of directors. The

first issue of the *Virginia Farm Bureau News* appeared in February of 1941 and continued monthly ever since. When the United States entered World War II, the Farm Bureau opposed Daylight Savings Time and the forty-hour workweek, and favored ceilings on wages and a deferred draft status for experienced farm laborers and extension agents. In the forties, the Farm Bureau began to question the price support system of the Roosevelt New Deal and also began to move away from being a merchandizing organization in order to concentrate on making and implementing farm policy. By 1944, membership had increased fifty percent to 12,712.[58]

Hereford cattle await transport in stockyards along the Norfolk and Western Railroad in Tazewell County.

By the time President G.F. Holsinger retired in 1948, the Farm Bureaus in Virginia had increased from one to sixty-seven. Under the brief presidency of his successor, Howard S. Zigler, a fruit grower and poultryman, the state Farm Bureau re-organized its finances and organized the Virginia Farm Bureau Mutual Insurance Company. In the presidency of Horace Guy Blalock a dairyman and tobacco farmer of Mecklenburg County, the state organization reformed its board selection method and began operating its insurance company.[59] The fifth president was Roy B. Davis, Jr., a livestock and tobacco farmer from Halifax County. Under his leadership, the Virginia Farm Bureau Federation offices moved to the 200 block of West Grace Street into a building that the affiliated Farm Bureau Insurance Company had purchased. T.T. (Terry) Curtis, an Orange County dairyman, County Extension Agent, and director of the Maryland-Virginia Milk Producers Association, was president from 1959 to 1962. He encouraged political involvement of farmers through "Measure the Candidate" meetings and served during the important time that the organization reviewed its earlier stand in favor of price supports and increased its emphasis on the importance of marketing and of expanding foreign markets. The Virginia (Farm Bureau) Agricultural Marketing Association resulted from these efforts. In addition, the board initiated the appointment of commodity committees, including one each for dairy and for livestock. Membership had increased to 23,000.[60]

Robert B. Delano, a former VPI Extension Service staff member and a dairyman and grain farmer from Richmond County, took over the leadership reins in 1962. With the help of the capable executive secretary Maury A. Hubbard, a highly skilled lobbyist, the Virginia Farm Bureau Federation mobilized its county bureaus in an effort to defeat the "Wheat Referendum" program of U.S. Secretary of Agriculture Orville Freeman. This initiative called for the creation of a quota system of production on the nation's farms. In the referendum on May 21, 1963, Virginia farmers voted a majority of negative votes, and nationwide the proposal failed to receive the necessary two-thirds majority.

In Virginia, the state federation built its own large office complex that occupied an entire city block on West Grace Street. Delano appointed a committee to investigate expanded services to the membership. In its study, the committee organized a study tour of state and county Farm Bureaus in Michigan, Illinois, and Tennessee, in which 168 state and county Farm Bureau leaders from sixty-seven counties participated. As a result of the study, an extensive program of expanded services, by-laws revision, legislative emphasis, educational programming, and expanded marketing was adopted by delegates to a special Virginia Farm Bureau Federation convention in Roanoke on June 1, 1965. The favorable vote resulted in a reorganization of the administrative structure of the organization, with Delano becoming the federation's first full-time chief executive officer.[61]

Matters that engaged the organization in the 1970s included increased political lobbying over issues, rather than endorsement of a party or a candidate; environmental concerns that affected farming, such as the impact of Environmental Protection Agency regulations; the effects of the new Occupational Safety and Health Administration (OSHA) regulations on farmers; health service delivery to Farm Bureau members; and marketing expansion. The Farm Bureau created a marketing association that many cattle producers thought should become directly involved in buying and selling cattle through qualified marketing agents.

The marketing association was funded with interest-bearing certificates of indebtedness that were purchased by farmers intending to use and benefit from the marketing services. Another timely program was the creation of Farm Bureau Young Farmer Committees to encourage leadership potential in the nineteen to thirty-year-old age group. By the end of the decade the membership had reached 55,000 families and the annual budget was over a million dollars.[62]

The decade of the 1980s saw further expansion in the organization, with membership passing 65,000 and the annual budget exceeding $1.5 million. Robert Delano, the longtime and successful president of the state organization was chosen vice-president of the American Farm Bureau Federation in 1975 and president in 1980. In 1981 and 1982, *U.S. News and World Report* named this Virginia dairyman one of the three most influential agricultural leaders in the United States. Samuel Thomas Moore, Jr., an agricultural engineering graduate of VPI and a livestock and tobacco farmer of South Hill, Mecklenburg County, succeeded to the presidency of the state federation in 1980. Under his leadership the organization of eighty-seven county Farm Bureaus counted 79,000 families across the Commonwealth as members.[63]

Behind the Scenes

These organizations that function "behind the scenes" each play a significant role in forming the network that supports the beef and dairy farmers of Virginia. One of the most important means by which they carry on their work is through the highly developed system of education that stretches from childhood through graduate school and the ongoing lifetime adult education. Educational efforts have evolved from the modest programs of agricultural high schools in the early years of the twentieth century to the remarkably complex and technical graduate education of the opening years of the twenty-first century. Outside the walls of the schoolroom and the university is the informal education of the 4-H clubs for youth and of the extension service for adults. The range of fairs, from county to state, provide a competitive and fun way to bring farmers together to learn from each other through friendly rivalry. The Farm Bureau also forms underpinning for the everyday business of operating a farm, with its need for services, insurance, purchasing power, marketing, and lobbying on issues of importance to the farming community. Each institution, organization, or business involved has played a significant role in supporting the beef and dairy farmers of Virginia, championing their needs, and preparing them to handle the challenges of a rapidly changing industry. ◗

Milk Goes Modern

Three hundred years after the first permanent settlement at Jamestown, the citizens of Virginia and of the entire country came together for a grand celebration of history and progress at the 1907 Jamestown Exposition. With the nation watching, the Virginia Polytechnic Institute dairy department, under the direction of Professor W.D. Saunders, hatched a bold idea. The professor, affectionately called "Cheese" and "Buttermilk," was known for his habit of carrying cheddar cheese in his pocket. Upon encountering friends, he would cut off a piece of it and offer it to them. This eccentricity aside, he was dedicated to promoting the modern dairy industry in the state. Saunders knew that the Jamestown Exposition would help prove that Virginia could be a major player in that industry. His plan was simple but revolutionary: taking fresh whole milk from the dairy herd at VPI, which was milked daily, he would store it in ten-gallon cans. The cans would be placed inside insulation bags, covered with ice, loaded on railroad cars, and shipped greater than 250 miles by rail from Blacksburg to the exposition dining hall in Newport News. The successful sanitary handling, refrigeration, rapid shipment, and direct delivery of the milk every day of the exposition would prove that Virginia's dairy industry had come of age.[1]

Because of the vision of men like Professor Saunders, the daily delivery of milk was commonplace in Virginia by the 1920s.

187

An Association for Virginia's Dairymen

Saunder's milk shipment was certainly a sensational gambit to promote Virginia as a milk-producing state, but a second, more-important result emerged from the Jamestown Exposition. While at the exposition, a number of individuals interested in the state dairy industry conducted a series of meetings to explore cooperative efforts that would benefit all in the industry. The enthusiasm spilled over into more meetings, organized in November of 1907 by Professor Saunders and Dr. Walter J. Quick, Dean of Agriculture at VPI. Before the end of the year the Virginia State Dairymen's Association (VSDA) had been organized and chartered. It was one of the earliest organizations of its kind in the United States.[2] Charter members in addition to Drs. Quick and Saunders were: James Bellwood, Manchester; T.L. Blanton, Richmond; T.J. Davis, Lassiter; Westmoreland Davis, Leesburg; Dr. J.G. Ferneyhough, Burkeville; Dr. A.W. Freeman; Richmond; A.W. Haxall, Middleburg; C.W. Holdaway, Blacksburg; J.F. Jackson, Richmond; D.S. Jones, Newport News; Professor Lane, Washington, D.C.; H.T. Pancoast, Purcellville; Benjamin L. Purcell, Richmond;

T.O. Sandy, Burkeville; A.R. Scott, Richmond; J.O. Scott, Richmond; B. Morgan Shepherd, Richmond; C.L. Stahl, Lynchburg; Joseph A. Turner, Hollins; Major A.R. Venable, Farmville; Frank S. Walker, Orange; and Joseph Wilmer, Rapidan.[3] T.O. Sandy was elected president, Westmoreland Davis was chosen vice-president, and Saunders was secretary-treasurer.[4] Davis, whose Morven Park estate exemplified the most modern and productive agricultural operations in the state, went on to become governor of Virginia from 1918 to 1922.

The creation of the USDA did not mark the beginning of dairying in Virginia, but it did signal the entrance of the state's dairy farmers into the modern dairy industry. Virginia's dairy farmers did not take a giant step overnight in 1907, rather, they had taken a series of small steps over the previous half century. The formation of the VSDA marked the coming together of breed development, technology such as the railroad, scientific advances that led to better understanding of animal diseases, the push for agricultural education and agricultural quality control, and a strong, cooperative marketing sense by some of Virginia's most forward-thinking farmers.

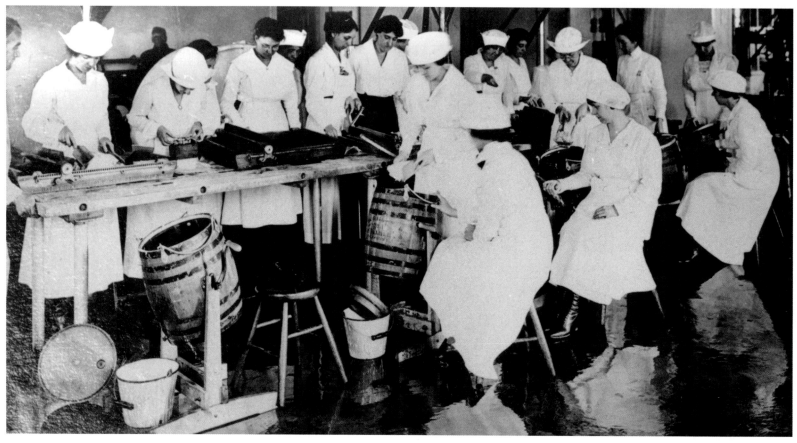

Women making butter in a factory-type setting, possibly in the basement of Price Hall at VPI, in the early twentieth century.

Old Dominion Cheesemakers

By the 1840s and 1850s, farmers often produced more milk and butter than could be consumed at home. Large amounts of butter were shipped to the more urban areas of the state. Heavily salted butter was also sold to the Caribbean sugar plantations, where it was an important part of laborers' diets. Later in the century, farmers moved fresh milk short distances by wagon to sell

W.D. "Cheese" Saunders

to city dwellers who did not have the luxury of a family milk cow. Without reliable refrigeration, however, shipping whole milk or cream by railroad remained impractical. In 1871, an effort to ship milk from Augusta County to Richmond by locomotive failed.[5] Unlike fluid milk, hard cheese could be shipped long distances, but with a few notable exceptions cheesemaking never became a commercially important component of the Virginia dairy industry. Perhaps the most successful antebellum commercial cheesemaking venture arose in Prince William County in 1845. Samuel Look of that northern Virginia county decided to sell his month-old spring calves for veal at four dollars apiece and turn his milk into cheese from April through November of each year. The venture proved so profitable that the idea spread to the surrounding counties of Loudoun and Fauquier. The numbers were appealing: each of the farmer's thirty cows produced enough milk to make two pounds of cheese a day. Cheese sold in the city of Washington, D.C. for ten cents a pound. Additionally, the whey left over from

Photos at right are of Virginia's cheese production factories (from top) Elk Creek, Spring Valley, Independence, and Eureka. In the photo above, a truck is loaded with cheese for delivery. All photos are ca. 1930.

cheesemaking, together with corn, could fatten twenty hogs. Although profitable three ways – veal, cheese, and pork – the novice cheesemakers found it hard to break into a business that was flooded with well-known cheesemakers from the northern states.[6]

Late in the century, a cluster of cheesemaking enterprises arose in Rockingham County. In the 1890s, Gottlieb Ritz, a German-Swiss cheesemaker from Wisconsin, and his brother-in-law, Adolph Wolters, opened the Linville Cheese Company. The two men revamped an old stone barn into a storeroom and began buying milk from neighboring farmers. They also marketed their cheese to local stores. In 1900, while peddling their wares, they located a building in Broadway that would serve as a site for expansion. Eventually the Linville cheese factory relocated to Edom in order to be closer to the second cheese making branch in Broadway. The Edom and Broadway branches made cheese on differing days and shared laborers. Apparently the cheese business was lucrative; another entrepreneur opened a similar business in Lacey Spring around 1900. The Rockingham cheese makers eventually marketed their product throughout the Valley of Virginia and even to Richmond, Norfolk, and Charlotte, North Carolina. Wholesale prices at the time were between nine and twelve cents per pound. By 1920, however, all three operations had become victims of tough marketing tactics from northern and western cheese producers. They closed their doors or converted to creameries.[7]

Early in the twentieth century, the United States Department of Agriculture encouraged cooperative cheesemaking in the Appalachian Highlands. The first cheese factory was established in Sugar Grove, North Carolina, in 1915. Others soon followed in Tennessee, West Virginia, and Virginia. By 1917, more than $125,000 worth of cheese was produced in thirty-four factories in the mountainous areas of those states. The USDA yearbook noted that "cheese making brings prosperity to the farmers of the southern mountains."[8] VPI's "Cheese" Saunders promoted small-scale cheese making enterprises around the state. He always carried the blueprints for a simple cheese making building and pushed

Sidney Thomas Beam of Swoope stands with a dairy heifer.

the idea of cheese production as a cottage industry. As a result of his work, remarkably similar looking cheesemaking factories sprang up all over the state.

Despite notable failures and small successes in the early twentieth century, it was clear that a division of labor between farm and factory had occurred in the dairy industry. Increasingly, the production of butter, cheese, and even ice cream took place off the farm, in a factory that used whole milk or cream sent from the farm.

Dairying Comes of Age

Specialization also occurred on the farm where farmers raised either dairy or beef animals, purchased machinery and tools specifically for either dairy or beef farming, and chose animals that exemplified either the ideal beef or dairy animal. An agricultural manual published in 1909 made the point clearly that specialization was the wave of the future:

Just as there are two distinct types of horses, the roadster and the draft horse, so there are two distinct types of cattle, – the dairy and the beef breeds. In both cases, there are many common animals that do not belong to either class. As a horse cannot be best for both speed and draft purposes, so a cow cannot excel for both meat and milk. A few cattle are bred for both purposes. These are called dual-purpose breeds, but none of these breeds is extensively raised, as they cannot compete with either the dairy or the beef breeds. The effort to develop a great dual-purpose breed must always fail.[9]

Dairy producers were encouraged to improve their herds by using purebred sires.

Dairy Cows vs. Beef Cows
What are the differences?*

	DAIRY	BEEF
Form	Wedge-shaped	Rectangular
Head	Small, long, narrow	Small, but thick
Neck	Fine, medium length, thin	Short, thick
Shoulders	Thin, lean, bony	Heavy, well-fleshed, wide between front legs, wide on top just behind shoulders
Back	Crooked	Straight
Loin (back)	Not fleshy	Broad, thick, fleshy
Flank	High	Low
Hindquarters	Thin	Full, heavy
Udder and milk veins	Large, prominent	Not prominent

*(Source: *Elements of Agriculture* by G.F. Warren, New York: The MacMillan Company, 1914, 322-323)

The author went on to explain that the dairy animal was wedge-shaped with a small, long, and narrow head; thin, lean, and bony shoulders; a crooked back; a high flank; and thin thighs. A beef animal frame was rectangular with a small, thick head. The shoulders were heavy and well-fleshed; the back was straight; the flank low; and the thighs full and heavy.[10]

The rise of dairy breed associations and stringent record keeping for purebred herds made a dramatic impact on production. By the mid-twentieth century, Virginia's dairy animals, infused with blood from Jersey, Guernsey, Ayrshire, Shorthorn, and Holstein cattle, had reached production levels never dreamed of in the nineteenth century. Progressive farmers such as Westmoreland Davis joined breed organizations and worked hard to keep their herds pure. Davis was also a member of the voluntary national organization known as The Pure Bred Sire League. Its members carried a card with the following pledge:

1) As soon and so far as possible to use only pure bred, registered sires in the production of all farm animals;
2) To advocate the general use of such sires;
3) To work for the betterment of pure bred sires in breed-character, individual excellence, quality, size, soundness and prepotence;
4) To discourage the use of grade, mongrel or scrub sires, and all sires and dams irrespective of breeding, that are diseased, hereditarily unsound, constitutionally unfit, or undesirable in conformation and character.[11]

The Simple Test that Changed Everything

FIG. 176. Putting the milk into the test bottle. The pipette is held at an angle with the test bottle and its point against the inside of the neck.

FIG. 177. Mixing milk and acid. A rotary motion with the bottle not pointed toward the face.

FIG. 178.
Whirling the samples

Although breeding practices and technology on the farm and in the factory revolutionized the dairy industry, nothing would have been possible without a simple test devised by the University of Wisconsin's Dr. Stephen Moulton Babcock in 1890. The professor theorized that sulfuric acid would dissolve solids in milk and release fats from the emulsion. He was right. With that test, the butterfat content of milk and cream could quickly be determined. Higher butterfat meant that more butter or cheese could be made from the milk. With the Babcock Test, the playing field was level. All milk could be evaluated and sold based upon butterfat content. The test also eliminated the dishonest practice of diluting milk with water in an attempt to gain more profit.[12]

Cooperative Herd Testing

The Babcock Test opened up a whole new world of testing consistency. In addition to improving animals through purebred programs, dairy herd improvement organizations could now judge animals on production and butterfat levels. It was no surprise that professors Saunders and Holdaway were at the forefront of the first cow testing project in Virginia. A VPI college field class in 1908 examined eight Montgomery County herds representing 130 cows and then reviewed the information with the herd owners. Project results were published in a VPI bulletin under the report title "Cooperative Herd Testing." Within a few years guidelines had been established for accurately testing milk using the Babcock Test. The system created a way to test each cow's milk production and feed consumption month-by-month and year-by-year. Both feed costs and production records based on the yield of butterfat and milk for one day each month were recorded. Local testing associations hired supervisors who would travel from herd to herd within the area, spending a day and a half a month with each herd. With rules in place, cows from any herd located anywhere in the nation could be compared. The supervisor's routine never varied. At afternoon milking he would:

1. Weigh and record milk from each cow.
2. Take a sample from each cow's milk.
3. Weigh the grain fed each cow.
4. Calculate accurately the amount of hay, silage and other roughage fed.
5. Identify each cow.
6. Secure calving dates on fresh cows and heifers.
7. Eartag new calves and make record of calf and eartag number.
8. Secure the price received for milk.
9. Determine costs to be charged for feeds.

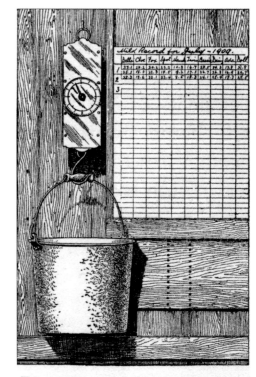

FIG. 172. Weighing the milk to find which cows pay

At the milking the next morning and for the remainder of the day he would:

10. Weigh and record milk from each cow.
11. Take a sample of milk from each cow and complete her composite sample.
12. If same amounts and kind of feed are fed as at night feeding, calculate on basis of record secured; otherwise get morning's feed record.
13. Run Babcock test for fat on each sample.
14. Calculate milk and fat production for month.
15. Calculate value of milk and fat.
16. Determine amount of feed for month.
17. Calculate value of feed for month.
18. Show amount of profit or loss over feed cost.
19. Determine herd summary for production and feed.
20. Record date in herd books.
21. Enter any new cows in herd book, listing name, registration or eartag number, date of birth, name and number of sire and dam, and when cow was fresh.
22. Summarize records that have been completed.
23. Prepare following reports to be sent to County Agent and Extension Agent: a. Monthly summary of association; b. Yearly herd summary when complete; c. Lactation records when complete, not to exceed 305 days; and d. Other records as required.
24. Discuss results of test with dairyman.
25. Participate in association affairs.[13]

Leon "Mose" Kiracofe followed the above steps nearly to the letter when he visited the twenty-one herds in Augusta County that he was hired to test. One of the reasons that Virginia had such a high quality of dairy herds lies in the fact that the state's dairy farmers encouraged dairy inspectors on their farms. That idea was reinforced by the Extension Agents across the state who coordinated the dairy herd improvement associations. Kiracofe followed that model. From 1958 until 1987, he traveled from farm to farm helping farmers improve their herds. When he first started, records were compiled "by pushing a pencil," but his methods became increasingly mechanized as the years went by. He laughs when he remembers that all of his trousers had holes in them from the sulfuric acid that splashed on him during the Babcock testing. "There has been a lot of change – going from flat barns to milking parlors. Then came better methods of feeding and forage testing," he recalled.[14]

The first Virginia group to organize and begin applying the test guidelines was the Loudoun Valley Cow Testing Association, organized in 1911. The founders included a number of prominent agriculturalists: H.T. Pancoast of Purcellville; John R. Hutcheson from VPI; Helmer Rabild from the U.S. Department of Agriculture; E.S. Hunter, the Loudoun County Extension Agent; and J.V. Nichols. The Loudoun cow testers were not only the first in Virginia, they were among the first in the nation. Another pioneer in testing was J.S. Roller of Rockingham County, who started his own testing in 1913 and the following year helped found the first Rockingham County association with seven members: Roller, J.O. Beard, Miller R. Rhodes, Ezra Minnick, W.C. Hoover, D.F. Roller, and Earl Kline. Kline served as the group's initial tester until Perry Wenger was hired in 1915. By 1916, Orange, Culpeper, and Prince William Counties had simi-

The Virginia State Epileptic Colony in Lynchburg had its herd on test.

lar organizations and 1,500 cows were enrolled.[15] By 1936, 23 dairy herd improvement associations were testing more than 14,700 cows in Virginia. In 1948, the Virginia Federation of Dairy Herd Improvement Associations was incorporated. Three years later, 57 local organizations, representing 1,042 herds and 45,303 cows were affiliated with the state group. In 1951, almost half of Virginia dairy herds of fifteen animals or more were under a testing program. That represented about ten percent of the state's milk cows. Having such concrete results made it much easier for farmers to decide which animals to breed and which to cull from the herd. The effects of different feeding programs were also reflected in the test results.

Cattle breeding organizations, which worked to improve herds through the use of bulls, sprang up alongside production testing associations. Bull exchanges, bull co-ops, and various bull lending programs were popular early in the century. After World War II, artificial breeding programs pushed bull exchanges to the background.

Massanutten Creamery in Penn Laird. The building currently serves as the community post office.

Milking Contraptions

Technological advances also rapidly pushed the industry into the modern age. In 1878, Dr. Carl DeLaval invented the first continuous discharge centrifugal separator. The machine skimmed cream off 300 pounds of milk every hour.[16] With the mass production of milk came the need to create a container in which to transport milk from the dairy to the customer door without spillage. Starting in the late 1870s and throughout the 1880s and 1890s, the market was flooded with patents on milk bottles and various types of lids. New Yorker Hervey Thatcher patented the first "modern" looking milk bottle with a tin closure and wire snap to hold the lid in place. By 1925 milk bottles sported a longer neck to display the cream line, in a more appealing way. In 1931 bottles with colored lettering, called

Bottling milk at Yoder Dairy

Pyroglaze, lined grocery shelves. As important as bottle type was, the machinery needed to fill containers was equally necessary. In 1886 an automatic bottle filler and capper was patented. By 1911 a rotary bottle filler was in use.[17]

Technology at the farm end of the milk production line progressed less swiftly. In 1898 a patent was issued to two employees at the DeLaval Company on a mechanical milker that operated by a vacuum. It proved unsuccessful. In 1903 experiments were under way on a mechanical milker that imitated hand motions, but it, too, was not practical. In 1910 a patent was issued on a better milking machine with teat presses that worked like human hands and used pneumatic pressure. It was not until 1918, after twenty-four years of research, that a practical mechanical milker was finally patented. The DeLaval Milker combined the best ideas from earlier machines developed by more than eight individuals.[18]

Even before automatic milkers had been perfected, Westmoreland Davis became enamored with them. In 1913 he purchased a six-unit machine. After it was installed in his dairy, he invited every dairyman in Virginia to see the contraption that did the work of seven men in half the time and freed up those men for other chores. According to period accounts, many of the men took Davis up on his offer, probably as much to visit the politician's estate as to see the machine.[19]

Electricity Turns on Mechanical Milkers

The adoption of the milking machine by the average Virginia farm took more time. Often it was the arrival of electricity that allowed the switch. In 1938, young Nelson Gardner of Rockingham County helped his family milk twenty-three cows by hand. When Nelson was nine years old in 1939, rural electrification brought power and milking machines to his parents' farm. "The day we got electricity, we started milking with an electric milker because my dad had it already fixed up," he recalled. The utility bill was $2.50 a month, but the labor saved was worth every penny, according to Gardner.[20]

Andrew Vincent Griffith operated Woodland Farm in Loudoun County from about 1915 until 1955. He had about 125 cows that were milked twice a day, seven days a week.

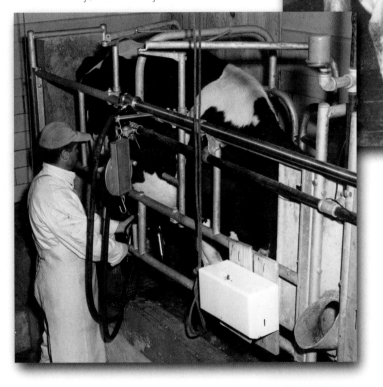

The milk was sent to Chestnut Farms Dairy in Washington, D.C. Not until the late 1940s that Griffith began using automatic milkers, but his cows were still stripped by hand. Milk was carried into the milk house, poured over a cooler, and collected in cans. Cans were picked up each day and transported to the dairy.[21]

Milking machines were by no means universal as late as 1949 when Paul M. Reaves, Professor of Dairy Husbandry at VPI, Roy H. Thomas, State Supervisor of Vocational Agriculture in North Carolina, and C.W. Pegram, Chief of Dairy Division for the North Carolina Department of Agriculture, teamed up to write a book on dairy farming in the South. The trio recommended that all dairy farmers consider acquiring such a labor saving device even if there were a few small drawbacks.

The advent of electricity revolutionized the dairy industry. Witness these dairy farms in Loudoun County: one still milking by hand (top) and one (at left) using a milking machine. In the photo below, John Middleton (standing) of Horsepen Farm, Herndon, and Neal Bailey, long-time employee, pose for a photo taken in the early 1970s for a June Dairy Month publication.

With labor being drawn away from the farm, dairymen must of necessity look to labor saving machinery. The milking machine is one that can be used every day in the year. It lessens the job of milking tremendously. There are a number of machines on the market that will do a good job of milking. Some dairymen eliminate most of the hand stripping by pulling down on the teat cups and massaging the udder just as the milking of the cow is being finished. This is called machine stripping and has proved satisfactory. Good hand milkers will do a better job than the milking machine, however the machine properly handled will do a better job than average hand milkers.[22]

By 1963, Reaves co-authored another book on dairy practices. By this time, the shift to automatic milkers was almost complete. "All commercial herds and many small herds are now milked with machines," he wrote. With machines, labor is reduced, high quality milk is produced, high production levels can be maintained, and "the milking task is made less objectionable."[23]

An Eye on Quality

By 1907 the time had been right for the creation of the state dairy association in 1907. By joining forces across the state, the industry finally had lobbying clout in Richmond. Success was immediate. The Virginia State Dairymen's Association (VSDA) asked for an appropriation of $7,500 to create a regulatory agency to safeguard the purity and sanitation of human and animal feeds. The new law, which passed unanimously, created the Dairy and Food Division in 1908 with Professor Saunders at the helm as the first commissioner. Saunders went to work right away with a large agenda. At that time, Virginia butter had a reputation for low quality. With the exception of some butter in the Shenandoah Valley and northern Virginia, most farm butter from the Commonwealth was bought by wholesalers who shipped it out of state, reprocessed it, and returned it to Virginia as "renovated butter." Saunders knew, additionally, that eighty-five percent of all dairy products sold in Virginia came from outside the Old Dominion. He believed that by enforcing standards, incorporating tests to analyze products, and, perhaps most importantly, by educating people who worked in the industry, he could make Virginia a dairy state.[24]

Growing Together

The strong dairy element, high standards, and effective educational outreach at Virginia Tech's agricultural department garnered respect from Virginia's farmers and dairy producers and created an unusual closeness not always seen between agricultural colleges and farming communities in other states. Saunders, a native of Franklin County, Virginia, came to Blacksburg as Agriculture Experiment Station Director in 1890. In 1895 he became Assistant Professor of Dairy Husbandry and Superintendent of the Creamery. He served simultaneously as VPI's Head of Animal and Dairy Husbandry and as the Virginia Commissioner of Dairy and Food Division from 1908 to 1914 and, after leaving the state position, he continued as head of the animal husbandry department until 1922. Saunders also patented a high-acid milk process for making cheese. The effect of his work was

so great that in 1949 a building that housed the dairy department at VPI was named in his honor. Another early dairy pioneer at VPI and a founder of the VSDA was C.W. Holdaway, a native of New Zealand. He joined VPI in 1905 as a creamery assistant. In 1923 he became Head of the Dairy Husbandry Department, a position he held until 1952.[25]

The inclusion of dairying in the VPI agricultural program is intertwined with the school's history. In 1893, just three years after Saunders was appointed director of the experiment station, a creamery and cheese plant were built on campus. This was the first plant to pasteurize milk in Virginia. The desire to set the standard for the state dairy industry was obvious. The construction of modern dairy barns in 1900; the establishment of the state's first dairy herd improvement tests in 1905; the completion in 1906 of the $85,000 Price Hall with a creamery, laboratories, of-

Augusta County Creamery in Waynesboro, ca. 1915

fices, and classroom space; and the addition of Guernseys to the college herd in 1907; were all examples of the leadership given the dairy industry by VPI.

Closer to the hearts of today's Virginia dairymen is Professor Paul M. Reaves who joined the VPI dairy faculty in 1928 from Tennessee. Over the next four decades he taught twenty-two different dairy classes to over 700 students and served as faculty advisor to more than 500 students. There was hardly a facet of Virginia dairying in which Reaves was not involved. He served on the Virginia-North Carolina Select Sires Board of Directors for seventeen years and on the Holstein Sire Selection Committee for a dozen years. He helped found the Virginia State Feed Association and chaired that group for twenty-two years. He developed nationally recognized programs in dairy nutrition and feed formulas. His involvement in the Holstein, Guernsey, and Jersey associations was long-standing, and he chaired the committee that wrote the seventy-fifth anniversary history of the Virginia State Dairymen's Association. Within the VSDA he was a major presence in myriad activities including serving many years on the group's resolutions committee. VSDA honored him by electing him as its first-ever life member.

More than anything else, Reaves gained permanent remembrance for practicing on the farm what he preached in the classroom and for instilling in the next generation a high standard. Upon his retirement in 1968, a dairy science scholarship to Virginia Tech was established in his name. In 1989 Reaves gave the dedicatory address at the Litton-Reaves building at VPI. The state-of-the-art teaching facility was named in honor of him and another revered Tech professor, George W. Litton.[26]

Sunlight, Sanitation

Through work in the classroom and at VPI's experiment station and with the messages learned there taken to the local farming groups by county extension agents, the rural countryside was radically altered in just fifty years. No longer did milking take place in damp, dank, dark barns where disease ran rampant and sanitation was non-existent. Educational bulletins issued by the USDA, the Virginia Department of

Fig. 171.
Milk pails. Compare the chances for dirt to drop into the different pails.

Agriculture, and the Virginia Agricultural Experiment Station, publicized new dairy facilities in plain terms accompanied by simple drawings and basic floor plans. Even the smallest and poorest farms could incorporate some of the ideas. Barns with milking stanchions featured good ventilation systems and floor gutters to help remove animal waste. "Sunlight," explained a USDA bulletin published in 1923, "is considered essential to the health of the dairy cow, and it also tends to destroy disease germs which may be found in dark and dirty stables."[27]

Milk was to be removed from the barn as quickly as possible. Milk houses were located at least fifty feet away from the dairy barn. In 1921, the USDA published a flyer on constructing separate sanitary milk houses. It began:

> The nature of milk requires that the milk room be separate from the stable. Milk absorbs odors and is easily contaminated by stable dirt. If so contaminated it may become unhealthful for the consumer and the contamination may cause losses to the producer through souring and the development of bad flavors. The milk should, therefore, be removed promptly after milking, to a clean, well-ventilated place free from dust, insects, and odors.[28]

As the modern dairy industry developed, researchers paid a great deal of attention to the diet of dairy cows. This continues to be the case. The experiment stations proved the connection between a balanced diet and high production levels. However, finding the right mixture of feed and vitamins, took most of the twentieth century and included extensive labora-

The rural countryside was radically altered with the inception of modern dairy facilities.

tory analysis in addition to more traditional agricultural experiments. A 1949 dairy textbook explained the issue:

> A cow is well suited to utilize large quantities of roughage. For high production she needs grain or other concentrate feed in order that she may consume sufficient nutrients to supply her maintenance requirements and have enough more to produce a large quantity of milk and butterfat. In average producing herds about half of the ration is used by the cow for maintenance leaving the other half for milk production.[29]

Progressive farmers worked hard to formulate a feed mixture that maximized milk production. In the 1930s, the mix used by Westmoreland Davis included 200 pounds of corn and cob meal, 400 pounds of Loudoun Special (a grain mixture developed in Loudoun County for high dairy production), 200 pounds of bran, and 100-200 pounds of peanut meal.[30]

Loudoun County dairy farmer Mike Reardon feeds his dairy cattle.

Fifty Years of Changes

A 1900 dairy farmer visiting a 1950 dairy farm would probably have been overwhelmed by the changes. R.G. Connelly, VPI's Extension Dairyman, remarked on the difference a half-century made:

> Today one may inspect a typical Virginia dairy farm that produces milk for fluid consumption and find there a herd of thirty or more cows housed in standard dairy barns built to meet the milk production requirements of Virginia, the District of Columbia and neighboring states. He would find the facilities and methods of management to be modern in every detail and in stark contrast to Old Dominion

dairying at the beginning of the century. He would find improved pastures nearly everywhere, usually the standard Ladino clover-Orchard grass combination that does so well on Virginia dairy farms. He would find a crop rotation system with a well-planned soil improvement program in full operation. On inquiry he may learn that some of the more fertile farms produce a hundred or more bushels of corn per acre; sixty-five or more bushels of barley or eighty bushels of oats; and frequently as many as four cuttings of alfalfa annually; and that the cows may graze from one hundred eighty to two hundred seventy days each year.

Virginia dairy barns are built according to standard plans to comply with the State and municipal dairy laws and to provide for efficient management and labor economy in the routine care of the herd. It is not unusual for dairymen to invest the equivalent of $300 to $600 per stall in constructing a dairy barn, milk house, silo . . . [to provide] the necessary fixtures and equipment to meet the minimum fluid milk production requirements of Virginia and the District of Columbia. This investment, of course, is exclusive of the cows that occupy the barn and the farm land that bears the dairy structures.

A Virginia dairy farm milk house usually rivals a Dutch kitchen in cleanliness. These milk houses are equipped with running water, steam boilers, wash vats, steam sterilizers and modern milk cooling and refrigeration facilities that enable many fluid milk producers to maintain bacterial counts far below 10,000 per cubic centimeter.

Now the transition is towards cold wall-holding tanks with tanker pick-up service for the bulk handling of milk on the farm and en route to the city milk plant. The ten-gallon milk can is being supplanted by the stainless steel bulk holding tank. So dairy evolution continues in Virginia, creating an ever increasing contrast with the methods and facilities of fifty years ago.[31]

The Golden Anniversary Convention and Gala of the Virginia State Dairymen's Association was held at the Hotel Roanoke in 1957.

Change and More Change

Connelly's last words were indeed prophetic. Even as he wrote them, milking parlors and pipeline milkers were coming into vogue. The milking parlor allowed the dairyman to milk more cows at a faster rate. The milker often stood in a pit below the cow, thus eliminating the need to stoop. The parlor was clean and compact. By the 1950s, many milking parlors and a few traditional stanchion dairy barns were also installing pipeline milkers that took the milk directly from the milking machine into a cooling tank by means of a pipe. Not only was this more sanitary, but it eliminated the need for milk cans, and made pick-up by a tank truck much easier.

Advances continued to be made in bovine nutrition. Not only did feed co-ops have an impact on the nutritional health of the dairy herd but so, too, did the use of silage, the creation of better harvesting equipment, and sod planting. By the 1980s, total mixed rations (TMRs) were in place. All the proper feeds, vitamins, and minerals were mixed together for the animal. Today some milking parlors have computers that individualize the ration for each cow depending on production, general health, and body weight. Dairyman John Miller noted that the days of throwing out a little silage and a little grain have long been replaced by the balanced ration concept. "When the cows get a mouthful of feed now they get the maximum. We even have mixer wagons." Bill Blalock's herd might have been the first in the state to benefit from blended rations. In about 1970 he sponsored a field day on his farm to demonstrate this aspect of his operation. Ray Murley also helped lead the way in the use of TMRs.[32] Murley joined the staff at Virginia Tech in 1965 as the Project Leader for Dairy Extension in Virginia. He coached the dairy judging team at Tech, pushed for the adoption of TMRs, served on many statewide agricultural organizations, and was instrumental in creating the Virginia Set Aside program. His work with the industry and in particular his guidance of the next generation of dairy leaders was so important that he was given the Delaval Dairy Extension Award, the highest honor a dairy extension worker can receive in the United States. After his retirement in 1980, a Virginia Tech scholarship was established in his name.[33]

Just as instrumental as Murley in the dairy industry has been John L. Miller of Rockingham County. Miller, who has an animal husbandry degree from Virginia Tech, has served dairying in a variety of ways. At Virginia Tech he was a key adviser to the Dairy Science Department and held a post on the College of Agriculture and Life Science's Leadership Council. He is also past president of the Virginia 4-H Foundation and helped in the fund-raising efforts for Virginia Tech's new dairy facilities dedicated in 2004. For over thirty years, from 1967 until 2000, he served as executive secretary of the Virginia State Dairyman's Association. Prior to 1967 he worked for Shenandoah's Pride Dairy as a field service representative and in management positions within the plant. He was also a town councilman in Bridgewater. Always an eloquent spokesman for Virginia dairying, in 2000 Miller was honored for a lifetime of service with induction into the Virginia Tech Agriculture Alumni Organization's Hall of Fame.[34]

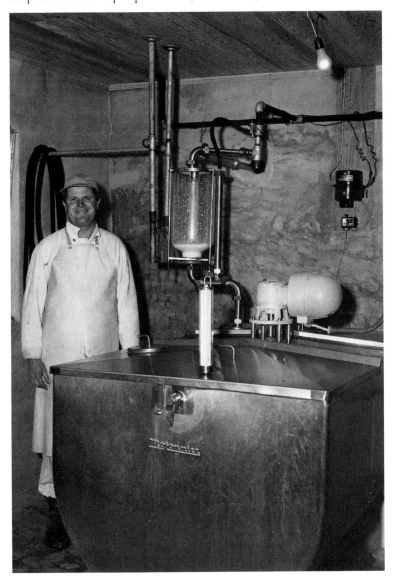

By the mid-twentieth century, many dairies had cooling tanks such as this one.

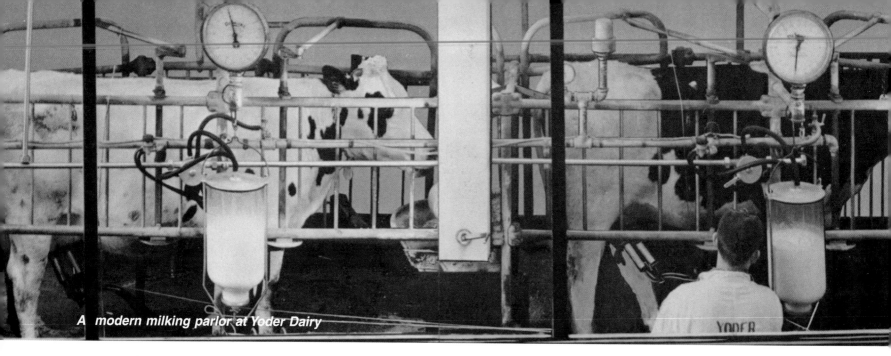

A modern milking parlor at Yoder Dairy

Building The Future

As today's cattle breeders look to the future, they are faced with the prospect of continuously increasing production on smaller farms and with fewer producers. It takes a specialist in livestock breeding to create the animals that will continue those strong production levels. In Luray, there is just such a person in Larry Kibler, who possesses an encyclopedic mind for animal pedigrees and an ability to breed premium, high quality registered cattle, primarily Holsteins, but also Angus. Kibler and his brother, Wayne, were raised in the world of 4-H animal judging. As youngsters the Kiblers bred and showed Ayrshires. As a result of his work with purebred dairy cattle, Larry won the National 4-H Boys Achievement Award in 1966 and was a member of the National 4-H Report to the Nation Team. In 1983 the brothers teamed up to win Premier Breeder and Exhibitor at the World Dairy Expo. That same year they received All American Producer of Dam honors. The year their cow, KenWan Jada, was Reserve Senior and Reserve Grand at Madison their herd classification score was over ninety-one points. Together the Kiblers have shown their Ken-Wan Farm animals for nearly fifty years and during that time have exhibited champions at shows and fairs

A 1920 show on Main Street in Orange

across the Mid-Atlantic. In their thirty-seven years of showing at the West Virginia State Fair, they can count over 100 champions in two breeds.[35]

Two animals have emerged as predominant in the Ken-Wan line. Brookfield Elevation Pretty hailed from Bill Harrison's Loudoun County farm with an ancestry that included the famous sire Elevation. Pretty, an Excellent ninety-four, sold for a world record price at private treaty. She produced nine Excellent daughters and more than thirty Excellent offspring in the next generations. Today over sixty percent of the Ken-Wan herd traces to the Pretty cow. The other predominant cow is Marlu Elevation Esther, to which thirty-five percent of the current Ken-Wan herd can be traced. More recently Kibler has taken his expertise in bovine breeding into the beef arena where he is involved in the breeding and development of the Maple Lead Angus herd in Harrisonburg. Working in cooperation with George and Lo Aldhizer, the herd is being developed in the tradition of cow family breeding by being built around two main matriarchs.[36]

Marketing Co-op

The decade from 1907 to 1916 had proved to Virginia's dairymen that cooperation was the key to success. More could be achieved together to improve the industry and market their products than could ever have been accomplished individually. Year after year the state dairymen and the local cow testing associations came together and discussed concerns and issues and looked toward the future. The piece still lacking in the cooperative puzzle was marketing. That changed in 1916 when the dairymen of northern Virginia and Maryland united to sell their product more successfully in the District of Columbia. The Maryland and Virginia Milk Producers' Association, Inc, with a motto of "Capital Milk for the Capitol," became a force to be reckoned with in the region around the nation's capital. Within a few years a dozen or more cooperatives had been formed across the state. The Valley of Virginia Cooperative Milk Pro-

The original Early Dawn Dairy, ca. 1928

ducers Association began in 1922, Roanoke Co-operative Milk Producers in 1924, and the Richmond and Norfolk Co-ops in 1930. Others that organized in the next three decades included larger co-ops like Southside Milk Cooperative, Albemarle Dairymen's Association, and Early Dawn Cooperative Dairy in Waynesboro and smaller groups in Lynchburg, Winchester, Southside Virginia, Pulaski-Montgomery Counties, and Southwest Virginia.[37]

Capital Milk

Virginia and Maryland, as the original state co-op came to be called, was a powerful organization in the capital region. Prominent men such as Westmoreland Davis were active members, but even the average farmer realized the value of cooperatives. In 1977 Thurston J. Potts who lived on the Snicker's Gap Road in Loudoun County remembered those early struggles before the formation of the co-op.

I remember when the people all milked the cows by hand and strained the milk into ten-gallon cans. They'd have vats of water with ice in it. They would cool this milk that way; with these vats. Haul it with horses and wagons maybe five miles to the railroad, ship it into

Washington. Usually had to get there by six o'clock in the morning. That meant they had to get up two or three o'clock to start milking. They'd return [the cans] with ice, if they didn't have ice of their own. Some of them had their own ice houses. They couldn't be very far from the railroad if they'd get there with horses. Way back they'd have thirty, forty, maybe seventy-five [cows], the big dairies. The people who had two or three cows, they didn't ship. They'd try to make butter; feed the milk to the hogs....It was a hard life until they got organized and got those co-ops like the Maryland-Virginia Milk Producers' Association.[38]

Production within the region increased steadily from about ten million gallons in 1926 to about thirty-three million on the eve of World War II. Despite the Depression of 1929, production soared in 1930, 1931, and 1932 before dipping slightly in 1933 and then moving steadily upward again.[39] In those early years a great concern of all dairy farmers was competition from butter substitutes, like oleo. At the 1931 annual meeting of the co-op, that challenge was presented to the producers.

We want to continue this drive for the increased consumption of dairy products, beginning first at home. Think of a milk producer expecting the Association to get a living price for his product when he himself

W. Pat Jennings leads the Grand Parade at Virginia Tech Dairy Day.

A dairy cow in the Maryland and Virginia "milkshed"

is using butter substitutes on his table. What do you think of a dairyman who will give oleomargarine to his children when he knows that he is depriving them of the vitamins so necessary for their growth? Use butter and support your industry.[40]

Gearing up for War

With the advent of World War II, dairymen worked to meet the milk demands of a growing metropolitan population. The population's needs were reflected in the association's steady growth which bordered on being unmanageable. The leadership of the Maryland-Virginia Milk Producers at the time consisted of Frank S. Walker of Orange, president; J. Homer Remsburg, first vice-president; V.B. Harding, second vice-president; and B.B. Derrick, secretary-treasurer. Sitting on the board of directors from Virginia were: J.L. Bristow, George R. Bready, and E.L. Popkins from Fairfax County; A.R. Glaettli and C.H. Bowen from Fauquier; H.L. Gregg and V.B. Harding from Loudoun; A. Gordon Willis from Culpeper County; and E.H. Marsteller from Prince William. The 1941 membership stood at an all-time high of 1,348 and produced an average of 92,500 gallons daily. Despite the 1941 daily figure surpassing the 1940 figure by 20.3 percent, production exceeded sales only two or three months of the year. But even that quantity would prove too little to meet the demands of a highly-motivated population intent on building a war machine in the nation's capital. In 1930 the district and

surrounding area population stood at about 621,000. From 1941 to 1942, estimates were that the metropolitan area's population would increase enough to 1.2 million. The pressure was on. The leadership of the milk producers promised the Department of Agriculture that their association would increase production and provide Washington with an adequate milk supply. Members were urged to buy more cows and feed more grain. In a letter dated June 5, 1942, the secretary-treasurer described the situation for the producers.

Our old producers have increased their production about 6% over last year, month by month. New producers have increased our total production 9%, making a total increase of 15% in production, whereas our sales have increased 25%. Due to the War Production Board's restrictions on building new barns, the problem is squarely in the laps of our present producers.

What can you do to produce more milk? I am enclosing a self-addressed post card for you to tell your Association WHAT YOU CAN AND WILL DO to give immediate relief by increasing your total delivery.[41]

Success in the Future

Capital-area milk producers emerged on the other side of the war knowing what could be accomplished by pulling together. In the sixty years since then, Maryland and Virginia has continued to expand. Today the milk marketing and processing cooperative represents nearly 1,500 dairy farmer-owners in eleven states from Pennsylvania to Alabama. The cooperative owns two fluid processing plants: Marva Maid in Newport News and Maola Milk and Ice Cream in New Bern, North Carolina. It also has two manufacturing plants, one in Laurel, Maryland, and one in Strasburg, Virginia, and an equipment and farm supply business in Frederick, Maryland. In 2003 co-op sales reached $668 million with a net income of more than $3 million.[42]

Through the years a number of Virginians have been prominent in the association. One who ranked high on the list of influential men in the dairy industry was Edward C. Norman who spent a lifetime of ninety years on Longmoor Farm near Purcellville, in Loudoun County. Norman combined talents in dairying and finances. Having been raised on a dairy farm, his natural inclination when he studied at Virginia Tech was dairy science. In addition to operating a dairy farm for sixty-two years, he served for a time as Loudoun's Deputy Commissioner of Revenue and was a director of the Loudoun National Bank. The family-operated dairy operation, Longmoor Farms, Inc., consisted of 780 acres and 90 milking Holsteins in 1979. The reputation of Longmoor earned Norman the Man of the Year in Agriculture Award from the Loudoun Chamber of Commerce in 1964. Too, he garnered Master Farm Family honors in 1952 from the Virginia Extension Service and Progressive Farmer Magazine, and earned the VPI Dairy Science Club production achievement award in 1968. Norman realized the importance of support organizations such as the Maryland and Virginia Milk Producers Association where he served as a director for thirty years, from 1951 to 1981, and as president from 1964 to 1973. During his long career he also served variously as vice-president, secretary-treasurer, and executive committee member of the American Dairy Association of Virginia and as both president and director of the Dairy Council of Greater Metropolitan Washington, D.C. For ten years he was also director of the Southeast United Dairy Association based in Atlanta and was president of the Virginia State Dairymen's Association. He held positions on boards or served as an officer in the National Milk Producers Association, the National Dairy Council, the Loudoun DHIA, Loudoun Farm Bureau, United Dairy Industry Association, and Virginia's Board of Agriculture and Commerce.[43]

Jack Hardesty of Berryville, yet another example of a person who dedicated a lifetime to the dairy industry, served on the Maryland and Virginia board from 1981 until his retirement in 2004 and was president from 1997

until 2003. For his work with the association, Hardesty was honored in 2001 with the national "Farmer Cooperative Director of the Year Award" given by the National Council of Farmer Cooperatives. As president of Maryland and Virginia from 1997 to 2003, Hardesty set the eighty-year-old organization on a solid course for the future. He oversaw the consolidation with Carolina Virginia Milk Producers and helped create two joint projects, Valley Milk Products LLC and Advantage Dairy Group. He never forgot that he was a member as well as president. He and his family own and operate Harvue Farms, a 1,731-acre operation where they milk 400 registered Holsteins and have 400 heifers and bulls. The Harvue prefix is internationally known with cattle being exported to eighteen different countries. Harvue has had bulls in most of the major United States breeding studs, including Select Sires, American Breeders Services, and Landmark Genetics. Hardesty's record of service to the dairy industry and the community is outstanding. He has served as president, vice president, board member and delegate to the national convention for the Virginia Holstein Association, and was finance chair and steering committee member for the National Holstein Convention. He was on the board of the Virginia Agribusiness Council, the Mid-Atlantic Milk Marketing Association, and the Virginia State Dairymen's Association, the latter of which he also served as president. In the greater community he served on the board of the Bank of Clarke County and for thirty years was an elected member of the Clarke County Board of Supervisors. Awards recognizing such a lifetime of service include: Outstanding Young Farmer for the Northern District and the State of Virginia (1955), Virginia Dairy Industry Achievement Award Winner (1985), Virginia Distinguished Dairyman (1986), Clarke County Citizen of the Year Award (1987), and World Dairy Expo Dairyman of the Year Award (1992).[44]

Another example of fine leadership in the dairy industry may be found in the work of William French of Woodstock, who is currently on the Maryland and Virginia board. W.W. "Monk" Sanford of Orange and Kenneth Smith of Remington have also been active board members with the former also serving on the Virginia Agribusiness Council.

Consistency in membership has been a hallmark of the

Lindsey-Robinson and Co. of Roanoke provided the FAIR-ACRE PROFIT-MEASURE DAIRY TAPE to farmers for estimating the live weight of a cow.

association's success. In 2003, the J.W. Eustace family of Willowlyn Farm in Catlett was honored for seventy-five years of membership. Fifty-year members from Virginia included the Shrock family on the Diamond T. Joy Farm in Catlett, the Roberts Family on Fairfield View Farm in Somerset, the Burton family on High-Hope Farms in Calverton, the Ingram family operating Little River Dairy in Floyd, and L.L. Yancy in Keezeltown. Typical of such loyal members is Al-Mara Farm, Inc., operated by Ronald and Pat Leonard in Midland. Al-Mara began shipping milk in 1953 when Ronald's parents owned the farm. At that time ten cows were being milked. By 2003 the operation had grown to 330 cows. The family farms about 1,800 acres and has worked hard to take the business into the future by opening a corn maze and dairy farm tour business. Also typical is Jordan Brothers Dairy operated by brothers John and Bill in Mt. Crawford. The two men own 200 cows and farm 300 acres on the same farm that their parents began operating in 1942. In Rixeyville, four generations of the Compton family live on Sunnyside Farm which has been in the family for ninety-five years. During that time the number of milk cows has ranged from 15 to 300.

Commitment to the co-op has been from farm to factory. Making the connection between the two for more than fifty years was milk hauler Carlyle Long of Bealeton. Long's uncle and father launched a milk hauling business in 1927 and Carlyle joined the two men when he was old enough. The brothers hauled milk in cans until 1952 when they switched over to tanker trucks. Carlyle purchased the business in 1984. In 2000 he sold the family business to his brother-in-law Charles Frazier. Carlyle began hauling for Maryland and Virginia in 1949 and the company continues to haul milk for several association members in the Old Dominion.

Shenandoah's Pride

War, in this case World War I, played a key role in the formation of another milk cooperative. During that war milk prices and production soared in the upper and central Shenandoah Valley, but collapse came with the end of the conflict. Wartime milk prices climbed as high as three dollars per hundred pounds, but by 1921 overproduction pushed prices down to only ninety cents per hundred. When a survey showed that prices were lower in the Harrisonburg area than anywhere else in the state, county agent Charles W. Wampler, Sr.; and extension marketing specialist G.B. Warber knew something had to be done. A series of meetings and planning sessions resulted in the chartering of the Valley of Virginia Cooperative Milk Producers Association on May 1, 1922. Miller D. Rhodes was elected president; Thomas G. Herring, first vice-president; R.F. Thompson, second vice-president; Fred A. Driver, secretary; and D.E. Shank, treasurer.[45]

Within a year the membership comprised 422 producers owning over 3,000 cows. Just as significantly, the association had, after extensive negotiations, acquired its own milk plant. The former Milner Dairy Company, located in Harrisonburg, employed seven or eight workers.[46] During its first year, the Valley Cooperative produced 7.6 million pounds of milk for a sales total of $154,000. In the 1920s, the total sales receipts never dropped although the pounds of production fluctuated slightly from year to year. In 1926 the co-op joined forces with the National Milk Producers Federation.

Depression and War

The advent of the depression in 1929 and low milk prices hurt the association. In 1929-1930, despite a record 13 million pounds of production, the association lost $17,600. That would prove to be the last year that the organization ever suffered a loss.[47] In 1930 the association was recognized as the largest and most successful dairy co-op in the South.

Because it was the largest dairy cooperative in the entire South and because its directors had expanded operations and modernized equipment, the association weathered the economic storm. But the storm was a tough one to survive. A financial depression and a withering drought hit the Valley simultaneously. In a two-year period, milk prices dropped

Shenandoah's Pride, ca. 1920

from $2.40 per hundred of First Grade Milk to $1.70 per hundred. But the association continued to move forward nonetheless. In 1930 members successfully lobbied the Rockingham Board of Supervisors for funds necessary to provide free tuberculosis testing for the county's 13,300 cattle. New testing requirements from Pennsylvania and New Jersey meant only TB free cattle could cross those state lines. This had hurt local livestock producers. Additionally, Washington, D.C. required that only milk from TB free herds enter the city. Through the efforts of the co-op, the supervisors' appropriations, and the leverage of federal funds, the incidence of TB in Rockingham soon dropped to less than half of one percent and valuable markets were reopened.[48]

In the midst of their darkest hour Valley of Virginia Co-op members had selected the brand and trade name of "Shenandoah's Pride," and persevered. By 1934 milk prices were climbing upward. In 1935, Shenandoah's Pride sales increased by 400 percent.[49]

The management of Shenandoah's Pride was what made the co-op such a shining success. Dave Shenk, at the helm for forty years from 1924 until 1964, put the association on the map. Shenk knew how to support the co-op's members and create a smooth path for the next generation. Under his direction, Shenandoah's pride loaned money to farmers to start one of the first artificial insemination units in Virginia in 1946 and to upgrade their dairy equipment. The association generously supported FFA and 4-H clubs in the purchase of calves as well.[50] Those club members went on to become the next generation of co-op members.

Wartime brought an end to the depression, but added new concerns for the association. With shortages looming on vehicles, tires, and gasoline, the association purchased three horse-drawn milk wagons and appropriate harnesses. Public service advertisements were aired in order to instruct customers on how to keep milk safe during every-other-day milk delivery periods. Ironically, even as Shenandoah's Pride was considering horse and wagon milk delivery, it purchased two 2,500-gallon tank trucks. The impetus for such a purchase was the troop build-up in the Hampton Roads area and the federal government urging Valley milk producers to help supply that need. Tank trucks eliminated the use of cans, the need for can washing, and ice.[51]

Despite fluctuating prices after the war and into the 1950s, Shenandoah's Pride continued to expand, test new

markets, and be worthy of its name. Homogenized milk and the more familiar square milk bottles were introduced in the 1940s. In the 1950s, advances in breeding and herd testing were lauded, and reciprocal agreements were reached with the Norfolk Cooperative Milk Producers' Association. On the fortieth anniversary of the founding of the organization, members produced 143 million pounds of milk and realized product sales of $13.5 million.[52]

Over the years the association purchased many small distributors and many larger plants all over Virginia. Included were Eastern Dairy Products Co., Highs Dairy Products Corporation in Alexandria, and Birmingham Dairy Products Co. in Manassas. With the vision that has marked Shenandoah's Pride history, in 1964 these plants were consolidated into an ultra modern plant constructed on nine rural acres in Springfield, just outside of Washington, D.C. In 1981, the co-op purchased the Sealtest plant in Roanoke and added the Monticello Dairy in Charlottesville in 1984. The latter has been converted into a distribution center.[53]

Through three-quarters of a century, a select group of visionaries guided the future of Shenandoah's Pride. The association's first manager, Fred Driver, stayed from 1922 to 1924. Dave Shenk, a dynamic individual who remained at the helm through depression and two wars, succeeded him. Harvey Scott who "apprenticed" under Shenk as assistant manager and then took over as manager from 1965 until 1988, followed Shenk. Scott carried on the Shenk tradition, but he did not let that tradition get in the way of modernization. He, and his son Fred who succeeded his father in 1989, put the people of the organization above all else.

Only six men have led the co-op board as presidents: Miller D. Rhodes from 1922 to 1938, S.L. Cline from 1938 to 1942, Frank Harrison from 1942 to 1959, Henry Bowman from 1959 to 1960, Clarence Whissen from 1960 to 1972, and Nelson Gardner from 1973 until 2000.

Nelson Gardner was involved as a producer with Shenandoah's Pride long before he went on the board in 1963. He eventually became president in 1973 and was chairman of the board when the co-op was purchased by Suiza (now Dean Foods) in 2000. During his involvement, the association became one of the largest milk producing cooperatives on the East Coast. Under his guidance, Shenandoah's Pride moved into the upper echelon of milk production with a gamble as bold as that made by "Cheese"

Saunders back in 1907. What put Shenandoah's Pride on the map was the building of a new plant that could produce milk with an extended shelf life of seventy-five to one hundred days. Extended shelf life can only be achieved with a different pasteurization process that requires specialized equipment. To that end, Gardner and the father-and-son Scott team oversaw the construction of a $20 million plant in Mt. Crawford capable of producing extended-life products. Gardner's efforts moved Shenandoah's Pride to the forefront of the industry. When the line that produced extended-life milk opened in 1988 it was one of only two places in America that could produce such a product.[54]

Rockingham Still Leads

The twenty-first century is a long way from 1922, but some things have not changed. Rockingham County is still a leader in the dairy industry and Shenandoah's Pride is still a trademark. With its 275 dairy farms, Rockingham leads the state in dairy production, in overall agricultural production, and ranks in the top twenty-five agricultural counties nationally. Farmers in the county realize about $100 million in milk income annually. Today at Mt. Crawford in Rockingham County there stands an expan-

sive 151,000-square foot Shenandoah's Pride dairy plant. There is nothing out-dated at the Mt. Crawford plant. It features the latest, newest technologically advanced equipment for converting fluid milk into consumable dairy products. The bottle-making machine, using patented rotary blowers, can turn out 110 bottles a minute. Another machine fills 300 bottles in the same sixty seconds. Value added products such as extended-life milk and flavored bottled milk are produced there. The plant operates round the clock, producing 8.5 million pounds of plain and flavored liquid milk, ice cream, shake mixes, eggnog, dairy creamers, and soy drink every week. In February 2000 when Dean Foods bought the plant, the co-op dissolved.[55]

The grand opening and dedication of the Shenandoah's Pride Mt. Crawford Dairy Plant was held September 15, 1989. Guest speaker was Virginia Governor Gerald L. Baliles.

The Gardner Connection

The influence of Nelson Gardner in the dairy industry has been felt around the world. Through the use of artificial insemination (AI) and embryo transfer, his Rocby Holsteins have international bloodlines. The fame of his herd was such that in 1980, Nelson sold 103 of his cows to John Lennon of Beatles Fame and his wife Yoko Ono. The sale made national news but, true to his word to John and Yoko, Gardner refused to reveal details of the sale to the press. Gardner, who grew up on his family's dairy farm, entered the business for himself at the age of nineteen when he bought out his dad's share of seventy-five head of Guernsey cattle. He gradually switched to Holsteins and built a

Former Beatle John Lennon and his wife, Yoko Ono, have purchased 103 Holstein dairy cows, but the man making the sale refuses to say where they are to be delivered, complete privacy being part of the sales contract.　(AP Laserphoto)

Nelson Gardner

herd with one of the finest reputations in the country. His work as a dairy farmer, Holstein breeder, and a milk market leader has earned him a number of honors. Through the years he has served as president of the Virginia Holstein Association and as a director with the National Holstein Association. In the national organization he served as chairman of both the finance and milk marketing committees. He also served on the Select Sires board and sat on a Virginia Tech Dairy Science Department advisory committee. In 1985 he was named the Distinguished Dairy Cattle Breeder by the National Dairy Shrine. The following year the Virginia State Dairymen named him Dairyman of the Year and in 1990 he was given the Virginia Holstein Association's Meritorious Service Award. Also in 1990, he was named Southeastern Farmer of the Year at the Lancaster/Sunbelt Expo. At that time he had 130 registered Holstein cows, fifty bull calves, and 280 replacement heifers on his 650-acre dairy farm.[56]

Why did John Lennon buy Bridgewater farmer's cows?

BRIDGEWATER (AP) — Former Beatle John Lennon and his wife, Yoko Ono, have bought 103 Holstein dairy cows from a Rockingham County farmer.

But they made farmer Nelson Gardener of Bridgewater promise not to tell what they're going to do with the bovines.

"You'll have to ask him about that. I'm bound by contract not to divulge details of the sale," Gardener said Tuesday.

Legal papers describing the sale filed in Rockingham County court-

house list Lennon's address as W. 72nd St., New York City.

The only thing resembling a pasture near there is the city's Central Park.

The legal papers carry of the name of Lennon's attorney, which is illegible, and they do not say how much Lennon paid for the cows.

Gardener said the Holsteins have not yet left his farm, one of the biggest dairy operations in the Shenandoah Valley.

When asked about the plans for the cows, the farmer said, "I can't say."

Mennonite children feeding Holstein calves their bottles.

Milk Cooperatives Supply Tidewater

Largely because of the efforts of the VSDA, milk co-ops across the state enjoyed working relationships rather than wasting time in unproductive competition over markets. Strong cooperatives, like those that developed early in northern Virginia and the Shenandoah Valley, eventually emerged across the state. The pressures of World War II created a need to supply large amounts of fluid milk to urban areas whose populations were boosted by military personnel. The baby boom that followed the war only increased the need for cooperative marketing. Probably no better example can be found of this trend than the Southside Milk Producers who organized in 1949 under the guidance of Tom Stark.[57]

The outlet for the association's milk was Norfolk, an area that witnessed an explosion of military personnel during the war. Supplying much of the fluid milk to the area was Birtcherd Dairy, but the demand for fresh, local milk was more than any one dairy could meet. Birtcherd became the marketing conduit through which the Southside group shipped a steady supply of milk in cans.

Under the guidance of men such as D.P. "Pete" Wilkinson and Edward B. "Ned" Tucker, Southside grew. In the early 1950s the producers made the switch from milk cans to bulk tanks. By 1954 an office was established in Blackstone.

Meanwhile, two other milk producer associations within the same market area, Richmond and Norfolk, were organizing simultaneously. The three groups had always worked cooperatively in supplying and pricing milk for military personnel in the area. Eventually the three became Tidewater Milk Sales.

In 1953, a group of producers in Southwest Virginia, called Tri-State Milk Producers, operated under the management of Ben F. Morgan, Jr. Tri-State began as a small cooperative headquartered in Bristol, but with members in Tennessee and West Virginia as well as Virginia. Virginia senator Woodrow Bird from Bland and Charlie Allison from Glade Spring were among the co-op's early leaders. Around 1960, Tri-State merged with Carolina Milk Producers to form Southeast Milk Producers and add more members, including some from North Carolina. In 1969 mem-

Godly Gals Make Good Gouda

Every ten days from mid-January until early November a truck carrying more than 6,000 pounds of milk from Mennonite farms in Rockingham County winds its way out of the Shenandoah Valley, crosses the Blue Ridge Mountains and pulls up to a complex of red barns nestled in the lush rural Albemarle countryside outside the town of Crozet.

The milk's arrival signals the preparation for another cheesemaking day at Our Lady of the Angels Monastery, a community of nine nuns garbed in black-and-white habits. To them, turning out 300 yellow Gouda cheeses every ten days or so is just a part of their regular, simple, prayerful monastic life. It was not always so.

Our Lady of the Angels Community belongs to the Cistercian monastic order founded in France in 1098. In 1949 a Cistercian monastery was formed in Massachusetts. From that "mother house" six nuns were chosen in 1987 to bring the monastic life to Virginia. Among those six was Sister Barbara, a lively nun nearing seventy who has assumed the role of chief cheesemaker.

The Roman Catholic nuns did not come to Crozet for the purpose of making cheese. However, their order has traditionally supported itself through some agricultural or cottage industry. Because the property in Crozet came with cheesemaking equipment

bers convinced the Richmond and Norfolk producers as well as several others to join together and form Dairymen, Inc. (DI). A total of eleven co-ops merged to create the association of between 8,000 and 10,000 members. DI was headquartered in Louisville, Kentucky. Morgan remembered the significance of that merger. "It got the dairy farmers into the market system. We could move milk from production areas to consuming areas and it got dairy farmers from one area to work with those from another area to move the milk where it was needed." Morgan managed the Southeast Division of DI from his Bristol office. In 1971, however, he was transferred to Louisville where he was promoted to CEO. Expansion continued under Morgan's guidance. At one time DI was the third largest dairy co-op in the country and owned fourteen plants. "We were part of the dairy picture of the United States," said Morgan. "At that time we were very active in promoting legislative issues and in dairy promotion and advertising." Morgan retired from DI in 1988.[58] In the mid-1990s, DI was absorbed by Dairy Farmers of America, Inc. (DFA), the world's largest dairy cooperative with nearly 23,000 members in forty-eight states. Thirty-three percent of the nation's milk supply comes from the DFA cooperative that is based in Kansas City, Missouri. Virginia members belong to the regional branch of DFA called the Southeast Area Council. The region has approximately 3,500 member farms with a combined annual milk production of 5.8 billion pounds.[59]

The historical path of the Southside co-op went in a different direction than Tri-State in 1969 when members decided that their interests would best be served by joining with Maryland and Virginia as a division with a contract agreement. The arrangement between the two groups worked, both because of the leadership of each – James E. Click at Maryland and Virginia and Ned Tucker at Southside – and because of Southside's need for a milk supply balancing program. Maintaining the balance between supply and demand in the market is particularly difficult for farmers in southeastern Virginia. Natural breeding and reproduction cycles combined with the heat and humidity of the area mean that milk is more plentiful in the spring than in the summer or fall. Unlike milk production, milk sales remain steady throughout the year, forcing farmers to dispose of surplus milk in the spring and buy supplemental milk in the fall. Maryland and Virginia had enough members to warrant a manufacturing/balancing plant in Laurel, Maryland, which helped maintain a steady supply of fluid milk to the region throughout the year. Joining forces with Maryland and Virginia

Sister Mary David at prayer

from a wholesale business the previous owners had, the match seemed perfect.

"We were so naïve," Sister Barbara says with a twinkle in her eyes. "We thought we could just get a few lessons and then go make some cheese!"

"Well it was one challenge after another. If we had known then what we were in for, I don't know if we would have had the courage. The first cheesemaking day was eighteen hours. It was like a circus in the beginning, but little by little it worked itself out," she explained.

The nuns not only had to master the art of cheesemaking, they had to tackle government regulations, build a customer network for what has become a booming mail-order business, and learn the best techniques for packaging and shipping. Many people contributed to the process and the nuns have not been shy about rolling up their sleeves and asking questions. Three of the women recently attended a dairying course at the University of Wisconsin in order to keep abreast of the latest techniques in the industry.

Now, fourteen years after that first eighteen-hour day, the milk truck arrival simply signals a regular part of monastic life. "In our everyday routine we ordinarily have five-and-a-half hours of physical work," explains Sister Barbara. That work could include grounds keeping or working in the sisters' vegetable garden. "On cheesemaking day, it's about seven hours of physical work. Everybody knows several jobs. The day after is usually quieter and a little more relaxing, but cheesemaking day is intense and the physical labor is good."

Cheesemaking day begins in the immaculate cheese barn at 4:15 a.m. when two nuns arrive to begin pasteurizing the milk.

equally in the cost of supplying the market and the revenue generated by the market. Five employees, one fieldman, one laboratory technician-milk dispatcher, two bookkeepers, and one manager coordinate CMPA's organization. The organization is ably operated by Bill Blalock, president, and Michael Myatt, manager. The firm balances its milk supply through the powder and condensed milk operation in Strasburg, Virginia, known as Valley Milk Products.[62]

made economic sense for the much smaller Southside Cooperative. Maryland and Virginia benefited as well by incorporating a new market and gaining the help and expertise of the Southside members.[60] That arrangement worked for twenty-four years, but fell apart in a dispute over payments for excess milk. In 1994, after an out-of-court settlement, the Southside Dairymen went independent as the Cooperative Milk Producers Association (CMPA).[61]

CMPA today has eighty Virginia members from Chesapeake to Galax to Harrisonburg who produce approximately sixteen million pounds of milk monthly. Producers share

Bill Blalock of Baskerville was named the Lancaster/Sunbelt Expo Southeastern Farmer of the Year for Virginia.

More nuns arrive at 8 a.m. to begin turning the milk into cheese. They stir in culture and add vegetable rennet. Soon little yellow chunks of curd bob in an ocean of milk. Whey is drained and the cheeses are pulled together into a large basket and pressed under weights for an hour.

Then comes hooping time – when the new cheese is placed into special round bowls that give Gouda cheese its distinctive shape. Each bowl, made only in Holland, holds two pounds of cheese. Following the hooping, cheeses are floated in salt brine for twelve to fourteen hours and then hand-painted with a polymer that allows them to breath as they cure. Twelve days later the cheeses are given a traditional red wax coating. Every three weeks until they are shipped to customers, the nuns turn the cheese.

Although the nuns have become experts at the technical and mechanical portions of the cheesemaking, it is the spiritual work they find most fulfilling. Because the cheese barn is a

Working in the cheese lab

Northern Virginia Dairies

The story of dairy production in Northern Virginia began as an unqualified marketing success story at the turn of the twentieth century and peaked around World War II. Farmers in Fairfax, Prince William, Fauquier, and Loudoun were leaders in herd improvement, production, safe milk supplies, and marketing.

The key to combining all the successful ingredients for profitable dairying is transportation. Without an efficient system to move milk from the farm to the consumer household, the best milk cow in the world is worthless. The earliest dairy operations in Virginia transported milk by the railroad. The line from Bluemont to Alexandria was known as the "Milk Train" because all the dairymen in Loudoun and Fairfax brought their milk cans to the local train depots so that the milk could be sent for processing and retailing in the Washington, D.C. "milkshed." By the 1930s, however, the train had been replaced by the truck. Foley Rust of Purcellville, Virginia, started a Northern Virginia milk hauling company in 1936.

The business of picking up milk cans in Loudoun and transporting them into the District of Columbia was so lucrative that he soon bought a second truck and expanded his pick-up routes. When stainless steel bulk milk tanks arrived, Rust upgraded to tank trucks. Eventually Rust's son, Tom, took over the business and today Loudoun Milk Transportation includes a third generation, Adam, assisting with the business. Although Loudoun Milk Transportation has continued to prosper, dairy farming is a thing of the past for Loudoun County so the Rusts use their thirty milk trucks to haul milk from the Shenandoah Valley to Washington, D.C.[63]

As is evidenced by the shift in hauling routes for the Rust family, the story of Northern Virginia dairying does not have an entirely happy ending. The same population growth that spurred the need for milk supplies became a double-edged sword as development enveloped farmland. Fairfax County was the first to go. In the 1920s, Maryland and Virginia counted 121 members milking over 15,000 cows in the county. In 1924, the average milk cow in Virginia produced 2,511 pounds of milk annually, significantly less than the national average of 3,527. Cows in testing associations in Fairfax, however, were well above national average at 6,077 with the county's

Cheese ages in a cooler and is turned regularly by the nuns. Fresh milk for cheesemaking is delivered to the monastery in Albemarle County. Early in the morning the cheesemaking process begins with milk flowing into the vats.

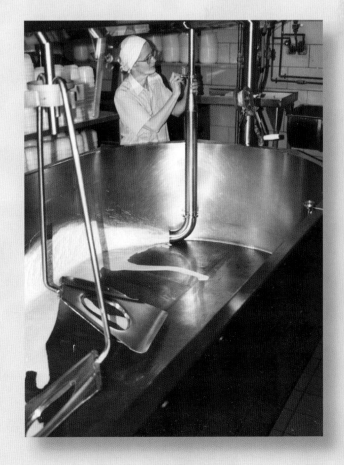

place of prayer as well as a place in strict compliance with government regulations concerning sanitation, the nuns would rather not have visitors on cheese day.

"We keep a tight ship and we never get bad marks when the inspectors come in," notes Sister Barbara with a touch of pride.

So every ten days for almost ten months of the year the community turns out hundreds of Goudas. Depending on the butterfat of the milk, the yield of cheese is around ten percent of the milk that is delivered — 6,000 pounds of milk produces about 600 pounds of cheese. Most of the milk the nuns use is Holstein which has a butterfat percentage of 3.5 to 3.7. In the

Early in the twentieth century, a Shenandoah County farm woman brought her prized milk cow and calf into the yard to be photographed.

first few years of operation, their supplier tried hard to deliver Guernsey milk to the nuns. Guernsey milk has high butterfat content, which allowed the women to produce greater quantities of cheese. Unfortunately there are no longer any Guernsey farms close enough to supply the monastery with milk.

In a year the nuns turn out between ten and eleven tons of cheese. All cheesemaking ceases at the beginning of November so that the next two months can be spent packaging and shipping cheese for Christmas gift giving. The mail order business suits them perfectly — they can control their product and simultaneously develop personal relationships with customers.

Sister Kay holds a wheel of Gouda ready for sale.

"Over the years, the people have become much more than customers. They have become friends. They often enclose requests for prayers and we take those very seriously," says Sister Barbara.

By Christmas all the cheeses are gone. They always sell out. In January the routine begins anew. Back in the 1990s when the community was first gearing up its business, the nuns were the only people in Virginia making cheese from cows milk. Today, thanks in part to the outreach and sharing of people like Sister Barbara, a handful of other farmers are experimenting with this cottage dairy industry.

Still, even though the nuns in Crozet are no longer unique, they are special. They have found a niche market in the dairy world. And because they have no cattle of their own, the success of their business has depended on an agricultural network that stretches from Mennonite farms of the Shenandoah Valley to what was then the

top herd producing an amazing 11,764 pounds per cow annually. A University of Virginia report noted that Fairfax County has "twenty percent of the cow testing associations operating in Virginia, and these and other considerations (including easy access by trolley to the Washington markets) have combined to give Fairfax first place in the State in the value of its dairy products."[64]

Ironically even as Fairfax milk production was in its heyday, the sun was setting on the county's rural life. In 1925 Fairfax dairyman Ben Middleton exhibited the champion Holstein at the state fair. According to many accounts, "Sadie" was the "best known Holstein in the world." In three years she had produced 60,000 pounds of milk and 2,000 pounds of butterfat. But in 1925 most of Fairfax County's 22,000 residents had already abandoned the farm for life in town. When lightening struck and killed Sadie in that year, some took it as a sign that agriculture was no longer a part of the county's future.[65] Fifty years later, in 1973, county planners noted that only thirty-seven viable farms remained as they declared: "Commercial agriculture in Fairfax County is the remnant of an earlier economy. . . ."[66]

The relentless march of suburbanization crept outward from Washington, D.C. in the final decades of the twentieth century. It marched until it hit Loudoun County, once the leading dairy producing county in the state. In 1963, dairy farmer Bill Harrison came to work in Loudoun County as its Extension Agent. Ironically, that same year an airport, located far out in the countryside, opened its doors. Few could have imagined the changes that Dulles International Airport would bring to the area's agricultural economy, but by the time Harrison retired in 1991 farming in Loudoun was only a shadow of what it had once been. In 1997, the *Loudoun Times-Mirror* featured Orchard Crest Farm, a working dairy operated by the sixth generation of the Potts family. The seventy-five Holsteins milked at Orchard Crest are a rarity in Loudoun today where only two dairy farms survive in 2004.[67]

Institutional Dairies

All but forgotten in the history of Virginia's dairy industry are the institutional dairies that used to be scattered across the Commonwealth. Colleges, facilities for special populations such as the mentally ill, and prisons, all operated dairies. Supplying their own populations was the primary concern of these institutional dairies, but many sold excess fluid milk to the general population.

The Virginia State Epileptic Colony was established on a farm in Amherst County in 1910. From the beginning, the operation of the colony included the continuation and

dairy cooperative known as Shenandoah's Pride, and to a small group of nuns committed to living a spiritual life and making a living from the land. The story of how that network was established back in 1990, as told by Sister Barbara, makes a strong statement about the strength of Virginia's agricultural roots.

"When we first got started, we began looking around for a place that could supply us with 6,200 pounds of milk every ten days. That is not easy because most places are dealing with millions of pounds every day. Finally we called Shenandoah's Pride (in Rockingham County) and talked to Harvey Scott and he said, 'I think we can do something for you, Sister.' Then six months went by before we were ready to start. Harvey Scott's son, Fred, sent Wendell Smith over to look at our operation. Then two sisters went over there to look at their place. While we were over there I said to Fred Scott, 'Would you like us to sign a contract?' I will never forget

what he said: 'Sister, if the word between two Christians isn't enough then we ought to fold up and go home.' Shenandoah's Pride has always bent over backwards for us. They even got us Guernsey milk when it was still available and that gave us a higher yield." ~

upgrade of the farm activities in order to feed the patients and to provide job skills. The 1910 annual report for the facility noted that "as a beginning for a dairy herd a registered Holstein-Friesian bull and two young grade heifers have been added to the herd of cattle, and it is our purpose to sell all of the scrub cattle on hand next spring and buy purebred and grade Holstein-Friesian cows."[68] In 1911 the director of the colony reported that plans were being formulated to improve the farm buildings. "The institution is without any barn for its cattle, the milch cows are without shelter except for a temporary open shed. A silo is a necessary part of the barn and dairy outfit. Such a barn and silo as would meet the needs of the institution would cost not less than $1,000."[69] By 1913 the modern dairy barn and silo were complete. "The barn has cement floors with sanitary dairy equipment and accommodates twenty-six cows, while the silo is of the best cypress and has a capacity of 104 tons."[70]

The superintendent of the colony made it a priority to develop a fine purebred herd. In late 1913 Superintendent A.S. Priddy wrote to Herbert Hutcheson of Boydton in regard to a cow that had recently been purchased from Hutcheson.

My dear Herbert:-

The cow came all right Friday night and is certainly a beauty and the Board and myself are very proud of her, as she is quite an addition to our herd of four registered ones and forty-five high grades. I am expecting to hear from the Department of Animal Industry every day and will have the test made and send you [a] check. However, I do not apprehend that there will be any trouble on that score as she seems perfectly healthy. . . .[71]

By 1915 the colony boasted a herd of sixty Holsteins, a dozen of which were registered purebreds. Several of the animals had even taken ribbons at the Lynchburg agricultural fair. Included among the herd was a registered bull, Pontiac, which had been acquired at a greatly discounted price from the State Hospital in Pontiac, Michigan.[72] A few years later Pontiac would be sold to avoid inbreeding and another prize-winning bull was brought in from the Pontiac herd. In 1918, the annual report stated that "the livestock of the institution has during the year yielded substantial and profitable returns." The fifty head of Holsteins (twenty-seven of which were registered) produced over 23,000 gallons of milk.[73]

Around 1930 a modern dairy barn was erected and in 1935 the herd of forty-nine milk cows came under the direct supervision of VPI's Dairy Extension Service.[74] Despite

the hard work to create a prize-winning, high producing herd, however, the colony still had to purchase milk from the nearby institutional dairy at Sweet Briar College. The colony produced 150 to 180 gallons a day from its herd of around fifty, and usually purchased another 100 gallons a day from the college in order to supply the patients with one-and-a-half pints of milk daily.[75]

The colony, which by this time was known as the Lynchburg Training School and Hospital, continued to operate a dairy until 1958. In the final years of operation, annual reports had complained of rising feed costs and the need for more farmland. In its nearly fifty years of operation, the institution had built from scratch one of the finest herds of its size in the state, while contributing to the physical, emotional, and vocational needs of the patients. The end was rather inglorious: the dairy barn was converted to a temporary dormitory and the cow barn was demolished.[76]

Sweet Briar College, which supplied milk to the colony, was not unique in having a dairy on campus. A number of other colleges, including Hollins at Daleville, had very profitable dairies. Eventually, most ceased to operate. Ownby Auction, located in Richmond, handled most of the major insti-

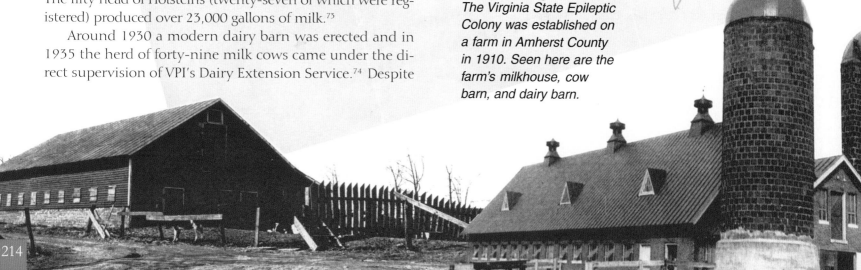

The Virginia State Epileptic Colony was established on a farm in Amherst County in 1910. Seen here are the farm's milkhouse, cow barn, and dairy barn.

tutional herd dispersals as public and private colleges and other institutions gave up producing milk for their residents and for commercial sale. These included the 1969 dispersal of the herd at Hollins College, which had been one of the earliest Virginia herds featuring registered Holsteins, the Elks National Home in Bedford in 1970, Virginia State College in Petersburg in 1972, and Sweet Briar College in 1994.[77]

Other special facilities with dairies included Eastern State Hospital in Williamsburg and Western State Hospital in Staunton. Both had large Holstein dairies. Ownby was involved in the complete dispersal of both farms in 1958. At the time of the sale, Eastern State owned 108 cows and heifers, nine DeLaval milkers, one DeLaval milking machine, a pasteurizing unit, two milk pumps, a galvanized sink, a sweet water tank, a refrigeration system, pumps, a boiler, hot water tanks, milk scales, sixty stanchions, ninety ten-gallon milk cans, four five-gallon cans, drying racks, a can washer, and numerous carts.[78] Over 500 people attended the Western State dispersal auction that included 184 cows, calves, and open heifers. The farm had developed an artificial breeding program and was on test with a DHIA herd average of 12,450 pounds of milk and 457 pounds of butterfat – the best record in Augusta County. Also sold was refrigeration equipment, a boiler, cooling unit, milk holding tank, milk pumps,

an in-line filler, a can washer, a milk pipe, milk scale, milk pails, a strainer, milk cans, a cooler, milker units and pumps, and a 300-gallon pasteurizer.[79]

In the twenty-first century there are still a number of institutional farms across the state operated by the Virginia Department of Corrections. One such farm is the James River Correctional Center (JRCC) located on 6,400 acres spanning the James River in Goochland and Powhatan Counties. At JRCC, a mixed farming operation is not only thriving, but is saving Virginia taxpayers thousands of dollars annually. The Grade A Holstein dairy herd has a 92.5 pounds per cow average for the 90 animals being milked. The pasteurization plant located on site turns out 75,000 gallons every month with the milk then consumed by inmates across the state. The resulting food cost savings for the Department of Corrections is estimated to be $576,000 annually. A commercial cow-calf operation and sire proving program are also located at the correctional center. The 650 crossbred brood cow herd produces a significant calf crop that returns hundreds of thousands of dollars to the state's general fund. The inmates within the agribusiness program also raise bees (for honey and pollination), vegetables, and feed crops (soybeans, corn, barley, oats, and crimson clover). Cutting-edge technology and state-of-the-art land stewardship practices have earned the facility both praise and awards.[80]

Dairy animals on the 6,500-acre James River Correctional Center Farm

215

WESTERN STATE HOSPITAL HOLSTEIN HERD
STAUNTON, VIRGINIA
COMPLETE DISPOSAL AT AUCTION
AUGUST 1ST, 1958 — 10:00 A. M.
also DAIRY EQUIPMENT

AUGUST 2ND, 1958 — 10:30 A. M.

SHOATS • PIGS • BROOD SOWS

FARM EQUIPMENT

APPLE CROP   **FEED**

W. Hugh Ownby
Auction and Realty Co., Inc.
HERMITAGE ROAD RICHMOND, VA.
PHONE ELgin 9-0649

WESTERN STATE HOSPITAL HOLSTEIN HERD
and DAIRY EQUIPMENT

DISPOSAL BY AUCTION — FRIDAY, AUGUST 1ST — 10:00 A. M.

184 — COWS, CALVES and OPEN HEIFERS — 184

REGISTERED HERD SIRE – 3 YEARS OLD
CATTLE TO BE SOLD IMMEDIATELY FOLLOWING DAIRY EQUIPMENT

A really good herd of Holsteins with type, quality, and production.

The herd has been well cared for with a well planned program of selective breeding.

An artificial breeding program has, and is being used for the cows, with a herd sire used for breeding heifers.

Last year's DHIA herd average— 12,450 lbs. of milk and 457 lbs. of butter fat—the best record in Augusta County.

REGISTERED AND GRADE — BANGS AND TB TESTED WITHIN 30 DAYS OF SALE

SALE OF DAIRY EQUIPMENT — 10:30 A.M. — FRIDAY, AUGUST 1st

9 Surge Milker Units, 1953
2 Surge Milker Pumps
Surge RV Pump—Type BB3 With ¾ hp electric motor. Good Condition.

Refrigeration Equipment—complete with lines, attachments and units. Universal Cooler, Model E 500 FH, Serial 782-940-0, has 5 hp electric motor.

Boiler, complete with Burner and 2,000 gal. Storage Tank—(Tank in ground at Dairy Barn, asphalt coated before being installed.) Scotch Marine Boiler. Winkler Oil Burner Model H.8. Boiler 100 psi working pressure.

Cooling Unit—4' x 6' wall type, Creamery Package, Serial No. 4025. Constructed with copper tubes. Complete with shields.

Milk Holding Tank—Creamery Package Serial No. 851, Stainless Steel, 70 gal. capacity.

Roto-Seal Milk Pumps—(2) Creamery Package Serial No. 2756 and 2761. Size RS-1.

Milk In-Line Filter — 3" x 2', with stainless steel milk strainer.
Can Washer-Steamer—Creamery Package No. D-273, Rotary, has 3 hp electric pump attached.
Stainless Steel Table—2' x 5' x 2' high.
Milk Pipe—34', in sections, 1⅞", Stainless Steel with fittings.
Milk Scale, 1956
2 Rolling Can Racks, 1956
5 Stainless Steel Milk Pails
6 Stainless Steel Milk Pails with tops
Milk Strainer
Aluminum Gate, 12 ft.
Milk Cans, Assorted Sizes
10 Milk Cans, Dispensers
Cooler
Can Washer (Rotary)

Pasteurizer with Recorder — 300 Gal. Capacity, round, Creamery Package Serial No. 6236. 1 Curtis Compressor size 2 x 1¾, Model V-101, operates recording mechanism.

THIS EQUIPMENT IS IN EXCELLENT CONDITION

Correctional officer Danny Simms works in the milk processing plant at the James River Correctional Center.

State Milk Commission

The modern dairy industry, featuring vibrant milk cooperatives like Maryland and Virginia and DFA, and a global industry leader such as the milk processing plant in Mt. Crawford, did not appear overnight. It took decades of work and leadership on the farm, in the legislature, and in the cooperative associations. With the onset of the Depression, members of both the Virginia State Dairymen's Association and the Virginia Dairy Products Association became concerned about wildly fluctuating prices and issues relating to supply and demand. Together the two organizations outlined an act that was proposed to the Virginia General Assembly by Rockingham Delegate J. Owen Beard and Augusta Sena-

tor J. Stewart Moffett. After intense political maneuvering, the Virginia Milk and Cream Act passed in the final hours of the 1934 session. The law provided for the regulation, supervision, and control of the production, processing, transportation, storage, and distribution, and sale of milk and cream. It also created the State Milk Commission and other local agencies.[81]

Today, Virginia is one of the few states to have a viable milk commission. That has been the result of proactive efforts on the part of VSDA. For instance, in the 1960s it was decided that half of the increase of each year would be assigned to new producers, which opened up markets to non base-holding producers.

The modern mission of the agency is to ensure "that the citizens of the Commonwealth have a constant, available, and reasonably priced supply of milk and assures the industry that the supply of milk is equitably priced." In 1974, the original Milk Act was amended so that the commission board contained four consumer members, two milk producers, one milk processor-distributor, and a non-voting administrator. On July 1, 2003, the commission was merged into the Virginia Department of Agriculture and Consumer Services. The tasks of the commission are spelled out in Virginia law. They are to: assure Virginians a constant supply of fresh and wholesome grade "A" milk at fair and reasonable prices; maintain an allotment (base) system sufficient to satisfy the demand for fluid milk in Virginia; license all milk processors and distributors that sell fluid milk products in Virginia; and assign milk allotments (bases) to all licensed processing distributors, entitling them to an equitable share of the milk supply to satisfy their requirements for fluid milk sales in Virginia. The commission does not control retail and wholesale pricing, nor does it set prices that guarantee a profit. Also it is not involved in setting health and nutritional requirements and it does not regulate, control, or supervise non-fluid milk products such as cheese, cream, or ice cream. The commission is funded solely by the dairy producers, processors, and distributors and does not receive state funds. In 2004 the Virginia Milk Commission held licenses for seventy-three general distributors, forty sub-distributors, thirty-five non-processing general distributors, and four producer general distributors. Fourteen of those distributors are Virginia companies. There were also 1,176 licensed producers, including 559 from Virginia.[82]

Set Aside Program Supports Industry

An idea launched by Virginia Tech's Ray Cragle and Jim Nichols in the early 1970s has ensured a bright future for Virginia's dairymen. In 1972 they asked farmers to voluntarily dedicate .14 percent of their milk sales money to a fund that would support the industry. Cragle, in particular, accepted the challenge of signing up every milk co-op and every dairymen. He criss-crossed the state, stopping at co-operatives and sitting across from farmers at their kitchen tables as he led the charge. As a result of his crusade, nearly $9.2 million has been raised in the last three decades and

important facets of the industry, such as research at Virginia Tech, have thrived. No other state university in the country can boast of a college dairy program supported by the state's dairymen. Although the Set Aside Program is voluntary, it is not unrealistic to think that in the future 100 percent of Virginia's dairymen could be in the program. This high rate of participation results largely from those early efforts of Cragle and Nichols, whose work gave the state's farmers the opportunity to witness the program's success and directly benefit from it.

Dairy Council Promotes Products

The marketing and advertising of dairy products has always concerned the dairymen. In 1925 the state dairymen helped organize the Virginia Dairy Council, which had as its mission "to teach the general public the value of milk and dairy products as health foods." Marketing and education-minded councils were eventually in place all over the state: in Washington in 1928, Richmond in 1933, Roanoke in 1936, the Shenandoah Valley in 1949, Appalachia in 1960, and Tidewater in 1961. In 1963 the American Dairy Association (ADA) was formed in Virginia. Within a year a set aside program was established to raise funds for promoting milk products, for educational outreach, and for dairy scholarships.

Successful marketing originally focused on the local and state level, but in more modern times it takes place on the national level as well. In Newport News the Yoder Dairy, founded in 1914, produced its own marketing campaign around mid-century. Yoder specialized in daily truck deliveries with the memorable motto "Today's milk Today." A storybook was given out with pictures tracking the milk from farm to baby bottle. "This is the empty bottle that held the milk the baby drank from the man who delivers Today's Milk Today from the pasteurizing and bottling plant that adjoins the Parlor in front of the green pastures near the spot where the man empties the silos that hold the food the men grow (right on the Yoder Farm) to feed the

Cows Milked in the Parlor at the Yoder Dairy, right here on our Peninsula," read the last page of the booklet.[83]

Obviously the Yoder advertising campaign was aimed at a regional audience. Other marketing efforts aspired to loftier goals. In America, June was declared Dairy Month as early as 1937. In 1940 the VSDA, the Virginia Dairy Council, and the VPI Dairy Department began actively promoting a June Dairy Month Program. In the 1960s, money from the ADA set aside program also helped to pay advertisement costs in June.[84] The sophistication of national dairy marketing, from the "Got Milk?" to the "Milk Mustache" campaigns, has increased dramatically. Perhaps no marketing campaign is better known than the Milk Mustache advertising scheme that features celebrities sporting a line of milk over their upper lips. Hundreds of famous athletes, movie stars, and politicians have posed for the campaign photos that began in 1994.

In Virginia the "Got milk?" people are the Southeast United Dairy Industry Association (SUDIA). SUDIA promotes dairy products in Alabama, Georgia, southern Indiana, Kentucky, Louisiana, Mississippi, North Carolina, Tennessee, and South Carolina in addition to most of Virginia. The group is funded by 5,000 dairy farmers and is affiliated with Dairy Management, Inc., the American Dairy Association, and the National Dairy Council. SUDIA gives programs and provides information to consumers, media, school and health professionals, and dairy farmers.[85]

Dairy's Youth

Training the next generation in Virginia's dairy industry has always been important. Through programs conducted and sponsored by the 4-H and various breed organizations, youth have learned responsibility, leadership, and cooperation, which they have applied in their family, community, and professional lives. Many of the youth activities exhibit real creativity, for instance, the world's most expensive gallon of milk. In 1981 the Loudoun County 4-H Dairy Club initiated the sale of the Golden Gallon of Milk. That gallon was "donated" by the Supreme Champion Dairy Cow at the annual Loudoun County 4-H Fair and auctioned off to benefit the fairgrounds. In 1988 the Golden Gallon, taken from C Rose Vega Certosa Viola who was owned by 4-Her Kathy McComb, sold for $20,000. In dairymen's terminology that translates into $2,325.58 per pound.[86]

The Dairy Quiz Bowl marked another fun way of training the next generation in the industry. The first multi-state 4-H Dairy Quiz Bowl was held at the Atlantic Rural Exposition/State Fair of Virginia in 1977. The idea for the contest was conceived by Dr. Carl Brown, Extension Dairy Youth Specialist at Virginia Tech. The contest eventually became regional and is held annually at the North American Livestock Exposition in Louisville, Kentucky. In 2002 and 2003 Virginia 4-H teams won the contest. The 2002 team was the first Virginia team ever to win the national contest. Josh and Sarah Clemons from the Madison 4-H Dairy Club, Brian House – a Virginia Tech student from Nokesville – and Sarah Leonard with the Fauquier-Prince William 4-H

Who says dairy cattle are only for milking? These two Holstein oxen were raised and trained by Bill Speiden of Orange. Speiden uses the oxen to demonstrate how early colonists might have harnessed bovine power to assist with farm work.

Dairy Club made up the winning team that was coached by Virginia Tech dairy scientist David Winston, and 4-H volunteers Patty Leonard and Julie Clemons.[87]

Since 1980, the Holstein organization has hosted a similar contest on the junior and senior level at its national convention. In 1988 the Virginia Holstein team consisting of Kathy McComb, Brandie McDonald, Brent Eaton, and Chris Vest won the competition. In 1999 Holstein Dairy Jeopardy was launched by junior Holstein

leaders Patty Leonard of Fauquier County and Carol McComb of Loudoun. Ms. McComb, who serves on the national Holstein Junior Advisory Committee, convinced the Holstein Foundation to sponsor the contest on a national level. The first national competition was held at the 2000 convention.[88] Dairy Jeopardy has proven so popular in the national level as a competition to showcase industry knowledge that the creators put the game on a CD. The Dairy Jeopardy CD can be used as an activity at 4-H and FFA meetings.[89]

Dairying Tomorrow

Technological developments on the farm and in the factory coupled with innovative marketing strategies in the corporate board room have made it possible for the farm family to live comfortably from the income generated by a dairy operation. VPI Dairy Husbandry Professor Paul M. Reaves championed dairying for decades. A book that he co-authored lauded the profession at mid-century. "Dairying promotes thrift as it makes it possible for farmers to live on a cash basis rather than on a credit basis which sometimes carries high interest charges. Then, too, a good dairyman usually has a desire for better cows, barns, or equipment which furnish incentive to save."[90]

Fifty years later those words still ring true. However, as Virginians prepare to celebrate the 400th anniversary of Jamestown, the Old Dominion's dairy industry bears little resemblance to the one "Cheese" Saunders helped launch in 1907 at Jamestown's 300th celebration. Today's dairy cows wear computer chips and eat scientifically mixed rations, and consumers can buy a carton of milk and drink from it three months later with no ill effects. Milk production is at an all-time high even as the number of cows and dairy farms continues to drop. Today's world of milk production and dairy processing was unimaginable one hundred years ago. Who knows what the next century will bring to Virginia's dairy industry?

Roanoke County dairy farmer William Poage gives Virginia Governor Mark R. Warner a drought tour in July of 2002.

Addie Shirey
Meyerhoeffer of
Goods Mill in
Rockingham
County feeds
her calf.

When the Robert Hartman family of Waynesboro sold their dairy herd, they couldn't bear
to part with their favorite Holstein named Goof. When the personable cow finally passed
on, her likeness was painted on the garage as a permanent reminder of her presence.

Dairy Turns to Milk Specialists

As with beef cattle, the popularity of different dairy breeds has shifted over time, although there are fewer dairy breeds than beef breeds. These shifts in breed popularity are reflected in the membership and strength of the national and state breed associations.

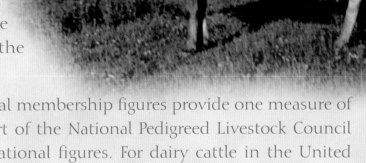

Between 1850 and 1870 the gradual switch began from dual-purpose cattle to specialized breeds – one of the most significant developments in livestock improvement in America. This can be seen most clearly in the growth in popularity of two dairy breeds, Ayrshires and Jerseys, and the decline of dual-purpose cattle, especially the Devon and the Kerry.[1]

Registration figures and national membership figures provide one measure of breed popularity. The annual report of the National Pedigreed Livestock Council includes a compilation of those national figures. For dairy cattle in the United States in 2000-2001 the figures were as follows:

Association	Members	Registrations
American Guernsey Association	890	5,890
American Jersey Cattle Association	2,353	62,812
American Milking Shorthorn Society	298	2,465
Ayrshire Breeders' Association	532	5,170
Brown Swiss Cattle Breeders' Association	970	10,031
Holstein Association, U.S.A.	17,394	311,393[2]

*Gari Melchers, **Belmont**, 1931, oil on canvas, Belmont, The Gari Melchers Estate and Memorial Gallery, Mary Washington College, Fredericksburg, Virginia*

Ayrshire

An Early Dairy Breed

One of the earliest dairy breeds was the Ayrshire, named for its county of origin in southwestern Scotland, near Glasgow. The extensive colonial trade between Glasgow tobacco merchants and colonial Virginia plantations resumed in 1783 after the American Revolution and could well have included some of these cattle. However, the first record of Ayrshire importation into America occurred in Connecticut and New York in the 1830s. The Massachusetts Society for the Promotion of Agriculture, organized in 1792, imported Ayrshire cattle in 1837. Club members publicized the breed so successfully that others were imported in the 1840s.

A New York City convention on October 17, 1843, appointed "committees to report on the points of excellence in the several breeds of Durhams, Herefords, Ayrshires, Devons, and native stock." The Association of Breeders of Thorough Bred Neat Stock grew from that meeting. It published the *Herd Record–Ayrshires*, the first Ayrshire herd book, in 1863. By then, herd books had already been established and published for Shorthorns, Herefords, and Devons.[3] When the herd book was published, only nineteen men were listed as importing one or more animals. Only one, R.D. Shepherd, came from Virginia.[4]

Nearly a century after the first Ayrshire meeting in New York, an Ayrshire organization was founded in Virginia. Meanwhile several dairymen developed Ayrshire herds. H.C. Groome of Warrenton, B.S. Horne of Keswick, and A.R. Venable of Farmville owned Virginia's first registered Ayrshires. C.E.

This 1956 photo shows the classic Ayrshire horns.

Griffith of Brandy joined the national Ayrshire group in 1935, and his son F.D. Griffith helped form the Virginia association. Bill Carpenter of Rutherfordton, North Carolina, was the source of foundation animals for the herds of important Ayrshire breeders in Virginia in the 1940s such as Jack Perrow of Big Island, Carter Elliott of Lynchburg, and Norwood Wilson of Hopewell. Jane Gamble Heyward of Charlottesville inherited the Laneway herd from Taunton, Massachusetts, and had served as a director of the national Ayrshire association. She also served for many years as secretary of the Virginia Ayrshire Association.[5] Another prominent Ayrshire farm was that of the Douglas Forrest family near Culpeper. Forrest had developed a fine herd at Anchor Mere farm in Litchfield, Connecticut, wrote a column for the *Ayrshire Digest*, and managed Mrs. Heyward's Ayrshire herd at Laneway farm.[6]

On August 6, 1952, sixteen persons met at the Virginia Hotel in Lynchburg and founded the Virginia Ayrshire Breeders Association. R.G. Connelly, VPI Extension Dairyman, gave the keynote address. The officers elected were F.D. Griffith of Western View Farm in Brandy, president; Jack M. Perrow, Big Island, vice president; Norwood Wilson, Greenbank Farm, Hopewell, secretary-treasurer. Of the five dollars annual dues, one dollar was to go to the Virginia State Dairymen's Association (VSDA). The other organizing members present were and Mr. and Mrs. George Baker of Lithia, Sam Bivens of Chase City, R.E. Daniel, Jr., of Chase City, Clayton Douglas of Big Island, Mr. and Mrs. Henderson Heyward of Charlottesville, Lawrence Stewart of Evergreen, and Roger P. Denny of Frederick, Maryland, national representative.[7] At the second meeting in January 1953, held at the Jefferson Hotel in Richmond in conjunction with the Virginia Dairymen's Association meeting, H.D. Hevener of Fishersville was added to the board of directors. The group discussed ways of promoting Ayrshires and of holding a state sale.

The third annual meeting, at the Hotel Roanoke, produced a constitution and by-laws, and added as members of the board J.W. East of Gretna, Lawrence Stewart, Jr. of Evergreen, Dr. G.M. Good of Hillsville, and George Baker of Lithia. Jack M. Perrow was the second president. The group planned two purebred sales at Staunton, one in April of 1954 and another in the fall. They managed money well, spending only for postage, membership cards, sales advertisements, and commissions. One can only guess the purpose of two plastic cows purchased for fourteen dollars.[8]

Other presidents of the Ayrshire Association were Carter Elliott, Richard Lahman, Larry Kibler, and David Jones. Virginia Tech had been given the Strathglass Memorial herd, which it sold to raise money for students interested in Ayrshires. David Jones purchased the herd and also started the

1979 Junior and Open A-A Champion at the Virginia State Fair, Anchor Mere Mars Grapette, shown by Julie Forrest of Culpeper.

young sire program. Board members and officers in the 1970s included Justin Dovel, Gary Forrest, Wayne Kibler, Margaret Hevener, Jane Heyward, Paul Terrell, A.F. Weaver, Mrs. E.P. Guest, Jack Perrow, and Henderson Hevener. Honorary members were Professors W.N. Patterson and R.A. Sandy of Virginia Tech. The roster included seventy-two members and sixteen junior members.[9] The Virginia Ayrshire Breeders Association sponsors an annual scholarship for a dairy science student at Virginia Tech, among its other current activities.[10]

Jersey

Soft Eyes and Crumpled Horns

This ancient breed, which originated on the Island of Jersey in the English Channel off the north coast of France, has been purebred for almost six centuries in its homeland. The soft-eyed, fawn-colored cows with the crumpled horns and high butterfat content of their milk were often called Alderneys when first brought to America. Alderney is a Channel Island along with Jersey and Guernsey. The first Jersey cow probably arrived in Virginia in 1657 with George Poingdestre and his family when they left Jersey and settled at Middle Plantation, now Williamsburg. The Poingdestre (Poindexter) family home, Swan Farm, still stands on the Island of Jersey.[11]

Richard Morris of the Philadelphia Society for the Promotion of Agriculture, wrote in 1817 of his recently imported Alderney cow, whose milk produced eight pounds of butter in a week. High productivity by a small animal that consumed less food than Morris' ordinary stock explains the attraction of the breed. Hundreds of Jerseys were imported into the United States from the 1850s to the 1870s, mostly to the northeastern states. The first Jersey in Virginia was recorded in 1872, according to records of the national association.[12]

The Royal Jersey Agricultural and Horticultural Society, founded in 1833, only saw the need for a herd book in 1866, when members concluded it would protect the identity and market value of cattle that were rapidly becoming an important export. The American Jersey Cattle Club began with importers and breeders in Pennsylvania, Connecticut, and New York who recruited George E. Waring, Jr., of Rhode Island, as secretary-treasurer and the editor of the first herd book. The American Jersey Cattle Club (AJCC) was formally organized in 1868, with forty-three members in various northeastern states. It was based in New York until 1946 when it moved to Columbus, Ohio. In 1994 the name changed to the American Jersey Cattle Association (AJCA), and the organization is now based in Reynoldsburg, Ohio.[13]

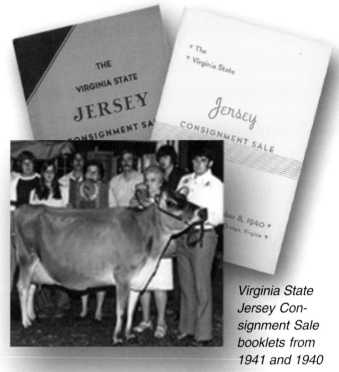

The Stiles family of Clearbrook, Virginia, receives the Supreme Champion Dairy Animal Award at Maryland's Montgomery County Fair in this 1975 photo.

Virginia State Jersey Consignment Sale booklets from 1941 and 1940

An early Jersey herd in Virginia was that of Major Henry E. Alvord at Spring Hill Farm, Fairfax County, created in 1871. He joined the American Jersey Cattle Club in 1883 and became a director. A.M. Bowman of Salem, a lieutenant governor of Virginia, also became a director of the AJCC. His herd continued under his son, A.M. Bowman, Jr., and was dispersed in the 1960s. In 1887 several Richmond area Jersey breeders formed a state association with M. Erskine Miller of Henrico as president, but it did not thrive.[14] J.S. Roller of New Market purchased his first registered Jerseys in Tyler, Tennessee, in 1913 and transported them by train to Virginia.[15]

The Virginia Jersey Cattle Club was organized in 1916, a banner year that also saw the debut of the Virginia Guernsey Breeders Association and the Virginia Holstein Breeders Association. The original officers were William B. Gates of Rice, A.M. Bowman, Jr., of Salem, and Frank C. Baldwin, of Fredericksburg. The club's first sale at Fredericksburg in 1920 included cattle from Dr. J.S. Andrew, Orange; Frank C. Baldwin of Clover Hill Farm, Manassas; James McGee, of Spotsylvania; M.B. Rowe, Fredericksburg, R. Conroy Vance, of VPI, and J.S. Roller and Son, Timberville.[16]

The club actively promoted the breed from 1938 until 1963 with an annual consignment sale at the fair grounds in Orange. In 1940, fifty-two animals from eighteen breeders were sold. Included among the Jersey breeders were Dr. J.S. Andrews, R.E. Brown, Cleaveland Dairy Farm, T.T. Curtis, R.F. Hill, Jr., Jack Sanford, W.W. Sanford, and Margaret S. Walker, of Orange; Clover Hill Farm of Manassas; Carter Glass of Lynchburg; Montpelier Dairy of Montpelier Station; H.T. Patrick of Rustburg; J.S. and Paul Roller of Timberville; C.L. Speiden of Somerset, and C.W. Worley and B.F. Wyatt of Honaker.[17] The highest price recorded for a Jersey in a Virginia sale was paid by Major F.B. Owlsey for Sybil's Gipsy King for $6,600 in the early 1920s. In 1970 Yatton Farm in Orange sold Supreme Virginian for $5,100, the most ever paid for a Virginia-bred Jersey.[18]

Others who were actively involved with Jerseys in the 1960s included Fred R. Whipple of Brownsburg, Rockbridge

County, and George W. Miller of Bridgewater, in Rockingham County, and his son John L. Miller. The development of an All-Jersey Milk program at Bristol in the 1960s encouraged the breed in southwest Virginia, where Fred Brown of Rural Retreat and Claude DeBusk of Saltville were among leaders. In the 1970s Virginia Jerseys produced several Hall of Fame records for Yatton farm in Orange County; for the Huffard Jersey Farm in Crockett founded by James S. Huffard, Sr., and continued by his son and grandson, J.S. Huffard, Jr. and J.S. Huffard III; and also for the Kendale Jerseys, owned by the Harold Roller family at Weyers Cave, Augusta County.[19]

Virginians who served the national association as directors in the latter half of the twentieth century included T.T. Curtis, 1951-1954, Wyatt A. Williams, 1957-1960, R.F. Hill III, 1963-1968, and Harold W. Roller, 1972-1975. Roller was one of the first to be elected to three terms as director, continuing until 1982. In that period, the AJCC developed its performance program and Roller chaired that key committee. The Virginia Jersey Cattle Club had the honor of hosting the AJCC All-Jersey meeting in 1976 at Hotel Ingleside, Staunton, with the largest attendance ever, and with a successful sale at Expoland in Fishersville. Wyatt Williams received the AJCC Distinguished Service Award at this meeting. Williams also served as president of the National All-Jersey Milk Marketing Organization.[20]

For much of the twentieth century the Stiles family of Waverly Farm at Clearbrook, Frederick County, has championed Jerseys, and continues to do so. Breeding Jerseys for four generations, since 1906, they won the American Jersey Cattle Association's Master Breeder Award. Brothers Ken, Mike, and Paul currently operate Waverly Farm, established by Marylanders Robert and Hazel Stiles in 1967. Their sister, Deborah Callison of Augusta County, National Junior Achievement Winner in 1980, also has an interest in the farm. In the 1970s, the herd had fifteen nominations in the All American Contest, and exhibited the grand and reserve grand champion cows at both the Virginia and Maryland state fairs and the Montgomery County, Maryland, fair for seven consecutive years. The cows at Waverly produce more than 11,000 pounds of milk a day, with an average of fifty-seven pounds per cow. By 1999, more than fifty Waverley-bred sires had been proven, with about twenty entering active AI service. One of their bulls is so highly regarded that his semen has been used for artificial insemination around the world.[21] The Robert Stiles Family won the Premier Breeder Award fourteen times and the Premier exhibitor Award six times at the All-American Jersey Show and has exhibited five national grand champions. Cows, bulls, heifers, and embryos from Waverley are featured at national consignment sales, with customers from Canada, Latin America, South Africa, and Den-

Tracking the facts

J.C. Penney's Foremost Bull

Virginia has produced some outstanding sires of both beef and dairy cattle. Among the foremost was a Guernsey bull named Foremost – Langwater Foremost to be exact. He was named the fourth-most influential bull of the Guernsey breed. This animal gave his name to Foremost Dairies, a company

founded in Jacksonville, Florida, which during World War II was called "the longest milk run in the world." Through mergers and acquisitions, the company became the third largest dairy company in the world in the 1950s and operated from its San Francisco headquarters. That name continues into the twenty-first century in one of America's great dairy cooperatives, Foremost Farms USA, from a midwestern base.

Langwater Foremost belonged to one of America's legendary retailers, the self-made multi-millionaire, J.C. Penney. But before Penney acquired the splendid bull, the animal lived happily on the J.C. Courter, Sr., farm near Maplewood in Amelia County, Virginia. How this bull, born on the Langwater Farm in Massachusetts, came to graze in Amelia County pastures is a story in itself.

Langwater Foremost

mark. The Stiles were recognized in the 1990s as a Virginia Distinguished Dairy Farm Family and The National Dairy Cattle honored the Stiles Family in 1999 with its Distinguished Breeder Award at its Fiftieth Anniversary Awards Banquet held in Madison, Wisconsin. [22]

An important Jersey breeder in the Stiles family has been recognized through the creation of the Tracy Stiles Memorial Scholarship of the Virginia Tech Dairy Science Alumni Association. Virginia Tech had recognized Tracy, who died in November of 2000, for his work with the Virginia State Dairymen's Association, and the American Jersey Cattle Association, as well as for his outstanding milk production and genetic advancement work at Waverley Farm and, just prior to his death, at the Shenandoah Jerseys Farm in Maryland. He had the fourth highest Jersey herd in milk production in the nation. [23]

Other Virginia Jersey breeders have achieved distinction in recent years. James Huffard III of Huffard Dairy Farms, Crockett, served as a director of the American Jersey Cattle Association from 1988 to 1994 and was president of AJCA from 2001 to 2004. In 2001 the AJCA honored Harold W. Roller of Weyers Cave for his years of service to the dairy industry and to the Jersey breed with the distinguished service award. Dr. Joe Lineweaver is a Virginian serving currently on the national AJCA board.

Guernsey
Championed by a Virginia Governor

This dairy breed originated on the Isle of Guernsey in the English Channel off the north coast of France. In about 960 A.D. Robert, Duke of Normandy, sent monks to teach and convert the islanders. The monks brought with them Norman Brindles from the province of Isigny and the Froment du Leon breed from Brittany. The Guernseys were developed from these breeds. Like the Jerseys, the Guernseys were sometimes called Alderneys. The breed made its American debut in 1840, when a sea captain brought three cows to New York. Another sea captain soon brought a bull and two heifers from Guernsey. These animals are the original stock for most American Guernseys today. [24]

The exceptionally high butterfat and high protein content of Guernsey milk attracted American dairymen in the early twentieth century. The high betacarotene content gave the milk a rich yellow appearance much prized in fashionable hotels and resorts in an era less conscious of weight gain. Another advantage of Guernseys is that they produce their rich milk while consuming twenty to thirty percent less feed per pound of milk produced because they are smaller animals than the Holsteins that were popularized later in the twentieth century.

Courter began his married life in 1911 as a tobacco farmer who soon switched to raising horses and sheep, with a few cows to produce butter and milk for his growing family. The horses and sheep did not prove profitable, but some influential neighboring farmers interested Courter in Guernsey cows in 1914. One of the first two Guernsey cows he purchased produced over 9,000 pounds of milk and 481 pounds of butterfat in 1915, a remarkable record. Courter added other cows and began to visit sales and shows.

At the dispersal sale of the estate of Lowell Goble in Wyebrook, Pennsylvania, Courter purchased a bull named Langwater Foremost, for $4,000 on his personal note, an unusually high price. Back in Virginia, his banker would not lend him the money, so Courter sold a one-quarter interest in the bull to each of two friends for $1,000.

As daughters sired by this bull in New York and Pennsylvania came into production and proved themselves exceptional

milkers, breeders wanted to know where the bull was located. Word soon got out that the bull was in a remote part of rural Virginia and breeders from all over America began to visit the Courter farm to buy some of Langwater Foremost's daughters. Courter and his partners organized production sales that attracted buyers from all over the country, many of them interested in acquiring the bull, not just his daughters.

Finally, in 1922, Langwater Foremost was sold to J.C. Penney for $20,000, a record figure at that time. Even as the bull was being loaded on the train, a New York car drove up with a buyer who offered $25,000 for Langwater Foremost.

J.C. Penney, the son of a farmer-preacher, was born in Hamilton,

J.C. Penney

Virginia Tech's Guernsey herd is seen at rest in this early twentieth-century photo.

Missouri, in 1875, learned merchandizing in the west, and opened his first "Golden Rule" store in Kemmerer, Wyoming, in 1902. By 1914 he owned 71 stores, and 197 by 1917. Because he built his personal fortune in the business based on Christian principles and a cash-and-carry policy, Penney became concerned about some American farming practices that he considered harmful.

First, he was concerned about the low quality of beef and dairy cattle, and second, he was concerned that great herds were broken up at their owners' deaths, rather than remaining together and continuing to improve over generations, as occurred on some British estates. In his own effort to combat this problem, Penney bought Emmadine Farm at Hopewell Junction, New York, and on the advice of leading Guernsey breeders, he bought Langwater Foremost from J.C. Courter and partners for the record price of $20,000. Penney then provided the herd a financial

endowment that would continue after his death, because a lifetime was "not long enough to develop a great herd of cattle."

Langwater Foremost's progeny did not disappoint. He had ninety-eight registered daughters, eighty-four registered sons, and thirty-nine advanced registered daughters. The average production for those thirty-nine advanced registered daughters was 10,667 pounds of milk and 555.5 pounds of butterfat.

Langwater Foremost met an unfortunate end in 1928. He and another bull got into a fight on Penney's Emmadine Farm. His back was broken and he had to be put down. Penney was so attached to the bull that he had its head mounted and hung in his den, and the body buried in his front yard, where the great merchandiser erected a large stone to Langwater Foremost's memory.

A few years later, Penney memorialized the bull in another way. He purchased a creamery in Jacksonville, Florida, and named

John B. Davis of Richmond owned the first registered Guernsey in Virginia. M.B. Rowe of Fredericksburg, C.R. Paxton of Leesburg, and Davis all purchased Guernseys in 1884. Dr. G.M. Wallace of Spotsylvania County was another Guernsey breeder in Virginia by the 1880s. Judge R.H.L Chichester of Glencairne Farm, Spotsylvania County, who established his herd about 1908, was an advocate of the breed and raised a number of class leaders and record holders at the Virginia State Fair. Through wise purchases and careful management, Judge Chichester established himself as a Virginia Guernsey breeder with an outstanding national reputation.[25] In 1908, Thomas Fortune Ryan's Oak Ridge Guernsey herd in Nelson County was the first to begin advanced registry testing. Other early breeders included Dr. G.M. Wallace of Falmouth, C.K.G. Billings of Richmond, R.B. Mallory of Williamsburg, M.K. Stroud of Herndon, Charles F. Burroughs of Bayville Farms, Virginia Beach, and J.C. Courter of Jetersville.[26]

One of Virginia's great proponents of Guernsey cattle was Westmoreland Davis, Governor of Virginia from 1918 to 1922. Son of an old but impoverished Virginia planter family with distinguished colonial roots, the young Virginia Military Institute graduate worked his way through law school at Columbia and became a successful corporate lawyer in New York. He married a wealthy young woman and in time they returned to Virginia to purchase Morven Park, a magnificent house and farm in Loudoun County. For his dairy, Davis purchased 150 cows straight from the Isle of Guernsey. He was so pleased with the early results of the breed that he purchased fifty-two more Guernsey cows in 1906.[27] Davis became a leader among progressive farmers in Virginia, publishing often in the *Southern Planter*, a popular agricultural newspaper founded in the 1840s, preaching a gospel of the scientific breeding of livestock. In 1909 he succeeded the progressive farmer T.O. Sandy of Burkeville as president of the Farmer's Institute. Davis transformed the organization into a powerful political lobby for farming interests.[28]

Gentlemen farmers like Davis in Virginia's hunt country were attracted to Guernsey cows. Guernsey clubs formed on the Eastern Shore and in Augusta and Loudoun Counties. The Loudoun County Breeders' Association held its sixth Guernsey Sale in 1919, the most successful to that time. In 1917 County Agent Brame

Westmoreland Davis

it Foremost Dairies. *Originally operating in twelve Southern states, Foremost Dairies expanded dramatically during World War II and in the postwar years, so that by 1954 it operated in twenty-three states. Further expansion brought it to the attention of the Federal Trade Commission, which required Foremost to divest itself of some of its operations. In 1995, the Wisconsin Dairies Cooperative and the Golden Guernsey Dairy Cooperative merged into Foremost Farms USA, keeping the name of the legendary bull before the public. Today, Foremost Farms is one of the five largest U.S. dairy cooperatives in milk volume.*

In 1952, the Penney herd moved to the College of Agriculture at the University of Missouri-Columbia. Although most of the cows in that herd are now Holstein, there are still some Guernseys, and every one of them is a descendant of Langwater Foremost.

And what happened to the Courter family that sold Langwater

J. Carlton Courter, III

Foremost to J.C. Penney? J.C. Courter, Sr., was killed when a tornado, sweeping through a narrow strip of Amelia County in 1924, caught him in his barn milking the cows, tore the barn apart, and injured him fatally. He left a widow and eight children, who were sustained economically in the difficult years ahead by the offspring of Langwater Foremost. Two of the Courter sons went into the dairy business and, until recently, one of them kept on his farm a great-great-great granddaughter of Langwater Foremost. Her record production was 13,270 pounds of milk and 526 pounds of butterfat in 329 days. And a grandson of J. Carlton Courter, J.C. Courter, III, carries on the farming tradition of his family and serves all farmers in the Commonwealth as Commissioner of the Virginia Department of Agriculture and Consumer Services. ~

Pamela J. Karg, "Foremost Farms traces its name to J.C. Penney," *Rural Cooperatives*, May-June 2000, 29-31; written material from the J.C. Courter family provided by J.C. Courter, III.

brought Mecklenburg County farmers together to form a breeders' association. The group chose Guernseys as the breed they would handle cooperatively and so they purchased some of Judge Chichester's stock for their dairy experiment in that heartland of Virginia tobacco country. A field day at Oak Ridge Farm in 1915 led to the formation of a Virginia Guernsey Breeders Association, whose first president was C.H. Yates, the manager at Oak Ridge. The 1916 field day featured speakers John R. Hutcheson, Extension Livestock Specialist with VPI, former Governor William H. Mann, Professor R.E. Hunt of V.P.I., and gubernatorial hopeful and Guernsey breeder Westmoreland Davis. [29]

The milk of this breed gained great popularity through the success of the marketing of Golden Guernsey Milk. Frank Rennie of the Virginia Dairy Company in Richmond began selling it by that name in 1923 and signed a contract to do so in 1924, continuing for a half century – a national record. A successful aggressive marketing campaign for Golden Guernsey Milk in central Virginia in 1930 was later expanded to the entire state. In 1928 Bayville Farms of Virginia Beach decided to make the production and distribution of Golden Guernsey milk its major enterprise. A dairy plant was built and delivery service expanded until there were 4,000 customers.

The size of the milking herd increased to 400. By the time of World War II the operation was so busy that it was necessary for a potential new customer to have a physician's prescription in order to begin delivery from Bayville. [30]

In 1920, the American Guernsey Cattle Club placed W.W. Fitzpatrick as its first fieldman in Virginia and the South. When he resigned in 1928 to manage Quail Roost Farm, Harvey Bates succeeded him. More than a dozen others served as fieldmen and Golden Guernsey representatives over the years. R.A. McLaughlin served a number of years and was succeeded by Edward J. Wright.

In 1947 the Virginia Guernsey Cattle Club transformed into the Virginia Guernsey Breeders Association, Inc. (VGBA). Kenneth M. Mace served as its executive secretary for twenty years until 1967. The presidents of the association from its founding to 1981 were C.H. Gordon, Alfred Mistr, E.C.C. Woods, W. Clark Fleming, Jr., W.N. Angle, Herman Haga, George W. Palmer, W.E. Jefferson, Rowland R. Beauvais, R. DuVal Dickinson, Dr. A.V. Bartenslager, L.E. Sly, J.F. Chase, Jr., B. Calvin Bass, Jack H. Newbill, and Ivan W. Byers. Since that time, presidents have included E. Cline Brubaker, John Crowgey, Jr., and Dan W. Brubaker. The current president in 2004 is Clinton L. Pease, Jr., of Leesburg.

Virginia Gov. Westmoreland Davis and his wife are shown with a Guernsey cow at Morven Park.

The association recognizes outstanding service to the breed with a Certificate of Honor annually. It encourages the interest and work of young people in exhibits at the state fair and the National Guernsey Show, through college scholarships, and through an annual trophy sponsored by the Southern States Cooperative for the highest milk production record by a Junior-owned Guernsey. In the 1970s and 1980s Virginia junior herds went to national shows in Harrisburg, Pennsylvania, and Louisville, Kentucky. In 1986 Shenmont Admiral Amber, consigned by Lisa Brubaker, was the top selling junior-owned animal in the National Convention Sale at $30,000.[31]

The Southern Quality Sale began in 1964 among Guernsey associations in southern states and took place at the State Fairgrounds in Richmond in 1976. The Bayville Farms herd rose to prominence under the management of W. Clark Fleming, Jr., and was shown extensively at state fairs in the 1960s. Bayville showed the Grand Champion female, Bayville Royale Lavinia, at the National Guernsey Show,

NOTICE

Use the following abbreviations to indicate the color of the animal sketched.

W........... *White*
F........... *Fawn*
LF........ *Light Fawn*
DF........ *Dark Fawn*
RF........ *Red Fawn*
B........... *Brown*
Br......... *Brindle*

Right Side

The American Guernsey Cattle Club voted December 21, 1881, that the sketch on this form shall be drawn showing the outline of the white markings of the animal and that the colored parts shall be shaded or indicated by letters.

This sketch is a part of the data certified to on the other side of this application.

FEES

To Members — Entry Fee $2.00 for animals under six months. $10.00 for animals over six months. Transfer fee $2.50.
To Non-Members — Entry Fee $3.00 for animals under six months. $10.00 for animals over six months. Transfer fee $2.50.
Entry and Transfer applications furnished free. A charge is made for bound application forms.

MAKE ALL REMITTANCES PAYABLE TO

THE AMERICAN GUERNSEY CATTLE CLUB, PETERBORO, N. H.

Establishing a uniform method for registration of purebred cattle was important for the integrity of each breed.

and also garnered a Three Best Females, a Produce of Dam, and a Premier Breeder Award.[32] In June of 1965, Shenmont Farms presented to Virginia's Governor Albertis Harrison a Guernsey calf on the second floor of the John Marshall Hotel in Richmond as part of the June is Dairy Month celebration. Some of the leading Guernsey farms and breeders in the recent past have been John Crowgey, Jr., of Ham Farm, James Heizer of Sunny Top Farm, Jack Newbill of Forest Lake Farm, Goggin Jamison of Rockland Farms, and Wayne Wampler of Enyaw Farm. Blackwater Lord Amen, bred by Cline Brubaker, has been the number one Guernsey bull in the nation in recent years.[33]

In 1966 the association hosted the national convention of the American Guernsey Cattle Club in Norfolk and in 1982 in Roanoke.[34] Three leading Guernsey breeders in Virginia have played an active role in recent years in the national Guernsey association, Dan Brubaker of Dayton and W. Clark Fleming, Jr., of Bayville Farms, Virginia Beach, as directors on the national board, and E. Cline Brubaker of Blackwater Valley Farm, Rocky Mount, as director from 1989 to1997 and as president of the American Guernsey Association from 1991 to 1997. Brubaker also received the AGA Distinguished Service Award in 2003 and was president of the World Guernsey Federation from 1995 to 1998. Dan Brubaker currently serves as trustee of the American Guernsey Foundation.[35]

Milking Shorthorns

Beef Breed Crosses Over

Although the Shorthorn had declined considerably in popularity as a beef cattle breed by the 1920s, the dairy Shorthorns moved slowly and steadily in the twentieth century to become established as an important dairy breed by mid-century. Their heyday has since waned, having been outpaced by the higher-producing breeds, especially the Holsteins.

The American Milking Shorthorn Breeders' Association, founded in 1915, merged in 1920 with the Milking Shorthorn Cattle Club of America to form the American Milking Shorthorn Society. That group, incorporated in 1948, has published its own herd book since 1949. The society's motto was "The Breed That Fills Every Need." The association established its national office in Springfield, Missouri, in 1950, then moved it to Beloit, Wisconsin, in 1986. In 1969 Milking Shorthorns were recognized officially as a dairy breed and in 1972 the Purebred Dairy Cattle Association recognized them. Genetic improvement of the breed has been made possible by the breed's official production testing, gain performance, and trait appraisal programs, by national shows, and by programs to provide semen from the breed's best proven bulls and young sires.[36]

A Milking Shorthorn is among the livestock kept on the mid-nineteenth century American farm at the Museum of American Frontier Culture in Staunton, Virginia.

Northern and Piedmont Virginia and the Valley were the areas in which Milking Shorthorn interest was the strongest in the 1940s and 1950s, the heyday of the breed in the Old Dominion. Some of the most prominent early breeders were R.G. Pierce of Maidstone Farm at Rectortown, Fauquier County, and G. Ray and Holden Harrison of Dairylou Farm, Herndon, who had exhibited cattle at the Great International Show in Indiana in the 1940s. Colonel J. Churchill Newcomb, owner of the Dunvegan Herd near Purcellville, brought what was thought to be the first polled Milking Shorthorn to Loudoun County in June of 1944. Newcomb had bought Fairy Queen, who held the breed Record of Merit in milk production, at a midwestern sale. Dunvegan also had the polled champion Milking Shorthorn bull, Tyfarms Supreme, who sired only polled offspring.[37]

Other important Milking Shorthorn breeders in Virginia were Z.R. Lewis of Rock Hill Farm, Madison; H.D. Newcomb's Wavertree herd of Greenwood; Philip Connors of Middleburg; R.G. Pierce of Rectortown; D.M. Dawson of Lovettsville; Carl Grove of Waynesboro; Terry Kibler of Woodstock; D.C. Bowman and Sons of Boones Mill; and Dr. R.L. Simons of Lexington.[38]

Brown Swiss

A German-Austrian Crossbreed

This breed is not an ancient one, for it seems to have originated in the mid-nineteenth century in the German-speaking cantons of northern Switzerland, where the first efforts were made to improve native brown cattle. Large cattle were brought in from Germany and the Pinzgauer breed was brought in from Austria. The latter contributed the light dorsal stripe that many Brown Swiss have. The Swiss were slow to promote the breed, and did not have a herd book until 1911. A herd book for Brown Swiss had appeared in the United States twenty years earlier.

Henry M. Clark of Belmont, Massachusetts, visited the canton of Schwyz and imported the first Brown Swiss, a bull and seven heifers, to the United States in 1869. When the Brown Swiss Breeders Association was formed, this bull was registered as William Tell I, named for Switzerland's great national hero. In 1882, Scott and Harris of Wethersfield, Connecticut, imported nineteen Brown Swiss cows. Five other importations occurred in the next decade,

Old Mill E Snickerdoodle, owned by the Allen Bassler family of Upperville, Virginia, was Supreme Champion at the 2003 World Dairy Expo.

including those of L.J. McCormick, of Chicago, brother of reaper inventor Cyrus McCormick, both natives of the Augusta-Rockbridge area of Virginia. In 1906, E.M. Barton of Hinsdale, Illinois, imported thirty-four cows and five bulls. An outbreak of hoof and mouth disease caused importation to cease, and only three cattle have been brought from Switzerland since then. Consequently, all Brown Swiss in the United States come from the 155 brought from Switzerland up to 1906 and recorded in the herd book.[39]

The first Brown Swiss came to Virginia through Henry J. Guest of Culpeper, but no records survive of their offspring. General J.W. McIntosh established a herd at Overlook Farm at The Plains, Fauquier County, after World War I. In 1923, Colonel E.M. Brown, developer of Endless Caverns at New Market, established a Brown Swiss herd at his New Market farm.[40]

J.H. Carwile of Hillbrook farm in Charlotte County introduced the breed to Southside in 1938. Three other Carwile farms in that county featured Brown Swiss. A second flurry of activity in the breed in Virginia occurred at the end of World War II. In 1945, sisters Judith and Julia Shearer chose Brown Swiss from Wisconsin for their Madison County dairy herd at Meander Farm near Locust Dale. In that same year, Joseph E. Wright, Sr., moved from Connecticut and established a herd at Lucky Hill Farm in Fauquier County. Three years later, General B.E. Allen put together a herd at Meadow Farm, near Gainesville, in Prince William County. In 1954 J.T. and Alma Williamson established their prize-winning herd at Chic-a-Wil farm in Brightwood. William M Hackman and his son James developed a fine large herd at Orange Hill, Middleburg. In 1960 Mr. and Mrs. Shirley Smith of Breezy Hill Farm, Weyers Cave, assembled an outstanding herd. One of their cows made a National Honor record in 1966 and was the dam of Breezy Hill Virginian, a U.S.D.A. Proof

Bull sold to American Breeders Service, Inc. in 1970 for one of the top prices ever paid for a Brown Swiss bull.[41]

The outstanding Brown Swiss in Virginia today is Old Mill E Snickerdoodle, the 2003 Grand Champion Female of the Central National Brown Swiss Show at the thirty-seventh World Dairy Expo in Madison, Wisconsin. She also won Grand Champion and Reserve Supreme Champion at the Eastern National Show in 2003 for her owners and exhibitors, Tammy and Allen Bassler, Jr., of Old Mill Farm, Upperville. Snickerdoodle is descended from the third Brown Swiss animal to be imported into America back in 1867. Her impeccable breeding attracted the attention of *Braunvieh*, the magazine of the breed association in its native land, Switzerland, which published a two-page color spread on her twenty-five-generation genealogy.[42]

The Virginia Brown Swiss Breeders Association held its first meeting at Warrenton. Unfortunately, with the exception of a secretary's book for 1952-1953, all the early records of the association were lost when fire destroyed the Shirley Smith home at Weyers Cave in 1965. The organization met annually from at least the early 1950s at a different farm each summer. From 1971 to 1980 host breeders were Shirley Smith, Willand and James Hackman at Middleburg, Ian Prydes of Washington, Ed Titmus at Sutherland, Allen Hertzler at Grottoes, the Williamsons at Brightwood, Robert Heizer at Middlebrook, Vernon Hull at Strasburg, and Rolf Paulson at Port Republic. In that same decade, presidents of the association were J.T. Williamson, LeRoy Banks, and Vernon Hull.[43] The current president in 2004 is Barbara Paulson of Port Republic.

Holsteins

A Rise to Dominance

Although a relative latecomer on the dairy scene, Holsteins achieved such dominance that about ninety percent of American dairy cattle were Holsteins by the turn of the twenty-first century. The breed traces its origins to the black cattle and the white cattle that accompanied the Batavians and the Friesians, two migrant European tribes who settled in the Rhine delta area some two thousand years ago. These developed into the black-and-white cattle of the two northern provinces of the Netherlands, North Holland, and Friesland.

The first Holstein cow in America arrived in Boston on a Dutch ship in 1852, where Winthrop Chenery, a Massachusetts breeder, purchased her. He was so pleased with her production that he purchased additional Dutch cows in 1857, 1859, and 1861. Chenery worked hard to popularize the breed, so that about nine thousand had been imported when cattle disease broke out in Europe and importation ended.[44]

The first registered Holstein came to Virginia in the early 1870s. This bull was Highland Chief, bred by Chenery.

Its owner was William Fullerton, a New York City judge who had a farm at Clifton Station in Fairfax County. Fullerton added two cows. Another important early Virginia breeder of Holsteins was J.R. Beuchler of Leesburg.[45] The heifer Lakeside Belle, No. 568 H.H.B., was probably the first cow in Virginia to have her yearly milk production recorded. Cattle from these two pioneer herds were the foundation for many Virginia herds, including those at VPI.[46]

There were two national breed organizations, The Holstein Breeders' Association and the Dutch-Friesian Association. These joined in 1885 to become the Holstein-Friesian Association of America. Virginia had only four members listed that first year, Fullerton, Beuchler, Hubert Dilger of Front Royal, and Thomas R. Smith of Lincoln. There were other breeders in Virginia, however, for 1885 was also the first year that Holsteins were exhibited at the Virginia State

Agricultural Society Fair in Petersburg. Two exhibitors were T. Loveland of Gordonsville and W.E. Grant of Henrico.[47] In the late 1880s and early 1890s, Mrs. William Cameron of Petersburg purchased animals registered by the Holstein-Friesian Association of America.[48]

Work by Joseph Turner at Hollins Institute and Frank S. Walker at Woodberry Forest in building outstanding Holstein dairy herds for their schools attracted attention to the breed. Another early Holstein proponent and honorary member of the association was T.O. Sandy of Burkeville, first director of the Virginia Agricultural Extension service at VPI. The first Holstein bred at VPI was born in 1895. The first Holstein breeder in eastern Virginia was D.S. Jones of Beacondale Farm, Newport News, a mayor of that city around 1900. His farm and productive herd was later acquired by Dr. G.L. Smith. By 1910 there were fifteen Vir-

ginia members of the national association, but a decade later the number had risen to 121.[49]

The rise in popularity of Holsteins in the decade of World War I led to the formation of the Virginia Holstein-Friesian Club during the Virginia State Dairymen's Association convention at Harrisonburg in February of 1916. Frank S. Walker of Woodberry Forest was president, Joseph Turner of Hollins Institute (now University) and J.S. Haldeman of Winchester were vice presidents, and R.V. Martindale of Sweet Briar College was secretary-treasurer. The first directors were Dr. G.L. Smith, Newport News; W.G. Hoover, Timberville; T.O. Sandy, Burkeville; W.H. Newman, Woodstock; F.E Bowman, Remington; and J. Aubrey Clarkson, Brookwood. Twenty-one Holstein breeders were present at the meeting, and a total of thirty-two became charter members of the club. In 1923 the club invited the national association to hold its 1924 convention in Richmond, the first time the association met in the South.[50]

A young girl and her Holstein heifer pose in this Shenandoah County early twentieth-century photo.

The success of that national convention in 1924 and of the National Holstein sale held in conjunction with it did much to publicize the breed in Virginia. The story of Holsteins in Virginia for a quarter century until the next national convention in the Old Dominion is one of steady progress and success. The association had excellent leadership during those early years in its presidents: Frank S. Walker, Orange; C. Nelson Beck, Charlottesville; George T. Carr, Charlottesville; J. Owen Beard, Linville; L.J. Crowgey, Wytheville; John M. Willis, Culpeper; H. W. Craun, Roanoke; and J.C. Eller, Culpeper. The secretaries in those years were R.V. Martindale, Sweet Briar;

C.H. Crabill, Richmond; P.M. Reaves, Blacksburg; H.W. Craun, Roanoke; and L.A. Drewry, Ferrum.

Among the most successful of the programs of the Holstein-Friesian Club was the annual Field Day, held at a different breeder's farm each year. J.P. Taylor's Meadow Farm at Orange was the site of the first field day in 1933. Some of the others have included F.W. and R.E. McComb, Bluemont in 1937; Curles Neck Farm, Richmond, in 1939; The Frank Walker Family at Rosni Dairy in Orange; the Myers Family at Walkup Holstein, Harrisonburg; Whippernock Farm at Sutherland; Temple Slaughter's at Culpeper in 1947; Charles R. Hope and Sons of Purcellville. In 1951; L.J. Crowgey and son, Richdale Farm, Wytheville in 1954, and H.H. Kelley, Woodgrove Farm, Round Hill in 1955.[51] In 1966 John Archbold's Foxlease Farm near Upperville in Fauquier County hosted a very successful field day. Among the special guests was a prominent U.S. Congressman named Gerald Ford.[52]

In the past decade the annual field day has been hosted by Kenneth Smith's Cool Lawn Farm, Dave Yutzy's Windcrest Holsteins, Dave Johnson's Highland Dairy, C.W. McNeely III's Early Dawn Dairy Farm, Carter Elliott, Jr.'s Seven Oaks Farm, the Nuckols Family's Eastview Farm, James and Jennifer Cook's Jareco Farm, and the George Alvis Family's Alvis Dairy.[53]

The annual meeting in the winter and sales in spring, summer, and fall highlight the annual activities of the association. Virginia hosted its second national Holstein convention and sale in 1952 at Roanoke, including a visit to VPI in Blacksburg. Harold W. Craun and R.G. Connelly were responsible for the convention in the Hotel Roanoke, while Paul M. Reaves chaired the sale held at Victory Stadium.[54]

In 1955 the Virginia Holstein Club was incorporated and the name was changed to the Virginia Cooperative Holstein Breeders Association, Inc. This encouraged a division of the state into ten districts in 1960 with the formation of district clubs with their own twilight meetings and black and white shows. Two types of membership were established, standard for purebred breeders and associate for owners of grade Holsteins. The association also contributed in 1960 toward the construction of a Holstein Show Barn at the state fair. It joined with the North Carolina club in 1961 to publish the *North Carolina-Virginia Holstein News.* This was a forerunner of *Southeastern Holstein News,* serving a five-state area currently. In 1962 Virginia hosted its third national convention with Richmond as the site, the seventy-seventh for the national association. Harold W. Craun, a national director, chaired the convention and George A. Miller the sale.[55] A further change in 1969 produced the name Virginia Holstein Association, Inc., a non-profit, non-stock corporation. In 1972 the association passed the 400-member mark; by 1981 it had 481 members, and 539 in 1987.

In 1965 the Virginia Meritorious Service Award was instituted, with a suitably engraved silver tray presented each year to an outstanding member. From 1965 to 1973 the

Stuart Land and Cattle Company sponsored the award. In 1974 Foxlease Farm became the sponsor. Winners of this award (in chronological order from 1965-2002) have been: George A. Miller, Frank Walker, Sr., Leonard J. Crowgey, Professor Paul M. Reaves, Frank McComb, I. Fred Stine, Dr. Wyndham B. Blanton, Jr., J.W. "Wag" Eustace, Harold W. Craun, William Alexander "Zan" Stuart, Jr., Grayson Bowers, John Middleton, William N. Patterson, Ronald A. Hope, Ralph Fields, Sr., William H. Logan, Sr., Dr. William Etgen, Dr. John White, John A. Hunt, Hershel H. Gardner, E. Theo Haberland, Mrs. Margaret Adams, L. "Buddy" Trigg, Margie Ann Dick, J. Dennis Ownby, Nelson S. Gardner, Charles F. Moyer, Jr., Edgar R. Tillett, Daniel J. Myers, and James L. Tait. Under the sponsorship of George and Pippen Miller's Round Oak-Select the recipients were J.D. "Jack" Hardesty, Riley and Barbara Wagner, Charles N. "Chuck" Miller, Jimmie N. Eustace, Carol and Robert McComb, George Edgerton, and Walter V. McClure, Sr. The current sponsor is Riley and Bar-

bara Wagner's Rilara Holstein. The latest recipients are Jerry Swisher, Joseph and Pat Houck, and, in 2004, Dr. James "Jim" Nichols.[56]

George A. Miller

The Trailblazer Award, created by George A. Miller, has been received by John M. Willis, Douglas B. Child, Virginia Artificial Breeding Association, William B. Blalock, William H. Harrison, Paul Smith, and Dr. James R. Nichols.

Presidents who have served the association in the past four decades include Charles F. Moyer, Jr., William H. Logan, Wyndham B. Blanton, Jr., Jimmie N. Eustace, Nelson S. Gardner, Dwight Peck, Hershel Gardner, William R. Kingery, J.D. Hardesty, W.E. Blalock, Edward B. Titmus, Joseph A. Houck, Daniel J. Myers, Larkin D. Moyer, Charles N. Miller, David Barns, Robert Pemberton, Larry Timbrook, and Barbara Wagner. In addition to the presidents a number of persons have ably filled the position of secretary-treasurer of the Virginia Holstein Association,

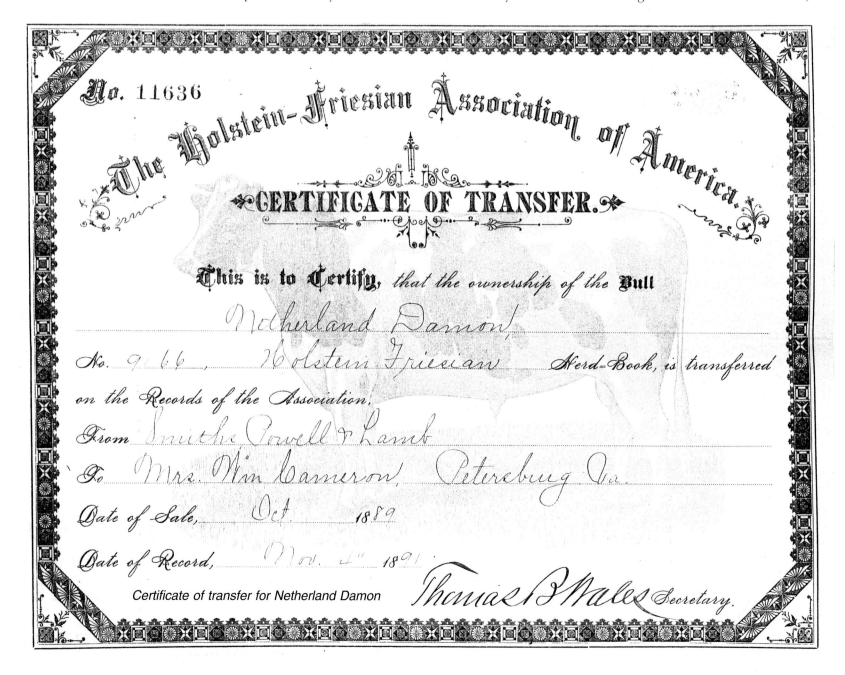

Certificate of transfer for Netherland Damon

beginning with Jack Hunt and including John M. Willis, Daniel J. Myers, Harold W. Craun, Harvey Crabill, Paul M. Reaves, Aubrey Drewry, I. Fred Stine, R.V. Martindale, Walter McClure, R.P. Keithley, and coming down to Margie Ann Dick serving in the position in 2004.

Three leaders of the state association to achieve national status were Harold W. Craun, Dr. Wyndham B. Blanton, Jr., and Nelson Gardner of Rocby Farm, Bridgewater. Craun, who was general chairman of the 1962 national convention, became a director, vice-president, and president of the national association. Dr. Blanton, who served as president of the Virginia association, was the featured guest speaker at the 1970 national convention in Boston. Nelson Gardner, who in 1981

Rilara Mars Las Ravena
Excellent 91 and Top Cow on the Super Donor cow list
Bred by Riley and Barbara Wagner of Bridgewater, Virginia

was elected a director of the Holstein-Friesian Association of America, served in that position for eight years. His additional honors have included Virginia Distinguished Dairyman in 1987, the Dairy Industry Award from the Virginia Tech Dairy Club, and selection thirteen times for the Progressive Breeder Award. He was honored by the National Dairy Shrine as Dairy Shrine Breeder of the Year in 1986.[57]

A junior Holstein breeder who achieved national recognition long before the Virginia association had established its junior program was William H. Harrison of Herndon, whose path to excellence was through 4-H. While still in high school he built his own herd of thirty-two registered Holsteins, served on the county dairy judging team, won the 1956 Virginia 4-H Dairy Achievement Award, and saw his Holsteins win sixty-six championships, 572 ribbons, and nine trophies, as well as prize money to finance his college education. His success story was featured on the Voice of America program, and won him the 1958 national Holstein Junior Champion award at the national convention in Boston.[58]

In 1972 the *Virginia Holstein News* became the *Southeastern Holstein News*, covering North Carolina, Maryland, West Virginia, Delaware, and Virginia, originating under the editorship

of Robin and Jane Agee of Farmville, Virginia. Other Virginia editors have included R. Bentz Rhoads, Joan A. Peck, Ella Rhoads, Walter V. McClure, and Margie Ann Dick. The News is an excellent vehicle for spreading word of sales. These began as winter convention sales in 1969, but in 1976 became the Spring Sale. The Twilight Sale, another important activity of the association, changed later to the Sale of Stars.[59]

In 1979 another important Virginia Association award was instituted under the chairmanship of William H. Harrison of Leesburg. This is the Founding Fathers Award, which recognizes persons who have aided Holstein development in the Old Dominion through their work with 4-H, FFA, and local leadership roles, and for which Meri-

Rocby Ivanhoe Dina Charm
Excellent 93
Bred by Nelson Gardner of Bridgewater, Virginia

torious Service Award winners are not eligible. The first award was presented at the Field Day at Whippernock Farm in July of 1980. Persons whom the board has honored with the Founding Fathers Award have included Howard Sprague, E. Theo Haberland, Joe Dillion, Ned and Florence Sutphin, Frank Walker, Jr., John Hunt, Margaret Adams, Paul Craun, J.E. Goode, A.K. Hardy, Charles Miller, L.B. Trigg, W.L. Dickenson, and W.H. "Buddy" Hill.[60]

In 1976 the Virginia Junior Holstein Association was formed with officers and two directors from each district. Some who have served as president of this group have been Johnny Hardesty, Melinda Johnson, David Hardesty, Patricia Ann (Dick) Leonard, Rosanne Koontz, Charles H. Streett, IV, Teresa Myers Calender, Amy Wagner, Patti Roudabush Craun, Kathy McComb Swift, Matthew Eustace, Karen McComb McClellan, Sarah Foley, Kristy McComb, Aaron Shiflett, Sarah Leonard, and Daniel Hardesty. The Virginia Holstein youth, Kathy McComb, Brandie McDonald, Brent Eaton, Chris Vest, and coach Carol McComb, won the Senior Dairy Bowl at the 1988 National Convention in San Diego. The major honor available in Holstein youth work is to be named National Holstein Boy or Girl, as it

Costume classes at local fairs are popular events among youngsters whose families breed and raise Holsteins. Michelle Skeen of Mount Sidney was a participant in one such class at the Augusta County Fair.

Norfolk in conjunction with the convention, set an all-time record. Three of the 124 animals brought over $100,000 and there was a record gross of over $2.2 million for the entire sale. Two animals sold on that occasion are still in the news today through their progeny, Walkup Valiant Lou Ella and Kinglea Mars Daisy.[64]

Hunter McCray, grandson of James Tait of Gloryland Holsteins, shows off a red and white Holstein calf at his family's farm in Grottoes, Virginia.

was originally called, but is currently known as Distinguished Junior Member. Five Virginians have received this award, Ben P. Middleton, William H. Harrison, Thomas Fletcher, Allan McClure, and Kathy McComb.[61]

The Virginia Junior Holstein Association sponsors calf raffles and a variety of contests such as "Dairy Jeopardy" and a speech contest.[62] An important component of the junior division is the Virginia Junior Holstein Scholarship available to members. Each year the Virginia Dairy Princess and her court of Virginia Dairy Maids help to promote the dairy industry around the state. The Princess for 2004 was Ashley Shiflett of Augusta County. Advisors to the juniors have included William Harrison, Rhoda Johnston, Barbara Streett, Carol McComb, Debbie Hardesty, Lois Skeen, Nancy Potts, and Donna Kerr, among many other dedicated volunteers. Young people who have been presidents have included Johnny Hardesty, Melinda Johnston, David Hardesty, Patricia Ann (Dick) Leonard, and Teresa D. Myers. Advisors for the group have included William H. Harrison, Rhoda Johnston, Barbara Street, Katy Roudabush, Dianne Wall, and Juanita Hazlegrove. Officers for 2004 were Danny Hardesty, president; Sarah Leonard, vice president; Katy Leonard, secretary; Ashley Shiflett, treasurer; and Michelle Skeen, reporter.[63]

In 1983 Virginia had the honor of hosting the National Holstein Convention in Norfolk, the fourth to be held in the Old Dominion. This is still considered to have been one of the best national conventions that the organization ever held. The National Convention Sale, held in

Red and White Cattle
Combining the Best of Two Worlds

The most recent entrant into the dairy breeds in Virginia is the Red and White. This breed has its origins in the cross of Red Holsteins, a genetic variant of the traditional black and white Holsteins, with Milking Shorthorns. One of the pioneer breeders was John C. Gage of Duallyn Farm, Eudora, Kansas. He was typical of the developers of the breed: basically a Milking Shorthorn breeder who sought to infuse needed new blood by the mix with Red Holsteins. Initially, this mix was entered into the registry of the Milking Shorthorn Society. As differences arose over the direction of development of this cross, Gage and others laid the foundation for a new national association.

In February of 1964, the American Red and White Dairy Cattle Society was incorporated as a non-profit organization. Two years later, in 1966, the group changed its name to the Red and White Dairy Cattle Association. The goals of the society include the encouragement and promotion of the new breed; provision for the registration and transfer of pedigrees; the recording of milk records; the support of scientific studies of milk production of the breed; the improvement through artificial insemination from high quality bulls; and to create publications that will promote the breed.

By the late 1960s, with its growing pains over, the national association initiated an annual autumn national show and sale. Official recognition as a separate breed came from the United States Department of Agriculture. The national office, originally in Kansas City, migrated to Green Bay, Wisconsin, then Elgin, Illinois, before settling at Crystal Spring, Pennsylvania, where it built its own building in 1988.[65]

In that same year, 1988, the Southeast Red and White Dairy Cattle Association was formed. Mark Clark took a leadership role in this, contacting dairy associations in the various states, and learning from them of persons interested in an organization. Twelve attended the first meeting, coming from Virginia, Maryland, West Virginia, and the Carolinas. Charter members from Virginia were Leon Rhodes, Steve Rhodes, Lester "Buck" and Carol Cobb, and Franklin Good.

Mark Clark was the president from 1988 until 1993. Steve Rhodes followed in that position, serving the decade from 1993-2003. Leon Rhodes is the current president. Carol Cobb has filled the secretary/treasurer position since 1988.

Meanwhile, the Maryland members later formed their own club, and Steve Rhodes of Harrisonburg, became a director of the national association, with a term to expire in 2005.

In 2004 the club has fourteen members who milk about 600 Red and White cows. Activities of the Southeast group

Kimder Treasure Ronny-Red, owned by Staka Holsteins Harrisonburg, Virginia, topped the Second Southeast Red and White Classic in 1991.

have included six sales of Red and Whites and four events that were combination shows and sales. They hold two field days annually. Favorite activities include cow-milking contests at local ball games. The group has donated funds to help purchase milking equipment and fans at the Rockingham County Fair, to help a family injured in an automobile accident, and to help new Red and White clubs get started.[66]

Breed Associations Important to Industry

There is no doubt that the national breed associations and their state affiliates have played a critically important role in the development and promotion of each breed of dairy cattle as it appeared in America. They have all worked diligently and well in developing marketing strategies that will work to the greatest economic benefit of their members. Their shows and sales have encouraged breeders to produce the best cattle possible. In recent decades, the work of the various associations in encouraging and sponsoring genetic research and the implementation of the latest knowledge and technology have enabled the beef and dairy cattle industries to make astonishing strides in breeding the most remarkable cattle the world has ever known.

Beef Industry Comes of Age

All roads for breeders and producers of beef cattle lead to market. The successful marketing of beef is the bottom line, the end result of all the attentive breeding, feeding, and care that go into producing livestock. For much of the history of beef cattle in Virginia, the road to market was a simple one: the individual farmer sold his cattle to a local buyer who assembled droves of cattle and drove them to an urban market. In the eighteenth and early nineteenth centuries, those cattle were literally driven to places such as Alexandria, Baltimore, or Philadelphia. With the coming of railroads, the cattle were driven to the nearest railhead and shipped on cattle cars. The increasingly complex economy of the twentieth century and competition from midwestern and western cattle producers required that Virginia's breeders and producers develop more sophisticated methods of marketing their product and of uniting to develop their individual and group well-being. The individual breed associations formed in the early years of the twentieth century were an important step in that direction. But further united action was necessary.

The Bidding Begins

Organized, cooperative marketing efforts for Virginia cattle through beef cattle sales and auctions were developed only in the middle third of the twentieth century. Virginia lamb producers pioneered this method of marketing. In the early 1930s, prior to the livestock auction era, lamb pools were organized in which lambs were graded by state graders and then co-mingled by grade, not by individual farm, and shipped to central urban markets for sale through producers' cooperative marketing associations. The success of this effort was not lost on cattlemen, many of whom raised lambs. As auction markets developed in Virginia in the 1930s, the grading of lambs took place there. Soon, veal calves were added to these auctions. This paved the way for developing feeder calf auctions and for organizing producers of feeder calves.[1]

The first Virginia breeders' Aberdeen Angus sale was held in 1934 and it improved in quality and importance each subsequent year. By the seventh sale, held at Warrenton in October of 1940, fifty head averaged $313, five bulls averaged $586, and forty-five females averaged $270. Wintonian 5th consigned by Col. J.B. Dillard of Winton Farm, went to Col. A.E. Pierce of Canterbury Farm for the top price of $1,100. Lewis Strauss' Brandy Rock Farm of Culpeper bought Broadview Farms' Epponian 3rd for $1,000. Five other significant sales were scheduled for Virginia that fall. Kenneth Litton, of VPI, was manager for two sales of Hereford calves on successive days at the Tazewell stockyards. Both of these sales were sponsored by the Virginia Hereford Breeders Association. Litton managed two sales at the Union Stockyards in Staunton on successive autumn weeks, the Shorthorn sale and the purebred Aberdeen Angus sale sponsored by the Augusta Breeders' Association. Both sales consisted mainly of yearlings and calves. Another Staunton sale held that fall was the Hereford dispersal of Mrs. S.S. Young's herd from Bowling Green, Virginia.[2]

By the middle of the twentieth century, livestock auctions such as this one were common in Virginia.

Some auctions were organized and sponsored at individual farms. Bud Snidow recalled an auction at Indian Trace Farm at Locust Dale, held In October of 1940, at which he was too new at the business to be a ring man, and so was given the job of clerk. A vivid picture of this early Hereford sale appeared in *The Virginia Breeder*. Buyers from seven states were present, including former Nebraska Governor Samuel R. McKelvie, who advised Virginia breeders to breed the best cattle, as they would be in great demand when the war ended. A constant downpour and the bawling of cattle nearly drowned the voice of auctioneer Col. E.F. Gartin. Besides young Snidow, Paul Swaffar and George Litton assisted with the sale.[3]

A three-farm sale of Aberdeen Angus took place at Brandy Rock Farm at Brandy in Culpeper County in April of 1940. Strauss played the role of genial host, greeting guests from as far as Nebraska and Kentucky. His sale co-sponsors were Edward Jenkins of Red Gate Farm, Millwood, Clarke County, and Charles T. Neale of Gordonsville in Orange County. The animals were of excellent quality, but had not been fattened for the show and auction ring, so offered fine value for purchasers.[4]

Along with auctions came a colorful and talented group of auctioneers. Col. Fred Reppert of Decatur, Indiana, auctioneer of the three-farm sale at Brandy Rock, was in great demand. In addition to his skill in calling the sales, Col. Reppert was highly knowledgeable and often gave short talks on aspects of cattle breeding as part of the auction program. Col. G.R. Chaffee sometimes substituted for Col. Reppert, as he did for the 1939 Staunton dispersal sale for Mrs. Young. Col. Earl F. Gartin called a large number of these early Virginia cattle auctions, as did Col. Coleman Dunn of Berryville, and Col. Roy Johnston. Col. Reppert operated a school of auctioneering and counted among his graduates H.H. "Benny" Terry of Mustoe, who advertised his services to Virginia cattle breeders.[5] A.W. "Ham" Hamilton of Lewisburg and Mike Jones, a VPI graduate, were nationally known auctioneers at many Virginia sales, as was Morris Fannon, who was also a cattleman.

Other familiar figures in and around the ring for these important early Virginia cattle auctions would continue to play significant roles in Virginia cattle associations and educational activities. These included Kenneth Litton, who left a position as assistant Extension Animal Husbandman at VPI to become manager of the outstanding Morlunda Farms of Lewisburg, West Virginia, and his brother George Litton, Extension Animal Husbandman, as well as Paul Swaffar, Robert Carter, and B.C. "Bud" Snidow.

Most of these early cattle auction sales took place at individual breeders' farms or at the stockyards located on railroad property. Front Royal, Harrisonburg, Staunton, Abingdon, and Bristol were among the towns where the earliest livestock auctions were held. Culpeper, Winchester, and Tazewell also became auction centers.

Virginia cattle auctions moved into a more sophisticated and organized mode with the arrival of the Ownbys from Sevier County, Tennessee. E.P. Ownby had pioneered livestock auctions in Knoxville, Greenville, Morristown, and Cookville, Tennessee. His influence brought his son, Roy Ownby, and his nephew, W. Hugh Ownby, who was in the

Ringmen look for bids during an Angus seedstock sale. The gentleman standing in the center at the auctioneer's podium is G. Dayton Hodges, an Augusta County Angus breeder.

wholesale and retail meat business in Tennessee, to Virginia. The big, ruddy-faced, slow-talking Roy and the slighter, fast-moving, glib talking Hugh moved to Richmond in 1936 to open the South Richmond Stockyards on Petersburg Pike. At the time of their first auction in 1937, they lacked a clerk. H.M "Dick" Campbell, who had clerked at country auctions, was in the audience and offered to fill the post. Twelve years later they closed that operation and in 1948 formed two new corporations, Richmond Livestock Company, Inc., at Richmond, and Southside Stockyards, Inc., at Petersburg. Campbell, who had stayed on as clerk, became a partner and treasurer of Southside Stockyards at Petersburg. In 1948 when the two corporations were formed, Thomas F. Hardesty, who was in the livestock business in Winchester, joined the Ownbys as secretary-treasurer of Richmond Livestock Company and president of Richmond Union Stockyards.[6] In 1951 Hugh took over operation of the Richmond Union Stockyards and added the auction division. He developed a specialty in graded feeder calf sales in Richmond, for which he received the Martin F. Strate Service Award from the Virginia Beef Cattle Association in 1978.[7] Brother Leo Ownby was also a participant in the operation and showed his mastery in the ring. Other prominent auctioneers included Col. Mike Jones of Georgia, Col. Paul Good of Ohio, the late Col. Hamilton "Ham" James of Illinois, and Col. Tom Gammon who split his time between Oklahoma and Virginia. They cried many of the top Angus sales from the 1950s until the 1970s. Jones, the son of Clarence Jones who managed Crow Harris Farm in Forest for F.H. Ludington, continues to auction Angus

This framed cattle photograph and thermometer served as an advertising piece for a Richmond stockyard.

sales in the state and across the nation. Gammon continued selling until his death in the late 1990s.[8]

The ten-acre complex of the Richmond Livestock and Richmond Union Stockyards was ideally situated on Hermitage Road about six blocks from Broad Street and adjacent to railroad tracks and trucking companies. Nearby were two slaughterhouses, Richmond Abbatoir, Inc., and Union Abbatoir, Inc., and three meat packing firms, Kingan and Company, Inc., George H. Meyer Sons, and Joseph McSweeney. Private chutes at the stockyards led directly to each of the firms above, but the auctions also attracted butchers and packers from Maryland, Pennsylvania, and

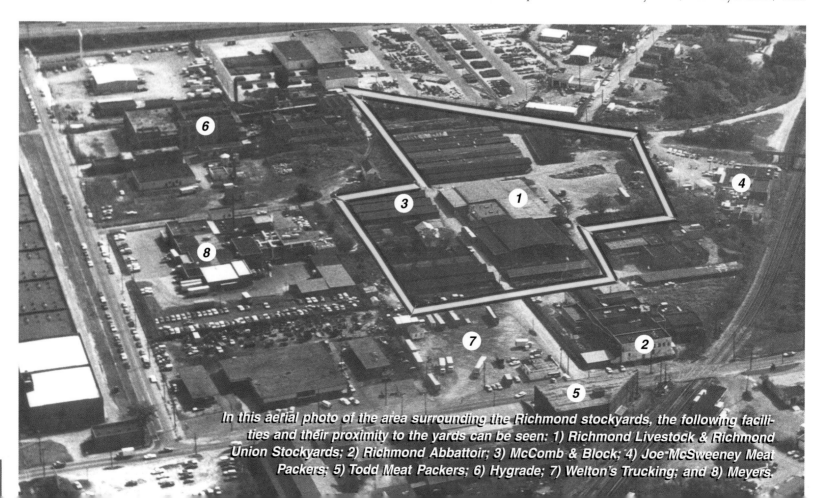

In this aerial photo of the area surrounding the Richmond stockyards, the following facilities and their proximity to the yards can be seen: 1) Richmond Livestock & Richmond Union Stockyards; 2) Richmond Abbattoir; 3) McComb & Block; 4) Joe McSweeney Meat Packers; 5) Todd Meat Packers; 6) Hygrade; 7) Welton's Trucking; and 8) Meyers.

One of the founders of the Virginia Cattlemen's Association was Senator Harry Carter Stuart whose cattle interests included these Angus.

New Jersey. In 1952, for example, the Monday and Thursday auctions at Richmond netted around $100,000 a week, while the Tuesday auctions at Petersburg brought from $80,000 to $110,000 at a time that calves were selling for around $15 to $16 per hundredweight. The combined annual volume at both locations amounted to about $10 million in 1951, making the Ownby firms among the most important of their kind in Virginia.[9]

In 1968, Barbara Clary, a Brunswick County native, returned to her home state from Los Angeles and joined the Ownby firm. By that time, Ownby had developed a significant livestock export business in both horses and cattle and Clary handled the mountains of paperwork for these international transactions. For more than three decades, working in cataloging, clerking, cashiering, bookkeeping, and even as a cowgirl, she watched the firm develop and respond to the changing times in the beef and dairy cattle business. She recalls that a dairy dispersal sale was held nearly every week in either Culpeper or Norfolk during those early years. She now drives by shopping malls, golf courses, and developments with million-dollar homes where cows grazed just thirty years ago.

The amount of record keeping has risen exponentially since the 1960s when some herds appeared for sale with only a breeding chart, and others did not have even that. Herds have increased sharply in size over the years as well. Clary recalled that the firm had numerous dispersal sales for the same people. Dennis Ownby asked one very good dairyman whom they had sold out several times if he was really sure he wanted to sell. The man assured Ownby that this was definitely his last sale, and that even "if the Good

Lord called and asked him to milk His herd, he wouldn't go." He was true to his word – that was his last sale.

Among the significant sales Clary remembers over the years have been those for I. Fred Stine of Winchester; selling the "Joanna" cow for $25,000 for Dr. Wyndham Blanton, Jr., in the 1970s; sales for the Butler Brothers of Bealeton, J. Franklin of Herndon, and Ed Norman of Purcellville in the 1980s; and the dispersal sales for several college herds.[10] Today, the firm continues the services to the cattle industry that the Ownby brothers pioneered more than half a century ago, but with modern equipment and methods that would amaze its founders.

Cattlemen Organize

Although the various cattle breed associations were doing a fine job of helping breeders to market their stock through auctions, by the late 1930s, some leading Virginia cattlemen felt the need for an organization that went beyond the concerns of a breed association.

Because the early minutes of the cattle association have been lost, many details of the development of the organization remain murky. Sometime in the latter part of 1939 several leading cattlemen formed the Richmond Cattle Producers Association with A.W. Buhrman of Richmond, a cattle producer and John Deere dealer, as its president and "ramrod." Senator Harry Carter Stuart of Elk Garden was vice-president, William T. Reed, Jr., of Sabot was the treasurer, and additional founders included R.E.B. Blanton and C.C. Reed, both of Richmond.[11]

The organization took on some significant battles in its first five years. One was a successful fight against freight rate hikes on feeder cattle proposed by southern and western railroads. Another effort was the sponsorship of significant shows and sales. In 1939 they started the Annual Fat Cattle Show, which they hoped would be an educational tool to improve the quality of Virginia stock, and later they began an annual feeder and stocker grading demonstration and sale. They organized the first 4-H Baby Beef Sale. A third victory was their campaign for government grading of beef and acceptance of U.S. carcass grades. Also, they lobbied successfully to have the state legislature require all state institutions to purchase only graded beef, and they convinced chain supermarkets to purchase graded beef.[12] The impetus for this latter move actually came from the supermarket. In speaking to the James River group that made up the Richmond Cattle Producers Association in 1940, Hunter Phelan, president of Colonial Stores, Inc., encouraged the organization to "get your dressed beef graded, and sell it to our stores in uniform, high quality lots."[13]

Funds Propel Effort

An important step occurred in January of 1944 when the Virginia General Assembly appropriated $10,500 that would be available to the Richmond Cattle Producers Association on July 1, on the condition that they transform it into a statewide organization. It is likely that Senator Stuart played a significant role in gaining that appropriation, for in 1948 Allen Randolph, when he was executive secretary of the organization, noted that "in 1944 Harry Stuart and others fathered the Virginia Beef Cattle Producers Association."[14]

The newly-minted Virginia Beef Cattle Producers Association (VBCPA) employed Paul Swaffar as its first executive secretary, luring him away from his position as Assistant Extension Animal Husbandman at VPI. Swaffar was hired mainly to carry out a plan of the association to create a major livestock exposition for the east coast that could rival those in Denver, Chicago, Kansas City, and Fort Worth. With significant contributions from breeders around the state, $75,000 was raised to purchase the stock of the old Virginia State Fair Association and its 460 Strawberry Hill acres north of Richmond. The plan was to construct a purebred sales pavilion to attract the principal purebred livestock shows and sales for the entire Atlantic seaboard. The Atlantic Rural Exposition (ARE) was the name selected for the enlarged fair. On April 25-26, 1946, the first fat stock show took place on the grounds of the new Atlantic Rural Exposition, with a total of 434 head of fat cattle, 268 of them 4-H club steers.[15]

For half a year, from April to November, 1945, William B. McSpadden (VPI '40) was on the staff of the VBCPA as executive secretary while Swaffar devoted his efforts to the ARE. During McSpadden's brief tenure, his assignment was to work on developing the statewide association and to get county associations organized. In his travels around the state, he sensed some resentment of the control of the organization by "the Richmond crowd." McSpadden made a strong plea in *The Eastern Breeder* for expanding the membership beyond the 500 who belonged in 1945 until it included every cattleman in the state and could be a voice for beef producers as strong as labor unions had become for industrial workers. When the Atlantic Coast Line railroad made him a good offer to become their livestock development agent, McSpadden accepted it.[16]

In May of 1946, Henry E. Hutcheson, Extension Agent for Henrico County, joined the VBCPA staff as executive secretary. As Hutcheson looked to the future for the association, he saw the need for several major initiatives. His first priority was to provide better markets for live and dressed cattle at a time when markets needed great physical improvement and when beef supply exceeded slaughtering and processing capacity in the state. Another priority was control of cattle disease. The third area was in government regulation and laws affecting the beef industry.[17] Hutcheson oversaw the association's role in Paul Swaffar's first Atlantic Rural Exposition beef cattle show held in October of 1946, with over 500 cattle from Massachusetts to Florida exhibited.[18]

Under Hutcheson's leadership, the first VBCPA convention was held in Richmond in December of 1946 with more than 200 cattlemen attending. Keynote speaker Fernand E. Mollin of the National Live Stock Association in Denver discussed successful efforts to keep foot and mouth disease out of the United States, but warned of the necessity for constant vigilance. Topics addressed by a dozen other

Four men important to early Virginia feeder cattle marketing were James Shelburne, Virginia Department of Agriculture livestock grader; C.P. McClaugherty, supervisor for Virginia Department of Agriculture livestock grading; Allen K. Randolph, secretary of the Virginia Beef Cattle Association; and Morris Fannon, auctioneer.

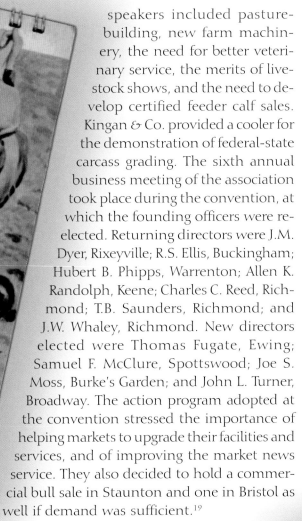

speakers included pasture-building, new farm machinery, the need for better veterinary service, the merits of livestock shows, and the need to develop certified feeder calf sales. Kingan & Co. provided a cooler for the demonstration of federal-state carcass grading. The sixth annual business meeting of the association took place during the convention, at which the founding officers were re-elected. Returning directors were J.M. Dyer, Rixeyville; R.S. Ellis, Buckingham; Hubert B. Phipps, Warrenton; Allen K. Randolph, Keene; Charles C. Reed, Richmond; T.B. Saunders, Richmond; and J.W. Whaley, Richmond. New directors elected were Thomas Fugate, Ewing; Samuel F. McClure, Spottswood; Joe S. Moss, Burke's Garden; and John L. Turner, Broadway. The action program adopted at the convention stressed the importance of helping markets to upgrade their facilities and services, and of improving the market news service. They also decided to hold a commercial bull sale in Staunton and one in Bristol as well if demand was sufficient.[19]

Filling the position of executive secretary of the VBCPA was not easy. Hutcheson, who had done well in the job, died in June of 1947, leaving a serious void. This was filled in September of that year when R.C. "Bob" Carter of Jonesville in Lee County accepted a joint position as executive secretary and also of secretary of the Virginia Hereford Breeders' Association. Carter, a 1931 VPI graduate, worked with the extension service in three counties and worked with his father raising purebred Herefords. He remained in the position for a year, then left in the spring of 1948. In September of 1948 Carter joined the animal husbandry department at VPI to conduct research in animal breeding.[20]

The Randolph Years

Allen K. Randolph, a cattle breeder at Keene in Albemarle County and a member of the VBCPA board, became the executive secretary of the organization by May of 1948. He highlighted for the board several accomplishments of the organization between 1945 and 1948. These included working with bankers and the legislature for better credit laws for farmers needing to borrow, promoting acceptance of

calfhood vaccination by the state for control of Bang's disease, and instituting a state-wide system of veterinary diagnostic laboratories to control animal diseases and parasites. Other significant accomplishments were lobbying the General Assembly for increased funding for the agricultural experiment stations and improved services from VPI for farmers, and organizing purebred bull sales for commercial cattlemen in addition to those already existing for fancy purebred bulls.[21] L.B. Dietrick, Director of Virginia Agricultural Extension Work, wrote to A.W. Buhrman, president of VBCPA, in March of 1948, thanking him for "the work which you and other members of your organization did in securing these increases" in state funding.[22]

When the VBCPA held its state convention in Richmond in February of 1949 the focus of the several excellent speakers was on the marketing of beef. John C. Milton from the American Meat Institute stressed that national organization's advertising campaign to convince the public to eat more meat. The work to create a meatpacking cooperative in the Shenandoah Valley was discussed, as were methods of preparing cattle for railroad shipment to maximize their sale price. Attendees also discussed plans to use Virginia feeder calf sales as a marketing strategy. Bud Snidow (VPI '40), editor of *The Eastern Breeder*, who attended nearly all the Virginia

Feeder calves at the Abingdon Livestock Market in 1954.

sales, discussed merchandizing purebred cattle, with special emphasis on the growing importance of auctions. Snidow left his editor's pen behind in 1951 when he became eastern fieldman for the American Hereford Association, covering all of the thirteen original colonies.[23]

As the VBCPA developed organizational strength, the various individual feeder calf sales continued to operate fairly independently from 1938 until 1952. Each locality where sales took place had a committee that developed the rules and regulations for its sale. Coordination among the local sales organizations occurred informally through the efforts of men like VPI Extension specialists Paul Swaffar, Lester Dalton, and especially Curtis Mast, who would offer demonstrations on castrating, dehorning, and vaccinating to complement the organizations' local calf sales. In February of 1952 the local groups, meeting at the Patrick Henry Hotel in Roanoke, organized as the Virginia Feeder Calf Sales Association, a separate entity from the VBCPA.[24] Part of their separateness came

from some existing skepticism between commercial cattle producers and purebred producers, from differences between cattle producers and market operators, and in sectional rivalry – and perhaps even distrust – between Southwest Virginia cattlemen and those in Northern Virginia.[25]

Feeder cattle sales had begun with the first officially graded calf sale held in Lee County, in the fall of 1939 and a three-county Orange-Greene-Madison feeder-calf sale that same year. Nine sales took place in 1940. *The Eastern Breeder* in April 1941 noted that "a movement is now under way to get the feeder and stocker-calf sales which are to be held in Virginia this fall kind of standardized." Proposals included the idea of a statewide organization, size and disease standards, and sales by graded lots. The article noted that "probably no other event has aided Virginia's cattle industry more than these calf sales which grossed over $91,000 for calf producers last fall."[26] Other examples of these sales included the first yearling steer sale, held at A.K.

Gilmer's Abingdon Livestock Market in 1950 and four graded yearling sales there the following year. In 1953, Bristol and Abingdon were sites of yearling steer sales, and spring feeder calf sales occurred at Lynchburg, Culpeper, and Winchester.[27] At that formative meeting of the Feeder Calf Sales Association, Dalton also had appointed a committee to work out the sales dates for the coming year. Included on this committee was Allen K. Randolph, executive secretary of VBCPA. From the beginning of the Feeder Calf Sales Association its leaders worked for a strong relationship with the VBCPA. The VFCSA president, Lester Dalton, appointed a committee, chaired by John Camm, Jr., of Lynchburg, to investigate cooperating with the VBCPA for sales. Those members included Rufus Copenhaver of Dublin; Emmet Doyle, Culpeper; Rhodes Brown, Sperryville; William S. Adkisson, Clover; and Kenneth C. "K.C." Williamson, livestock marketing specialist with the animal science department at VPI. The VFCSA engaged the VBCPA to advertise and promote its calves and sales at fifty cents a head in 1952 and 1953.[28] The VFCSA encouraged the VBCPA to incorporate. In the agreement between the two organizations, seven of the ten directors of VBCPA were to be the state Feeder Calf-Yearling Committee.[29]

This cooperative venture was significant. Among the earliest archives of the Virginia Cattlemen's Association are the letters to Allen K. Randolph, still in their original envelopes with three-cent stamps on them, from the managers of the various regional calf sales, enclosing their checks for fifty cents a head on the calves sold. The writers included Garland V. Ely for the Lee Farmers Cooperative in Jonesville; George C. Rawlings, Fredericksburg attorney, for the Fredericksburg Feeder Calf Sale; John Hyatt for the Bedford Feeder Calf Producers Association; Marvin Bates, County Agent for the Culpeper Feeder Calf Sale; John C. Estes, Orange County Agent for the 15th annual Orange-Madison-Greene Feeder Calf Sale; and P.E. Byrd, County Agent in Wytheville for the Wythe-Bland calf sale. Often more than 800 calves sold at these events. I. Fred Stine, who managed the Northern Virginia Livestock Producers' Association sale of 2,781 calves at Winchester, noted that eighty percent of the sales were from out of state. Expressing his pleasure with the results, he wrote, "We feel that we made satisfactory inroads into the midwest markets of Ohio, Indiana and Michigan, as well as retaining our big market in Pennsylvania and other eastern states. We appreciate your cooperation and assistance in this year's sale."[30]

Meanwhile, VBCPA had undertaken an important recommended organizational restructuring; they had cut ties with the Atlantic Rural Exposition. The officers met in February of 1953 to set Randolph's salary at $6,500 per year, and to charge the Atlantic Rural Exposition $1,250 for Randolph's services as Livestock Superintendent at the fall show. They also instructed Randolph to take immediate

steps to have the organization incorporated.[31] On April 10, 1953, the organization was issued a certificate of incorporation as a non-profit corporation, retaining the name Virginia Beef Cattle Producers' Association. The stated purpose of the organization was "to better the conditions of those engaged in the producing of beef cattle in the State of Virginia and encourage the development of better beef products." The group was authorized to study, consult, advise and act in seven specific areas: improving beef cattle breeding, feeding and care; solving transportation problems; "broadening, perfecting, facilitating and stabilizing the marketing of livestock and beef;" encouraging official grading of live animals and dressed meat; increasing beef con-

K.C. Williamson (Extension animal scientist), E.C. Grigsby (Extension agent in Pulaski), Tom Mallory (Extension agent in Bland), Rufus Copenhaver (beef producer in Pulaski), Jimmy Shelburne (Head of the Virginia Department of Agriculture's grading), Morris Fannon (auctioneer), and Ed Eller (marketing agent for the Virginia Department of Agriculture) gather at the Dublin Stockyard.

sumption; coordinating all aspects of beef industry from producer to consumer; and cooperating with other organizations in aiding the welfare of Virginia farmers. The directors named in the charter were A.W. Buhrman, Richmond; Harry C. Stuart, Elk Garden; W.T. Reed, Jr., Sabot; W.S. Addisson, Clover; R.E.B. Blanton, Richmond; Lee Boatwright, Sommers; Dr. R.L. Booth, Middleburg; J.H. Cunningham, Marshall; C.C. Funkhouser, White Post; Samuel F. McClure, Spottswood; George C. Palmer, Charlottesville; R.R. Renalds, Timberville; J. Hubert Wheeler, Ewing; John Camm, Jr., Lynchburg; and J. Rhodes Brown, Sperryville. In addition to officers Buhrman, Stuart, and Reed, Allen Randolph was named secretary.

Allen K. Randolph, VBCA executive secretary, (second from left); Jim Warner, Ohio State University beef specialist, (third from left); and K.C. Williamson, VPI Extension beef specialist, (far right) are seen in this photo taken during a Virginia Feeder Cattle promotional trip to Ohio in the 1950s.

The newly incorporated organization plunged into its mission of marketing Virginia beef and livestock, especially through the successful feeder calf program. In so doing the group followed an important national trend. In 1953, the respected publication, *The National Live Stock Producer*, titled a lead article in its March issue "Corn Belt Feeder Buyers Go South" and featured a Winchester Hereford feeder sale in a photograph. Noting the revolution in southern agriculture from row crops to beef cattle in the preceding decade, the article advised buyers to head south for quality cattle. The 5,000-acre R.S. Graves and Brothers farm near Syria in Madison County, Virginia, operated by the brothers R.S. "Bob," F.M., and Elvin, was singled out as an excellent Angus operation, and Allen Randolph and the sales efforts of the VBCPA received favorable attention as well.[32]

Allen Randolph reported that in 1953 he attended fourteen in-state sales meetings and made nine trips out of

state to call on customers and attend sixteen sales. Twenty-nine members of the organization participated in these trips, but crucial to their success was the work and presence of K.C. Williamson, VPI's livestock marketing specialist. Destinations included Lenawee County, Michigan, where the 4-H program had bought eighty Virginia calves. A trip to Maryland and Pennsylvania offered the opportunity to follow-up on 1,700 calves sold there in 1952 and review the remarkable accuracy of their original grading. These trips also offered the opportunity to listen to expressions of disappointment with calves purchased or with shipping problems and shipping fever. A complaint that the organization took to heart and worked for years to solve was the elimination of dairy cattle crosses in beef cattle sold. Allen Randolph's log of these visits is full of pithy comments. Buyers who found a stag (a male animal castrated after sexual maturity) in their lots said "Certainly

YESTERDAY

TODAY

VIRGINIA COWMEN AND COMPUTERS TAKE
"GUESS WORK" OUT OF BEEF PRODUCTION

TODAY BEEF IS BETTER

wish you fellows had never started using rubber bands; I just don't like them." A more direct Maryland purchaser told Randolph, "Damn the day the man invented the rubber band! They don't show staggey until late January or February, after I've got all that feed in 'em, and it's hell!"[33]

Wood County, Ohio, the cattle Feeders Roundup at Kenton, Ohio, and Indiana were 1953 summer destinations. In reporting on the great contact value of these trips, Randolph noted that "the project of exhibiting a pen of Herefords and a pen of Angus at the Lenawee County Fair in Adrian, Michigan, proved successful beyond our greatest expectations" in the large crowds attracted. The group had some excellent publicity opportunities from the *Toledo Blade*, got a free half hour of radio publicity in Findlay, Ohio, and through Williamson's efforts appeared on a popular radio program, the "National Farm and Home Show." A scheme hatched by George Rawlings of Fredericksburg to send a Virginia Feeder Calf to the national Jaycee Convention in Minneapolis was another great publicity ploy. The board voted Williamson a generous gift in gratitude for his work.[34] A decade of work with the feeder calf sales had excellent results. From nine sales in 1940 featuring 1,980 calves that grossed $91,047 or $45.98 per head, the figures had risen in 1951 to twenty-two sales at which 17,278 calves sold for $3,047,916 or an average of $176 per head.[35]

The VBCPA also acted swiftly to fulfill its obligation to work for the well being of Virginia farmers and especially beef cattle producers by exerting political pressure. In the face of a drought in 1953 and declining cattle prices because of saturated markets, the association at its convention in April of 1953 adopted a resolution to contact Virginia Senators and Congressmen as well as Secretary of Agriculture Ezra Taft Benson, opposing any program of subsidies, supports, or controls. The group recommended instead the provision of additional cattle feed to drought-affected areas through the Commodity Credit Corporation. State Senator Harry Stuart, vice president of VBCPA, presented the resolution to the Agriculture Committee of Congress when it met at Bristol, Virginia, on September 19, 1953.[36] That same month the VBCPA board passed a resolution commending the Honorable Parke C. Brinkley, Commissioner of Agriculture, for his efforts to get additional hay into the drought-stricken areas of Virginia, and urging his assistance in the effort to

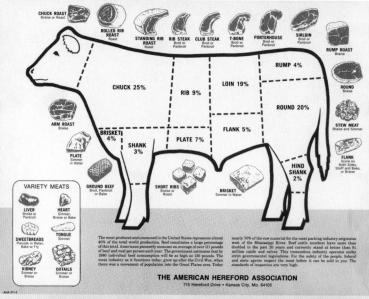

This chart shows the break out on a beef carcass and cuts of meat yielded by various parts of the carcass.

Beef Industry Sets a Standard

The idea of grading beef to indicate its quality probably came from the Progressive Movement, a social and political reform movement in the early twentieth century. It also owed much to the desire of the United States Department of Agriculture (USDA) to be able to report market prices by grade. In 1918 the USDA initiated market reporting by grades. In the Roaring Twenties two federal agencies that purchased large quantities of meat – Veterans Bureau hospitals that had been created after World War I and the United States Shipping Board – requested standards for grading meat. When the USDA published tentative standards for market classes and grades of cattle in 1925, the editor of the Breeders Gazette took up discussions about the idea in an editorial. This led to a meeting in Kansas City in 1926 in which 250 prominent cattlemen considered the necessity

of grading. They formed the National Better Beef Association to promote the grading and stamping of meat.

Initially packers resisted the idea of government grading, preferring to use their own house grades – names such as Swift Premium or Armour Star that are familiar today. Unfortunately there was no standardization in this, so cattlemen tended to back the idea of government grading. In 1928 the official United States Standards for Graders of Slaughter Cattle were published.

Tracking the facts

get the CCC to release surplus grains and cattle feed. In December of 1953, the board lobbied Governor Thomas Stanley for the re-appointment of Brinkley.

With its increasing experience in sales and in representing the industry at the state level, the VBCPA board, meeting in Richmond in December of 1955, elected George C. Palmer II as its new president and appointed a committee of senior board members to work on a state appropriation. In addition, the president appointed a budget committee to develop a plan for the VBCPA to be financed on a statewide, self-sustaining basis. The annual meeting in Natural Bridge in February 1956 was held in conjunction with the Virginia Feeder Calf-Yearling group. This meeting symbolized a new level of cooperation between the two organizations.[37]

The board of the VBCPA took a strong stand on several political issues at its meeting in December of 1957. These included favoring the retention of one cent in the Virginia gasoline tax to be used for agricultural research. The board opposed a proposal of the Commissioner of Agriculture, acting on instruction from the governor, to levy

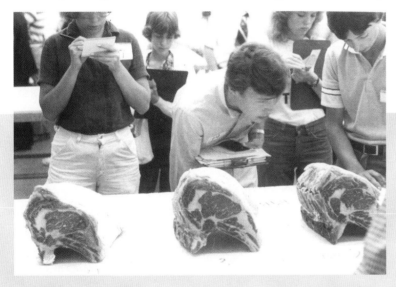

4-H teams compete in a meats judging contest

The idea of grading livestock came to Virginia in the spring of 1931 with J.H. Meek, Virginia's Director of Markets. Lamb grading was the focus that first year, with demonstrations held in cooperation with staff from both federal and state departments of agriculture, the Extension Service at VPI, experiment stations, and the Virginia Department of Vocational Agriculture. At that time there was only one auction market in Virginia. In the 1930s, livestock producers experimented with cooperative marketing in central markets such as Jersey City, selling through commission merchants there. The idea of grading fit well with such co-

mingled sales of animals from various small producers. The men who traveled to make this possible were George Herring, Kenneth Litton, Paul Swaffar, and George Litton for the Extension Service and Roy Thompson, Buster Barnes, Jake Shelburne, and Ray Buchanan for the Division of Markets in the Virginia Department of Agriculture. But it was an expensive and time-consuming operation to travel all over the Commonwealth to grade the animals.

In 1937, slaughter sheep and veal were added to the classes of livestock graded, and the first auction market, Staunton Union Stockyard, requested and received grading service. The next year, hogs were added to the animals graded, and market grading was taken to Abingdon, Orange, Roanoke, and Buena Vista.

The first stocker and feeder-calf grading in Virginia occurred in 1940, but only in the fall of 1941 did this expand to co-a charge on livestock at auctions to cover the cost of a veterinarian that federal law now required be present at sales. The board considered this a public health issue that should be covered out of general revenue rather than by a tax on Virginia's livestock producers. The board also opposed a measure for state licensing of livestock dealers. It was further upset by the USDA ruling that county agents could no longer handle and sell blackleg bacterin and instructed Randolph to take steps to prevent distribution of certain drugs by veterinarians only.[38]

William T. Reed, Jr., who had served as treasurer of the state organization for nearly two decades from its formation, resigned in 1958 and was replaced by P.T. Fitzhugh, Jr., of Culpeper. Hargrave Cunningham was president of the VBCPA that year. Events that received the backing of the organization in 1958, in addition to the regular program of sales, included the Virginia Beef Congress at Natural Bridge in February, which brought all elements of the cattle and beef industry together, and a demonstration meeting in Richmond by the American Livestock and Meat Board, which the VBCPA co-sponsored with the Farm Bureau. Of concern to the board in 1959 was the resignation of fieldman Morris Fannon, who had served successfully as auctioneer for so many of the feeder-calf and yearling sales. The board hoped to convince him to continue. Ear-tags for cattle, an issue

that Rufus Copenhaver had pushed as a board member, came up for discussion at most meetings in 1958 and 1959, and their use increased among the cattlemen. Representatives of the State Department of Agriculture visited the board to explain the necessity of increasing grading fees and were granted a brief spot at the annual meeting to explain the need to the membership.[39]

In 1959 the VBCPA board members gave increasing attention to three key areas of concern. One was to continue promoting cooperation among concerned organizations. They encouraged the Virginia Beef Cattle Improvement Association and the Virginia Feeder Calf Association to hold their annual meetings at Natural Bridge at the same time as the VBCPA. Another growing concern was the transportation of cattle. The board was aware of the apparent disinterest of railroads in expanding cattle shipping to meet the increasing need. This caused problems in moving cattle when there were several cattle sales closely scheduled. It seemed clear that more cattle shipping would be taking place through the expanding

Graders evaluate beef carcasses to determine a yield grade.

mingling of ownership. This came at a time when the beef industry in Virginia was changing dramatically. The export steer market had dwindled and producers were switching from finished to feeder-cattle and cow-calf herds. To assure midwestern buyers that they could obtain quality feeders in Virginia, graded feeder-calf and cattle sales emerged. In 1950, feeder-cattle, mainly yearling steers, were added to the list of graded bovines in Virginia. Meanwhile, in 1946, the USDA published its "Official Standards for the Grades of Feeder Cattle" as part of the Agricultural Marketing Act of 1946.

In 1954, the Division of Markets in the Virginia Department of Agriculture joined with the Extension Service and Experiment Stations in grading beef-breed calves and yearlings in their Record of Performance (ROP) program under the leadership of Dr. T.J. Marlowe of the VPI Department of Animal Science. Bull grading began in 1955 and the first graded slaughter cattle sales took place in 1957. By the mid-1950s, the Virginia graded

feeder-calf sales program and the excellence of grading at Virginia sales was recognized nationally as unsurpassed. By 1958, more than 50,000 calves and cattle were being graded for these sales, all according to the revised USDA standards.

In September of 1979 the USDA issued new grade standards for feeder cattle. The Virginia Department of Agriculture and Consumer Services announced that the new standards would be used starting with the spring of 1980 feeder-cattle sales. Henceforth, three characteristics would be evaluated to determine grade: frame size, thickness, and thriftiness. Frame size refers to the animal's skeletal size – its height and length in

trucking industry in Virginia. To that end, the board considered the use of posters on trucks bearing the message "Another Load of Virginia Feeder Cattle" and bumper stickers for cars advertising that "I attended a Virginia Feeder Calf Sale." A third area of concern was finding the means to expand midwestern markets for Virginia feeder cattle. The board suggested various avenues of increasing contacts in key cattle-feeding counties, using advertising, breed association contacts, Extension Service personnel, chambers of commerce, and an active campaign of personal letter writing.[40]

The statistics for beef cattle in Virginia in 1960 do much to tell the story of the remarkable transformation of the beef cattle industry in the state, as gradually beef cattle replaced dairy cattle as the predominant type in the Old Dominion.

	Beef Cows	Total Cattle
1927	33,000	727,000
1940	52,000	896,000
1950	300,000	1,129,000
1960	371,000	1,394,000

This growth represented more than a tenfold increase in beef cows since the eve of the Great Depression, and a sevenfold increase in the years since the founding of the cattle association.[41] Thus, the number of beef cows in Virginia increased dramatically during the middle third of the twentieth century.

The much-admired and very colorful Allen K. Randolph died in 1964. This was a great loss to the association, as he had been with it from its earliest days and had done much to shape the organization and to develop the beef cattle industry in Virginia. The VBCA board voted to establish an award in Randolph's honor, the Cattleman of the Year, with a cane handsomely mounted on wood. *The Livestock Breeder Journal* joined forces with VBCA in sponsoring the award. The honoree may be a cattle producer, extension agent, livestock grader, or livestock market operator. Nominations are sought annually by the association, and a special committee selects the honoree, who receives the award at the annual convention.[42]

The VBCPA chose as Allen Randolph's successor Martin F. Strate, a Nebraska native who had worked abroad in agricultural aid work with the Heifer Project International, then settled in Virginia after his marriage to Margaret Wampler of Rockingham County. He was an auctioneer from 1950 to 1959, then in the latter year joined the staff of the Virginia Beef Cattle Association as a field representative. His years with the

Earl Kindig stands beside his champion Charolais-Angus cross steer that won the carcass class at Richmond in 1966.

relation to its age. Large, medium, and small were the categories. Thickness was the muscle system in relation to skeletal size. There were three thickness categories in each frame size. Thriftiness referred to the health of the animal and its ability to grow and fatten normally. These standards have been in effect, with periodic amendments, ever since, with the most recent amendments becoming effective in October of 2000.

The USDA has revised its standards for grades of slaughter cattle periodically since they were first published in 1928.

Changes were published in 1939, 1950, 1956, 1966, 1973, 1976, 1987, 1989, and 1997. In some years the changes were minor, in others greater. Changes in 1966, for example, reduced the marbling requirements in Prime, Choice, Good, and Standard carcasses and established five yield grades to identify differences in cutability of yield of boneless, closely trimmed retail cuts.

With nearly three-quarters of a century of cattle grading experience to draw upon, it is clear that grading was one of the factors that enabled the beef cattle industry in Virginia to expand so dramatically and successfully by offering to buyers a reliable source of quality cattle to finish. ~

Especially helpful was material supplied by K.C. Williamson from his many years of experience in the field, including "Report on Early Development of Cooperative Cattle Marketing in Virginia," "A Historical Review of Virginia's Livestock Industry for the 13th Annual Animal Industry Day, 1976" and C.P. McClaugherty, "History of Livestock Grading in Virginia," and C. P. McClaugherty, "Adjusting Livestock Grading Programs to Meet Changing Marketing Conditions," 1956; Charles E. Ball, *Building the Beef Industry: A Century of Commitment* (Denver: The National Cattlemen's Foundation, 1998); *USDA United States Standards for Grades of Slaughter Cattle*, 1996; and USDA, *United States Standards for Grades of Feeder Cattle*, 2000.

association were heavily invested in developing the growing feeder calf sales program, which included not only work in the state with the feeder calf associations and livestock markets, but also an active travel program to potential buyers in Maryland, Pennsylvania, and in the Midwest.

The number of cattle in Virginia continued to rise as the VBCA worked to expand markets and build the beef industry. In 1971 there were 511,000 beef cows in the state and 1,171,000 total cattle. The VBCA urged more of its members to join the American National Cattlemen's Association, noting that there were eighty-two Virginia members that year, a growth from thirty only a few years before, but still not enough in proportion to the significance of the cattle industry in the state.

Another important development that Strate oversaw was the move of the association from its office on South Main Street in Harrisonburg into a new building on Rt. 33 east of the city. The building, dedicated in September of 1973, also served the state's poultry association and the Virginia State Dairymen's Association. A Charolais bull representing the beef industry and a Holstein cow representing the dairy industry did the ribbon cutting. The "ribbon" was not red satin – it was an alfalfa rope, decidedly tastier to the unusual pair doing the ceremonial honors.[45]

Unfortunately, Strate was not present to enjoy the occasion. His sudden death in August of 1973 as the result of a heart attack was a serious loss to the association, as George Litton made clear in his tribute in *The Virginia Cattleman*. The association memorialized its executive leader in the creation of the Martin F. Strate Service Award, to be given at the discretion of the board to a person who had provided outstanding service to the beef cattle industry.

In October of 1973 the board announced the appointment of Reginald B. "Reggie" Reynolds as executive secretary of the VBCA. Reynolds was raised on a farm near Troutville in Botetourt County and graduated in animal sciences from Virginia Tech 1964. He was an area marketing agent with the Virginia Department of Agricul-

Key to Virginia's cattle industry are those who haul livestock, including Millard W. Turner of Broadway.

ture in Roanoke prior to accepting the VBCA position, and had been active with the Virginia Slaughter Cattle Marketing Association's Tel-O-Auction sale program and the National Livestock Marketing and Grading Association. At the time of his appointment, he was serving a

Members of an early board of directors for the Virginia Beef Cattle Association were, front row, left to right, K.C. Williamson, Roy Meek, Tuck Janney, Rufus Copenhaver, Carl LaOrange, Bob Burris, and Martin Strate. Back row, Jim Bailey, Owen Thomas, Jr., Silas Aylor, Harold Bailey, and Bob Chilton.

term on the VBCA board as the representative of the Virginia Department of Agriculture and Commerce.[44]

One of the marketing tools that became widely implemented by the VBCA in 1973 and 1974 was the Tel-O-Auction – telephone bidding through a conference call that connected directly with and included the auctioneer. The concept had been around for more than a decade, and the practice became standard in slaughter-hog auctions as early as 1960. Dublin, Tazewell, and Abingdon were using Tel-O-Auction for slaughter lambs in 1963 and in 1969 it was tried at Dublin for slaughter cattle. Roy Meek tried it for feeder cattle at Dublin in 1972 but experienced some problems. He tried it again with greater success in 1973, selling 720 of 6,142 head in that fashion. The appeal to out-of-state buyers, who saved the expense and time of travel, was considerable. *The Virginia Cattleman* predicted to members in December of 1973, quite accurately, that the practice was likely to expand.

In July of 1974 the VBCA moved its office to Daleville, near to where Executive Secretary Reynolds lived and more conveniently located for the majority of cattle producers in the state. The two areas of Virginia that had shown the greatest increases in beef cattle since 1965 were the southwest (fifty-four percent) and the southside (forty-three percent). The association has occupied the same site for thirty years. The VBCA expanded its board to include representatives from the veterinary, banking, and cattle-feeding segments of the industry in addition to the traditional breed, Virginia Tech, and regional representatives. That same year also saw the debut of the Cow Belles, a women's auxiliary to the VBCA to help with promotional projects at a time of low prices for beef. Nancy Hess and Lucinda Reynolds were among its organizers.

The education of its members was always a goal of the VBCA. The monthly publication, *The Virginia Cattleman*, was

In this newspaper clipping photo, a Charolais bull, representing the beef industry, and a Holstein cow, representing the dairy industry, performed the ceremonial "ribbon cutting" at the dedication of the Agri-Industries Center in Harrisonburg in 1973. The "ribbon" was not red satin – it was an alfalfa rope, decidedly tastier to the unusual pair performing the honors.

an essential educational tool. Several matters in the 1970s became the focus of association efforts to inform the membership of new developments and initiatives. The VBCA pressed hard for the adoption of the self-help, or checkoff, plan in 1974 with a special focus on the plan in the December issue of *The Virginia Cattleman*. In spite of this, the referendum failed the following spring. Virginia's new cattle brand-

Whitestone Miss Skymere K046 won reserve grand champion female at the 1999 Maryland State Fair Angus Show. She is sporting the nationally recognized brand of Whitestone farm in Aldie, Virginia.

ing law went into effect in 1974 and the association made its provisions clear to members so that they could select a brand and register it with the state if they chose.[45] As the proposal for a regional veterinary school to be located at Virginia Tech took shape in the mid-to-late seventies, the VBCA put its support squarely behind the plan, passing resolutions to the legislature, and urging all its members to pressure their legislators to support the measure.

Bruce Bainbridge, standing, Extension livestock marketing specialist of the Virginia Tech animal science department, gives directions to Joe Meek, fieldman, (seated, left) and Reggie Reynolds, executive secretary, Virginia Cattlemen's Association during a satellite auction.

Victor M. duPont, former president of the VBCA, chaired a successful membership drive for the American National Cattlemen's Association (ANCA) in Virginia that netted the VBCA a $2,000 award. The 1975 Allen K. Randolph Cattleman of the Year Award went to duPont, a Loudoun County stockman, who was a regional vice president of ANCA, director of BCIA, and president of Northern Virginia Livestock, Inc.[46]

The decade of the 1970s was difficult for the beef cattle industry in many respects. Prices were sluggish during much of the decade, and drought was a problem in Virginia. Also, significant shifts were taking place in the Virginia cattle industry. The total number of cattle increased sixteen percent to 1,653,000 between 1970 and 1975. Dairy cattle decreased in numbers by at least five percent, sheep and lambs decreased twenty-five percent, and swine were down also, while beef cows increased thirty-three percent from 1969 to 1975. At the same time, the number of farms decreased by nearly thirteen percent. While the next year saw a decrease in cattle numbers, the trend toward consolidation of farms into larger units of production and a concentration on beef cattle was significant for Virginia agriculture.[47] As the decade neared its end, the VBCA welcomed the formation of the Virginia Forage and Grasslands Council in 1977 and watched with hopeful anticipation the plans for Old Dominion Beef, a private enterprise that was to have custom feeding facilities and a modern slaughtering plant. Though a slaughter plant was built at Jarratt, it never became operational as a beef plant.

The VCA exhibited at the 2003 NCBA Annual Convention and Trade Show.

	Dairy Cows in Virginia	Beef Cattle Sold in Virginia Graded Sales
1960	382,000	59,771
1970	224,000	78,988
1980	170,000	117,588
1990	141,000	164,643 (in 1994) [49]

The Virginia Cattleman, which since 1970 had been published as a supplement to the *Livestock Breeder Journal*, became its own separate quarterly publication in 1978 by vote of the VBCA board, with plans to make it bi-monthly when financially feasible. In the 1980s the board voted to simplify the name of the organization to the Virginia Cattlemen's Association (VCA). It is remarkable that as the organization marks its sixtieth year, in a world vastly changed from that of the 1940s in the scientific and technological information available to the cattle breeder and producer, it still devotes most of its time and resources to working in the seven areas specified in its charter, and that has served Virginia's cattle industry so well.

Calf Associations Form

As early as 1940 while he was still the extension livestock specialist at VPI, Paul Swaffar had begun work on a program of feeder-calf marketing. The emphasis was on group sales of graded calves in pen lots by grade, breed, and weight. Lee County in the far southwest has the distinction of holding the first feeder-calf sale in Virginia, according to Dave Gilbert, whose family operated a dairy farm in Lee County from the 1930s to 1950, and who has been raising beef since 1958. He has taken an active role in the local feeder-calf association, which holds it sales at the Lee Farmer's Livestock Market.

C.P. McClaugherty, head of the Virginia Department of Agriculture Grading Service, was among the leaders of the early movement to develop specialized feeder-calf sales, along with R.C. Carter and George Litton, who were county agents in Lee and Tazewell Counties, respectively, around 1940, and who later went on to important faculty positions at VPI.[50] Another pioneer of the feeder-calf sales movement was M. Lester Dalton. As an extension specialist from 1944 to 1952 he developed the idea of selling "Virginia Certified Calves" that had been sired by a registered purebred bull, and that had been dehorned (or were naturally polled), castrated, and vaccinated. He also worked with the state veterinarian on rules for issuing health certificates for moving cattle across state lines – essential if the feeder-calf sales were to appeal to out-of-state buyers.[51]

As the popularity of feeder-calf sales expanded, local associations were formed. Amherst and Campbell County cattle producers held their first feeder-calf sale in 1942, with 103 steers and 77 heifers sold at an average price of twelve

New trends in marketing during the 1970s all encouraged and employed at the sales sponsored by VBCA, included the Tel-O-Auction and "special sales" that focused on one gender or one breed at a time. The early success of the Tel-O-Auction caused the U.S. Department of Agriculture to grant $106,708 to the Virginia Department of Agricultural Economics to assist the cattle industry in developing a more effective Tel-O-Auction system, through the use of sophisticated electronic equipment. The VBCA urged attendance at the Southern Beef Council's Southern Beef Conference in Roanoke in November of 1978. That meeting addressed improving graded feeder- calf sales and the new developments in electronic marketing. Both initiatives had enormous appeal to Virginia cattlemen. A third new development affecting the cattle industry in Virginia was the dramatic change in American beef consumption. In the 1970s hamburger fast-food chains began to transform American eating patterns. The sharply increased demand for hamburger meat was a major national trend.[48]

The decline in the number of dairy cattle continued as the twentieth century progressed. Meanwhile, the number of beef cattle rose steadily, reaching an all-time high by 1994.

dollars per hundredweight. By 1948 consignors from eight counties participated in these sales at Lynchburg. In July of 1948 the Lynchburg Feeder Calf Producers Association, Inc., was chartered as a cooperative non-profit organization. The original officers were Rowland Lee, Amherst County, president; Charles W. Wood, Nelson County, vice president; O.B. Ross, Amherst, secretary; and John Camm, Lynchburg, treasurer. The association remained active until its dissolution in 1964, but was replaced by the Lynchburg Feeder Cattle Association as a continuation of the original group.[52] By the 1970s it served producers in an eleven-county area and was marketing around 5,500 feeder cattle annually, placing emphasis on producing calves sired by bulls that had met performance standards.[53]

The Fredericksburg Feeder Calf Association started when a group of local producers banded together for a sale at the Fredericksburg Livestock Market in October of 1948. Local extension agents Dayton Crosby from Essex and Frank Tullos from Stafford assisted the producers with setting rules and inspecting calves, emphasizing quality to attract Maryland and Pennsylvania buyers. The agents managed the sale. Over the winter of 1949 the association took shape and in 1950, after another sale, its officers filed articles of incorporation. Hunter Greenlaw from Stafford, George D. Williams from King George, Crosby, and Tullos, were the original directors. The association set firm rules from the earliest years, including the requirement that calves be dehorned, that herds be Bangs-tested, heifers vaccinated, and that animals showing dairy breeding be rejected.[54] Another active northern Virginia group was the Marshall Feeder Cattle Association in Fauquier County, which sold its cattle at the Fauquier Livestock Exchange in Marshall. This group was formed in 1964. In its first year it sold 2,766 head for $266,685, and in the tenth anniversary year, when Earl Browning was outgoing president and James N. Fletcher, Jr., was president, the group sold 6,478 head for a $2,236,169.[55]

In the valley, the Rockingham Feeder Cattle Association held several annual sales in the 1970s when John L. Turner was its president. In Highland and Bath Counties the feeder association had as its leaders in the 1970s John Trimble of Warm Springs and A.L. Shepherd of Monterey. The Rappahannock producers, who sponsored the feeder calf sales for Rappahannock County, held sales at the Front Royal Livestock Market. Newbill Miller served as the group's president in the early 1970s.

The Dublin Feeder Cattle Association was formed in 1953, according to retired extension agent Tom Tabor of Pulaski County, who grew up on a Guernsey dairy farm there and now raises Angus. He has been active with the Virginia Feeder Cattle Association and, like so many Virginia producers, applauds these sales because they make it possible to generate trailer-loads of cattle to ship west and bring Virginia producers a good return on their investment.[56] In 1974 the Dublin Feeder Cattle Association, under the leadership of its president, Roy Meek, became the first in the nation to sell cattle that were still on the farm through its Tele-Auction.[57] Another of the feeder cattle organizations in southwestern Virginia was Galax Feeder Cattle Sales.

The Albemarle Feeder Cattle Association was typical of many similar county organizations in turning out nearly one hundred producers and their wives for its annual banquet in Charlottesville in December of 1971. As did many of the associations, the Albemarle group used the occasion as an educational opportunity for its members. Representatives of chemical companies, feed companies, and the Beef Cattle Improvement Association, presented a program on pre-conditioning of feeder-calves, while K.C. Williamson, the Livestock Marketing Specialist at VPI, gave an overview of feeder-cattle marketing. Leaders of the organization at that time included Larned Randolph, Fred Scott, Jr., and M.Y. Sutherland.[58] Nearby Madison County had a Feeder Yearling Association.[59]

Besides the individual local feeder-cattle associations, a statewide organization was formed. A driving force in creating this group was M. Lester Dalton, who organized the local feeder-cattle groups into districts with an elected

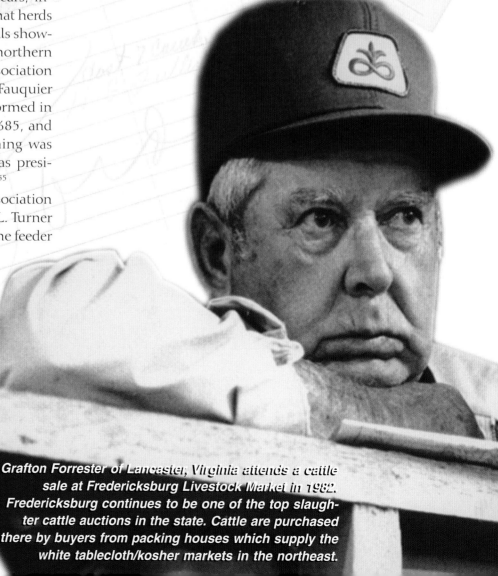

Grafton Forrester of Lancaster, Virginia attends a cattle sale at Fredericksburg Livestock Market in 1982. Fredericksburg continues to be one of the top slaughter cattle auctions in the state. Cattle are purchased there by buyers from packing houses which supply the white tablecloth/kosher markets in the northeast.

representative from each. That committee later evolved into the Virginia Feeder Cattle Association.[60]

Livestock Markets

The number of livestock markets in Virginia began to expand as the auction movement and the feeder calf sales movement took off in the 1940s. The Lee Farmers Livestock Market, site of Virginia's first feeder-calf auction, is owned by John William and operated by Wayne Markham, both of Jonesville.[61]

Luther Hamilton owned four early livestock markets, Bristol, Abingdon, Wytheville, and Tazewell, in the late 1930s. The Tazewell market had been built in 1935 with Works Progress Administration (WPA) labor, a New Deal federal employment program in the Great Depression.[62] A young VPI graduate who had worked for the Eastern Livestock Marketing Cooperative Association in Jersey City returned in 1939 to his native Russell County and began to grade livestock at Hamilton's four markets. This was Aaron Kemper Gilmer, Jr., who joined with two partners in 1940 and purchased the Tazewell Livestock Market. The following year he became the principal stockholder in the Abingdon Livestock Market and the market operator. Fire destroyed the market in 1974, but Gilmer built at a new location in 1976 and sold it in 1980. The market had the largest volume of any livestock market east of the Mississippi, and is still operating today.[63] Another important southwest market is the Pulaski Livestock Market at Dublin, which Roy Meek managed in the 1960s and 1970s and is today managed by his son Joe Meek. The Narrows Livestock Market, Inc., owned by R.S. Morris and J.L. Morris, Jr., in Pearisburg, and E.L. Lowry, served producers in Giles County and across the border in West Virginia. Gerald Gardner of Hillsville and James C. Williams of Galax owned the Galax Livestock Market serving Grayson and Carroll Counties and some producers in adjacent North Carolina.

In Lynchburg a group of stockholders, including Lawson Turner, David Hugh Dillard, Dr. W.M. Cardwell, Frank Gilliam, and Herbert Thompson, built the Lynchburg Livestock Market on Mayflower Drive in 1939. Bernard Camden was the general manager, John Amanett the assistant manager, and Jack Howell the ring master. Harry Turpin was manager in the 1970s. In 1976 the location changed when a new sale barn was built in Campbell County. The partnership of Metcalf, Gilliam, and Fariss, L.L.C. now owns this market.

In Charlotte County the Phoenix Livestock Market was started by B.F. Dodd in 1948 and operated until 1985. The Bedford Livestock Market had a similar lifespan. It was started in 1947 by E.M. Hewitt of Staunton and Harry Turpin of Bedford County and closed in the early 1980s. North of the James in Amherst County, Rufus Edwards and the Jack Howell family (including Rob, Glenn, and Tommy Howell) built the Amherst Livestock Market in March of 1976. This market held its last auction in December of 2001. Today the facility is a limited buying station and pre-conditioning barn.[64]

Culpeper Agricultural Enterprises was a livestock marketing center for that important cattle county and handled special graded feeder sales and purebred cattle sales. In the 1970s, the Orange Livestock Market held sales every Wednesday under the management of Haywood Darnell. J.B. Stephens managed the nearby Albemarle Livestock Market, just outside Charlottesville near I-64 and Virginia Rt. 20.

In Northern Virginia, the Leesburg Livestock Market was an important location for feeder-calf sales until it was destroyed by fire. The Fauquier Livestock Exchange in Marshall, managed by J.G. Simpson from its opening in 1962, until 1973, and then by John Heyl, served that northern cattle county. In 1971, this was the first market in Virginia to install a closed circuit television to display information about

A.K. Gilmer

the animals in the ring – their kind, weight, and number – to help prospective buyers.[65] Monterey Livestock Market serves the producers in Bath and Highland Counties, most of whom are members of the Highland-Bath Cattle Association. Lester Dalton, extension agent in Bath County, was a major promoter of this market that was managed by George Swecker.

In the Shenandoah Valley the important livestock markets were at the Farmers Livestock Exchange at Winchester, managed by Lindy Hieronimus, Staunton Union Stockyards, operated by the Hewitt family, and Shenandoah Valley Livestock Sales, Inc. at Harrisonburg operated by Bill Joseph. Charles W. "Charlie" Lawson, who began as an employee at the Staunton Union Stockyards in 1935, was, by the 1970s, the chief executive officer not only of that market, but also of Rockingham Livestock Sales, Inc., and Monterey Livestock Sales, Inc.[66] In the Roanoke area, Joe Graham was manager of the Roanoke-Hollins Stockyard at Hollins in the 1970s, with a sale every Monday, often featuring feeders.

The operators of these various livestock markets formed their own organization, the Virginia Association of Livestock Market Operators, which held its annual meeting in conjunction with several breed associations, the cattleman's association, and other groups in what had come to be known by the 1970s as the Virginia Beef Cattlemen's Convention. For a number of years, this was held at the Natural Bridge Hotel, and then moved to the Homestead and several other locations. The organization had settled on Virginia Livestock Markets Association as its name by 1975 when A.K. Gilmer III was its president.

George Swecker, long-time manager of Monterey Livestock Market

Virginia Beef Cattle Improvement Association

What the Babcock test for butterfat in milk did for advancing the dairy industry, the introduction of performance testing did for the beef industry, by demonstrating that properly managed cattle could gain weight rapidly. The introduction of central bull testing in Texas in 1941 offered a successful demonstration of competition based on performance. A cattle production records program had been developed at the USDA Station at Miles City, Montana, by 1936 but performance programs did not become widespread until the 1950s. The performance movement in Virginia drew on research discoveries that growth rate in cattle is an inherited trait. Significant early beef cattle breeding work took place at the research station at Front Royal operated by VPI and the USDA, beginning in 1947. Leaders in this work were Dr. Charles M. Kincaid and Dr. Robert C. Carter of VPI and Dr. T.C. Byerly and Dr. Everett Warwick of USDA, with Bob Priode and Dr. Ken Bovard supervising the pioneering onsite breeding work.[67]

From 1945 to 1950, beef cattle improvement programs were introduced into many southwestern and western states, usually through state extension services. A significant field research project began in Virginia in 1953 at the instigation of Charles W. Wampler of Dayton, president of the Virginia Angus Association, who had learned of the Front Royal research. Wampler also involved Dr. Kincaid, Curtis Mast, the beef extension specialist, and Professor George Litton, head of animal husbandry at VPI, in the data gathering. The program, which began with nine herds, had grown to seventy herds by 1955, using first a portable scale that Wampler had built, then experimenting with other types of scales. The group developed an index for growth rate and type score. The data were related to sire and dam and shared with the breeder. The study concluded that it was possible to develop a program for improved growth and quality of cattle on Virginia farms. This led to a legislative appropriation to VPI in 1954 to employ a breeding and genetics specialist to direct the program, Dr. Thomas J. Marlowe, and to employ an experienced grader to grade the calves in the program. Joe Graham, who undertook this difficult job, was later honored at the state and national level for his pioneering work. This on-farm performance testing program continued with great success until the 1980s.[68]

In January of 1955, Virginia had the distinction of being the first state to establish a statewide beef cattle improvement association. The founders, Marlowe, Mast, W.L. Cover, D.W. Mason, R.H. Matthiessen, Fred W. Scott, and Hank Davis, met at the Virginia Angus headquarters in Charlottesville.[69] The Virginia Beef Cattle Improvement Association (VBCIA) was the name chosen. Clover, the first president, served for three years and was succeeded by David E. Brower, manager of Still House Hollow Farm at Hume. The VBCIA performance testing program, out of which the organization grew, has been housed in the Animal Science Department at Virginia Tech, where computers and experts are available for analyzing the statistics. Organization memberships and fees for services have funded the program and its secretary's salary. The Animal Extension Specialist at Virginia Tech has supervised the work. Dr. Marlowe left the supervision of these efforts in 1959 and was succeeded by Henry H. Dickenson, Jr., then by Charles R. Cooper until 1961. From 1961 to 1998 A.L. "Ike" Eller, Jr., Extension Animal Scientist, supervised the program.[70]

The VBCIA has been an important factor in the remarkable improvement of the quality of Virginia cattle in the past half-century. Its primary stated purposes are: "to foster the improvement of beef cattle in Virginia through improved genetics and management with major emphasis placed on selection criteria for traits of economic importance," and "to carry on educational and promotional work in connection with the production of improved beef cattle."[71] Beef cattle improvement associations were founded in that same decade in nearly every major cattle-producing state in the nation. From 1968, the VBCIA and these other state organizations have been guided by the Beef Improvement Federation, the national organization that sets the guidelines and standards for beef cattle genetics.

The early leadership of the VBCIA was closely connected with the leadership of the VBCPA, so that the same names often appear in board and officer lists of the two organizations. VBCIA officers in 1959 were Dave E. Brower, Jr., of

Hume, president; F.W. Scott, North Garden, vice president; W.B. McSpadden, Chilhowie, treasurer; T.J. Marlowe, secretary; and W.L. Clover, Charlottesville, past president. Other board members were W.A. Davidson, Marshall; P.C. Duckworth, Lynchburg; H.R. Greenlaw, Fredericksburg; W.C. Jones, Franklin; Allen K. Randolph, Keene; and C.W. Wampler, Harrisonburg. The technical advisors were George W. Litton, T.J. Marlowe, and C. Curtis Mast.[72]

An important early program of the VBCIA was the ROP Bull Feeding Test. This began in October of 1958 with seventy-five of the top indexed bull calves (fifty Angus, twenty-two Hereford, and three Shorthorn) from thirty-seven Virginia herds and one from Maryland on a 140-day gain test. Those bulls were then sold at public auction in April of 1959 at Culpeper Agricultural Enterprises. All had been fertility tested and given a clean bill of health to be shipped anywhere in the world.[73] This was just the kind of program and public offering designed to fulfill the organization's mission to improve Virginia cattle.

VBCIA held its fourth annual meeting in Culpeper on February 17, 1959, coinciding with the official weighing of the bulls on the feeding test program, and an exhibit of the bulls and feed samples. The organization was engaged in a performance testing program for beef cattle in cooperation with VPI and with the Virginia Division of Markets. This program involved 5,097 calves and 1,423 yearling cattle sired by 4,089 bulls in seventy-eight Angus, fifty-two Here-

An Angus, Hereford, and Shorthorn are seen at the Front Royal beef cattle research station in 1949. Records of their growth from birth and of their feed rations were carefully measured to determine their respective development.

ford, and four Shorthorn herds in forty-five Virginia counties. In reviewing the results of the study, the VBCIA leaders noted the great variation in performance of cattle in the same herd under the same management practices. This caused them to emphasize and recommend to Virginia cattle producers "the opportunity to improve the performance of your herd by removing the poor producers and replacing them with outstanding individuals which are out of high producing cows and sired by bulls with high average performance for all of their calves."

In 1972 the VBCIA decided to open a test station on James D. Bennett's Knoll Crest Farm at Red House. The Bennett family built a new facility for the project. The first bulls entered the test that fall and the first senior bulls were sold the following spring. For a quarter century, Ralph

VPI Extension beef specialist Curtis Mast, far left, gives a type demonstration in the 1950s.

Mr. and Mrs. William Wampler accept the Bartenslager Award from Dr. Arthur Bartenslager at the 1996 Virginia Angus Association's annual meeting. The honor was bestowed on Charles Wampler and Sons of Harrisonburg for being the consignor of top-performing Angus bulls at Virginia BCIA bull test sales. The Wampler family has been instrumental in performance testing of cattle.

Tucker, Floyd Dominy, and Charles Fariss chaired the test and sale committee. From then until 1998, when the Bennett operation needed the facility, the Red House Bull Evaluation Center filled a need in central and southern Virginia and performed outstanding service for breeders.

Roy Meek was active in organizing and managing the BCIA bull test station at Dublin in the late 1960s and in the 1970s was an advisor to the new Foster Falls test station.[74] From 1980 to 2002 a test station was located at Brent Moore's farm just east of Wytheville; it was purchased by E.D. Umberger in 1986. Jack Poole managed the station until 2002.[75]

The bull tests have been the mainstay of the organization since they were established and in a typical year some 400 bulls are tested. About two-thirds of them are sold at

the organization's sales for strong prices, as the sales have earned a reputation as sources of reliable genetics. Currently, the VBCIA manages five test groups and three sales at two test locations, Culpeper and Wytheville. The Culpeper test station is at Tom and Kim Nixon's Glenmary Farm at Rapidan and the Southwest Virginia test station is at Tim Sutphin's Hillwinds Farm at Dublin. In April of 2004 the forty-sixth annual VBCIA Culpeper Junior Bull Sale saw fifty-five Angus bulls, representing the top sixty percent of the eighty-eight bulls tested, sell for a record average of $2,081 per head. The Virginia Cattlemen's Association co-managed this sale with Dale Stith serving as auctioneer.[76]

Over the years, the VBCIA developed a range of annual awards to offer to persons and farms of exceptional achievement. These include the Outstanding Seedstock Producer Award, the BCIA Superior Service Award, the Commercial Producer Award, and the Premier Breeder Award for various breeds. In 2003, for example, Bill Powell received the Superior Service Award; Dave Caldwell, owner, and Tommy Clark, manager, accepted the Outstanding Seedstock Producer Award for Mystic Hill Farms; Mike Goldwasser was named Outstanding Commercial Producer; Simmental Breeder of the year was Smith Reasor; the Charolais honors went to Leo and Annette Muncy; and James Willis' Green Acres Angus Farm accepted the award for that breed.[77] In addition, the two test stations also give awards to their winners. In 2004 the winners at the Wytheville test station were Fred Gent, Mike Griffith, Freddie Mullins, Ann Ogle Rambo, Harold Hawkins, Smith Reasor, and Jason Pratt. At the Culpeper test station the winners were Bo Walther and C.W. Pratt.

Officers of VBCIA in 2004 are Dennis Pearson, president; John Wilkins, vice president; Carl Lindgren, secretary-treasurer; and Scott Greiner, educational advisor. Current board members are Randy Mink, Roger Morris, Ray Simms, Leo Muncy, Charles Rosson, Terry Slusher, and Hank Maxey, past president. The technical directors are W.E. Beal and Norman Vincel.[78]

Beef Improvement Federation

As the idea of performance testing spread in the 1950s and early 1960s, leaders in the movement began to consider the necessity of standardizing performance criteria and measurements. Among the leaders of this movement was C. Curtis Mast of Virginia when he chaired the Extension Beef Improvement Committee of the American Society of Animal Science. Joining with Charlie Bell, Everett Warwick, and Frank Baker, Mast helped formulate a plan for national standardization and coordination. A meeting of representatives of extension services, research groups, and breed associations in which Mast participated gathered in Kansas City, Missouri, in May of 1964. From their

work came a report in February of 1965 that recommended the procedures for measuring traits of economic value in beef cattle. Central to this seminal report were ideas on handling records according to the sex of animals, the measurement of weaning weight at 205 days, measurement of yearling weight (365 days) or long yearling weight (550 days), and the importance of central testing stations, conformation evaluation, and carcass evaluation. This report laid the foundation for the formation of a national organization, but that did not occur for three more years.[79]

A meeting in Denver in January of 1967 of the "International Conference of Beef Cattle Performance Testing As-

James Bennett of Red House has had many beef industry honors come his way, including Lancaster/Sunbelt Expo Southeastern Farmer of the Year. He has also been placed on the Seed Stock Breeder Honor Roll of Excellence and has served on numerous state and national cattle industry boards.

sociations" brought representatives from breed associations, Performance Registry International, some Extension Services, and some state BCIA groups. All agreed on the need for a national organization, but working out its nature – whether it should be a council of member organizations or a direct membership organization – took many meetings over the next year. The outline of the organization was a blending of the ideas of Ferry Carpenter of Hayden, Colorado, and Frank Baker. The Beef Improvement Federation (BIF) was chosen as its name, and by-laws were written. In January of 1968, again in Denver, the organizational meeting took place. Virginia's own C. Curtis Mast had the distinction of delivering the keynote address. The Virginia BCIA was one of the organizations that applied for charter membership in BIF. Besides Mast, other Virginians who attended this organizational meeting were A.Y. Stokes and A.L. "Ike" Eller, Jr., of the VBCIA, J.M. O'Bannon, Charolais breeder of Woodville, and Henry Matthiessen, president of the American Hereford Association. Matthiessen was elected to the board of directors. The work carried out at that founding meeting set guidelines for beef producers around the world.[80]

Meetings in 1969 resulted in influential reports on the operation of Central Testing Stations; on standards for reporting Pre-Weaning and Post-Weaning Testing on Farms and Ranches; on working with the American Meat Science Association in developing Beef Carcass Evaluation standards; on Performance Pedigrees; and on National Sire Evaluation programs. At the 1970 annual meeting in Kansas City, Missouri, the BIF released a significant publication produced with the help of the Federal Extension Service, USDA, entitled *Guidelines for Uniform Beef Improvement Programs*. At the workshop for state BCIAs and extension beef cattle specialists, Eller, representing Virginia Tech, was one of those presenting papers. Eller appeared on the program in a similar capacity at the 1972 annual meeting at Omaha, Nebraska. The focus of the Research Symposium that year was on reproduction, with papers on heterosis, heritability, dystocioa, fertility, and use of reproductive techniques.[81]

BIF returned to Omaha for its 1973 annual meeting and research symposium. This event saw some important contributions by Virginians. Eller was named as one of the three regional secretaries, a new ex officio position to aid the secretary and program director, and James Bennett of Knoll Crest Farm, Red House, was elected to the board of directors. At the 1974 meeting in Denver, Eller served as chair of the Reproduction Committee, and the following year that committee reviewed research that Eller and two others conducted. At the 1976 meeting in Kansas City, Bennett was elected vice president of BIF and was also

Steve Hopkins, Orange County Extension Agent, left, and Tom Nixon, Culpeper Bull Test Station Manager, stand with senior bulls on test at Glenmary Farm.

named chair of a new committee to study calculating adjusted yearling weight, a subject that had caused such intense discussion that the central test committee report could not be accepted. At the 1977 meeting in Bozeman, Montana, the Record Utilization Committee that Eller chaired recommended that BIF publish a brochure on "Recommended Improvement Programs for Commercial Producers" and another on "The Beef Industry and Performance Records."[82]

In 1978 for the first time the BIF held its annual meeting in the east, at Donaldson Brown Continuing Education Center at Virginia Tech, on May 22-24. It was especially gratifying that at this meeting a Virginian, James Bennett, was elected president of the BIF. At the 1979 meeting, over which Bennett presided, another Virginian, Roger Winn, was elected to the board of directors. At this meeting, the BIF drafted a resolution in favor of the Beef Referendum. Winn was chosen vice president at the 1980 meeting, and president in 1981, at which time a revision of the *Guidelines* was published. An accomplishment of Winn's second year as president was the development of the standard frame score chart. When the group met in Sacramento in 1983, Eller was serving as executive director of the BIF, and could report at the next annual meeting in Atlanta in 1984 that there were thirty-two BCIA members, sixteen breed associations and eleven other organizations paying dues to BIF. The next year, however, Eller asked that the directors begin a search for his replacement, and in 1986, Roger McGraw took over the post and Eller was once more presenting research results to the symposium. In 1985 another Virginian, Al Smith, was elected to the board of directors, and in 1989 Paul Bennett, son of James, became the first second-generation board member and president.[83]

Like nearly every other major state or national cattle organization, the BIF developed a program of awards. Among the hundreds of persons from all over the nation honored with these awards is a handful of outstanding Virginia cattlemen. In 1972, and again in 1978, James Bennett was named to the Seed Stock Breeder Honor Roll of Excellence. In 1980 Floyd Dominy made the list, in 1981 Dwight Houff, in 1984 Jerry Chappell and Earl Kindig, in 1985 J. Newbill Miller, in 1988 Scott Burtner, in 1990 T.D. and Roger Steele, in 1991 Nicholas Wehrmann and Richard McClung, and in 1992 Tom and Ruth Clark. In 1976 C. Curtis Mast was honored with the Pioneer Award for Education. In 1978, two of the three Pioneer Awards went to Virginians: R. Henry Matthiessen, for breeder, and Bob Priode of Virginia Tech for research. In 1978, James Bennett was chosen Seed Stock Breeder of the Year. Named to the Commercial Producer Honor Roll of Excellence in 1980 was Roger Winn, Jr., of Virginia. In 1984 Norman Coyner and Sons received the commercial honor, in 1985 Ernie Reeves, in 1986 Charles Fariss, in 1990 Lewis T. Pratt,

and in 1992 Clinton E. Martin and Sons. For the award of Commercial Producer of the Year, Al Smith was honored in 1983 and Charles Fariss in 1986.

Livestock Council

Another influential organization with an impact on the cattle industry was the Virginia Livestock Council. This organization was established in the early 1950s to serve the VPI Animal Husbandry Department in an advisory and developmental capacity under the direction of department head, George W. Litton. It was composed of representatives of various organizations concerned with the breeding, raising, feeding, marketing, medical care, and processing of all kinds of livestock in the Commonwealth. Annual dues in the 1950s were twenty-five dollars per organization.

George Litton

The members of the council in 1959 were S.C. Aylor of Brandy Station, representing the Virginia Angus Association; J. Paul Williams of Richmond, for the Virginia Feed Manufacturers Association; S.F. McClure, Jr., of Spottswood, for the Valley-Northern Virginia Sheep Breeders Association; Dr. J.H. Burr of Covington for the Virginia Veterinary Medical Association; J.S. Moss of Burke's Garden, Southwest Virginia Sheep Association; L.P. Prillaman, Martinsville, Virginia Hereford Cattle Association; C.C. Funkhouser, White Post, Northern Virginia Livestock Association; A.L. Glasscock, Chuckatuck, Virginia Peanut and Hog Growers Association; A.J. Jessee, Timberville, Virginia Meat Packers Association; W. Clyde Koontz, Elkton, United Wool Growers Association; R.H. Matthiessen, Hume, Beef Cattle Producers Association; R.S. Ellis, IV, Alcoma, Purebred Swine Breeders Association; Turner A. Gilmer, Jr., Lebanon, Southwest Virginia Agricultural Association; and A.K. Gilmer, Lebanon, Virginia Association of Livestock Auction Markets. The council functioned very effectively for about ten years as the animal husbandry department expanded to serve the state's growing livestock industry.[84]

A Dollar a Head

The check-off concept of a required contribution to be pooled for promotional purposes came about in the 1920s, about the time that grading became an accepted practice. The National Livestock and Meat Board was founded in 1922 in an effort to bring more amicable relations between producers and packers. The first check-off

Promoting Beef at the Virginia Capitol in Richmond in the mid-1970s are (left to right) Reggie Reynolds, executive secretary of the Virginia Cattlemen's Association; Bob Delano, Virginia Farm Bureau president; Ray Vaughn, VDACS deputy commissioner of agriculture; and R. Bruce Hogue, of Charlottesville. Reynolds holds a "black baldie" steer with the primal cuts marked.

program began that same year with an assessment of five cents per train carload of cattle. The receipts from this program made possible the first national promotional campaign in 1923 with the slogan "Meat for Health."[85]

A national beef check-off idea surfaced in the late 1960s at a time of political and economic unrest in the nation. An unpopular war, a weak economy, and an oil crisis were some of the issues that made American consumers uneasy. In 1973 a plan for a value-added check-off of three-tenths of one percent of the price of each animal sold, to be collected by state beef councils, was introduced in Congress. The resulting funds would be used to promote beef and educate the public about it.

Meanwhile, in Virginia, the idea of a state beef check-off had advanced to the point of enabling legislation being passed by the General Assembly in 1969. R.S. Ellis IV of Buckingham and Roy A. Meek of Draper led this successful lobbying effort on behalf of the cattle industry. However, when a proposal was put to Virginia cattle producers in 1970, it failed by forty-seven percent favorable to fifty-three percent opposed.

Remaining optimistic, cattle industry leaders met in Staunton in June of 1974 with Ellis as moderator, to dis-cuss a strategy to get a check-off plan adopted. Representatives of the purebred beef associations, market operators, the Virginia Beef Cattle Improvement Association, the Virginia State Dairymen's Association, the Virginia Meat Packers Association, and the Virginia Beef Cattle Association, agreed unanimously to request a second vote among cattle producers on that 1970 ballot enabling legislation that would form a Virginia beef cattle commission. This check-off plan would entail a fifteen cents per head payment by the first handlers on all cattle sold. The estimated $100,000 to be generated annually from this check-off would be used to promote Virginia feeder cattle sales; to educate consumers on the cooking of the newer, leaner beef; to inform government leaders and to lobby legislators about cattle industry needs; to advertise beef; and to fund short-term research.[86] A fifteen-member Virginia Beef Cattle Commission was to be appointed by the governor from names recommended by cattle industry organizations. The voters were those who owned ten or more beef or dairy cattle on July 1, 1974 or January 1, 1975. Two-thirds of those voting on April 15, 1975 had to approve the check-off for it to become effective.[87]

The vote was so close when counted on April 22 that a recount was requested. The recount, held on April 25, confirmed that those voting "yes" were 66.59 percent, while those voting "no" were 33.41. The measure failed by 00.07 percent, but clearly sentiment in the Virginia cattle industry was swinging toward check-off.[88]

Virginia cattle producers finally approved a statewide referendum in August of 1984. Virginia's first beef promotion efforts began on July 1, 1985, with an assessment of twenty-five cents per head sold. The body named to oversee this effort, the Virginia Cattle Industry Commission, met initially in Richmond in January of 1985. Ellis chaired the commission, Meek was vice-chairman, and Reggie Reynolds was secretary. Board members were Phillip Morris, Jim Chambers, Dave Walker, Bob Kerr, Gene James, Dwight Houff, Ernie Reeves, Jim Latane, G.D. Gilliam, Cookie Milton, Russell Inskeep, Floyd Childress III, and Doug McIntire. The state re-appointed the board at the end of 1985 and changed the name of the commission to the Virginia Cattle Industry Board (VCIB). The VCIB contracted with the Virginia Cattlemen's Association for administrative services, and named Reynolds, executive secretary of VCA, as the executive director and secretary of the VCIB.[89]

On the national level, a similar program was enacted as part of the Beef Research and Information Act that Congress passed and that President Gerald Ford signed in May of 1976. "Keep Beef King" was the motto for this national value-added check-off, which also required a two-thirds majority. When the referendum took place in July of 1977, the vote was only 56.6 percent in favor. The act was revised slightly and in spite of widespread support by cattle industry organizations, a second "Beeferendum" that took place in February of 1980 saw only 34.6 percent of producers voting for it. Undaunted, Jo Ann Smith, president of the National Cattlemen's Association, led the campaign for a third "Beeferendum."

The act, by then revised as the Beef Promotion and Research Act, provided that half of the collections of one dollar per head of cattle marketed would remain with state beef councils, that half of the twenty members of the Cattlemen's Beef Board committee that controlled expenditures would be from the BIC of the Meat Board, and that imported cattle would be included in the check-off. Although the check-off went into effect in October of 1986, the vote did not take place until May of 1988. After cattlemen had seen the early results of the check-off, and with the assistance of "the most extensive and professional campaign ever staged by a commodity organization," they went to their polls and gave the measure an astounding seventy-nine percent "yes" vote.[90] The Virginia program, adopted earlier for a twenty-five cent check-off, became part of the one dollar federal program.[91]

This program placed enormous financial resources at the disposal of the industry to use in promoting beef. The group created under the law to handle this was the Cattlemen's Beef Promotion and Research Board, popularly known as the Beef Board. Its 113 members were nominated by beef and dairy industry organizations and appointed by the Secretary of Agriculture of the United States. Collec-

Former Virginia governor and current U.S. Senator George Allen, far left, Charlie Potter, and Reggie Reynolds fix dinner for participants in the Legislative Trail Ride.

tions amounted to about $80 million per year. One half of the total was to remain in the states where it was collected, to be used by the state beef council. In the first eight years, $638 million was collected, of which $392 million went to the BIC of the National Livestock and Meat Board. A portion of the check-off funds went to the National Cattlemen's Association, increasing its annual income by $4 or $5 million dollars. A 1991 study showed that a 2.24 percent increase in the demand for beef was directly attributable to the check-off and a 1996 report indicated a $5.80 return to producers for every dollar invested. In a move to reorganize the operation on a more equitable basis, a consolidation plan in 1996 created the National Cattlemen's Beef Association (NCBA) separate from the Beef Board.[92]

While the activities of the NCBA and the Beef Board might appear remote to Virginians, that is far from the case. The national advertising program, with its logos and slogans such as "Beef – It's What's for Dinner," were all made possible through check-off funds and have a direct impact on beef advertising in Virginia as well. Beginning in May 1999 the Virginia Cattle Industry Board created by the state "Beeferendum" has operated as the Virginia Beef Industry Council. Part of the council's duties include collecting one dollar per head on all cattle sold in Virginia. Half of the money collected remains in the Commonwealth for use in beef promotion, research, education, and information. The remaining fifty cents on the dollar goes to the national Cattlemen's Beef Board for the same purposes on a nationwide level. Serving on Virginia's Beef Industry Council in 2004 are Jack Bulls, Amelia, chair; Lewis Pratt, Draper, vice-chair; Raymond Buchanan, Saltville; Ernest Reeves, Mt. Solon; Jim Brumback, Winchester; William Oliver, Woodville; Kevin Powell, Somerset; Betty Jo Hamilton, Middlebrook; Charles Drumheller, Swoope; Robert Kube, Broad Run; Richard McClung, New Market; Linda Leech, Lexington; Laura Jackson, Boyce; Albert and Susan Epperly, Moneta; and Fenton Corker, Richmond, ex-officio. Cindy Boggs, director of consumer education; Anne Cardwell, director of promotions; and Joi Saville, director of producer communications, make up the VBIC support staff. Their work takes them throughout the state promoting the Virginia beef cattle in-

> *A 1991 study showed that a 2.24 percent increase in the demand for beef was directly attributable to the one-dollar-a-head beef check-off and a 1996 report indicated a $5.80 return to producers for every dollar invested.*

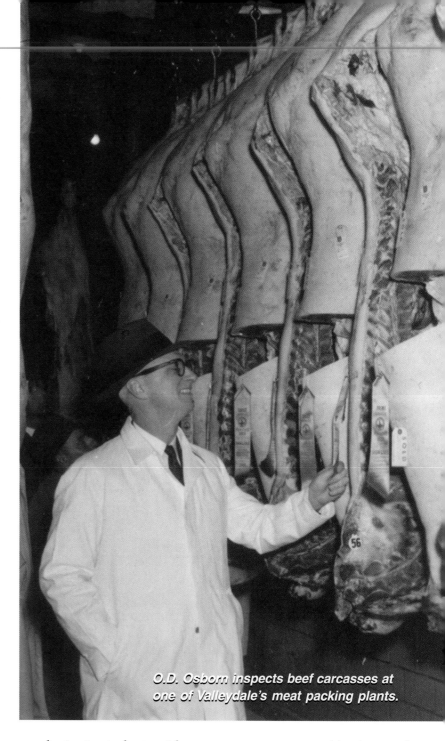

O.D. Osborn inspects beef carcasses at one of Valleydale's meat packing plants.

dustry to students, girl scouts, consumers, nutritionists, and health care professionals. VBIC programs mount campaigns on two fronts – educating beef cattle operators about the quality of their product and promoting these same products to consumers eager to prepare nutritious, affordable, and delicious entrees for their families' dinner table.

Quality assurance from farm lot to the dinner table is important to Virginia cattle producers. Beef Quality Assurance (BQA) programs were launched in the early 1980s to address government concerns about harmful residues in food. Through careful study, national Beef Quality Assurance guidelines were developed by the National Cattlemen's Beef Association. Cattlemen wishing to be BQA certified must adhere to guidelines pertaining to feedstuffs, feed additives and medications, processing/treatment and records, injectible animal health products, and herd health care and management. With the prospects of a national animal identification system looming on the horizon, Virginia cattle producers have

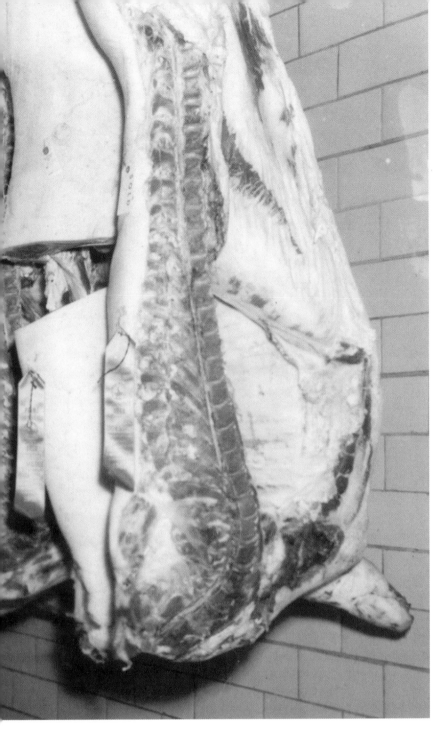

itability, and industry acceptability for their animals. Participating producers send five or more animals weighing between 550 and 800 pounds to an Iowa feedlot operator. Nearby sources of low-cost grain offer an economical means to finish out the cattle to slaughter weights. Detailed records are kept on each animal from arrival to sale and slaughter. Statistics on average daily gain, estimated feed conversion, detailed carcass data, cost of gain analysis, and profit/loss are sent back to Virginia owners who then use that information to increase the marketability of their cattle.

Virginia Cattle Feeders

Slaughter cattle production has changed dramatically since the days of Southwest Virginia's fat cattle kingdom. Consumer demand for meat produced by young, well-finished cattle encouraged cattle producers to incorporate feed programs consisting primarily of grain when feeding out slaughter cattle. These animals are usually started on feed when they reach 800 pounds and then fed a grain-based ration for 150 to 180 days. Slaughter cattle are harvested when they are less than 24 months of age and weigh about 1,300 pounds. While midwestern states traditionally have set national market trends for slaughter cattle, Virginia's proximity to northeastern packinghouses puts producers in an enviable position to market slaughter cattle. The Virginia Cattle Feeders Association organizes state-graded sales of slaughter cattle offering Virginia slaughter cattle producers a marketing mechanism for their product. Sales are held twice a month in Front Royal and once a month in Staunton, Fredericksburg, and Marshall.

Meat Packing Plants

In the years from about 1950 into the late 1970s, Virginia had a lively cattle feeding and slaughtering business. Consequently, meat packers played an important role in this and the state had nine packing plants that were active at the height of the period. These were Hygrade (formerly Kinghan), in Richmond, Virginia Packing Company in Norfolk, Suffolk Packing Company in Suffolk, George H. Meyer in Richmond, Valleydale with plants in Salem and Bristol, Shen-Valley Meat Packers in Timberville, Joseph McSweeney of Richmond and Dinner Bell Packing Company in Lynchburg.

An important packing company was the cooperative, Shen-Valley Meat Packers, Inc., with 1,700 farmer stockholders. In 1953 the president of the company was R.S. "Bob" Graves, a commercial cattleman from Syria in Madison County.[93] Valleydale Packers, Inc., was the business of the Neuhoff family, also a major cattle producer. Neuhoff farms, Inc., on some 5,000 acres in Botetourt and four southwest counties, had more than 2,600 brood cows.

put themselves in a proactive stance to incorporate such a system into their herd management programs.

Beef producers who earn BQA certification are eligible to raise the bar by seeking Virginia Quality Assured (VQA) certification for their feeder cattle. VQA feeder cattle are marked with a special ear tag certifying them to be of superior health and genetics. VQA certification offers buyers, many of whom buy cattle sight unseen, a quality seal, assuring buyers the cattle they are purchasing meet specific health and genetic standards.

Retained Ownership

Many Virginia cattle producers have participated in a cooperative venture with several feedlots in southwest Iowa. The Retained Ownership Program connects Virginia cattle operaters with the large, nationwide industry and provides valuable feedback on feedlot and carcass performance, prof-

The standards and demands of recent environmental legislation as well as competition from larger national meat packing houses in the Midwest eventually caused most of these packers to go out of business in the late 1970s and into the 1980s. Currently only one packinghouse remains active in Virginia. This is Dinner Bell in Lynchburg. This plant had been owned by the McKinnon family, then by Bill Jameson. G.D. Gilliam of Concord, who had worked with Swift in the west, acquired Dinner Bell and still operates it successfully.

A subsequent effort was made to establish a new packing plant in eastern Virginia. Organizers met in Jarratt. Called Old Dominion Beef, members of the beef industry involved in this effort included Victor duPont, Norm Coyner, William H. Perkinson, and J. Harwood Cochrane, among others. Several feasibility studies were done, most of which indicated that the plant operation would need to own about twenty percent of the kill to be successful, but another study indicated that if the plant were built, the business would appear. The organizers accepted that advice and built the plant, but found that they were under-financed and could not make it succeed.

Virginia Beef Expo

One of the most recent promising developments in the cattle industry has been the founding of the Virginia Beef Exposition, better known as Beef Expo. Leaders of the various beef breed organizations, representatives from the Virginia Department of Agriculture and Consumer Services, and members of the seedstock council of the Virginia Cattlemen's Association had talked of creating such an organization to sponsor a major show and sale for all breeds. The organization was chartered on September 1, 1988 and held its first board of directors meeting days later. The initial board included fourteen members, with Roger D. Steele representing the seedstock council and becoming the first president. John Mitchell, representing Salers, was vice president; and Reggie B. Reynolds of VCA was secretary-treasurer. Breed representatives were George R. Aldhizer, Jr., and Paul Hill for Angus; James Bennett for Gelbvieh; Mary H. diZerega and Ralph M. McDanolds, Jr., for Charolais; Edward L. Heartley and Dwight Houff for Polled Herefords, Henry Sanders for Herefords; Gerald Schiermyer and I.D. Walker for Shorthorns; and J. Steve Wright for Simmentals.

Funding to start the organization and plan for its first annual event came as contributions by member associations and individuals, as well as from the Commonwealth of Virginia. Representatives of the Department of Agriculture had hoped the event would take place in Richmond, but the board, most of whose members were located in northern and west-

Youngsters compete in the Youth Cattle Working Contest at a recent Beef Expo.

A Simmental cow-calf pair go through the sale ring at the 1992 Virginia Beef Expo.

ern Virginia, believed that the Shenandoah Valley should be the location. When the initial exposition took place on Friday and Saturday, April 27 and 28, 1990, the Rockingham County Fairgrounds near Harrisonburg was the site, and it has remained there since except for three years when it was held at the Virginia Horse Center in Lexington.[94]

The breed associations participating and holding sales have expanded since 1990 by the addition of Tarentaise, Limousin, and Red Angus. Beef Expo offers something for everyone in the beef cattle industry. There are purebred cattle sales, each managed separately by members of that breed association. There is a commercial replacement heifer sale, and a sale of bulls available by private treaty. Beef Expo also offers a special opportunity for young people, as each breed organization holds a youth show, the Junior Beef Roundup. An important part of Beef Expo is the trade exhibit hall, where new products, vaccines, equipment, and services are introduced to help cattlemen make their businesses more profitable. By 2004 Virginia Beef Expo was the largest event of its type on the East Coast, with nearly 400 head of seedstock cattle exhibited. The approximately 100 commercial replacement heifers for sale were certified through the Virginia Premium Assured Heifer Program. Bill McKinnon currently manages the event for the Virginia Cattlemen's Association. Earlier Expo managers include Joe Meek, A.L. Eller, Jr., and Jim Johnson. Approximately 7,000

visitors now attend or participate in the annual event. An educational aspect of Beef Expo is the demonstration of skills ranging from cooking beef to cattle working. Competitive tests of knowledge in topics such as hay evaluation and forage production, and the sight of teams competing in the youth cattle working contest, all provide fun for participants and spectators alike. One young woman is chosen annually to reign over the event as the Beef Queen.[95]

The beef industry in Virginia was totally transformed in the second half of the twentieth century into a modern, multi-million dollar force in the economy of the Old Dominion. Marketing was the power that drove the transformation, because the effort to improve ways to sell beef went hand-in-hand with the search for ways to produce it. Specialty cattle sales, new methods of selling that incorporate technological advances, sophisticated means of gathering and disseminating statistics, appealing new advertising methods, and the financial wherewithal to invest in sophisticated national advertising, are all components of modern marketing. These methods, coupled with the remarkable scientific advances that have been applied to the production of beef cattle, have produced a flourishing modern beef industry in Virginia as the Old Dominion prepares to celebrate the four hundredth anniversary of European settlement and of the introduction of cattle to Virginia. ◖

EXPO SALES

SALE	NO. LOTS	GROSS	AV.
LIMOUSIN	50	44,800	896
ANGUS	61	129,300	2119
SIMMENTAL	47	59830	1273
RED ANGUS	32	30465	952
P. HEREFORD	30	36960	1232
SHORTHORN	25	17420	696
CHAROLAIS	43	48575	1130
SALERS	22	18465	839
COM. HEIFER	109	64670	593
TOTAL	419	450,485	
PUREBREDS	310	385,815	1245

Results are posted following sales at Beef Expo.

A Charolais cow-calf pair are exhibited in a breed class during festivities at Beef Expo.

Promoting Quality in Seedstock

Breed associations have been critically important to the cattle industry. The national associations maintain the herd books and registration process, as well as the production data to popularize and market a particular breed. They disseminate information through publications and educational programs, encourage research and improved breeding practices, and organize national and regional shows and sales.

The state breed associations, in addition to sponsoring shows, sales, seminars, and schools, also promote a sense of community and fellowship in the midst of healthy competition among beef producers of the state. Often, associations created communities in which lifelong and even multigenerational bonds of friendship, respect, and mutual support are forged among producers who share a belief in the virtues of a particular breed of cattle.

Local fairs are fine examples of breed associations and exposition organizers working hand-in-hand to promote the state's agricultural industry. A government survey in 1928 reported of the local exposition in Staunton and Augusta County:

> One of the main reasons for starting the local fair was to improve the livestock in the county. It has been eminently successful in this respect. When the fair was started, thirteen years ago, there were less than 100 registered, purebred cattle in Augusta County and no local breeders' associations. Today there are over 4,000 such cattle and several of those associations. It is the policy of the fair to give no prizes except to registered stock. When the first fair was held, there were only 17 cattle exhibited, while now there are usually 600 head shown. This fact makes our fair the largest cattle show in Virginia.[1]

Shorthorns

America's First Official Breed

The first breed to be clearly recognized in the English-speaking world was the Shorthorn, an animal that can be red, white, red and white, or roan. This breed developed over time in the Teeswater area between Counties Durham and Yorkshire in northwest England.[2] In the early years these cattle were often called Durhams rather than Shorthorns.[3] The Shorthorns came to America as dual or triple-purpose animals, although within the breed the differences between those bred primarily for meat and those bred for milk appeared early.

The first recorded American importation of Shorthorns was by Henry Dorsey Gough of Maryland in 1783. Matthew Patton and Henry Miller were importers of early Shorthorn-type cattle to Virginia. Both of these breeders had moved to Kentucky before 1800.[4] Thomas Bates developed the "Milking Shorthorn" that became popular in America by the Civil War.[5] With Durham heifers, Scottish farmer Amos Cruickshank built one of the largest and best Shorthorn herds in Britain with emphasis on beef. His calves became the foundation of numerous Shorthorn herds in North America.

Publican the Seventh, owned by the Byers brothers, took top honors wherever he went, whether in his home county of Augusta or in another state.

Meanwhile, George Taylor of Cranford, near London, is credited with developing the modern dairy Shorthorn from 1878 until his death in 1912.[6] In 1905 the Dairy Shorthorn Association was founded and in 1907 the organization produced the first Dairy Shorthorn Year Book.[7]

Lewis F. Allen of New York founded the American Shorthorn Herd Book in 1846. In 1855, eighty-four percent of the registered cattle in America were Shorthorns. The American Shorthorn Association was founded in 1872, almost a century after the first Shorthorns were imported into America. At that time, the Shorthorn was still the principal registered breed, accounting for nearly seventy-four percent of the total of all registered bovines in the United States.[8] Registrations peaked at 118,039 in 1918. They dropped to 27,663 in 1932, probably because so many breeders had switched to Herefords. Registrations rose in World War II in the push to produce more beef in wartime, then dropped in the 1960s as

In southwestern Virginia, Mary Barns sits atop the Shorthorn bull owned by her father, W.O. Barns.

the "exotic" European breeds were introduced to America. Among capable secretaries of the national association, C.D. "Pete" Swaffar, served as the secretary from 1961 to 1979, Roger E. Hunsley, served from 1979 to 2003, and Ronald P. Bolze, Jr., now fills that position.[9]

At the height of the breed's popularity at the end of World War I, several Virginia counties formed Shorthorn associations. One such example was the Augusta County Shorthorn Breeders Association, with H.E. Coiner as the president. Some sixty-five members met at the Beverley Hotel in Staunton in early September 1919 in conjunction with the state agricultural fair. John R. Hutcheson, director of the extension division of VPI, was present. At this meeting the organization of the Virginia Shorthorn Association took place.[10] The Reverend Henry Woods McLaughlin, D.D., pastor of New Providence Presbyterian Church near Brownsburg and owner of a Rockbridge County farm, was elected president. A compassionate man with a wide range of interests, Dr. McLaughlin had helped start a bank in Brownsburg to give local farmers easier access to credit.[11] Unfortunately, Dr. McLaughlin found that the demands of his church, his large family, and his farm made it impossible for him to continue in the cattle association office, so he resigned. Dr. J.B. Tuttle was chosen as his successor. The other original officers of the state association were E.H. Tyler of Dublin, vice president and John C. Cather of Winchester as secretary-treasurer.[12]

A leading Shorthorn breeder in the 1920s and 1930s with close business ties to western Virginia, was Oscar Nelson of Morlunda Farm, Lewisburg, West Virginia. Prominent Shorthorn breeders in Virginia from the 1950s to the 1980s included Harvey Fishpaw of Berryville and Harry McCann of Winchester. James Fielding Lewis of Lewisfield Farm, Free Union, was a leading breeder in the 1960s. Other prominent breeders in the 1960s to 1980s were Raymond and Carl Bowman at Boones Mill, Joan McKay Smith at Farnley Farm, White Post, and Griselda Cunningham of Montana Hall Farm, White Post. Harry Peters of Windholme Farm at Orange was active as a Shorthorn breeder in the 1970s to 1990s. A Shorthorn graded, co-mingled feeder calf sale was held regularly at Winchester in the late 1950s and early 1960s.[13]

Unfortunately, no history of the Shorthorn association in Virginia exists, and current officers of the association are not certain of its continuity and history. The organization has been active for at least the past twenty years, during which time Otis L. Fisher, formerly of Craigsville and now of Churchville, has served as the secretary-treasurer. Fisher, a retired Presbyterian minister, has also published two books on the history of Shorthorns as a cattle breed. At the present time the association is an interstate organization known as the Virginia and West Virginia Shorthorn Association. The president is elected at the annual meeting, which takes place at the Virginia Beef Exposition (Beef Expo), in Harrisonburg. The past president is Dr. John V. Pratt of Moorefield, West Virginia, and the current president is William Heizer, who

Otis Fisher of Augusta County is a Shorthorn seedstock producer. He has compiled information about the breed in his book *Shorthorns Around the World*.

Farmers listen to a lecture about dwarfism in Herefords presented by specialists from VPI.

Too much of a good thing

Perhaps the greatest significance of the rise of Herefords is that they revolutionized beef production in America. Prior to their widespread acceptance, the typical slaughter animal was a four-year-old. Herefords matured early, becoming the ideal "baby beef." To enhance the early maturity, breeders in the late 1930s and the 1940s sought animals that were low-set, short, and both wide-and-deep-bodied. This was a remarkable change from the 2,000 to 3,000-pound animals desired in the mid-nineteenth century. These new compact Hereford cattle continued in popularity into the 1950s, but then popular taste made another shift. The demand for beef tallow was declining just as the American housewife began to prefer beef cuts with less fat and more muscle. Many breeders began to turn to other breeds for that purpose.

One unfortunate aspect of the push to produce the small Herefords was the introduction of the gene that produced dwarfism. Dwarfism is caused by a recessive gene, meaning perfectly normal looking animals might carry the gene. Even some very popular herd sires of the time carried the gene. Whereas a normal Hereford might have reached a mature weight of 1,800 pounds in the mid-twentieth century, a dwarf animal would only be 600 pounds at

farms near Middlebrook in Augusta County. In earlier years when Shorthorns were more numerous in Virginia, the organization held a state sale. Although it no longer conducts a sale, it does carry out an active program of advertising. One important activity is the junior program, which holds a show. In the most recent junior show, fifty-five Shorthorns were shown, second only to Angus in numbers among breeds. Many adult association members attend the national show in Louisville, Kentucky, at the North American International Livestock Exposition, successor to the old international show in Chicago.[14]

The establishment of a Shorthorn Performance Records program in the 1980s and the development of genetics research in Shorthorns have done much to strengthen the standing of the breed. The Shorthorn Performance Records program began in 1983. In this program, all bred heifers, cows, and bulls were enrolled and all calves reported. This data enabled the association to publish a Shorthorn Sire Summary beginning in 1987.[15]

Polled Shorthorns, a branch of the Shorthorn breed that was developed in America, resulted from cross-breeding Shorthorns with naturally polled animals. This work began in the late nineteenth century and in 1889 those interested in the work founded the American Polled Durham Breeders' Association. This group established its own Herd Book. In 1923, the American Shorthorn Association began to list the Polled Shorthorns in their Herd Book with an "x" beside the entry. Their numbers increased so that by the 1990s, the largest numbers of Shorthorns were of the polled type.[16]

Hereford

White-Faced, Red Cattle Bred for Beef

These white-faced, red cattle were created deliberately in the English county of Herefordshire in the mid-eighteenth century. Benjamin Tomkins is credited as having been the pioneer in developing Hereford cattle, beginning in 1742 with a bull and two cows inherited from his father's estate. Others followed Tomkins until the white-faced breed was well-developed and established as a good source of beef for the growing population of the industrialized island of England. It was not unusual for those early Herefords to tip the scales at 3,000 pounds.[17]

Herefords arrived in the United States in 1817 when Kentucky's great statesman, Henry Clay, imported a bull and two cows. While they attracted attention, they did not reproduce in sufficient numbers to form a herd, and in time they were absorbed into the other cattle on Clay's plantation. The distinction of establishing the first breeding herd in America belongs to William H. Sotham and Erastus Corning of Albany, New York, who did so in 1840. In 1844, eleven Herefords were exhibited at the New York State Fair. In the east and Midwest they were gaining in

popularity as the Civil War approached. After the war they achieved prominence at the 1876 Centennial Exposition in Philadelphia and spread rapidly in the developing areas of the Great Plains, Rocky Mountains, and Southwest.[18]

The ability of the Hereford to fatten and mature early made it especially popular with cattlemen. Until 1880 only 200 Herefords had been imported into the United States. Suddenly, between 1881 and 1889, some 3,500 Herefords were imported directly from England to America. These included the remarkable young sire, Anxiety 4, the common ancestor of most American Herefords today. In 1881 a group of breeders met in Chicago to found the American Hereford Association to keep the breed's records and to promote the interests of breeders.

The cattle preceded the associations, of course. A pioneer breeder in Virginia was Murray Boocock of Keswick, Albemarle County, who paid the top price of $3,000 in 1888 at Emporia, Kansas, for the imported English bull, Salisbury. Another early breeder, Charles E. Clapp of Berryville, Clarke County, paid $3,500 in Kentucky for Acrobat 68460, who left many descendants in Virginia. In the early twentieth century the largest herd, with eighty-eight head, belonged to Graham F. Blandy of White Post, Clarke County. Lucio W. Hill of Locust Dale, who acquired his foundation stock from Murray Boocock in 1905, became a Hereford leader. In 1913 he organized the Atlantic Hereford Breeders' Association. His son Lester Hill was managing the herd in the 1940s. Hill provided the foundation stock for another important early Hereford herd, that of W.O. Smith & Sons of Locust Dale.[19] Other early breeders included T.B. Davis, Dinwiddie Farm, Middleburg, and J.T. Frazier, Jr., of Chilhowie. An early Hereford of record in Virginia was a bull in Lee County in 1901. The success of his cross on Shorthorns led to the importation into Virginia of additional Hereford cows and bulls, especially registered ones from Kentucky.

The first recorded Hereford sales in Virginia took place in Orange and in Lee County in 1914. *The Hereford Journal* indicated that the Atlantic Hereford Breeders Association was formed in Orange on November 5, 1913, with twenty members, sixteen of them from Virginia.[20]

Dr. John R. Hutcheson, at that time livestock specialist for VPI but later president of the college, and W.H. Burruss, County Agricultural Agent, helped organize the Lee County Hereford

maturity. *Before 1940, dwarfism was not recognized as a problem in Herefords, but within ten years the problem was serious enough that many stockmen were searching for other breeds to raise. This caused the beef cattle industry and especially the Hereford Association to work hard to identify cattle bearing the gene and prevent them from passing it along.*

Because of some long-standing genetic work at the ARS Fort Keogh Livestock and Range Research Laboratory in Miles City, Montana, dwarfism has disappeared. Researchers at the center, where on-going genetic research has been conducted since 1934, had developed a herd of Herefords, known as Line I, which were free of the dwarfism gene. Line I became a pure breeding resource to use in purging the dwarfism gene. By the 1970s, dwarfism was no longer seen in Herefords and today two-thirds of the registered Herefords in the U.S. have Line 1 lineage. ~

Information for this sidebar came from the Virginia Tech archives and photo collection and Kathryn Barry Stelljes, "Beefing up Herefords with Line 1," *Agricultural Research*, August 1996.

A Hereford exhibiting dwarf traits stands next to a normal Hereford.

Association in February of 1915 at Pennington Gap. The twenty-one members elected Frank Litton their president. The group held sales every year until the Great Depression.[21]

The Virginia Hereford Association (VHA) became active in 1915, apparently taking over for the inactive Atlantic Association that Lucio Hill had founded. The new group may have languished in the war years, for it apparently had to be re-activated in 1919. In 1922 at the fourth annual meeting held in Roanoke, Dr. Ashby C. Byers of Harrisonburg was elected president, E.B. Keeley of Richmond, vice-president, and R.S. Orr of Pennington Gap, secretary-treasurer. Among the meeting's topics of discussion were plans to enter forty Herefords in the Southern Cattlemen's Convention to be held in Roanoke the following month.[22]

The Byers family of Augusta and Rockingham were also among the most important Virginia Hereford breeders in the 1920s. Dr. Ashby C. Byers and Sam Byers, Jr., owned and operated the registered Hereford enterprise known as Byers Brothers. The pride of the brothers' operation was "Publican the Seventh," a $10,000 bull that had garnered the prize of champion and grand champion of the East as a two-year-old and three-year-old. He had also finished

second in two other prestigious stock shows, the American Royal Stock Show and the International Stock Show.[23] Publican was a gentle giant who resided on the family farm in Burketown along the Augusta-Rockingham line. The children in the family rode the prize bull as if he were a pony and loved giving him baths – something Publican also apparently enjoyed immensely.[24]

Throughout the 1920s the Byers Brothers, together with Harrison & Gatewood of Rectortown, Fauquier County, hosted a Hereford breeders sale at the Staunton fairgrounds. The sale usually drew buyers from up and down the East Coast. One sale in April of 1922 saw twenty-nine lots of cattle sold for a grand total of nearly $10,000. The average sale price per animal was $331 with the top heifer bringing $910. Calves by and cows bred to Publican brought, on average, $510. Among the prominent buyers were Indiana Governor Warren T. McCray and Southern Railway president, Fairfax Harrison.[25] Harrison was credited with doing much to improve the quality of cattle in the area served by his railway. His cattle operation partner, E.C. Gatewood, was a director of the Hereford Association. Other Hereford breeders prominent in Virginia in the 1920s and 1930s in-

Forest Duncan, left, and Joe Graham stand with Duncan's herd sire at his farm in Nelson County.

cluded W.B. Bogert of Keswick; A. Frank Litton, J.T. Musick, and Robert S. Orr of Pennington Gap; C. Phipps & Son and J. Paul Bryant of Bridle Gap; the Misses Crenshaw of Rapidan; H.C. Wesson of Lawrenceville; J.B. Bryant of Independence; the Cameron Brothers and Curles Neck Farm near Richmond; J.H. Clark & Son of Proffit; J.O. Susong of Bristol; H.C. Lunsford of Monterey; and W.A. Cash of Kindrick.

An important Hereford breeding herd established in the 1920s was that at Virginia Polytechnic Institute. This was founded in 1923 with the purchase of females from Senator J.N. Camden's farm at Versailles, Kentucky. Professor R.E. Hunt headed the animal husbandry department and supervised the university's beef cattle management project that used Herefords.[26] In 1935, Lexington physician Dr. F.M. Leech established a herd of seventy registered Herefords at Stone Castle, his family's 1,400-acre farm in Rockbridge County, where he held private auctions.[27] About the same time, Tyler Snodgrass, a Virginian who had done well in a major western supermarket chain, returned to his native Virginia and purchased 2,700 acres of blue grass land near Elway, in the heart of Russell County. Having purchased registered stock at major western dispersal sales such as the Rothschild and Red Deer Ranch, by the early 1940s Snodgrass developed one of the finest Hereford breeding herds on the Atlantic seaboard. His 250 to 300 animals were generally of the shorter "Painter" type, many descended from old Prince Domino, often considered "the bull of the breed."[28]

Fred Bailey Gent of Honaker sold these two Hereford heifers at Roanoke for $2,425 in April 1943.

> Breeders worked to create a new Hereford that was larger and converted feed to muscle rather than fat.

One of the important large operations that made the shift to Herefords from Shorthorns was the Stuart Land and Cattle Company, owned by Governor Henry Carter Stuart in Russell County. Other important breeders included Fred Bailey Gent of Honaker, who showed five animals at the annual Virginia Hereford show and sale in Roanoke on April 20, 1943. Gent won two first places, two second places, a third place, and a reserve championship. From neighboring Tazewell County Dan Lynch and Harvey Ascue were prominent Hereford producers.[29] Another important Hereford herd established in 1945 was that at Bundoran Farm in Albemarle County, currently owned by Fred Scott, Jr.[30]

Some breeders made the shift to Angus in the 1950s and 1960s, but on a national basis, Hereford registrations remained high. In 1960 Virginia had 384 members of the American Hereford Association who were actively registering cattle, a sharp increase from the 111 Virginia members registering in 1930.[31] Others remained with Herefords, but worked to create a new Hereford that was larger and converted feed to muscle rather than fat. Hereford breeders were consequently interested in the latest developments in genetics, and in sire testing and evaluation.[32] One Hereford breeder who personified that modern approach was James Bennett of Knoll Crest Farm at Red House. Bennett has been engaged in the operation of this farm since 1951, and by the late 1970s had 400 registered Polled Herefords. His herd, widely recognized and considered by many to be the best in the region, produced the record yearling weight bull for British breeds in Virginia and also the record selling bull. As a cattleman interested in the latest developments in the field, Bennett was also interested in Angus, and began adding them to his stock. Bennett served as president of the Virginia Hereford Association and of the Virginia Beef Cattle Improvement Association, and on the national level was president of the American Polled Hereford Association and of the Beef Improvement Federation. Bennett was a leader and innovator in the concept of bull testing. He founded the Red House Bull Evaluation Center in 1972, an official Virginia Beef Cattle Improvement Association central bull test station. In addition, Bennett pioneered the idea for the first registered female test and sale, which was held at the Red House station in 1978.[33]

Even though many beef breeders switched to Angus, the VHA remained a strong organization. In 1950 to 1951 Morris

Fannon served as the first VHA professional staff member. Fannon, based in Pennington Gap, went on to become one of Virginia's best known cattle auctioneers. W. Edmond "Ned" Tyler followed Fannon from 1951 to 1955, with the title secretary-fieldman. The office was in Warrenton. George Simmerman held the position briefly from1955 to 1956, then Owen Thomas III came aboard as secretary-fieldman in 1956, serving until 1964. It was during his tenure that the association office moved from Warrenton to the Echols Building on Courthouse Square in Staunton.[34]

Dave Leonard, former executive secretary of the Virginia Angus Association and a professional cattle sale manager, recollected that early in his career, Thomas hired him for the Virginia Hereford Association at what Leonard thought was a princely salary of $4,800. Leonard had learned of a planned sale at the Virginia Circle K Ranch in Bedford County, owned by Charles Kepley, a Roanoke bookstore operator, and asked Thomas to allow him to manage it. The experience of horn-branding those Circle K cattle on a hot summer day was a trial by fire for the young Leonard. It was surely a turning point in his development as one of the best promoters of Virginia cattle, first for VHA and later for the Virginia Angus Association. Later, he managed the dispersal sale for Virginia Circle K, an event cattleman John Mitchell

of Bath County remembers attending at about age seventeen when he was in FFA. He recalled seeing cars from all over the United States whose owners had come to bid, as well as the sight of eighteen tractors lined up for the sale.

The Cattlemen's Capitol Bull Sale at Winchester was another major sale the VHA sponsored. One of these, in February 1961, turned into a bad dream come true for Owen Thomas, secretary-fieldman of the association and manager of the sale. With 225 bulls all graded by Friday and ready for the auction block the next day, Thomas awoke on Saturday to find that a blizzard had laid seventeen inches of snow on Frederick County. Cool-headed in the face of a crisis, Thomas and his crew carried on with the sale and carried the day. They got on the phone to let everyone know it was business as usual. Fortunately, many buyers had already come to town the day before. At the end of a long and difficult Saturday, every one of the 225 bulls had been sold, and at prices that were respectable, considering the circumstances of the sale.[35]

After Thomas left the VHA in 1964 to sell real estate and raise his own cattle, J. Burton Eller succeeded him as secretary-fieldman from 1964 to1970. From that post, Eller went on to an executive position in the National Cattlemen's Association. Another Virginia Hereford man who made a name

for himself on the national scene was H.H. "Hop" Dickenson, Jr., a 1955 classmate of Owen Thomas at VPI, who became the Executive Secretary of the American Hereford Association.[36] After 1972, as the rise of the Polled Herefords and the Virginia Polled Hereford Association made inroads into the membership of VHA, the organization no longer employed a full-time staff member.

The Virginia Hereford Association honored an outstanding member annually with the Mills Award, a handsome bronze statue called "Smoking Up" by the Montana cowboy artist, Charles Marion Russell (1865-1926). Mr. and Mrs. James P. Mills of Winyah Herefords, Middleburg, donated the sculpture to the association at its 1959 annual banquet for the award. Its winner is the Hereford cattleman in the VHA who "has done the most during the year to promote, improve, and encourage the growth and prosperity of the whiteface." The stringent qualifications, developed with the help of George Litton, head of the animal science department at VPI, included work with the association, with marketing and feeder cattle sales, and with improvement programs such as BCIA; the use of an active advertising program; a high business reputation; commitment to a quality breeding program, and the standing of the winner's herd over the years. Winners of the award have been Robert S. Orr, Maple Grove Stock Farm, Dryden; Ralph H. Matthiessen, Sr., Still House Hollow Farm, Hume; James K. Givens, Inwood Farm, Newport; Henry D. Sanders, Cobbler Mountain Farms, Delaplane, winner

in 1962 and 1969; R. Henry Matthiessen, Jr., Still House Hollow Farm, Hume; J. Glenn Brown, Blakeley Farm, Charles Town, West Virginia; A. Leland Clark, Spring Valley Hereford Farm, Poolesville, Maryland; Hunter R. Greenlaw, Albion Farm, Fredericksburg; Dave E. Brower, Jr., Still House Hollow Farm, Hume; Harry Cassell Wyatt, Crestline Hereford Farm; George W. Litton, Virginia Tech; Harold Henderson Dice of Dice Stock Farm, Warm Springs; and Morris Fraley Fannon, Pennington Gap.[37]

The Matthiessens, whose family firm made the famous Big Ben alarm clocks, bred and showed two Denver champion bulls at their Still House Hollow Farm. The elder Matthiessen was brought to Virginia by Col. John Tyssowski, and became his partner in putting together the Cobbler Mountain Farms at Hume in Fauquier County in the 1920s, before forming his own farm. Some of the other prominent Hereford breeders in Virginia have been the Marriott Family, Fairfield Farm, Hume; Hargrave Cunningham, Marshall; Charles and Richard Middleton, Birdwood Farm, Charlottesville; Cyrus Osborne, Mill Run Farm, Warm Springs; C.E. Richardson, Pulaski; Hidden River Farm at Mt. Jackson; T. George Vaughan, Galax; L.P. Prillaman, Martinsville; Russell Johnson, Salem; Herbert Thompson, Ivy Hill Farm, Forest; Bill Burruss, Burruss Land and Cattle, Charlotte Court House; Dan Lynch, Lynch Hereford Farm, Tazewell; T. Kent Loving at Columbia; Harve T. Ascue at Cedar Bluff; Forest T. Duncan , Faber; and Jessee L. Williams, Jr., Pine Pastures Farm, Suffolk.[38]

In 1966, the Virginia Junior Hereford Association was the first state junior Hereford Association to hold an All-American Junior Field Day. About 1,500 people attended, including teams from eleven states. First-place winners at the event posed for this photo after the competition.

So popular were Herefords in Virginia that a number of local Hereford associations were founded, each with its own active leadership, and each working to promote the breed and hold sales in its locale. The Bland-Giles Hereford Association included as leaders Olin Muncey, Meek Bowen, Chapman Straley, Bill Bird, Junior Wheeler, and Jim Givens. The Star Hereford Association had Russell Johnson and Charles Kepley as its leadership backbone. The Wythe Hereford Association leadership included Dr. Wagner, Jack Crockett, Rush Crockett, Joe Hounshell, and A.J. Lawrence. Men who worked on behalf of the Tri-State Hereford Association included H.H. Worrell, Love Rouse, Robert S. Orr, and Carson Trivett, while the New River Hereford Association luminaries included C.C. Wiseman, Jim Givens, and W.B. Vincel. The Tazewell Hereford Association had especially strong leadership in Dan Lynch, Rufus Sanders, H.H. Lineberry, Bowen Meek, Jim Hoge, Harve Ascue, G.I. Brown, Garnett Surber, and Guy Martin. In the lower Shenandoah Valley, Sidney Rogers and Robert Boyd were shining lights for the Northern Virginia Hereford Association.[39]

The Virginia Hereford Association, with 200 farm memberships and an active junior group, continues its successful work – including sponsorship and sales – with farmers and breeders across the Commonwealth. Robert K. "Bob" Schaffer of Deer Track Farm, Spotsylvania, and Rodney Phillips of Bay Brook Hereford in Dabneys are the most recent past presidents. Officers for 2004 to 2006 are Col. Sidney D. Rogers of Rolling Hills Farm, Winchester, president; Robert F. Kube, Fauquier Farm, Broad Run, vice president, and Kim Kube Crow of Warrenton, secretary-treasurer. Current directors are Kenneth Worley, Diamond "W" Farm, Abingdon; Dave McDaniel, Greenberry Manor Farm, Waynesboro; Alton Willingham, Remington; Jasper Persinger, Potts Creek Farm, Covington; Chester Turner, C & J Farm, Patrick Springs; Patti Price, Luray; Tom Underwood, Reva; Dr. Don Richardson, Dunrovin Farm, Crozet; and A.W. Garner, Plainfield Farm, Newburg, Maryland. Keith Heizer of Kendy Knoll Farm, Staunton, and Jerry Gustin, Gloucester, recently rotated off the board.[40]

The strength of the Virginia Hereford Association meant that its leadership was in a position for recognition at the national level as well. Virginia has provided two presidents of the American Hereford Association: Hargrave Cunningham of Marshall and Henry Matthiesson, Jr., of Hume.

Polled Hereford

Rarity emerges to become standard

When the American Hereford Breeders Association was formed in the 1880s, such a thing as a polled Hereford had not been imagined. Yet in the early 1900s, scientific research and breeding experiments with rare, naturally hornless purebred Herefords by the Iowa lawyer, Warren Gammon and the Canadian, Mossom Boyd, produced the unheard of. By 1911 the two early Polled Hereford organizations had merged into a national association. When the first volume of the American Polled Hereford Record was closed in 1912, there were 2,250 entries. Registrations nationwide were growing by 3,000 to 5,000 annually in the 1920s and 1930s.[41]

In 1956 the first-ever export of Herefords to England, their country of origin, took place. It was a group of twenty-three Polled Herefords assembled from some of America's leading herds. Among the dozen breeders represented were three from Virginia: George C. Palmer II, of Riverdale Farms, Charlottesville; John H. Royer, Jr., of Bushy Park Farm, Esmont; and Hubert Phipps of Rockburn Farm, Marshall.[42]

Although horned Herefords made up the great majority of the breed in Virginia in the 1940s and 1950s, Polled Herefords gained strength in the 1960s and 1970s causing a loss in membership and breeders in the VHA. The Virginia Polled Hereford Association (VPHA) formed in 1968 for breeders of the polled variant, after the American Polled Hereford Association (AHA) was organized nationally apart from the American Hereford Association. Henry Matthiesson was president of the AHA at the time. One of its founding members was Dr. Clayton Ernest Holmes, a poultry science professor at Virginia Tech, who also raised purebred polled Herefords at his Holmes Farm at Blacksburg.[43] The original officers of the VPHA were Harry A. Knabe, Jr., Winterfield Farms, Dillwyn, president; Don Kelly, vice president; Reid T. Putney, Ottervue Farm, Forest, secretary; and Robert Alger, Robin Roost Farms, Broadway, treasurer. Others who served as presidents to 1980 included Charles Combs, Homespun Farms, Bristol; Ray Rudacille, Flint Run Farms, Bentonville; R. Marvin Minor, Jr., Old Hundred Farm, Midlothian; and James Bennett, Knoll Crest Farm, Red House.

By 1974, when it published its first directory, the new organization had seen a thirty percent increase over the founding membership. The officers for the new Virginia Polled Hereford Association for 1974 were Nelson Hess, Hess Farms, Harrisonburg, president; John H. Royer, Jr., Bushy

The Bennett brothers, seven-year-old Paul on the left and six-year-old Jim, exhibited the Grand Champion Beef Animal at the Five County Farmville Fair in 1968.

Park Farm, Esmont, vice president; Dwight Houff, Holly Hill Farm, Weyers Cave, secretary; and Robert S. Alger, treasurer. Members of the board of directors were Claude Van Dyke, Van Dyke Hereford Farms, Tazewell; E.J. Mason, Red Bank Farm, Hollins; Ray Rudacille; Hughes Swain, Castle Hill Farm, Afton; Alton Willingham, Remington; Marvin Minor, Jr.; and T.Y.L. Steppe, King George.

In 1974, a Virginian served as a member on the board of directors of the American Polled Hereford Association. This was George C. Palmer, II, of Riverdale Farms, Charlottesville.[44] Palmer, a Georgia native, had established his farm with horned Herefords, but soon switched to polled. His herd sire, a son of ALF Choice Domino 6th did much to establish the reputation of his cattle. Palmer went on to become president of the APHA. The other Virginian who served as director of the APHA board and also president of the association was James Bennett of Knoll Crest Farm, Red House.

The VPHA's 1976 directory, produced with an American Bicentennial theme, carried a letter from Franklin D. Roosevelt, Jr., son of the late President of the United States, and a director of the American Polled Hereford Association. He congratulated the Virginia organization on its successful sales, field days, and the Standard of Perfection (S.O.P.) Show in Richmond, and noted that Virginia had more beef cattle than all the states north of her combined, a splendid opportunity for the Polled Hereford breeders of the Old Dominion.[45]

By 1980 the membership of the VPHA had grown to 136 individuals, families, or farms. By this time, Polled Herefords had the majority of the market in Virginia and the east. Dwight Houff was the manager for many Polled Hereford sales in the 1970s and early 1980s. The organization's activities included an Annual Appreciation Award. In 1988, for example, Charles H. Combs of Homespun Farms, Bristol, won the honor. The VPHA had an active junior division as well, with 102 individual members by 1980 who took part in showing their animals at the annual Junior Beef Roundup.

In 1995 the American Polled Hereford Association and the American Hereford Association merged. State organizations, including those in Virginia, followed that path as well.[46]

Prominent Polled Hereford breeders in Virginia include George C. Palmer, II, Riverdale Farm, Charlottesville; Hidden River Farm, Mt. Jackson; John Holland, Careysbrook Farm, Careysbrook; T. Kent Loving, Granite Hill Farm, Columbia; Forest T. Duncan, Lovingston; James F. Powell, Bivismont Farm, North Garden; Fred W. Scott, Jr., Bundoran Farm, North Garden; Oscar Nelson Sr. and Jr., Morlunda Farm, Lewisburg, West Virginia; William Mullen, Nutmeg Farm, Charlottesville; Robert Kube, Warrenton; Don Richardson, Dunrovin Farm Crozet; Col. Sidney Rogers, Rolling Hills Farm, Winchester; Ray Rudacille, Bentonville; the Bennett Family, Knoll Crest Farm, Red House; and Dwight E. Houff, Holly Hill Farm, Mt. Sidney.[47]

Angus

Turning Virginia's Hills Black

Possibly, the origins of Angus cattle are traceable to Vikings of coastal Britain in the eighth century. These Norse invaders brought small, hornless, dun-colored cattle with them that interbred with the black, horned native Celtic cattle. These black cattle were remarkably like Aberdeen Angus today, except smaller. In order to breed larger draft oxen, English longhorns, mainly red, were brought to Scotland for cross-breeding. This introduced the gene that produces Red Angus.[48]

The first Aberdeen Angus herd book was published in Scotland in 1862 and included reds as well as blacks. The Aberdeen Angus first came to America in the 1870s. Originally called Aberdeen Angus for the two Scottish counties where the breed originated, the name has been shortened in the twentieth century to Angus. The first American herd books, published in 1886 and 1888, included reds along with blacks, but in 1917 reds were barred from the American herd book.

A pioneer purebred Angus breeder in Virginia was J.E. Sheets, a grocery merchant in Staunton, who raised what were then called Aberdeen Angus on his farm outside the city as early as 1906.[49] Many who became prominent early Angus breeders in Virginia in the generation after Sheets grew up with Shorthorns or Herefords then made the switch in the period from the 1930s to the 1950s. For example, C. Whitney Grove and his brother Conrad Grove learned about Angus cattle through J.C. Coiner, Augusta County Agent and Angus breeder. In 1937 the Augusta County Livestock Judging Team went to the International Livestock Show in Chicago. The young Groves fitted the show cattle for two great pioneering Angus breeders in Augusta County, G. Dayton Hodges and Glen Yount, and became converts to the breed. The entire Grove family switched to Angus cattle in 1943. Another early promoter of the breed in Virginia was Lawson Turner of Old Elkton Farm at Forest.[50]

When a group of American Aberdeen Angus Association officials visited Virginia in May of 1940 they visited the farms of some of the prominent early Angus breeders in the northern part of the Commonwealth. These included George Cutting's Fenton Farm in Fauquier; David Sutherland's Broadview Farm where the International grand champion, Epponian 8th of Rosemere, was the pride of the place; the Pierce family's Canterbury Farm, managed by L.L. Little; Paul Llewellyn's Pen-Y-Bryn Farm and R.E. Johnston's Holiday Farm, both at Rectortown; and Amandale Farm at Upperville, owned by the "rootin'tootin'" Texan Thomas Cromwell Holliday. Also visited were three farms in Clarke County: Edward Jenkins' Red Gate Farm near Millwood; Graham Daugherty's new herd, and the William Bell Watkins' farm at Berryville. Finally the group visited the herd of W.S. Fox of Highland Farm at Round Hill.[51]

Other important early Angus breeders elsewhere in Virginia included Charles B. Feagans, senior and junior, at their farm between Lynchburg and Appomattox, L.W. Turner at Forest, Colonel James B. Dillard at Winton farm, and Ray Graham at Edgehill. Charles T. Neale, at Gordonsville, Fred H. Walton at Woodley Farm, Miss Julia Shearer at Meander Farm, and S.H. Garnett were well known in Orange County. In Culpeper County, Lewis L. Strauss at Brandy Rock Farm and Robert Tinsley at Rapidan were outstanding breeders.[52] In 1940, Strauss had purchased the second Grand Champion in the state, Bandolier Anoka 6th.[53]

A Virginia Angus Association was formed in 1926 with A.F. Buchanan of Glade Spring as president, but the group apparently did not gather strength and faded away. As the numbers of Angus breeders grew, the idea of forming a Virginia Angus Association (VAA) was born again in the cattle barn at North Wales Farm, Warrenton, in the fall of 1933, as a few of the early breeders sat around on bales of straw. The first president was Herbert McKelden Smith of Staunton, a prominent coal man and member of the Virginia House of Delegates.[54]

An early accomplishment of the VAA was to hold three bull sales in different parts of Virginia under sponsorship of county agents and livestock specialists. They sponsored cow sales as well. An early cow sale took place at C.T. Neale's Rockland Farm at Gordonsville in the mid-1930s, featuring stock from Canada and North Dakota. Staunton, Orange, and Amherst were the centers for the early sales. In 1937 the VAA organized its Angus Spotlight Show and Sale, now the second oldest consignment sale in the nation.

In 1948 the VAA had the good fortune to engage Dave Canning, a former resident of the Red River Valley in Min-

nesota, who had come to Virginia to manage the Ravenswood Farm at Warrenton, as its first full-time employee and executive secretary. C. Whitney Grove called Canning "probably the best promoter and salesman of Angus cattle I have ever known." One important accomplishment in Canning's second year with the association was the establishment of the Junior Angus Heifer Show. Lawson Turner donated the $1,000 in prize money that enabled this project to achieve instant success.[55]

Canning also played an important role in encouraging stockmen of southwest Virginia to invest in Angus. He persuaded Senator Harry C. Stuart of Elk Garden in Russell County to attend the National Western Stock Show in Denver in the early 1960s. There, Senator Stuart purchased a herd of Angus and shipped them to Elk Garden by rail. There had been much speculation in livestock magazines and papers as to whether Stuart would switch from Herefords to Angus. The appearance of his herd on the cover of *Livestock Breeder Journal* did much to turn the hilly pastures of southwest Virginia black.[56]

In April of 1952, when Julian Adams of Lynchburg, owner of Adams Plantation and a Ford automobile dealership, was VAA president, the association dedicated its first headquarters building in Charlottesville. To make that land purchase and building construction possible, about forty Angus breeders around the state each donated a heifer to be sold to raise the funds.[57] Charles W. Wampler, Sr. of Rockingham County was president in 1953. Under his leadership the VAA purchased the first set of portable scales for weighing calves. The scales were made by Layman's Machine Shop in Dayton, Virginia, and had their trial on Wampler's Sunny Slope Farm. Wampler joined with nine

other Angus breeders to lay the foundation for cattle performance testing in Virginia. In 1993, Wampler's son, William, followed in his father's footsteps as president of the VAA, the pair being one of only two father-son combinations to serve in that role. The other was T.D. Steele of Catawba and his son Roger D. Steele of Daleville.[58]

In 1954 the VAA founded *Angus Topics* which included a program of selling advertising monthly to association members. The editor and later the publisher was Charles M. "Chilly" Peery. The Virginia Angus Breeders Show was developed later in the 1950s as another means of promoting the breed. Sam Spangler succeeded Canning as executive secretary from 1954 to 1956; he, in turn, was followed by W.T. "Bill" King from 1957 to 1959. Bill Powell followed King.

Dave Leonard, executive secretary of the VAA from 1963 to 1970, played an important role in the expansion of Angus popularity in Virginia. Like many others who became Angus advocates, Leonard, a Russell County native, had grown up on a Hereford farm. A significant Angus event that VAA sponsored and Leonard managed in these years was the annual Brandy Rock and Eisenhower Farms production sale, held at Brandy Rock Farm at Brandy Station, Culpeper County. Leonard's vivid recollections include the 1965 sale, which former President Dwight D. Eisenhower and Mamie Eisenhower attended as guests of Brandy Rock's owner, Admiral Lewis L. Strauss. Strauss had been a member of Eisenhower's cabinet.[59]

An example of the successful educational outreach of the VAA was its sponsorship of the forum held in conjunction with the annual meeting at Blacksburg in January of 1968. In addition to welcoming addresses by the president of Virginia Tech, T. Marshall Hahn, and the dean of agriculture, Dr. Wilson B. Bell, ten speakers presented papers. These included professors from leading midwestern agriculture schools, members of Tech's faculty such as Dr. Robert Carter, leading Angus breeders, meat packers, and extension specialists such as A.L. "Ike" Eller.[60]

Another important development of the VAA under Leonard's direction was the creation of an export program that made Virginia the only Angus association in the United States shipping to foreign countries. That export program, and others such as the "Field Day on Wheels," the "Limelight Show and Sale," the Virginia Gentleman Bull Show and Sale (started in 1965), and Cow Country Commercial Sales in Southwest Virginia, did much to increase the popularity of Angus cattle. It was estimated that by 1970 sixty percent of the beef cattle on Virginia farms were Angus and Angus-cross cattle, whereas in 1960 sixty percent had been Hereford.[61]

The promotion of Virginia beef cattle extended across the Atlantic with the help of the Virginia Department of Agriculture. In 1969, for example, David Leonard, Executive Secretary of the Virginia Angus Association, met C.T. Barnes and Conrad Lutz with the export department of the Virginia Department of Agriculture in Madrid, Spain. They at-

First-day issue envelope commemorating the centennial anniversary of Angus in the United States

Angus notables Clara and Bill McSpadden, Lyle Springer, Paul Good, George Canning, and Dale Runnion are shown in this 1952 photo. McSpadden was an *Angus Journal* representative at the time.

ROBERT FARLEY, JR.　　　MARGARET WAMPLER　　　GARY LINEWEAVER

These heifers, Grand and Supreme Champion, Reserve Champion and 3rd prize, along with one of their brothers was 1st get-of-sire at the Rockingham County Fair 1960, in competition with a large and creditable exhibit of A n g u s. Sire Eileenmere A 100. These 3 heifers at 2½ years are now raising four fine calves. (Margaret's has twins) Their official grade is: 2.04-15-139, 2.12-14-137, 2.14-15,143, 2.79-14-164. Two years out of three we have had the fastest growing bull in the Culpeper Feeding Test. If interested in fast growing, good type, Record of Performance Angus Cattle come to see us. *Visitors Always Welcome.*

An advertisement from the Wampler farm in Rockingham County shows some of the prize stock bred at the purebred operation.

Eileenmere's Model T.H., a prize Angus bull owned by Charles W. Wampler Sr., is shown in this photo from the 1960s.

tended an agricultural fair and toured farms. As a result of these contacts, fifty choice Angus cows and two bulls were selected from twelve Virginia Angus herds and gathered in Richmond for the necessary export paperwork. Leonard accompanied the animals to Montreal, where they boarded a ship bound for their new home in Spain.[62]

The VAA experienced hard times in the mid-1970s with a turnover of three executive secretaries in four years, James L. Stork, Francis Updike, and Pete Lohr. By 1975 the board learned that the association had lost considerable money. To understand the problem, the entire board underwent an audit, and dedicated members like the new president, William S. Stokes of Upperville, John R. Mrotek of Madison (the new treasurer), and Paul Grinde, William McSpadden, and others spent many hours at the Charlottesville headquarters unraveling the story and developing the means to return the association to a sound financial position. Their careful stewardship of finances succeeded and the association has been fiscally sound ever since. The board engaged J. Vernon Kindig as executive secretary from 1975 to 1980. Mrotek became president of the VAA in 1982.[63]

Thomas M. Templeton's long and successful tenure as executive secretary extended from 1981 to 1995. Templeton recollected that the VAA was nationally recognized as one of the top state cattle organizations, especially for marketing members' products. The association managed as many as twenty-five auction sales per year all across the Commonwealth. In addition, it assisted members in private treaty sales and managed the Virginia Beef Cattle Improvement Association (VBCIA) Test Station Bull Sales to which all beef breeds were consigned. Templeton remembered the remarkable amounts of volunteer time that went into the Ladies Auxiliary, the Junior Angus Association, the area associations, preparation of the handbook, and organizing the annual meeting, as examples of the outstanding fellowship and cooperation in the organization.[64]

The Ladies Auxiliary held its meetings in conjunction with the VAA annual meeting. In 1968, for example, the officers elected were Mrs. Sam Spangler of Fredericksburg, president; Mrs. Charles Anderson, president-elect; Mrs. Paul Grinde, treasurer; and Mrs. William McSpadden of Chilhowie, secretary. Their fundraising project was the sale of Angus matchbook covers.[65]

In 1993, the VAA moved its headquarters from Charlottesville to Fishersville in Augusta County, where it purchased an attractive two-story colonial style office with parking space on the grounds. Dick Spader, executive vice president of the American Angus Association, dedicated the building on Sunday, October 17, 1993, with an address. On hand were many of the past presidents and former directors of the VAA. The officers at that time were William D. Wampler, president; C. Whitney Grove, president–elect; Jonathan P. Repair, treasurer; and Kenneth Barnhart, III, past president. Directors were John E. Hostetler, George T. Johnstone, Jr., Michael H. McDowell, A. Douglas Dalton, Jr., James Mark Duffell, J. Vernon Kindig, Dwight E. Houff, J. Newbill Miller, Jr., James W. Saunders, and Roger D. Steele. The staff members were Thomas M. Templeton, executive secretary, Patricia K. Douglas, office manager, and Silver J. Shifflett, secretary.[66]

Other Angus breeders who have served as president of the VAA include Tom Stokes, Ayrshire Farm, Upperville; F.H. Ludington, "Crow Harris Farm, Forest; Bill Perkinson, Harmony Grove, Lawrenceville; Gen. W.C. Crane, Kingdom Farm, Leesburg; Lee Butler, Kinloch Farm, Supply; Doug McIntire, P.T. McIntire & Sons, White Post; Greg May, Maymont Farm, Timberville; Preston Swecker, Rolling Hill Farm, Hillsboro; Paul Grinde, Charlottesville; Bill McSpadden, White Oak Spring Farm, Chilhowie; and J. Carlton "Zeus" Clore, Zeuswyn, Culpeper; and also its manager, John Pyne, Jr. The VAA has had three women presidents, Patty Douglas (Mrs. Gar), Tartan Angus Farms, Max Meadows; Rita Nicklas (Mrs. George), MeadowBrooke Angus, Afton; and Katherine Meadows (Mrs. Andy), Springwood Livestock Management, Inc., Buchanan. In addition, there has been a father-daughter leadership pair, Harold Entsminger, Jr., Springwood Angus, and Katherine Entsminger Meadows, both of Buchanan. A former president who has been generous with his legal expertise for decades in behalf of VAA is George R. Aldhizer, Jr., Maple Leaf Farm, Harrisonburg.[67]

Since Templeton's retirement in 1995, the VAA has had three executive secretaries, Mike Gothard, Kaye Weaber, and Ken Brubaker. The VAA continues to be a significant force in Virginia's cattle industry. Its spotlight sale has been continuous since 1937. For thirty years it had managed the VBCIA bull sales at Test Stations. The association's goal is to "promote the merits of the Angus breed of cattle as well as the education of breeders in the qualities and care of such animals." Schools, forums, meetings, publications, shows, and sales are the means by which it accomplishes these goals. The VAA is affiliated with the American Angus Association and seeks to incorporate its goals.[68] The state association is proud to have contributed three of its own prominent leaders, T.D. Steele, John C. Gall, and Dr. Arthur Bartenslager, as presidents of the American Angus Association.

By 2001 the VAA numbered 530 memberships, most representing a farm and a family.[69] Jerry Crenshaw was president; Albert Epperly, president elect; Mark Duffell,

Angus at the Wamplers' Sunny Slope Farm

Dr. Arthur Bartenslager

The Virginia Angus Association celebrated the opening of its new location in Fishersville, Virginia October 17, 1993. Those on hand for the event included Thomas M. Templeton, VAA executive secretary; William D. Powell, American Angus Association regional manager; Virginia Senator Frank Nolen; Patricia K. Douglas, VAA office manager; C. Whitney Grove, VAA president-elect; William D. Wampler, VAA president; Kenneth Barnhart, VAA past president; Jonathan P. Repair, VAA treasurer; James W. Saunders, VAA director; and Richard Spader, AAA executive vice president.

1994 Virginia Angus Association officers and directors were (front row, from left) Tom Templeton, Waynesboro, executive secretary; Whitney Grove, Forest, president; Doug Dalton, Altavista, vice president; and Jon Repair, Natural Bridge, treasurer; (directors, back row, from left) Bill Wampler, Harrisonburg; Keith Matney, Cedar Bluff; Jim Saunders, Piney River; Roy Simmons, Bridgewater; Scott Weller, Staunton; Roger Steele, Daleville; and Vernon Kindig, Lawrenceville.

past president; and Kaye Weaber executive Director. The board consisted of Domingo Alfaro, Robert Anderson, Paul M. Coleman, Jeff Kaufman, Vernon Kindig, Allen Strecker, Katherine Meadows, Chuck Alexander, Jay Fulk, Julian Heron, Jr., and Mike McDowell.[70]

Several major leaders in the production of Angus cattle in Virginia have been recognized for their outstanding work over the years by election to the Angus Heritage Foundation. Dave Canning, the talented secretary-fieldman of the Virginia Angus Association, who built that organization into one of the most active in the nation, was inducted into the foundation in 1983. Kenneth Litton of Hamilton, Virginia, was an organizer and first secretary of the Virginia Angus Breeders Association. He started spotlight sales, worked tirelessly to involve young people in 4-H Angus projects, and judged the first All-American Angus Breeders' Futurity. The Angus Heritage Foundation inducted him into its ranks in 1986. The following year, 1987, saw the induction of Charles M. Peery of New Market, Virginia, into the foundation. As publisher and editor of *Angus Topics* from 1958 to 1990, Peery championed the Angus breed and its breeders in his excellent editorials and drew from his lifetime of practical experience as a manager and breeder of Angus. In 1996, Dr. Bartenslager, a distinguished elder among Angus leaders, was inducted into the Foundation. A veterinarian with a bovine reproduction specialty, Dr. Bartenslager began breeding An-

gus in 1947 and established his Bellemonte herd in Virginia. He was president of the Virginia Angus Association, served two terms on the board of the American Angus Association, and was the national president in 1976.[71]

Recently honored by the Angus organization was Dwight Houff of Holly Hill Farms in Mt. Sidney who was named the VBCIA Outstanding Seedstock Producer for 2002. In 1982 the first Angus were added at Holly Hill, which had specialized in Polled Herefords. Today the herd consists of 130 registered Angus cows and seventy commercial cows used as embryo recipients. An annual fall sale features about fifty bulls.[72]

Other leading past and present Angus breeders in Virginia include Lawson Turner, Old Elkton Farm, Forest; G. Dayton Hodges, Arbor Hill Farm, Staunton; G. David Canning, Sugar Loaf Farm, Staunton; Glen Yount, Green Hill Farms, Staunton; J. Prescott Carter, Estouteville Farm, North Garden; Fred and James Carter, Skyview Farm, Buena Vista; Kenneth Litton, manager, Highlands Farm, Round Hill; Joe Schwerin, Creswell Farm, Forest; Ray Graham, Edgehill Farm, Shadwell; Lee D. Butler, Kinloch Farm, Supply; Jimmy Keister, Craiglands Farm, Maggie; J.B. Hodges, Elk Hill Farm, Forest; William B, McSpadden, White Oak Spring Farm, Chilhowie; Leon Cotnareanu, LeBaron Farm, Warrenton; John Gall, Amandale Farm, Upperville; Charles T. Neale, Rocklands Farm, Gordonsville; Ellen and Billings Ruddock, White Hall Farms,

Dorothy Rosen of Mt. Crawford in Rockingham County with some of her replacements heifers.

Keene; Sidney Shannon, Lee Hill Farm, Fredericksburg; Charles W. Wampler, Sunny Slope Farm, Harrisonburg; Marvin and Katheryn Robertson and George Lemm, Whitestone Farm, Aldie; A. Douglas Dalton, Daltons on the Sycamore, Altavista; T.D. Steele and his son Roger , originally at Lynn Brae, Daleville; Ed Jenkins, Red Gate Farm, Millwood; J. Carlton Clore, Zeuswyn Farm, Culpeper; Alphonse Stroobants, Northcote Farm, Forest; William Perkinson, Harmony Grove Farm, Lawrenceville; J. Gray Ferguson, Sugar Loaf Farm, Arbor Hill; Harry Grandis, Triple J Farm, Glen Allen; J. Newbill Miller, Ginger Hill Farm, Washington; John Kluge at Morven; Nick Wehrmann and Richard McClung of Wehrmann Angus Farm in New Market; T.K. and Mike McDowell at Locust Level Farm; the Bennett Family at Knoll Crest Farm, Red House; and Johnny Asal, Oak Hill Farm, Farmville.

Enthusiasm for Angus was so strong in Virginia by the 1970s that a regional group, the Shenandoah Valley Angus Association, was formed and held its first annual meeting and election of officers in January of 1975. Carl Craig, Jr., was chosen president; Bob Deputy, vice president; and Anita Parkinson, secretary-treasurer. Directors were Doug Livesay, Carroll Grove, Charles Curry, G. Dayton Hodges, Mrs. Paul Zimmerman, Frank Feymer, T.O. Reed, Russell May, and M.R. Myers.[73] There have been several other regional Angus associations across the state, including Southside, Roanoke Valley, Southwest, Central Virginia, and Northern Virginia. All have had dedicated and enthusiastic local board members, and all have sponsored auction sales and educational events.

1997 Virginia Beef Expo
Reserve Champion Red Angus heifer

Red Angus
Different color, adaptable to climate

Angus cattle have always carried the red gene but, because black dominated and was favored, the incidence of red calves was kept low. Although many countries register red and black purebred Angus together, in the United States from 1917, reds were barred from registration and breeders were advised to send reds to slaughter in order to increase the likelihood of black Angus. However, some producers did not heed the advice and found reds in demand in South America and Australia where their coloring was well adapted to the climate. In 1954 Waldo Forbes of Wyoming and others established the Red Angus Association of America, the first group to require performance data on each animal as a condition for registration.[74]

Red Angus herds were rarely found in Virginia before the 1970s. Among the earliest breeders in the state were Peter Goltra of Middleburg and James Keeler of Timberville. Keeler's Moreland Farms was the largest Red Angus farm east of the Mississippi at one time.

Red Angus herds were rarely found in Virginia before the 1970s.

In 1980, following a Red Angus production sale at New Market, some twenty-five breeders from Virginia, Maryland, West Virginia, New York, North Carolina, and Tennessee organized the Mason-Dixon Red Angus Association. The charter members from Virginia were Lloyd and Ruby Newland, New Market; Eugene and Beverly Nesselrodt, Harrisonburg; Jim and Sandra Keeler, Timberville; Alton and Betty Rinker, Fort Valley; Eddie Yancey, Broadway; George and Judy Miller, Harrisonburg; Forrest Dellinger, Mt. Jackson; T.G. and Kay Faulkner, Harrisonburg; and Jessie Gilley, Bassett.[75] Other important Red Angus breeders in Virginia are Leo Scott of Ferrum; James P. Massie of Goochland; and George and Joyce Tice of Boones Mill. Joyce Tice served on the board of the Red Angus Association of America.

The association now has about eighty memberships and has added Florida, Pennsylvania, Georgia, Michigan, and Ohio to its list of states involved. The group holds an annual Red Angus sale at the Virginia Beef Expo and participates in cattle shows in various states. In 1996 Deerwood Farm of Boones Mill produced "John Wayne," the Grand Champion Junior Bull in the Virginia and North Carolina state fairs. He went on to become the National Champion at Denver. The Mason-Dixon Red Angus Association officers for 2003 were Leo Scott of KC Farms, Ferrum; Gary Ramsey of Pelton Hills Farm, Fort Valley; and George Tice of Deerwoodie Farm, Boones Mill.[76]

Earl Kindig of Stuarts Draft with two Kinmont Charolais bulls at the 1966 Culpeper BCIA sale.

Charolais

The Great White Breed

Charolais cattle originated in west-central and south-eastern France in the old provinces of Charolle and Nievres. There white cattle had been found by 900 A.D. and were common in markets in the 1500s and 1600s. The breeding work of Count Charles de Bouille led to the first herd book in 1864 and the formation of a strong society in 1919.[77]

Jean Pugibet, a young Mexican industrialist of French background, was the first to import Charolais to North America. He had seen the breed in France while serving as a volunteer with the French army in World War I, and brought two bulls and ten heifers to Mexico in 1930 and additional shipments in 1931 and 1937. The first importation of Charolais into the United States occurred in 1936 when the King Ranch in Texas bought two bulls, Neptune and Ortolan, from Pugibet.[78]

A severe outbreak of hoof and mouth disease in Mexico in the early 1940s led to joint action against that disease and Rinderpest. The United States and Canada agreed to cover the costs of eliminating that outbreak of hoof and mouth (*Aftosa* in Spanish) disease in Mexico if all three nations would sign the Tripartite Quarantine Treaty for livestock imported into North America from Europe, and would refuse to import livestock from any nation where those two diseases were known to exist.[79]

This halted Charolais imports from France until 1965, which meant that the Charolais in the United States were crossed with other cattle. One result of the crossing with Angus, which are polled, was to produce polled Charolais. American Charolais are "purebred" if they carry 31/32 or more Charolais blood, and "recorded" if they carry less.[80]

In Virginia, the rise of Charolais breeders owes much to Lyle and Earl Kindig of Stuarts Draft and a string of life-changing events in 1959. Earl was keeping a few milk cows to help pay his farm bills. His brother, Lyle, in the orchard business, saw a spring freeze destroy his crop, forcing him to take an outside job. In September their father, John Kindig, passed away suddenly leaving about 1,000 cattle to be fattened, which he had placed around in the neighboring counties and West Virginia. "This put me in the cattle business real fast – a little faster than I really wanted to be, but since he had bought the cattle, I felt I was obligated to pick them up," noted Earl.[81]

In the meantime, while on a duck hunt in New Jersey with his new employer, Lyle had seen some Charolais-Hereford cross calves and pronounced them the largest for their age that he'd ever seen. Lyle Kindig returned to New Jersey and came home with a 7/8ths Charolais bull. This bull was possibly the first Charolais in Virginia. Once that bull's calves started coming, he made quite a stir. One of the neighbors, Stanley Furr, had heard about some purebred Charolais in Texas and he asked Lyle to drive the Kindig's truck to Texas to haul some Charolais cattle he planned to buy. Most of the Charolais in the United States at that time were descended from a group smuggled across the Mexican border into Texas during the 1930s.

Lyle Kindig and Stanley Furr started south after Christmas to the Rafter S. Ranch near Clarksville, Texas, which had the Charolais cattle they were seeking. Furr was disappointed with the rough-looking range cattle they found, but he bought a few after Lyle decided to purchase two heifers and a purebred bull.

With that the Kindigs became Charolais pioneers in Virginia. This new breed differed from the more traditional breeds in a number of ways. Their disposition was different, for example. "You can't drive them, but they'll follow, so we learned to call cattle," explained Earl with a laugh. "The Charolais were noted for their growth and the fact that they put on more lean than fat. We sold freezer beef. People wanted it because we fed with hay and grain but the meat had less fat," he explained.

The herd developed by the Kindigs soon gained quite a reputation in the Virginia Beef Cattle Improvement Association (VBCIA) central bull test program. In 1966 three Kinmont bulls were consigned in the BCIA Culpeper Test and Sale. They had yearling weights of 1,300, 1,271, and 1,132 pounds; the average of the British breeds was about 900 pounds. The real sensation occurred when the three animals brought $2,025, $1,800, and $1,250 at a sale where the average sale price was $792. Years later the Kindigs sold a record-priced $20,000 bull at a VBCIA sale in Culpeper.

In July of 1970, Earl and his son James Lee traveled to Oregon hoping to find a good polled Charolais bull with just enough Angus blood to retain the polled gene. They selected the six-week-old ACR Alfalfa John 075. The "Poller Bull," as they nicknamed him, became their sire of choice. He was homozygous polled, which meant that his offspring would all be polled. He never sired a horned calf.

The Poller Bull's calves began to attract attention. Some of his heifers began bringing prices of $1,200 or $1,300 in the early 1970s. A Kinmont heifer at a sale in Pennsylvania commanded $8,000. The argument has been made that the Poller Bull has influenced the American Charolais breed more than any other animal. Without a doubt that statement is true in Virginia. The Kindigs sold valuable interests to two other breeders at very substantial prices.

The Kindigs were not the only Charolais pioneers in the state. Other leaders in introducing Charolais to Virginia included Mary Howe diZerega. She inherited her family's Upperville farm when she was a recent Wellesley graduate and in 1964 started a purebred Charolais herd. She built Oakdale Farm into one of America's leading Charolais farms, and was nationally recognized for her expertise by selection to numerous positions and boards, including that of president of the American International Charolais Association.[82] In 2003, Mrs. diZerega was posthumously inducted into the Charolais Hall of Fame. The award was accepted by her daughter, Mrs. Mary Bryant deBerry.[83]

By the early 1970s widespread interest in producing Charolais across Virginia meant that plans could be laid for the creation of the Virginia Charolais Association. Until that time a four-state coalition of breeders known as the Virginia-Carolina Charolais Association had been the only

Three generations of the Wampler family of Rockingham County show off their prize-winning Charolais bull. Family members from far left are Charles, Bill, Melissa, Charles Sr. and Charles Jr.

breed organization in Virginia. Such a decentralized group was not meeting the needs of the cattlemen so Charolais breeder Tommy Gayle sent out a letter to Virginia breeders requesting that they meet to form their own organization. On February 8, 1974, nine people gathered at the Homestead Resort and set down a list of goals and reasons for forming a state organization.[84] Those organizational efforts launched an initial Virginia Charolais breeders meeting in March. Forty Charolais breeders were in attendance and an organizational committee consisting of William Wampler, Tommy Gayle, Bruce Hogue, Raymond Fox, and Earl Kindig was formed. Those five were charged with dividing the state into regions for the selection of directors, writing bylaws, and creating a slate of officers.[85] On June 29, 1974, the association was officially formed, and bylaws were adopted. Wampler was elected as the first president with Kindig serving as vice president, and Charles Mitchell as secretary-treasurer. Sixty-four charter members each paid a twenty-five-dollar annual membership fee.[86]

The organization's mission was to promote the breeding of better Charolais cattle in the state and to represent the interests of the Charolais industry. To that end, the group organized a consignment sale in Abingdon in September of 1975. There were forty-one entries in the sale, which was managed by Buzz Garey. The sale grossed $44,175 for an average of $1,077. The second Virginia National sale was held the following year in Waynesboro and returned $42,295 for an average of $1,208. In 1981, the association embarked on a series

of sales called The Virginia Heritage Sale. The initial event was managed by Ralph McDanolds of Madison.[87]

Through the years, Charolais Association members have actively promoted the breed through advertising, the publication of a member directory, the sponsorship of field days, the payment of premiums at shows, and the encouragement of youngsters in such events as the Virginia Junior Beef Roundup held each year at the Rockingham County Fair Grounds.[88] The state organization as well as the national organization recognizes members' contributions with annual awards as well.

In 1978 the Virginia Charolais Association gave Earl Kindig the Mr. Charolais Promotion Award. Two years later his wife Betty became the first and only woman to receive the Mr. Charolais Promotion Award. In 1984 Kindig was given the American International Charolais Association's Seedstock Producer Award. That was followed by the Allen K. Randolph Cattleman of the Year Award. In 2001 the Kindigs were recognized for their "pioneering and enthusiastic efforts in promoting the Charolais breed."

Another Virginian who rose to national prominence in Charolais circles was Edward P. Shurick, the owner-operator of Nutmeg Farms of Virginia at Charlottesville. He was a past president of the American-International Charolais Association when he was named in 1972 to the board of directors of the International Livestock Exposition, Chicago. He was the first Charolais breeder ever named to the governing board of the International.[89] When the first American-International Junior Charolais Foundation Memorial

Scholarships for agriculture students were announced by the national association in 1974, one of eight students selected across America as recipients was a Virginian. This was Ernest Sanderson Reeves from Mt. Solon, an eighteen-year-old animal science major at VPI & SU.[90] Reeves went on to become a leading cattle breeder in Augusta County, leader of the cattle industry in Virginia, and through his seat on the board of the National Cattle Association, a national cattle industry leader.

Following William D. Wampler's election as the first Virginia Charolais Association President in 1974, the following individuals have served two-year terms as VCA president: Eugene S. Hurst, Charles R. Mitchell, R.M. McDanolds, Jr., Walter Winkler, Frank M. Fisher, Mary Howe diZerega, Zane Pierce, Doug Hughes, William P. Anderson, Winston Streeter, Ralph Reynolds, R. Wayne Patteson, and William Thomason.[91] The current leadership of the association includes Robert G. Clowdis, Jr., of Longview Farms, Saxe, president, and his wife Annette F. Clowdis, secretary; Wayne Patteson, of Grandview Farm, Amherst, treasurer; and Bill Thompson, Mountain Meadows Farm, Clifton Forge, past president. Directors are Brent Crews, Crews Charolais Farm, Chatham; Dr. Dan Eversole, Blacksburg; Walt Winkler, Colonial Farms, Waynesboro; William Cole, Cherry Lane Farm, Amelia; Ralph Reynolds, R&R Charolais, Appomattox.[92]

Representative of successful and enthusiastic young Charolais breeders in Virginia today is Dr. F.B. Gent II of Abingdon, a small animal veterinarian, who is "Producing Charolais Bulls for the Commercial Cattleman's Needs" on his FBGII Farms. Gent is a third generation breeder of purebred cattle, following a pattern that has exemplified developments in cattle production in Virginia. In the 1930s and 1940s, his grandfather raised purebred Herefords. His father and his uncles bred Angus in the 1950s, 1960s, and 1970s. The family cows were introduced to Charolais bulls with pleasing results in hybrid vigor. When Gent entered the business of breeding cattle in the 1980s, he determined to acquire purebred Charolais heifers in order to produce his own bulls.[93]

J.L. McComas, his granddaughter, Emily, and JL Farms' herd sire Maximus

Limousin

The French Connection

Limousin is one of the most recent breeds introduced into the beef cattle industry in America, with the first importation in 1968. This breed of golden red cattle from the Haute Vienne region of France had been winning Grand Championship awards in its native land since 1886 when the breed's famous sire, Conquerant, won the Grand Prix d'Honneur at the International Agricultural Show in Paris.[94] In that year the first Limousin herd book was established. The origins of this strong, large-boned breed, which adapted well to harsh climate and difficult terrain, are clearly documented back into the 1600s, but these cattle also bear a striking resemblance to the famous prehistoric cave drawings in the Lascaux caves nearby.[95]

This cow is representative of stock on JL Farms in Raphine, the largest Limousin breeder in Virginia.

The first Limousin bull imported to North America was Prince Pompadour NIM 1, by Baron, who was bred at Domaine de Pompadour in France and imported by Adrien de Moustier of BOV Import, a founder of the Canadian Limousin Association. This bull left around 60,000 offspring in the United States and Canada. His daughters were the basis for many of the foundation herds all over North America.[96]

Richard Goff of Colorado was a leader in bringing the breed to the United States. He had been closely associated with the Pan-Charolais Association that was organizing to be the first beef cattle breed to have approved AI calves for registry. Up to that time in 1967, only dairy cattle had done this. The first Limousin bulls imported directly into the United Sates arrived in 1971, although Prince Pompadour semen was available in 1969. In 1968, fifteen cattlemen interested in Limousins met in Denver and formed the North American Limousin Foundation. Bob Purdy of Wyoming, a strong advocate of performance testing from his work with Charolais, was the first president. Dick Goff served as the executive vice-president who ran the office.[97]

During the first fifteen years of this breed's history in the United States it was associated primarily with the Great Plains states from Texas north to the Dakotas and into Colorado. For the first twenty years, from its formation in 1968 through 1987, there was not a Virginian represented as a national officer or board member of the North American Limousin Foundation. The first Virginian to receive national recognition from the foundation was Jennifer Eileen Platts of Culpeper, Virginia, who was the second young woman to receive a Limouselle Scholarship, a special scholarship for young women interested in studying agriculture.[98]

As Limousin cattle became Americanized, the polled trait has come to dominate, and a growing number of Limousin are black. In fact, black has become the color of choice for Limousin in most U.S. commercial markets. However, the breed has not been heavily used in Virginia commercial markets. Gradually the breed gained acceptance in Virginia so that enough breeders were active in the Commonwealth to form an association. The Virginia Limousin Breeders Association had as officers in the year 2000: W. Lane McComas of JL Farms, Raphine, president; Roger Winn of Dogwood Farms, Axton, vice president; and Ann Longenecker of Stony Meadows Farm, Troy, secretary-treasurer. The owners or managers of twenty-four farms across central Virginia, the Valley, and the southwest were members of the association. Prominent among Limousin breeders in Virginia are Eugene Worrell of Worrell Land & Cattle Company, Charlottesville, Patrick deBarros of Charlottesville, and Roger Winn, Jr, of Axton.[99]

The first Salers cattle to be registered in Virginia were owned by John B. Mitchell of Falling Springs Farm in Hot Springs.

Salers

Old Breed is Virginia Newcomer

One of the newest beef cattle breeds in Virginia is another old French breed, the Salers. One of the oldest and most genetically pure breeds, Salers come from the Auvergne region of south-central France. Their name comes from the fact that these large, hearty cattle closely resemble cave paintings from 7,000 years ago found near the French village of Salers. In their isolated native region of rocky terrain and harsh weather, they became foragers who could thrive almost solely on native grasses in summer and hay in winter. Typically Salers are a dark mahogany red and are horned, but polled black Salers are also available in increasing numbers.[100]

Valliant, the first Salers bull in North America, was imported to Canada in 1972. His semen was sold in the United States. From 1975 to 1978, fifty-two heifers and six bulls came to the United States and more than one hundred to Canada. These animals are the foundation of the breed in North America. Currently some 10,000 Salers are registered annually.[101]

The first Salers animal to be registered to a Virginia farm was Miss 7 Half Diamond 169M. She had been imported from Gordon Lansdale's 7 Half Diamond Ranch in Turner Valley, Alberta, Canada, and transferred to John B. Mitchell of Falling Springs Farm, Hot Springs, in October of 1984. Mitchell did not come upon Salers by accident. While he was raising Angus, a buyer told him that he needed more frame in his cattle. A Charolais cross was a natural to add that frame, but Mitchell was concerned over the calving problems that Charolais sometimes exhibit. He did research and liked what he read about Salers. In 1983 while on a family vacation in the west he visited some commercial operations that were using Salers. He was impressed enough to purchase Miss 7 Half Diamond 169M.[102] The first Salers calf born in Virginia was her son, Magnum 41T, born in April of 1985. The following year Robert Boyd and his son Bob of Cloverdale Farm, Winchester, and Dr. Jerry Engh of Cedar Creek Ranch, Alexandria, registered the next Salers in Virginia.[103]

In 1987 Mitchell was elected to the board of the American Salers Association and in 1991 he became president of the association. He is one of only a handful of Virginians ever to head a national breed organization. By April of 1990, interest in the breed in Virginia had increased enough that the first registered Salers were offered at auction in Virginia at the First Virginia Beef Expo at the Rockingham County Fairgrounds. Consigners were J.E. Brockman and sons of Berry Plains Farm, Amherst; Wallace Byer, Covington; Mark Slusher of Char Anne Ranches, Altavista; Bob Boyd, Cloverdale Farm, Winchester; Dr. Jerry Engh of Effingham Plantation Salers; Brad Miller, Mt. Crawford; and Mitchell. Since 1993, Mitchell has held a bull and heifer sale annually in March. In 2000 a bull in which William and Wanda Brockman held part ownership was named National Grand Champion in the Denver Stock Show.[104] Adventure Farm at Earleysville in Albemarle County, owned by Mary J. Chisholm and managed by Carl Tinder, is actively involved in the production of Salers commercial cattle.[105]

Simmental

A Swiss Arrival

One of the "newer" breeds that came to the attention of American cattlemen in the 1970s is actually one of the world's oldest, the Simmental. These large red and white animals have their origin and name in the Simme Valley ("Tal" in German) of western Switzerland, where

A Simmental entry at the 1977 Herd Bull Premier in Jackson, Mississippi

monastery records from centuries ago mention them. They were outstanding triple-purpose animals originally, valued for their early maturity, large milk volume, and draft power. The Swiss parliament limited their export as early as 1785 and the first herd book was established in Berne in 1806. The Swiss founded the Red and White Spotted Simmental Cattle Association in 1890.[106]

In the nineteenth century, Simmental spread throughout western and central Europe. In Germany they are called *Fleckvieh* and in France, *Pie Rouge*. They reached South Africa in 1895, Guatemala in 1897, and Argentina in 1922. There are scattered references to a few Simmental in the United States from 1887 to the 1920s, but they did not catch the attention of large commercial breeders until the late 1960s. A Canadian imported a bull in 1967 and in that same year Simmental semen was imported to the United States. The American Simmental Association was formed in 1968 and the first purebred bull was imported in 1970. Simmentals spread to Great Britain, Ireland, and Scandinavia in the early 1970s.[107]

Although fullblood Simmentals are red with white spots and a white face and are horned, most American Simmentals today are polled and solid red or black. The American Simmental Association has allowed grading up by top crossing on other breeds to arrive at a purebred status.[108]

The first Simmentals in Virginia were half bloods from semen that produced calves by Bismark at the Stuart Land and Cattle Company. W.A. "Zan" Stuart was one of the early promoters of the breed in Virginia. Other enthusiastic early breeders and promoters of Simmental cattle in Virginia included Tom Clark; Vernon Figgins at Mt. Crawford; Scott Burtner at Bunker Hill Farm, Mt. Solon; Jerry and Buddy Burner at Luray; Roy Meek at Draper; and McDonald Farms in Blacksburg. The 1988 National Western Grand Champion Simmental Bull came to reside at Donald Virts' Meadow Hill Farm at Purcellville, Loudoun County.

The American Simmental Association (ASA) is headquartered at Bozeman, Montana, where early breed leadership in the United States resided. Jess Kilgore, a Hereford breeder, took the lead. The first executive secretary was Don Vaniman.[109] Virginia contributed two members to the ASA board, W.A. "Zan" Stuart of Rosedale and Roy Meek. The latter also served as treasurer of the ASA.

The Virginia Simmental Association (VSA), founded in 1974 at Staunton with A.L. "Ike" Eller of VPI serving as temporary chairman of the group, was the twenty-seventh state association formed. The first officers elected were Stuart, president; Ligon Clark, Roseland, vice president; and Don Joyner, Staunton, secretary-treasurer. Under the leadership of Forrest Mars, owner of Mars Candy Bars and of the Forrest Mars Ranch at The Plains, a founder member club was organized and raised over $2,000 to put the new organization on sound financial footing.[110] By 1978 the VSA had held six successful state sales that attracted out-of-state buyers as well as Virginians. The state had been divided into five membership districts, and an active junior association had been formed with fifty members. The officers that year were W.B. Knott, Jr., Bonneville Farm, Dinwiddie, president; Wesley Wilkerson, Bannister Simmental, Charlottesville, vice president; and Robert Alger, Robin Roost Farms, Broadway, secretary-treasurer.[111]

The Virginia Simmental Association is an active group with a membership of sixty-eight Virginia farms stretch-

A Simmental heifer class at the Virginia State Fair

ing from Loudoun County to the far southwest of the state, and a juniors group with twenty-eight individual young members, many of them the children of adult members. The VSA officers in 2004 were Joey Doyle of Doyle & Doyle Farm, Emporia, president; Eric Keene, of Shallow Brook Farm, Dugspur, vice president; and Betty Campbell of Deer Creek Farm, Lowesville, secretary-treasurer. Directors of the Virginia Simmental Association in 2004 are Matthew Miller, Huckleberry Hill, Rural Retreat; Barbara Wright, Harmong Farm, Purcellville; Mark Campbell, Madison; Sprue Craig, Amherst; Douglas Layne, Monroe; Billy Seay, Calico Farm, Church Road; Carol Ambler, Ernie-Brooke Farm, Waynesboro; Jesse Webster, D.V.M., Sunny Heights Simmentals, Vinton; Jerry Burner, Trio Farms, Luray; and Lisa Zirkle, Shenandoah Valley Simmentals, Quicksburg.[112]

Steven Whelan of Mt. Solon, shows off his Tarentaise cow, CHF Cotton Candy, which won Grand Champion Heifer of Other Breeds at the Virginia State Fair.

Tarentaise

Mountain-Climbing French Cattle

The Tarentaise is another of the exotic European breeds that captivated so many American cattlemen in the 1960s, 1970s, and 1980s. In this case, they are dual purpose cattle, in contrast with so many of the other imports raised exclusively for beef. These cattle, which only received a name in 1859 and a herdbook in 1888, come from the Tarentaise Valley in the French Alps, in the regions known as Savoie and Haute Savoie. Two other French breeds, Charolais and Limousin, come from lush lowland areas, while Salers come from the regions of low mountains. Tarentaise, by contrast, graze at elevations from 1,000 to 8,000 feet in their native land, and over time developed excellent muscling as well as the high milk production desirable in that cheese-producing region.[113]

The first Tarentaise cattle in America arrived as the result of work by Dr. Ray Woodward of Miles City, Montana, director of the beef program of the American Breeders Service. He was seeking a breed to cross with commercial cows while retaining milking ability and avoiding fertility and calv-

ing problems of some Continental breeds. In 1972 his first bull calf, Alpin, arrived in Canada, and created much interest and high semen sales. The American Tarentaise Association was founded in 1973.[114]

Dr. H.Q. Tucker, a veterinarian in Orange, known as "Doc," brought the first Tarentaise to Virginia. He had been raising Angus cows bred to Shorthorn bulls on his Orange County farm since 1966. He first learned of Tarentaise in an ad in the *Drover's Journal* and first saw them on the Kissinger farm where he hunted out-of-state. In the late 1970s "Doc" bought one full-blood bull and six seven-eighths bulls from the Kissingers and bred them to five-eighths heifers. He was soon breeding his Angus cows to Tarentaise. He interested others in the breed, including his brother-in-law, Bill Fannon, and George Ashmund. In 1982, Doc became the 524th person to join the American Tarentaise Association (ATA). In 1985 he helped to found the Virginia Tarentaise Association, serving for several years after 1987 as its vice president. He served two terms on the American Tarentaise Association board, between 1989 and 1995. In that time, he began to show Tarentaise cattle to promote the breed at meetings such as the Virginia Beef Expo, NAILE, FFA convention, and the Southeast Herd Builders Sale. In 1993

Rob Bloch of Virginia served on the board of directors of the American Tarentaise Association in 1997.

he and his wife represented the United States at the World Tarentaise Federation meeting at Moutiers, France, and toured the native region of the breed. In 1994, Dr. Tucker was elected president of the American Tarentaise Association, one of the few Virginians to head national breed associations. In 2003 he was inducted into the ATA Hall of Fame.[115]

Gelbvieh

German 'Yellow Cows'

Another of the new breeds that have so dramatically changed cattle production in America is the Gelbvieh, German for "yellow cow." The breed is thought to have developed in Bavaria in the late eighteenth century from Bernese and Swiss Brown cattle used on the local red and red spotted cattle.[116]

The breed was virtually unknown in the United States in the late 1960s and was "discovered" accidentally by Leness Hall, an executive of Carnation Genetics, who was visiting Germany hoping to obtain a better supply of semen for the newly introduced Simmental breed. At Neustadt an der Aisch, Bavaria, he encountered his first Gelbvieh bull, Hass, the longest animal from head to tail that he had ever seen.[117]

Hickory Hill Farm of Blacksburg, Virginia, stepped into the winner's circle at the 1998 North American International Livestock Exposition with the reserve grand champion Gelbvieh female. HHF X14 was a polled purebred daughter of Polled Express.

Hall returned to Bavaria with a colleague the following year and found Hass just as large and fine a bull as he remembered. The two Carnation executives examined Gelbvieh in packing plants and at the experimental station and were highly impressed with their beef production capacity. They decided to import Gelbvieh semen and introduce the breed in America, even though there was no association as yet to help promote it. Enough influential American cattlemen had heard of Gelbvieh or seen them by 1971 that there was a brisk demand for the 43,000 ampules of semen.[118]

The American Gelbvieh Association was organized in 1971. The registration program recognized females as purebred at seven-eighths Gelbvieh and bulls at fifteen-sixteenths. Because of the AI performance testing and records program in Germany the breed has had an excellent performance heritage from the start. Consequently, performance records are required for registration. The national association has backed an aggressive commercial marketing program as well.[119]

James Bennett of Knoll Crest Farm, Red House, Campbell County, a leader in the Hereford Association and nationally in the Beef Improvement Federation (BIF), brought the first Gelbvieh to Virginia in 1982. Bennett, Ike Eller, and Larry Cundiff went to the Clay Center USDA Research Center in Nebraska following a BIF meeting. There they saw some of the early Gelbvieh in this country, and Bennett liked what he saw. He purchased eight bred heifers from the Garst operation in Coon Rapids, Iowa. They were successful, so Bennett later bought 100 more Gelbvieh from them.[120] Another early proponent of Gelbvieh in Virginia was Marshall Hahn, former president of Virginia Tech. His first animals were acquired for him by Ike Eller in Alberta, Canada.

Hahn's Hickory Hill Farm at Blacksburg stepped into the winner's circle in 1988 at the North American International Livestock Exposition with the reserve grand champion Gelbvieh female, HHF X14. Along with Bennett's Knoll Crest, Hickory Hill has become a leading Gelbvieh breeder. Their cattle sell well at the annual Southern Dream Sale at Clemson and the long-established VBCIA sales.[121] Another active Virginia breeder is Greg Keeler of Mooreland Farms, New Market. As Gelbviehs gained acceptance in the Old Dominion, the Virginia Gelbvieh Association was formed. Its president in 2003 was Roger Morris of Appomattox, vice president was Greg Keeler, and the secretary-treasurer was Charles Atkins of Atkins, Virginia.

Many other cattlemen are interested in Gelbvieh as balancers, which are Gelbvieh-Angus hybrids with very specific requirements regarding pedigree. They must be one-quarter to three-quarters Gelbvieh and one-quarter to three-quarters Angus or Red Angus. The sire and dam must be recorded by an organization such as the American Angus Association or the Red Angus Association of America. The Gelbvieh breed brings highly desirable traits of growth efficiency, muscling, calving ease, and high fertility. These qualities may be seen as a continental contribution to a blend formed mostly of British stock.[122]

Polled Express was bred and owned by Knoll Crest Farm, Inc. of Red House, Virginia. Express was tested through the Red House Bull Evaluation Center in 1984 and received the Virginia brand. The bull was one of the early homozygous polled Gelbvieh bulls used extensively throughout the Gelbvieh breed. Twenty years later, this photo of Polled Express continues to be used by the American Gelbvieh Association in its logo.

Highland Cattle

A Minor Breed Seeks a Niche

Another import that has gained favor in some quarters is the Scottish Highland, a minor breed that is valued for its ruggedness, disease resistance, calving ease, longevity, ability to graze well on poorer land, and its lean, well-marbled meat. Although red and black are the traditional colors of this shaggy-haired breed, yellow, dun, and silver-white are also common among Highland cattle today.

The herd book for the breed was established in 1884. Early imports of Highland cattle into western herds in the United States occurred about that time. The national organization is the American Highland Cattle Association, based in the Livestock Exchange Building in Denver, Colorado. Virginia breeders affiliate with the Appalachian Highland Cattle Society, a multi-state organization whose current president is Renee Dyer of Lashmeet, West Virginia. Among avid breeders of Highland cattle in Virginia are the Adams family of Tazewell County, whose members

were significant breeders of export fat cattle when that market dominated the agricultural economy of Tazewell in the early-to-mid-twentieth century.[123] While Highland cattle have their advocates, the breed has not yet become commercially significant in Virginia.

Scottish Highland cattle are kept at the Museum of American Frontier Culture in Staunton.

Beef Breed Associations Enrich Cattle Industry

In Virginia, the state affiliates of the national organizations for the various cattle breeds have played a central role in the success of the cattle industry. Although a handful of far-sighted breeders are generally responsible for introducing each "new" breed into Virginia, it has been the breed associations that have taken on the responsibility of making that breed popular and successful in the Commonwealth. The associations, in turn, have been able to succeed at their mission because they have had dedicated board members and creative, competent staff members. State breed associations' early endorsement of such significant concepts and programs as performance testing and data, performance pedigrees, sire summaries, and blood type records (DNA) are examples of the educational leadership they have provided for their members. Such efforts have steadily improved the quality of Virginia's cattle and have played an important role in helping Virginia to become a leader in the beef cattle industry.

The Future is Now

For three hundred years the story of cattle in Virginia was, for the most part, gradual and incremental. Nearly every farm family owned a few head of cattle, including a milk cow, and many families in villages, towns, and smaller cities kept a milk cow too. The rapid pace of urbanization, industrialization, and scientific advance as the twentieth century dawned offered a challenge to these traditional ways. A clash in Roanoke served as a harbinger of the dramatic changes that marked the twentieth century.

Great Cattle Battle

In the city of Roanoke, the situation turned ugly when, in 1902, a proposed law requiring cattle to be penned was billed as an issue between the "haves" and "have nots." In that year, Councilman Blair Antrim, supported by citizens who complained of cows dining on prize geraniums, mucking up city streets, and creating an impure milk supply from eating rotting garbage, proposed an ordinance to confine cattle kept within the limits of this city of 25,000 inhabitants. Howls of protest were substantial. Some claimed that the councilman was turning his back on history and tradition, while others couched the debate as a class war, noting that the proposed legislation would "impose a hardship on my neighbor by forcing him to hire a boy. . . and pay pasturage on a cow." The harried council put the matter to the people with a referendum. Voters turned out in droves – four times more than in the next presidential election – and the freedom of the cows was preserved by one vote.[1]

A year later a different city council voted to exclude cows from the city streets beginning January 1, 1904, however, the mayor refused to sign the ordinance. That summer, citing the public health issue, Councilman Antrim again pushed the legislation forward and a reluctant mayor signed the ordinance.[2]

Modern technology has enabled scientists to unlock secrets of cattle production on a cellular level. Genetic data provides information which allows farmers to predict progeny traits with a high degree of accuracy. Microscopic views of bovine reproductive systems, portrayed by the artwork above, provide a window into previously uncharted animal physiology.

The "Great Cattle Battle" in Roanoke was symbolic of the change occurring across Virginia. Those who argued that penning cattle violated tradition were right; in the face of dramatic social and economic change, people's attitudes about cattle were shifting rapidly. By this period, numerous breeds of cattle had been introduced to Virginia, railroads were transforming the marketing of cattle, and the specialization of dairy and beef industries was just developing. In a few more decades that steady record of advancement rolled into high gear. The application of science, in particular the new window of insight offered through the microscope, revolutionized both cattle industries. Transportation advances made the world a smaller place while allowing the rapid exchange of ideas and inventions and opening up new global markets. Were seventeenth-century Virginia farmers able to visit a farm in 1907, they would have recognized much of what they saw, certainly more than farmers from 1907 would in visiting a Virginia farm in the twenty-first century. The change in one century has been that great.

Evolution Revolution

One of the most important advances spurring that change occurred in the laboratories and barns of Russia. There, E.I. Ivanoff spent the years prior to World War I perfecting methods for the artificial insemination of farm animals – the mechanical introduction of semen into the genital tract of a female. His successes with horses, sheep, and cattle were eventually repeated in Denmark. It was not until the late 1930s that those European ideas were brought to America. In 1938, with the successful impregnation of ninety-eight cows at the North Central School of Agriculture and Experiment Station at Grand Rapids, Minnesota, the face of animal husbandry in the United States began to change. Also in 1938 Professor Enos Perry, an extension dairyman in New Jersey, traveled to Denmark to study artificial insemination techniques. When he returned, he helped form the nation's first cooperative artificial breeding association in May of 1938.[3]

Perfecting artificial insemination (AI) changed the face of the cattle industry, most immediately in dairying where most of the early AI research took place, but later in the beef industry as well. AI was the key to dairy herd improvement and thus to increased production. Because of AI and other advances such as embryo transfer, overall numbers of dairy cows in Virginia and the nation continue to drop while production continues to rise. The semen of proven sires can be collected and distributed across the world in the way that a bull never could be physically transported. Not only can larger numbers of cows be bred from one sire than could ever have been bred naturally, but the need to have costly and perhaps dangerous bulls on the farm has been eliminated. Also eliminated is the risk of sexually transmitted diseases, particularly those that cause spontaneous abortion.

Virginia Test Tube is born

Virginians immediately recognized the potential of AI. The Virginia State Dairymen invited Professor Perry to speak at their annual meeting in January 1939. It was not long before a few breeders purchased the basic collection and inseminating equipment and practiced inseminating a few animals. The honor of having the first AI calf in Virginia fell to a Holstein cow in the Virginia Tech herd. The appropriately named calf, Virginia Test Tube 2165078, was born on October 17, 1939.[4]

Nelson Gardner, a prominent dairy farmer in Rockingham County, remembers the shift of technology during that time period and the part that his home area played in the new era of the dairy industry.

Every farm had its own bulls until the mid-1940s. When AI was introduced into the United States, the skeptics said it would never work, but it did. One of the first four or five bull studs in the United States was here in Rockingham County. Two others were in Culpeper and Franklin County, also in Virginia. The large barn still standing in Reherd Acres in Rockingham County served as the local housing for the bulls. Any farmer who wanted to participate just put five dollars per cow into the project plus paid five dollars per cow each breeding. Dr. Tom Koudelka, as a young veterinarian, was hired to manage the bulls, collect the semen, and breed the cows out on the farms with the fresh semen.[5]

Across the state interest in AI was immediate, but few of the fledgling AI units survived for very long. In Galax, where Carnation Milk Company had established a milk condensing plant in 1934, a small AI station was set up in 1939 with two Holsteins, one Guernsey, and one Jersey. The company wanted to speed up the use of proven, registered bulls to increase their production and profit. Two men collected and processed semen and inseminated cows in the area. However, the AI work at Carnation ceased permanently during the World War II when the technician was drafted in 1942.[6]

At least one other AI unit was organized before the war. Three Holstein bulls and later one or two Guernsey bulls were located at Wilmer Kline's barn in Manassas. A veterinarian and a senior dairy student supplied semen to farms

The Blue Ridge AI Association facility near Rocky Mount is seen in this ca. 1960 aerial photo.

in the Fairfax, Prince William, and Spotsylvania area. This business also did not survive the war, partly because of shortages in gasoline and tires.[7] Another early unit opened in Nansemond County in 1944 with the help of VPI Extension Service Agent Parke C. Brinkley. After only two years, the Tidewater Artificial Breeding Association at Chuckatuck decided to purchase semen from the Southeastern Artificial Breeding Association rather than collecting it on site. The latter, formed in Asheville, North Carolina, took over the Tidewater facilities in 1946 and eventually expanded into other parts of Virginia. The organization was the forerunner of the American Breeders Service.[8]

Curtain rises on AI

The conclusion of the war brought renewed interest in AI as a whole generation of farm boys who had served in the war were now home and ready to make a living from the family farm. In Franklin County, a pre-war cooperative bull association evolved into an AI business after WWII. In the 1930s Holstein and Guernsey breeders there had formed two cooperative bull associations. Young bulls were purchased by the groups and moved from farm to farm. In 1947 the two breed associations formed the nucleus of the newly-formed Franklin County Artificial Breeding Association. An office, laboratory, and bull housing facilities were built on forty acres near Rocky Mount.

Roy E. Flora and J. Harlan Bowman operated the service that soon expanded into the Blue Ridge AI Association. By 1950 Blue Ridge operated in the counties of Bedford, Floyd, Franklin, Montgomery, Nottoway, Appomattox, Amherst, Campbell, Roanoke, and Botetourt.[9]

A number of other small AI services opened in the years immediately after the war. In Pulaski a small Guernsey and Holstein unit was created on the Cabel Massie farm and in the northern part of the Shenandoah Valley the Shenandoah AI Association was established. In northern Virginia, the Northern Virginia AI Association, headquartered in Culpeper, was founded in 1946. Eventually the northern Virginia and the Shenandoah units were consolidated in Culpeper. The Curtiss Breeding Service, headquartered in Illinois, offered AI service to farms in the northern Shenandoah Valley and Piedmont.[10]

By 1950 Virginia's top dairymen recognized the inefficiency of scattering small AI units across the state. A survey of the Virginia facilities concluded that efforts should be consolidated at the Blue Ridge Artificial Breeding Association in Rocky Mount. In February of 1950, J.C. Eller, president of the Northern Virginia Cooperative Breeding Association, and W.M. Angle, president of the Blue Ridge Artificial Breeding Association, asked their membership to merge. This was accomplished and W.N. Angle became president of the newly-formed Virginia Artificial Breeding Association (VABA). The name was changed to Virginia Animal Breeders Association in 1965.[11]

VABA Grows to Serve Virginia

With William H. Armstrong as manager, local units were organized and became federated with the VABA. With the consolidation, the three top dairy breeds in Virginia – Holstein, Guernsey, and Jersey – were all being represented from one organization and thus served the twenty-two existing breeding associations in the state. The aim, according to the state dairymen's journal, was to use artificial breeding "to increase the production of calves and milk, and to help the small producers with small herds to obtain facilities for herd improvement."[12] The bulls were moved from Culpeper to Rocky Mount, giving that facility four or five proven sires from each breed and two or three highly selected young bulls to help replace the old ones. Eventually the Rockingham bulls were also moved to the Franklin headquarters. Liquid semen was originally shipped six days a week by parcel post and by bus, a frequency that was reduced to three days once the use of frozen semen became widespread. In its first year, VABA had 21,035 services. By its twentieth year, that number had risen to over 85,000.[13]

It did not take long for the success of AI to be reflected in the quality of Virginia's dairy herds and production records. Soon VABA added semen from two other dairy breeds, Ayrshire and Brown Swiss. In 1950 Angus bulls were included and Hereford semen became available in 1958. To improve the beef program, the Armour Beef Improvement group was added to VABA membership.

Renowned VPI dairy instructor Paul Reaves described VABA's first years:

The cost of semen was $1.75 per first service to the local associations who employed the technicians and set per first service breeding fees. Locals billed and collected for services rendered. These associations and their technicians became the building blocks for growth over the next twenty years. New units joining were Central, Frederick, Clarke, and Richmond in 1950; Charlotte, Pittsylvania, Bland, and Wythe in 1951; Tazewell and Loudoun in 1952; Patrick, Brunswick, Rappahannock, Lee, and Wise in 1953; Russell, Mattaponi, R&W in 1954; Shenco 1955; Louisa and Highland, 1957; Washington-Smyth and Carroll/Grayson 1962-1964.[14]

Reaves had more than a casual interest in VABA. The close association that had always existed between Virginia Tech and the state's dairymen was only strengthened as AI became the wave of the future. Reaves used his college classes as a laboratory to experiment with freezing semen using dry ice and alcohol. As a result, on August 13, 1955, V.P.I. Jessie Katrinka Defrost 4098698 became the first Vir-

While the dairy industry was first to capitalize on breeding through artificial insemination, it wasn't long before beef cattle producers recognized the value of the practice and began to incorporate it into herd management programs. Two Virginia-bred Angus bulls that have had a significant impact throughout the United States because of their large number of progeny by artificial breeding are Rito 6I6 of 4B20 6807 (left) and Paramont Ambush 2172. Rito 6I6 has greater than 13,000 progeny recorded with the American Angus Association and Paramont has over 12,000. Paramont Ranch in Abingdon bred the Ambush bull and Wehrmann Angus in New Market bred the 6I6 bull.

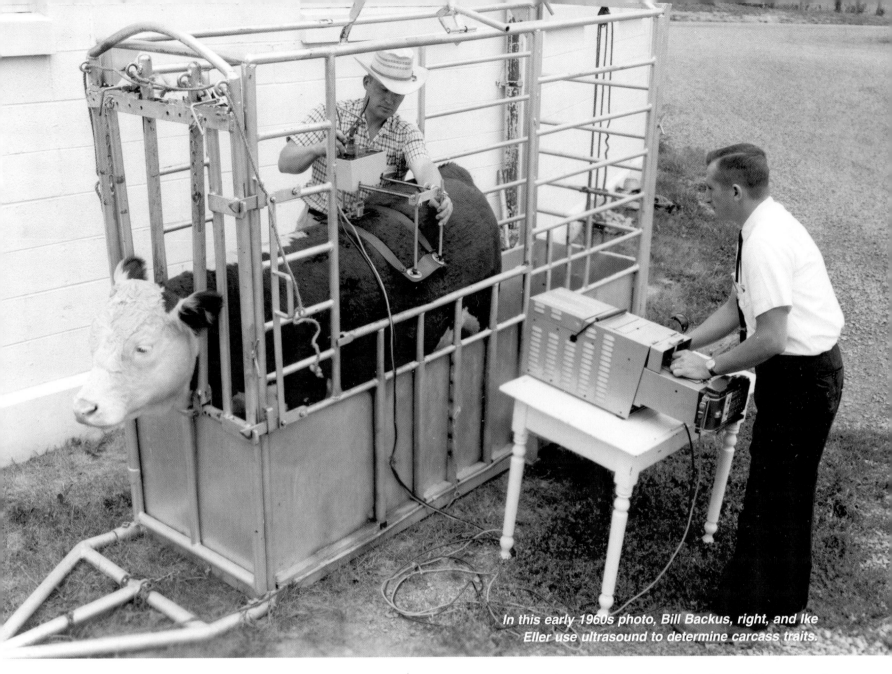

In this early 1960s photo, Bill Backus, right, and Ike Eller use ultrasound to determine carcass traits.

ginia calf born from the use of frozen semen. Almost simultaneously, VABA was getting positive results with frozen semen use in the Roanoke and Botetourt areas.[15] Dr. Richard Saacke at Tech was instrumental in perfecting the frozen semen method. The use of frozen semen advanced production levels in the industry because more cows could be bred per bull with the very best semen producers breeding in excess of 100,000 cows annually. By 1965 the majority of the field technicians across the state were offering frozen as well as liquid semen.

Networking Resources

The cooperative work between the state's local AI groups, state units, and the cutting edge technology being promoted at Virginia Tech, are evidenced in a single Staunton newspaper article from 1960. Under the headline, "1959 Achievements, 1960 Objectives Outlined by Artificial Breeders," the article detailed the annual meeting of the Augusta Artificial Breeders Association. At the meeting, approximately 100 members elected R.G. Heizer

as a new board member and reelected A.F. Weaver and J.N. Jackson to the board. Weaver, manager of Early Dawn Dairy in Waynesboro, continued the presidency he had held for over a decade and was again asked to represent the group in the state association, VABA.[16]

The group then heard a presentation by VABA manager, William Armstrong, who noted that his group hoped to supply 75,000 first services in 1960, which was 12,000 more than the previous year. He added that his Rocky Mount group hoped to "Give better service, provide more modern facilities, provide superior sire batteries, provide a greater sire selection, help produce offspring with national appeal, and strengthen the organization." He boasted of the progress made by his organization that now offered thirty different varieties of semens. His assistant manager, George A. Miller, used slides to show the group some of those animals, noting that "the breeding program and battery of bulls now available can help correct the weakness in your herds, and this denotes outstanding progress. . . [Our aim] is to get the best bull we can and make it available to you."[17]

Miller and Brubaker – Industry Leaders

In 1956, six years after the formation of VABA, George A. Miller, the assistant manager who spoke to the Augusta County club, started work for the organization as a fieldman. Prior to attending Virginia Tech, Miller, a Loudoun County native and 4-H All-Star, had spent five years working on his Uncle Charles R. Hope's Round Oak Farm. Who would have guessed how intertwined the life of Miller, Round Oak Farm, and the future of the Holstein breed would eventually become? Round Oak Farm was the birthplace of the Holstein Bull of the Century, Elevation, whose "career" as a sire was managed by Miller.

That story would not unfold, however, until years later. Miller earned a B.S. in dairy science in 1952 and spent three years as the VPI Dairy Herdsman while earning his masters degree. In 1965, VABA's original manager, William Armstrong, resigned, leaving behind a legacy of quality and success in cattle genetics. Miller replaced him and continued on the course Armstrong had established. While at VABA, he founded the Program for Genetic Advancement sire sampling and proving system, which became the most respected random sampling program in the industry. He was also instrumental in purchasing Round Oak Rag Apple Elevation and developing the breeding program that made him the most influential AI sire in history.[18] Under the leadership of Miller and VABA secretary-treasurer Emory Brubaker, VABA began a series of discussions with other AI units across the nation.

"Those discussions eventually led to the formation of Select Sires in 1969," recalled Nelson Gardner, past VABA president. "We had many meetings, with discussions as to the best way to join together for the benefit of dairy and beef farmers over the United States and the world. We succeeded in putting Select Sires together as a federation, with each unit keeping its identity."[19] Also instrumental in the creation of the federation was Rowland Hill III and Dr. Jim Nichols, dairy science professor at Virginia Tech. The new Select Sires, Inc. organization was headquartered in Ohio, the site of the Central Ohio Breeding Association.

In 1973, Miller resigned as manager of VABA in order to move to Ohio as Director of Marketing for Select Sires. His record of service to the AI industry and to the Holstein breed continued unbroken during the next eighteen years. "During his tenure, Miller has presided over a tripling of the marketing of semen at Select," noted Select Sires General Manager Richard Chichester at Miller's retirement in 1991.[20] "His devotion, leadership, and honesty have made him a leader in the AI industry." Miller's career brought world renown to Select Sires and numerous honors on the national and state level. He continued to serve as an analyst and consultant for Select Sires even in retirement and in 1993 was given the Distinguished Service Award by the National Association of Animal Breeders. Among his other honors are the Virginia Tech Agriculture Alumnae Distinguished Service Citation and an Honorary Life Membership in the Virginia Holstein Association.[21]

When Miller left VABA for Select Sires in 1973, Emory Brubaker succeeded him as manager. A Franklin County native, Brubaker followed in his father's footsteps with a career in the cattle industry. His father, Riley E. Brubaker, was instrumental in forming both the Franklin County Guernsey Bull Association and then the Franklin County Artificial Breeding Association. Like Miller, Brubaker was a 4-H All-Star and earned a bachelor and masters in dairy science at Virginia Tech but, unlike Miller, he chose to specialize in Guernseys. He came to VABA as a fieldman in 1957, the year after Miller. After being named secretary-treasurer in 1965, he supervised the finances and administration of the organization. For twenty years, from 1973 to 1993, he led the organization through a period of amazing growth. During his first year,

The Brubaker family of Rocky Mount has supplied several generations of leaders in the cattle industry. In this 1948 family portrait, front row, left to right, are Galen B. Brubaker, Janie B. Brubaker, E. Cline Brubaker, and Riley E. Brubaker. On the back row are R. Emory Brubaker, Frances B. Wampler, and Daniel W. Brubaker.

VABA marketed 145,680 units. In 1992, Virginia-North Carolina Select Sires (the name was changed in 1977) recorded 599,029 units. During that time, staff numbers rose, new facilities were added, training and educational opportunities expanded, and the organization extended its market into Florida, Maryland, West Virginia, and Delaware.[22]

Tradition Continues

Filling Brubaker's shoes upon his retirement in 1992 was C. Wayne Dudley, a Rocky Mount native. His resume bears remarkable resemblance to his predecessors: placed first in judging Guernseys in national competition, recipient of the Paul M. Reaves Award, Virginia Tech dairy science graduate, and staff member of VABA since 1973. His first assignment was shipping semen, but he quickly became promotion and finance director and was then named VABA Secretary-Treasurer in 1977.

In July of 2000, Virginia-North Carolina Select Sires became Select Sire Power, Inc. and the territory was extended northward to include all of New England. Today Select Sires is the largest AI organization in the world with a genetics program for dairy and beef cattle that is second to none. But it might be the company's reputation outside of AI that has created a deep-rooted sense of respect for it throughout the cattle industry. Just seven years after its inception, in 1957, the organization began spon-

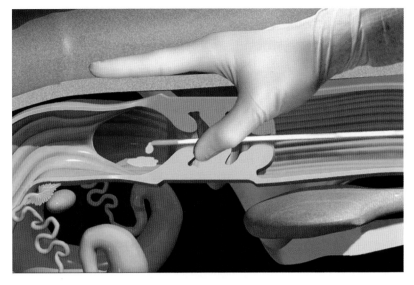

This diagram shows the technique used in artificial insemination. Semen is introduced into the cow's uterus via a tube inserted through the cervix.

soring the participation of the Virginia 4-H Dairy Judging Team in the national contest. Now FFA teams and 4-H teams in both dairy and beef receive sponsorship in all states served by Select Sires. Financial support has also been freely given to numerous other cattle shows, publications, judging teams, and related programs. Through the support of Select Sires, a collegiate training course in AI has been developed for agriculture and veterinary students. Research in genetics and reproduction, both in-house and in cooperation with Virginia Tech, has a decades-old history of sponsorship as well.[23]

Virginia Genetics, Inc., members in 1980 were, left to right, William Harrison, Bill Blose, Bill Blalock, Douglas Child, Richard Harris, Dwight Peck, Jack Hardesty, Joe Crowgey, and Jim Eustace.

The Early Days of AI

In the 1950s AI technicians operated on a new frontier. They had to be part veterinarian and part health inspector while working under the constraints of time with a highly perishable product. At that time AI technicians used glass insemination rods and wore rubber sleeves. There were no disposable items used in early artificial insemination. Everything had to be cleaned and sterilized between inseminations.

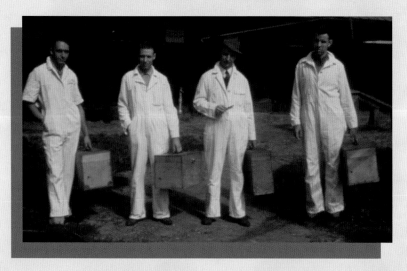

Artificial insemination technicians in the 1950s are carrying boxes containing insemination equipment and the insulated liquid semen cooled with alcohol and dry ice.

During this period only trained professional technicians inseminated cows. Training was usually carried out by faculty at land grant universities such as Virginia Tech. Later, AI stations began to train technicians and large herd owners. Now anyone can receive AI training.

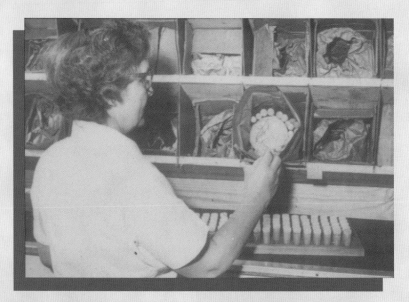

This insulated insert for an insemination box was designed to hold liquid semen at forty degrees Fahrenheit. The can of ice in the center was the coolant and the vials containing the liquid bull semen surround it.

Virginia Genetics, Inc.

By the 1970s the future of the cattle industry was being changed at the cellular level. In 1972 a group of ten progressive Holstein breeders decided to pool their resources for the purpose of proving young bulls and collectively promoting Virginia Holsteins. Further, they wanted a means of sharing farming experiences and to use their collective knowledge to improve their agricultural enterprises. The group consisted of Richard Harris of Culpeper, Douglas Child of Brodnax, William Harrison of Leesburg, Bill Blose of Penn Laird, Bill Blalock of Baskerville, Jim Eustace of Catlett, Dwight Peck of Fredericksburg, Jack Hardesty of Berryville, Dennis Ownby of Richmond, and Joe Crowgey of Wytheville.

The group's founders, all highly respected dairymen, came to the conclusion that dairy farmers needed to use bulls with a higher repeatability of their proof and that they could accomplish this with Virginia Genetics' cooperative venture. In the twenty years of the organization's existence, the men purchased and proved fifty bulls. Eight of the bulls were leased to bull studs, the most successful being Diamond Grove Chip, a Sunnyside Stardust son that was bred by Douglas Child and leased to American Breeders Service.[24]

Another Leap Forward

Even as AI was coming into its own, research at Virginia Tech was helping launch another great scientific leap forward – embryo transfer. Again the advances resulted from the continuous nudging and vision of the Virginia Dairymen's Association. At its seventy-first convention in 1978, members summed up this desire to constantly raise the bar: "Management, labor, genetics and production are closely tied together. Accurate records are the basis for most decisions on dairy farms. Feeding and proper nutrition determine possible production, and genetics limits the level of production."[25]

Embryo transfer made the world a market place for Virginia cattle starting in the early 1980s. "This was a great tool to use," said Nelson Gardner. "We could super ovulate our best cows to furnish bull studs in the U.S. and over the world," he said in pointing out that Virginians were some of the first to ship fresh embryos to Europe. "Emtran's Dr. Alan McCaully and Dr. John Hassler from Pennsylvania would fly into Bridgewater Airpark, owned by Karl Stoltzfus, early in the morning, come to the farm, flush the embryos and then leave for Washington or New York destined for Europe. These trips were coordinated with other farms to lessen the costs. In less than twenty-four hours the embryos were surgically implanted in recipient cows in Europe. It was quite an ordeal."[26]

Blue Ridge Embryos

Dr. Joe Lineweaver of Blacksburg recognized early on the promise of genetic herd improvement that embryo transfer held. In 1978 he helped organize a group of dairymen, known as Blue Ridge Embryos, for the purpose of enhancing the genetic base of top cows in Virginia. Since that time, the organization has conducted 8,970 flushes as of July 2004. Seven thousand and ninety of those flushes have been with dairy animals and the remainder were beef animals. Today Lineweaver is the sole owner of the company that continues to supply both frozen and fresh embryos and participates in the export of frozen embryos.[27]

Pioneers

The true pioneers in the export of bovine embryos were those involved in American Marketing Services, Inc. International (AMS). The Richmond company, reorganized from Ownby Export in 1978 and incorporated in 1979. Key players were C.T. Barns, Oscar W. Kennedy, Dennis Ownby, Conrad Lutz, and Robert D. Heilman. The business plan for the company was to export all breeds of livestock from the United States to world markets. However, the organization of the company came just as the scientific world was perfecting the technique of embryo transfer and as the European Union threatened the U.S. with an embargo on live animals. Although the concept of embryo transplant had been incorporated into the AMS marketing plan in 1978, early efforts were focused on a thriving AI bull market with the European Union. Then in February of 1982 the embargo materialized and the embryo transfer program was activated.

"Marketing efforts required securing pedigrees, cow family genetic information, and photographs of the potential donors. The donors had to be in similar stages of gestation and reproductively healthy. The potential clients and products were easily identified – current AI center clients. The products were Holstein embryos to replace Holstein bulls," recalled Robert D. Heilman, one of the AMS partners.[28]

Assembling a Team

While the concept was workable, the logistics of removing an embryo from one cow, flying it across the ocean, and implanting it in another cow within twenty-four hours, were daunting. Coordinating connecting air flights and the required governmental paperwork was enough to dampen the enthusiasm for the project, not to mention the finan-

These men are loading liquid bull semen into vials, readying it for shipment. Vials contained doses from three to fifteen cubic centimeters depending upon the demand in certain areas for certain bulls.

Cooled liquid semen was put in plastic bags and packaged around a can of ice, then placed in corrugated cardboard shipping containers. This arrangement maintained the forty-degree Fahrenheit temperature required for shipment to the technician. The technician usually received the semen within twenty-four hours of collection. He transferred the vials to the refrigerator where it remained until used. Liquid semen had a life of three to four days. Roy Flora, the Director of Virginia Artificial Breeding Cooperative Semen Productions Lab, perfected a method of extending the viability of the semen by adding chicken egg yolks and sodium citrate. Flora was employed by VABA and then later Select Sires.

Cooled liquid semen was transported from the bull sires to the technicians by automobile, bus, train, or, in special circumstances, by air.

Technicians often received the liquid semen at the bus station. At other times, technicians picked up the semen at the post office, as is depicted here.

cial risk involved in such a venture. Over the course of many months, the AMS staff undertook the challenge. The first hurdle involved securing the embryo rights from breeders. The second involved assembling a veterinary team skilled in non-surgical embryo recovery. A team from Pennsylvania (Emtran) and a team from New Jersey (Huff n Puff) both agreed to be involved. AMS then had to venture into more unexplored territory to negotiate the terms of a sale the complexity of which was unprecedented.

"In addition to the potential donor information, the terms of sale had to be negotiated. AMS was to provide the ET Team for implantation and be fully responsible for implantation. AMS technical personnel were to offer educational instruction to the buyer's technical team during and following implantation. AMS was to provide all technical equipment and required drugs. The buyer was to prepare potential recipients under the direction of AMS for estrus synchronization," recalled Heilman.[29]

Once sales terms were hammered out, AMS worked out details to ensure that herd health on both ends of the deal was certified. Finally, there remained but one small detail to fall into place – securing the financial risk of international travel with live embryos. As this was a venture that no insurance company had ever before been asked to insure, AMS representatives thought it best to make a personal visit to Lloyd's of London and explain the enterprise. Lloyd's agreed to underwrite risk coverage due to delay or missed flight connections, but would not cover any guarantee of pregnancy results.[30]

Launching the Plan

With a full plan in place, Heilman traveled to Europe to meet with Mike Nador of Terimpex and the Hungarian Breeding Institute of Budapest and show them the assembled documentation of Holstein embryo donors. They accepted the offer. On October 1, 1981, two veterinary teams recovered thirty-six fresh embryos from three Pennsylvania farms. The embryos were placed in test tubes which were then taped to members of the traveling team who were Dr. Walter Logan, veterinarian, Dr. John Hasler, embryologist, and Heilman as a representative of AMS.

The team knew that every minute counted as they had a mere twenty-four hours from embryo harvest in Pennsylvania to embryo implantation in Hungary. Fortunately, Swiss Air had been notified in advance and a connecting flight was held so that the men with their valuable test tubes taped to their bodies and the important equipment in the cargo hold could all be transferred without delay. The advanced preparations paid off in Hungary when they were whisked through customs and driven to the village of Ullo. There the AMS team had to wave aside the pleas of the Hungarians who wanted the weary travelers to sit down for a meal before finishing their task. But the Americans were focused on their goal and immediately prepared for surgical implantation. After all thirty-six embryos were implanted, they relaxed and enjoyed the fellowship of their Hungarian hosts.[31]

Just over three months later the AMS team received a telex advising them of seventeen pregnancies from the thirty-six cows for a 47.2 percent success rate. The first venture had been a success all around.

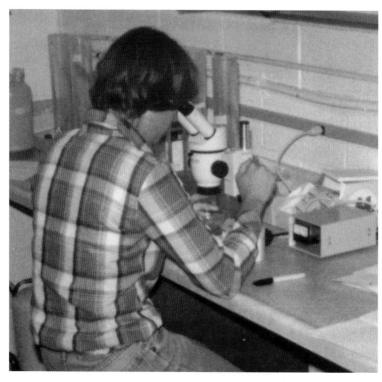

An embryologist in the United States determines if the embryos are of a quality to be sent to Hungary with the AMS embryo implant team.

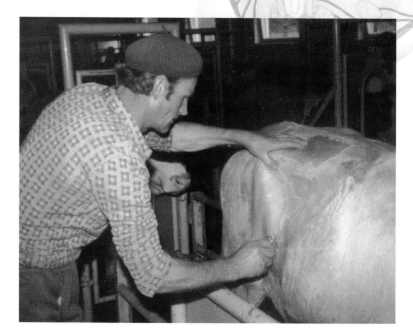

A Hungarian farm worker prepares the site where surgery will be performed to implant the imported embryos.

Hatching Eggs

Within a short time, a second embryo shipment took place – this one to France. Interrupting the champagne celebration dinner that followed the successful implantation was a call from a customs official to Heilman. The French official insisted that Heilman return the imported items to customs at the airport immediately. Fortunately the head of the French Veterinary Service was at the celebratory dinner and he advised the customs agents to come and collect all the cows if they really wanted the embryos returned because the embryos had already been implanted. The customs official then explained that the difficulty lay in the identification number on the custom form. That, explained the veterinarian, was because no identification number had been established for bovine embryos because none had ever been imported before. Thus, he had confused the customs personnel by identifying the first bovine embryos to ever enter France as "hatching eggs." Those "hatching eggs" resulted in a forty-eight percent pregnancy; making the second AMS journey to European equally successful.[32]

The Freeze Factor

In the late 1950s the switch from fresh to frozen semen was seen as an important milestone in AI as the perishibility and the time factor were eliminated from the equation. The influence of a single bull could be greatly expanded with the use of frozen semen. At that time the technical advances were arising out of Virginia Tech's animal science department. Three decades after Paul Reaves' students helped perfect the use of frozen semen, significant scientific and technical advances were still being made in Dr. Richard Saacke's dairy science laboratory at Virginia Tech. This time the mission was more complicated. An embryo has live cells and has to be frozen over a long period of time or the cells will crystallize and be destroyed. The benefits of perfecting the technique were obvious. If a cow produced more embryos on a given day than there were recipients, the extra embryos could be frozen for later use or sale.

The initial success experienced by AMS with shipping fresh embryos overseas was not duplicated with the first frozen embryo shipment. That attempt, in 1983, was a financial disaster and resulted in a zero pregnancy rate. Two years later, however, a simultaneous shipment of fresh and frozen embryos resulted in a higher pregnancy rate (sixty-one percent) from the frozen embryos than from the fresh (fifty-one percent).[33]

As techniques for freezing and thawing improved throughout the 1980s, the need for fresh embryo shipments declined rapidly. The road toward exclusive use of frozen embryos did encounter one speed bump on the tarmac of the Charles D'Gaulle Airport, however. When a container holding AMS frozen embryos broke open after falling from an aircraft cargo door onto the pavement, the liquid nitrogen created a cloud of smoke and an explosion-like noise. The airport was closed

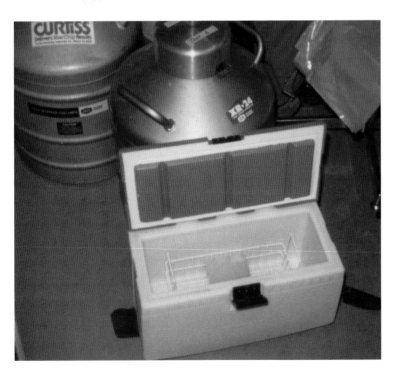

This temperature controlled box and a transporting medium were used in Hungary to store the embryos until implantation.

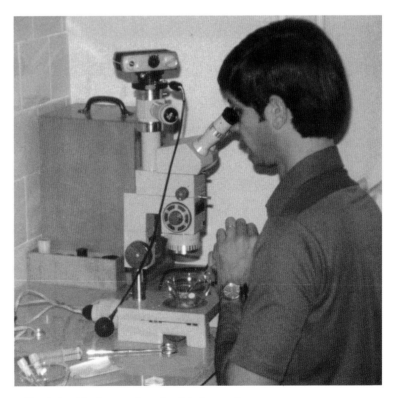

Dr. John Hasler, embryologist, inspects embryo quality and state of development in Hungary prior to implantation.

for an hour and the incident created the first embryo insurance claim. The breeders having embryos in the damaged shipment received the first and only 100 percent pregnancy payment as a result of the insurance claim.[34]

Despite the failure of initial efforts and the incident at the French airport, frozen embryos were the wave of the future. Markets were expanded from cooperatives and governments to individual breeders and the gene pool of donors was enlarged across the country. As markets expanded exponentially, so too did government regulations. With a larger pool of genetic material, embryos could be flushed from the very best animals, creating a need to rank animals according to genetic quality. Eventually AMS rolled over into AMS Genetics, Inc. under the guidance of Heilman and his wife, Nancy. In 1999 the company was sold to Corey C. Wolff who now bases the business in Pennsylvania. From that first journey in 1981 when three men traveled to Hungary with test tubes taped to their bodies, the advance has been remarkable. Through the years the company sent embryo shipments to thirty-four countries on five continents.[35]

Despite the unqualified success of frozen embryo transfer, however, there is still ample room in the industry for AI and for live cattle sales. In late 2003, 600 pregnant Holsteins waited out the winds and rough water from Hurricane Isabel before embarking on a Turkish-bound

ship anchored in the Richmond port. The animals belonged to American Marketing Services which continues to ship cattle overseas on an irregular basis. Only two international shipping companies, one Belgian and the other Flemish, specialize in ocean carrier livestock trade.[36]

A New World

Global markets, world-wide health threats, government regulations, and scientific advances never dreamed of just a few short years ago, have see-sawed modern dairy and beef farmers' hopes for the future and offered challenges to twenty-first century agribusinesses.

Of all the challenges, the biggest headliner is Bovine Spongiform Encephalopathy, also known as BSE or simply mad cow disease. The fatal disease, which is spread by cattle eating feed contaminated with meat and meal from scrapie-infected sheep or BSE infected cattle, causes complete degeneration of the central nervous system. Physiologically the culprits are prions – proteins gone awry – which eat holes in the victims' brains. Humans eating beef that has been tainted with infected central nervous tissue such as that from the spine or brain can contract the disease. Scientists first became aware of BSE in England in 1985. Since

Tracking the facts
Good Genes, AI "Create" Bull of the Century

Round Oak Rag Apple Elevation

In the annals of Holstein history, the date of August 30, 1965, should be encircled with gold stars. On that day at Round Oak Farm in Purcellville, Virginia, a black and white bull calf named Round Oak Rag Apple Elevation entered the world. There was no doubt that he held promise, for he was the result of more than two decades of careful herd improvement by Charles Hope and his son Ronald to Virginia's Holstein bloodlines. The two men had been introducing Canadian cows and bulls from the Rag Apple bloodline.

Elevation, as the Round Oak bull came to be called, boasted a strong pedigree. His sire

that time approximately 200,000 infected cattle from twenty-three countries have been located. Cattle embargos, the slaughter of 3.5 million cattle worldwide, and the revamping of feed and slaughter laws have been the result.[37]

In addition to establishing safeguards in feed programs and at slaughterhouses, some scientists are seeking ways to simply do "an end around" the mad cow gene through cloning. Ever since Dolly the cloned sheep was introduced to the world by her Scottish creators in 1997, cloning has raised ethical debate. Today at least three research teams worldwide are attempting to create cloned cattle that are genetically immune to BSE. One of those teams, under the direction of Virginia Tech's Will Eyestone and William Huckle, will probably have such a cloned calf by the end of 2004 or early 2005. Successful cloning is nothing new to the Virginia Tech biologists, who produced a cloned calf – Mr. Jefferson – in 1998. Now they want to deactivate the prion-producing gene in the bovine cell. An animal with such a "switched-off" or "knockout" gene as the scientists call them, would theoretically be immune to mad cow disease, but proof will come only after years of testing. Eyestone feels that by combining research in cloning, knockout genes, and AI, the threat from BSE could be curbed within six or seven generations of cattle.[38]

Looking for New Ways

Ernie Reeves, the owner and operator of Mossy Creek Farm in the Shenandoah Valley is always looking for ways to meet the challenges of the future head-on. Reeves operates a 650-head commercial cowherd and a 2,000-head backgrounding enterprise on the 2,500-acre family farm. He has managed to stay atop of the most current scientific advances with about forty percent of his Angus-based animals serving as surrogate mothers for a custom embryo recipient service. At the same time he practices several soil conservation and environmental management techniques.

In 2002, in the wake of BSE concern, Reeves decided to begin raising all-natural beef as well. Although he uses some chemical fertilizers, none of his animals receive hormones or antibiotics. Their feed consists of a mixture of hominy, corn silage, and corn gluten meal. "It's an all-vegetarian diet. Just feed and water," notes Reeves. With these farming practices, Reeves has not left the mainstream farming arena, however. For example, he represented the National Cattlemen's Beef Association as regional policy vice president when he testified before Congress in the summer of 2003 regarding international trade barriers being placed on cattle exporters. His work has earned him a number of

was Tidy Burke Elevation and his dam was Osborndale Ivanhoe Eve. From his earliest public appearances, he earned a reputation as the cream of the crop, but no one could have predicted his incredible legacy to the world's Holstein population. His standing, both as representative of the classic breed standard and as a proven sire, never diminished in a lifetime of almost fourteen years. As a calf he finished second in three shows, received a Very Good rating of eighty-six as a two-year-old, and was scored ninety-six, Excellent, as a mature bull.

Fate sent Elevation to an even higher level of fame in July of 1966 when Foxlease Farm in Loudoun County hosted the Virginia

Teresa Ann Myers with Walkup Astronaut Lou Ann

honors including the National Cattlemen's Beef Association Region I Environmental Stewardship Award (1997) and the Beef Improvement Federation's Commercial Producer of the Year in 1999. Reeves is representative of the generation of farmers who strive to incorporate all the best techniques and information so that an industry that is four centuries old in Virginia will be viable in the future.[39]

Environmental stewardship and safe food sources are two of the most pressing issues facing producers in both the beef and dairy industry. In Virginia, dairy farmers like the Grove family (John and Crystal Grove and their son Mark) in Augusta County are using best management practices (BMPs) to address both issues. BMPs on a dairy farm mean

1. Being aware of all farm resources for dairy prod-uct production, including manure as well as chemical fertilizers.

2. Controlling and directing those resources for a profit while protecting surface and ground water re-sources for those who depend on them.

For the Groves, who milk 120 Holsteins, this meant working closely with soil and water conservation district personnel to construct an open-air milking parlor and an open-air resting shed with dirt floors and fans. It also meant developing a nutrient management plan for using both the liquid and dry manure gathered from the farm; creat-

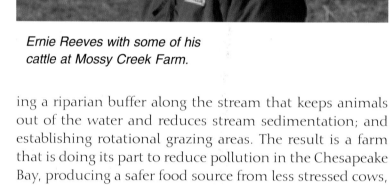

Ernie Reeves with some of his cattle at Mossy Creek Farm.

ing a riparian buffer along the stream that keeps animals out of the water and reduces stream sedimentation; and establishing rotational grazing areas. The result is a farm that is doing its part to reduce pollution in the Chesapeake Bay, producing a safer food source from less stressed cows, and providing a good living for the family.[40]

At Oak Grove Farm in Marshall, Katherine McLeod is following a different route with a small herd of Ayrshire

Holstein Field Day. The crowds gathered to hear featured speakers, including a U.S. House of Representatives majority leader named Gerald Ford, but many in the crowd were all abuzz with conversation about the yearling bull just up the road at Round Oak Farm.

A visit was paid to the Hopes and soon a consortium of men developing an artificial insemination (AI) breeding program for proven bulls paid $2,800 for Elevation — $1,800 more than had ever before been paid for a Holstein bull in Virginia. That investment turned golden for the original group. AI offered a way to spread Elevation's superior genes across the country and even internationally. Soon, through the performance of his progeny, Elevation's reputation become legendary. His daughters were not only beautiful, but they were champion milkers. His genes were so superior that even mediocre cows produced cham-pion offspring when Elevation was the sire.

For seven years, starting in 1970, Elevation lived the life of a pampered king, including the use of an air-conditioned pen in the summertime. In return, three times a week he mounted a dummy animal or a specially outfitted steer and his semen was collected, frozen, and sold around the world. All told, more than 522,000 straws of his semen were sold for millions of dollars.

Time and again, Elevation's progeny were champions. His daughters brought tens of thousands of dollars at sales. Eight times Elevation was named the Leading National Honor List Sire for Production and he was named an All-American Get of Sire three times.

Elevation died in 1979, but his genes have become the foundation on which the world's Holstein population now stands. It is a rare Holstein bloodline that doesn't include one or more Elevation listings. Through the miracle of modern

dairy cows. There on the 560-acre Virginia certified organic farm in the Blue Ridge foothills, farm manager Ryan Hagenston, herd manager Joe Witscher, and cheesemaker Ross Gagnon, turn McLeod's dream into reality. Their goal is to show how a small, organic farm can be both profitable and mainstream. They are certified through the Virginia Department of Agriculture and Consumers Services and are working cooperatively with Virginia Tech. Quality and profitability are their main focuses. The herd, approaching ninety animals, is on official DHIA test. The top cows in the herd should make records of 14,000 to 15,000 pounds of milk. Each animal gets two to three pounds of organically raised rolled corn per day in addition to fresh pasture during the warmer months and hay in the colder season. Managing the herd is multifaceted. Not only do Hagenston and Witscher delve into the genetics of the Ayrshires, but they monitor changes in weather, food, and animal health, which all factor into the premium butter and cheddar and ricotta cheese that are produced on the farm and marketed locally.[41]

In 1966, then-House Majority Leader Gerald Ford spoke at Foxlease Farm in Loudoun County at Virginia Holstein Field Day.

Environmental Issues

Environmental and water quality issues, especially for those living in the Chesapeake Bay watershed, are a reality of farm life in the twenty-first century. Since 1987 the states with waters draining into the Chesapeake Bay have entered into an initiative to reduce the amounts of nitrogen, phosphorus, and sediment that enter the bay, a portion of which comes from agriculture. Although progress has been made, recent studies have shown that there is still a long road ahead for those who want a healthier Chesapeake Bay. Realizing that the issues must be met directly and that all parties affected by the pollution and clean-up must come together for a solution, a group of Shenandoah Valley dairy farmers traveled in late 2003 to Port Isobel Education Center and Tangier Island on a trip sponsored by the Chesapeake Bay Foundation. For two days they learned about the issues involving overfishing, erosion, and declining water quality. They met with fishermen whose livelihoods are negatively impacted by the declining health of the Bay, and they were able to share some of their own frustrations of trying to cut through government red tape and overcome rising costs while struggling to meet environmental regulations, nutrient management requirements, and implement BMPs. Although no solutions were found to the problems

the few bulls in the world to have a special museum exhibit created in his honor, but that is the case at the Loudoun Heritage Farm Museum located not far from Elevation's birthplace. At the dedication to that museum, J. Carlton Courter III, the Virginia Commissioner of Agriculture, noted: "Elevation was the most influential domesticated animal in the New World."

Proof of Elevation's greatness, of course, is in his daughters. Countless descendants of Elevation appeared at the annual Virginia Sale of Stars hosted by the Virginia Holstein Association. The sale, started in 1973, showcases the brightest stars of the state and the pedigrees are as blue-blooded as can come from a black-and-white dairy cow.

In 1974, a young girl in Harrisonburg, purchased an Elevation descendant named Willowlyn Elevation Lou. On January 16, 1976, Walkup Astronaut Lou Ann was born of

science, Elevation's semen left a legacy of 60,000 daughters and 10,000 sons. To put that another way, five million of the world's 50 million Holstein's are Elevation descendants. It is for that reason that in the year 2000, Holstein International named Elevation the Bull of the Century. He is probably one of

In 2003, the Grove family of Augusta County followed best management practices when designing new dairy buildings. The farm's 120 Holsteins enjoy an open-air milking parlor and an open-air resting shed, seen here, with dirt floors and fans. The Groves also developed a nutrient management plan for using both the liquid and dry nutrients generated by their dairy herd.

Willowlyn and the sire Astronaut. Soon Teresa Myers (now Callendar) and her heifer became a team, garnering fistfuls of ribbons and honors on the state, regional, and national level. In six years, they received Junior All-American three times, were twice reserve champion, once honorable mention, and twice Nominated All-American. Within the state, Lou Ann was All-Virginia from 1977 to 1982 and during that period was grand champion at the Virginia State Show four times and reserve champion once. Willowlyn and Lou Ann together were named All-Virginia Daughter-Dam in 1982.

Lou Ann's breeding held true and many of her progeny garnered championship honors. The team of Lou Ann and Teresa was unstoppable. Teresa excelled in both 4-H and FFA and was named the winner of the Virginia Distinguished Holstein Youth Award. She also sat on the state's championship Dairy Bowl Quiz Team and the FFA Dairy Judging team that won the national contest.

An article in Holstein World, described the dazzling dairy duo in this way: "Lou Ann's owner, Teresa Myers Callendar, would have been a successful youth without Lou Ann, but it wouldn't have been nearly as much fun. They worked beautifully well together over the years, proving to be nearly unbeatable in the show ring."

Lou Ann died in May of 1992. Although Lou Ann never earned Cow of the Century honors, the genetic material of her famous ancestor put her among a select group of Holsteins most influential in the breed's future.

Loudoun Heritage Farm Museum, www.loudounfarmmuseum.org, Seedstock article, pp. 218-224; "Reflections of Round Oak," by George A. Miller in *Holstein-Friesian World*, April 10, 1978; "DNA Trail Began in Va.," by Michael Laris, *Washington Post*, June 30, 2002; "Virginia Sale of Stars," by George A. Miller; and "Terrific Team: Lu Ann and Teresa," *Holstein World*, July 1991.

Hog Island roundup subject of TV show

It was in April that the wild cattle of Hog Island were last in the news. That was when a group of North Carolina cowboys made their second trip to the Eastern Shore barrier island in an attempt to remove the cattle from the area.

The cattle had roamed free across the marshes and dunes for years, ever since the last families which had inhabited the island left in the 1930s.

The North Carolina cowboys had tried to remove the cattle during the fall of 1985 but found the wild animals were more of a task than they had planned on.

Then in the spring of this year, the National Geographic Society provided funding to help with a second attempt. The cattle, it was believed, needed to go in order to protect the bird nesting areas and salt marshes on the island.

This time the cowboys were successful in their roundup and National Geographic was there to record all of the action.

Now, on Sunday, Sept. 7, that filmed recording of the roundup will be a featured segment of the television show National Geographic Ex-

plorers scheduled for broadcast at 8 p.m. on WTBS.

The show will be rebroadcast on WTBS Saturday, Sept. 13, at 9 a.m.

Locally, WTBS is received by cable subscribers on channel 9.

Scenes of the roundup on Hog Island shown being filmed here are scheduled for broadcast on Sept. 7.

A 1986 newspaper story tells about the conservation efforts on Virginia's Hog Island.

facing the Bay, partnerships were forged and all parties came away from the trip with a better understanding of the complexities involved in cleaning up the Chesapeake Bay for future generations of Virginians.[42]

Resource Management

Seventeenth-century settlers found Virginia's coastal islands good places to send their cattle to graze safely without the fear that they might wander off. The land was sparsely settled then. Conservation was not an issue. By the late twentieth century, cattle on coastal islands had become a threat to rare species of birds and to the sand dunes that are critical to protecting the rapidly-disappearing marsh lands.

In an excellent example of wise resource management, conservationists and cowboys joined forces to save Hog Island, a barrier island off Virginia's Eastern Shore, from the damaging effects of an expanding herd of feral cattle. The cattle descended from stock owned by some of the 400 people who lived on Hog Island in the 1930s. When sand erosion destroyed the settlement, the people moved to the main-

land, leaving a few cattle behind. As they multiplied, these "bulls in nature's china shop" trampled nests of rare water birds in this protected habitat and chomped the grasses that hold the dunes in place to protect the island and the adjacent mainland salt marshes from the power of the ocean.

When The Nature Conservancy acquired Hog Island, it decided that the cattle threatening the natural habitat there had to be removed. In 1986, Naturalist John Hall of the Conservancy, Director of the Virginia Coast Reserve, worked with a group of seven cowboys from North Carolina who were experts at roping wild cattle. The men, their fourteen horses and twenty-four dogs, traveled the twelve miles by water to Hog Island, where Hall and volunteers created noises that drove the cattle from their brushy hiding places toward the island's beaches There the swift-riding cowboys could round up the cattle and get them in pens for transport to the mainland. Most of the cattle went to the stockyard, but some were relocated, appropriately, to join a North Carolina herd.

The successful operation is an example of wise management practices that employed a scientific understanding of the interrelationship of man, beast, birds, and land to achieve a solution that protects the ecosystem.[43]

A Tasty Gene

No dairy farmer, cattleman, or scientist involved in those first AI experiments in the 1940s could ever have imagined the cattle industry of the twenty-first century. Whereas those men and women looked to improve the future by building a more efficient and cleaner milking parlor, today's industry leaders look in a microscope and talk of building a better cell. Scientists mapping the cow genome are now looking at particular traits on the cellular level when matching animals to be bred. One company recently announced the discovery of the genetic markers that make for good-tasting meat. If they are correct, then breeders can screen cattle for their genetic potential on the human dinner plate. The project identified genetic characteristics for producing well-marbled meat (important for tenderness) as well as for the ability to convert food into muscle. Some feel that the discovery could lead to a safer food source. If the scientists are correct, animals that have inherited the tasty gene could be fattened more gradually and given fewer growth hormones because the need to artificially increase their size is no longer there.[44]

Clearly it is an increasingly complicated and global world that industry leaders live in, but the farmers of tomorrow will continue to move forward just as their counterparts of four centuries ago did, armed with the best knowledge, tools, and vision available. Who knows where the future will lead now that those tools are available, including the capacity to manipulate DNA – the very stuff of life itself.

Dorothy Rosen was honored with the 1997 Virginia Environmental Stewardship Award for her leadership and accomplishments in resource conservation as owner and manager of Grove Church Farm in Mt. Crawford. The award was presented at the 1997 Virginia Beef Industry Convention.

With the implementation of best management practices and soil and water conservation programs, Virginia's beef cattle and dairy producers help keep the state's streams and rivers flowing clean. Their efforts protect the fragile balance of the Chesapeake Bay's ecosystem.

Epilogue

Four hundred years ago the first English settlers established their tentative foot-hold in North America at the place they called Jamestown and the colony they named Virginia. That began a transformation of the continent and, indeed, the world.

From the beginning, the large-eyed, four-legged beasts they called "neat cattle" and "kine" accompanied them. These cattle were a necessary part of their way of life – an important source of the meat and dairy products on which they based their foodways, for the draft power to pull cart and plow, and for leather that was essential for shoes, harness, saddles, and military needs.

Together, man and beast developed ways of adapting to the new world, so that within half a century, both were thriving and multiplying. Virginia thus became the pioneer region in which the methods of developing a cattle industry that ultimately became the modern beef and dairy industries were pioneered.

The free range management of cattle that the Virginia settlers adapted, so opposite to their livestock management practices in England, foreshadowed the open range of the western Great Plains of the nineteenth century. Virginia cattle drives of the eighteenth and nineteenth centuries – for military needs in the Revolution and Civil War and for agricultural market development as settlers pushed into the rich Valley of Virginia and lands beyond the Alleghenies – foretold cattle drives of a later era from Abilene to Kansas City.

The export of cattle was one of the earliest sources of trade income in Virginia. By the 1650s, Virginia shipped live cattle to northern colonies and salted beef to the West Indies. This was a small beginning that pointed to a significant later trade in the dramatic story of fat cattle exported from lush bluegrass pastures of southwest Virginia to London and Liverpool in the six decades between the Civil War and World War I.

Virginia farmers were always among the leadership in producing better beef and dairy cattle. Pioneer importers of Shorthorns, Herefords, Angus, and Holsteins and George Washington's interest in improved breeds pointed the way to industry leaders of the late twentieth century who have worked so successfully with Continental breeds.

These recent pioneers have effected a total transformation of the beef and dairy industries in Virginia. On the cutting edge of new developments, these men and women have experimented with new breeds of beef and dairy cattle, ever seeking stock that can produce more and better beef and milk for a greater return on investment and a more efficient use of agricultural resources. Their interest in quality seedstock has meant that Virginia animals have garnered top prizes in major national shows.

Virginia leaders in the beef and dairy industries have played an important leadership role on boards and as officers of national breed and improvement organizations.

Their work in areas of artificial insemination and embryo transfer have placed a number of Virginia's breeders and agricultural scientists among the leading experts in the nation, with their skills in demand internationally as well.

The consistent support of the Commonwealth of Virginia and the Virginia Department of Agirculture and Consumer Services from the late nineteenth century to the present has had a dramatic impact on the growth and strength of the state's cattle industry. The outstanding relationship between Virginia Tech, Virginia State, the experiment stations, and the network of county agents is a model for the nation.

The large cast of characters who have created, supported, and led the major beef and dairy organizations, who have developed more effective means of marketing livestock and marketing milk, who have labored to educate Virginia's farmers and upcoming generations of farmers through agriculture classes, clubs, market shows, judging teams and projects, are unsung heroes in the drama of cattle in Virginia.

The authors, editor, designer, and sponsors hope that this book draws together the entire cast of characters who have created and developed the beef and dairy industries of Virginia. From shaky beginnings four hundred years ago, through struggles of settlement, tribulations of war, threat from drought, disease, and depression, these industries have emerged in strength today.

Virginia's cattle story is America's cattle story. Just as the two have been linked in the past, it seems clear that Virginia leaders of these industries will continue to be on the cutting edge of new trends, developments, and technologies. Many frontiers in beef and dairy cattle production remain to be explored. The tradition of successful growth and adaptation initiated at Jamestown will continue as the twenty-first century unfolds. These first four centuries are only the beginning of *Virginia's Cattle Story*. 🄌

Many frontiers in beef and dairy cattle production remain to be explored. Future generations of Virginians will chart the courses for the state's beef and dairy industries.

Donors to the
Virginia Cattle History project

Platinum

Ayrshire Farm, Sandy Lerner
Mary Howe diZerega
Garland & Agnes Gray Foundation and
      Florence Gray & Thomas H. Tullidge, Sr.

Dwight E. Houff
Debbie Snead
The Titmus Foundation, Inc.
Virginia Cattlemen's Association

Gold

Clifford A. Cutchins, III
Dublin Feeder Cattle Association
Huntley Farm
William A. Hazel
Little River Foundation
Harry & Harriet Grandis Family Foundation
John & Patsy Liskey

John B. Mitchell
The Ohrstrom Foundation, Inc.
Bill & Lucy Oliver
Virginia Farm Bureau Federation
Virginia State Dairymen's Association
William D. & Bonnie Lou Wampler

Silver

Abingdon Feeder Cattle Association
Roy L. Ash
Bayville Farms Association
William E. Blalock
Robert W. Brooks
CFW Communications Foundation
Paul & Virginia Coleman
F. Joseph Copenhaver, Jr.
A. Douglas Dalton, Jr.
Dairy Farmers of America, Inc.
A. L. Eller, Jr.
Edward B. Eller
First Bank and Trust Co.
First and Citizens Bank
Charles T. Foster
Nelson Gardner
William H. Groseclose
William & Polly Harrison
Pete & Connie Henderson
J. Earl Kindig
Knoll Crest Farm, Inc.

Lawrence Transfer, Inc.
David A. Leonard
William H. McDonald
Mead-Westvaco, Inc.
Mossy Creek Farm
Ownby Auction Co.
George G. Phillips, Jr.
Monira Rifaat
Samuel G. Spangler
W.A. Spillman, Jr.
A.C. Spotts, III
Stoney Run Farms, Inc.
Stuart Land and Cattle Co.
W.A. Stuart, Jr.
Warren G. Teates
Virginia Beef Industry Council
Virginia Livestock Marketing Association
Virginia State Feed Association
Nicholas Wehrmann
Whitesel Brothers, Inc.

Bronze

George A. Allen, Jr.
William Backer Foundation
Donald R. Benner
Robert K. Bennett
W.B. Blanton, Jr.
Blue Ridge Embryos
William A. Bratton
R. Emory Brubaker
C & C Farmers Supply Corp.
Ernest T. Carter
Charles Cassell
Richard H. L. Chichester
Louis & Claudia Chisholm
Cooperative Milk Producers Association
Copper Creek Corporation
Gray Coyner
Norman Coyner
Sidney Crockett
John H. Crowgey, Jr.
Dairymen Specialty Co., Inc.
Robert C. Davenport
Justin W. Dove
Richard S. Ellis IV Family
Carlton L. Emmart
Charles E. Fariss
John Faulconer
George E. Fisher
Watt L. & Jennifer B. Foster, Jr.
Fredericksburg Feeder Calf Association
Duane D. Gilliam
Glover D. Gilliam
Allan Graybeal
Sidney Grove
Harvue Farms
Harold D. Hawkins
Gerald Heatwole
Robert Heilman
Donald F. Herbst
Julian Heron
George A. Horkan, Jr.
James H. Huffard III
W. Martin Kegley, Jr.
Theresa & Donald Key
Gordon C. Keys
Walter Kingrey
Robert F. Kube

G.C. Luck, Jr.
Lynchburg Feeder Cattle Association
Joe H. McConnell
Mike McDowell
P.T. McIntire
William B. McSpadden
Maryland & Virginia Milk Producers Cooperative Assoc., Inc.
Frank H. Maxey
T. Carter Melton
George A. Miller
J. Clifford Miller, III
Charles, Larkin & Damon Moyer
John & Bernice Mrotek
W. Ray & Ruby M. Murley
Tim Neale
James R. Nichols
Rita & George Nicklas
Delbert O'Meara
Carl E. Polan
C.W. Pratt
Lewis Pratt
S.W. Rawls, Jr.
Jeff G. Reeves
Don Richardson
Roanoke-Hollins Stockyard
E.D. Robertson
RMC - Rockingham Mill
Rockingham Cooperative, Inc.
Harold W. Roller
Rolling Hills Farm
Fred H. Scott
Select Sire Power, Inc.
Chip & Debbie Snead
T.D. Steele
George R. Swecker
Charles W. Thomas
Randall Updike
Valley Feed Co.
Virginia Jersey Cattle Club
Virginia Limousin Breeders Association
Wall Brothers Dairy, Inc.
Wampler Farm
Leon C. Warner
Jessee Webster
K.C. Williamson

Endnotes

Virginia's First Cattle

1 Lewis Cecil Gray, *History of Agriculture in the Southern United States to 1860* (Washington, D.C.: The Carnegie Institution of Washington, 1933), vol. 1, 140. 2 Jamestown Yorktown research files. The two accounts are from Captain John Smith. The first, early in 1609, mentioned only pigs and chickens, while the second, later in the year, provided a more complete inventory. 3 Harry Sinclair Drago, *Great American Cattle Trails* (New York: Bramhall House, 1965), 82. 4 Beverley Straube, curator, Jamestown Rediscovery Project, e-mail and telephone conversation with Nancy Sorrells, 6 January 2003. 5 Ferrar Papers: Document #32, "Provision for the Planters in Virginia. 20 February 1611." 6 Virginia DeJohn Anderson, "Animals into the Wilderness: The Development of Livestock Husbandry in the Seventeenth-Century Chesapeake," *William and Mary Quarterly*, 3:59 (April 2002), 381. 7 John Rolfe, *A True Relation of the State of Virginia Lefte By Sir Thomas Dale Knight In May Last 1616* (Charlottesville, Va., University Press of Virginia, 1957), July-August 1619, 14-15. 8 *The Records of The Virginia Company of London: The Court Book, from the Manuscript in the Library of Congress*, ed. Susan Myra Kingsbury (Washington, D.C.: Government Printing Office, 1906), 171-172. 9 Ibid., January 1619/20, 243. 10 Ibid., 30 September 1619, 221. 11 Ibid., 3 November 1619, 257. 12 *Declaration of the State of the Colonie and Affaires in Virginia* (Force, Tracts, III, No. 5), 5. 13 Wesley N. Laing, "Cattle in Seventeenth-Century Virginia," *Virginia Magazine of History and Biography*, 67(April 1959): 150. 14 Ibid. Laing drew his information about Gookin from Frederick William Gookin, *Daniel Gookin, 1612-1687, His Life and Letters and Some Account of His Ancestry* (Chicago, 1912). 15 List of cattle importations compiled from Virginia Company of London records by research staff at Jamestown Settlement. 16 *The Records of The Virginia Company of London*, 24 October 1621, 535. 17 Ibid., 13 March 1622, 618. 18 *The Records of the Virginia Company of London*, 19 June 1623, 233. 19 Ibid., 235. 20 Ibid., October 1623, 284. 21 Ibid., 19 June 1623, 238. 22 *The Records of the Virginia Company of London*, 28 March 1623, 66. 23 Colonial Williamsburg Past Portal database, Harvey 1630, in Muraca and Heillier 1992:40. 24 Ibid. 25 *The Complete Works of Captain John Smith*, ed. Philip L. Barbour (Chapel Hill, N.C.: The University of North Carolina Press for The Institute of Early American History and Culture, 1986), vol. 2, 264. 26 Virginia DeJohn Anderson, 384. 27 Ibid., 385. 28 Ibid., 382. 29 Hening I, 199. 30 Virginia DeJohn Johnson, 389. 31 Ibid., 389-390. 32 Ibid., 390. 33 Interview with Joanne Bowen, Director of Agricultural Archaeology, Colonial Williamsburg, March 2003. 34 Ibid., 383. 35 Chinard 1934: 119. 36 Lewis Cecil Gray, 198-199, 217, 606, 801-802 and G. Melvin Herndon, *William Tatham and the Culture of Tobacco, including a facsimile reprint of an historical and practical essay on the culture and commerce of tobacco by Tatham* (Coral Gables, Fla.: University of Miami Press, 1969, originally London: 1800), 6, 474. 37 Virginia DeJohn Anderson, 377. 38 Susie M. Ames, *Studies of the Virginia Eastern Shore in the Seventeenth Century* (Richmond: The Dietz Press, 1940), 16-20. 39 Ibid., 20-24. 40 Quoted in Ames, 56, from *Northampton County Records*, II, 67, a letter from Lady Dale dated August 12, 1636. 41 Ibid., 32-33. 42 Jon Butler, "Thomas Teackle's 333 Books: A Great Library on Virginia's Eastern Shore, 1697," *William and Mary Quarterly,* 3rd series, 49(July 1992): 450-452. 43 Ames, 61, citing DeVries, *Voyages from Holland to America,* 64 and Hening, I, 227. 44 Gray, 209. The observers quoted were Ligon and Oldmixon. 45 Ibid., 135. 46 Anderson, "Animals into the Wilderness," 393-395. 47 Darret B. and Anita H. Rutman, *A Place in Time: Middlesex County, Virginia, 1650-1750* (New York and London: W.W. Norton and Company, 1984), 44-45. 48 James Horn, *Adapting to a New World: English Society in the Seventeenth-Century Chesapeake* (Chapel Hill and London: Published for the Institute of Early American History and Culture, Williamsburg, Virginia, by the University of North Carolina Press, 1994), 282. 49 Anderson, 397. 50 Ibid., 49. 51 Deed from Sir John Harvey to Bartram Obert, 3 May 1640, recorded 11 July 1660, Lancaster County Deed Book 2:379. By the time this deed was recorded, Obert had died, so its recordation may have been related to the settlement of his estate. 52 Bartram Obert will, Lancaster County Deeds & Wills, 1654-1661: 72-74. 53 Rutman, 150-151. 54 Warwick County Cattle (Livestock) Accounts 1658-1685, originals in Library of Virginia 22057c. Transcribed in Richard Dunn, editor, *Warwick County, Virginia, Colonial Court Records in Transcription* (Williamsburg, Va.: The Jones House Association, Inc., 2000), 590-591. 55 Ibid. 56 Deed of gift by Francis Graves, (Old) Rappahannock County, 28 November 1678. Copy courtesy of Virginia Historical Society, Mss2G7845a1. Old Rappahannock County existed from 1656 until 1692, at which time it ceased to exist, being divided into Richmond and Essex Counties. Many years later another Rappahannock County was created in the foothills of the Blue Ridge Mountains.

Cattle and the Colonists

1 Interview with JoAnn Bowen, Director of Agricultural Archaeology, Colonial Williamsburg, March 2003. 2 Ibid. 3 Maude H. Woodfin and Marion Tingling, *Another Secret Diary of William Byrd of Westover for the years 1739-1741, with Letters & Literary Exercises, 1696-1726* (Richmond: The Dietz Press, 1942), 25 March, 23 August 1740; 24 March 1741. 4 William Byrd to Lord Tipparari [Lord Dunkellen], 18 February 1718, Woodfin and Tingling, *Another Secret Diary. . .Letters and Literary Exercises*, 324-325. 5 Ibid., passim. 6 Ibid., 22 December 1739; 22n1. Braxton's son Carter, named for his maternal grandfather, Robert "King" Carter, was born in 1736, so he would only have been a toddler at the time of this dinner. 7 Hannah Glasse, *The Art of Cookery made Plain and Easy* (London: 1747), 23. 8 Ibid., passim. 9 Ibid., 4, n2 indicates that Byrd's Hanover lands, Middle Quarter and two Quarters, were processioned (the boundaries were walked) by the St. Paul's Parish vestry. 10 Ibid., 25 July 1741. Byrd noted, "We had a beef brought in the cart." 11 Ibid. 12 ,16 August 1739. 12 Ibid., 17 December 1739. 13 Ibid., 31 December 1739. 14 Ibid., 17, 19, 20 November 1740. 15 Ibid., 2, 4 February 1741. 16 27 Jan 1772, 3 Feb 1772. Jack P. Greene, editor, *The Diary of Colonel Landon Carter of Sabine Hall, 1752-1778*, Volume II (Charlottesville: Published for the Virginia Historical Society by The University Press of Virginia, 1965), 2:646-648. 17 Charlene McIntire Talcott, "Tidewater Virginia Farmers, 1760-1805: An Analysis of Assets in a Pre-Revolutionary and Post-Revolutionary Economy," masters thesis, Virginia Commonwealth University, Richmond, 2000, 25. 18 Ibid., 407-408. 19 Ibid., 415. 20 Amy Speckart, "Small Planters in York County, Virginia, 1780-1800," A report for the Yorktown Victory Center, Jamestown-Yorktown Foundation, 1998-1999, 11. 21 Ibid., n.p. 22 Rosemary Brandau, "Small Milkhouse on Wythe Property," A report for the Colonial Williamsburg Foundation, 1984. 23 Robert D. Mitchell, *Commercialism and Frontier: Perspectives on the Early Shenandoah Valley* (Charlottesville: University Press of Virginia, 1977), 139-140. 24 Phillip Vickers Fithian, ed. R.G. Albion and L. Dodson, *Journal, 1775-1776* (Princeton, N.J.: Princeton University Press, 1934), 145, 151. 25 Mitchell, *Commercialism and Frontier*, 147. 26 Ibid., 148-149. 27 William Crow and Charles Lewis vs. Daniel Smith et al, November 1763, Augusta County Judgments. 28 Sarah S. Hughes, *Surveyors and Statesmen: Land Measuring in Colonial Virginia* (Richmond: Va.: The Virginia Surveyors Foundation, Ltd., 1979), 160. 29 Gray, 841. 30 Augusta County Judgments, Andrew Greer vs. Israel Christian, 1766, May – B – 411. 31 Mitchell, *Commercialism and Frontier,* 142. 32 Lewis Cecil Gray, *History of Agriculture in the United States to 1860* (Washington, D.C.: Published by the Carnegie Institution of Washington, 1933), 210. 33 Edward Wakefield, *An Account of Ireland, Statistical and Political* (London: Longman, Hurst, Rees, Orme, and Brown, Paternoster-Row, 1812), 315. 34 Arthur Young, *A tour in Ireland; with general observations on the present state of that kingdom; made in the years 1776, 1777, and 1778, and brought down to the end of 1779* (Dublin: Whitestone Sleater, 1780), 126. 35 Ibid., 222, 233. 36 Amos Long, Jr., *The Pennsylvania German Family Farm* (Breinigsville, Pa.: The Pennsylvania German Society, 1972), 25. 37 Oscar Kuhns, *The German and Swiss Settlements of Colonial Pennsylvania* (New York: 1914), 90, quoting an extract from Governor Thomas Pownall's Journal in 1754. 38 Long, *The Pennsylvania German Family Farm*, 25. 39 Mitchell, *Commercialism and Frontier,* 183. 40 Ibid., 185. 41 Letter from the Reverend H. Toulmin to Mr. James Leigh, Winchester, Va., 20 November 1793, *The Western Country in 1793: Reports on Kentucky and Virginia* by Harry Toulmin, edited by Marion Tinling and Godfrey Davies (San Marino, Cal., 1948), 58. 42 Carter Burwell was the son of Robert Carter's daughter, Elizabeth Carter, and her first husband, Nathaniel Burwell of Fairfield, Gloucester County. Robert Carter provided the land on which his grandson built the handsome plantation house and dependencies. 43 Lorena S. Walsh, *From Calabar to Carter's Grove: The History of a Virginia Slave Community* (Charlottesville and London: University Press of Virginia, 1997), 119-121. 44 6 November 1771. *Diary of Landon Carter,* 2:638-639. 45 1 September 1774. *Diary of Landon Carter,* 2:855. 46 Walsh, *From Calabar to Carter's Grove*, 122. 47 The new overseer was Leonard Hill, at Carter's Park Quarter. 9 May 1776. *Diary of Landon Carter*, 2:1035. 48 13 July 1771 My quarter at the Park in fine order. . . The overseer writes for butter pots. 12 August 1771 John Beale from my Northumberland quarters sent up a pot of butter weight 30 pounds. I send down 2 pots of about 20 pounds each to be more handy. Ibid., 2:591, 2:611. 49 Ibid., 123. 50 25 June 1777. *Diary of Landon Carter*, 2:1100. 51 Undated entries 1773, *Diary of Landon Carter,* 2:786 52 17 May 1772. Greene, *Diary of Landon Carter,* 2:685-686. 53 The long diary entry assessing his feeding and breeding patterns was made on 29 May 1772. *Diary of Landon Carter,* 2:697. 54 Mount Vernon website: www.mountvernon.org/pioneer/first.html. 55 Alan and Donna Jean Fosonie, *George Washington: Pioneer Farmer* (Mount Vernon, Va.: Mount Vernon Ladies' Association, 1998), 23-25. 56 Ibid., 31. 57 Ibid., and www.mountvernon.org/pioneer/sun/oxen.html. 58 Fosonie, *George Washington*, 32. 59 George Washington to William Pearce, 23 September 1793, found at www.Mountvernon.org/pioneer/sun/george.html. 60 BBC Homepage, "Historic Figures: Robert Bakewell (1725-1795)," www.bbc.co.uk/history/historic_figures/bakewell_robert.shtml.

Revolutionary Times

1 Patricia Givens Johnson, *William Preston and the Allegheny Patriots* (Pulaski, Va.: B.D. Smith & Bros., Inc., Printers, 1976), 35-36. 2 Ibid., 37 3 Ibid., 40. 4 Ibid., 42-43. 5 Robert D. Mitchell, *Commercialism and Frontier: Perspectives on the Early Shenandoah Valley* (Charlottesville: University Press of Virginia, 1977), 139-143. 6 Otis K. Rice, *The Allegheny Frontier: West Virginia Beginnings, 1730-1830* (Lexington, Ky.: University of Kentucky Press, 1970). 41. 7 Ibid., 145-146. 8 Johnson, *William Preston, 119-120.* 9 Ibid., 120-123. 10 Ibid., 125-128. 11 Reuben Gold Thwaites and Louise Philips Kellogg, eds., *Documentary History of Dunmore's War, 1774* (Madison, Wis.: The State Historical Society of Wisconsin, 1905, reprinted Harrisonburg, Va.: C.J. Carrier, Co., 1975), passim; Johnson, *William Preston*, 138-9, 142. 12 See for example several ads in *The Virginia Gazette* (Purdie) 16 June 1775. 13 Landon C. Bell, *The Old Free State: A Contribution to the History of Lunenburg County and Southside Virginia,* Two Volumes in One (Baltimore: Genealogical Publishing Co., Inc., 1974), 1:212. These special groups included infantry regiments raised by Nathaniel Gist, Grayson, and Thurston; a rifle company of Mosts Rawlings; Harrison's artillery; dragoons raised by Bland and Baylor, and legions enlisted by Lee and Armand. 14 Ibid., 232 from his letter to the President of Congress, 23 December 1777. 15 Ibid., quoted from Beveridge, *John Marshall,* citing Marshall's own biography of his commander-in-chief, *Life of Washington,* I, 215. 16 Jack P. Greene, editor, *The Diary of Colonel Landon Carter of Sabine Hall, 1752-1778* (Charlottesville: Published for the Virginia Historical Society by The University Press of Virginia, 1965), 2:1012. 17 Ibid., 1061. 18 Rice, *Allegheny Frontier,* 102. 19 Lewis Cecil Gray, *History of Agriculture in the Southern United States to 1860* (Washington, D.C.: Carnegie Institute of Washington, 1933), I:585. 20 *Virginia Gazette* (Dixon & Hunter), 24 April 1778, 3:1. 21 Hening's *Statutes at Large*, X (1779-1781), 189. 22 Ibid., Chapter LIII, 218. 23 Quoted in Maude Carter Clement, *The History of Pittsylvania County, Virginia* (Baltimore: Regional Publishing Company, 1987), 189-190. 24 Ibid., 190-193. 25 Bradshaw, *The History of Prince Edward County,* 122. 26 Janice L. Abercrombie and Richard Slatten, compilers and transcribers, *Virginia Revolutionary Publick Claims in three volumes,*(Athens, Ga.: Iberian Publishing Company), 1: vi. 27 Bradshaw, 124-127. 28 Ibid., 127. 29 These survive in the state archives for sixty-nine of the then seventy-five counties that cover present Virginia, West Virginia, and Kentucky. They constitute a remarkable resource about agricultural productivity in Virginia, about price fluctuations, and are even useful genealogical sources for placing persons in a particular county or even section of a county at a specific time. Abercrombie & Slatten, *Virginia Publick Claims,* I, *introduction.* 30 Abercrombie & Slatten, *Virginia Publick Claims,* II. 31 Ibid., II: 533. 32 Ibid., 533-537. 33 Ibid., I: 94. 34 Ibid., I: 97. 35 Ibid., I: 98-99. 36 Ibid. 37 The original records of the York County claims have been photocopied and collected for research use by the staff of Yorktown Victory enter. We are grateful to Dr. Edward Ayers for making these available to us. 38 Ibid.

The New Republic

1 Lewis Cecil Gray, *History of Agriculture in the Southern United States to 1860* (Washington, D.C.: The Carnegie Institution of Washington, 1933), 217, 606. 2 G. Melvin Herndon, *William Tatham and the Culture of Tobacco, including a facsimile reprint of an historical and practical essay on the culture and commerce of tobacco by Tatham* (Miami: University of Miami Press, 1969, original Tatham published in London, 1800), 6. 3 Gray, *History of Agriculture*, 198-199. 4 John T. Schlebecker, "Farmers in the Lower Shenandoah Valley, 1850," *The Virginia Magazine of History and Biography* 79, no. 4, October 1971, 476. 5 *Thomas Jefferson's Farm Book, with commentary and relevant extracts from other writings*, ed. Edwin Morris Betts (Charlottesville, Va.: University Press of Virginia, 1976), 194. 6 Ibid., 194. 7 Ibid., 314-316. 8 Gray, *History of Agriculture*, 848. 9 *American Farmer*, ed. John S. Skinner, no. 18 (27 July 1821), 137-141. 10 Gray, *History of Agriculture*, 848-849. 11 Otis L. Fisher, *Shorthorns Around the World* (Harrisonburg, Va.: published by the author, printed by Campbell Copy Center, Inc., 1993), 32. 12 *The Art of American Livestock Breeding*, exhibition catalog by the American Minor Breeds Conservancy (Pittsboro, N.C.: published by the American Minor Breeds Conservancy, 1991), 14, 70, 46. 13 *American Minor Breeds Notebook*, compiled by Laurie Heise and Carolyn Christman (Pittsboro, N.C.: The American Minor Breeds Conservancy, 1989), 15. 14 "Cattle," *The Southern Planter*, vol. 1, no. 7 (August 1841), 134-135. 15 Christmas Duke flyer, *Valley Democrat* 12 March 1858, Rosenberger Collection, MS 387, Virginia Military Institute special collections library. 16 J.M. Sherwood to George W. Rosenberger, 23 April 1860, Rosenberger Collection. 17 Christmas Duke flyer, *Valley Democrat* 12 March 1858, Rosenberger Collection. 18 John W. Sowers to George W. Rosenberger 25 July 1854, Rosenberger Collection. 19 *American Farmer*, ed. John S. Skinner, no. 37 (6 December 1822), 289-292. 20 In the nineteenth century, this was the most popular way to spell the word "milk." There was no difference in the way the word "milch" was pronounced and the way we pronounce the word "milk." 21 "Premiums," *The Southern Planter*, vol. 1, no. 3 (April 1841), 48. 22 "Premiums," *The Southern Planter*, vol. 2, no. 1 (January 1842), 16. 23 "Virginia State Agricultural Society," *The Southern Planter*, vol. 8, no. 8 (August 1853), 227-230. 24 James F. Hoy, *The Cattle Guard: Its History and Lore* (Lawrence, Kansas: University Press of Kansas, 1982), 72-73, 187-189. 25 James Hoy, "Plains Folk: Cattle Guard Pilgrimage, *Marion County Record* (Kansas), 4 November 1996, 2. 26 *The Garden and Farm Books of Thomas Jefferson*, ed. Robert C. Baron (Golden, Colo.: Fulcrum, 1987), 322. 27 *The Southern Planter*, vol. 1, no. 2 (February 1841), 25; vol. 1, no. 3 (April 1841), 45; vol. 3, no. 4 (April 1843), 94-95. vol. 4, no. 12 (December 1843), 278. 28 Nan Netherton, Donald Sweig, Janice Artemel, Patricia Hickin, and Patrick Reed, *Fairfax County, Virginia: A History* (Fairfax, Va.: Fairfax County Board of Supervisors, 1978), 254-255, 265. 29 Calculations are for the years 1787 and 1788. Charlene McIntire Talcott, "Tidewater Virginia Farmers, 1760-1805: An analysis of assets in a pre-revolutionary and post-revolutionary economy," masters thesis, Virginia Commonwealth University, Richmond, 2000, 417. 30 Ibid., 407. 31 Ibid., 409-410. 32 Johann David Schoepf, *Travels in the Confederation*, translated and edited by Alfred J. Morrison (Philadelphia: William J. Campbell, 1911), 100. 33 R. Archer, "Report to the State Board of Agriculture," *The Farmers' Register*, vol. 10 (1842), 339. 34 Talcott, "Tidewater Virginia Farmers," 413. 35 Ibid., 418-419. 36 An excellent biographical account of Médéric-Louis-Elie Moreau de Saint-Méry (1750-1819) is found in the introduction written by Stewart L. Mims to the journal of his five years in America, Kenneth Robert and Anna M. Roberts, translators and editors, *Moreau de St. Méry's American Journey [1793-1798]* (Garden City, N.Y.: Doubleday & Company, Inc., 1947), ix-xxi. St. Méry's grandfather was an important official on Martinique, but the young man established his legal reputation on Santo Domingo (now Haiti) the richest French island, and wrote extensively about that and other French Caribbean possessions. He settled in Paris in 1784 and became a leading writer about French law, then a significant participant in the French Revolution. He fled France when Robespierre came to power, and came with his family to Norfolk to become a shipping agent, then settling in Philadelphia for five years before returning to France in 1798. 37 Roberts, *Moreau de St. Méry's American Journey,* 61. 38 Ibid. 39 Lorena S. Walsh, "Report on selected agricultural and food related items in York County, Virginia, and St. Mary's County, Maryland inventories, 1783-1820, Prepared for the Yorktown Victory Center, 5 March 1991, 4-5. 40 *American Farmer*, ed. John S. Skinner, no. 18 (27 July 1821), 137-141. 41 Leila Skipworth Tucker to Frances Bland Coalter, 30 May 1809, Tucker-Coleman Collection in the Colonial Williamsburg Collection. 42 "Wintering Cows," *Staunton Spectator*, 10 January 1860. 43 Thomas Ross Pirtle, *History of the Dairy Industry* (Chicago: Mohonnier Brothers Co., 1926), 27. 44 Sam Bowers Hilliard, *Hogmeat and Hoecake: Food Supply in the Old South, 1840-1860* (Carbondale, Ill.: Southern Illinois University Press, 1972), 135. 45 *Report of the Commissioner of Patents for the Year 1851* (Washington, D.C.: Robert Armstrong, 1852), 284, 288. 46 U.S. Agricultural Census, 1860, Augusta County. Information used to determine home consumption and surplus amounts is from Joan M. Jensen, *Loosening the Bonds: Mid-Atlantic Farm Women, 1750-1850* (Westford, Mass.: Yale University, 1986), 85. 47 The Inflation Calculator, www.westegg.com/inflation/. 48 *The Southern Planter*, vol. 10, no. 7 (July 1847), 161-162. 49 Wilma Dunaway, "Rethinking Cherokee Acculturation: Agrarian Capitalism and Women's Resistance to the Cult of Domesticity, 1800-1838, *American Indian Culture and Research Journal*, vol. 21, 156. 50 *The Southern Planter*, vol. 7, no. 5 (June 1850), 4

A War on All Fronts

1 David Phillips, *A Soldier's Story: The Double Life of a Confederate Spy* (New York: Friedman/Fairfax Publishers, 1997), 47. 2 G. Terry Sharrer, *A Kind of Fate: Agricultural Change in Virginia, 1861-1920* (Ames, Iowa: Iowa State University Press, 2000), 3. 3 The Inflation Calculator, www.westegg.com/inflation. 4 Alexandria is actually Alexandria County, which was renamed Arlington County in 1920. 5 *The Agriculture of The United States in 1860; compiled from the original returns of the Eighth Census under the direction of the Secretary of the Interior*, Joseph C. G. Kennedy, Superintendent of Census. 6 Sharrer, *A Kind of Fate*, 19. 7 Ibid. 8 William B. Gallaher to Clinton and Charles Gallaher, 29 May 1861, Augusta County, Valley of the Shadow website, http://etext.lib.virginia.edu/etcbin/civwarlett-browse?id=A2003. 9 Report of Union Brig. Gen. T.A. Morris, Indiana Militia, 16 July 1861, *Official Records of the Union and Confederate Armies*, series 1, vol. II. 10 William C. Marsh, "Food and Rations In The Civil War," the Cincinnati Civil War Round Table, 2000, http://members.aol.com/CintiCWRT/food.html. 11 Report of Union Brig. Gen. Irvin McDowell, 16 July 1861, General Orders, No. 17, *Official Records of the Union and Confederate Armies,* series 1, vol. II. 12 William Hewitt, *History of The Twelfth West Virginia Volunteer Infantry* (Published by The Twelfth West Virginia Infantry Association, 1892), 321. 13 Robert E. Lee to P. St. George Cocke, 24 April 1861, *Official Records of the Union and Confederate Armies,* series 1, vol. II. 14 Report of Union Brig. Gen. Irvin McDowell, 18 July 1861, General Orders, No. 19, *Official Records of the Union and Confederate Armies,* series 1, vol. II. 15 Ibid. 16 *Hanging Rock Rebel*, ed. Dan Oates (Shippensburg, Penn.: Bard Street Press, 1994), 98-103. The authors are grateful to Patricia Turner Ritchie for pointing out this information. 17 William J. Miller, "Scarcely any Parallel in History: Logistics, Friction and McClellan's Strategy for the Peninsula Campaign," The Peninsula Campaign of 1862: Yorktown to the Seven Days, ed. William J. Miller (Campbell, Calif.: Savas Woodbury Publishers, 1995), 132, 150, 163. 18 John H. Ruckman to Jefferson Davis, 10 June 1861, *Official Records of the Union and Confederate Armies,* series 1, vol. II. 19 S. Cooper to Joseph E. Johnston, 18 June 1861, *Official Records of the Union and Confederate Armies,* series 1, vol. II. 20 Charles P. Stone to E.D. Townsend, *Official Records of the Union and Confederate Armies,* series 1, vol. II. 21 "West Virginia Civil War Map of Battles," www.destinationdurbin.com/civilwar.html. 22 Robert E. Lee

to James A. Seddon, 1 June 1863, *Official Records of the Union and Confederate Armies,* vol. 25, 847. 23 *A Civil War Diary from French Creek: Selections from the Diary of Sirene Burten,* ed. Stephen Cresswell, vol. 48 (1989), 131-141, www.wvculture.org/history/journal. 24 "Civil War Hero Joseph Lonsway recounts his story," *Observer,* Clayton, N.Y., 23 April 1908. 25 "A Moment in Time with Dan Roberts: The Beefsteak Raid," www.ehistory.com. 26 Ibid. 27 William B. Gallaher to Clinton and Charles Gallaher, 29 May 1861, Augusta County, Valley of the Shadow website, http://etext.lib.virginia.edu/etcbin/civwarlett-browse?id=A2003. 28 Tinsley L. Allen to James Henry Allen, 22 November 1861, *The Allen Family of Amherst County, Virginia: Civil War Letters,* ed Charles W. Turner (Berryville, Va.: Rockbridge Publishing, 1997). 29 Jesse Rolston to Catharine Rolston, 23 November 1861, *"until seperated by death": Lives and Civil War letters of Jesse Rolston, Jr. and Mary Catharine Cromer,* ed. Joyce DeBolt Miller (Bridgewater, Va.: Good Printers, Inc., 1994), 6. 30 Jesse Rolston to Catharine Rolston, 24 November 1861, *"until seperated by death,"* 7. 31 A.E. Rolston to Sister Sarah, 1 June 1862, *"until seperated by death,"* 17. 32 Jesse Rolston to Catharine Rolston, 21 June 1862, *"until seperated by death,"* 19. 33 Jesse Rolston to Catharine Rolston, 8 April 1863 and 27 September 1863, *"until seperated by death,"* 31, 47. 34 Jacob R. Hildebrand, *A Mennonite Journal, 1862-1865: A Father's Account of the Civil War in the Shenandoah Valley,* ed. John R. Hildebrand (Shippensburg, Pa.: Burd Street Press, 1996) 16, 19, 30, 31. 35 Ibid., 30. 36 Ibid., 41. 37 Sharrer, *A Kind of Fate,* 9. 38 Ibid., 18. 39 Ibid., 19, 21. 40 Civil War letters of Stephen Buckson, www.kyledesign.com/civil2.html. 41 Ibid. 42 Ibid. 43 Diary of Francis McFarland, 6 June 1864, Washington and Lee University special collections. 44 The Diary of Nancy Emerson, Valley of the Shadow website, http://etext.lib.virginia.edu. 45 David Hunter Strother, *A Virginia Yankee in the Civil War: The Diaries of David Hunter Strother,* ed. Cecil D. Eby, Jr., (Chapel Hill, N.C.: University of North Carolina Press, 1961), 254. 46 John L. Heatwole, *The Burning: Sheridan in the Shenandoah Valley* (Charlottesville, Va.: Rockbridge Publishing, 1998), xi. 47 Ibid., 34, 36. 48 The Inflation Calculator, www.westegg.com/inflation. 49 Heatwole, *The Burning,* 121. 50 Ibid., 25-26. 51 Ibid., 116-117. 52 Ibid., 187. 53 Ibid., 174-175. 54 Ibid., 192. 55 Ibid., 213. 56 *Unionists and the Civil War Experience in the Shenandoah Valley,* compiled and transcribed from The Southern Claims Commission Records, 1871-1880, The National Archives, Washington, D.C., by David S. Rodes and Norman R. Wenger (Dayton, Va.: Published by The Valley Brethren-Mennonite Heritage Center and The Valley Research Associates, 2003), vol. 1, 281-308. 57 *The James E. Taylor Sketchbook,* (Dayton, Ohio: The Western Reserve Historical Society, 1989), 578. 58 A Civil War Chronology of Loudoun County, Virginia, www.waterfordva-wca.org/history/loudoun. 59 Family story written by Ida Blanche Haley. Manuscript and watercolor painting privately owned by John A. Taylor. 60 The Statistics of the Wealth and Industry of the United States, Ninth U.S. Census (Washington, D.C.: Government Printing Office, Francis A. Walker, Superintendent of Census, 1872).

The Great Cattle Drives

1 Porte Crayon (David Hunter Strother), *Virginia Illustrated* (New York: Harper and Brothers, 1871) 131-133. 2 Maria G. Carr, *My Recollections of Rocktown, Now Known as Harrisonburg* (originally printed in 1926 by Frank L. Sublett, reprinted in 1959 by John W. Wayland, reprinted again in 1984 by the Harrisonburg-Rockingham Historical Society), 41. 3 Waldo Whistleman, August 2002. 4 *Winchester Republican,* 29 November 1823. 5 Alma Hibbard[?] Journal, 1854-55, in Special Collections Library, Duke Univ., Durham, N.C.. 6 Ibid. 7 Henry Smals diaries, James Madison University Special Collections, SC 2059, Box 1, 18 bound notebooks, extracts are from volume one. 8 Gray, 840. 9 Henry Boswell Jones letter, *Report of the Commissioner of the Patents for the Year 1851* (Washington, D.C.: Robert Armstrong Printer, 1852). 10 *Journal of Agriculture,* ed. John S. Skinner (New York: Greeley and McElrath), July 1847-June 1848 volume, 105-106, 367. 11 Hibbard Journal. 12 David Flook from Caswell Freeman in Jacksborough, Tenn., letter 16 June 1842, James Madison University Special Collections, Virginia Wise Breen collection SC 2084, compiled March 1990 by Chris Bolgiano 13 Levi Pitman diary (Shenandoah County), 1844-1882, University of Virginia, Alderman Library, special collections, 67078. 14 Jedediah Hotchkiss, *Virginia: A Geographical and Political Summary* (Richmond: Prepared and published under the supervision of the Board of Immigration, 1876), 72. 15 Folly Farm papers, loose page in James C. Cochran Cashbook from 1860-1872, University of Virginia University of Virginia, Alderman Library, special collections, 9380. 16 All of the information obtained from Leon "Mose" Kiracofe came from a March 2002 interview conducted with Kiracofe in New Market, Virginia, and published in the "Summer grazing" article in *Augusta Country,* April 2002. 17 Interview of John V. Heatwole of Rockingham County, Va., conducted by John Heatwole, 4 July 1980. The author would like to thank John Heatwole for sharing his interviews concerning Valley grazing practices. 18 Interview of Willard Miller of Mossy Creek, Va., conducted by John Heatwole, 15 December 1997. 19 Interview of William H. Sipe of East Rockingham County, Va., conducted by John Heatwole, 21 January 1997. 20 Whistleman interview. 21 "Cattle drives from Nichter/Meyerhoeffer Farm – Goods Mill, Va.," e-mail from Janet Downs to Nancy Sorrells, 19 October 2003. 22 Darwin Lambert, *The Undying Past of Shenandoah National Park* (Lanham, Md.: Roberts Rinehart, Inc., in cooperation with the Shenandoah Natural History Association, 2001), 131. 23 Ibid, 132-133. 24 Ibid., 135. 25 Ibid., 137-139. 26 There is at least one known exception – the Cash family of Montebello, in Nelson County. The story of the Cash cattle drive, which has persisted for at least four generations, was documented by journalist Lynn Coffey in an issue of her *Backroads* publication. She accompanied the Cash family on their annual drive in May of 1999. Lynn Coffey, "Driving the cattle to the summer grazing fields," *Backroads,* 1999. The author is grateful to Lynn Coffey for sharing her article about the Cash family and for putting her in touch with one of the last remaining families still practicing the old cattle drives and summer grazing traditions.

Riding the Rails of Progress

1 "A History of American Agriculture, 1776-1990," USDA timeline, www.usda.gov. 2 Jedediah Hotchkiss, *Virginia: A Geographical and Political Summary* (Richmond: R.F. Walker, Superintendent of Public Printing, 1876), 119. 3 Ibid., 251-258. 4 "A History of American Agriculture, 1776-1990," USDA timeline, www.usda.gov. 5 *Country Life in Virginia* (Published by the Real Estate Department of the Chesapeake and Ohio Railway Company, 1913), 20. 6 Al Kresse, "Early C&O Livestock Cars," *Chesapeake and Ohio Historical Magazine,* September 1999, 4. Special thanks must be given to the staff at the C&O Historical Society in Clifton Forge for help in researching much of the railroad information and for supplying accompanying images. 7 Ibid., 5. 8 Acker Family Diaries, Special Collections #2050, Carrier Library, James Madison University. Box 1, Folder 1. 9 Ibid., Box 1, Folder 3. 10 Ibid., Box 1, Folder 2. 11 *Country Life in Virginia* (Richmond: Published by the Industrial Department of the Chesapeake and Ohio Railway Company), 1913 vol. 20, and 1914 vol. 16. 12 Elisabeth B. and C.E. Johnson, Jr., *Rappahannock County, Virginia: A History* (Berryville, Va.: Virginia Book Company, 1981), 259. 13 Al Kresse, "C&O Livestock Facilities," *Chesapeake and Ohio Historical Magazine,* December 2000, 11. 14 Ibid. 15 Ibid., 9-10. 16 Ibid., 11. 17 Ibid., 3-4. The increase in tonnage also included a significant rise in the numbers of hogs being shipped to market. 18 "Official Industrial and Shippers Directory," (C&O), Vol. II, 1919, 1925. 19 Revenue tonnage classified, The Chesapeake and Ohio Railway Company, 1932, 28. 20 *Norfolk and Western Railway Industrial and Shippers Guide,* (Compiled by the Agricultural and Industrial Department N.&W. Ry., Roanoke, Va., 1916), 147-174. 21 Personal reminiscences of Leslie L. McCracken, 20 December 2002. 22 Nan Netherton, Donald Sweig, Janice Artemel, Patricia Hickin, and Patrick Reed, *Fairfax County, Virginia: A History* (Fairfax, Va.: Fairfax County Board of Supervisors, 1978), 552. 23 The creamery cooperatives were Kingsley Brothers in Fauquier, and three located in the towns of Lincoln, Lovettsville, and Leesburg in Loudoun County. Sharrer, *A Kind of Fate,* 100. 24 Sharrer, *A Kind of Fate,* 102-103. 25 Robert Beverley and Essex County Farmers Educational and Cooperative Union, Beverley Family Papers, Virginia Historical Society. 26 "Twelfth Annual Report of the Commissioner of Agriculture," *Report of the State Board of Agriculture of Virginia* (Richmond, 1890), 18. 27 Sharrer, *A Kind of Fate,* 138-139. 28 Nancy Sorrells, "Stuarts Draft's Kindig family paved way for Charolais breed in Virginia," *Augusta Country,* Summer 2002. 29 Kresse, "C&O Livestock Facilities," 5, 9. 30 Sue Simmons, "Sea cowboy tells of voyage to deliver livestock," and "Project provides livestock to needy nations," *Augusta Country,* February 1995. 31 Childs Family Papers, Virginia Historical Society. 32 Jeanne N. Logue, *Beyond the Germ Theory: The Story of Dr. Cooper Curtice* (College Station, Texas: Texas A&M University Press, 1995), 49. 33 Virginia Agricultural and Mechanical College, Agricultural Experiment Station, Bulletin No. 61, February 1896, vol. V, Blacksburg, Va., 19-24. 34 Logue, *Beyond the Germ Theory,* 91. 35 Sharrer, *A Kind of Fate,* 117. 36 Ibid., 134. 37 Sharrer, *A Kind of Fate,* 118. 38 Virginia Agricultural and Mechanical College, Agricultural Experiment Station, Bulletin No. 61, April 1901, vol. X, Blacksburg, Va., 35. 39 Virginia Agricultural and Mechanical College, Agricultural Experiment Station, Bulletin No. 103, August 1899, vol. VIII, Blacksburg, Va., 155. 40 William F. Rhea Papers, mss 12094, University of Virginia, Special Collections Library. 41 Heather Smith Thomas, *Storey's Guide to Raising Beef Cattle* (Pownal, Vt.: Storey Books, 1998), 154. 42 Virginia Agricultural and Mechanical College, Agricultural Experiment Station, Bulletin No. 13, February 1892, Blacksburg, Va., 15. 43 U.G. Houck, *The Bureau of Animal Industry of the United States Department of Agriculture: Its Establishment, Achievements and Current Activities* (Washington, D.C., printed by the author, 1924), 64. 44 Thomas, *Raising Beef Cattle,* 154. 45 Walter Robinson interview with Debbie Garrett, 25 July 2002.

Folk Artist Brought Yankee Dairying to Virginia

1 "Grandma Moses in Augusta County, Virginia, 1887-1905," unpublished research paper by Frank Johnston of the Shenandoah Valley Rural Heritage Foundation. The authors wish to thank Johnston for gathering and sharing the information used in this sidebar. 2 Anna Mary Robertson Moses, *My Life's History* (New York: Harper & Brothers, 1952), 63-64. 3 Ibid., 66-70. 4 Ibid., 77. 5 Ibid., 95.

Caring for Cattle

1 Peter Wallenstein, *Virginia Tech, Land Grant University, 1872-1997: History of a School, a State, a Nation.* (Blacksburg, Va.: Pocahontas Press, 1997), 12; G. Terry Sharrer, *A Kind of Fate: Agricultural Change in Virginia, 1861-1920* (Ames: Iowa State University Press, 2000), 115. 2 Wallenstein., 12-13. 3 Jenkins Mikell Robertson, "VPI Historical Data Book," *Bulletin of the Virginia Polytechnic Institute* 57 (Jan. 1964):4-5. 4 Ibid., 5-6; Wallenstein, 14-15. 5 Sharrer, 114-115. 6 Robertson, 5-6. 7 Wallenstein, 37-38. 8 Robertson, 7; Duncan Lyle Kinnear, *The First 100 Years: A History of Virginia Polytechnic Institute and State University* (Blacksburg: Virginia Polytechnic Institute Educational Foundation, Inc., 1972), 58-59. 9 Robertson, 6-7 10 Ibid., 10. 11 Quoted in Kinnear, 93. 12 Kinnear, 77-86. 13 Sharrer, Table 3.1 Food Production Compared, 1860 and 1880 from U.S. census data, 89. 14 Ibid., 100-103. 15 Ibid. 115. 16 Ibid., 114. The quotation is from the text of the Hatch Act. 17 Ibid., 117. 18 D.O. Nourse, "Feeding Experiments," *Virginia Agricultural and Mechanical College Experiment Station Series of 1889-90, Bulletin,* 3 (November 1889): 3-10. 19 D.O. Nourse, "Steer Feeding," *Virginia Agricultural and Mechanical College Experiment Station Bulletin,* 10 (June 1891): 4-13. 20 D.O. Nourse, "Silos and Silage," *Virginia Agricultural and Mechanical College Agriculture Experiment Station Bulletin,* 53 (June 1895): 74-80. 21 D.O. Nourse, "Hay Substitutes," *Virginia Agricultural experiment Station Bulletin,* 148 (May 1903): 83-90. 22 Andrew M. Soule and John R. Fain, "Gluten and Cotton-Seed Meal with Silage, Hay and Stover for Dairy Cows," *Virginia Agricultural Experiment Station Bulletin,* 156 (July 1905): 4. 23 Lyman Carrier, "Silo Construction," *Virginia Agricultural and Mechanical College Agriculture Experiment Station Bulletin,* 182 (June 1909). 24 Robertson, 30-34. 25 Kinnear, 195-197. 26 "Seaman Ashael Knapp," *The New Columbia Encyclopedia* (New York & London: Columbia University Press, 1975), 1488; Robertson, 35-37; Kinnear, 197. 27 Kinnear, 197-198; Robertson, 37. 28 Quoted in Kinnear, 232.

A Fat Cattle Kingdom

1 Contagious Bovine Pleuropneumonia (CBPP) is a highly infectious, subacute or chronic cattle disease that affects the lungs and joints. It is caused by *Mycoplasma mycoides mycoides* small colony type. It is spread by inhaling droplets from an infected, coughing animal. Its incubation period is two to three weeks. It does not survive in the meat or in exposure to air, and can be eradicated with disinfectants. It had spread to the United States in the 1880s, and the federal government created the Bureau of Animal Industries (forerunner of the USDA's Animal and Plant Health Inspection Service) in 1884 to eliminate CBPP. That task was completed by 1893. www.vet.uga.edu/vpp/gray_book. See also www.nda.agric.za/vetweb for information about the spread of the disease from Europe to South Africa. 2 J.R. Dodge, "The Cattle Plague in Europe," in *Report of the Commissioner of Agriculture for the Year 1865* (Washington: Government Printing Office, 1866), 550. Dodge, a staff member in the U.S. Department of Agriculture, estimated the loss at £3 million sterling or $15 million dollars, and amount equivalent to $165 million in 2002 dollars. 3 Laurie Winn Carlson, *Cattle: An Informal Social History* (Chicago: Ivan R. Dee, 2001), 123. 4 Mad Cow Disease is bovine spongiform encephalopathy (BCE) and a variant, Creutzfeldt-Jacob disease. Foot and Mouth Disease (FMD), one of the most contagious animals diseases, is caused by a virus. Good internet resources for these two diseases that left disastrous effects on British cattle are: www.mad-cow.org, and www.aphis.usda.gov/lpa/issues/find, and www.oie.int/eng/maladies. 5 Jamie A. Grady, *Bowens of Virginia and Tennessee,* 1969. We are grateful to Irene Bowen Wendell of Rosedale, Virginia, for providing this important evidence of early export cattle trade in Tazewell. 6 Authors' interview with a group of descendants of the early Cove settlers and the later fat cattlemen at the home of William Gillespie, 9 July 2003. 7 Bickley's "History of Tazewell County", [1856] ; W.H. Moss, "Early Beef Production," in Louise Leslie, *Tazewell County* (Radford, Va.: Commonwealth Press, 19XX), 470-471. 8 "Stuart Estate is Largest 'Ranch' East of the Mississippi," *Crawford's Weekly* (1927), 8. The bluegrass that flourished throughout southwest Virginia was one of three forages introduced from the Old World, the other two being orchard grass and fescue. Warm season grasses such as bluestem and switch grass were native grasses of Virginia. 9 Transcription of oral history interview of Sam Baylor of Wardell Farm, Tazewell County, by Mary Adams on 1 June 1976. The authors are grateful to Nick Adams of Cedar Bluff, Virginia, for sharing this transcription. 10 *Virginia: A Geographical and Political Summary* (Richmond: R.F. Walker, Superintendent of Public Printing, 1876), 71. 11 *First Annual Report of the Commissioner of Agriculture of the State of Virginia* (Richmond, Va.: James E. Goode, Printer, 1877), 44-45. 12 Sam Baylor interview. 13 George W. Litton, "Early Tazewell Agriculture," in Leslie, *Tazewell County,* 462. Litton was County Extension Agent in Tazewell, and used records in possession of the late Robert Lincoln Moss for his research. Those records are still held on the Lawson farm by Moss's widow, Kathryn Gillespie Moss Huffman. The 1850s date that Litton gives to the beginning of Lawson's export cattle trade must be erroneous. Lawson was still living in 1920, and was not likely a developer of an export cattle business seventy years earlier when he could only have been a teenager or in his early twenties. Mrs. Huffman says that 1885 was the year Lawson came to Burke's Garden. 14 William C. Pendleton, *History of Tazewell County and Southwest Virginia, 1748-1920* (Richmond: William C. Hill Printing Co., 1920) 15 Most of the families that developed the fat cattle/export cattle business in the late nineteenth century continued with it until its end, and are still in other aspects of cattle farming three or four generations later. Although Lawson had children, only one married, late in life, and had no children, so there were no descendants to carry on his pioneering importation of stock and exportation of fat cattle. 16 H. Jackson Darst, *The Darsts of Virginia: A Chronicle of Ten Generations in the Old Dominion* (Williamsburg, Va., 1972), 134-136, 155. Bell, who already owned land, acquired two additional farms from members of the related Darst and Glendy families, "Sunny Side" and "Alcove House, " and part of another, "Ash Brook." 17 Ibid., 255. The sources that Darst used about the Martin cattle being shipped included *Southwest Times, Milestones Edition,* 21 July 1968, 55 and *Southwest Times, Centennial Edition.* 18 J.R.K. Bell, account of the first shipment of cattle to England, 1878. The authors are grateful to Robbie Brown of Swoope and Mrs. Francis Bell IV of Harrisonburg, who has published a family history for distribution only to family members, for allowing them to see this document. For information about Bell and Major Martin, see Darst, *The Darst Family,* 255. Efforts to authenticate the information about the ship, called the *"Beuratentuna"* in the transcription of the J.R.K. Bell letter, but this may be a misreading of *Bonaventura.* No ship of either name has been located in Spanish American War records of the Spanish Navy or of merchant vessels taken as prize and sold. Each ship in the Spanish Navy is named and described on the website www.spanamwar.com, as well as those private vessels taken as prize and sold. No ship named either Beuraventuna or Bonaventura appears on any of these detailed lists. Nonetheless, there could have been other ships unaccounted for among merchant vessels, or possibly the ship had changed its name. 19 J.R.K. Bell account. 20 Ibid. 21 Material courtesy of Mrs. Francis Bell IV, of Harrisonburg, from family papers. 22 Recollections of Joseph S. Gillespie's nephew;

from the family papers of Mrs. X Bell. 23 *Staunton Spectator,* 17 July 1877. 24 Interview with James Hoge of Burke's Garden, 8 July 2003. 25 Sam Baylor interview. 26 *Second Annual Report of the Commissioner of Agriculture of the State of Virginia* (Richmond, Va.: R.E. Frayser, Superintendent of Public Printing, 1878), 47-48. The Inflation Calculator figures $746,830,852 for the 2002 value of $46 million in 1877, and $795,537,212 for the $49 million in 1878. www.westegg.com/inflation 27 "Beautiful Elk Garden Estate," *Bluefield Daily Telegraph,* Sunday, 10 July 1927. 28 "Stuart Estate is Largest 'Ranch' East of Mississippi," *Crawford's Weekly,* 1927. 29 Sam Baylor interview, 1976. 30 Ibid. 31 Ibid. 32 Sam Baylor interview. 33 "Sheep for Europe" *Staunton Spectator,* 31 July 1877. 34 Interview with Marvin Meek, Burke's Garden, 8 July 2003. 35 "Beautiful Elk Garden Estate," *Bluefield Daily Telegraph.* 36 George W. Litton, "Early Tazewell Agriculture," in Leslie, *Tazewell County,* 463. 37 Carlson, *Cattle: An Informal Social History,* 124-125. 38 Sam Baylor interview; Authors' interview at Bill Gillespie's. 39 Sam Baylor interview.40 Oral tradition from oral history interviews in Tazewell. See also "Beautiful Elk Garden Estate," *Bluefield Daily Telegraph,* Sunday, 10 July 1927. 41 Authors' interview at Gillespie's. The standard first class postage stamp was three cents at that time.

In Pursuit of Excellence

1 Nancy Sorrells, "Schools Promoted Agricultural education," *Daily News Leader,* n.d. 2 Ibid., 286. 3 Ibid. 4 "Key Moments in FFA History," www.ffa.org. 5 Ibid. 6 The authors are grateful to Nelson Gardner for this information. 7 "Items on Polled Herefords," *The Virginia Cattleman,* July 1974:7; "Trivette Named National Future Farmer President," *The Virginia Cattleman,* November 1974: 1. 8 "4-H in Virginia," www.ext.vt.edu/resources/4h/. 9 Mills Award Album provided to the authors by Morris Fannon. 10 See various issues of *Head, Heart, Hands, and Health in Virginia* 1957, 1960, 1962, 1965, 1983. 11 *The Virginia Cattleman,* January 1972, cover, 7. 12 "Loudoun 4-H'er Glynn Moreland Advances in Livestock Project," *The Virginia Cattleman,* March, 1975: 15. 13 Ibid. 14 Ibid. 15 William Harrison recollections shared with the authors. Harrison was a member of the editorial board for this book. 16 Betty Jo Hamilton, "Bill Simmons recalls growth, success of Market Animal Show," *Augusta Country.* 17 Ibid. 18 Chris Earhart presentation to Staunton Rotary Club, 18 May 2004. 19 Duncan Lyle Kinnear, *The First 100 Years: A History of Virginia Polytechnic Institute and State University* (Blacksburg, Va.: Virginia Polytechnic Institute Educational Foundation, Inc., 1972), 221, 230. 20 Ibid., 232. 21 Ibid., 342. 22 Ibid., 357-358. 23 Ibid., 372, 380. 24 Ibid., 374. 25 Ibid., 374-375, 385, 387. 26 Ibid., 388, 389. 27 Ibid., 407. 28 Ibid., 419, 422. 29 Ibid., 424, 426-429. 30 Ibid. 438-440, 449, 452-453. 31 Interview with a dozen retired leaders of the dairy industry, Holiday Inn, Blacksburg, 15 July 2004. 32 *The Chronicle: News for Members of National Dairy Shrine,* August 2000; www.americanfarm.com/Beef; www.universityawards.vt.edu/public. 33 Information supplied by John L. Miller, Bridgewater. 34 Ibid., 448. 35 www.ext.vt.edu/offices. 36 www.csrees.usda.gov. 37 www.technews.vt.edu/Archives. 38 www.cdcd.vt.edu/pjd/const.status/main.html. 39 www.dasc.vt.edu/youth/2004sedyr.html and www.VATechAlumni.com. 40 "History of the State Fair of Virginia, 1994," provided by Atlantic Rural Exposition. 41 Jay Lugar, Marketing Director, "The State Fair of Virginia 2003 Fact Sheet." 42 Nancy Sorrells, "Augusta Fair has Long History," *Augusta Country,* Vol. 2:8 (summer 1995), 16-17. 43 "History of the State Fair of Virginia, 1994." 44 Mills Award Album, courtesy of Morris Fannon. 45 Paul Swaffar, "Livestock Rambles," *The Eastern Breeder,* December 1944: 19-21; notes provided to the authors by K. C. Williamson. 46 "First Annual Atlantic Fat Stock Show," *The Eastern Breeder,* May 1946. 47 "First Atlantic Rural Exposition Provides High Quality Beef Cattle Show," *The Eastern Breeder,* November 1946:9. 48 Sorrells, "Augusta Fair." 49 Mills Award Album. 50 "State Fair Sept. 19-28," *The Virginia Cattleman,* August, 1974:7. 51 "History of the State Fair of Virginia, 1994." 52 www.statefair.com. 53 Ibid.; phone conversation with Jay Lugar, publicity director of the State Fair of Virginia. 54 "The American Farm Bureau Federation," *The National Republican,* 25 June 1921. 55 Ibid., J. Hiram Zigler, *The Virginia Farm Bureau Story: Growth of a Grassroots Organization,* (published by the Virginia Farm Bureau, 1982), 50-55. 56 "The American Farm Bureau Federation." 57 Zigler, *The Virginia Farm Bureau Story,* 57-60, 162-165. 58 Ibid., 67-74. 59 Ibid., 87-91. 60 Ibid., 170-173. 61 Ibid., 97-112. 62 Ibid., 112-116. 63 Ibid. 116-117, 174-178.

Milk Goes Modern

1 Paul M. Reaves, Harold W. Craun, Hershel H. Gardner, and John L. Miller, *History of The Virginia State Dairymen's Association: 1907-1982* (Published by the Virginia State Dairymen's Association, 1982), 14; and group interview by Katharine Brown and Nancy Sorrells with individuals involved with the Virginia dairy industry, 21 October 2003. 2 The Wisconsin Dairy Association was formed in 1872. Sara Ruth, *About Cows* (Stillwater, Minn.: Voyageur Press, Inc., 2000), 80. 3 Reaves, et al., *History of the Virginia State Dairymen's Association,* 14. 4 Ibid., 9-10. 5 Ibid., 7. 6 Russell L. Stultz, *Forty Years of "Shenandoah's Pride" 1922-1962* (Published by the Valley of Virginia Cooperative Milk Producers Association, Harrisonburg, Va., 1963), 9. 7 Stultz, *Forty Years,* 13-14. 8 John C. Campbell, *The Southern Highlander and his homeland* (Kentucky: The University Press of Kentucky, 1969), 257. 9 G.F. Warren, *Elements of Agriculture* (New York: The Macmillan Company, 1914), 323. 10 Ibid. 11 Morven Park archives. 12 Ruth, *About Cows,* 83 and Thomas, et al., *Dairy Farming,* 47-48. 13 Roy H. Thomas, Paul M. Reaves, and C.W. Pegram, *Dairy Farming in the South* (Danville, Ill.: The Interstate, 1949), 380-384. 14 Interview with Leon "Mose" Kiracofe by Nancy Sorrells, 19 March 2002. 15 R.G. Connelly, extension agent, VPI, "The Development of Dairying in Virginia," Blacksburg, unknown publication, 43. 16 Ruth, *About Cows,* 80-83. 17 Ibid., 82. 18 Ibid., 84-87. 19 Carolyn Green, *Morley – The Intimate Story of Virginia's Governor & Mrs. Westmoreland Davis* (Leesburg, Va.: Goose Creek Productions, 1998), 45. 20 Nelson Gardner, "A Lifetime of Dairy – A Historical Perspective," address delivered 6 May 2002 and interview of Nelson Gardner by Jeremy Knopp, 14 August 2000, transcript in Bridgewater College Library, Bridgewater, Va. 21 Interview of John A. Taylor (grandson of Griffith) by Nancy Sorrells 23 March 2002. 22 Roy H. Thomas, et al, *Dairy Farming,* 254-255. 23 Paul Reaves and H.O. Henderson, *Dairy Cattle Feeding and Management* (New York: John Wiley and Sons, Inc., 1963), 417. 24 Reaves, et al., *History of the Virginia State Dairymen's Association,* 15. 25 Carl E. Polan, "Highlights of Dairy Science Department," expanded and updated in December 2002 and combined with a PowerPoint presentation. 26 "Litton-Reaves Hall Dedicated," *The Virginia Dairyman,* November 1989. 27 *Dairy-Barn Construction,* U.S. Department of Agriculture Farmers' Bulletin No. 1342 (Washington, D.C.: 1923), 3. 28 *Dairy Farm Houses,* U.S. Department of Agriculture Farmers' Bulletin No. 1214 (Washington, D.C.: 1921, rev. 1932), 1. 29 Roy H. Thomas, et al, *Dairy Farming,* 163. 30 Morven Park archives. 31 Connelly, "The Development of Dairying," 43. 32 Group interview by Katharine Brown and Nancy Sorrells with individuals involved with the Virginia dairy industry, 21 October 2003. 33 *Milky Way 2003,* 75th Anniversary Edition, 1. 34 "Former Leader of Virginia Dairymen's Association Inducted Into Virginia Tech Ag Hall of Fame," 9 October 2000, www.technews.vt.edu. 35 Thanks to Larry Kibler for providing biographical information as well as information about Ken-Wan Farm. 36 Ibid. 37 Reaves, et al., *History of the Virginia State Dairymen's Association,* 140-141. 38 Interview with Thurston J. Potts by Eugene M. Scheel, 28 June 1977. Interview transcript in the Balch Library, Leesburg. 39 Maryland and Virginia Milk Producers' Association, Inc., 1941 Annual Report, Morven Park archives. 40 "The Annual Meeting and Banquet of the Maryland and Virginia Milk Producers' Association, Inc.," *The Loudoun-Fauquier Breeders' Magazine,* vol. 3, Spring 1932, 30. 41 Letter from B.B. Derrick, Secretary-Treasurer, Maryland and Virginia Milk Producers' Association, Inc., to member producers, 5 June 1942. 42 *The Pipeline,* news releases from the Maryland & Virginia Milk Producers Cooperative Association website, www.mdvamilk.com. 43 Thanks to the family of Edward C. Norman for providing his biographical information. 44 Thanks to Jack Hardesty of Harvue Farms for supplying his biographical information. 45 Stultz, *Forty Years,* 22-24. 46 Ibid., 25-27. 47 Ibid., 136. 48 Ibid., 43-45. 49 Ibid., 56-57. 50 Thanks to Nelson Gardner for providing historical notes about Shenandoah's Pride. 51 Stultz, *Forty Years,* 71-74. 52 Ibid., 128. 53 Gardner's historical notes. 54 Interview with Nelson Gardner by Nancy Sorrells. 55 Pan Demetrakakes, Pamela Smith, "Dean milks the single-serve trend: the facility in Mt. Crawford, Va., bottles much of Dean Foods' cutting-edge single serve flavored milks – Dean Foods," *Food & Drug Packaging,* January 2003 and David Phillips, "Location Leads to Innovation: Former co-op plant has become the launch site for a new aseptic venture – Plant of the Month – Morningstar Foods," *Dairy Foods,* May 2002. 56 "Nelson Gardner Named Dairy Shrine's Distinguished Breeder," "Local Man State Farmer of the Year," and "Nelson Gardner Named Southeastern Farmer of the Year." Thanks to Nelson Gardner for supplying the information and miscellaneous newspaper articles. 57 Unpublished history of the Cooperative Milk Producers Association. Thanks to Michael Myatt for pulling together this valuable information. 58 Interview with Ben F. Morgan, Jr. 27 August 2004. 59 Dairy Farmers of America, Inc. website, www.dfamilk.com. 60 Ibid. 61 Interview with Bill Blalock in Blacksburg, 15 July 2004. 62 Cooperative Milk Producers Association history. 63 Thanks to William Harrison for assembling the material on Loudoun Milk Transportation. 64 Nan Netherton, Donald Sweig, Janice Artemel, Patricia Hickin, and Patrick Reed, *Fairfax County, Virginia, A History* (Fairfax, Va.: Fairfax County Board of Supervisors, 1978), 516-517. 65 Ibid., 541. 66 Ibid., 566. 67 Deborah Fitts, "Potts family takes a realistic look forward," *Loudoun Times-Mirror,* Fall 1997. 68 *First Annual Report of the Board of Directors and Executive Officer of the Virginia State Epileptic Colony,* Richmond, 1910, 18. Special thanks to Burckhard K. Blöb, Human Resource Manager II for the Central Virginia Training Center of the Virginia Department of Mental Health, Mental Retardation and Substance Abuse Services. Blöb has researched the history of the colony and supplied the authors with a substantial amount of information relating to the colony. 69 *First Annual Report of the Board of Directors and Executive Officer of the Virginia State Epileptic Colony,* Richmond, 1911, 14. 70 Ibid., 1913, 21. 71 A.S. Priddy, Virginia State Epileptic Colony, Madison Heights, Virginia, to Herbert F. Hutcheson, Boydton, Virginia., 21 October 1913. 72 *First Annual Report of the Board of Directors and Executive Officer of the Virginia State Epileptic Colony,* Richmond, 1915, 22. 73 Ibid., 1918, 18, 42. 74 Ibid., 1929, 1936. 75 Ibid., 1938. 76 Burckhard K. Blöb to Nancy Sorrells, 9 January 2003. 77 The authors are grateful to Barbara Clary, current owner of Ownby Companies, for sharing her recollections at two oral history sessions and in writing. 78 Eastern State Hospital Complete Dispersal by Auction booklet, 4 April 1958. 79 Western State Hospital Complete Disposal at Auction booklet, 1 August 1958 and "Sale at Western State Hospital," *The Staunton News-Leader,* 1 August 1958. 80 Thanks to Carolyn Peterson, Quality Assurance-Agribusiness, JRCC, the spokespeople with the Virginia Department of Corrections, and www.vadoc.state.va.us/facilities/institutions/jamesriver.htm. 81 Stultz, *Forty Years,* 54-55. 82 Commonwealth of Virginia State Milk Commission website, www.state.va.us/milk. 83 Yoder Dairy booklet, c. 1950. Booklet made available by Christine S. Yoder of Newport News. 84 Reaves, et al., *History of the Virginia State Dairymen's Association,* 146-148. 85 www.southeastdairy.org. 86 Thanks to William Harrison for providing the information on dairy activities for youth in Virginia. 87 "Farm News," www.onthefarmradion.com. 88 Ibid. 89 "Dairy Jeopardy now available to anyone," unknown newspaper source, 27 August 2004. 90 Roy H. Thomas, et al, *Dairy Farming,* 25.

Dairy Turns to Milk Specialists

1 Leonard William Brinkman, Jr., "The Historical Geography of Improved Cattle in the United States to 1870," Ph.D. dissertation, University of Wisconsin, 1964, 17. 2 National Pedigreed Livestock Council, Annual Report, Directory & Career Opportunities, 200-2001, (Brattleboro, Vermont, 2001). 3 Bowling, History of Ayrshire Cattle, 24-27. 4 George Augustus Bowling, A History of Ayrshire Cattle in the United States, (Parsons, W.Va.: McLean Printing Company, 1975), 16-21. 5 Manuscript notes on the history of Ayrshires in Virginia by Mrs. Douglass Forrest. 6 Bowling, A History of Ayrshire Cattle, 264; Mrs. Douglass Forrest, mss notes. 7 Minutes of the Virginia Ayrshire Breeders Association, 6 August 1952, courtesy of Mrs. Douglass Forrest. 8 Ibid., 20 January 1954. 9 Mrs. Douglas Forrest mss notes, Virginia Ayrshire Breeders' Association membership list. 10 www.dasc.vt.edu/scholarships. 11 Hans Nørgaard, "Historical Review: To Improve and Promote the Breed," www.syd.fyn.dk/historic. 12 Ibid. 13 Ibid. 14 Paul M. Reaves, Harold W. Craun, Hershel H. Gardner, and John L. Miller, History of The Virginia State Dairymen's Association: 1907-1982 (Published by the Virginia State Dairymen's Association, 1982), 127. 15 Authors are grateful to Nelson Gardner of Bridgewater for supplying this information. 16 Ibid. 17 Catalog The Virginia State Jersey Consignment Sale, 8 October 1940. 18 Reaves, et al., History of the Virginia State Dairymen's Association, 128. 19 Ibid. 20 Ibid. 21 Linda McCarty, "A Century of Agriculture," Winchester Star, 12 August 1998. 22 "Dairy Shrine Recognitions Will Go to Stiles Family," September 1999: 89. 23 "Tracy Stiles Memorial Scholarship," Virginia Tech Department of Dairy Science, www.dasc.vt.edu/stiles. 24 "Guernsey," www.ansi.okstate.edu/breeds. 25 Guernsey Breeders' Journal, 1917, 1919, 1920. 26 Reaves, et al., History of the Virginia State Dairymen's Association, 123. 27 Carolyn Green, Morley – The Intimate Story of Virginia's Governor and Mrs. Westmoreland Davis (Leesburg, Va.: Goosecreek Publications, 1998), 5-11. 28 Jack Temple Kirby, Westmoreland Davis: Virginia Planter-Politician, 1859-1942 (Charlottesville: The University Press of Virginia), 30-39. 29 Reaves, et al., History of the Virginia State Dairymen's Association, 123. 30 The authors are grateful to Nelson Gardner for obtaining this information about Bayville Farms from Allister MacKay. 31 Authors are grateful to E. Cline Brubaker of Rocky Mount for this information. 32 Ibid. 33 Authors are grateful to E. Cline Brubaker for this information. 34 Ibid., 124. 35 Authors are grateful to Harold W. Roller of Weyers Cave and to E. Cline Brubaker for supplying this information. 36 "Milking Shorthorn Cattle," www.ansi.okstate.ed/breeds. 37 "Sale's Top Milking Shorthorn Cow Purchased by Loudoun Breeder," *Loudoun Times-Mirror,* 12 June 1944. 38 Authors are grateful to William Harrison of Leesburg for this information. 39 "Brown Swiss," www.ansi.okstate.edu/breeds. 40 Reaves, et al., History of the Virginia State Dairymen's Association, 121. 41 Ibid., 121-122. 42 "Virginia Cow Repeats as Grand Champion," World Dairy Expo News Releases, 3 October 2003, www.world-dairy-expo.com; the authors are grateful to Allen Bassler for information on Snickerdoodle. See also, "Snickerdoodle—zurück bis 1867," Braunvieh (April 2003): 52-53. 43 Ibid., 122. 44 "Holstein," www.ansi.okstate.edu/breeds. 45 Paul M. Reeves, "Early Holstein History in Virginia," Holstein-Friesian 67th Annual Convention. Program, (Roanoke, 1952), 27. 46 Reaves, et al., History of the Virginia State Dairymen's Association,, 125. 47 Ibid., 28. 48 Certificates of transfer to Mrs. William Cameron of Petersburg, Va., of one bull and one cow. Certificates issued by The Holstein-Friesian Association of America, Virginia Historical Society, Richmond, MSS1 C3467a26566-26624. 49Reaves, et al., History of the Virginia State Dairymen's Association, 29. 50 R.G. Connelly, "A History of Virginia Holsteins and Holstein Breeders, Virginia Holstein Directory. 51 Ibid. 52 Virginia Cooperative Holstein Breeding Association, Inc., "Field Day Program," 20 July 1966. 53 The authors are grateful to George A. Miller for this information. 54 John O. Hardesty, "Some Historical Items of Holstein Interest." 55 Ibid. 56 Hardesty, "Some Historical Items of Holstein Interest." 57 The authors are grateful to Harold W. Roller of Weyers Cave for this information. See also "The 1987 Virginia Distinguished Dairyman," *Holstein World* (June 10, 1987): 73. 58 "National Junior Champions Named," *Holstein News,* 19 (April 1958): 1-2; *North Carolina Holstein News* 15 (July-September 1958): 1. 59 Reaves, et al., History of the Virginia State Dairymen's Association, 127; George A. Miller, "Virginia Holstein Association's First 75 Years," *Holstein World* (July 1991): 11. 60 Paul Reaves, Joan Peck, and Margie Ann Dick, "Virginia Holstein History," *Holstein World,* (June 10, 1987): 58. 61 Miller, "Virginia Holstein Association's First 75 Years." 62 Ibid., 126. 63 "Virginia Junior Holstein Association," www.vaholstein.org. 64 The authors are grateful to Walter McClure for this information. 65 "History of the Red and White Dairy Cattle Association," www.redandwhitecattle.com. 66 Notes provided to the authors by Carol Cobb of Dayton, secretary/treasurer of the Southeast Red and White Dairy Cattle Association.

Beef Industry Comes of Age

1 K.C. Williamson provided the authors a very helpful mimeograph copy of a speech or article about the formation of the Virginia Cattlemen's Association that contained the link with the lamb pooling and grading. The author of this paper is not known, but Williamson thinks it may have been C.P. McClaugherty, head of the livestock grading section of the Virginia Department of Agriculture at one time. 2 Bud Snidow provided the authors with a good selection of articles from *The Virginia Breeder* about sales held around Virginia in 1940 when he was just entering the sales business. These provide a good overview of the significant role that these auctions had developed in marketing Virginia cattle. See for example "Six State Sales of Pure-Bred Cattle to See Best of Breeds on Block," *The Virginia Breeder,* September, 1940, 4-5. 3 "Indian Trace Farm's Herefords Bring Average of $180 in Successful Farm Auction." *The Virginia Breeder,* October, 1940, 41. 4 "Three Farm Sale of Aberdeen-Angus at Brandy Rock Proves Big Success," *The Virginia Breeder,* June, 1940, 36-37. 5 Reports on the various sales often name the auctioneer, sale manager, pedigree reader, and ring assistants. Benny Terry, a graduate of the Reppert auction school, advertised his services in *The Virginia Breeder,* October, 1940, 40. 6 Jim Jenkins, Jr., "Who'll Start the Bidding? The story of Two of Virginia's Outstanding Livestock Auction Companies and How They Work." *Virginia and the Virginia County* (March 1952): 27-29. 7 "Honored by Beef Industry: Ownby, Service Award," *The Virginia Cattleman,* (March 1978): 14. 8 The authors are grateful to Patricia Douglas for supplying the auction information and for her careful search for content accuracy in this chapter and others. 9 Jenkins, "Who'll Start the Bidding?," 56-57. 10 The authors are grateful to Barbara Clary, current owner of Ownby Companies, for sharing her recollections at two oral history sessions and in writing. 11 Notes prepared for the authors by K.C. Williamson. An oral history interview conducted by Ike Eller with Bill McSpadden produced the observation that it was Buhrman who spearheaded the organization. 12 Information about these early accomplishments comes from two sources. One is a letter from Allen K. Randolph, executive secretary, Virginia Beef Cattle Producers Association, to Senator Robert Y. Button, Culpeper, Virginia, 11 May 1948, Virginia Cattlemen's Association (VCA) archives. The other is a tongue-in-cheek article by Paul Swaffar, "Livestock Rambles," *The Eastern Breeder,* September 1944, 19-21, which mentions these accomplishments of the first five years in a humorous vein. 13 Henry E. Hutcheson, "The Future Program of the Virginia Beef Cattle Producers Association," *The Eastern Breeder,* August, 1946, 43. 14 Allen K. Randolph, to Senator Button, 11 May 1948, VCA archives. 15 Paul Swaffar, "Livestock Rambles," *The Eastern Breeder,* December, 1944, 19-20; K.C. Williamson notes on the history of the VCA; "First Annual Atlantic Fat Stock Show Brings Entries from Five States," *The Eastern Breeder,* May, 1946. 16 K.C. Williamson account; oral history interview notes with Bill McSpadden; William B. McSpadden, "Virginia Beef Cattle Producers' Notes," *The Eastern Breeder,* May 1945, 44. 17 Hutcheson, "Future Program," 43. 18 "First Atlantic Rural Exposition Provides High Quality Beef Cattle Show," *The Eastern Breeder,* November 1946, 9. 19 Henry E. Hutcheson, "Virginia Cattlemen's' Convention Widely Acclaimed," *The Eastern Breeder,* January, 1947, 14-15. 20 "R.C. Carter Named Secretary Virginia Beef Producers' and Hereford Associations" *The Eastern Breeder,"* September 1947, 43; K.C. Williamson account. 21 A.K. Randolph to Senator Button, 11 May 1948. 22 L.B. Dietrick to A.W. Buhrman, 18 March 1948, VCA archives. 23 "Merchandizing is Theme of Virginia Beef Producer's Annual Meeting," *The Eastern Breeder,* March 1949, 65-69; manuscript recollections of Bud Snidow prepared for the authors. 24 Notes on the feeder calf sales organizations provided by K.C. Williamson. 25 Historical overview of the cattlemen's association, possibly by C.P. McClaugherty, contributed by K.C. Williamson. 26 *The Eastern Breeder,* April 1941, 45. 27 K.C. Williamson, notes on "Cattle Marketing Developments in Virginia since 1939." 28 Minutes of Organization Committee Meeting State feeder Calf Sales Organization, Lynchburg, 20 June 1952, by K.C. Williamson, secretary; additional recollections/notes on feeder calf sales organizations provided by Williamson. After polling representatives of twenty-four feeder calf sales organizations around the state on proposed charges of one dollar per head and fifty cents per head, thirteen voted for fifty cents. 29 Allen Randolph [?] to P.T. Fitzhugh, Jr., 31 March 1958. The second page of this letter with the writer's name is missing, but internal evidence indicates Randolph, VBCPA executive secretary, as author. In

this letter he clarifies the relationship between the VBCPA and the Virginia Feeder Calf-Yearling Association, noting that the latter "absolutely owns, controls, and operates" the former. VCA archives. 30 I. Fred Stine, Northern Virginia Livestock Producers' Association, Inc., to Allen K. Randolph, Virginia Beef Cattle Producers Association, 12 November 1953. VCA archives, Daleville. 31 Minutes of meeting of Burhman, Blanton, and Reed, Richmond, 3 February 1953, filed with VBCPA minutes book, 1953-1959, VCA archives. 32 C.G. Randell (Farm Credit Administration), "Corn Belt Feeder Buyers Go South," *National Live Stock Producer,* March, 1953: 8, 17, 22. 33[Allen Randolph], Log of Feeder Calf Promotional Trip to Maryland-Delaware-Pennsylvania, June 22 through 25, '53. VCA archives. 34 [Allen Randolph] report to the VBCPA board on feeder cattle promotional efforts, 1953, filed with minute books 1953-1959, VCA archives. 35 "Summary of Beef Calf Sales," filed in VBCPA minute book, 1953-1959, VCA archives. 36 Harry C. Stuart, "Statement of the Virginia Beef Cattle Producers Association before the Agricultural Committee of the Ways and Means Committee, 19 September 1953, filed with minutes of the VBCPA, VCA archives. 37 Minutes of the Annual Meeting of the VBCPA at Natural Bridge, 6 February 1956, filed with minutes of VBCPA, VCA archives. 38 Minutes of the directors of the VBCPA and the VFCYC at the Thomas Jefferson Inn, Charlottesville, 9-10 December 1957, VCA archives. 39 Minutes of the VBCPA Board, Charlottesville, 12 May 1958 and State Feeder Cattle Sale Committee Meeting, Natural Bridge, 15 February 1959, VCA archives. 40 Minutes of Feeder Cattle Sales Committee, Thomas Jefferson Inn, January 8-9, 1959. VCA archives. 41 The authors are grateful to Reggie Reynolds of the Virginia Cattleman's Association for his compilation of statistics on beef and dairy cattle in Virginia that we have used in this chapter. 42 "Make Nominations Now for Cattleman of the Year," *The Virginia Cattleman,* (August 1971): 7. 43 "Association Moves to New Headquarters," *The Virginia Cattleman,* (September 1973): 8. 44 "Reynolds Named to VBCA Executive Secretary Post," *The Virginia Cattleman,* (October 1973): 1. 45 A.L. "Ike" Eller, Jr., "Virginia Beef Topics," *The Virginia Cattleman,* (December 1974): 6. 46 "Win $2,000 from ANCA" and "1976 Cattleman of the Year," *The Virginia Cattleman* (March 1976): 4. 47 A.L. "Ike" Eller, Jr., "Virginia Beef topics," *the Virginia Cattleman,* (January 1977): 12 and (March 1977): 6. 48 "Southern Beef Conference," *The Virginia Cattleman,* (October 1978): 12. 49 Reggie Reynolds, "Happy Birthday Virginia Cattlemen's Assoc." *The Virginia Cattleman,* (April 2003): 2. 50 K.C. Williamson, "Group Effort has made Virginia Feeder Sales Big Business," *The Virginia Cattleman,* (September 1972): 4. 51 "Lester Dalton: Strate Award," *The Virginia Cattleman,* (March 1975): 9. 52 Excerpts from notes of a talk about the evolution of cattle marketing in Buckingham given to the Lynchburg Feeder Cattle Association in 1987 by Richard S. Ellis, III. 53 R.S. Ellis IV, "'Growth Feeder Sale' is First of Its Kind," *The Virginia Cattleman,* (September 1972): 8. 54 The authors are grateful to Kelly Liddington who provided a written account of the early history of the Fredericksburg Feeder Calf Association. 55 Photo caption, *The Virginia Cattleman,* (April 1974): 1. 56 Interview with Tom Tabor, 25 July 2002. 57 "Roy Meek: Cattleman of the Year," *The Virginia Cattleman* (March 1975): 8. 58 "Good Attendance Seen at Albemarle Feeder Assn. Meet," *The Virginia Cattleman,* (January 1972): 5. 59 "Russell Yowell is President of Madison County Assn.," *Virginia Cattleman,* (April 1974): 1. 60 "Lester Dalton: Strate Award," *The Virginia Cattleman,* (March 1975): 9. 61 Interview with Dave Gilbert, 18 July 2002. 62 Williamson, "Group Effort has made Virginia Feeder Sales Big Business," 4. 63 Authors are grateful to Cornelia Gilmer Estep of Lebanon for providing information about her father, Aaron Kemp Gilmer, Jr. 64 The authors are grateful to Edmund Metcalf of the Lynchburg Livestock Market for putting together information about markets in that Southside area. 65 "Instant Monitoring Gives Buyer Facts," *The Virginia Cattleman* (January 1972): cover and 15. 66 "Director in Action: Charles W. Lawson," *The Virginia Cattleman,* (September 1971): 3. 67 A.L. "Ike" Eller, Jr., "Beef Cattle Improvement in Virginia" unpublished paper made available to the authors by Dr. Eller. The authors would also like to thank Bill Wampler for sharing information about his family's extensive involvement in the beef industry. 68 Ibid. 69 Beef Improvement Federation, *Ideas Into Action: A Celebration of the First 25 Years of the Beef Improvement Federation,* (Stillwater, Ok.: University Printing Services, 1993) 9-10. 70 Eller, "Beef Cattle Improvement in Virginia." 71 http://bcia.apsc.vt.edu/history.html. 72 Sixth Annual Report, Virginia Beef Cattle Improvement Association. VCA archives. 73 "Progress Report, VBCIA's First ROP Bull Feeding Test," VCA archives. 74 "Roy Meek: cattleman of the Year," *The Virginia Cattleman,* (March 1975): 8. 75 Eller, "Beef Cattle Improvement in Virginia." 76 http://bcia.apsc.vt.edu. 77 http://bcia.apsc.vt.edu/news.html. 78 http://bcia.apsc.vt.edu/officers.html. 79 BIF, *A Celebration of the First 25 Years,* 10-12. 80 Ibid., 13-17. 81 Ibid., 20-23. 82 Ibid., 27-32. 83 Ibid., 37-40 84 Turner A. Gilmer, Jr., Treasurer, Virginia Livestock Council, dues notice, 9 December 1959. VCA archives; information supplied by A.L. "Ike" Eller, Jr. 85 The authors are grateful to Reginald Reynolds of the Virginia Cattleman's Association for preparing materials on beef check-off for use in this chapter. 86 Reginald Reynolds, "Current Problems Show Battle is Not Won When the Calf Leaves the Farm," *The Virginia Cattleman,* (October 1974): 2. 87 "Virginia's 'Self-Help' Plan," *The Virginia Cattleman* (November 1974): 1. 88 "Vote to Create Cattle Commission Negative," *The Virginia Cattleman,* (May 1975): 1. 89 Reynolds material on check-off cited above. 90 Charles E. Ball, "A Dollar A Head," *Building the Beef Industry: A Century of Commitment* (Denver: The National Cattlemen's Foundation, 1988), 231-232. 91 Reynolds material. 92 Ibid., 232-233. 93 Randell, "Corn Belt Feeder Buyers," *National Live Stock Producer,* March, 1953: 17. 94 The authors are grateful to George R. Aldhizer, Jr., Esq., of Harrisonburg, for writing his recollections of the formation of Virginia Beef Exposition. 95 Bill McKinnon, "Beef Expo Update," *The Virginia Cattleman* (April 2003): 16.

Promoting Quality Through Seedstock

1 Clay Catlett and Elliott G. Fishburne, *An Economic and Social Survey of Augusta County* (University of Virginia Record Extension Services, 1928), vol. XII, #7, 143. 2 Otis L. Fisher, *Shorthorns Around the World* (Harrisonburg, Va.: published by Otis L. Fisher, 1993), 7-9. 3 Fisher, 10-12. 4 Fisher, 30. 5 Fisher, 12. 6 Fisher, 15-17. 7 Fisher, 17. 8 Leonard William Brinkman, Jr., "The Historical Geography of Improved Cattle in the United States to 1870," Ph.D. dissertation, University of Wisconsin, 1964, 16. The authors are grateful to Ken Koons for bringing this unpublished study to their attention. 9 Fisher, 32-33. 10 "Short Horn Breeders Organize," *Staunton Daily News,* 5 September 1919. 11 Katharine L. Brown, *New Providence Church: A History, 1746-1996* (Raphine, Va.: New Providence Presbyterian Church, 1996), 200. 12 "McLaughlin quits as President of Breeders' Asso'n," *Staunton Daily News,* 30 September 1919. 13 The authors are grateful to A.L. "Ike" Eller for supplying this information. 14 Telephone interview with Otis L. Fisher of Churchville, Virginia, April 2004. 15 Fisher, *Shorthorns Around the World,* 36-37. 16 Ibid., 34. 17 "Hereford," www.ansi.okstate.edu/breeds. 18 Ibid. 19 *History of Hereford Cattle,* 91. 20 George W. Litton, "A Historical Review of Virginia's Livestock Industry," manuscript prepared for 13th Annual Animal Industry Day, 16 July 1976. Provided by the Virginia Cattlemen's Association Office, Daleville, Virginia. 21 Ibid. 22 *Staunton News-Leader,* 22 April 1922, "Dr. Byers President of Hereford Breeders." 23 *History of Virginia,* 286, Byers family papers in private collection. 24 Byers family recollections provided by Conrad Byers. 25 *Staunton News-Leader,* c. 1922, "$10,000 Sale of Herefords; Notable Gathering of Breeders from Eastern States Attend." 26 *History of Hereford Cattle,* 91. 27 "Investment in Herefords in Rockbridge Proves Profitable to Physician," *The Virginia Breeder,* March 1940, 45-46. 28 Addy Muncy, "Tyler Snodgrass Started with Herefords on the Hook, Now has Them on Hoof," *The Virginia Breeder,* July 1940, 35. 29 "Russell Cattle Make Record" article from Lebanon [?] newspaper provided by Dr. F.B. Gent III. 30 "Polled Hereford Cattle," www.bundoranfarm.com/herefords.html. 31 Donald R. Ornduff, *The Hereford in America: A Compilation of Historic Facts about the Breed's Background and Bloodlines* (Kansas City, Missouri: privately published, 1960), 311. 32 "Hereford Heritage," American Hereford Association website, www.hereford.org. 33 "Bennett, Tucker Breeders of the Year," *Beef Improvement Federation Update,* No. 8, July 1978. 34 Interview with Owen Thomas, 2 June 2004. 35 Ibid., group interview at Virginia Cattlemen's Association offices, 13 May 2004. 36 Owen Thomas interview. 37 The authors are grateful for the use of the photo album with photographs and biographical sketches of all Mills Award winners from 1959 to 1974, provided by Morris Fannon. 38 The authors are grateful to A.L. "Ike" Eller for assistance in compiling this list. 39 The authors are grateful to Eller for making them aware of the work of these local Hereford organizations. 40 Virginia Hereford Association www.virginiahereford.org. 41 Ornduff, *The Hereford in America,* 314-318, 363-365. 42 Ibid., 310. 43 "Nunc Dimittis: Clayton Ernest Holmes," www.poultryscience.org/psa/ndim. *44 Virginia Polled Hereford Association Directory, 1974.* The authors are grateful to Owen Thomas, III, for making this publication available. 45 "A Message from APHA Director, Franklin D. Roosevelt, Jr.," *1776-1976 Virginia Polled Hereford Association Directory.* The authors are grateful to Owen Thomas, III, for making this directory available. 46 www.wvagriculture.org. 47 Comstock Cattle Services, sale flyer, May 13, 1988; the authors are grateful to A.L. "Ike" Eller for information provided on the Polled Herefords; Ike Eller, "Culpeper BCIA Bull Sale Averages $1,630" Livestock Update, May 1997, www.ext.vt.edu/news/periodicals/livestock/aps-97_05/aps-778.html. 48 "A History of Red Angus," (Denton, Texas: Red Angus Association of America, nd). 49 *Staunton Dispatch and News Historical and Industrial Edition,* January 1906, 44. 50 C. Whitney Grove recollections manuscript prepared for this book and collected by Patty Douglas. 51 "Officials and Mid-West Breeders of Angus Inspect Virginia and Maryland Herds," *The Virginia Breeder,* June 1940, 34. 52 Paul Swaffar, "Looking Over the Angus for Warrenton Sale," *The Virginia Breeder,* July 1940, 30. 53 "Aberdeen Angus Herds in State are Rated Tops," *The Virginia Breeder,* (c. 1940), 25. 54 Virginia Angus Association Open House Program, 17 October 1993. 55 C. Whitney Grove recollections. 56 Dave Leonard recollections manuscript prepared for this book and collected by Patty Douglas. 57 "Virginia Angus Association: A Brief History" in program for Open House and Dedication at the new VAA headquarters in Augusta County, 17 October 1993. 58 William D. Wampler to Patty Douglas, 8 July 2003. 59 Culpeper newspaper clippings, 20 October 1965. 60 *Virginia Angus News,* Vol. 35, No. 1 (February 1968). 61 "Virginia Angus Association," *Angus Topics,* June 1970, 12. 62 The authors are grateful to Dave Leonard for providing this information. 63 John R. Mrotek recollections manuscript prepared for this book and collected by Patty Douglas. 64 Thomas M. Templeton recollections manuscript prepared for the book and collected by Patty Douglas. 65 *Virginia Angus News* , Vol. 35, No. 1 (February 1968). 66 Program for Open House and Dedication, 17 October 1993. 67 The authors are grateful to Patty Douglas for providing identifications for so many leaders of VAA. 68 Virginia Angus Association website, www.vaangus.org. 69 *Virginia Angus Association Handbook* 2001. 70 *VAA Handbook,* 9. 71 *Angus Heritage Foundation* (published by the Angus Heritage Foundation, 1999). 72 www.ext.vt.edu/news/periodicals/livestock. 73 "Shenandoah Valley Angus Assn. Formed," *The Virginia Cattleman,* February 1975:7. 74 Red Angus in Virginia manuscript notes from Joyce Tice. 75 Ibid. 76 Ibid. 77 "Charolais," www.ansi.okstate.edu/breeds. 78 Ibid. 79 Dale F. and June A. Runnion, editors, *The History of Limousin in North America* (Fountain Hills, Ariz.: Dale F. Runnion, 1987), 8. 80 "Charolais," www.ansi.okstate.edu/breeds. 81 Nancy Sorrells, "Stuarts Draft's Kindig family paved way for Charolais breed in Virginia," *Augusta Country,* Summer 2002. All of the information about the Kindig family and their contribution to the Charolais breed is contained in the article, which is the result of an interview in 2002 with Earl and Betty Kindig. 82 Virginia Charolais Association, www.breedersworld.com/beef/vacharolais. 83 Robert Clowdis, "Virginia Charolais Association Newsletter," *The Virginia Cattleman,* 25 (April 2003): 26. 84 "History of the Virginia Charolais Association," prepared for this book by Walter Winkler. 85 Ibid. 86 Ibid. 87 Ibid. 88 Ibid. 89 "Virginia's Edward Shurick is Appointed International Director," *The Virginia Cattleman,* January 1973: 11. 90 "Mt. Solon Youth Awarded Scholarship by Charolais," *The Virginia Cattleman,* January 1974:21. 91 Ibid. 92 "Charolais," www.ansi.okstate.edu/breeds. 93 F.B. Gent, D.V.M. to Fellow Cattle Breeders, 4 November 1998. 94 Runnion, 6-8. 95 "Limousin," www.ansi.okstate.edu/breeds. 96 Runnion, 9, 21. 97 "Limousin," www.ansi.okstate.edu/breeds. 98 Runnion, 176-177. 99 Virginia Limousin Breeders Association website, www.limousin.org/pages/vlbamem.html. The authors are grateful for additional Limousin information provided by A.L. "Ike" Eller. 100 "Salers," www.ansi.okstate.edu/breeds. 101 Ibid. 102 Interview with John Mitchell at Virginia Cattleman's Association offices, Daleville, 12 May 2004. 103 John B. Mitchell manuscript notes on Salers. 104 Ibid. 105 www.bundoranfarm.com/herefords.html. 106 "Simmental," www.ansi.okstate.edu/breeds. 107 Ibid. 108 Ibid. 109 The authors are grateful to A.L. "Ike" Eller for this information. 110 "Virginia Forms 27th State Simmental Group," *The Virginia Cattleman,* September 1972: 14-15. 111 *The Virginia Simmental Association Breeders Guide, 1978* (insert booklet in *The Virginia Cattleman,* August, 1978). 112 www.breedingcattlepage.com/vsa. 113 "Tarentaise," www.ansi.okstate.edu/breeds/cattle. 114 Ibid. 115 "Doc Tucker, Hall of Fame Inductee," www.usatarentaise.com/latest_news.htm. 116 "Gelbvieh," www.ansi.okstate.edu/breeds. 117 Leness Hall, "How Gelbvieh First came to the United States," American Gelbvieh Association fax to James Bennett, 11 December 2003. 118 Ibid. 119 "Gelbvieh," www.ansi.okstate.edu/breeds. 120 James Bennett in oral history interview session at Virginia Cattleman's Association offices, Daleville, Virginia, 12 May 2004. 121 www.cattletoday.com/salesreports and www.ext.vt.edu/news/periodicals/livestock. 122 www.gelbvieh.org. 123 Promotional flyers from American Highland Cattle Association, #200 Livestock Exchange Building, 4701 Marion Street, Denver, CO 80216 and the Appalachian Highland Cattle Society, P.O. Box 190, Lashmeet, WV 24733.

The Future is Now

1 Beth Macy, "The Late Great Cattle battle," *The Roanoke Times,* 17 August 2003. 2 Ibid. 3 *The Artificial Insemination of Farm Animals,* Edited by Enos J. Perry (New Brunswick, N.J.: Rutgers University Press, 1955), 5-7. 4 Paul Reaves, Harold W. Craun, Hershel H. Gardner, and John L. Miller, *A History of the Virginia State Dairymen's Association, 1907-1982* (Published by the Virginia State Dairymen's Association, 1982), 136. 5 Nelson Gardner, "Dairy Impact in Rockingham County," 6 May 2002. 6 Ibid. 7 Ibid. 8 Ibid. 9 *50 Years: A Golden Anniversary, 1950-2000* (Produced by the Virginia-North Carolina Select Sires, Inc., 2000). 10 Paul Reaves, et al, *A History,* 137. 11 *50 Years.* 12 "Artificial Insemination," G.W. Hicks, *Milky Way,* 6 May 1950. 13 Paul Reaves, et al, *A History,* 137. 14 *50 Years.* 15 Paul Reaves, et al, *A History,* 137. 16 "1959 Achievements, 1960 Objectives Outlined By Artificial Breeders," *Staunton News-Leader,* 7 February 1960. 17 Ibid. 18 "George Miller Retires," *S.E. News,* 15 July 1991. 19 *50 Years.* 20 "George Miller Retires," *S.E. News,* 15 July 1991. 21 Personal recollections supplied by George Miller. 22 Ibid. 23 Ibid. 24 Information provided by William Harrison. 25 Paul Reaves, et al, *A History,* 92. 26 Nelson Gardner, "Dairy Impact." 27 Information provided by William Harrison. 28 Robert D. Heilman, "The History of American Marketing Services, Inc.: International Involvement in Bovine Embryo Exporting," February 2004. 29 Ibid. 30 Ibid. 31 Ibid. 32 Ibid. 33 Ibid. 34 Ibid. 35 Ibid. 36 Karen E.Thermer, "After Isabel, 600 head of Cattle ship Out of Richmond, VA for Turkey Onboard the M/V Cimbria," *The Virginia Dairyman* (reprinted from *AJOT, Mediterranean/Middle East/African Trade*), January 2004, 25. 37 Duane Mickelsen, "Mad Cow Disease," *The Pinzgauer Journal,* March 2004, 16-18. 38 A.J. Hostetler, "Cloning Studied As Means to Block Mad-cow; Virginia Tech Scientists Turn to Genetics to Ward Off Brain-destroying Infections," *Richmond Times-Dispatch,* 8 January 2004. 39 "Scott Greiner, "Giles Rand and Mossy Creek Farm Names Beef Improvement Federation Commercial Producers of The Year, July 1999, www.ext.vt.edu/news/periodicals/livestock; "Cattle Industry's Future Growth Dependent On Ability To Export," Government Affairs Center, National Cattlemen's Beef Association, 18 June 2003, www.hill.beef.org; and Bonnie Naumann, "What cows eat, before we eat them," *The Daily News Leader,* 14 January 2004. 40 Headwaters Soil and Water Conservation Tour, 17 August 2004 and "Dairy BMPS for farm profit and water quality improvement," Virginia Department of Conservation and Recreation. 41 "This Small Farm Succeeds The Organic Way," *Ayrshire News,* January 2003 and Judith Weinraub, "The Oak Grove Experiment: The small, innovative dairy farm in Virginia has big talent, big bucks and big ideas," *The Washington Post,* 7 August 2002. 42 Eric S. Bendfeldt, "Of Blue Crabs, Oysters, Rockfish, and Eels: Dairy Farmers and the Chesapeake Bay Foundation Discuss the Complexity of Cleanup Efforts, *The Virginia Dairyman,* January 2004. 43 Michael Olmert, "The Cowboy and the Conservationist," National Geographic Society television presentation, 7 September 1986. 44 Antonio Regalado and Scott Kilman, "Better-Tasting Beef Through Genetic Testing?", *Wall Street Journal,* 7 June 2004.

Steven Whelan of Augusta County and his Tarentaise cow, Cotton Candy

Authors' Acknowledgments

Authors of all history books incur many debts in the course of their work. Their writing does not spring out of their imaginations as the work of a novelist might. Their raw material is found in many different public and private manuscript collections, archives, historic photographic collections, archaeology and material culture collections, and public records repositories. These are found in universities and colleges, historical societies, state archives, museums, and in public and private libraries as well as in family scrapbooks and dust-covered shoeboxes. In every instance, whether through a personal visit to the institution or someone's home, or through telephone and internet connections, skilled professionals, volunteers, and friends have been on hand to make those materials available to the researcher. The personal recollections of older persons who have experienced some of that history are also another rich source that historians tap. This requires a generosity of their time and a generosity as well with treasured family materials on the part of the persons interviewed.

Dairy industry persons who met with us in two oral history sessions, one in Staunton and the other in Blacksburg, were: John L. Miller, George A. Miller, Nelson S. Gardner, C.T. Barnes, Ray Murley, Bob Heilman, Carl E. Polen, Emory Brubaker, Harold W. Roller, Richard Chichester, Jim Nichols, Barbara Clary, William H. Harrison, W.E. "Bill" Blalock, Dale Gardner, Michael Myatt, John O. Hardesty, and Walter McClure.

Cattlemen who met with us in a day-long oral history session at the Virginia Cattlemen's Association headquarters in Daleville were Reggie Reynolds, James Bennett, A.L. "Ike" Eller, Dave Leonard, K.C. Williamson, Bill McKinnon, and John Mitchell.

K.C. Williamson and Ike Eller for beef cattle and George A. Miller and Nelson Gardner for dairy cattle deserve special thanks for the large body of material they shared with us for the mid-twentieth century developments in those two industries. The staff and members of both the Virginia Cattlemen's Association and the Virginia State Dairymen's Association have been helpful from start to finish in supplying us with contact information and industry materials.

We are grateful to Debbie Garrett of Buena Vista, who conducted numerous interviews of people important to the cattle industry. We are also indebted to Tom Tabor of Carroll/Grayson Counties, William H. Harrison, Leesburg; Joe Graham, Goshen; Turner A. Gilmer, Jr., Lebanon; Jon Repair, Rockbridge County; and Dave Gilbert. We must also thank John Heatwole for allowing us to use his own oral history research in the Shenandoah Valley.

Various persons whom the authors interviewed, including Otis Fisher, Lyle and Betty Kindig, Leon "Mose" Kiracofe, the late Dr. Arthur Bartenslager and his wife Delila, Dr. James Nichols, Bill and Betty Wampler, and Bill and Polly Harrison were gracious in welcoming us to their homes and sharing their knowledge with us.

Ike Eller accompanied us to Tazewell County in the summer of 2003 for fascinating interviews about the fat cattle business. There we spent two delightful days with Jim Hoge, Marvin Meek, Catherine Moss Huffman of Burke's Garden and in The Cove with Bill Adams, Nick Adams, Will Adams, William and Cindy Gillespie (who hosted the group for a luncheon), A.P. "Al" Gillespie, Rees Bowen VII, Irene "Cecil" Bowen Wendell, Clinton Bell, Walter "Brownie" Elswick, and Mike Harris, Tazewell County Extension Agent.

Others who provided valuable material about the fat cattle business were Mrs. Francis Bell IV, Harrisonburg; Betty E. Spillman, Radford; Emilie T. Lyckman, Pulaski; Lee Stuart Cochran, Staunton; W.A. "Zan" Stuart and his wife Lynda; and Robbie Brown, Swoope.

Persons who sent family materials, photographs, recollections, breed association items, or miscellaneous cattle materials or who allowed us to take photographs for use in the book include: George R. Aldhizer, Jr., Robert Earl Alley, Billie Jean Banks, Gordon Barlow, Allen Bassler, Laten Bechtel, Dave Beyeler, Jean Bosserman, E. Cline Brubacker, Emory Brubaker, Conrad Byers, Debbie Stiles Callison, Carol Cobb, Lynn Coffey, Barbara Corse, Margie Ann Dick, Ann Dorsey, Patty Douglas, Earl and Janet Baugher Downs, Sandra Elkins, Cornelia Gilmer Estep, Patt Fitzhugh, Mrs. Douglas Forrest, Nelson and Kathleen Gardner, Fred W. Gent II, C. Whitney Grove, Mary Crockett Hill, Atwood Huff, Earl and Betty Kindig; Marvin Kokes, Dave Leonard, Kelly Liddington, Gene McIlwee, Walter McClure, Les McCracken, Allister McKay, J.L. McComas, George A. Miller, John R. Mrotek, Rodney Phillips, Reggie Reynolds, Lois Rhodes, Dr. Richard Saacke, Joi Saville, Charles Shoffer, John Henry Smith, Bill Speiden, Betty Spillman, John A. Taylor, Owen Thomas III, Charlie Thompson, Shaun Thurman, Norm Vincel, Barbara Wagner, William D. Wampler, Neal West, Samuel, Kipp, and Steven Whelan, Walt Winkler, Waldo Wistleman, and Tyre and Jane Yancey.

Staff Members of various museums, libraries, and archives who provided research materials, photographs and other illustrations are Edward S. Ayres, Dan Hawks, Nancy Egloff of the Jamestown-Yorktown Foundation; Chris Bolgiano of James Madison University Special Collections; Anne Sindelar and Anne Salsich, Western Reserve Historical Society Library and Archives; Barbara Adamson, Shenandoah County Historical Society; Lucinda Stanton, Robert H. Smith International Center for Jefferson Studies; staff at Morven Park; staff at Loudoun Heritage Farm Museum; Stephanie Jacobe and Joseph Ruggles, Virginia Historical Society; Joanne Bowen, Andrew Edwards, and Marianne Martin, Colonial Williamsburg Foundation; Angelika Kuetlner, Washington and Lee University; Margo Oxendine, Bath County Historical Society; Tami Ramsey, New River Historical Society; Margaret T. Whittington and staff at the C&O Historical Society; Kathy Roncarati, Plimoth Plantation; Catherine Dean, Curator of Collections, APVA-Virginia Preservation; Bly Straube, Paula Neely, Catherine Correll-Walls of APVA/Jamestown Rediscovery; Ginger Peterman, Picture Collection Specialist, The Library of Virginia; Robert Teagle, Foundation for Historic Christ Church; Ray Swick, Blennerhassett Island State Historical Commission, Parkersburg; Dawn Bonner, Mount Vernon Ladies' Association; Mary Fishback, library assistant, LaVonne Markham, tech specialist, Jane Sullivan, library manager, and Jerry Michael, local researcher and dairy farmer, all of the Thomas Balch Library, Leesburg; Burckhard K. Blöb, Human Resource Manager II for the Central Virginia Training Center of the Virginia Department of Mental Health, Mental Retardation and Substance Abuse Services; Rick Wills, Western State Hospital; Carolyn Peterson, James River Correctional Center – State Farm; staff at the Virginia Military Institute Archives, Preston Library; Joyce McMullin, Alexandria Library; staff at the University of Virginia special collections; Chris C. O'Brien, Office of the President and Melissa Matchett, In-House Research Co-ordinator, National Geographic Television and Film; staff at Humpback Rocks Interpretive Center, Wilderness Road Museum staff and Susan Wilkinson of Historic St. Mary's City.

Virginia artists who graciously contributed the use of their work or pieces of art in their possession to add color and beauty for illustrations in the volume are Linda Patrick, Lyndurst; Mia LaBerge, Harrisonburg; Nancy Bass, Albemarle County; Patricia Thomas, Lexington; June Mullins, Blacksburg; Joni Pienkowski, Blacksburg; Paul M. Willouer, Harrisonburg; and Robert Stovall, Lynchburg, for his mother, artist Queena Stovall. In addition, the staff at Belmont, the Gari Melchers Museum, Fredericksburg, Kirsti Blom of the Grandma Moses Foundation, George Horvath of the Virginia Tourism Corporation, and Linda Staley, Sara Bemiller, and Kim Pulicre of the O. Winston Link Museum, Roanoke, assisted us with images of the artists for whose heritage they are custodians. Pam Harshbarger Smith and John Alvin Taylor graciously gave permission for private pieces of artwork in their possession to be reproduced in the book.

Peggy Dillard, as an intern for Lot's Wife Publishing, and Sarah Clarke, as a research assistant for Lot's Wife, both contributed enormously to the body of research used in this history.

A project of this magnitude could never happen without those persons who know far more about the world of computers than we even imagine: Sam Warren who provided the technical layout assistance needed for us to tackle such a project, John Riley, owner of John's Computers, who kept busy running between the computers of Nancy, Katharine, and Betty Jo in an effort to move the project along in a timely fashion, and the staff at Good Printers for making this all happen. Other persons who provided us with help along the way are: Kevin Barnes; Charlie Borst, *The Free-Lance Star*; Dorothy Boyd-Bragg; Leila Boyer, Museum of the Shenandoah Valley; Cindy Correll, *The News Leader*; Ed Covert; Jim Hoy; Jeff Ishee; Frank Johnston; Patrick Jones, Tessi Lamb; Richard MacMaster, Bill Miller; Ernie Miller, Pat Ritchie; Norman Wenger and David Rodes (Southern Claims Commission Papers); Al Stuart, Robin and Linda Williams; Lisa Craig, Augusta County 4-H and FFA Market Animal Show Media Committee; Frank Wood, Christine Yoder, and Bobby Whitescarver, Bob Ford, and Sandy Greene at USDA's Natural Resource Conservation Services.

Fran Carrington provided clerical assistance and Stephen Nickerson, head of Dairy Science at Virginia Tech, shared helpful editorial suggestions. Thoughtful proofreading came from both the editorial and advisory boards, but particular thanks must be given to Patty Douglas and Nelson Gardner on the editorial board, and non-board members George A. Miller, Harold W. Roller, and John L. Miller. Kathleen Gardner helped in taking and tracking down photographs. O. Beverley, B. Randolph, and Jason Roller were kind enough to take time to pose for a FFA photograph.

Graphic design credits are due to two talented women who have given this book its handsome appearance, Cheryl Lyon of LDA Creations, Dayton, for the dustjacket and the sophisticated template for the book's interior, and Betty Jo Hamilton, who raises beef cattle in Middlebrook and sits on the VCA board and VBIC, for translating the template into a beautiful book in her patient and thoughtful work on the layout.

The book would not have been complete without a photograph of the authors posing with their favorite subjects for the last three years – cattle. Thanks to Bill, Suzanne, Cole, and Ben Heizer of Middlebrook for arranging an exciting photo shoot in their barn one Sunday afternoon and to Betty Jo Hamilton for taking the pictures. The result is far more appropriate than a studio shot. Additionally, thanks to Middlebrook 4-H Livestock Club members and their parents for enduring a photo session, also in the Heizer barn, and to Sarah Heizer for the loan of her Angus heifer, Sally.

Our editor, Professor Ken Koons, an agricultural historian in the history department at Virginia Military Institute, has been the most gracious and helpful editor that writers could want. His thoughtful criticisms and suggestions through three readings of the entire manuscript clarified our thinking when it got muddied and helped this book to read much more smoothly.

To the editorial and advisory boards of the cattle history project we owe an enormous debt. To John Mitchell and Ike Eller, whose brainchild this entire project was, and to all other members of the editorial board, James Bennett, William Harrison, Nelson Gardner, Debbie Snead, and to Patty Douglas, its secretary, we can only offer our heartfelt gratitude. We are grateful for their courage to undertake the project, for the thousands of miles they have traveled to meetings over the past three years, the countless hours of their time invested, their generosity with their own materials and contacts, and for their faith in two women historians who are neither dairy nor cattle people and for their patient coaching of us through every stage of the work. We hope that the resulting book is one in which they can feel justly proud.

To the nuns of Our Lady of the Angels Monastery in Crozet we must thank you for the cheese, and for all of your help both materially and spiritually. Finally, we must give humble thanks to our support staff on the homefront who could only sigh when told that the cattle history book would once again take precedence over dinner or laundry or family gatherings. Thanks to Madison, Randy, Bob, and Deb for hanging in there. We hope you enjoy the book.

Nancy T. Sorrells
Katharine L. Brown
September 2004

About the Artists in *Virginia's Cattle Story*

Charlottesville-area artist *Nancy Bass,* whose husband operates a cattle farm, has painted Virginia landscapes for over twenty years. She admires the quiet elegance of cows as animals that exhibit uniquely human characteristics. "The cows of my paintings meet the viewer's eye in an inquisitive confrontation. Often my cows are searching, whether for food or their calves, or shelter from a storm. The varied seasons and times of day in my paintings celebrate the unique beauty of the pastoral Virginia landscape," she explains.

Edward Beyer was born in the Rhineland in 1820, studied at the Royal Prussian Academy, painted in Dresden, then came in America in 1848, living in Newark and Philadelphia, where he worked on panoramic painting. From 1854 to 1857 Beyer was in Virginia painting landscapes, towns, spas, and technology. Thirty-nine of his works were published as lithographs in Album of Virginia. The Peaks of Otter painting is a result of his work during that period and was part of that book.

Casimir Bohn, a Washington, D.C., artist, whose scene of antebellum Lexington is depicted in the New Republic chapter, visited Lexington in 1856 to make sketches. He returned the following year to open a business selling colored lithographs for five dollars each.

The watercolor painting of John Milton Reed's burned mill was painted by *Ida Blanche Haley* to preserve the family story about Union troops in Fauquier County in 1864. Ida's mother, Ida Etta (Reed) Haley, was a teenager when the North launched that campaign of destruction. Years later Ida chose to write her mother's story and to paint the ruins of her grandfather's mill. Not only did she make sure that the memories of those times were never forgotten by Reed descendants, but she provided a valuable bit of historical information for her great-great-niece, Nancy Sorrells, to use in *Virginia's Cattle Story.*

Sir Joshua Reynolds originally painted the portrait of Virginia's last colonial governor, Lord Dunmore. In 1929 Mr. and Mrs. Alexander Wilbourne Weddell presented an exhibition of Virginia historical portraiture, organized under the auspices of the Virginia Historical Society, at Virginia House in Richmond. Mrs. Weddell commissioned *Charles X. Harris* (1856-ca. 1930) to make this copy of the borrowed exhibition portrait for the society's collection.

Mia LaBerge was raised on a Rockingham County farm and often paints landscapes of her native county. She holds a Bachelors in art with teacher certification from James Madison University (1992), and has taught art in Loudoun County and Harrisonburg public schools and Hunter McGuire School, as well as in numerous camps and special programs. A self-dubbed "art teacher turned artist," she has painted in oil for over fifteen years. She has twice earned the James Madison Art Achievement Award.

O. Winston Link, born in 1914 in Brooklyn, New York, learned photography from his father, graduated from the Polytechnic Institute of Brooklyn and entered public relations. After WWII he became a freelance photographer specializing in complicated industrial and commercial lighting scenes. In Staunton on a commercial shoot in 1955, he discovered that the Norfolk & Western Railway in Waynesboro still operated steam engines and so impressed railway management with his train pictures that he received permission to photograph on its property. By 1960 in twenty trips to Virginia, West Virginia, North Carolina, and Maryland, he produced about 2,400 images. His most memorable photographs, including Cow 13 in the "Riding the Rails of Progress" chapter, were taken at night with radio-controlled devices involving dozens of flash bullbs, yards of wire, and multiple cameras. In the 1980s these photos were recognized as works of art and in 2004 The O. Winston Link Museum opened at the historic Norfolk & Western Passenger Station in Roanoke.

Julius Garibaldi "Gari" Melchers, born in Detroit in 1860, was the son of a Prussian sculptor. He studied at the Dusseldorf Academy in 1877 and the Ecole de Beaux-Arts in Paris. He helped found an art colony in Holland, painted Dutch peasant life there, and won a Grand Prize at the 1889 Paris Exposition. He was a professor at Grand Ducal Saxony School of Art from 1909 to 1914. He returned to America, painted in New York, and at his Fredericksburg home, Belmont, depicted in this book as the opening spread for the "Milk Specialists" chapter, and where he died in 1932. Mary Washington College operates Melchers' Belmont Museum.

Hugh Morrison, Jr., learned photography from his father, Hugh Starke Morrison, who set up a photography studio in Harrisonburg in 1859. Hugh, Jr., became a travelling photographer in 1886. In 1895 he opened a permanent studio in Woodstock where he remained until his death in 1950. Morrison's glass plate negatives were given to the Shenandoah County Historical Society.

Grandma Moses was simply Anna Mary Robertson Moses when she came to Augusta County from her native New York as a bride in 1887. She and her husband farmed and raised milk cows. She made and sold butter to local general stores and fancy hotels. Later the Moses family sold whole milk in Staunton. The family returned to New York in 1905. At age seventy Grandma Moses began to paint her memories of rural American life in a primitive style that achieved instant popular acclaim in the 1940s. At least thirty-eight paintings depict scenes from the two decades she lived in Virginia. She died at 101 in 1961.

Kathleen June Mullins received a BS in the physical sciences from Colorado State University and an MS in reproduction physiology from the Department of Dairy Science at Virginia Tech. Illustrations of the bovine reproductive tracts were accumulated during a career in dairy science at Virginia Tech, and culminated in the 2003 production of the "Illustrated Anatomy of the Bovine Male and Female Reproductive Tracts - From Gross to Microscopic" by Mullins and Virginia Tech Dairy Science professor, Dr. R.G. Saacke. She is currently a free-lance artist and scientific illustrator in Blacksburg.

Lyndhurst watercolor artist *Linda Patrick* uses her skills as a painter to preserve rural images of Virginia's landscape. Livestock and western Virginia architecture are her specialities. Patrick was born in Charlottesville and grew up in the Nelson County village of Beech Grove. Although she developed an interest in art by the age of eight, she has had very little formal training. She was introduced to watercolors in a YMCA art class in the 1970s. Most of the paintings and their subsequent prints are real scenes and have real stories behind them.

Joni Pienkowski was born in Stoughton, Wisconsin, received a BS in art education and an MS in fine art, graphics, and painting at the University of Wisconsin in 1961. Growing up in Wisconsin exposed her to dairying from an early age. Her work has been featured in six special travelling exhibitions in Virginia and ten publications. She has had one person shows in leading museums, universities, and galleries in Virginia, New York, Wisconsin, and Washington, D.C. She lives and paints in Blacksburg.

The nineteenth century lithograph featuring the church ruins at Jamestown was the work of *F.B. Schell* and *H.S. Beckwith.* Schell was born in Philadelphia in 1838 and died in Chicago in 1905. Most of his time was spent in Pennsylvania where he became known for his land and seascapes.

Several folksy paintings in *Virginia's Cattle Story* that depict rural life from the more recent past are the work of *Queena Stovall.* Born in 1887, she lived in Virginia and began painting at the age of sixty-two when she enrolled in an art class at Randolph-Macon Woman's College in Lynchburg. She painted places, people, and activities she knew best from rural Virginia. By 1969 she had completed forty-seven paintings. Mrs. Stovall died at the age of ninety-three in 1980.

The New York artist who depicted the destruction by Union troops of the Virginia countryside during the Civil War was *James E. Taylor,* a visual reporter for *Frank Leslie's Illustrated Newspaper.* He accompanied Union General Philip H. Sheridan on his military campaigns in the fall of 1864. The sketch used to open the chapter "A War on All Fronts" came from Taylor's diary kept during those military activities.

Patricia Matson Thomas is a native Glencoe, Illinois, but has resided in Lexington since the 1970s. She received a BA degree from Mount Holyoke College, studied art at the Rhode Island School of Design, and earned a Master of Fine Arts in Painting at the University of Iowa. She has taught studio art at Hollins University and Randolph-Macon Woman's College. Her work has been exhibited in numerous shows, including the Lynchburg Fine Arts Center and the Art Institute of Chicago.

The painting "Seven Bends on the Shenandoah River" by *William Winston Valentine* was completed about 1890. Valentine, a Richmond artist, was the older brother of the more famous artist Edward Valentine. William Valentine travelled and studied in Europe, where he learned the tradition of the picturesque and was influenced by the French artist Claude Loran.

Pennsylvanian *Paul M. Willouer* came to the Shenandoah Valley in 1962. He and his wife settled near Harrisonburg and raised three daughters. Willouer only began to paint his watercolors at the age of fifty. The scenery of the Valley inspired most of his pieces, like "Cook's Creek Crossing" that is featured in *Virginia's Cattle Story.* Now retired, he and his wife enjoy their eight grandchildren, and Willouer admits to spending more time on the golf course than at the easel.

Credits for Photos and Other Illustrations

We are grateful to the following persons and institutions for granting permission for their photographs, paintings, drawings, prints, maps, and documents to be used as illustrations in this volume.

Title page: Courtesy Nancy Sorrells (NTS); Title page verso: Courtesy Betty Jo Hamilton; Dedication page: Courtesy Nancy Bass (NB).

Virginia... at Daybreak: 0-1 Courtesy APVA Preservation Virginia; 2-3 Grubb Photo Service, Inc.; 4-5 Courtesy NTS; 6-7 Courtesy NTS; 8-9 Great Falls National Park (Fairfax County), Courtesy Virginia Tourism Corporation (VTS), Richard T. Nowitz; 10-11 Southwestern Virginia, Courtesy VTC; 12-13 Blue Ridge Highlands, Courtesy VTC, Tim Thompson; map, Department of Geography & Earth Sciences, University of North Carolina at Charlotte (UNC-C); 14-15 Skyline Drive (Shenandoah Valley), Courtesy VTC, Buddy Mays; 16-17 Big Walker Mt. Lookout (Wytheville), Courtesy VTC, Bob Krist.

Virginia's First Cattle: 18-19 Courtesy Plimoth Plantation (PP); 20 Courtesy Marvin Kokes, The National Cattlemen's Foundation; 21 Courtesy of APVA/Jamestown Rediscovery; 22 Courtesy NTS; 23 map, (UNC-C); and Courtesy NTS; 24 Colonial Williamsburg Foundation, Williamsburg, Va. (CWF); 25 Courtesy Historic St. Mary's City, St. Mary's City, Md., (HSMC); 26 Virginia Historical Society, Richmond, Va. (VHS); 27 Courtesy PP; 28 Courtesy Jamestown-Yorktown Foundation (J-YF); 30 The Clip Art Book; 31 Courtesy HSMC; 32-33 Courtesy Loudoun Heritage Farm Museum.

Cattle and the Colonists: 34-35 CWF; 36 Virginia map – (UNC-C); Michel's map, courtesy Virginia Magazine of History and Biography; 37 Courtesy Augusta County Courthouse; 38 CWF, photographer Andrew Edwards; 39 photo – CWF; woodcut – courtesy J-YF; 40 photo – CWF; clip art – Dover clip art book; 41 Dover clip art book; 42 Courtesy Foundation for Historic Christ Church, Irvington, Va. with permission of Wellford family, Sabine Hall; 45 Dover clip art book; 46 Courtesy Mount Vernon Ladies' Association (MV); 47 Courtesy MV; 48 both MV; 49 CWF.

Revolutionary Times: 50 CWF; 51 Courtesy NTS; 52 painting – VHS; 52-53 powder horn – courtesy Gordon Barlow; 53 Courtesy NTS; 54 Courtesy Augusta County Courthouse; 55 Courtesy NTS; 56 UNC-C; 57 Courtesy NTS; 58 Courtesy J-YF.

The New Republic: 60 Courtesy Washington and Lee University, Lexington, Va.; 61 Courtesy NTS;

62 Courtesy NTS; 63 National Geographic Magazine; 64 Courtesy Virginia Military Institute Archives, Preston Library (VMI); 65 Courtesy VMI; 66 Courtesy Earl Kindig (EK); 67 Courtesy VMI; 70-71 Courtesy Blenner-hassett Island State Historical Commission, Parkersburg, W.Va.; 71 Courtesy Bath County Historical Society; 72 Courtesy NTS; 73 Courtesy Catherine Moss Huffman (Huffman); 74 University of Virginia Special Collections Library; 75 Courtesy VMI.

A War on All Fronts: 76-77 The Western Reserve Historical Society, Cleveland, Ohio; 78 Courtesy Alexandria Library, Special Collections (AL); 79 Courtesy AL; 80-81 Courtesy Neal West; 82-83 Frank Wood, The Picture Bank; 84 Public domain; 85 Courtesy VHS; 86 Courtesy John Alvin Taylor; 87 Library of Congress; 88-89 National Archives, courtesy Norman Wenger and David Rodes; 92-95 UNC-C; 96-97 Courtesy Linda Patrick (LP).

Great Cattle Drives: 98-99 Courtesy Leslie L. McCracken; 100 Courtesy NTS; 101 Courtesy Schmid's Printery, Staunton, Va.; 102 Top – courtesy James Madison University Library, Special Collections; Painting – Courtesy the Harshbarger family and Pamela Harshbarger Smith, photo by Ron Blunt for the Museum of the Shenandoah Valley, Winchester, Va.; 103 Courtesy Robert E. Alley; 104 Courtesy the Stuart family; 105 Courtesy Jim Hoge; 106 Courtesy Darwin Lambert; 107 Courtesy Virginia Cattlemen's Association (VCA); 108 Courtesy NTS; 110-111 Courtesy Cattle History Editorial Board (CHEB).

Riding the Rails of Progress: 112-113 Courtesy Library of Virginia; 114 Top - courtesy Fred W. Gent II (Gent); Second – Chesapeake & Ohio Historical Society, Clifton Forge, Va. (C&O); Third – courtesy Katharine L. Brown (KLB); Fourth – Courtesy Huffman; 115 Courtesy NTS; 116-117 C&O; 118 Top – National Archives; Bottom – courtesy Ike Eller (Eller); 119 Courtesy O. Winston Link Museum, Roanoke, Va.; 120-121 Courtesy Eller; 122 Courtesy VCA; 123 Courtesy Virginia Tech Archives (VT); 124 Courtesy Massanutten Regional Library, Harrisonburg, Va.; 125 Left – courtesy NTS; Right – Courtesy VT; 126 Left – courtesy Morven Park, Leesburg, Va. (Morven); Right – courtesy Dr. Snowden Hunter, photograph BJH; 127 Courtesy VT; 128 Grandma Moses Properties, New York City, N.Y.

Caring for Cattle: 130 VHS; 131 Courtesy Clinten Bell; 132 Courtesy John B. Mitchell; 133 Courtesy VT; 134-135 Courtesy VT; 136 Silo photos – Courtesy Tyre and Jane Yancey; Bulletin – courtesy NTS; 137 Courtesy VT; 138 Top – courtesy VT; Bottom – courtesy NTS; 139 Courtesy NTS; 140-141 Courtesy Mia LaBerge (ML); 141 Courtesy Carl Polen.

Fat Cattle Kingdom: 142-143 Courtesy Eller; 144 Courtesy Eller; 145 Courtesy Huffman; 146 Top – Courtesy Huffman; Bottom – courtesy NTS; 147 Both courtesy NTS; 148 Courtesy Emilie T. Lyckman; 149 Top – Irene Wendell (Wendell); Bottom – courtesy NTS; 150 Courtesy Wendell; 151 Courtesy Huffman; 152 Top – courtesy Bill Gillespie; Bottom – courtesy Huffman; 153 Courtesy Marvin Meek; 154 Courtesy Eller; 155 Top – courtesy Mike Harris; Bottom – courtesy LP; 156 Courtesy Robert Stovall (Stovall); 157 Map – courtesy The Nature Conservancy; letterhead – courtesy John Henry Smith; 158 Courtesy the Stuart family; 158-159 Courtesy The Nature Conservancy.

In Pursuit of Excellence: 160 Ribbon courtesy Dave Beyeler (DB); top – courtesy Thomas Balch Library, Leesburg, Va. (Balch); Middle – courtesy DB; Bottom – courtesy the Dr. H. Lynn Moore family; 161 Courtesy Jim Nichols; 162 Courtesy NYS; 163 Courtesy John Henry Smith; 164 Courtesy NTS; 165 Courtesy New River Historical Society; 166 National Archives; 167 National Archives; 168 Top left – courtesy VCA; Bottom three – courtesy Bill Wampler (Wampler); background courtesy of the national 4-H organization; 169 Logo courtesy National FFA; Bottom – Courtesy VT; 170 Left – courtesy CHEB; Right – courtesy Atwood Huff; 171 Courtesy CHEB; 172 All courtesy VT; 173 Courtesy VT; 174 Top – courtesy VT; Smithfield photos courtesy John Henry Smith; 175 Top courtesy VT; bottom – courtesy John Henry Smith; 177 Courtesy Bill Harrison (BH); 178 Courtesy Bill Gillespie; 179 Left – courtesy NTS; Top right – Courtesy DB; Bottom right – Courtesy Richard Hamrick; 180 Courtesy Huffman; 181 Courtesy VCA; 182 Courtesy Huffman; 184 Courtesy Balch; 185 Courtesy Balch.

Milk Goes Modern: 186 Courtesy Stovall; 187 Courtesy Christine S. Yoder (Yoder); 188 Top – courtesy Virginia State Dairymen's Association (VSDA); Bottom – courtesy VT; 189 All courtesy VT; 190 Left – courtesy Morven; Right – Courtesy Janet and Earl Downs (Downs); 192 Courtesy NTS; 193 Courtesy The Central Virginia Training Center of the Virginia Department of

Mental Health, Mental Retardation and Substance Abuse (CVTC); 194 Left – courtesy Roger Pence, Rockingham Construction, Harrisonburg, Va.; right – courtesy Yoder; 195 Top – courtesy John Alvin Taylor; Middle – Courtesy Balch; Bottom – courtesy BH; 196 Courtesy Virginia Department of Agriculture and Consumer Services (VDACS); background – VT dairy barns, courtesy VT; 197 Top – courtesy Downs; Middle – courtesy NTS; Bottom – courtesy Balch; 198 Left – Courtesy Harrison; Right – Courtesy Dale Gardner; 199 Left – courtesy Balch; Right – courtesy DB; 200 Top — courtesy Yoder; Bottom – courtesy CHEB; Milk cap – courtesy DB; 201 Top – courtesy DB; Milk cap – courtesy DB; Bottom – courtesy VT; 202 Courtesy Balch; 203 Top – Courtesy BJH (tape); Courtesy VSDA (ad); 204 Courtesy Nelson Gardner (NG); 205 Courtesy NG; 206 Courtesy NG; 207 Head shot – courtesy NG; Newspaper – courtesy NG; Photo – Charles Chiffonier Photography (Chiffonier); 208 Courtesy Our Lady of the Angels Monastery (OLAM); 209 Background (Chesapeake Creamery) – courtesy Downs; Bottom – courtesy OLAM; 210 Top left – courtesy VT; Top right – Courtesy VCA; Bottom two – Courtesy OLAM; 211 Courtesy OLAM; 212 Top – Shenandoah County Historical Society, Morrison Studio Photography Collection (SCHS)); Bottom – Chiffonier; 213 Courtesy OLAM; 214 All photos – courtesy CVTC; Background letter – courtesy NTS; 215 Courtesy Virginia Department of Corrections, James River Correctional Center-State Farm (JRCC); 217 Courtesy Barbara Clary, Ownby Auction; 217 Courtesy Ownby; 218 Courtesy JRCC; 219 Courtesy VCA; 220 Courtesy VSDA; 221 Top – courtesy NTS; Bottom – courtesy Yoder; 222 Courtesy VCA; 223 Top – Courtesy Downs; Bottom – Courtesy Brenda Knea and Goof; 224-225 Courtesy Stovall.

Dairy Turns to Specialists: 226 Courtesy The Gari Melchers Estate and Memorial Gallery, Mary Washington College, Fredericksburg, Va.; 227 Courtesy Downs; 228 Courtesy the Forrest family; 229 Left and photo – courtesy Debbie Callison; two Jersey books courtesy CHEB; 230 Courtesy J. Carlton Courter III (JCC); 231 Courtesy JCC; 232 Courtesy VT; 233 Top – courtesy Morven; Bottom – courtesy VCA; 234 Courtesy Morven; 235 Courtesy Morven; 236 Courtesy NTS; 237 Courtesy BH 238 Courtesy Joni Pienkowski; 239 Courtesy SCHS; 240 Top – courtesy George Miller; Bottom – courtesy

Index

Symbols

1876 Centennial Exposition 285
4-H 165, 221, 241; 4-H All-Stars 318; 4-H Angus projects 296; 4-H Baby Beef Sale 252; 4-H educational centers 167; 4-H teams 259
7 Half Diamond Ranch 303

A

Aberdeen Angus 292
Abingdon 155, 167, 290, 300, 301
Abingdon Livestock Market 254, 267
Accomack County 5, 16,17, 30, 57
Acker, Isaac 115; John 116
acorns, problems with 107, 108
Acrobat 68460 285
Adams, Bill 152, 153; family 307; Julian 293; Margaret 240, 241;
Adams Plantation 293
Adkisson, William S. 255
Advantage Dairy Group 203
Adventure Farm 303
advertising, dairy 220
African Americans 77, 87, 100
Afton 291, 295
AGA Distinguished Service Award 235
Agee, Jane 241; Robin 241
Agnew, Ella G. 139, 165; Margaret 69
Agri-Industries Center 263
agricultural advances 61, 66, 68; economics 172; education 133, 137
Agricultural Experiment Station 119, 124, 125, 126, 135, 136, 170, 171, 173, 174, 196, 197, 198, 253; director 196
Agricultural Extension Service 125, 137, 165, 173, 174, 176, 193, 238; extension agents 193, 197, 213
Agricultural Hall 137, 138
agricultural journals 65, 66, 68, 71, 74, 75, 102
agricultural manuals 45
agricultural practices, enlightened 45, 46, 47
agricultural production 206; during war 55
agricultural revolution 66, 69, 73
agricultural schools 162
agricultural societies 131
agriculture, diversification 44
agriculture, early 11
agronomy 137, 172
Airfield 4-H Educational Center 167
Ajacan 19
AJCC All-Jersey meeting 230
AJCC Distinguished Service Award 230
Al-Mara Farm, Inc. 204
Albany, N.Y. 284
Albemarle County 56, 62, 67, 75, 78, 102, 177, 208, 211, 253, 285, 287
Albemarle Dairymen's Association 201
Albemarle Feeder Cattle Association 266
Albemarle Livestock Market 267
Alberta, Canada 306
Albion Farm 166, 289
Alderman, E.A., 137
Alderneys 229, 231
Aldhizer, George 200; George R., Jr. 278, 295; Lo 200
Aldie 264, 297
Alexander, Chuck 296
Alexandria 69, 71, 78, 80, 133, 164, 205, 211, 248, 303
ALF Choice Domino 6th 291
Alfaro, Domingo 296
Alger, Robert S. 291, 304
All American Contest, Jersey 230
All-American Angus Breeders' Futurity 296
All-American Get of Sire 326
All-American Junior Field Day 290
All-Jersey Milk 230
Alleghany County 17

Allegheny Glades 70, 71
Allegheny Mountains 8, 69, 100
Allen, B.E. 237; George 275; Hudson 58; Isham 58; Lewis F. 282; Tinsley 83; William Jr. 58;
Allen K. Randolph Cattleman of the Year Award 300
Allison, Charlie 208
Alphin, Horace E. 177; Mrs. Horace E. 177
Alphin-Stuart Multipurpose Livestock Arena 177
Alpin 305
Altavista 295, 297, 303
Alvis, George 239
Alvord, Henry E. 229
Alwood, William B. 135
Amandale Farm 292, 297
Amanett, John 267
Ambler, Carol 305
Amelia County 16, 57, 139, 140, 230, 301
American Aberdeen Angus Association 292
American   Angus   Association 295, 296, 306
American Breeders Service, Inc 203, 237, 305, 315, 320
American Dairy Association 220
American Dairy Association of Virginia 203
American Farm Bureau Federation 181, 182, 183
American Farmer 71
American Farmer Degree 164
American Gelbvieh Association 306
American   Guernsey   Association 227, 235
American Guernsey Cattle Club 234, 235
American Guernsey Foundation 235
American   Hereford   Association 254, 272, 285, 287, 289, 290, 291
American   Hereford   Breeders Association 290
American Highland Cattle Association 307
American International Charolais Association 299
American Jersey Cattle Association 227, 229, 231
American Marketing Services, Inc. International 321, 324
American Milking Shorthorn Breeders' Association 235
American Milking Shorthorn Society 227, 235
American National Cattlemen's Association 262, 264
American Polled Durham Breeders' Association 284
American Polled Hereford Association 287, 291
American Red and White Dairy Cattle Society 242
American Royal Stock Show 286
American Salers Association 303
American Shorthorn Association 63
American Simmental Association 304
American Society of Animal Science 271
American Tarentaise Association 305
American-International Charolais Association 300
American-International Junior Charolais Foundation 300
Amherst County 17, 56, 83, 213, 214, 265, 292, 301, 303, 305,315
Amherst Courthouse 55
Amherst Livestock Market 267
ammunition, collection 57
AMS Genetics, Inc 324
Anchor Mere Mars Grapette, 228
Anderson, Mrs. Charles 294; Robert 296; William 43; William P. 301
Andrew, J.S. 229

Angle, W.M. 234, 315
Angus 155, 158, 169, 200, 269,287, 292, 295, 303, 305, 306, 316; Angus Heritage Foundation 296; bull 294; Junior Angus Association 294
Junior Angus Heifer Show 293;
Angus Journal 294
Angus Spotlight Show and Sale 292
Angus Topics 293, 296
animal health laboratories 141
animal husbandry 137, 173; colonial 38, 43, 45; German 42; nineteenth century 73; Scotch-Irish 42
Animal Science Farm 177
animal science department 155, 137, 171, 172
Annual Appreciation Award 291
Antrim, Blair 311
Anxiety 4 285
Appalachian Mountains 8
Appalachian Highland Cattle Society 307
Appalachian Highlands 190
Appalachian Plateau 4, 14
Appalachian Power Company 168
Appomattox 167, 292, 301, 306
Appomattox County 315
Appomattox Courthouse 78
Arbor Hill 297
Arbor Hill Farm 296
archaeology 15, 20,21, 24, 25, 36, 38
Archbold, John 239
Armour 154
Armour Beef Improvement group 316
Armstrong, William H. 316, 317
Arnold, Benedict 57
ARS Fort Keogh Livestock and Range Research Laboratory 285
artificial breeding associations 313
artificial insemination 205, 207, 242, 313, 319, 320, 326; technicians 320; bull market 321; service, Jerseys 230
Asal, Johnny 297
Ascue, Harvey T. 287, 289, 290
Ashe County, N.C. 149, 151
Asheville, N.C. 315
Ashmund, George 305
Association of Breeders of Thorough Bred Neat Stock 228
Association of Livestock Auction Markets 273
ATA Hall of Fame 305
Atkins, Charles 306; Virginia 306
Atlantic Coast 8
Atlantic Hereford Breeders' Association 285
Atlantic, Mississippi and Ohio RR 115
Atlantic Ocean 10
Atlantic Rural Exposition 166, 179, 180, 252, 255
auction sales 248, 294, 297
auctioneers 288
Augusta Agricultural Society 178
Augusta Artificial Breeders Association 317
Augusta County 9, 16, 37, 40, 43, 52, 53, 58, 59, 62, 68, 71, 74, 78, 82, 83, 84, 86, 87, 92, 100, 108, 109, 111, 129, 134, 139, 146, 162, 164, 165, 193, 215, 230, 282, 283, 292, 294, 326, 328
Augusta County Court 41
Augusta County Creamery 196
Augusta County Fair 178, 242
Augusta County Livestock Judging Team 292
Augusta County Shorthorn Breeders Association 283
Augusta Parish Church 59
Augusta Springs 109
Australia 297
Auvergne, France 302
Axton 302
Aylor, S.C. 273; Silas 262

Ayrshires 63, 191, 200, 227, 228, 316, 326; herd record 228
Ayrshire Breeders' Association 227
Ayrshire Digest 228
Ayrshire Farm, 295

B

Babcock, Stephen Moulton 192
Babcock Test 192, 193, 268
Babesia bigemina 124
baby beef 284; baby beeves show 169, 178
Backer, Henry 58
Backus, Bill 317
Bailey, Harold 262; Jim 262; Lewis, Jr. 68; Lewis, Sr. 68; Neal 195
Baileys Cross Roads 68
Bainbridge, Bruce 264
Baker, George 228; Mrs. George 228
Bakewell, Robert 22, 47, 48, 62
Baldwin Frank C. 229; John Briscoe 178
Baldwin-Augusta Fair 178
Baliles, Gerald L. 206
Baltimore 71, 75, 115, 123, 147, 248
Baltimore & Ohio RR 115, 164
Bandolier Anoka 6th 292
Bang's disease 126, 140, 253; Dr. Bang 127; Bang's Free certification 126; vaccine for 127
Banks, LeRoy 237
Bannister Simmental 304
Baptist, Edward 58, 59
Barbados 30
Barbee, Gabriel 119
Barger, Daniel H. 182
Barger estate 109
Barnes, C.T. "Buster" 154, 259, 293, 321; Kenneth 295; Kenneth III 295
Barns, David 240; Barns family 145; Mary 282; Robert 145; W.O. 282
barrier islands 5, 24, 30
Barringer, Paul 137
Bartenslager, Arthur V., 234, 270, 279, 295, 296
Bartenslager Award 270
Barton, E.M. 237
Baskerville 210, 320
Bass, B. Calvin 234
Bassett 297
Bassler, Allen Jr. 237; Tammy 237
Bates, Harvey 234; Marvin 255; Thomas 282
Bath County 9, 53, 54, 100, 288
Baugher, Leannah 109; Louise 109; Scott 109; Wayne 109
Bavaria 305
Bay Brook Hereford 290
Baylor, Sam 145; family 145; Sam 146, 149, 151
Bayville Farms 233, 234, 235
Bayville Royale Lavinia 235
BCIA Culpeper Test and Sale 299
BCIA Superior Service Award 270
Beacondale Farm 238
Beal, W.E. 270
Beam, Sidney Thomas 190
Beard, J. Owen 193, 218, 239
Beattie, A.C. 126
Beauvais, Rowland R. 234
Beck, C. Nelson 239
Bedford 215
Bedford County 62, 134, 288, 315
Bedford Feeder Calf Producers Association 255
Bedford Livestock Market 267
Beef Cattle Center 177
Beef Cattle Improvement Association 266
beef check-off , Virginia 263, 273, 274, 275
Beef Expo 278, 279, 283
Beef Improvement Federation 271, 272, 287, 306, 326
Beef Promotion and Research Act 275

Beef Quality Assurance (BQA) 276
beef trade 39, 69
"Beeferendum" 275
Bell, David 58; Francis 147, 148; Frank 148; J.R.K. 148; Jim 148; Joseph 58; Wilson B. 173, 174, 293
Bellemonte herd 296
Belling 106
Bellwood, James 188
Belmont 227
Belmont, Mass. 236
Belvidere 129
Bennett, James D. 270, 271, 272, 273, 278, 287, 291, 306; Bennett family 270, 292. 297; Maitland 162; Paul 273, 291
Bennett School 162
Benson, O.H. 165
Bentonville 291
Berkleys Hundred 22
Berry Plains Farm 303
Berryville 203, 249, 292, 320
best management practices 326-328, 332
Beuchler, J.R. 238
Beverley Manor High School 164
Beverley, Robert 119, 134
Beverly, W. Va. 81
Bicentennial Farms 174
Bicentennial of American Independence 174
Big Island 228
Billings, C.K.G. 233
Binghamton, N.Y. 181
biotechnology 123
Bird, Bill 290; Woodrow 208
Birdwood Farm 289
Birmingham Dairy Products Co. 205
Birtcherd Dairy 208
Bismark 304
Bivens, Sam 228
Bivismont Farm 291
blackleg 125-126, 139, 260; kit 126; vaccine 126
Blacksburg 124, 135, 137, 187, 188, 291, 293, 301, 304, 306, 321
Blackwater Lord Amen 235
Blackwater River 83
Blackwater Valley Farm, 235
Blakeley Farm 289
Blalock, Bill 199, 210, 319, 320; Horace Guy 182; W.E. 240; William B. 240
Bland 208
Bland-Giles Hereford Association 290
Blandfield 134
Blandy, Graham F. 285
Blanton, R.E.B. 251, 255; T.L. 188; Wyndham B., Jr. 240, 241, 251
Blennerhassett, Harman 69–71, 70
Bloch, Rob 305
blood type records 307
blooded stock 65
Blose, Bill 319, 320
Blue Grass 180
Blue Ridge AI Association 315
Blue Ridge Artificial Breeding Association 315
Blue Ridge Embryos 321
Blue Ridge Mountains 4, 6, 8, 9, 10, 40, 100, 108, 109, 111, 208
bluegrass 145, 149, 151, 152, 157
Bluemont 211
Board of Agriculture and Immigration 139
Boatwright, Lee 255
Bogert, W.B. 287
Boggs, Cindy 276
Bolze, Ronald P., Jr. 283
"Bonaventura" 147
Bonneville Farm 304
Boocock, Murray 285
Boones Mill 236, 283, 297
Boophilus 124
Booth, R.L. 255
Borst, Peter 87
Boston 237
Botetourt County 9, 41, 52, 56, 262, 315
bottles, milk 194, 205, 206; bottle-making machine 206

BOV Import, 302
Bovard, Ken 268
bovine reproductive systems 311
Bovine Spongiform Encephalopathy 144, 324
Bowen, C.H. 202; Joanne 38, 39; Meek 290; Rees, 144; Rees V 150; Rees VI 150, 154; Rees VII 144, 154; Rees VIII 144
Bowers, Grayson 240
Bowman, A.M. 229; A.M. Jr. 229; D.C. 236; F.E 239; Henry 205; J. Harlan 315; Raymond 283
Boyce 166
Boyd, Bob 303; Mossom 290; Boyd, Robert (Bob) Jr. 290, 303
Boykins 78
Boys' Corn Club 139
Bozeman, Mont. 304
Braddock, Edward 52
brands 46, 102, 106; on horns 288
Brandy Rock Farm 292, 293
Brandy Station 293
Braunvieh 237
Breadbasket of the Confederacy 87, 101
Bready, George R. 202
Breeders Gazette 258
breeds, associations 282; development of 22, 23, 47, 63; specialization 190
Breezy Hill Farm 237
Brethren 90
Bridgewater 87, 101, 108, 119, 230, 241, 295
Bridgewater Airpark 320
Briery Branchers 108
Brightwood 237
Brindles, Norman 231
Brinkley, Parke C. 258, 315
Bristol 169, 230, 287, 291
Bristow, J.L. 202
British breeds 287, 299
British Longhorn 63
Broad Run 290
Broadview Farms 248, 292
Broadway 115, 190, 291, 297, 304
Brockman, J.E. 303
Brockman, Wanda 303; WIlliam 303
Brock's Gap 80
Brodnax 320
Brookfield Elevation Pretty 200
Brooks, William 164
Brower, Dave E. Jr. 166, 268, 269, 289
Brown, Carl 221; E.M. 237; Fred 230; G.I. 290; J. Glenn 289; J. Rhodes 255; R.E., 229;
Brown Swiss 236, 316; grand champion 237; herd book 236
Brown Swiss Breeders Association 236
Brown Swiss Cattle Breeders' Association 227
Browning, Earl 266
Brownsburg 229
Brubaker, Daniel W. 234, 235, 318; E. Cline 234, 235, 318; Emory 318; family 318; Galen B. 318; Janie B. 318; Ken 295; Lisa 235; R. Emory 318; Riley E. 318
Brumback, Jim 276; L.O. 164
Bryant, J.B. 287; J.Paul 287
Buchanan 56, 295
Buchanan, A.F. 292
Buchanan County 16, 146
Buchanan, Raymond 259, 276
Buckingham 253
Buckson, Stephen 85
Buena Vista 296
Buhrman, A.W. 251, 253, 255
bulls, associations 315; evaluation center 306; sales 270, 294, 295; test program 260, 268, 299; test sales 270; test station 271, 272, 287; to improve herds 194
Bull Cove 17
Bull Run Creek 16
Bulletin 135, 136
Bullpasture Mountain 17
Bullpasture River 100
Bulls Dock 17
Bulls, Jack 276

Bulls Landing 17
Bundoran Farm 287, 291
Bunker Hill Farm 304
Bureau of Animal Industry 124, 125, 126, 140
Bureau of Plant Industry 181
Burke's Garden 142, 145, 146, 147, 149, 152, 253
Burketown 286
Burkeville 139, 188, 233, 238
Burner, Buddy 304; Jerry 304, 305
Burning Springs 81
Burning, the 86, 87, 88
Burr, Aaron 71; J.H. 273
Burris, Bob 262
Burroughs, Charles F. 233
Burruss, Bill 289; W.H. 285
Burruss Land and Cattle 289
Burtner, Scott 273, 304
Burton family 204; Sirene 82
Burwell, Carter 44; Nathaniel 57; Nathaniel II 44
Bushy Park Farm 290, 291
butchering 39, 44, 70; techniques 38
Butler Brothers 251
Butler, Lee D. 295, 296
butter, production 73, 129, 188, 189, 196; markets 116; print 129; renovated 196; substitutes 201; trade 70, 73, 78
butterfat 192, 211, 215
Byer, Wallace 303
Byerly, T.C. 268
Byers, Ashby C. 286; family 286; Ivan W. 234; Sam Jr. 286
Byers Brothers 282, 286
Byrd, P.E. 255; William II 36, 37, 38

C

C & J Farm 290
C Rose Vega Certosa Viola 221
C. Phipps & Son 287
Caldwell, Dave 270
Callendar, Teresa Myers 241, 325
calf parties 168
Calfpasture River 100
Calfpen Bay 17
Calico Farm 305
Callison, Deborah 230
Calverton 204
Camargue 23
Camden, Bernard 267; Senator J.N. 287
Cameron Brothers 287
Cameron, Mrs. William 238
Camm, John 266; John Jr. 255
Camp Union 53
Campbell Arena 177
Campbell, Betty 305; H.M (Dick) 250; Mark 305
Campbell County 78, 315
Canada 292, 302, 305
Cannaday, James 58
canning clubs 165
Canning G. David 292, 296; George 294
Canterbury Farm 248, 292
Cape Charles 5
capital crimes 21
carcass evaluation 271
Cardwell, Anne 276; W.M. 267
Careysbrook Farm 291
Carnation Genetics 305
Carnation Milk Company 314
Carolina Milk Producers 208
Carolina Virginia Milk Producers 203
Caroline County 56, 67, 78, 181
Carpenter, Bill 228
Carr, George T. 239; Maria 100
Carter, Dale 157; family 31; Fred 296; J. Prescott 296; James 296; Landon 38, 44, 45, 55; Mary Taylor 157; R.C. "Bob" 253, 265, 268, 293; Robert 38, 42, 44, 249;
Carter's Grove 39, 44, 57
carts 38, 44, 57, 71, 72, 87, 132
Carwile, J.H. 237
Cary, Archibald 62
Cash, Doris 111; family 111; Ralph 111; W.A. 287

Cassell, Bennet 177
Castle Hill Farm 291
Castlewood 157
Catawba 293
Cather, John C. 283
Catlett 203, 320
cattle camps 107
cattle cars 114, 115, 117
cattle dealers 41
cattle, as gifts 32; barriers 74; breeding organizations 194; Celtic 292; collection of 55, 56; descriptions of 104; digestive systems 127; diseases 132, 139, 153, 313; early characteristics 22; early twentieth century descriptions 106;export trade 148, 149, 150, 152, 178; first 19, 20, 21, 38, 52, 53; hiding 87; humor 72; importation 21, 116; laws 131; military uses 77; moving 38; names 32, 63, 64, 66–68; plague 144; prices 103, 154; seventeenth-century descriptions 33; size of 28; trade 21, 30, 39, 42; treatment of 117; uses of 16, 49, 53, 62, 115; working 279
cattle drives 28, 37, 40, 41, 43, 52, 53, 56, 58, 69–71,75, 78, 84, 99, 100, 101, 102, 103, 104, 107, 108, 109, 110, 111, 116; damage from 100, 101, 102; in towns 121; military 90, 91; Revolutionary War 56; Sabbath problems 100; Trans-Allegheny 70
cattle guards 67
cattle placenames 16, 54, 71
cattle producers, 52, 102; colonial 29, 30, 35, 40, 43
cattle raids, military 80, 81, 82, 83, 84, 85, 86
Cattleman of the Year Awards 261, 264
Cattleman's Capitol Bull Sale 288
Cattlemen's Beef Promotion and Research Board 275
Cedar Bluff 289, 295
Cedar Creek Ranch 303
Cedar Falls 108
census, agriculture 92
census, cattle 22, 28, 40, 43, 74, 78, 93, 97, 103, 134, 146, 194, 211, 261, 264, 265
Central Virginia Angus Association 297
Century Farms 174
Certificate of Honor, Guernsey 235
Chaffee, G.R. 249
Chambers, Jim 275
Chandler, Paul 175
Chappell, Jerry 273
Char Anne Ranches 303
Charles City County 37
Charles, Count de Bouille 298
Charles Town, W. Va. 289
Charlotte County 170, 237, 267
Charlotte Court House 289
Charlotte, N.C. 115
Charlottesville 78, 117, 205, 228, 239, 289, 290, 291, 293, 294, 295, 300, 302, 304
Charolais 68, 165, 262, 263, 270, 279, 298, 300, 302, 303, 305; Charolais-Angus cross 261; Charolais-Hereford cross calves 299
Charolais Foundation Memorial Scholarships 300; Mr. Charolais Promotion Award 300
Charolais Hall of Fame 299
Charolle, France 298
Charolle, France 298
Chase City 228
Chase, J.F. Jr. 234
Chatham 301
cheese, factories 74, 189, 190, 196; high acid process 196; hooping 210; lab 210; making 189–190, 209, 211, 212; marketing 190;
Chenery, Winthrop 237
Cherokee Nation 75
Cherry Lane Farm 301
Chesapeake & Ohio RR 114, 115, 117
Chesapeake Bay 3, 5, 10, 24, 69, 169, 327, 332

Chesterfield County 57, 62, 165
Chestnut Farms Dairy 195
Chew family 67; Roger 67
CHF Cotton Candy 305
Chic-a-Wil farm 237
Chicago 292
Chicago International Livestock Show 166
Chichester, John H. 177; R.H.L. 233, 234; Richard 318
Chichley, Henry 32
Chief Cornstalk 53
Child, Douglas 240 319, 320
Childress, Floyd III 275
Chilhowie 126, 154, 285, 294, 295, 296
Chilton, Bob 262
Chisholm, Mary J. 303
cholera 123
Christian, William 53
Christmas Duke 65, 68
Chuckatuck 315
Church of England 30
Church of the Brethren Volunteer Service 123
Church Road 305
Churchville 283
churning 129
Civil War 77, 78–79, 79–80, 80–81, 85, 86, 96, 131, 139, 145, 146, 150, 178
claims, Civil War 88, 89, 90; Revolutionary 57, 58, 59
Clapp, Charles E. 285
Clark, A. Leland 289; C.C. 154; Henry M. 236; Mark 243; Ruth 273; Tom 270, 273, 304
Clark ranch 180
Clarke County 84, 101, 103, 166, 285, 292
Clarkson, J. Aubrey 239
Clarksville, Texas 299
Clary, Barbara 251
Clay Center USDA Research Center 306
Clay, Henry 284
Clayton, John 28
Clearbrook 229, 230
Cleaveland Dairy Farm, 229
Clemons, Josh 221; Julie 221; Sarah 221
Clemson 306
Cleveland, Grover 135
Click, James E. 209
Click's Hacking 106
Clifton 177
Clifton Farm 157, 159, 175
Clifton Forge 116, 117, 301
Clifton Station 238
Clinch Mountain Wildlife Management Area 159
Clinch River 144, 157, 175
Cline, S.L. 205
cloning 325
Clore, J. Carlton 295, 297
Clover Hill Farm 229
Clover, W.L. 269
Cloverdale Farm 303
Clowdis, Annette F. 301; Robert G. 301
co-mingled sales 259
Coalter, Frances Bland 73
coastal islands 329
Coastal Plain 2, 3, 5, 7
coastline 4
Cobb, Carol 243; Lester "Buck" 243
Cobbler Mountain Farms 179, 289
Cochrane, J. Harwood 278
Cocke, Philip St. George 79
Coffey, R.L. 169
Coiner, H.E. 283; J. C. 292
Cole, Dean 154; Digges 58; William 301
Coleman, Paul M. 296
Colonial Farms 301
Colonial Williamsburg 38, 44
Columbia 289, 291
Columbus, Christopher 19, 20
Combs, Charles H. 291
Commercial Producer Award 270, 326
commissaries 78, 79
Commissioner of Agriculture (and Consumer Services) 138, 140, 177, 258, 259, 327

compensation for property losses 79, 89
competition, with Midwest 119
Compton family 204
Confederacy 77
Confederate army 150
confiscation of property 79, 82, 84, 85, 86, 90, 91
conformation evaluation 271
Congressional District Agricultural Schools 162
Connelly, R.G. 198, 228, 239
Connors, Philip 236
Connoway, Eltonhead 32
Conquerant 301
Conrad, Arthur 168
Conservation Forestry Program 157, 159
conservation practices 326
consignment sale booklets 229
contagious bovine pleuropneumonia 144
Continental breeds 305
Continental Congress 54
Cook, James 239; Jennifer 239
Cool Lawn Farm 239
cooling milk 199, 201
Coon Rapids, Iowa 306
Cooper, Charles R. 269; Peter 114
Cooperative Extension Service 174, 196
cooperative herd testing 192–194, 205
cooperative marketing 259
Cooperative Milk Producers Association 210
Cooperative State Research Service 176
cooperatives 119
Copenhaver, Rufus 255, 260, 262
Corbin, Charlie (Buck) 110
Corker, Fenton 276
corn clubs 165
corn production 101
Corning, Erastus 284
Coronado 20
Corotoman 44
Corps of Cadets 174
Cotnareanu, Leon 296
Courter, J. Carlton III 140, 177, 327; 230, 233
Cove, The 144, 149, 150, 151, 154
Cover, W.L. 268
Covington 290, 303
cow barn 214
Cow Belles 263
cow bells 100, 102, 106
Cow Country Commercial Sales 293
cow family breeding 200
Cow Gut Flat 17
Cow Island 17
Cow Swamp 17
cow-calf feeder operation 158, 215
Cowan's Station 116
Cowbone Ridge 17
Cowcamp 17
cowkeeper 20
Cowpasture River 9, 100
Cowpen Neck 17
cowpenning 28, 29, 47, 61, 62, 313
Coyner, Norm 278
Crabill, C.H. 239; Harvey 241
Cragle, Ray 175, 220
Craig, Carl Jr. 297; Sprue 305
Craig County 146
Craiglands Farm 296
Craigsville 283
Crane, W.C. 295
Craun, E.B. 164, 169; Harold W. 239, 240, 241; Lurty 164; Patty Roudabush 241; Paul 241, W.H. 239
cream separator 194
creameries 196
Crenshaw, Jerry 296; the Misses 287
Crestline Hereford Farm 289
Creswell Farm 296
Crews, Brent 301
Crews Charolais Farm 301
Crimora-Dooms area 109
Crockett 230
Crockett, Jack 290; Rush 290
Croghan, George 52

crop rotation system 198
Crosby, Dayton 266
Cross Keys, Battle of 80
crossbreeding 158
Crow Harris Farm 250, 295
Crow, Kim Kube 290; William 41
Crowgey, Joe 319, 320; John Jr. 234; L.J. 239; Leonard W. 240
Crozet 208, 290, 291
Cruickshank, Amos 282
Culbertson, James 58
Culpeper 116, 237, 239, 260, 295, 297, 302, 315, 316, 320
Culpeper Agricultural Enterprises 267, 269
Culpeper Bull Test Station 272
Culpeper County 56, 193, 202, 248, 292, 293, 314
Culpeper Feeder Calf Sale 255
Cumberland County 57, 85
Cundiff, Larry 306
Cunningham, Griselda 283; Hargrave 260, 289, 290; J.H. 255
Curles Neck Farm 239, 287
Curry, Charles 297
Curtice, Cooper 124, 125
Curtis, J.W. 79; T.T. (Terry) 183, 229, 230
Curtiss Breeding Service 315
Custer, George Armstrong 87
Custis, John 30
Cutting, George 292

D

Dabneys 290
Dairy and Food Division 140, 196
dairy animals 190; barns 196, 197, 198, 214; equipment 40, 215; facilities 197, (Virginia Tech) 199; husbandry 137, 172; industry, beginnings 187, 198; inspection 140; judging 165, 241; plants 206; production 211; regulations 196; tape measure 203
Dairy Cattle Center 177
Dairy Council of Greater Metropolitan Washington, 203
Dairy Extension Service 214
Dairy Farmers of America, Inc. 209
dairy herd improvement tests 196
Dairy, Holstein Jeopardy 221
Dairy Industry Award 241
Dairy Management, Inc. 220
Dairy Month 195, 220, 235
Dairy Quiz Bowl 221
Dairy Show 169
dairying, colonial 26, 39, 40, 43, 44, 47; nineteenth century 73; early twentieth century 129; New Republic 70, 73; in the South 195
Dairylou Farm 236
Dairymen, Inc. 209
Dale, Elizabeth 29; Thomas 20, 29
Daleville 214, 263, 293, 295, 297
Dalton, A. Douglas 297; A. Douglas, Jr. 295;
Dalton, Lester 254, 255, 265, 266, 267
Daltons on the Sycamore 297
Daniel, R.E. Jr. 228
Danish Red 24
Danville 78, 169
Darnell, Haywood 267
Daugherty, Graham 292; W.H. (Bill) 171; William 174
Davidson, W.A. 269
Davis, Hank 268; Jefferson 81; John B. 233; Roy B. Jr. 182; T.B. 285; T.J. 188; Westmoreland 108, 126, 188, 191, 194, 198, 201, 233, 234
Dawson, D.M. 236
Dayton 68, 293
de St. Méry, Moreau 70
dean of agriculture 171
deBarros, Patrick 302
deBary, Anton 123
DeBusk, Claude 230
Deer Creek Farm 305
Deer Track Farm 290
Deerwood Farm 297
Deerwoodie Farm 297

DeHart, P.H. (Pat) 173, 174
Delano, Bob 274; Robert B. 183
Delaplane 289
DeLaval, Carl 194
Delaval Dairy Extension Award 199
DeLaval Milker 194
Delaware and Lackawanna Railroad 181
Dellinger, Forrest 297
Delmarva Peninsula 5
deMoustier, Adrien 302
Denmark 313
Denney, Roger P. 228
Denver 302, 307
Denver Stock Show 303
Department Reorganization Act (1994) 176
Depression, Great 164, 204, 218, 261, 267, 286
Deputy, Bob 297
Derrick, B.B. 202
destruction, military 77, 85, 86, 87, 90, 91
Detroit 69
Devon cattle 24, 63, 145, 227
Dewlapping 107
DHIA herd 215
Diamond Grove Chip 320
Diamond T. Joy Farm 203
Diamond "W" Farm 290
diBerry, Mrs. Mary Bryant 299
Dice, Harold Henderson 289
Dice Stock Farm 289
Dick, Margie Ann 240, 241
Dickenson County 16
Dickenson, H.H. "Hop" 289; Henry H., Jr. 269; W.L. 241; R. DuVal 234
diet, colonial 35, 37, 38, 40; colonists' needs 20; military 51, 79; New Republic 70; Revolutionary War 55; slaves 36, 38, 44, 189
Dietrick Hall 173
Dietrick, L.B. (Deet) 171, 253
Dilger, Hubert 238
Dillard, David Hugh 267; J.B. 248; James B. 292;
Dillion, Joe 241
Dillwyn 291
Dinner Bell Packing Company 277
Dinwiddie County 57, 165, 304
Dinwiddie Farm 285
Dinwiddie, Robert 51
disease 85; livestock 123; resistance to 123; result of Civil War 123
dispersal auctions 215, 216, 217
Distinguished Breeder Award 231
Distinguished Junior Member 242
Distinguished Service Award 318
diZerega, Mary Howe 278, 299. 301
Dodd, B.F. 267
Dogwood Farms 302
Domaine de Pompadour, France 302
domestication 23
Dominy, Floyd 270, 273
Douglas, Clayton 228; Patricia K. 295
Dovel, Justin 229
Downs, Janet Baugher 109
Doyle & Doyle Farm 305
Doyle, Emmet 255; Joey 305
draft animals 26, 40, 46, 70, 77, 84, 221
Draper 304
Drewry, Aubrey 241; John 39; L.A. 239
dried beef 51
Drinkard, A.W. Jr. 171
Driver, Fred 204, 205
drought 106, 118, 204, 222
drovers 71, 79, 100, 101, 104, 105, 109, 116, 117; routes 56, 110
Drover's Journal 305
Drumheller, Charles 276
Dry River 108
Dryden 289
dual-purpose cattle 227, 305
Dublin 78, 267, 270, 283
Dublin Feeder Cattle Association 266
Dublin Stockyard 255
Duckworth, P.C. 269
Dudley, C. Wayne 319
Duffell, James Mark 295, 296
Dugspur 305

Dulles International Airport 213
Duncan, Forest 286; Forest T. 289, 291
Dunford, Anne 40
Dunkellan, Lord 37
Dunmore's War 51–55
Dunn, Coleman 249
Dunrovin Farm 290, 291
Dunvegan Herd 236
duPont, Victor M. 264, 278
Durand of Dauphiné 29
Dutch-Friesian Association 238
dwarfism 284
Dwyer family 106; Jake 106, 110; Jeff 110
Dyer, J.M. 253; Renee 307

E

Eagle Bridge, N.Y. 129
Eakle, Mr. 129
ear crops 102, 107, 108
ear tags 108, 260
Earleysville 303
Early Dawn Cooperative Dairy 201, 317
Early Dawn Dairy Farm 239
Early, Jubal 83
East, J.W. 228
Eastern Breeder 252, 253, 254
Eastern Dairy Products Co. 205
Eastern National Livestock Exposition 166
Eastern Shore 3, 5, 17, 24, 29, 30, 35, 57, 78, 233
Eastern State Hospital 215
Eastview Farm 239
Eaton, Brent 221, 241
economic recovery 114
Edgehill Farm 292, 296
Edgerton, George 240
editorial board 147
Edom 190
Edwards, Rufus 267
Effingham Plantation Salers 303
Eggleston, Joseph D. 137, 139, 162, 170
Eileenmere's Model T.H.(Model T) 68, 294
Eisenhower, Dwight D. 129, 293; Mamie 293
Eisenhower Farms 293
elective breeding 63
electricity 195
Elevation 200, 318, 324
Elie, Robert 107
Elizabeth City County 39, 69
Elk Creek 189
Elk Garden 145, 150, 176, 182, 293
Elk Garden Creek 174
Elk Garden Farm Products Company 158
Elk Hill Farm 296
Elks National Home 215
Eller, A.L. (Ike) 107, 269, 272, 279, 293, 304, 306, 317; Ed 255; J. Burton 288; J.C. 239
Elliott, Carter 228; Carter Jr. 239
Ellis, R.S. 253; R.S. IV 274
Elswick, John Henry (Jack) 358
Elway 287
Ely, Garland V. 255
embryos, custom recipients 325; export 321; flushes 321, 324; fresh 321, 323; frozen 321, 323; importation 322; insurance 324; recovery 322; shipment 323; storage 323; transfer 207, 313, 320; transplant 321-322
Emerson, Nancy 86
Emmadine Farm 232
Emory and Henry College 150
Emporia 305
Emporia, Kansas 285
Emtran 322
Endless Caverns 237
Engel, R.W. (Charlie) 172
Engh, Jerry 303
England 144, 148, 153, 154, 157, 177, 290, 324; dispute with 52; plantation culture 11; traditions 28
Entsminger, Harold Jr. 295
environmental issues 327
Environmental Protection Agency 183

Environmental Stewardship Award 326; Virginia Environmental Stewardship Award 332
Enyaw Farm 235
Epperly, Albert 276, 296; Susan 276
Epponian 3rd 248
Epponian 8th of Rosemere 292
Ernie-Brooke Farm 305
Esmont 290, 291
Essex County 134
Essex County Farmers Education and Cooperative Uni 119
Estes, John C. 255
Estouteville Farm 296
estray books 43, 105, 108
Etgen, William 240
Eureka 189
Europe 320
European Union 321
Eustace, J.W. (Wag) 203, 240; Jim 319, 320; Jimmie N. 240; Matthew 241
Evergreen 228
Eversole, Dan 301
export program 293
export sheep market 152
extended shelf life 205
Eyestone, Will 325

F

Faber 289
Fain, John R. 136
Fairfax County 68, 119, 202, 211, 229,238
Fairfax, Lord 31, 35
Fairfield Farm 289
Fairfield View Farm 204
fairs 131, 133, 166, 178, 282, 291, 304, 305; premiums 66
Fairy Queen 236
Fall Line 6, 7, 56
Falling Springs Farm 303
Falmouth 233
Fannon, Bill 305; Morris 166, 249, 252, 255, 260, 287; Morris Fraley 289
Fariss, Charles 270, 273
Farm Bureau 181, 260; agricultural marketing association 183; Farm Bureau Associated Women 182; Farm Bureau Insurance Company 183; Farm Bureau Young Farmer Committees 183
farm life, during war 78, 83, 84; statistics 139
Farmer's Alliance 135
Farmers' Assembly 119
Farmers Cooperative Demonstration Work 137, 139
Farmers Livestock Exchange 267
Farmville 188, 228, 241, 297
Farnley Farm 283
Farrar, F. Southall 139
fat cattle 144, 146, 151, 153; export business 115; fat cattle show 252; trade 151
Faulkner, Kay 297; T.G. 297
Fauquier County 16, 56, 66, 74, 77, 79, 91, 134, 145, 146, 149, 172, 179, 189, 189, 202, 211, 222, 236, 237, 239, 266, 286, 289, 292
Fauquier Farm 290
Fauquier Livestock Exchange 266, 267
Fauquier-Prince William 4-H Dairy Club 221
FBG II Farms 301
Feagans, Charles B., Jr. 292; Charles B., Sr. 292
Federal Board of Vocational Education 164
feed, animal 69; cattle 22, 28, 31, 44, 68, 70, 73, 102, 104, 105, 111, 116, 120, 127, 192, 197, 198, 199; co-ops 199
feeder calves 254; Feeder Calf Sales Association 255; graded sales 254, 258, 260, 261, 265; grading 259; marketing 265
Feeder cattle 151, 153, 256, 261; sales 263
Feeder Yearling Association 266
Felty, Jesse 154
fencing 20, 24, 27, 42, 43, 61, 96
Fenton Farm 292

Ferguson, J. Gray 297
Ferneyhough, J.G. 188
Ferrum 239, 297
fertilizer companies 119
Feymer, Frank 297
FFA 164, 165
field days 290; Guernsey 234; Holstein 239, 241; on Wheels 293
Fields, Ralph Sr. 240
Figgins, Vernon 304
financial crisis 119
Fincastle County 52
fiinchback 25
Fisher, Framk M. 301; Otis L. 283
Fishersville 100, 164, 228, 294, 295
Fishpaw, Harvey 283
Fishwaters, Mr. 80
Fitzhugh, P.T., Jr. 260
Fitzpatrick, W.W. 234
Five County Farmville Fair 291
Fleckvieh 304
Fleets Bay 31
Fleming, W. Clark Jr. 234; W. Clark Jr. 235; William 52, 53
Fletcher, James N., Jr. 266; S.W. 136, 137; Thomas 242
Flint Run Farms 291
Flook, David 103
Flora, Roy 315, 321
Florida 19
Floyd 204
Floyd County 315
Foley, Sarah 241
food supply, military 51, 52, 53, 54, 55, 56, 57, 78, 79, 80, 85; prisoners of war 58
foodways, at cattle camps 107; colonial 35, 37, 38, 40; mutton broth 108
foot and mouth disease 144, 237, 252, 298; research project 158
Forage research 171
Forbes, Waldo 297
Ford, Gerald 239, 275, 326, 327
Foremost Dairies 230
Foremost Farms USA 233
Forest 289, 291, 292, 295, 296, 297
Forest Lake Farm 235
Forrest, Douglas 228; Gary 229; Julie 228
Forrest Mars Ranch 304
Forrester, Grafton 266
forts: Fort Dinwiddie 52; Fort Dunmore (Pittsburgh) 53; Fort Frederick 51; Fort George 54; Fort Prince George 51; Fort James 21; Fort Randolph 55; Fort Sumter 132
Fort Valley 297
Foster, Bob 154
Foster Falls test station 270
Foster, Sherman 154
Founding Fathers Award 241
Fox, Raymond 300; W.S. 292
Foxlease Farm 239, 240, 327
France 229, 231, 323
Frank Walker family 239
Franklin County 196, 314, 315, 318
Franklin County Artificial Breeding Association 315, 318
Franklin County Guernsey Bull Association 318
Frazier, Charles 204; J.T., Jr. 285
Frederick County 40, 230, 288
Frederick, Md. 203
Fredericksburg 41, 169, 227, 229, 233, 289, 294, 297, 320
Fredericksburg Agricultural Society 66
Fredericksburg Feeder Calf Association 266
Fredericksburg Feeder Calf Sale 255
Fredericksburg Livestock Market 266
free range system 24, 27, 28, 29, 30, 42, 96, 102, 111
Free Union 283
Freeman, A.W. 188; Caswell 103
Fremont, Gen. 80
French and Indian War 51, 52, 54, 55
French Creek, W. Va. 82
French Veterinary Service 323
French, William 203

Frissell, H.B. 137
Front Royal 167, 238
Front Royal beef cattle research station 268, 269
Front Royal Livestock Market 266
Fugate, Thomas 253
Fulk, Jay 296
Fullerton, William 238
Funkhouser, C.C. 255, 273
fur trade 70
Furr, M.B. 149; Stanley 299
Future Farmers of Virginia 162

G

Gage, John C. 242
Gagnon, Ross 327
Galax 289, 314
Galax Feeder Cattle Sales 266
Galax Livestock Market 267
Gall, John C. 295, 297
Gallaher, Charles 79; Clinton 79; William 83; William B. 79
Gammon, Tom 250; Warren 290
Garber, Maynard 123
Gardner, Dale A. 177; Gerald 267; Herschel A. 240; Hershel 240; Nelson 195, 205, 206, 207, 240, 241, 314, 318, 320
Garner, A.W. 290
Garnett, S.H. 292
Garst operation 306
Gartin, Earl F. 248, 249
Gates, Thomas 20; William B. 229
Gatewood, E.C. 286
Gay family 71
Gayle, Tommy 300
Geddy, William, Jr. 58
Gelbvieh 158, 305, 306; Gelbvieh-Angus hybrids 306
genetic research 285, 311, 325, 332; markers 332
Gent, F.B. II 301; Fred 270; Fred Bailey 287
geology 3
George H. Meyer 277
George H. Meyer Sons 250
George, King 291
Gerken, John 166
germ theory 123, 124
Germany 305
Giles County 267
Gillespie, Al 154; Bill 153; Jeff Sr. 358; Joseph S., Sr. 148; Nancy 144; Thomas 145; William M. 152
Gilley, Jessie 297
Gilliam, Frank 267; G.D. 275, 278
Gilmer, A.K. III 254, 267, 273; Aaron Kemper Jr. 267; Turner A., Jr. 273
Ginger Hill Farm 297
Gitchell, Byers H. 181
Givens, H.C. 140; James K. 289; Jim 290
Glade Spring 208, 292 Southwest Research Station 135
Glaettli, A.R. 202
Glasgow 10, 228
Glasse, Hannah 37
Glen Allen 297
Glencairne Farm 233
Glenmary Farm 270, 272
Gloryland Holsteins 242
Gloucester County 17, 24, 57, 290
Gloucester Point 78
Glover, Thomas 27
Goff, Richard 302
Golden Gallon of Milk 221
Golden Guernsey Dairy Cooperative 233
Golden Guernsey Milk 234
Goldwasser, Mike 270
Gondwanaland 3
Goochland County 57, 215, 297
Good, Franklin 243; G.M. 228; Paul 294
Goode, J.E. 241
Goodlatte, Robert 177
Goods Mill 109
Goof the Cow 223
Gookin, Daniel 21, 22
Goolsby Sod 106
Gordon, C.H. 234

Gordonsville 238, 248, 292, 297
Got Milk? 220
Gothard, Mike 295
Gouda cheeses 208
Gough, Henry Dorsey 282
government regulations 209
grading beef 258; lamb 259
Grading Service 265
Graf, G.C. 172
Graham, Albert B. 165; Joe 267, 268, 286; Ray 292, 296
grain cultivation 28, 39, 62, 101, 102
Grand Rapids, Minn. 313
Grandis, Harry 297
Grandview Farm 301
grange movement 119, 134
Granite Hill Farm 291
Grant, Ulysses 78, 91; W.E. 238
Graves and Brothers 256
Graves, Elvin 256; F.M. 256; Francis 26, 33; R.S. (Bob) 256, 277
Gray, Lewis Cecil 19, 20
Grayson County 149
grazing 10, 42, 43, 52, 69, 70, 84, 100, 102, 104, 105, 108, 110, 115, 116; fees 105; lands 106, 110, 111, 116; West Virginia 108
Great Wagon Road 11, 40
Green Acres Angus Farm 270
Green, George 69
Green Hill Farms 296
Greenbank Farm 228
Greenberry Manor Farm 290
Greenbrier County 82, 99
Greenbrier Valley 52
Greene, Nathanael 56
Greenlaw, Hunter R. 166, 266, 269, 289
Greenwood 236
Gregg, H.L. 202
Greiner, Scott 270
Gretna 228
Griffith, Andrew Vincent 195; C.E. 228; F.D. 228; Mike 270
Grigsby, E.C. 255
Grinde, Mrs.,Paul 294; Paul 294, 295
Groome, H.C. 228
Groseclose, Henry C. 162
Grottoes 237, 242
Grove, C. Whitney 292, 293, 295; Carl 236; Carroll 297; Conrad 292; Crystal 326; family 326, 328; John 326; Mark 326
Grove Church Farm 332
Guernsey 65, 191, 196, 207, 213, 231, 232, 314, 316; bull 230; clubs 233; Island of 231, 233; national convention sale 235; national show 235; sales 233
Guest, Henry J. 237; Mrs. E.P. 229

H

ha-ha 67
Haberland, E. Theo 240, 241
Hackman, James 237; William M. 237
Haga, Herman 234
Hagenston, Ryan 327
Hahn, Thomas Marshall Jr. 172, 293, 306
Haldeman, J.S. 239
Haley, Ida Blanche 91
Halifax County 165, 182
Hall, G.W. 84; John 329; Leness 305
Hall of Fame, Jersey 230
Halstead, James 54
Ham Farm 235
Hamilton 296
Hamilton, Betty Jo 276; Luther 267; Ralph 164
Hamitic, Longhorn 23; Shorthorn 23
Hampshire sheep 151, 152
Hampton 69
Hampton Normal and Agricultural Institute 133, 137, 165, 181
Hampton Roads 57, 205
Hanover County 16, 38, 56,
Hardesty, Daniel 241, 242; David 177, 241, 242; Debbie 242; J.D (Jack) 203, 240, 329, 320; Johnny 241, 242; Thomas F. 250
Harding, V.B. 202
Hardy, A.K. 241

Harmony Farm 305
Harmony Grove 295
Harmony Grove Farm 297
Harpers Ferry 5, 9
Harpers Weekly 100
Harris, Richard 319, 320
Harrison & Gatewood 286
Harrison, Albertis 235; Fairfax 286; Frank 205; G. Ray 236; Holden 236; William B. Dr. 174; William H. (Bill) 168, 177, 200, 213, 240, 241, 242, 319, 320
Harrisonburg 11, 80, 100, 107, 141, 169, 200, 204, 262, 263, 279, 283, 286, 291, 295, 297
Harvey, John 24, 32
Harvue Farms 177, 203
Hasler, John 322
Hass, Gelbvieh bull 305
Hassler, John 320
Hatch Act 135
Hatch, William Henry 135
Haute Vienne, France 301
Hawkins, Harold 270; John 55
Hawksbill Creek 110
Haxall, A.W. 188
Hayes, Rutherford B. 178
Haymarket 145
Hazlegrove, Juanita 242
Heartley, Edward L. 278
Heatwole, John D. 108; John V. 108; Tom 108
Heifer Project 123
Heilman, Nancy 324; Robert D. 321, 322, 323, 324
Heizer, James 235; Keith 290; R.G. 317; Robert 237; William 283
hemmorhagic septicemia 139
Henrico 238
Henrico Agricultural and Horticultural Society 66
Henry, King 59
Henry, Patrick 157
herd books 63, 228, 282, 292, 301, 307
Herd Bull Premier 304
Hereford cattle 24, 65, 106, 107, 151, 152, 153, 155, 158, 173, 182, 269, 284, 285, 287, 292, 301; associations 285, 290, 306; Junior Hereford Association 290
Hereford Journal 285
Herndon 195, 233, 236
Herndon, George 56
Heron, Julian E. 296
Herring, George 259; Thomas G. 204
Hertzler, Allen 237
Hess Farms 291
Hess, Nancy 263; Nelson 291
Hevener, H.D. 228; Henderson 229; Margaret 229
Heversly, Virginia 108
Hevins, John 101
Hewitt, E.M. 267; family 267
Heyl, John 267
Heyward, Henderson 228; Jane Gamble 228, 229
HHF X14 306
Hibbard, Alma 103
Hickory Hill Farm 306
Hidden River Farm 289, 291
hides 69
Hieronimus, Lindy 267
Higginbotham, Dale 180
High-Hope Farms 204
Highland Cattle 307
Highland Chief 237
Highland County 9, 17, 100, 108, 116, 180
Highland Dairy 239
Highland-Bath Cattle Association 267
Highlands Farm 292, 296
Highs Dairy Products Corporation 205
Hildebrand, Jacob 84
Hill, Leonard 44; Lester 285; Lucio W. 285, 286; Paul 278; R.F. Jr. 229; Rowland F. III 230, 318; W.H. (Buddy) 241
Hillbrook farm 237
Hillsboro 295
Hillsville 228

Hillwinds Farm 270
Hodges, G. Dayton 249, 292, 296, 297; J.B. 296
hoe cultivation 27
Hog Island 30, 329
Hoge, James 147, 149, 290; Peter 58
Hogue, Bruce 300; R. Bruce 274
Holdaway 192
Holdaway, C.W. 172, 188, 196
Holiday Farm 292
Holiday Lake 4-H Educational Center 167
Holland, John 291; L. Bruce 141
Holliday, Thomas Cromwell 292
Hollins Institute (now university) 188, 214, 238, 239, 291
hollow tail 127
Holly Hill Farms 291, 296
Holmes, Clayton Ernest 291
Holmes Farm 291
Holsinger, Gabriel F. 182
Holsteins 158, 166, 191, 200, 203, 211, 213, 214, 215, 237, 262, 263, 314, 316, 318, 324; Holstein (Breeders) Association, U.S.A 227, 238; breeders 320; convention 242; sales 239; field day 177; Holstein Foundation 222; Holstein-Friesian Association of America 238, 241; heifers 239; Junior Advisory Committee 222; Junior Champion 241; Meritorious Service Award 239, 241; national convention 203, 241, 242; Sale of Stars 241; Sire Selection Committee 196; Virginia Holstein Junior Association 241
Holsten River 52
home demonstration agent 139
Homespun Farms 291
Homestead Resort 300
Honaker 229, 287
Hoover, John 116; W.C. 193; W.G. 239
Hope, Charles R. 239, 318, 324; Ronald A. 240, 324
Hopewell 83, 228
Hopkins, Steve 272
horn, uses of 53-55
Horne, B.S. 228; T.J. 164
Horsepen Farm 195
Hostetler, John E. 295
Hot Springs 303
Hotchkiss, Jedediah 104
Hotel Roanoke 173, 198
Houck Joseph 240; Pat 240
Houff, Dwight E. 165, 273, 275, 278, 291, 291, 295, 296
Hounshell, Joe 290
House, Brian 221
Howell family 267; Glenn 267; Jack 267; Rob 267; Tommy 267;
Hubbard, Maury A. 183
Huckle, William 325
Huckleberry Hill 305
Huff, A.J. 170; Arden 180; Ballard 154; Huff n Puff 322
Huffard Jersey Farms 230, 231
Huffard, J.S. III 230; J.S. Jr. 230; James S. Sr. 230
Hughes, Doug 301
Hughes' store 108
Hull, Vernon 237
humane treatment 117
Hume 180, 289, 290
Humped Longhorn 23; Shorthorn 23
Hungarian Breeding Institute of Budapest 322
Hungary 322, 323, 324
Hunsley, Roger E. 283
Hunt, Jack 241; John 241; John A. 240; R.E. 170, 171, 234, 287
Hunter, Archibald 41; E.S. 193; James 41
Huntington, W. Va. 115
Hurst, Eugene S. 301
Hutcheson, Henry E. 252; John R. 170, 181, 193, 234, 283, 285; T.B. 171
Hyatt, John 255
Hygrade 250, 277
Hylton, Mr. 62

I

Imboden, General 82
Independence 189, 287
Indian Trace Farm 248
Ingram family 204
inheritance patterns 32
Inskeep family 71; Russell 275
institutional dairies 213–215
International Livestock Exposition 166, 286, 292, 300
Inwood Farm 289
Iowa State University 172
Irish Kerry 23
Irish Moiled 24
Island Ford 108
Ivanoff, E.I. 313
Ivor 141
Ivy Hill Farm 289

J

J.H. Clark & Son 287
J.S. Roller and Son 229
Jackson, Miss. 304
Jackson, J.F. 188; J.N. 317; Laura 276; Thomas Jonathan (Stonewall) 84, 87, 104
Jackson River 9, 52
Jacksonville, Fla. 233
James City 22
James City County 17, 57
James, Gene 275
James River 6, 9, 24, 29, 37, 54, 56, 57, 215
James River Correctional Center Farm 215, 218
Jameson, Bill 278
Jamestown 20, 131, 222
Jamestown 4-H Educational Center 167
Jamestown Exposition 187
Jamestown Island 19, 20, 32
Jamison, Goggin 235
Janney, Tuck 262
Jareco Farm 239
Jarnigan, Milton P. 136
Jefferson, Thomas 59, 62, 67, 71; W.E. 234
Jenkins, Edward 248, 292, 297; Lizzie 165;
Jennings Gap 109
Jennings, W. Pat 201
Jersey cattle 24, 191, 227, 229, 314, 316; herd books 229; Island of 229
Jersey City 152
Jessee, A.J. 273
Jetersville 233
JL Farms 301, 302
Joanna 251
Joe McSweeney Meat Packers 250
John Wayne 297
Johnson, Dave 239; Jim 279; Melinda 241; Russell 289, 290;
Johnston, Joseph 79; Melinda 242; R.E. 292; Rhoda 242; Roy 249; Zachariah 58
Johnstone, George T., Jr. 295
Jones, Clarence 250; D.S. 188, 238; David 228; Henry Boswell 73; Jessie M. 165; Mike 249; W.C. 269
Jonesville 255, 267
Jordan, Bill 204; John 204
Jordan Brothers Dairy 204
Joseph, Bill 267
Jouett, Jack 59
Journal of Agriculture 102
Joyner, Don 304
junior associations 304; junior cattle groups 290; junior dairy shows 180

K

Kanawha River 53, 55
Kansas State University 172
karst geology 8
Kaufman, Jeff 296
KC Farms 297
Keeler, Greg 306; James 297; Jim 297; Sandra 297

Keely, E.B. 286
Keene 253, 297
Keene, Eric 305
Keezeltown 204
Keister, Jimmy 296
Keithley, R.P. 241
Kelley, H.H. 239
Kelly, Don 291
Ken-Wan Farm 200
Kendale Jerseys 230
Kendy Knoll Farm 290
Kennedy, Oscar W. 321
Kentucky 285
KenWan Jada 200
Kepley, Charles 288, 290
Kerr, Bob 275; Donna 242
Kerry cattle 65, 227
Keswick 228, 285, 287
Kibler, Larry 200, 228; Terry 236; Wayne 200, 229
Kile, George 58
Kilgore, Jess 304
Kilmacronan 170
Kimder Treasure Ronny-Red 243
Kincaid, Charles M. 268; Charlie 127, 172
Kindig, Betty 300; Earl 120, 261, 273, 298, 299, 300; family 68; J. Vernon 294, 295; James Lee 299; John 120, 298; Lyle 298; Vernon 295, 296
Kindrick 287
kine (cattle) 19
King Ranch 298
King, W.T. "Bill" 293
Kingan & Co. 250, 253, 277
Kingdom Farm 295
Kingery, William R. 240
Kinglea Mars Daisy 242
King's Mountain 145
Kinloch Farm 295, 296
Kinmont Charolais 298
Kiracofe, Leon (Mose) 105, 106, 193
Kittrell, Bill 159
Kline, Earl 193; John 116; Wilmer 314
Kluge, John 297
Knabe, Harry A., Jr. 291
Knapp, Seaman A. 137, 181
Knoll Crest Farm 270, 272, 287, 291, 297, 306
Knott, W.B., Jr. 304
Koch, Robert 123, 124, 125
Koiner, George Wellington 137, 138, 139
Kosher markets 153
Koudelka, Tom 314
Kube, Robert F. 276, 290, 291

L

Lacey Spring 190
Ladies Auxiliary VAA 294
Ladysmith High School 165
Lafayette, General 57
Lahman, Richard 228
Lakeside Belle, No. 568 H.H.B 238
Lancaster County 16, 32, 44, 68
land grant college 134, 165, 170
land regions (Va.) 12
Landmark Genetics 203
landscape, seventeenth century 27
Lane, Professor 188
Laneway herd 228
Langwater Farm 230
Langwater Foremost 230
Lansdale, Gordon 303
LaOrange, Carl 262
Lassiter 188
Latane, Jim 275
Laurel, Md. 203
Lawrence, A.J. 290
Lawrenceville 287, 295, 297
Lawson, Charles W. (Charlie) 267; Robert 57; Robert M. 147, 152
Layman's Machine Shop 293
Layne, Douglas 305
leather 77, 87
Lebanon Valley 149
LeBaron Farm 297
Lee County 166, 253, 254, 265, 285

Lee County Hereford Association 285
Lee Farmers Cooperative 255
Lee Farmers Livestock Market 265, 267
Lee Hill Farm 297
Lee, Robert E. 78, 79, 81, 178; Rowland 265
Leech, F.M. 287; Linda 276
Leesburg 188, 233, 238, 295, 320
Leesburg Livestock Market 267
legislation104; affecting agriculture 119; against TB 125; colonial 21, 22, 27, 29, 30, 31, 41, 42, 103; dairying 218; federal 117; Revolutionary War 56; twentieth century 106
Lemm, George 297
Lennon, John 207
Leonard, David 288, 293; Katy 242; Patricia Ann (Dick) 204, 221, 222, 241, 242; Ronald 204; Sarah 221, 241, 242
Lewis, Andrew 51, 52, 53; Charles 53, 54; G.F. 133; James Fielding 283; Joseph 70; Z.R. 236
Lewisburg, W. Va. 53, 283, 291
Lewisfield Farm 283
Lexington 61, 86, 87, 133, 236, 287
lime plants 139
Limelight Show and Sale 293
limestone soil 11
Limousin 279, 301, 305; Canadian Limousin Association 302; Limouselle Scholarship 302; Virginia Limousin Breeders Association 302
Lincoln Red 24
Lincolnshire sheep 48
Lindgren, Carl 270
Lindsey-Robinson and Co. 203
Line I 285
Lineberry, H.H. 290
Lineweaver, Joe 231, 321
Link, O. Winston 119
Linville Cheese Company 190
Linville Station 116
Lithia 228
Little Kanawha River 69
Little, L.L. 292
Little River Dairy 204
Litton, A. Frank 286, 287; George W. 153, 155, 171, 176, 197, 248, 249, 259, 265, 268, 269, 273, 289; Kenneth 172, 248, 249, 259, 296
Litton-Reaves Hall 176, 197
Liverpool 147, 158
Livesay, Doug 297
livestock 20; auctions 248, 249; breeding 200; dealers 118; facilities 177; grader 252; hauling 262; hiding 85; judging 165, 166; markets 261, 267; producers 205; shippers 118; shows 169
Livestock Advancement Project 166
Livestock Breeder Journal 261, 265, 293
Livestock Judging Pavilion 177
Llewellyn, Paul 292
Lloyd, Thomas 52
Lloyd's of London 322
Locust Dale 285
Locust Level Farm 297
Logan, Walter 322; William H. 240; William H. Sr. 240
Lohr, Pete 294
Lomax, Lunsford 135
London 147
London Company 20, 29
London Meat Importation Company 149
Long, Arthur 110; Carlyle 204; Louise Varner 110
Longenecker, Ann 302
Longhorn 23, 48
Longmoor Farm 203
Longview Farms 301
Lonsway, Joseph 83
Look, Samuel 189
Looney's Ferry 56
Loudoun 4-H Beef Club 166
Loudoun County 16, 56, 77, 79, 91, 109, 168, 177, 189, 195, 198, 200, 201, 202, 203, 211, 222, 233, 264, 304, 305, 318, 325, 327

Loudoun County 4-H Dairy Club 221
Loudoun County 4-H Fair 221
Loudoun County Breeders' Association 233
Loudoun DHIA 203
Loudoun Farm Bureau 203
Loudoun Heritage Farm Museum 327
Loudoun Milk Transportation 211
Loudoun Special (feed) 198
Loudoun Valley Cow Testing Association 193
Louisville, Ky. 284
Love, George 66
Loveland, T. 238
Lovettsville 236
Loving, T. Kent 289, 291
Lovingston 291
Lowesville 305
Lowry, E.L. 267; John 70
Lucketts 166
Lucky Hill Farm 237
Ludington, F.H. 250, 295
Lunsford, H. C. 287
Luray 87, 200, 290, 304, 305
Lutz, Conrad 293, 321
Lynch, Dan 287, 289, 290
Lynch Hereford Farm 289
Lynchburg 78, 141, 169, 188, 193, 201, 228, 292, 293
Lynchburg Feeder Calf Producers Association, Inc. 265
Lynchburg Feeder Cattle Association 266
Lynchburg Livestock Market 267
Lynn Brae, 297
Lynnhaven 168
Lynnhaven Mattoax Brook 168

M

Mace, Kenneth M. 234
Madison 236, 300, 305
Madison 4-H Dairy Club 221
Madison County 110, 237, 256
Madrid, Spain 294
Maggie 296
Magill, E.C. 162
Magnum 41T 303
Maiden Spring 144
Maidstone Farm 236
Mallory Hollow 176
Mallory, R.B. 233; Tom 255
Maltby, Robert 164
Manassas 79, 205, 314
Manassas Agricultural School 162
Manassas campaign 79
Manchester 188
Mann, William H. 234
manure 46, 47, 61, 62, 73, 78, 85; green 45, 62; value 39
Maola Milk and Ice Cream 203
map, Shenandoah Valley 36
Maple Grove Stock Farm, 289
Maple Lead Angus 200
Maple Leaf Farm 295
Marietta, Ohio 70
Marion 127
Market Animal Show 169, 178
marketing 220; 248; dairy 200
markets 43, 107, 114, 259; changes in 115; New Republic era 61; niche 212
Markham, Wayne 267
Marlowe, T.J. 260, 269
Marlu Elevation Esther 200
Marriott Family 289
Mars Candy Bars 304
Mars, Forrest 304
Marshall 169, 289, 290, 326
Marshall Feeder Cattle Association 266
Marshall, John 55
Marsteller, E.H. 202
Martha Washington Inn 155
Martin, Clinton E. 273; Guy 290; James E. 174; Robert Dickerson 147
Martindale, R.V. 239, 241
Marting, O.B. 165
Martins Hundred 22
Marva Maid 203

Mary Washington College 227
Maryland Agricultural College 133
Maryland and Virginia Milk Producers Association 183, 200, 201, 202, 203, 209, 211
Mason, D.W. 268; E.J. 291
Mason-Dixon Red Angus Association 297
Massachusetts Institute of Technology 172
massacre 22
Massanutten Creamery 194
Massanutten Mountain 9
Massie, Cabel 315; James P. 297
Mast, C. Curtis 254, 268, 269, 270, 271, 272
Master Breeder Award, Jersey 230
mastitis 125
Mathews County 16, 85
Matney, Keith 295
Matthiessen, R. Henry 268, 272, 273, 291; R. Henry, Jr. 180, 289, 290; Ralph H., Sr. 289
Maury, Matthew Fontaine 178
Max Meadows 295
Maxey, Hank 270
Maximus 301
May, Greg 295; Russell 297
Maymont Farm 295
McComb, Carol 240
McClung, Richard 276
McBryde, John McLaren 135, 136
McCann, Harry 283
McCaully, Alan 320
McClaugherty, C.P. 252, 265
McClellan, George 80; Karen McComb 241
McClung, Richard 273, 297
McClure, Allan 242; Samuel F. 253, 255; Walter 177, 241; Walter V. 241; Walter V., Sr. 240
McComas, Emily 301; J.L. 301; W. Lane 302
McComb & Block 250
McComb, Carol 222, 241, 242; F.W. 239; Frank 240; Kathy 221, 241, 242; Kristy 241; R.E. 239; Robert 240
McCormick, Cyrus 237; Cyrus Hall 173; family 172; L.J. 237
McCray, Hunter 242; Warren T. 286
McDaniel, Dave 290
McDanolds, R.M., Jr. 301; Ralph 300; Ralph M., Jr. 278
McDonald, Brandie 221, 241
McDonald Farms 304
McDowell, Battle of 17
McDowell, Irvin 79; Michael H. 295, 296, 297; T.K. 297
McFarland, Francis 86, 92
McGaheysville 182
McGee, James 229
McGillard, Dare 172
McGraw, Roger 273
McGuffey, Jane (McGuffe) 33
McIntire, Doug 275, 295
McIntire, P.T. & Sons 295
McIntosh, J.W. 237
McKinnon, Bill 279; family 278
McLaughlin, Henry Woods, Jr. 283; R.A. 234
McLeod, Katherine 326
McNeely, C.W. III 239
McSpadden, Clara 294; Bill 294, 295; Mrs. William 294; McSpadden, William B. 252, 269, 294, 296
McSweeney, Joseph 250, 277
Meadow Farm 237
Meadow Hill Farm 304
Meadow, The 181
MeadowBrooke Angus 295
Meadows, Katherine (Mrs. Andy) 295, 296; Katherine Entsminger 295
Meander Farm 237, 292
meat packing houses 78, 79, 154, 250, 276, 277; cooperatives 253
meats judging contest 259
Mecklenburg County 182, 183, 234
Meek, Bowen 290; family 152; J.H. 259; Joe 264, 279; Marvin 146, 153; Roy 262, 267, 270, 304; Roy A. 274

Melchers, Gari 227
Mellon, Paul 172, 176
Mennonites 90, 208
Merritt, Wesley 77, 91
Metcalf, Gilliam, and Fariss, L.L.C 267
Mexico 298
Meyers 250
Michael, R.D. 174
Michel, Franz Ludwig 36
Michigan State University 133
Mid-Atlantic Milk Marketing
        Association 203
Middle Peninsula 6
Middlebrook 237, 284
Middlebrook High School 164
Middleburg 172, 188, 236, 237, 285,
        289, 297
Middleburg Agricultural Research and
        Extension Center 176
Middlesex County 31
Middleton, Ben P. 213, 242; Charles
        289; John 195, 240; Richard 289
Midland 204
Midlothian 291
Miles City, Mont. 285, 305
Milford 78
military life 79; units 54
milk 208; cans 204, 208, 211; co-ops
        200, 204, 205,208; cooling
        198, 199; councils 220; delivery
        129, 187, 205; distribution cen-
        ters 205; fever 127; hauling 187,
        189, 195, 201, 204, 209, 211; ho-
        mogenized 205; marketing
        202, 207; milk houses (dairy
        house) 40, 47, 195, 196, 197, 198,
        214; Milk Mustache 220; plants
        204, 205; prices 204, 205, 218,
        219; processing plants 203, 218;
        production 198, 201, 202, 209,
        211; sales 219; supply 219; sup-
        ply balancing 209; wagons 205
Milk Train 211
milking, by hand 195, 201; machines
        194, 195, 215; parlors 199, 200;
        team 166
Milking Shorthorn 235, 236, 242, 282;
        Milking Shorthorn Cattle Club of
        America 235; Milking Shorthorn
        Society 242; polled 236;
Mill Run Farm 289
Mille, William 147
Miller, Brad 303; Charles 241; Charles
        N. (Chuck) 240; George 297;
        George A. 239, 240, 318; George
        W. 230; Henry 62, 282; J. Newbill
        273; J. Newbill, Jr. 295; John
        199; John L. 177, 199, 230; Judy
        297; M. Erskine 229; Matthew
        305; Newbill 266; Pippen 240;
        William 108
milling 101
Mills Award 166, 289
Mills, James P. 289; Mrs. James P. 289
Millwood 248, 292, 297
Milner Dairy Company 204
Milton, Cookie 275
Mink, Randy 270
Minnick, Ezra 193
Minor, Charles Landon Carter 134;
        Marvin, Jr. 291; R. Marvin, Jr.
        291
Miss 7 Half Diamond 169M 303
Mitchell, Blair 132; Charles 300;
        Charles R. 301; John 278, 288;
        John B. 303; Maurice 132; Nanie
        132; Robert A. 132
mixed farming 40, 75, 78, 115, 215
Moffett, J. Stewart 218; R.W. 164
Monroe County 82, 99, 305
Monroe Park 178
Montana 289
Montana Hall Farm 283
Montebello 111
Monterey 266, 287
Monterey Livestock Market 267, 268
Montgomery County 16, 126, 132,
        133, 134, 145, 182, 192, 201, 315
Monticello Dairy 205
Montreal 152, 294

Moore, Brent 270; Merritt 59; Ronnie
        166; Samuel Thomas Jr. 183
Moorefield, W. Va. 283
Mooreland Farms 306
Moreland Farms 297
Moreland, Glynn 166
Morgan, Ben F., Jr. 208
Morlunda Farms 249, 283, 291
Morrill Act 133
Morris, J.L. Jr. 267; Phillip 275; R.S.
        267; Richard 229; Roger 270, 306;
        T.A. 79
Morrow, George 180
Morven Park 109, 188, 233, 234, 297
Mosby, John 91
Moses, Anna Mary Robertson
        (Grandma Moses) 128, 129; Tho-
        mas 129
Moss family 152
Moss, Frank 149; George 149; Joe S.
        253
Mossy Creek 108
Mossy Creek Farm 325, 326
Mount Rogers 4
Mount Vernon 14, 46
Mountain Meadows Farm 301
Moutiers, France 305
Moyer, Charles F. 240; Larkin D. 240
Mrotek, John R. 294
Mt. Crawford 204, 206, 303, 304, 332
Mt. Jackson 289, 291, 297
Mt. Sidney 165, 291, 296
Mt. Solon 301, 304, 305
muley cattle 25, 106
Mullen, William 291
Mullins, Freddie 270
Multipurpose Livestock Arena 177
Muncey, Olin 290; Annette 270; Leo
        270
Murley, Ray 175, 199
Murray, John (Lord Dunmore) 52, 53
Museum of American Frontier Culture
        236, 307
Musick, J.T. 287
Myatt, Michael 210
Myers, Daniel J. 240
Myers family 239; M.R. 297; Teresa
        Ann 325; Teresa D. 242
Mystic Hill Farms 270

N

Nador, Mike 322
Nansemond County 315
Narrows Livestock Market, Inc 267
National All-Jersey Milk Marketing
        Organization 230
National Association of Animal
        Breeders 318
National Cattlemen's Association 276,
        288, 301
National Cattlemen's Beef Association
        325
National Council of Farmer Coopera-
        tives 203
National Dairy Council 203, 220
National Dairy Shrine 175, 207, 241
National Farmers' Alliance 119
National Grand Champion 303
National Guernsey Show 235
National Holstein Association 207
National Junior Achievement Winner 230
National Live Stock Association 252
National Livestock Judging Contest 164
National Livestock Judging Contest 164
National Milk Producers Association 203
National Milk Producers Federation 204
National Register of Historic Places 175
National Western Stock Show 293
Native Americans 2, 10, 22, 29, 51,
        52, 53, 55, 75, 105
native scrub stock 27, 62, 63
Natural Bridge 295
Nature Conservancy, The 157, 159, 329
NCBA Annual Convention and Trade
        Show 265
Neale, Charles T. 248, 292, 297
neat cattle 19
Nelson County 85, 233, 265, 286
Nelson, Oscar 283; Oscar, Jr. 291;
        Oscar, Sr. 291

Nelson, Thomas 56; William 44
Neptune 298
Nesselrodt, Beverly 297
Neuhoff family 277
Neuhoff farms, Inc. 277
Neustadt an der Aisch 305
New Bern, N.C. 203
New England 30
New Farmers of America 164
New Farmers of Virginia 164
New Leicester sheep 48
New Market 11, 87, 229, 237, 296,
        297, 306
New Netherlands 30
New River 10, 51
New River Hereford Association 290
New York 152, 153
Newbill, Jack H. 234, 235
Newburg, Maryland 290
Newcomb, H.D. 236; J. Churchill 236
Newland, Lloyd 297; Ruby 297
Newman, W.H. 239; Walter S. 162, 171
Newport News 123, 187, 188, 203,
        220, 238
Newport; 289
Nichols, J.V. 193; Nichols, James R.
        175, 220, 240, 318
Nicholson Hollow 110
Nicklas, Rita (Mrs. George) 295
Nievres, France 298
Niles, Edwin P. 135
Nixon, Kim 270; Tom 270, 272
No. 92 105
Nokesville 221
Nolen, Frank 295
Norfolk 69, 70, 78, 115, 132, 201, 208,
        235, 242
Norfolk & Western RR 118, 119, 137,
        182
Norfolk (cattle breed) 25
Norfolk Cooperative Milk Producers' As-
        sociation 205, 208
Norman, Edward C. 203, 251
North American International Live-
        stock Exposition 284, 306
North American Limousin Foundation 302
North Carolina-Virginia Holstein News 239
North Dakota 292
North Garden 291, 296
North River High School 169
North Wales Farm 292
Northampton County 5, 16, 30
Northcote Farm 297
Northern Neck 6, 14, 31, 38, 107
Northern Neck Proprietary 35
Northern Virginia 14, 211
Northern Virginia 4-H Educational Center
        167
Northern Virginia AI Association 315
Northern Virginia Angus Association 297
Northern Virginia Cooperative Breeding
        Association 315
Northern Virginia Hereford Association 290
Northern Virginia Livestock Association 273
Northern Virginia Livestock, Inc. 264
Northern Virginia Livestock Producers'
        Association 255
Nottoway County 139, 165, 315
Nourse, David Oliver 135, 136
Nuckols family 239
Nutmeg Farms of Virginia 291, 300
nutrition research 172

O

Oak Grove 147
Oak Grove Farm 326
Oak Hill Farm 297
Oak Ridge Farm 234
Oak Ridge Guernsey 233
Oakdale Farm 299
O'Bannon, J.M. 272
Obert, Bartram 32; family 32
observations, contemporary 69, 73,
        100, 101
Occoquan 78
Occupational Safety and Health
        Administration 183
O'Ferrall, Charles 124
Ohio Agricultural
        Experiment Station 135

Ohio River 69
Ohio Valley 53, 69, 71
Old Dominion Beef 264, 278
Old Elkton Farm 292, 296
Old Hundred Farm 291
Old Mill E Snickerdoodle 237
Old Mill Farm 237
Old World animals 35; plants 15, 28, 39
Olin & Preston Institute 133
Oliver, William 276
Ono, Yoko 207
oral histories 146; , cattle drives 109;
        grazing 108
Orange 188, 200, 202, 203, 221, 229,
        283, 292, 305
Orange County 56, 118, 193, 230,
        285, 292, 305
Orange Hill 237
Orange Livestock Market 267
Orchard Crest Farm 213
Oregon 299
organic farm 327
Orr, Robert S. 286, 287, 289, 290
Ortolan 298
Osborn, O.D. 276
Osborndale Ivanhoe Eve 325
Osborne, Cyrus 289
Ottervue Farm 291
Otwell, Will B. 165
Our Lady of the Angels Monastery 208–213
Outer Banks 19
Outstanding Seedstock Producer 296
Overlook Farm 237
Owlsey, F.B. 229
Ownby Auction 214, 215
Ownby, J. Dennis 240, 251, 320, 321;
        E.P. 249; Leo 250; Roy 249; W.
        Hugh 249
Ownby Export 321
ownership marks 102, 105–108
ox cheek 37
ox shoe 146
oxen 35, 40, 44, 46, 48, 70, 71, 221

P

pacifists 90
Page County 87, 110
painting 129
palisaded rings 24
Palmer, Amy 68; George C. 255; George
        C. II 259, 290, 291; George W. 234
Palo Alto Gap 108
Pan-Charolais Association 302
Pancoast, H.T. 188, 193
Panic of 1873 146
Paramont Ambush 316
Paramont Ranch 316
Parker Field 179
Parkersburg, W. Va. 69
Parkinson, Anita 297
partisan raids 91; soldiers 81
Pasteur, Louis 123
pasteurization 123, 125, 196, 206
pastures 198
Patrick, H.T. 229
Patrick Springs 290
Patrons of Husbandry 119, 134
Patterson, William N. 229, 240; R. Wayne
        301
Patton family 71; James 41, 144;
        Matthew 62, 282
Patton stock 62, 63
Paul M. Reaves Award 319
Paulson, Barbara 237; Rolf 237
Paxton, C.R. 233; John 58
Pearisburg 267
Pearson, Dennis 270
Pease , Clinton L. Jr. 234
Peck, Dwight 240, 319, 320; Joan A. 241
pedigrees 68
Peery, Charles M. (Chilly) 293, 296
Pegram, C.W. 195
Pelton Hills Farm 297
Pemberton, Robert 240
Pen-Y-Bryn Farm 292
Pendleton County 108
Peninsula, the 6, 85
Penn Laird 194, 320
Penn State University 133, 175

Penney, J.C. 230
penning cattle 313
Pennington Gap 286, 287, 288
performance data 297; pedigrees 272; programs 268; testing 268, 270, 271, 293, 302, 306, 307
Perkinson, William H. 278, 295, 297
Perrow, Jack M. 228
Perry, Enos 313
Persinger, Jasper 290
Peters, Harry 283
Petersburg 56, 169, 215, 250
Philadelphia 41, 78, 116, 144, 152, 248
Philadelphia Society for the Promotion of Agriculture 229
Phillips, Rodney 290
Phipps, Hubert B. 253, 290; Mary 68
Phoenix Livestock Market 267
Piankatank River 31
Pie Rouge 304
Piedmont 4, 6, 7, 8, 14, 56, 78
Piedmont, Battle of 86
Pierce, A.E. 248; family 292; J.B. 181; Paula 166; R.G. 236; Zane 301
Pine Pastures Farm 289
Piney River 295
pipeline milkers 199
Pitman, Levi 104
Pittsylvania County 56, 78
Plainfield Farm 290
plantations 43
planters 39, 42, 44; colonial 37
Platts, Jennifer Eileen 302
Pleasant Valley 91
pleuropneumonia 124, 125
Plimsoll, Samuel 152
plowing 26, 35
Plum Island, New Jersey 158
Poage, William 222
Pocahontas County 81, 105, 108
Poingdestre (Poindexter) family 229; George 229;
Polan, Carl 175
political reform 119
Polled, Charolais 298; Herefords 287, 289, 290, 296; Shorthorns 284
Polled Express 306
Poller Bull (ACR Alfalfa John 075) 68, 299
Pontiac 214
Poole, Jack 270
Poolesville, Md. 289
Popkins, .L. 202
Port Republic 80, 237
ports 14
Portsmouth 132
Potomac River 5, 9, 31, 70, 83
Potter, Charlie 275
Potts Creek Farm 290
Potts family 213; Nancy 242; Thurston J. 201
powder horns 53, 54–55; German tradition 54
powder magazine 51
Powell, James F. 291; Kevin 276; William D. 270, 293, 295
Powhatan County 57, 215
Powhatan Indians 22
Pratt, C.W. 270; Jason 270; John V. 283; Lewis T. 273, 276
pregnancy rate 323
Premier Breeder Award 270; Guernsey 235; Jersey 230
prenuptial agreement 26, 33
Preston, Robert 41; Robert T. 134; William 51, 53
Price, H.L. 171; Hall 137, 138, 188, 196; Patti 290
Priddy, A.S. 214
Prillaman, L.P. 273, 289
Prince Domino 287
Prince Edward County 57
Prince Pompadour NIM 1 302
Prince William County 16, 78, 79, 145, 162, 189, 194, 202, 211, 237
Priode, Bob 268, 273
production, dairy cattle 192
Proffit 287
Program for Genetic Advancement 318
property damages 90
property sales 54

provision trade 69
Prydes, Ian 237
Publican the Seventh 282, 286
Pugibet, Jean 298
Pulaski 165, 289, 315
Pulaski County 78, 145, 147, 148, 201
Pulaski Livestock Market 267
Purcell, Benjamin L. 188; family 118
Purcellville 188, 193, 203, 211, 236, 251, 304, 305, 324
Purdy, Bob 302
purebred animals 63, 65; bull sales 253; cattle 214
Purebred Dairy Cattle Association 235
Pure Bred Sire League 190, 191
Putney, Reid T. 291
Pyne, John, Jr. 295

Q

quarantine line 124, 125
Quick, Walter 119; Walter J. 188
Quicksburg 305
Quisenberry, J.S. 182; Sharron 177

R

R&R Charolais 301
Rabild, Helmer 193
Rafter S. Ranch 299
raiding parties 57
railroads 67, 87, 108, 109, 114-115, 120, 129, 152, 187, 211; advertising 116; beginnings 114; classroom 119; commission 119; depots 117; facilities 116, 117; 78, 114, 115, 118; legislation against 119; problems with 120
Rambo, Ogle 270
Ramsey, Gary 297
Randolph, Allen K. 252, 253, 255, 256, 261, 269; Larned 266; Thomas Mann 59
Raphine 301, 302
Rapidan 188, 287, 292
Rappahannock County 106, 110, 116
Rappahannock County (Old) 33
Rappahannock River 6, 31, 32, 44, 87, 119
Ravenswood Farm 293
Rawlings, George C. 255, 258
Reardon, Mike 198
Reasor, Smith 270
Reaves, Paul M. 174, 176, 195, 196, 222, 239, 240, 316
recipe 37; for cattle fever 85
recollections 105
Record of Performance (ROP) program 260
Rectortown 236, 286, 292
Red and White Cattle 242; Red and White Classic 243; Red and White Dairy Cattle Association 242
Red and White Spotted Simmental Cattle Association 304
Red Angus 158, 279, 292, 297, 306; Red Angus Association of America 297, 306
Red Bank Farm 291
red coloring 25
Red Deer Ranch 287
Red Gate Farm 248, 292, 297
Red Holsteins 242
Red House 271, 287, 291, 297, 306
Red House Bull Evaluation Center 270, 287, 306
Red Poll 24, 25
Reed, Charles C. 251, 253; John H. 103; John Milton 91; T.O. 297; William T., Jr. 251, 255, 260
Reeves, Ernest Sanderson 165, 273, 275, 276, 301, 325, 326
refrigerated cars 115, 118
refrigerated ships 152
registration of purebred cattle 235
Remington 203, 239, 290, 291
Remsburg, J. Homer 202
Renalds, R.R., 255
Renick family 71
Rennie, Frank 234
Repair, Jonathan P. 295

Reppert, Fred 249
Research Division 174
Retained Ownership Program 277
Reva 290
Revolutionary War 39, 51, 54, 54–57, 55, 57–59, 145
Reynolds, Lucinda 263; Ralph 301; Reggie B. 262, 264, 274, 275, 278
Reynoldsburg, Ohio 229
Rhea, William F. 126
Rhoads, Ella 241; R. Bentz 241
Rhodes, Fannie 91; John 88, 89, 91; Leon 243; Miller D. 193, 204, 205; Steve 243
Rhudy, Allen 166
Rice 229
Rich Mountain 159
Rich Mountain Farm 157
Richardson, C.E. 289; Don 290, 291; Gwyn 154; Kathy 166
Richdale Farm 239
Richland Mountain 108
Richmond 6, 10, 43, 56, 73, 75, 78, 87, 115, 132,177, 188, 201, 214, 228, 233, 234, 239, 253, 274, 287, 291, 320, 321
Richmond Abbatoir, Inc. 250
Richmond and Danville and Piedmont RR 115
Richmond and Norfolk producers 209
Richmond Cattle Producers Association 251, 252
Richmond County 38, 55, 183
Richmond Livestock & Richmond Union Stockyards 250
Richmond Livestock Company, Inc. 250
Richmond milk producers 208
Richmond stockyard 250
Richmond stockyard 250
Richmond Union Stockyards 250
Rilara Holstein 240
Rilara Mars Las Ravena 241
Riner 166
Rinker, Alton 297; Betty 297
Rito 616 316
Ritz, Gottlieb 190
Riverdale Farms 290, 291
Rixeyville 204, 253
road marking 151
Roanoke 8, 169, 183, 203, 205, 235, 239, 286, 287, 311
Roanoke Co-operative Milk Producers 200
Roanoke College 133
Roanoke County 222, 315
Roanoke Island colony 19
Roanoke River 10, 38
Roanoke Valley Angus Association 297
Roanoke-Hollins Stockyard 267
Robert Hartman family 223
Roberts Family 204
Robertson, Randal M. 174; Katheryn 297; Marvin 297
Robin Roost Farms 291, 304
Robinson, Alex 127; John 59; Walter 127
Rocby Holsteins 207, 241
Rocby Ivanhoe Dina Charm 241
Rochedale Hundred 24
Rock Hill Farm 236
Rockbridge County 9, 43, 56, 73, 102, 133, 229, 283, 287
Rockburn Farm 290
Rockingham Cooperative Farm Bureau 182
Rockingham County 16, 62, 65, 67, 68, 80, 87, 88, 89, 103, 108, 115, 119, 124, 134, 146, 166, 167, 182, 190, 193, 195, 205, 206, 208, 213, 230, 293, 294, 300, 314, 316
Rockingham County Fairgrounds 243, 279, 303
Rockingham Feeder Cattle Association 266
Rockland Farms, 235
Rocklands Farm 292, 297
Rockwood 148
Rocky Mount 177, 235, 315, 316, 317, 318, 319
Rogers, Sidney D, 290, 291
Rolfe, John 21
Roller, B. Randolph 164, 165; D.F. 193; Harold 230; J.S. 193, 229; Jason 164, 165; O. Beverley 164, 165; Paul 229

Rolling Hill Farm (Hillsboro) 295
Rolling Hills Farm (Winchester) 290, 291
Rolston, Jesse Jr. 84; Mary Catharine Cromer 84
Roosevelt, Franklin D., Jr. 291
ROP Bull Feeding Test 269
Rosedale 174, 304
Rosegill Creek 32
Roseland 304
Rosen, Dorothy 332
Rosenberger, George W. 65, 67
Rosni Dairy 239
Ross, O.B. 265
Rosson, Charles 270
Rotary Club 169
Rotunda 74
Roudabush, Katy 242
Round Hill 292, 296
Round Oak Farm 318, 324
Round Oak Rag Apple Elevation 318, 324
Rouse, Love 290
Rowe, M.B. 229, 233
Rowlsley, William 22
Royal Jersey Agricultural and Horticultural Society 229
Royer, John H., Jr. 290, 291
Royston, Jimmy 166
Ruckman, John 81
Rudacille, Ray 291
Ruddock, Billings 297; Ellen 297
Ruffin, Edmund 133; Frank 78
Ruffner, William Henry 133
Runnion, Dale 294
Rural Retreat 164, 230, 305
Ruritan Club 169
Russell, Charles Marion 289
Russell County 118, 134, 144, 146, 150, 158, 175, 182, 287, 293
Russell, William 53
Russia 313
Rust, Adam 211; Foley 211; Tom 211
Rustburg 229
Ryan, Thomas Fortune 233

S

Saacke, Richard G. 175, 317, 323
Sabine Hall 38, 55
Sadie 213
safety, in food 196
Salem 51, 289
Salers cattle 302; Angus cross 248
salting 103, 106, 109
Saltville 115, 157, 230
Sanders family 71; H.W. 162; Henry 278; Henry D. 289; Rufus 290;
Sandiges 180
Sandy Creek Expedition 51, 52
Sandy, R.A. 229; T.O. 139, 181, 188, 233, 238, 239
Sanford, Jack 229; W.W. 229; W.W. (Monk) 203
Sangerville 106, 169
sanitation 125, 197, 198, 211
Saratoga, Battle of 58
satellite auction 264
Saunders, James W. 295; W.D. 187, 188, 190, 192, 196; T.B. 253
Savage, Thomas 29
Saville, Joi 276
Savoie and Haute Savoie 305
Saxe 301
scales 101, 115, 116, 117
Schewel, Michael J. 140
Schiermyer, Gerald 278
Schoepf, Johann 69
Schwerin, Joe 296
Science Museum 178
scientific farming 127
Scotland 228, 292
Scott, A.R. 188; F.W. 269; Fred 213; Fred W. Jr. 266, 287, 291; Harvey 205, 213; J.O. 188; Leo 297
Scott County 151
Scottish Highland cattle 23, 307
sea cowboys 123
seafaring trade 39, 42, 69
Sealtest 205

Sears Roebuck Company 181
Seay, Billy 305
Secretary of Agriculture 140
Seddon, James 81
Seed Stock Breeder Honor Roll of
        Excellence 271, 273
Seedstock Producer Award 270, 300
seedstock sale 249
Select Sires 175, 196, 203, 207, 318, 319
selective breeding 48, 62, 63, 65
semen, collection 314, 326; fresh 314;
        frozen 316, 317, 323; importa-
        tion 304, 306; liquid 316, 317,
        320, 321; sales 305; shipping 321;
        straws 326; viability 321
Senior Dairy Bowl 241
Set Aside Program 175, 199, 220
settlement expansion 23, 29, 30, 33, 40
settlers 11, 21; ethnicity 35, 40
Seven Oaks Farm 239
Shadwell 296
Shaffer, Robert K. "Bob" 290
Shallow Brook Farm 305
Shank, D.E. 204
Shannon, Sidney 297
Sharrer, G. Terry 85
Shawsville 119, 182
Shearer, Judith 237; Julia 237, 292
sheep 151, 152
Sheets, J.E. 292
Shelburne, Jake 259; James 252, 255
Shen-Valley Meat Packers 277
Shenandoah Valley Angus Association 297
Shenandoah Valley AI Association 315
Shenandoah County 87, 104, 212, 239
Shenandoah Mountain 80, 107
Shenandoah National Park 106, 110
Shenandoah River 5, 9, 128
Shenandoah Valley 10, 58, 71, 128,
        129, 145, 169, 204, 208, 290, 325
Shenandoah Valley Livestock Sales, Inc. 267
Shenandoah Valley Research Station
        172, 176
Shenandoah Valley Simmentals 305
Shenandoah's Pride 199, 204, 205–
        206, 206, 211, 213
Shenk, Dave 205
Shenmont Admiral Amber 235
Shenmont Farms 235
Shepherd, A.L. 266; B. Morgan 188;
        R.D. 228
Sheridan, Philip 77, 87, 91, 132
Shetland 24
Shifflett, Silver J. 295
Shiflett, Aaron 241; Ashley 242
shipping cattle 116, 119; shipping fe-
        ver 139; statistics 117
shortages, wartime 84
Shorthorn cattle 24, 25, 48, 62, 63,
        64, 65, 67, 73, 105, 106, 107, 110,
        144-146, 151, 153, 157, 158,
        169, 178, 191, 269, 282, 287,
        292, 305; bulls 147; Performance
        Records 284; Sire Summary 284
Shorthorns Around the World 283
Shrock family 203
Shull's Sod 106
Shumate, Mr. 154
Shurick, Edward P. 300
Sigel, Franz 79
silos 111, 135, 198, 214
Silverthorn, Thomas 66
Silvey, J.J. 119
Simme Valley, Switzerland 304
Simmental 158, 270, 278, 304, 305;
        national champion bull 304
Simmerman, George 288
Simmons, Bill 169; Roy 295
Simms, Danny 218; Ray 270
Simons, R.L. 236
Simpson, J.G. 267
Sipe, William H. 108
sire evaluation 272; summaries 307;
        testing 287
Sister Barbara 208, 209
Sister Kay 212
Skeen, Lois 242
Skeen, Michelle 242
Skelton, William E. 174
Skiffs Creek farm 79

Skinner, John 71
Skyland 110
Skyview Farm 296
slaughter cattle auction 266; produc-
        tion 277
Slaughter, Temple 239
slavery 8, 38, 77
Slusher, Mark 303; Terry 270
Sly, L.E. 234
Smals, Henry 101
Smith, Al 273; Daniel 175; Eliza C.
        157; G.L. 238, 239; Harry 150;
        Henry 157, 175; Henry II 176;
        Herbert McKelden 292; James
        144; Joan McKay 283; John
        26, 31; John Henry Anderson 176;
        John Henry Anderson II 176; John
        Henry Anderson III 176; John
        Henry Anderson IV 176; John Tay-
        lor 176; Kenneth 203, 239; Mary
        James 175; Paul 240; S.S. 140;
        Shirley 237; Thomas R. 238;
        Wendell 213; William Gilkeson
        176; William Isaac 176
Smith Island 30
Smith Mountain Lake 4-H Educational
        Center 168
Smith-Hughes Act 162
Smith-Lever Act 139, 165, 181
Smithfield 174
Smithfield plantation 134
Smyth County 145, 150
Snicker's Gap Road 201
Snidow, B.C. (Bud) 248, 249, 253
Snodgrass, Tyler 287
sods 105
soil improvement program 198
soils 15
Somerset 204, 229
Somma, Charles A. 179
Sotham, William 284
Soule, Andrew McNairn 136
South America 297
South Boston 169
South Richmond Stockyards 250
Southampton County 78
Southampton Hundred 22
Southeast Herd Builders Sale 305
Southeast Milk Producers 208
Southeast Red and White Dairy Cattle
        Association 243
Southeast United Dairy Association 203
Southeast United Dairy Industry
        Association 220
Southeastern Artificial Breeding
        Association 315
Southeastern Holstein News 239, 241
Southern Cattlemen's Convention 286
Southern   Claims   Commission
        88, 89, 90
Southern Dream Sale 306
Southern Planter 68, 74, 75, 139, 170, 233
Southern Railway 286
Southside 6
Southside Angus Association 297
Southside Cooperative 209
Southside Milk Cooperative 201
Southside Milk Producers 208–210
Southside Stockyards, Inc. 250
Southwest Angus Association 297
Southwest Research Station 135
Southwest Virginia 14, 104, 208
Southwest Virginia 4-H Educational
        Center 167
Spader, Richard 295
Spangler, Mrs. Sam 294; Sam 293
Spanish-American War 147
specialization (beef or dairy) 63
Speiden, C.L. 229; Bill 221
Sperryville 255
Spiencop 106
Spillman, W.J. 181
Spitlar, Mr. 129
Spotlight Show and Sale 292, 296
Spotswood, Alexander 10
Spotsylvania County 229, 233, 290
Spotted Buck 150, 152
Spottswood 111, 253
Spottswood High School 164
Sprague, Howard 241

Spring Hill Farm 229
Spring Valley 189
Spring Valley Hereford Farm 289
Springer, Lyle 294
Springfield 205
Springwood Angus 295
Springwood Livestock Management,
        Inc. 295
St. George's Parish 30
Stafford County 166, 175, 266
Stahl, C.L. 188
Staka Holsteins 243
stampedes 100
stanchion dairy barns 199
Standard of Perfection (S.O.P.) Show 291
Stanley, Thomas 258
Star Farmer of America 166
Star Hereford Association 290
Stark, Tom 270
starvation, military 52
Starving Time 20
State Department of Agriculture and
        Immigration 137
State Milk Commission 218–219
State Supervisor of Agricultural Educa-
        tion 162
Staunton 11, 40, 41, 56, 58, 78, 86,
        87, 100, 107, 114, 115, 129,
        149, 178, 179, 180, 215, 228, 230,
        248, 282, 283, 288, 290, 292, 295,
        296, 304, 307, 317
Staunton Livestock Market facility 117
Staunton Spectator 73
Staunton Union Stockyards, 169, 259,
        267
Staunton-Parkersburg Turnpike 81
Steele, Roger D. 273, 278, 293, 295, 297;
        T.D. 273, 293, 295, 297
Steeles Tavern 176
Stephens, J.B. 267
Steppe, T.Y.L. 291
Stevenson, William 59
Stewart, David 51; Lawrence 228;
        Lawrence Jr. 228
Stiles family 229, 230; Hazel 230; Ken
        230; Mike 230; Paul 230; Tracy 231
Still House Hollow Farm 180, 268, 289
Stine, I. Fred 240, 241, 251, 255
Stith, Dale 270
Stock raising 115
stockyards 114, 115, 117, 119, 250
Stokes, A.Y. 272; Tom 295; William S. 294
Stoltzfus, Karl 320
Stone Castle 287
Stone, John 30
Stony Meadows Farm 302
Stork, James L. 294
Straley, Chapman 290
Strasburg 203, 210, 237
Strate, Martin F. 261, 262
Strauss, Lewis L. 292, 293
Strawberry Hill 179, 180, 252
stray cattle 43, 53, 61, 103, 131
Strecker, Karl 296
Street, Barbara 242
Streeter, Winston 301
Streett, Barbara 242; Charles H. IV 241
stripping (milking) 195
Stroobants, Alphonse 297
Strother, David Hunter (Porte Crayon)
        87, 99, 100
Stroud, M.K. 233
Stuart family 154, 157; Henry Carter
        (Governor) 150, 151, 153, 157,
        182, 287, 293; J.E.B. 150; Patricia
        Bonsall 177; Harry Carter (State
        Senator) 158, 251, 252, 255, 258;
        Walter 158; William Alexander
        150, 157, 158; William Alexander
        (Zan) Jr. 158, 240, 304
Stuart Land and Cattle Company of
        Virginia, Inc. 150, 157, 158,
        175, 240, 287, 304
Stuarts Draft 68, 120, 298
Stuarts Draft High School 164
Suffolk 289
Suffolk Dun 25
Suffolk Packing Company 277
Sugar Grove, N.C. 190
Sugar Grove Valley 106

Sugar Loaf Farm 296, 297
Suiza (Dean Foods) 205, 206
Sunny Heights Simmentals 305
Sunny Slope Farm 293, 295, 297
Sunny Top Farm 235
Sunnyside Farm 204
Sunnyside Stardust 320
Superintendent of Public Instruction
        in Virginia 137
supplies, collection of 56, 57; supply
        train 80
Supply 295, 296
Supreme Virginian 229
Surber, Garnett 290
Susong, J.O. 287
Sutherland 237, 239
Sutherland, David 292; M.Y. 266
Sutphin, Florence 241; Ned 241; Tim
        270
Swaffar, C.D. "Pete" 283; Paul
        180, 248, 249, 252, 254, 259, 265
Swain, Hughes 291
Swecker, Bobby 180; George 267, 268;
        Preston 295
Sweet Briar College 214, 215, 239
Swift 154
Swift, Kathy McComb 241
Swift Run 108
Swift Run Gap 10
Swisher, Jerry 240
Switzerland, 236
Swoope 129, 190
Sybil's Gipsy King 229

T

Tabor, Tom 266
Tait, James L. 240, 242
tallow 45, 69, 77
Tangier Island 5
tanker trucks 204, 205, 211
tanning 30, 84, 87, 116
Tarentaise 279, 305
Tarentaise Valley, France 305
Tarleton, Banastre 57
Tartan Angus Farms 295
tattoos 108
tavern keepers 110
tax, on cattle 56
Taylo, Jeremiah 58
Taylor, George 282; J.P. 239; John 31;
        Pinkethman 58
Tazewell 121, 144, 166, 289, 291
Tazewell County 134, 144, 147, 148, 150,
        158, 171, 178, 182, 287, 307
Tazewell Hereford Association 290
Tazewell Livestock Market 267
Tazewell stockyards 248
TB free herds 205
Teackle, Thomas 30
Tees River 25
teeth, of cattle 39
Tel-O-Auction sale program 262, 264
Templeton, Thomas M. 294, 295
tenant system 110
Tenth Legion 65
Terrell, Paul 229
Terry, H.H. (Benny) 249
test markets 205
test stations 270, 295; associations 213
Thatcher, Hervey 194
The Plains 237, 304
Thistleton on the Clinch 152
Thomas, Owen 288, 289; Owen, III
        288; Owen Jr. 262; Roy H. 195
Thomason, William 301
Thompson, Bill 301; Harry 154, 155;
        Herbert 267, 289; R.F. 204; Roy
        259; Sam 151;
Thompson's Valley 144
Thorofare Mountain 110
Thoroughfare Gap 78
threshing 44
Tice, George 297; Joyce 297
tick dipping 125; eradication 125
tick fever 124, 125; medicines for 124
Tidewater 6, 25, 35, 38, 39, 48, 78
Tidewater Artificial Breeding
        Association 315

Tidewater Milk Sales 208
Tidy Burke Elevation 325
Tillett, Edgar R. 240
Timberville 229, 239, 273, 295, 297
Timbrook, Larry 240
Timson, Mary 40
Tinder, Carl 303
Tinsley, Robert 292
Titmus, Edward 237, 240
tobacco 7, 14, 62; cultivation 14, 28, 29, 30, 39, 49, 69
Todd Meat Packers 250
toll collectors 110; tollhouse 109
Tomkins, Benjamin 284
total mixed rations 199
Toulmin, Harry 44
trade centers 7
Trailblazer Award, Holstein 240
Trans-Allegheny cattle drives 70
Trans-Allegheny region 52
transportation changes 73
Tri-State Hereford Association 290
Tri-State Milk Producers 208
Trigg, L.B. "Buddy" 240, 241
Trimble, John 266
Trio Farms 305
Tripartite Quarantine Treaty 298
Triple J Farm 297
triple-purpose animals 22, 24, 27, 304
Trivett, Carson 290
Trivette, Alpha Everette 165
Troutville 262
Troy 302
truck transportation 109, 120, 189, 211
tuberculosis 123, 125, 140
tuberculosis testing 204
Tucker, Edward B. (Ned) 208; H.Q. 305; Leila Skipworth 73; Ned 209; Ralph 270
Tullos, Frank 266
Turner, Chester 290; John L. 253, 266; Joseph 238, 239; Joseph A. 188; L.W. 292; Lawson 267, 292, 293, 296; Millard W. 262
Turner Valley, Alberta, Canada 303
Turpin, Harry 267
Tuttle, J.B. 283
Twilight Sale, Holstein 241
Tyfarms Supreme 236
Tyler, W. Edmond "Ned" 288; E.H. 283
Tyssowski, John 179, 289

U

U.S. Agriculture Census 92
U.S. Department of Agriculture 126, 137, 181, 190, 193, 258
U.S. Department of Education 164, 170
Umberger, E.D. 270
Underwood, Tom 290
Union Abbatoir, Inc. 250
United Dairy Industry Association 203
United Irishmen 69
United States Congress 133
University of Maryland 133
University of Virginia 74, 133, 150
Updike, Francis 294
Upperville 91, 237, 292, 295, 297, 299
Upshur County 82
urban markets 41, 47, 70, 73, 75, 101, 102, 107, 116, 208
urban sprawl 213

V

V.P.I. Jessie Katrinka Defrost 4098698 316
vaccines 123, 126, 127
Valley and Ridge Province 4
Valley Campaign 84
Valley Forge 54, 55
Valley Milk Products LLC 203, 210
Valley of Virginia 6, 8, 9, 11, 40, 52, 56, 69, 71, 78, 86, 100, 105
Valley of Virginia Cooperative Milk Producers Association 200, 204, 204–206
Valley Pike 90
Valley Railroad 115
Valleydale Packers 154, 276, 277
Valliant 302
Van Dyke, Claude 291
Van Dyke Hereford Farms 291

Vance, R. Conroy 229
Vaniman, Don 304
Varner family 110; Hamilton 110
Vaughan, T. George 289; Ray 274
veal 37
vector theory 124
Venable, A.R. 188, 228
Vernon, Jo 171
Versailles, Kentucky 287
Vest, Chris 221, 241
veterinary medicine 172; changes 127; traditional. methods 124; school 264;
Vikings 292
Vincel, Norman 270; W.B. 290
Vinton 305
Virginia (Farm Bureau) Agricultural Marketing Association 183
Virginia 4-H Dairy Judging Team 319
Virginia Agribusiness Council 140, 203
Virginia Agricultural and Mechanical College 133, 134
Virginia and Tennessee Railroad 147
Virginia and West Virginia Shorthorn Association 283
Virginia Angus (Breeders) Association 165, 268, 270, 273, 288, 292, 295, 296, 318; ladies auxiliary 294; show 293
Virginia Animal Breeders Association 315, 316
Virginia Artificial Breeding Association 240, 315
Virginia Artificial Breeding Cooperative Semen Pro 321
Virginia Association of Livestock Market Operators 267
Virginia Ayrshire (Breeders) Association. 228
Virginia Beach 169, 233, 234
Virginia Beef Cattle Association 123, 262
Virginia Beef Cattle Commission 274
Virginia Beef Cattle Improvement Association 260, 268, 274, 287, 287, 294, 299
Virginia Beef Cattle Producers Association 179, 252, 255
Virginia Beef Cattlemen's Convention 267
Virginia Beef Congress 260
Virginia Beef Expo 278, 283, 297, 303, 305
Virginia Beef Industry Convention 332
Virginia Board of Agriculture and Consumer Service 140
Virginia Board of Immigration 146
Virginia Breeder 248
Virginia Brown Swiss Breeders Association 237
Virginia Cattle Feeders Association 277
Virginia Cattle Industry Board 275
Virginia Cattle Industry Commission 275
Virginia Cattleman 262, 263, 265
Virginia Cattlemen's Association 165, 251, 265, 274, 278
Virginia Central RR 114
Virginia Charolais Association 299, 300; presidents 301
Virginia Circle K Ranch 288
Virginia Commissioner of Agriculture 137
Virginia Company 21, 24
Virginia Cooperative Extension 141, 165, 176
Virginia Cooperative Holstein Breeders Association 239
Virginia Dairy Company 234
Virginia Dairy Council 220
Virginia Dairy Princess 242
Virginia Dairy Products Association 218
Virginia Department of Agriculture (and Commerce; and Immigration; Mining, and Manufacturing; and Consumer Services) 134, 135, 138, 139, 140, 262, 278, 293, 327
Virginia Department of Corrections 215
Virginia Distinguished Dairy Farm Family 231; Distinguished Dairyman 231
Virginia Farm Bureau 174, 182, 274
Virginia Farm Bureau News 182

Virginia Federation of Dairy Herd Improvement Associations 194
Virginia Feed Manufacturers Association 273
Virginia Feeder Calf Sales Association 254, 260
Virginia Feeder Cattle Association 266
Virginia Forage and Grasslands Council 175, 264
Virginia General Assembly 59, 131, 134, 138, 139, 162, 174, 177, 252, 274, 292
Virginia Genetics, Inc 319-320
Virginia Gentleman Bull Show and Sale 293
Virginia, geography of 4
Virginia Guernsey Breeders Association 229, 234; Cattle Club 234
Virginia Hereford (Breeders) Association 166, 173, 248, 253, 273, 286, 287, 288, 289, 290
Virginia Heritage Sale 300
Virginia Historic Landmark 175
Virginia Holstein (Breeders) Association 168, 203, 207, 229, 239, 240, 318; Virginia Holstein-Friesian Club 239; Virginia Holstein Field Day 325, 327
Virginia Holstein News 241
Virginia Holstein team 221; Holstein youth 241
Virginia House of Burgesses 131
Virginia Jersey Cattle Club 229, 230
Virginia Junior Beef Roundup 300; Junior Hereford Association 290; Junior Holstein Scholarship 242
Virginia Livestock Council 273
Virginia Livestock Markets Association 267
Virginia Meat Packers Association 273, 274
Virginia Military Institute 87, 133, 233
Virginia Milk and Cream Act 218, 219
Virginia National sale 300
Virginia Packing Company 277
Virginia Polled Hereford Association 165, 289, 291
Virginia Quality Assured 277
Virginia School for the Deaf and Blind 178
Virginia Shorthorn Association 283
Virginia Simmental Association 304
Virginia Slaughter Cattle Marketing Association 262
Virginia State Agricultural Society 132, 133, 134, 178
Virginia State College 215
Virginia State Dairymen's Association 188, 196, 198, 203, 208, 218, 220, 228, 231, 239, 262, 274, 314, 320
Virginia State Epileptic Colony 193, 213, 214
Virginia State Fair 177, 180, 181, 221, 228, 230, 233, 238, 239, 297, 304, 305; Association 179, 252; fairgrounds 235
Virginia State Feed Association 196
Virginia State University 141, 176
Virginia Tarentaise Association 305
Virginia Tech (VPI, VPI &SU, Virginia Polytechnic Institute) 133, 134, 138, 139, 170, 287 140, 141, 155, 162, 165, 170, 171, 172, 173, 175, 228, 232, 238, 239, 252, 253, 255, 262, 264, 273, 284, 285, 289, 291, 293, 301, 304, 306, 314, 316, 320, 325, 327; animal science department 127, 172, 273, 323; Beef Cattle Shortcourse 172; Dairy Day 201; dairy department 196–197; dairy herd 196; Dairy Herdsman 318; dairy science department 173, 196, 207, 220; dairy science lab 323; herd testing 192
Virginia Test Tube 2165078 314
Virginia Veterinary Medical Association 273
Virginia-Carolina Charolais Association 299

Virginia-North Carolina Select Sires 319
Virginia's Beef Industry Council 276
Virginia's Board of Agriculture and Commerce 203
Virts, Donald 304
vocational agriculture 164
von Steuben, General 59

W

W.O. Smith & Sons 285
Wagner, Amy 241; Barbara 240, 241; Dr. 290; Riley 240, 241
Wakefield 167
Wakefield, Edward 42
Walker, Dave 275; Frank 240; Frank Jr. 241; Frank S. 188, 202, 238, 239; Gilbert 133; I.D. 278; John 58; Margaret S. 229; Thomas 59
Walkup Astronaut Lou Ann 325
Walkup Holsteins 239
Walkup Valiant Lou Ella 242
Wall, Dianne 242
Wallace, G.M. 233
Walnut Grove 172, 182
Walther, Bo 270
Walton, Fred H. 292
Wampler, Charles W. 268, 269, 297; Charles W., Sr. 204, 293, 294; family 68, 270, 300; Frances B. 318; Margaret 261; Wayne 235; William 270, 293, 300; William D. 295, 301
Wampler farm 294, 295
Warber, G.B. 204
Warburton, Benjamin 58
Ward, David 145
Wardell 154
Wardell Farm 145
Ward's Cove 155
Warm Springs 266, 289
Warner, Jim 256; Mark R. 222
Warrenton 141, 145, 166, 180, 228, 237, 248, 288, 290, 291, 292, 293, 297
Warwick County 32, 107
Warwick, Everett 268
Washington College 133
Washington County 145, 150, 168, 170
Washington, D.C. 5, 6, 14, 71, 75, 132, 162, 188, 189, 195, 200, 211
Washington, George 46, 52, 54, 55, 62, 67, 164
Washington, Virginia 297
water gaps 10
Watkins, William Bell 292
Waverly Farm 230
Wayne, Anthony 59
Waynesboro 87, 196, 201, 236, 290, 300, 301, 305, 317
Weaber, Kaye 295, 296
wealth, determination of 19, 29, 30, 32, 40
Weaver, A.F. 229, 317
Webster, Jesse 305
Wehrman Angus Farm 297, 316
Wehrmann, Nicholas 273, 297
weighing milk 192
weight measurement, weaning 271; yearling 271
Weller, Scott 295
Welsh Black 23
Welton's Trucking 250
Wendell, Irene Bowen 154
Wenger, Perry 193
Wesson, H.C. 287
West, Dan 123
West Indies trade 30, 69
West, Thomas (Baron De La Warr) 20; Thomas J. 67
West Virginia 116, 149
Western State Hospital 215, 216, 217
Western View Farm 228
Westmoreland 233
Westover 36, 38
Weyers Cave 164, 230, 237, 291
Whaley, J.W. 253
wheat production 14
"Wheat Referendum" 183
Wheeler, J. Hubert 255; Junior 290

Whelan, Steven 305
Whippernock Farm 239, 241
Whipple, Fred R. 229
Whissen, Clarence 205
Whistleman, Waldo 109
Whitacre, Mr. 80
White Hall Farms 297
White, Harlen 171; John 240
White Oak Spring Farm 295, 296
White Park 23
White Post 283, 285, 295
White Sulphur Springs, W. Va. 129
Whitehall 67
White's Ford 83
Whitestone Farm 264, 297
Whitestone Miss Skymere K046 264
Wilkerson, Wesley 304
Wilkins, John 270; Mr. 80
Wilkinson, Cary 58
Wilkinson, D.P. (Pete) 208
William, John 267
William Tell I, 236
Williams, George D. 266; J. Paul 273; James C. 267; Jesse L., Jr. 289; Wyatt A. 230
Williamsburg 51, 57, 73, 168, 215, 229, 233

Williamson, Alma 237; J.T. 237; Kenneth C. (K.C.) 255, 256, 262, 266
Willingham, Alton 290, 291
Willis, A. Gordon 202; James 270; John M. 239, 240, 241
Willowlyn Farm 203
Wilmer, Joseph 188
Wilson, Norwood 228
Winchester 11, 40, 41, 52, 53, 56, 67, 100, 169, 201, 239, 255, 283, 288, 290, 291, 303
Windcrest Holsteins 239
Windholme Farm 283
Winkler, Walter 301
Winn, Roger 273, 302
Winston, David 221
Winterfield Farms 291
Winton Farm 248, 292
Winyah Herefords 289
Wise, Henry A. 133
Wiseman, C.C. 290
Witscher, Joe 327
Wolff, Corey C. 324
Wolters, Adolph 190
women's work 31
Wood, Charles W. 265
Woodberry Forest 238
Woodbridge, Dudley 70

Woodgrove Farm 239
Woodland Farm 195
Woodley Farm 292
Woods, E.C.C. 234
Woodstock 171, 203, 236, 239
Woodward, Ray 305
World Dairy Expo 175, 237
World Guernsey Federation 235
World Tarentaise Federation 305
World War I 139, 153, 181, 204, 237, 239, 258, 283, 298, 313
World War II 154, 169, 170, 179, 182, 202, 205, 208, 211, 233, 234, 237, 282, 314
Worley, C.W. 229; Kenneth 290
Wormeley, Agatha Eltonhead 32; Ralph 32
Worrell, Eugene 302; H.H. 290
Worrell Land & Cattle Company 302
Wright, Barbara 305; Edward J. 234; J. Steve 278; Joseph E., Sr. 237
Wyatt, B.F. 229; Harry Cassell 289
Wythe County 182
Wythe Hereford Association 290
Wythe-Bland calf sale 255
Wytheville 141, 239, 320

Y

Yancey, Eddie 297; L.L. 204
yarders 117
Yates, C.H. 234
Yatton Farm 229, 230
Yeardley, George 29
Yoder Dairy 194, 200, 220
York County 17, 59, 69, 70
York River 6, 19, 24, 29, 31, 57
Yorkshire (England) 63
Yorktown 39, 44
Yorktown, Battle of 59; campaign 58
Young, Arthur 42; H.N. 171, 174; Harold 172
Yount, Glen 292, 296
Youth Cattle Working Contest 278; Dairy Competitions 181; youth programs 221
Yutzy, Dave 239

Z

Zane, Isaac 69
Zeuswyn Farm 295, 297
Zigler, Howard S. 182
Zimmerman, Jacob 105; Mrs. Paul 297
Zirkle, Lisa 305

John Henry "Jack" Elswick managing Jeff Gillespie, Sr.'s cattle in southwest Virginia during the 1930s.